ISLAM
OUTSIDE THE ARAB WORLD

ABSTRACT

David Westerlund & Ingvar Svanberg (eds), *Islam Outside the Arab World*. Richmond: Curzon Press, 1999. 488pp. ISBN 0–7007–1124–4 (Hbk). ISBN 0–7007–1142–2 (Pbk).

Today about 85 per cent of the world's Muslim population live outside the Arab world and due to population growth, 'missionary' (*dawa*) endeavours and migration, the number of Muslims in non-Arab nations is rapidly increasing. Yet many people in the West conceive of Islam as an 'Arab' religion and it is only recently that a more thorough scholarly interest in other parts of the Muslim world has emerged. This volume presents the spread and character of Islam in many non-Arab countries in Africa (south of the Sahara), Asia, Oceania, Europe and the Americas. It focuses particularly on the contemporary situation, but also presents an historical background. Much attention is devoted to Sufism, which appears to be the predominant form of Islam in most non-Arab countries, as well as to the growing significance of Islamism, which challenges both secularism and the Sufi forms of Islam. An extensive introduction provides a general background account of the origin, expansion and characteristics of Islam.

Key concepts: Islam, Sufism, Shia, Ahmadiyya, conversion, immigrant communities, minorities, folk religion.

ISLAM
OUTSIDE THE ARAB WORLD

edited by

David Westerlund
and
Ingvar Svanberg

CURZON

First Published in 1999
by Curzon Press
15 The Quadrant, Richmond
Surrey, TW9 1BP

Editorial Matter © 1999 David Westerlund and Ingvar Svanberg

Typeset in Sabon by LaserScript Ltd, Mitcham, Surrey
Printed and bound in Great Britain by
Biddles Ltd, Guildford and King's Lynn

British Library Cataloguing in Publication Data
A catalogue record of this book is available from the British Library

Library of Congress Cataloguing in Publication Data
A catalogue record for this book has been requested

ISBN 0–7007–1124–4 (Hbk)
ISBN 0–7007–1142–2 (Pbk)

Contents

Contents

Preface

In January 1998 the *Anchorage Daily News* reported that there is a growing presence of Muslims in Alaska and that there are now three Islamic centres in Anchorage. Increasingly, Islamic obligations like fasting during the month of Ramadan are observed by Muslims in places as far apart as Rio de Janeiro, Cape Town, Stockholm and Christchurch. This illustrates the fact that Islam is not only a religion of Arabs. In fact, the great majority of Muslims are neither Arabic-speaking, nor resident in the Middle East, but are spread across virtually all parts of the world, particularly in Central, South and Southeast Asia as well as in large parts of sub-Saharan Africa. Of the six most populous Muslim countries in the world – Indonesia, Pakistan, India, Bangladesh, Turkey and Iran – none is Arab, and in Africa sub-Saharan Nigeria has more Muslims than any of the Maghrib countries of North Africa. Furthermore, after the Second World War and decolonisation, labour immigration and refugees have given Muslims a significant minority position in Western Europe.

This book deals with the great variety and complexity that characterise Islam outside the Arab world. The case studies present Islam and the role of Muslims in a number of countries in Africa, Asia, Oceania, Europe and the Americas. The contributions provide a historical background to the growth of Islam in the respective areas but concentrate primarily and comprehensively on the contemporary situation. Among other things, much attention is focused on Sufism, which is the most significant form of Islam in many non-Arab parts of the Muslim world, as well as on the importance of the recent resurgence of Islam in the form of various Islamist movements and organisations. The introduction to the book provides a historical and theological background to the area studies and accounts for some important and recurring Islamic concepts.

The volume is partly a result of a research project at Uppsala university, sponsored by the Swedish Council for Research in the Humanities and Social Sciences. The contributors represent several disciplines, such as anthropology, ethnology, history of religions, Iranian Studies, Islamic studies, missiology, political science and sociology. This indicates that research on Islam and Muslims is today quite well-established in a great number of disciplines. Much of the authors' material is based on field notes and local sources. References to some scholarly books and articles, which may be recommended for further studies, are found in an annotated section at the end of each chapter. Since the volume is written for a wide circle of readers, there is a simplified system of transcription without diacritical marks, and the Islamic concepts used are briefly explained in each contribution.

David Westerlund and Ingvar Svanberg

Contributors

Muhammed Abdullah al-Ahari is a postgraduate in Linguistics and History at Northeastern Illinois University. His main research interest is Islam in the Western world. He has published extensively in American and other journals and is currently working on a multi-volume *Encyclopedia of Islam in the Americas and Europe* as well as translating slave narratives and Islamic works from Arabic to English.

Ishtiaq Ahmed is Associate Professor of Political Science at Stockholm University. His scholarly interests cover a wide range of contemporary issues and areas. He has written on the politics of South Asia and the Middle East, nationalism and ethnicity, religion and politics in Islam, human rights and international migration. Currently, he is working on the project 'Islam and human rights: a comparative study of Turkey, Egypt and Pakistan'. His recent publications include *State, Nation and Ethnicity in Contemporary South Asia* (1996).

Justin Ben-Adam is an Assistant Professor of Anthropology at Tulane University, New Orleans. His major research fields are China, Central Asia, urban anthropology and cultural studies of religion. He has carried out extensive field work in Chinese Central Asia. In addition to articles on Uighur culture, he has recently published the monograph *Uyghur Nationalism along China's Silk Road* (1997).

Sven Cederroth is a social anthropologist and Associate Professor at the Centre for East and Southeast Asian Studies, Gothenburg University. He has specialised in the anthropology of religion with a focus on Indonesia and Malaysia. His recent publications include *Survival and Profit in Rural Java: The Case of an East Javanese Village* (1995) and *Managing Marital Disputes in Malaysian Syariah Courts: Islamic Mediators and Conflict Resolution in the Syariah Courts* (1997).

Svante Cornell is a postgraduate in the Departments of Peace and Conflict Studies and East European Studies at Uppsala University. He has published a number of articles on politics and conflicts in the Caucasus and Transcaucasus regions in journals such as *Current History* and *Central Asian Survey*.

Eva Evers Rosander is Senior Research Fellow in Gender Studies at the Faculty of Theology, Uppsala University, and Associate Professor in Social Anthropology at Stockholm University. Her main scholarly interests are Islam, particularly Sufism, gender and development, currently with a focus on Senegal. She has carried out extensive field work in Morocco, Ceuta and Senegal and is the author of *Women in a Borderland: Managing Muslim Identity where Morocco Meets Spain* (1991) and the co-editor, together with David Westerlund, of *African Islam and Islam in Africa: Encounters between Sufis and Islamists* (1997).

Mattias Gardell is Assistant Professor and Research Fellow in the History of Religions at the Faculty of Theology, Uppsala University. His main fields of interest are African–American religion, political Islam, religious racism and radical nationalism. He recently published *In the Name of Elijah Muhammad: Louis Farrakhan and the Nation of Islam* (1996).

Ron Geaves is Lecturer in Religious Studies at the University of Wolverhampton. His main fields of interest are the religions of the Indian subcontinent, including the varieties of Islam that have developed in that region. As a result of migration processes, he is particularly interested in the transmigration and adaptation of subcontinental traditions into Britain. He has recently published the monograph *Sectarian Influences within Islam in Britain* (1996) and is currently working on a book entitled *The Sufis of Britain*.

Christer Hedin is Associate Professor of Studies in Faiths and Ideologies and teaches Islam and the History of Religions at the Universities of Uppsala and Stockholm. His main scholarly interest is Islamic theology, Quranic as well as contemporary. In addition to a number of articles in English, he has published several books and articles in Swedish, including an introduction to Islam entitled *Islam i vardagen och världen* (1994).

Bernhard Helander is Associate Professor at the Department of Cultural Anthropology, Uppsala University. His regional focus is Africa, and he has carried out research in Somalia since 1982. He has published extensively in the fields of local community organisation, medical anthropology and post-conflict management.

Michael Humphrey is Senior Lecturer in the School of Sociology at the University of New South Wales. His interests include issues of cultural identity and globalisation, especially in the context of the contemporary crisis of the nation-state. In this field he has recently published the volume *Ethnicity and Identity in a Globalizing World* (1998). He has also published extensively on Islam in Australia and Lebanon, including the new book *Islam, Multiculturalism and Transnationalism: From the Lebanese Diaspora* (1998).

Franz Kogelmann is Lecturer in the Department of Islamic Studies at Bayreuth University. Apart from Muslim communities in Europe, his scholarly work focuses on contemporary Islamist movements and pious endowments (*waqfs*) in modern Muslim societies. His recent publications include *Die Islamisten Ägyptens in der Regierungszeit Anwar as-Sadat* (1994) and *Islamische fromme Stiftungen und Staat: Der Wandel in den Beziehungen zwischen einer religiösen Institution und dem marokkanischen Staat seit dem 19. Jahrhundert bis 1937* (1998).

Abdulaziz Lodhi is Senior Lecturer in Swahili and East African Area Studies at the Department of Asian and African Languages, Uppsala University. He has published extensively in Swahilistics and on Zanzibar affairs. Currently he is working on the project 'Oriental influences in East Africa (with special reference to loanwords)'.

Kjell Magnusson is a sociologist and Assistant Professor at the Centre for Multiethnic Research, Uppsala University. His main scholarly interests are ethnic and national conflicts, sociology of religion and society and culture in the Balkan peninsula. In addition to numerous articles on Yugoslavian and Balkan issues, he has recently published the book *Attitudes and Values in Bosnia and Herzegovina: A Sociological Investigation* (1995).

Roberta Micallef is Research Fellow and teaches Turkish at the Department of Asian and African languages, Uppsala University. Her current research focuses on Uzbek and Middle Eastern literature. She recently published the volume *National Identity Construction: The Case of Uzbekistan* (1997).

Neal Robinson is Senior Lecturer in Islamic Studies at the Department of Theology and Religious Studies in the University of Leeds. His current major research interests are Quranic studies and Islam in France. *Discovering the Qur'an* (1996) and *Islam: A Concise Introduction* (1998) are two of his recent publications.

William Shepard is Associate Professor of Religious Studies at the University of Canterbury in Christchurch, New Zealand. His primary interest is in Islamic ideology in the modern world, particularly in Egypt. His most recent book is *Sayyid Qutb and Islamic Activism* (1996), an annotated translation of the last edition of Qutb's *Social Justice in Islam*, comparing it in detail with the earlier editions.

Christopher Steed teaches African history at Uppsala University. His current research interests are Christian missionary strategies towards African Islam, and the ecclesiatical history of Nigeria. He is joint author, with Bengt Sundkler, of *A History of the Church in Africa* (1999).

Ingvar Svanberg is an ethnologist and Senior Research Fellow at the Department of East European Studies, Uppsala University. His research interests include Central Asian culture, religion and history, ethnobiology and minority issues, particularly concerning Muslims. He has written numerous books and articles on a wide range of topics. Recently he published the monograph *China's Last Nomads: The History and Culture of China's Kazaks* (1998), together with Linda Benson, and the collective volume *Contemporary Kazaks: Cultural and Political Perspectives* (1999).

Abdulkader Tayob teaches Islam and Religious Studies at the University of Cape Town. Recently he has been studying the history and institutions of Muslims in South Africa and their transformation during the period of transition and democratic government. In 1995 he published *Islamic Resurgence in South Africa: The Muslim Youth Movement*, and another book, on South African mosques and sermons, is now in press.

David Westerlund is Associate Professor at the Department of Comparative Religion, Stockholm University, and Senior Lecturer in the History of Religions at the Faculty of Theology, Uppsala University. His main scholarly interests are indigenous African religions and Islam in Africa, religion and politics, Sufism in Europe and inter-religious relations, particularly between Christians and Muslims. He has recently edited *Questioning the Secular State: The Worldwide Resurgence of Religion in Politics* (1996) and co-edited, with Eva Evers Rosander, *African Islam and Islam in Africa: Encounters between Sufis and Islamists* (1997).

Bo Utas is Professor of Iranian Studies in the Department of Asian and African Languages, Uppsala University. His scholarly interests cover a field from the history of West Iranian languages (especially Persian) to the history of Persian culture, religion and literature, particularly Sufi poetry. He has published articles and books on a wide range of topics, including the recent *Arabic Prosody and its Applications in Muslim Poetry* (1994), which he co-edited with Lars Johansson.

Introduction

Christer Hedin, Ingvar Svanberg and David Westerlund

Say (O Muhammad): O people! I am the messenger of God to all of you.

(Sura 7:158)

At the beginning Islam was the religion of the Arabs, although non-Arab Muslims often point out that even some of the Prophet Muhammad's first disciples were not Arabs. During the Umayyad period (before 750) a particularist view was predominant, and there were hardly any attempts to convert colonised peoples to Islam despite the universalist features of the Quran, exemplified by the quotation above. It was not until the Abbasid period (after 750) that Islam to a considerable extent started spreading among non-Arab peoples. Even though the vast majority of the Muslims of the world are now found outside the Arab world, it is still common in the West to consider Islam as an Arab religion. Scholars of religion, whose work has concentrated primarily on the development of early Islam and who have often combined the research on Islam with studies of Semitic languages, have seldom wanted – or been able – to follow the enormous expansion of Islam in time and space, further and further out into the 'periphery'. It is primarily owing to other specialists such as historians, anthropologists, sociologists, political scientists and philologists who specialise in other 'Muslim' languages such as Urdu and Swahili that, particularly during the last few decades, a sounder knowledge of Islam outside the Arab world has been acquired. The substantial number of social scientists now involved in the study of Muslims in most parts of the world reflects the increased political influence of Islam.

The concept of the Arab world can be understood in various ways. Here it is not used in a geographical or ethnic sense but as language term. Currently the number of people whose mother tongue is some 'dialect' of Arabic is at least 175 million. Of these approximately 90 per cent are Muslims. However, the total number of Muslims in the world probably by far exceeds 1 billion. Thus, only some 15 per cent of all Muslims are Arabs. Moreover, the number of Muslims is growing more rapidly outside than inside the Arab world. The increase is primarily due to population growth in Muslim areas, but it is also caused by conversions to Islam. In particular,

1

conversion is an important additional reason for the expansion of Islam in Africa south of the Sahara. The purpose of this book is to present Islam and its current renewal among non-Arab Muslims. The volume includes a number of case studies on different parts of the world: Africa, Asia, Oceania, Europe and the Americas. These studies exemplify the rich variety that so often is obscured in stereotypic and monolithic accounts which are common in Western media. We have tried to avoid stereotypic simplifications not only in the texts but also in the illustrations that we have chosen. Hence, the latter are not dominated by Western standard pictures of, for instance, veiled women and praying men, which easily heighten prejudices about Muslims.

The multiplicity of Islam is largely associated with Sufism, which is the predominant form of Islam in many areas outside the Arab world. Yet, despite all the variety among Muslims, there are certain basic features, such as classical Arabic as a ritual language and Mecca as a ritual centre, which give the worldwide community of Muslims a feeling of togetherness. In particular, the basic creed (*shahada*) – 'there is no god except God and Muhammad is His Messenger' – unites all Muslims of the world. There has always been a more orthodox stream which has depicted Islam as a homogeneous entity. However, pan-Islamic and Arab-oriented tendencies can also be found within Sufism. Currently, it is above all the so-called fundamentalist or Islamist groups that stress the international issues and want to 'purify' Islam from the 'degenerate' influence of Sufism and Western secularism. In this introduction we will first provide a more general background to the regional studies that follow. Since the book is written not only for students of Religious Studies or specialists on Islam but for a wider circle of readers, there is a fairly detailed account of some basic elements of Islam, which will facilitate the reading of the following essays. In the latter there will, therefore, be only brief explanations of Islamic concepts used. Since Sufism is of great significance in areas outside the Arab world, we will pay considerable attention to introducing this type of Islam. Much attention will also be focused on the contemporary, and not least politically important, Islamic resurgence.

The foundations of Islam

In Western studies, Islam is often portrayed as a founded religion, whose origin can be dated back to the seventh century. Since Muhammad is regarded as the founder, the term 'Muhammadanism' has been used. According to Muslims, however, Muhammad was not the founder of Islam and, as a consequence, they reject the concept of Muhammadanism. Islam is the original religion of humankind, founded by God. For the same reason, Islam is the natural religion, the religion which is in perfect accordance with human nature and reason. The first human beings were

Adam and Eve. This Muslim belief has seldom led to any conflicts with the findings of the natural sciences concerning the age of the earth and the origin of the species. Adam and Eve may be seen as symbols of the emergence of humankind. For Muslims, Adam was not only the first human being but also the first Muslim and first prophet. Islam is not primarily a religion in a limited sense but a basic view on, and a whole pattern of, life. In Western handbooks, Islam is often translated 'submission'. Although this is not wrong, it becomes misleading if it is not seen in its proper context. Theologically trained Muslims do not use the term 'submission' to depict what is central in Islam. Islam is an Arabic word, and like other Arabic words it is based on three consonants with a basic spectrum of meaning. The consonants 'slm' are found in the term *salaam* too, which signifies piece, harmony, balance and righteousness. Living as a Muslim means living in a right relationship to God and fellow human beings. Today it is often added that it also means to live in a right relationship to nature. God's creation is good, and He has appointed the human being as His deputy. If humans live righteously, the world can develop its potential for perfection. The duty of human beings is to administer the creation so that all its opportunities are taken advantage of and all its gifts are shared in a righteous way.

From the beginning, the whole creation was in a state of Islam, an innocent and promising phase with a potential for a perfect life for all. Animals and plants still live in this original Islam – they live in accordance with the laws of nature, instituted by God, and consequently in a right relationship to their creator. The problem is humankind. Since humans are created in the image of God, they must have free will. Therefore, they can deviate from the natural order they were born into and grew up in. The adult human is the only created being that can refuse to live according to the will of God. Created in the image of God, a human being is not only free but also morally good and rational. In Islam there is no doctrine of a Fall and original sin. The optimistic view on humans is a necessary consequence of the concept of God. God is one, and He is wise and omnipotent. Nothing must be put on a par with Him. He would never accept that the evil power controlled His finest creature, the human being. To believe in such a possiblity would be to put Satan on a par with God. Satan is a spiritual being who refused to venerate the human being as God's most perfect creature. At the end of time Satan will be eternally punished, but until then he tempts human beings. The evil is rooted in lack of knowledge and insufficient wisdom. Humans can make faulty judgements that make them act in a wrong way. Since evil is associated with reason rather than will, it is generally argued that reason must control the basic instincts of human beings.

The fact that Adam is the first Muslim as well as the first prophet means that he has been commissioned by God to convey to other human beings the

3

message about God's will. However, this message was soon distorted by ignorant and unreasonable people. God then sent new prophets, whose message was also distorted. Before God sent the final prophet, Muhammad, there had been hundreds of thousands of prophets commissioned by God to teach the right way of life, that is, the meaning of Islam. Through Muhammad, God wanted to give humankind a revelation which corrected all previous misrepresentations and could not be distorted. It is the last revelation, perfect in all respects. According to the majority of Muslims, no-one can claim to be a prophet after Muhammad.

Muslims hold that the deity they worship is the same as the one worshipped by Jews and Christians, although there are various names in different languages. Allah (literally 'the God') is an Arabic word used by Christian Arabs too. Muslims believe that God revealed Himself to a vast number of Biblical persons like Noah, Abraham, Moses, David and Jesus, but their revelations were recorded in a distorted way, and it is these versions that were put together to form the Hebrew and Christian Bibles. The flawless, and thus impeccable, version of God's revelation was conveyed by Muhammed and recorded in the Quran. Its similarities with the Bible prove that it is the same God who has revealed Himself to all prophets, while the dissimilarities demonstrate that the older revelations have been misrepresented. Since animals and plants live unconsciously and involuntarily in Islam, we can learn about God's intentions by studying nature. Human beings, however, who have a free will, can in their actions deviate from the 'laws of nature' which apply to them, that is, from those norms that express the will of God. In order to counteract the possibility of human deviations, God has revealed His will not only in the Quran but also in the perfect life of Muhammad. In other words, there are two parts of the divine revelation: the Quran and the example of the Prophet, *sunna*.

The book called the Quran is a terrestial copy of a heavenly prototype, commonly called the Original Quran. It is the contents of that Quran which has been revealed to prophets at all times. Muhammad was an 'ordinary' human being in the sense that he was in no way divine. Muslims frequently believe that he could not read or write. Among scholars, this is a questioned belief, but for Muslims the crucial point is that the Quran came into existence through a miracle. The miracle being that an unlearned man could present a book which in all respects is the most perfect one that has ever existed. The perfect language of the Quran means that Arabic holds an exceptional position as the sacred language of Islam. As a rule, Muslims regard the learning of Arabic as a religious duty and, ideally, the Quran should be read in this language. Outside the Arab world, however, Muslims often memorise certain parts of or even the whole book without properly learning the language itself. In particular, memorising as much as possible of the Quran has been, and still is in many places, an important goal in the education of Muslim youth. Since Arabic has a special religious status,

A copy of an old Quran in the Muftiate centre of Tashkent, Uzbekistan (photo: David Thurfjell, 1998).

knowledge of that language has a legitimising function. However, this does not mean that all teachers in Quranic schools can explain how the principles of Islam are rooted in the sacred texts. This has proved important when, for instance, Muslim feminists in Pakistan have learnt Arabic 'properly' and opposed male religious leaders on issues concerning the role of women. Because of their superior knowledge of Arabic, they have been successful in such debates.

The life of Muhammad is largely known, although a number of uncertainties remain. He was about forty years old when he first presented his message in Mecca, calling for a reform of the old Arab religion. In the early seventh century there was social unrest in Mecca, with many young Arabs having lost the traditional bonds with their tribes. It was largely from this group of uprooted people that Muhammad started attracting followers. Very few of his adherents had a social standing in Mecca, and many of the city's leaders fought against him. Muhammad then moved his activities to Medina, where an Islamic society was established. A couple of years before his death, the people of Mecca became his followers too. When he died in 632 almost the whole Arab peninsula was united in one country based on affiliation to Islam. Since Muhammad's own life was associated with Mecca and Medina, these cities are of special significance to Muslims. Every year, millions of people make the pilgrimage (*hajj*) to present-day Saudi Arabia in order to visit them. With the old Meccan temple of Kaba as the ritual centre, a complex set of rites is performed by the pilgrims. There is, moreover, a Muslim tradition which says that Muhammad once made a nightly journey to Jerusalem. In that way, his deeds were connected to those of the old prophets. Mecca, Medina and Jerusalem are – in that order – the most important cities of Islam, although some theologians are critical of the veneration of Jerusalem.

Knowledge of Muhammad's life can be gained from a number of sources. Since the followers saw the Prophet as an ideal in all aspects of human life, they started recording those episodes that could in some way be used to regulate Islamic behaviour. As time went on, a vast number of brief stories about Muhammad's sayings and doings circulated among Muslims. In Arabic a report of this kind is called *hadith*. Eventually learned religious scholars made collections of stories which were considered authentic. On the basis of these collections they were able to depict the life of Muhammad and, as a consequence, the life of any righteous Muslim. This ideal is called *sunna* (custom, practice). Because only about 500 of the 6,000 verses in the Quran form a basis for laws about right and wrong, the most part of the legal regulations must be based on the Sunna. As a religious source of inspiration the Quran holds the central position, but as a source of law the Sunna is at least as important as the Quran.

Muslims often say that there is no distinction in Islam between doctrines and ethics. One cannot make a distinction between doctrine and pattern of life. Islam is a total way of life, often described with the Arabic term *tawhid*, which means oneness in several respects and concerns, above all, God Himself, who is One and Unique. This view of God, and the meaning of Islam, implies that one cannot distinguish between spiritual and non-spiritual, between religion and politics or between soul and body. Ideally, this means that a Muslim's whole life becomes a service of God, a 'worship'. The right worship is a life in Islam, and the guidelines for such a life are found in the Quran and Sunna.

Islamic law and organisation

As a historical religion Islam has, consequently, developed into a system of advice, commandments and prohibitions. This legal system is called the *sharia*. The Islamic law is based on the Quran and Sunna, but the principles of analogy and consensus (of the learned scholars), as well as new interpretations (*ijtihad*), have contributed to a great flexibility in terms of adjusting the regulations to new areas and periods of time. Although there are Muslims who argue that the 'gates of *ijtihad*' were closed about 1,000 years ago, the majority hold that new interpretations should be made.

During the first few centuries some so-called law schools or traditions developed. In part, these are based on various traditions of interpretation and have different 'founders'. The differences between them are, in general, fairly small, although they have been of some significance in terms of shaping the identity of Muslims in various parts of the world. The Maliki school is associated with Malik Ibn Abas, who died in 795, and predominates in North and West Africa. Abu Hanifa lived in Mesopotamia during the eighth century and became the originator of the Hanafi legal tradition. Most of its followers are found in Turkey, Central Asia and India. Al-Shafii worked in Egypt in the late eighth and early ninth centuries. His work was aimed at systematising the various methods for deriving new from old within Islamic jurisprudence and became the point of departure for the Shafii school of law, which is found mainly in East Africa and Southeast Asia. The fourth tradition is the one that differs most from the others. Its founder was Ahmad Ibn Hanbal, and his followers are found mainly on the Arabian peninsula. Outside the Arab world it has few adherents, but during several centuries reform movements calling for a return to the original Islam have been inspired by the Hanbali tradition. In that way its influence has spread far beyond the borders of the Arab peninsula.

There is no priesthood in Islam. The religious tradition is transmitted primarily by juridically and religiously trained scholars. A Muslim jurist is called *faqih* (plural *fuqaha*), and the activities of the *fuqaha* are called *fiqh*. Religiously learned scholars, who often also have a substantial knowledge of legal matters, are called *ulama* (singular *alim*, learned). The *ulama* can work at a university, a mosque or some other study centre. They have no special ritual functions in the mosque worship, even though, for example, they may preach at the main Friday service. With regard to their relationship to God, Muslims do not depend on the *ulama*. Each individual is directly answerable to God. Thus, there are no 'sacraments' that have to be administered by religious leaders.

All Muslims in the world belong to what they call *umma*, which may be translated as community or congregation. The *umma* has no decreed organisation. The learned scholars, *ulama* and *fuqaha*, are the most important 'functionaries' of Islam, but there is in principle no ordination for their roles and no hierarchy which gives one power over the other. In practice, certain local forms of organisation have developed, but there are few, if any, similarities to the strict hierarchy of, for example, the Catholic Church. Muhammad was an inspired preacher who received a number of revelations of a very practical kind. These contributed to the detailed regulation of organisational matters concerning, for instance, marriage, divorce and inheritance. The following of Islamic inheritance rules means that a deceased person's belongings are given to a considerable number of relatives. Thus, it has been difficult or impossible for individuals to accumulate great fortunes through inheritance. However, it has been possible for individuals or families to form a religious foundation (*waqf*). Many Muslim activities have been initiated and administered by such foundations. They can be involved in, for instance, education and health care, but they may also build mosques and shelters. This privately formed network of organisations has largely been able to function outside the control of religious leaders.

Theology of religion

The idea of Islam as the original and natural religion makes its relationship to other religions an inclusive one. What does it mean to be a Muslim? On the one hand, one can be a 'nominal' Muslim. There is no baptism in Islam, but it is commonly held that those who have said the creed in the presence of two witnesses have become Muslims. On the other hand, Muslim religious leaders may argue that it is possible to be a 'functional' Muslim despite nominal adherence to another religion. Following this line of thought, even a person who does not consider himself or herself to be religious at all may be regarded as a Muslim. When Muslims today discuss the difficulties of poor Muslim countries, they may say that the problem is the Muslims themselves: 'They are no longer Muslims'. Conversely, they may argue that a formally Christian European or American is 'a good Muslim'.

In all religions there may be people who live 'in Islam'. However, the religions of the so-called peoples of the Book are considered to be particularly close to Islam. As 'protected peoples' they should have the right to a considerable amount of independence in Islamic countries. First and foremost Jews and Christians, who received revelations from older prophets which are collected in books, belong to this category of peoples. When Muslims later encountered other believers with holy books, such as Zoroastrians in Iran, some of these were occasionally also included in the category of peoples of the book. By contrast, groups or individuals who have claimed to fulfil or supplement the revelations of the Quran have been strongly opposed by the vast majority of Muslims. Two examples of such movements are the Bahai of Iran and the Ahmadiyya of South Asia. At times they have been ruthlessly persecuted. There may have been several reasons for such persecutions, but the theological justification is that the revelation of Muhammad is complete and therefore cannot be supplemented.

Sunnites and Shiites

Muhammad managed to unite the Arab peninsula, but who should succeed him as the leader of this region after his death in 632? There was no revelation which made it clear how the *umma* should be lead or administered after that time. Eventually the struggle for power lead to the division of Muslims into two main groups, Sunnites and Shiites. The majority of Muslims favoured the appointment of the Prophet's father-in-law, Abu Bakr, as his successor (caliph). An opposing group argued that the rightful successor to Muhammad was his cousin and son-in-law, Ali. According to them, the Prophet had a unique position among human beings, and only those who were related to him could have the proper resources to succeed him. Those who favoured Ali may have had their own interests of power, and it is possible that they planned to take advantage of Ali's youth. When Muhammad died, Ali was only thirty years old. This was something held against him by his opponents.

Abu Bakr became the first caliph, and the supporters of Ali bided their time. When Abu Bakr died in 634, they had a new chance, but this time another of Muhammad's helpers, Umar, was elected. Following Umar's death ten years later, Ali was yet again passed over, and Uthman became the third caliph. It was not until the death of Uthman that Ali eventually became the prime leader of the Muslims. However, he had many enemies, especially among Uthman's relatives in the Umayyad family, and Ali was accused of being an accessory to the murder of the third caliph. In 657 Umayyad soldiers met Ali's supporters in the battlefield. Ali seemed to prevail over his enemies, but he accepted a cease-fire and arbitration. As a result, a large group of followers left Ali. These people, the Kharijites (seceders), formed their own congregation and exerted a considerable political influence during the first few centuries of Islam's history. According to the Kharijites, the prime leader of the Muslims should be the most pious person, regardless of descent. The leader must have the support of the congregation, and purity of life is the crucial test. The Umayyads continued to threaten Ali, and eventually he too was murdered. The leader of the Ummayads at that time (661), Muawiya, became the new caliph and established his headquarters in Damascus. The Shiites were now an opposition group lead by Ali's sons, first Hasan and later Husayn. In 680, Husayn's followers urged him to attack the new Umayyad caliph Yazid. Their forces met in the battlefield of Karbala, where the outnumbered army of Husayn suffered a devastating defeat. The battle of Karbala, and the idea of martyrdom associated with this struggle, have an immense significance in Shiite Islam. For many Shiites, Karbala is thus an even more important city than Mecca, Medina and Jerusalem.

The highest Shiite leader is called Imam. After the death of Husayn, his son became the fourth Imam; following whose death the Shiites split into two groups which supported different successors. The Zaydis, named after their candidate Zayd, were the minority group. However, at the end of the ninth century they managed to establish a Zaydi state in Yemen, which existed until 1963. After the death of the sixth Imam, Jafar al-Sadiq, in 765, another division occurred when a minority supported the elder son Ismail, while the majority held that Jafar al-Sadiq had designated his younger son, Musa al-Qazim, as his heir. The Ismaili Shiites later suffered further divisions. Some of the splinter groups still exist, while others have disappeared. A well-known branch of the Ismaili tree is the Nizaris (Khojas) led by the Aga Khan. The Druse are a non-Muslim offshot of

9

Ismailism. Theologically, Ismailis tend to be very eclectic, and their doctrines may deviate substantially from those of more orthodox forms of Sunni Islam. The largest group of Shiites, the followers of Musa al-Qasim and a series of subsequent Imams, are called Imamites or Twelvers. Their twelfth Imam, Muhammad al-Muntazar, disappeared or left the earth in the ninth century. The Twelvers believe that he went into seclusion but will return at the end of the world as a messianic figure, the Mahdi (expected one), and usher in the perfect society of Islam. In Iran, Imamite Shiism is now the politically established form of Islam. Ayatollah Khomeini (d. 1989) was called Imam, but in that case it was an honorific title. The returning Imam, the Mahdi, is still expected, and the Shiite leaders of Iran claim that their Islamic rule is paving the way for his reappearance.

The largest group of Muslims, who regarded the caliph as their prime leader, were called Sunnites. Among other things, this refers to their adherence to the *sunna* of the Prophet, which is considered more important than the leader's ties of consanguinity. The Shiites have always been a minority within Islam, usually between 10 and 15 per cent. Although the basic conflict has concerned the leadership question, other differences have also gradually developed, and Shiite Islam now differs in many respects from Sunnism. Since the Imams are conceived of as divinely inspired leaders, their interpretations and guidelines are of utmost importance. Ordinary Shiites can understand the exoteric aspects of the Quran, but the Imams have been entrusted with an additional esoteric message. Sunnites, who do not conceive of the caliphs in that way, emphasise more strongly the need for each Muslim to read the Quran and Sunna, the final revelations, in order to find out what is right and wrong.

In Shiite Islam, suffering and martyrdom is exalted as a duty and happiness. The prime model of Shiite suffering is the above-mentioned death of Husayn. The memory of Husayn's martyrdom at Karbala is recalled to mind every year through exquisite recitations, passion plays and street processions, which may include dramatic physical self-torment as the tragedy of Husayn is relived. Through ritual reenactment and identification with the experience of Husayn, Shiites seem to seek atonement for their sins and hasten the final triumph, which will be accomplished when the Mahdi returns. Somehow this hope for the future and the memories of the past may compensate for suffering here and now. In Shiite theology the view of man tends to be darker than in Sunnism. Shiites need their spiritual leaders for proper guidance, but their eschatology provides hope for a bright future.

The historical spread of Islam

The Islamic empire founded during the time of Muhammad proved to be militarily very strong. The powerful neighbouring countries Byzantium and Iran were soon defeated as were Egypt and Mesopotamia. One century after the death of Muhammad the caliphate covered a huge area from the Indus in the east to Spain in the west. Karl Martell's victory over the Muslims at Poitiers in 732 had a symbolic rather than a political significance, but it sealed the border of Muslim expansion in Western Europe.

As of 750 the caliph resided in Iraq, but as early as the ninth century he lost his real political power. Turkish military leaders and Iranian rulers became increasingly powerful. However, Islam thoroughly influenced Turkish and Persian culture. The Turks largely contributed to the further spread of Islam in Central Asia. In the thirteenth century Mongols invaded large areas with Muslim populations, but many of them soon converted to Islam. During the following centuries Islam spread further and further eastwards. The Shiite Safavid empire was established in the sixteenth century in Iran. The Mughul empire of South Asia was founded at the beginning of that century, and this region eventually became religiously divided, basically between Hindus and Muslims. The further spread of Islamic influence in South East Asia, mainly through trading activities, was a slow process. Now, in the late twentieth century, Islam is the politically dominant religion in Malaysia, and Indonesia has more Muslims than any other country. The most successful of the Turkish empires was the Ottoman empire, which was founded in the thirteenth century. It was the Ottomans who captured Constantinople in 1453, and conquered Egypt in 1516–17. The Ottoman sultan in Istanbul was called caliph at least from the eighteenth century until the caliphate was abolished in the early 1920s and a new secular Turkey was formed. Through Ottoman rule in the Balkan region, many people in those areas became Muslims. However, the Ottoman advance in Eastern Europe came to a halt when they were defeated at Vienna in 1683.

North Africa became a part of the Islamic empire early on. From the north, Berber and Arab merchants spread Islam in the Sudanic belt, and some kings in West Africa converted to Islam. Moreover, Islamic influence in Africa south of the Sahara spread from Egypt through traffic on the Nile and from the east towards the highlands of present-day Eritrea and Ethiopia. In East Africa, Arab traders established settlements along the coast and started intermarrying with Bantu women, eventually forming the eclectic Swahili culture. In most parts of sub-Saharan Africa, however, only very limited numbers of people converted to Islam before the modern period of European colonialism. Paradoxically, that period favoured the spread not only of Christianity but also of Islam.

Through the slave trade, some Muslims came to the Americas. In post-colonial decades, emigration from Islamic parts of the world has brought considerable numbers of Muslims to the Western world, particularly Europe. As immigrants, a limited number of Muslims also arrived in Australia, New Zealand and the South Pacific. In all these parts of the world only a few people have converted to Islam.

Sufism

In Western studies Sufism is often referred to as the mysticism of Islam, even though it involves much more than that. It has its roots in the earliest period of Islam, and grew gradually to become immensely important, especially in areas outside the Arab world. In the life of Muhammad, and particularly in his early message, there was an element of mysticism. He left for lonely places to pray and meditate, and as a prophet he had intense religious experiences. Sufis often refer to Muhammad, as well as to Jesus, as prime examples of mystical life. As a mystical movement, Sufism was also a reaction against the splendour and affluence that characterised the life of Muslim political and other leaders. The ideal of asceticism was an important aspect of early Sufism. Furthermore, Sufis were influenced by pious people in other religions, particularly Christians. Even some of the philosophical schools of late antiquity had elements of mysticism which influenced Sufi Muslims. During the earliest centuries of Islam, Sufi leaders frequently demanded a modest life style and stood up for 'spiritual' values. Their asceticism was combined with a strong trust in God (*tawakkul*). Love of God was the cardinal virtue, and could only be received as a gift. The Sufis turned against the predominant role of the jurists and wanted to replace obedience with love as the central aspect of people's relationship to God. Also, they tended to see sentiment as a more important religious element than reason.

The term Sufism is probably derived from the word *suf*, which refers to the simple wool garments worn by early ascetics. Although Christian monastery life was one of their sources of inspiration, Sufis did not live a celibate life. In the earliest period, they were not organised, but during the ninth century the communal aspects, in terms of spiritual exercises and religious discussions, became increasingly important. *Dhikr* (remembrance of God) seances, with repetition of God's names and passages from the Quran, litanies and deep meditation became characteristics of Sufi gatherings. Music and dance were important elements in these meetings. At the beginning they could take place anywhere, even in mosques, but gradually special buildings came to be used, and the Sufi gatherings became to some extent alternatives to the mosque services.

The rift between Sufism and 'official', or more orthodox, forms of Islam widened during the ninth century. Sufis established structures which resembled monasteries, and some of them withdrew from the world outside these compounds. The Shiite doctrine about the coming saviour of the world, the Mahdi, was incorporated even in the Sunni forms of Sufism. Sufi leaders walked about in towns and in the countryside, preaching and telling dramatic life stories, often influenced by other religions. In order to justify new elements in their message, they referred to *hadiths* which more orthodox religious leaders dismissed as spurious. Whole doctrinal systems soon developed within Sufism. By referring to these, Sufis defended themselves against accusations of religious anarchy. Spiritual life was regulated in detail, and Sufis passed through various stages towards greater closeness to God. In trance, some Sufis even identified themselves with God. Through the spiritual 'refinement', ideas of sainthood and veneration of saints became important elements within Sufism. In some respects, saints were regarded as even more important and holy than the prophets. Although Muhammad was the last prophet, that did not mean that an even greater saint could not appear later. There is a cosmic dimension of sainthood – the very existence of the world depends on the cosmic saint. Such a mysterious saint, who is called al-Khadir, is an invisible guardian saint who guides human beings to spiritual perfection.

As of the tenth century Sufism became more and more questioned by representatives of 'official' Islam. In 922, the Sufi al-Hallaj, who claimed some kind of mystical identification with God, was executed. Perhaps there were also political reasons for this execution. However, one branch of Sufism now came nearer to orthodox theology, and around 1100 a 'reconciliation' was brought about through the work of Abu Hamid al-Ghazali. He stressed the importance of mysticism for theology and created a synthesis which demarcated theology from philosophical speculations and mystical excesses. In that way one branch of Sufism became socially presentable, but – with a few exceptions – this also alienated the philosophically interested from theology. In other branches of Sufism, the influence of Gnostic, neo-Platonic and other philosophical currents continued to be important. In neo-Platonically inspired pantheistic Sufi speculations, a monistic view of reality developed. The strict cleavage between the Creator and the created was thus blurred, and it was argued that God is everything. The leading representative of this Sufi speculation was Ibn al-Arabi (d. 1240), who carried the monistic pantheism to its extreme. This form of Sufism became increasingly exclusive and lost its popular support, although its theological contents could be used to legitimise several traits in popular Sufism. Since there was a divine presence in the creation, things like music, dance, wine and sexuality could offer attractive ways to contact with God. In poetry and preaching such worldly pleasures were given a prominent place; and since nothing human could be completely void of divine contents, ideas from other religions were incorporated and regarded as expressions of Islam.

The twelfth century was important not only because of al-Ghazali's legitimation of certain forms of Sufism but also because of the formation of the first great Sufi orders or brotherhoods, *turuq* (singular *tariqa*, method, path), lead by spiritual masters or *shaykhs*. Sufism thus became transformed from loose associations to well-organised, distinctive institutions, which by the thirteenth century created international networks developing Sufism into a popular mass movement whose preachers became the great missionaries of Islam. The source of a *shaykh's* authority was spiritual reputation, lineage connections with predecessors and miraculous powers. A special blessing (*baraka*) was the product of their spiritual power. In Asia as well as in Africa the orders were influenced by other religions as they spread further and further away from their places of origin, and new orders or new branches of old orders were formed. Islam thus became more and more varied and complex. Increasingly, the orders also became socially and politically important, particularly during periods of unrest and oppression. As resistance organisations they fought against unfair treatment and exploitation of sultans and other rulers. Official Islam, lead by *ulama*, was in general closer to the representatives of political power, while popular protests could be chanelled through Sufism. Hence, the orders sometimes had the function of socio-political interest organisations or liberation movements, and the spreading of information, propaganda and plans for actions against various regimes could be a part of 'religious' gatherings. It must not be forgotten, however, that there are also examples of Sufi leaders and orders that have been closely allied to political rulers.

A Sufi master or *shaykh* was called *pir* in Persia and South Asia and *marabout* in North and West Africa, while a disciple could be referred to as *murid*, *dervish* or *faqir*. The whole Sufi community was often called *ikhwan* (brothers). Normally, there were two kinds of members. The inner circle lived in the compound or headquarters (*zawiya*, Persian *khanqah*), where the master usually lived too, while the outer circle lived elsewhere and met the *shaykh* more rarely. An order or *tariqa* is made up of several *zawiyas*. The brotherhoods are usually named after their founders. The oldest and most widespread of all Sufi orders is the Qadiriyya, whose founder was Abd al-Qadir al-Jilani (d. 1166). This *tariqa* was formed in Baghdad but has spread to virtually all parts of the Muslim world. In most places the Qadiri order is fairly close to more orthodox forms of Islam and opposed to popular excesses. It is now divided into several branches.

The oldest of the Turkic orders is the Yasaviyya, founded by Ahmad Yasavi in the twelfth century. It has been influenced by a number of Asiatic religious traditions of a shamanistic kind. Another eclectic order is the Bektashiyya, an early offshoot of the Yasaviyya, which is influenced by Shiite and Christian ideas. These orders are unusual in that women are strongly involved. The Naqshbandi *tariqa*, now one of the most widespread and important orders, was founded in the fourteenth century in Bukhara by Baha al-Din, called Naqshband, the painter. He was given the name Naqshband because he used to 'paint spiritual pictures in the heart'. His disciples do the same by silently reading certain words in the *dhikr* seance. Although there are some connections between the Naqshbandiyya and the Bektashiyya, they constitute separate orders. The Naqshbandi brotherhood is younger and a good deal closer to orthodox Islam. It has been successful particularly in Central and South Asia but more recently also in the West. Its best-known member in South Asia was the reformer Ahmad Sirhindi,

The *mazar* (tomb) of Muin al-Din Chisti, the founder of the Chisti brotherhood, at his shrine centre in Ajmer, India (photo: Ron Geaves, 1998).

who in the seventeenth century worked for the purification of Islam from pantheism and other elements derived from contacts with Hindus and the teachings of al-Arabi. In Sirhindi's view, Islam and Hinduism were mutually exclusive. The best-known among the primarily urban-based orders in Turkey is the Mawlawi, organised by the poet Jalal al-Din Rumi in the thirteenth century. Rumi's poetic work *Mathnawi* has been enourmously important and has been referred to as 'the Quran of Sufism'. Because of their whirling dance, the Mawlawis have been called 'the dancing dervishes'. They are found mainly in Turkey and other parts of the Middle East. In South Asia, not only the Qadiriyya and the Naqshbandiyya but also the Chistiyya play a particularly significant role. The Chisti order was founded in the thirteenth century by Muin al-Din Chisti, whose grave in Ajmer is an important pilgrimage centre. During the time of the great Mughul emperor Akbar (d. 1605) the Chistiyya flourished, and after a period of decay, it was reorganised in the nineteenth century by Kwaja Nur Muhammad and became again an influential part of South Asian Islam.

In Africa the Qadiri order has been, and still is, particularly strong. Less widespread in Africa is another order of Asian origin, the Shadhili *tariqa*, which was founded by Abu al-Hasan al-Shadhili, who lived in the thirteenth century and was strongly influenced by al-Ghazali. The now most widespread order formed in Africa is the Tijani, which was founded by Ahmad al-Tijani in Fez in the late eighteenth century. He held that good deeds are the most important form of divine service. The Tijanis thus tend to engage intensively in social activities of various kinds. In general, Sufi orders in Africa have been strongly influenced by indigenous African religions. Here, as elsewhere, their openness and flexibility have facilitated the mission work.

Through conquests and immigration, Sufi orders came to Europe. For instance, during the period of Ottoman rule in the Balkan region, several Sufi orders, notably the Bektashi, were introduced. In recent decades several Sufi orders have come with Muslim immigrants to the West. The Naqshbandi, for instance, is widely spread and has also been fairly successful in terms of converting Westerners to Islam. Among Western converts to Islam, intellectuals who have been attracted by Sufism are an important group. Their form of Sufism is often not tied to specific orders. A more general form of Sufism, to some extent connected to the New Age movement, is nowadays preached by Sufi missionaries such as Fadhlalla Haeri and the British convert Reshad Feild. In their work, Sufi preachers and organisations, as well as other Muslim leaders and associations, increasingly make use of the modern medium of the Internet.

Islamic culture

During its first few centuries Islam spread in regions with age-old cultures such as Egypt and Mesopotamia. When the caliph was installed in Baghdad (probably in 763), this city developed into the leading centre of Islamic culture. Since the tenth century, a competing caliph was based in Cordoba, but there was a lively cultural exchange between these centres. The Spanish–Arabic culture created buildings, adorned with arabesques, of lasting beauty. Architecture was the most encouraged art form.

Muslim scholars in Baghdad endeavoured to assimilate all available scholarly knowledge. The most important source of inspiration was classical Greek philosophy. Greece had been devastated by the Goths, but Greek scholarly works had been brought to Egypt and later translated into Syrian. In Baghdad such works were translated into Arabic. In Spain, Jewish and Christian scholars cooperated with Muslim academics in order to transfer as much knowledge as possible into this language. Not all scholars in Baghdad were Arab, but Arabic was the learned language until it was superseded by Persian around 1000. Here great works in for instance astronomy, medicine and mathematics were produced. The development of mathematics was influenced by scholarly discoveries in India. During the twelfth century, centres for translations from Arabic into Latin were established in Spain and Sicily. Around 1200 the Greek and Arabic achievements of science were thus available in the learned language of

Europe. This initiated a development that would not have been possible without the Muslim scholarly activities.

Muslims were not only interested in the natural sciences but studied language, history and religion too. Even music eventually developed despite the early lack of interest among more orthodox Muslims. Artisan products like carpets and metallic vessels were produced with great dexterity. A particularly important field of interest was law. The judicature was combined with a development of theology and politics. Islamic scholars thus studied statecraft, historical theories and economics. During the fourteenth century, however, Muslim scholarly and cultural creative power petered out and did not return until about half a millennium later. When Europeans met Islam in the modern colonial period it seemed to be inimical to culture and to have a retraining effect on scholarly work. Yet Muslims themselves are well aware of the glorious scholarly and cultural achievements of earlier Islamic periods, as well as their significance as a basis for the later development of science and culture in the West, which eventually gave Westerners a sense of superiority to, and contempt for, Islam.

Women

The Arabic culture in which Muhammad grew up was patriarchal, and Islam later spread in areas with predominantly patriarchal traditions. Hence, there has been a tendency to regard it as a religion that is particularly hostile to women. However, most other religions, including Judaism and Christianity, also have their roots in patriarchal cultures. In the normative Muslim texts, the Quran and the Sunna, there are certain parts that seem to discriminate against women but there are others that place all human beings on an equal footing. Many *hadiths* stress the decisive role of women as mothers. The pre-Muslim tradition of killing some newborn girls was outlawed by the Quran. Because many men died in the battlefields, it is possible that the (restricted) Islamic acceptance of polygyny was partly caused by the resulting surplus of women. The Quran states, however, that complete impartiality is a condition for polygyny. Since the Quran also says that only God is completely just, or impartial, it is frequently argued that implicitly the Quran forbids polygyny. Nowadays many Muslims are actively opposed to it. Those who defend it may argue that in exceptional cases it can give women and children the protection of living in a family.

In terms of, for instance, divorce and inheritance men and women are not treated equally in Islamic law. In practice, however, local traditions have tended to be more important for regulating the relations between the sexes than have the official regulations of the *sharia*. In some areas this may prove advantageous and in other areas disadvantageous to women. In a few regions, mainly of Northeast Africa, female 'circumcision' is practised by

Muslims. Essentially, however, it is a pre-Islamic custom which is practised not only by Muslims but also by Christians and adherents of indigenous African religions. It is difficult to defend by reference to the Sunna, and in most parts of the Muslim world it is not considered to be a part of the *sharia*. On the contrary, it is condemned by most Muslims of the world.

Today there is an intense debate about the position of women. In particular, Muslim feminists fight for a thorough implementation of the ideals of equality. Although there is general agreement that men and women are equal, the interpretations of the consequences of this principle differ. As in the West, some argue that equality means the right of women to be different from men in terms of, for instance, occupations and position in society, while others disagree. Many men obviously try to protect their own privileges. Women's issues have been interlaced with a wider discussion of, and opposition to, Western influences. Some argue that the changing roles of women in the West have lead to increasing promiscuity and a crisis in family life. In their view, traditional Islamic family values safeguard against such developments. Among Muslim feminists, some are influenced by various Western feminist thoughts and practices, while others champion more specifically Islamic solutions to the problems of gender inequality. Today there are many Islamist feminists who support their views on equality between the sexes by referring to certain passages in the Quran and Sunna. In general, it should be stressed that, both in terms of ideas and of practices, the varieties are so great that it is grossly misleading to speak about 'the role of the woman in Islam'. Like other world religions, Islam has been utilised to legitimise a wide variety of ideals concerning women, sexuality and family life.

Reform movements

The relationships between Christians in the West and Muslims have largely been hostile, and Western pictures of Islam have for propaganda purposes been darkly painted. During the colonial era, Muslim contacts with Westerners were intensified. At that time an incressingly gloomy picture of Islam as an oppressive religion and culture, which was inimical to culture and hindered or at least retarded development, legitimised the white man's 'responsibility' to administer Muslim regions. Among Muslims who cooperated with the purpose of opposing colonial rule Islam frequently became an ideological tool. When Europeans accused Islam of hindering modern development, Muslims increasingly responded that this was because of the degeneration of Islam caused by the influence of Sufism. A 'purified' Islam would be the strongest shield against Western imperialism.

Some Muslims who were inspired by the West abandoned Islam, but the majority of 'modernisers' opted for a reform of their religion. The complex

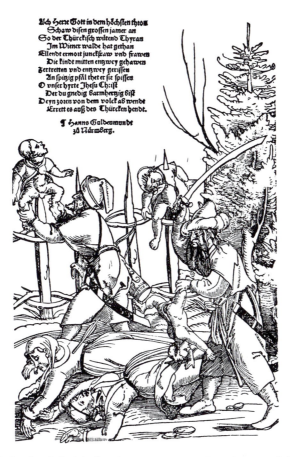

'The wicked deeds of the Turks'. In Europe negative views on Muslims have dominated throughout the centuries, as exemplified by this German propaganda leaflet from the sixteenth century.

and fixed legal tradition had to be re-examined in the light of new circumstances and through a rereading of the main sources, the Quran and the Sunna. During the nineteenth century a number of reform movements thus emerged in the Muslim world. One of the best-known examples is the Salafiyya of North Africa, founded by Muhammad Abduh (d. 1905) and others, which strongly influenced the development of anti-colonialism there and elsewhere. Abduh and other reformers such as Jamal al-Din al-Afghani (d. 1897) who lived in several parts of the Muslim and Western world accused more conservative or traditional Muslims of betraying Islam. By using the principle of *ijtihad*, old ideas and practices were reformed. In some cases the influence of Western models was more conspicuous than in others. When Muslim countries became independent in the mid twentieth century, many new regimes were controlled by reformist-oriented Muslims who tried to balance the Islamic heritage and new Western influences. In many countries Islamic socialism became the ideological guiding rule. This idealistic form of socialism is said to be based on Islamic values and principles, but secular legislation is largely accepted.

The more recent development of Islamism, or 'Islamic fundamentalism', may partly be seen as a reaction to the failures of Islamic socialism. In the West, the term Islamic fundamentalism became particularly topical in connection with the Iranian revolution in 1979, and at least in mass media it is still a popular concept. One reason for its popularity is that it is a derogatory term. It is accusatory rather than descriptive. Besides, Islamic fundamentalism has little in common with the proper fundamentalism which was formed among American Protestant Christians in the early twentieth century. In Muslim contexts, Islamism is a more appropriate term. At least partly it is a self-designation, and it emphasises the use of Islam as an ideology. The Islamist goal is that Islam and its revealed law, the *sharia*, shall permeate the whole society as well as the lives of individuals. In that way a just society is created. By utilising the principle of *ijtihad*, Islamists interpret Islam in the context of the modern situation. Historical examples can be important sources of inspiration, but the purpose is not to recreate old forms of Islam. Many Islamists are well-educated, often in the natural sciences, and they react not only against the Western tendency to privatise religion but also against the 'conservatism' of Sufism. In all respects – religious, political, economical, social, moral and cultural – they aim at a renewal and work out Islamic programmes for changing existing conditions. In a sense, thus, Islamism may be seen as a Muslim modernisation project.

In Western analyses of the rise of Islamism it is largely interpreted as a result of growing economic and social problems. However, this focus on negative factors needs to be supplemented by a study of the activities of the Islamists themselves. Why have Muslims increasingly chosen Islamism, rather than some other ideology, as their tool for expressing opposition against various regimes? One of the factors that have attracted people is the development effort of Islamists. While awaiting the foundation of Islamic states they build Islamic societies, and their activities in the fields of, for instance, education and health care have a modern character. The combination of modernisation efforts and the strong emphasis on the Islamic cultural and religious heritage attracts many Muslims at a time when the critique of what is seen as Western cultural imperialism and economic exploitation increases. When, due to economic and other problems, state welfare systems are facing serious problems, private initiatives become particularly important. The Islamist development work may be compared to the similar and long-standing work of Christian

A fast food restaurant in Kuala Lumpur, Malaysia, serving *halal* meat (photo: Ingvar Svanberg, 1989).

mission organisations, which has contributed to attracting new followers. To some extent Islamists are supported by petrodollars, especially the moderate wing, but the work is largely voluntary.

Another important aspect of the growth of Islamism is the modern organisations. New Islamist local, national and international organisations have mushroomed in virtually all parts of the Muslim world. Ironically, the rise of new 'religious' organisations is partly an effect of the Western secular influence, the separation between state and religion. There is also a Western influence in the way that Islamist associations are constructed. Unlike Sufi orders, with their more hierarchic and hereditary leadership, Islamist organisations usually have proper constitutions and elected leaders. In many Muslim countries, even where multi-party systems have been introduced, it is illegal to form political parties based on religion. However, as the example of the National Islamic Front, the political arm of the important Islamist organisation the Muslim Brotherhood (al-Ikhwan al-Muslimun) in Sudan, indicates, Islamist 'religious' associations may fairly easily be transformed into political parties should the opportunity arise. In general, Islamist organisations tend to be stronger on local and national than on international levels. However, the Muslim Brotherhood is an association which is spread throughout many Muslim countries. Besides, the leading spokesperson for the Muslim Brotherhood in Sudan, Hasan al-Turabi, one of the most influential theorists in the Islamist movement, has tried to increase the organised international cooperation between Islamists from various countries by establishing the Pan Arab and Islamic Conference (PAIC). This new international Islamist association is intended to be an Islamist oppositional counterpart to the Organisation of the Islamic Conference (OIC), which is an official 'commonwealth organisation' for the Muslim world.

The growth of Islamism is in a way associated with improved educational standards. In general, post-colonial regimes in Muslim countries have devoted much attention to the construction of a modern school system. A great interest in modern education, though more inspired by Islamic ideas, is also a characteristic of Islamist organisations. Their members fight against what they may call *neo-jahiliyya* – the new ignorance – which is actually worse than the ignorance that characterised pre-Islamic Arabia before Muhammad appeared because the Quran and Sunna, the revealed sources of enlightenment, are now available. Islamists argue that the governmental school systems are too one-sidedly focused on secular subjects, whereas Sufi Muslims are criticised for their trust in the spiritual power of their *shaykhs* and failure to learn classical Arabic which makes it impossible for them to study the Quran and Sunna in the language in which they were revealed. Many Islamists and other students from non-Arab countries study in Arab countries. Such studies, as well as international activities such as conferences and distribution of literature, improve the level of knowledge and often strengthen the Islamic orientation.

Islam's revitalisation has much to do with its potential for opposition against the state. It provides a political language, and its symbolic arsenal is available to all. In a sense, the current Islamist revival is nothing new. Movements of a similar kind have reappeared time and again like waves of history. One particularly important example is the Wahhabi movement, established by Muhammad Ibn al-Wahhab in the eighteenth century, which has influenced many modern groups of Islamists. It is hardly a coincidence that Islamist groups are particularly strong in countries such as Sudan and Nigeria, where mythicised reform movements and Islamic states in the past are important sources of inspiration for contemporary organisations. First and foremost, it is in Arab countries, where Islam is deeply rooted and the population most homogeneously Muslim, that Islamist groups gain wide support. Although the leaders of such groups frequently come from a middle class background, their message also appeals to followers in poorer social strata.

The growth of Islamism has attracted a great deal of attention among scholars and media, whereas other contemporary Muslim movements have been more overlooked. However, it should be emphasised that Islamism is only one, albeit a very important one, of several political forces in countries with a predominantly Muslim population. Although secularisation is weaker here than in the West, leaders who oppose the Islamist tendencies and favour a *status quo*, that is, a distinct separation of religion and state, are usually still in power. With the main exceptions of Iran and Sudan, Islamists thus form opposition groups. Moreover, support from economically strong Western countries favours political leaders who oppose Islamists, with varying degrees of severity. Time will show if the current Islamic wave has reached its peak or whether more modern Islamic states will be founded.

Africa

It is difficult to assess the number of Muslims in Africa. For political reasons, official statistics on religious affiliation is nowadays often forbidden. However, it is likely that almost half of the continent's appoximately 700 million people are Muslims. The number of Christians about equals that of Muslims, and there is in many areas an intense struggle between Christian and Muslim missionaries to convert those people who are still adherents of indigenous African religions. Such people are found mainly in certain parts of West and Central Africa. Some African peoples have proved quite 'resistant' to both Muslim and Christian attempts to convert them, but normally the conversion process is very rapid. In North Africa, as in Somalia and Mauretania, almost 100 per cent of the population is Muslim. Egypt has a Christian minority of at least 5 per cent. In West Africa, countries such as Senegal, Guinea, Mali and Niger are predominantly Muslim. The number of Muslims in Nigeria, with almost 100 million people the most populous country of Africa, is about 50 per cent. At least two thirds of Sudan's population are Muslims, while one third of Ethiopia's population is Muslim. Tanzania is exceptional in East Africa in that almost half the population is Muslim. In other parts of East Africa, as well as in Central and southern Africa, where Christianity is the predominant religion, Muslims form more or less substantial minorities. In these parts of Africa, the Muslim presence is particularly noticeable in Malawi and Mozambique.

The rapid spread of Islam during the modern colonial era was caused partly by improved communications, urbanisation and economic change. Sufi Muslims in particular were actively involved in missionary work. The European colonial reactions to Muslims varied from vigorous opposition to pragmatic cooperation. The colonial use of literate Muslims for local administration sometimes contributed to the consolidation and spread of Islam. One example of cooperation between colonisers and Muslims is the close contacts between the British and the emirs of northern Nigeria, which is depicted in the chapter by Christopher Steed and David Westerlund. The attitudes of Muslims towards the colonisers also varied a great deal. Some cooperated and took advantage of colonial rule. Unlike Christianity, however, which was largely associated with the colonial powers, Islam frequently became a religion of resistance, although open revolts were rare.

The traditional split between Sunnites and Shiites is not very conspicuous in Africa. Here the vast majority of people are Sunnites, although Shiites in earlier periods have been strong in some parts of North Africa. Particularly in Africa south of the Sahara the Shiites are normally only tiny minorities. Many of the West African Shiites have a West Asian origin, while most of the Shiites in East and southern Africa have their roots in South Asia. The Ahmadiyya have had some success, especially in West Africa, but their numbers are very limited. The great variety of Islam in Africa has above all been caused by the strength of Sufism and its ability to adapt to various local traditions. In, for example, the contribution by Bernhard Helander on Somalia there is a detailed account of the local character of Sufi Islam. Almost everywhere in Africa south of the Sahara, Sufism is the predominant form of Islam, and the Sufi orders contain virtually every kind of local variation. Even in South Africa, which is sometimes referred to as an example of a fairly strong orthodox Muslim presence in Africa, there is a considerable number of Sufi Muslims, possibly more than half of the population. An account of Islam in South Africa and some neighbouring countries is provided in the chapter by Abdulkader Tayob.

The Qadiri order is found in virtually all parts of Muslim Africa, whereas Tijanis live primarily in North and West Africa. In addition to these widely spread orders, which are divided into several sub-orders, there are other, more locally restricted orders, such as the Askariyya, which is mentioned in the contribution on Tanzania by Abdulaziz Lodhi and David Westerlund. The Mouridiyya in Senegal have many followers, but they are basically restricted to that country and to the Wolof people. Mouridism contrasts sharply with, for instance, the reformed branch of the Tijaniyya, founded by the Senegalese *shaykh* Ibrahim Niass, which has a much stronger international and pan-Islamic character. The chapter on Senegal, by Eva Evers Rosander and David Westerlund, provides another detailed account of Sufism, in this case particularly of the religious and political as well as social and economic significance of the Mouridiyya. Senegalese Islam is very strongly influenced by the Sufi orders. However, all the chapters on African countries illustrate the great importance of Sufism in this part of the world. Like other chapters in the book, they also show that Sufism involves much more than just 'mysticism'.

The new Islamist organisations are stronger in the homogeneously Muslim North Africa than in the religiously more diverse Africa south of the Sahara. In the latter part of the continent the message of the Islamists is often branded as 'foreign' or 'Arab', and here the Islamist groups are usually quite small. Even if the rise of Islamism has weakened Sufism in several areas, it is still strong enough to counteract efficiently the Islamist challenge, which in certain respects comes hand-in-hand with Arabisation

The old central mosque in Dakar, Senegal, which is controlled by the Tijani brotherhood (photo: Roman Loimeier, 1991).

tendencies. In some parts of sub-Saharan Africa there are strong memories not only of Western colonialism but also of the Arab slave trade which dampens any enthusiasm for the more 'Arab' forms of Islam. Furthermore, in markedly multi-religious contexts it is difficult to work for an Islamisation of the state. Lately the Sufi *shaykhs*, who have traditionally had their strongholds in the countryside, have developed their activites in the rapidly growing urban areas, where the Islamists have been most successful. In their competition with Islamists, the *shaykhs* also increase their efforts to provide, for instance, modern education and health care.

Nigeria is exceptional in sub-Saharan Africa in that more orthodox forms of Islam are fairly strong there. The background for the relatively strong orthodox traditions, especially the significance of the Sokoto caliphate, is described in the chapter on Nigeria. In Sudan, which is in the border area between the Arab and the non-Arab world, an Islamisation policy during the 1980s culminated after the military assumption of power in 1989. Here the Islamist Muslim Brotherhood has exerted great influence. However, certain Islamist tendencies have also been noticeable within the Ansar and the Khatmiyya, the two predominant Sufi orders in Sudan, showing that the borderline between Sufism and Islamism need not be that distinct. Like Nigeria, Sudan has an 'Islamist heritage', and the Ansar order is the heir to the Mahdist state that was formed at the end of the nineteenth century. In Somalia, Senegal and Tanzania the Islamist tendencies are clearly weaker than in Nigeria and Sudan. Zanzibar is to some extent an exception. Its population is virtually 100 per cent Muslim, and the Islamic roots and Arab contacts are old ones. In Central Africa, the small minority groups of Muslims have not shown much interest in the Islamist movement. In South Africa, where Muslims in general are more highly educated, its effects are felt more strongly, although Islamist associations such as the Iran-inspired Qiblah and the more Saudi-oriented Muslim Youth Movement are relatively small minorities here too.

Asia and Oceania

During the nineteenth century the Ottoman empire, which at its peak included most parts of North Africa, West Asia and the Balkan Peninsula, was divided into a number of nation states in which Christian minorities in particular redefined their identities in a spirit of nationalism. When the secular republic of Turkey was born in the 1920s, it included Anatolia and a small part of the Balkan Peninsula and became a geographical and cultural bridge between East and West, connecting Europe and Asia. The idea of nation-building in Turkey has been to replace Islam with Turkish nationalism as the integrative force. In a contribution by Svante Cornell and Ingvar Svanberg the survival of Islam in secular Turkey is discussed. The development since the 1980s has given religion a certain political role, and Turkey may function as a bridge between, on the one hand, the Islamic countries of the Middle East and, in particular, Central Asia and, on the other hand, the secular countries of the West. By and large the project of constructing a Turkish identity has succeeded in the western parts of the country, but in the eastern parts the Kurds fight for a national identity of their own and the foundation of an independent Kurdistan. Kurds are found in northern Iraq, northwestern Iran and as a small enclave in Syria too, where they oppose Arab supremacy.

During the sixteenth century Iran appeared as a regional super power with Shia Islam as its state religion. The Imamite form of Shiism is inseparably linked to the modern history of Iran. In the chapter by Bo Utas the case of Iran as well as of its neighbouring countries Afghanistan and Tajikistan, whose history partly coincides with the history of Iran, is studied. However, while Iran is dominated by Shiites, most inhabitants of Afghanistan and Tajikistan are Sunnites. The integrative significance of Sunni Islam was an important asset during the long war against the Soviet Union. The recent formation of several new states in Central Asia brings the role of Islam in nation-building to the fore. In the Turkic-speaking republics of Kazakstan, Kirghizstan and Uzbekistan, Islam has been used to strengthen and consolidate the national identity in opposition to Russians and others who nowadays are often regarded as strangers and intruders. In current views of history, Islam is a part of a process of creating a national identity. What role Islam may play in debates about domestic and foreign policies is dicussed in the chapter on Turkic Central Asia by Roberta Micallef and Ingvar Svanberg. Particularly for politicians in Kazachstan, where only about half of the population is Muslim, the issue of national identity may turn out to be crucial.

For a long time the Muslim population of China has been quite unknown outside this country, although they number at least 18 million. Islam has been an integrated part of China for more than 1,000 years. The Muslim religion reached China along the so-called silk road through Central Asia. The gaining of independence by the Central Asian republics in the early 1990s created a new uncertainty in China, where there is a fear that Chinese Muslims may become inspired by their fellow Muslims across the border. However, the majority of the Chinese Muslims are Hui who, in terms of language and culture, are very closely related to the Han majority of China. The Hui population is spread throughout China and has no territorial demands. Besides, some of the Chinese Muslim groups, like those in Shanghai and in Tainan on Taiwan, are quite isolated from the wider Muslim world, and their Islam is strongly influenced by non-Islamic ideas and practices. Nevertheless, the Islamic consciousness among China's Muslims has increased in recent years, partly because of improved contacts with Muslims outside China and partly due to the activities of some Sufi orders. The complexity of the Muslim presence in China is presented in this book by Justin Ben-Adam.

South Asia has played an important role in the development of Islam. During the modern period of European colonialism Muslims and Hindus had a common enemy in Great Britain, and they were united in the Sepoys revolt in 1857. Later on, however, Muslims and Hindus became divided in the nationalist struggle, and eventually the former created a new state in the Muslim-dominated parts of the north. Many Hindus therefore left West Pakistan, fleeing to India, while millions of Muslims fled in the other direction. Yet a substantial minority of Muslims (about 10 per cent) remained in India. A very large part of the world's more than 1 billion Muslims are found in South Asia, notably in Pakistan, Bangladesh and

India. In terms of population, Pakistan is, with about 100 million Muslims, the second largest Muslim country, after Indonesia, whereas Bangladesh with 94 million is the third. Ever since the time of independence Islam has continued to play an important role in the political development of South Asia, and due to Islamist as well as anti-secularist Hindu movements its significance has increased in recent years. In the longest essay of this book, which includes sections on Sri Lanka and the Maldives, Ishtiaq Ahmed provides a detailed account of the development and present role of Islam in South Asia.

In South East Asia adherents of indigenous religions, Buddhism, Islam, Christianity, Hinduism and Chinese religions meet each other. On the Mindanao island of the Philippines, Muslims have fought a war of liberation against the Catholic-dominated central government. Demands for independence have also been voiced by Muslims in southern Thailand. In Vietnam and Cambodia the Muslim minorities have been openly oppressed. The strongest Muslim presence in South East Asia is found in Malaysia and Indonesia, which have many similarities in terms of language and culture. The character and role of Islam in these two countries is discussed in a contribution by Sven Cederroth. For those who tend to identify Islam with the Arab world the encounter with Islam in Indonesia provides a particularly useful corrective. As in Africa south of the Sahara, for instance, Islam in Indonesia is largely characterised by local traits and is not a state religion. In Malaysia, by contrast, Islam is the state-established religion, and the Muslims, who constitute half of the population, are given certain advantages over the Chinese.

Further south, in Australia and New Zealand as well as on some of the South Sea Islands, notably Fiji, Muslims constitute small or even tiny minorities. An account of the arrival of Muslim immigrants and their contemporary situation in Australia and New Zealand is provided in the chapter by Michael Humphrey and William Shepard. The Muslim interaction with the majority population is gradually increasing. Thus, they tend to move from being Muslims 'in' Australia and New Zealand to becoming Muslims 'of' these countries. A similar process can be observed in several Western countries.

Europe and the Americas

Due to immigration of workers and refugees from the so-called Third World, Europe now has a substantial number of Muslims. However, Islam is not a new religion in this part of the world. The Ottoman Muslim presence on the Balkan Peninsula as well as the Arab Muslim presence on the Iberian Peninsula have already been mentioned. Besides, mosques from the Ottoman period have been found in southern Hungary, and there was an early Muslim presence in what is now southern Italy. In Eastern Europe

The mosque in Christchurch, New Zealand (photo: William Shepard, 1985).

Islam has existed since the tenth century when it reached the Volga area, and the town Ufa in present-day Bashkortostan in Russia is still an important Islamic centre. In the tsarist empire Muslims, who were mainly merchants, artisans and soldiers, were spread over most parts of Russia. In those areas of the empire that eventually became Lithuania and Poland, Muslims are still found whose traditions there are several centuries old. The impressive new mosque in Warsaw is a sign of the increased significance of the Muslim presence in contemporary Poland. Despite the emergence of new states in Central Asia, which were previously parts of the Soviet Union, there are still significant numbers of Muslims in Russia. In this book an account of Islam in this country is given in a contribution by Svante Cornell and Ingvar Svanberg.

Muslims are found in all the Balkan states, first and foremost in Albania and Bosnia and Herzegovina but also, as substantial minorities, in southern Serbia and Kosovo, Macedonia, Bulgaria and Greece. The predominant languages used by Muslims in these areas are Slavonic, Turkish and Albanian. Due to the recent devastating war in Bosnia and Herzegovina, there is now a greater international awareness of the situation of the Serbo-Kroatian Muslims in former Yugoslavia. In his chapter on Bosnia and Herzegovina, Kjell Magnusson shows how the Islamic identity after the

Second World War developed into a national identity, which was strengthened during the troubled period of the 1990s. In addition to the human suffering caused by the war, a great number of old mosques and other Muslim buildings, as well as churches, were destroyed.

In Western Europe the strongest Islamic presence is felt in France, where the Muslims number some 3 million. France also probably has the largest number of converts. Here, as elsewhere in Europe, however, the great majority of the Muslims are immigrants or children of immigrants, in this case primarily from the former French colonies of North Africa, particularly Algeria. The complexity of the Muslim situation in France is discussed in the chapter by Neal Robinson. Germany is another country with a substantial Muslim minority. After the Second World War many Muslim workers arrived, in particular from Turkey and North Africa. Some Turkish Islamist and traditionalist movements, which have been forbidden in Turkey, have had an opportunity to develop and attract followers in Germany. For instance, the Nurculuk and the Süleymanli movements, as well as Milli Görüş, have their European centres in Germany, even though they are also represented in most of the other nations of Western Europe too. An account of Islam in Germany, and the small Muslim minority in neighbouring Austria, is found in the chapter by Franz Kogelmann.

In Great Britain the heated discussions about Salman Rushdie's book *The Satanic Verses* in the late 1980s and early 90s contributed to the fairly high political profile of Muslims in this country. Muslims in Britain struggle, among other things, for Islamic schools and against racism. A radical Islamist position was represented by the Iran-inspired Kalim Siddiqui (d. 1996), who, in 1992, founded the Muslim parliament in London. Most of the Muslims in Great Britain came originally from former British colonies in South Asia and East Africa. Because of its colonial past Great Britain, like France, has old ties to Muslim cultures and societies, and the history of Islam is older in Britain than in other countries of Western Europe. The history and present conditions of Muslims in Great Britain is discussed in the contribution by Ron Geaves.

In the Nordic countries the Muslim presence is not as strong as in France, Germany and Great Britain. The Muslim minorities of Denmark and Sweden are composed of people from several different countries, notably Turkey, Iran and Bosnia. In Norway, Muslims with a Pakistani background are predominant. As early as 1925 a mosque, still used for religious purposes today, was built by Tatars in Finland's capital Helsinki. In Finland the Tataric minority now numbers about 1,000 people. Among other things, the recent immigration of refugees to the Nordic countries has contributed to an intensified debate about Islam. However, much of the discussion concerns an imaginary Islam created by mass media rather than the real Islam of present-day Muslims in the Nordic countries. The book's chapter on this part of Europe is written by Ingvar Svanberg.

The mosque in Malmö, Sweden (photo: David Thurfjell, 1998).

Islam came to the Americas with the slaves from Africa and with immigrants from various Muslim parts of the world. In North America almost half of the Muslims, presented by Mattias Gardell, are African Americans. In the United States the Nation of Islam, lead by Louis Farrakhan, has become a particularly important but also controversial element. The conversion of a number of well-known sportsmen and musicians has contributed to the publicity of this organisation, which has an interesting role in discussions about African American identity. Now there are – largely unknown – Muslim minorities dispersed in Caribbean and Latin American countries. Trinidad and Tobago, Surinam and Guyana are countries with substantial numbers of Muslims, most of whom have a South or South East Asian background. In the large countries of Brazil and Argentina the Muslim minority presence is quite strongly felt too. Muhammad al-Ahari provides a comprehensive account of Islam in the Caribbean and Latin America, far away from the ritual centre of Mecca.

Literature

John L. Esposito's book *Islam: The Straight Path* (New York and Oxford: Oxford University Press, revised edition, 1991) is a good introduction to Islam. The collective volume *Islam*, ed. Peter Clarke (London: Routledge,

1988), which is published in the British series The World's Religions, provides easily comprehensible overviews of Islam in different parts of the world. Ira M. Lapidus' *A History of Islamic Societies* (Cambridge: Cambridge University Press, 1988) is a broad and impressive historical introduction of more than 1,000 pages. Edward W. Said's book *Orientalism* (Harmondsworth: Penguin Books, 1978) is a critical discussion of Western research on Islam that has attracted much attention. Another interesting Muslim study of Western views on Islam is Akbar Ahmed's *Postmodernism and Islam: Predicament and Promise* (London: Routledge, 1992). *Muslim Peoples: A World Ethnographic Survey*, ed. Richard E. Weekes, 2 vols. (Westport: Aldwych Press, 1984) is an important handbook on the world's Muslim peoples. Essays on pilgrims and Islamic migrants from Africa, Asia and Europe are found in *Muslim Travellers: Pilgrimage, Migration, and the Religious Imagination*, eds. Dale F. Eickelman and James Piscatori (Berkeley 1990). A useful periodical called *Journal: Institute of Muslim Minority Affairs* is published biannually and includes essays of varying quality on Muslim minorities from virtually the whole world. Continuous bibliographical information is found in *Index Islamicus*, which is a quarterly publication.

Annemarie Schimmel's monograph *Mystical Dimensions of Islam* (Chapel Hill: University of North Carolina Press, 1975) is a classical study of Sufism. Among more recent introductions to Sufism, Julian Baldick's *Mystical Islam: An Introduction to Sufism* (London: Tauris, 1989), A.J. Arberry's *Sufism: An Account of the Mystics of Islam* (London: Allen and Unwin, 1990) and Jürgen Frembgen's *Derwische, Gelebter Sufismus: Wandernde Mystiker und Asketen im Islamischer Orient* (Köln: DuMont, 1993) may be mentioned. An overview of various orders is presented by J.S. Trimingham in *The Sufi Orders of Islam* (Oxford: Oxford University Press, 1971). A more recent and extensive work on orders is the French collective volume *Les voies d'Allah: Les ordres mystiques dans le monde musulman des origines à aujourd'hui*, eds. Alexandre Popović and Gilles Veinstein (Paris: Fayard, 1996).

Among books on Muslim women the following may be recommended: Fatima Mernissi, *Beyond the Veil: Male–Female Dynamics in Modern Muslim Society* (Bloomington: Indiana University Press, 1975, 1987); *Women in Islamic Societies*, ed. Bo Utas (London: Curzon Press, 1983); M.E. Combs-Schilling, *Sacred Performances: Islam, Sexuality and Sacrifice* (New York: Colombia University Press, 1989); Fatima Mernissi, *Women and Islam: An Historical and Theological Inquiry* (Oxford: Basil Blackwell, 1991); Leila Ahmed, *Women and Gender in Islam: Historical Roots of a Modern Debate* (New Haven: Yale University Press, 1992); Lila Abu-Lughod, *Writing Women's Worlds: Bedouin Stories* (Berkeley and Los Angeles: University of California Press, 1993); and Fatima Mernissi, *The Forgotten Queens of Islam* (Cambridge: Polity Press, 1993).

The increased political significance of Islam has been discussed in a great number of books. An interesting example of works focusing on the Middle East is Henry Munson's *Islam and Revolution in the Middle East* (London: Yale University Press, 1988). A large number of case studies from different parts of the world are found in 'Islam and Politics', a special issue of the journal *Third World Quarterly*, 10:2 (1988). The German volume *Islam in der Gegenwart*, eds. Werner Ende and Udo Steinbach (Munich: C.H. Beck, 1991) contains a general introduction to Islam's role in the development of anti-colonialism and nationalism with special emphasis on the contemporary situation. An overview and bibliography are found in Yvonne Y. Haddad, John O. Voll and John L. Esposito (eds.), *The Contemporary Islamic Revival: A Critical Survey and Bibliography* (New York: Greenwood Press, 1991). Current Western views on Islam are studied in Fred Halliday's *Islam and the Myth of Confrontation* (London: Tauris, 1995), and in a recent book entitled *Muslim Politics* (Princeton: Princeton University Press, 1996) Dale F. Eickelman and James Piscatori critically discuss, among other things, Samuel Huntington's well-known and controversial ideas about the 'clash of civilizations'.

A still useful, if somewhat outdated, introduction to Islam in Africa is J.S. Trimingham's *The Influence of Islam upon Africa* (London: Longman, 2nd edition, 1980, first published 1968). The more recently published *African Islam and Islam in Africa: Encounters between Sufis and Islamists*, eds. Eva Evers Rosander and David Westerlund (London: Hurst and Athens, Ohio: Ohio University Press, 1997), contains several broad overviews on both North Africa and sub-Saharan Africa. In *Les musulmans et le pouvoir en Afrique noire* (Paris: Karthala, 1983), which focuses primarily on West Africa, Christian Coulon discusses the political role of Islam. Sufism is presented in a number of case studies in *Charisma and Brotherhood in African Islam*, eds. Donal Cruise O'Brien and Christian Coulon (Oxford: Clarendon and New York: Oxford University Press, 1988). Mervin Hiskett's *The Development of Islam in West Africa* (London and New York: Longman, 1984) and Peter Clarke's *West Africa and Islam: A Study of Religious Development from the 8th to the 20th Century* (London: Edward Arnold, 1982) are fine introductions to the history of Islam in that part of the continent. Contemporary Muslim issues, primarily in West Africa, are discussed in *Muslim Identity and Social Change in Sub-Saharan Africa*, ed. Louis Brenner (London: Hurst, 1993). Concerning Islam among Swahili-speakers in the east, R.L. Pouwels' *The Horn and Crescent: Cultural Change and Traditional Islam on the East African Coast, 800–1900*, African Studies Series, 53 (Cambridge: Cambridge University Press, 1987) can be recommended. The French collective volume *Les voies de l'islam en Afrique orientale*, ed. François Constantin (Paris: Karthala, 1987), presents contemporary aspects of Islam in East Africa. A useful French journal on Islam in sub-Saharan Africa is *Islam et sociétés au sud du Sahara*.

The range of introductory and comparative literature on Islam east of West Asia is limited. However, there are some important overviews with detailed statistical information on Muslim peoples in the former Soviet Union, namely Shirin Akiner's *Islamic Peoples of the Soviet Union* (London: Routledge and Kegan Paul, 1986) and the volume *Muslims of the Soviet Empire: A Guide*, by Alexandre Bennigsen and S. Enders Wimbush (London: Hurst, 1985). In the series Studies of Nationalities, published in Stanford by the Hoover Institution of War, Revolution and Peace, several monographs on Muslim peoples in the former Soviet Union have appeared. Some examples are: Edward A. Allworth, *The Modern Uzbeks* (Stanford: Hoover Institution Press, 1991); Audrey L. Altstadt, *The Azerbaijani Turks: Power and Identity under Russian Rule* (Stanford: Hoover Institution Press, 1992); Alan W. Fisher, *The Crimean Tatars* (Stanford: Hoover Institution Press, 1987); Azade-Ayse Rorlich, *The Volga Tatars: A Profile in National Resilience* (Stanford: Hoover Institution Press, 1986); and Martha B. Olcott, *The Kazakhs* (Stanford: Hoover Institution Press, 1987). Valuable essays on Islam in Central Asia are found in *Muslims in Central Asia: Expressions of Identity and Change* (Durham: Duke University Press, 1992). The collective volumes *Contributions to Islamic Studies: Iran, Afghanistan and Pakistan*, eds. Christel Braae and Klaus Ferdinand (Aarhus: Aarhus University Press, 1987), and *Islam in Asia*, ed. John L. Esposito (Oxford: Oxford University Press, 1987), contain a number of useful studies on Muslims in Central, South and Southeast Asia. The Moro Muslims of the Philippines and Muslims in Thailand are presented in detail in W.K. Che Man's *Muslim Separatism: The Moros of Southern Philippines and the Malays of Southern Thailand* (Singapore: Oxford University Press, 1990).

Since the 1980s an increasing number of works on Islam in Europe have been published. *The Islamic Presence in Western Europe*, eds. Tomas Gerholm and Yngve G. Lithman (London: Mansell, 1988) discusses the situation of immigrant Muslims. A broad overview of Muslims in European countries is found in Jorgen Nielsen's monograph *Muslims in Western Europe* (Edinburgh: Edinburgh University Press, 1992), while *L'islam et les musulmans dans le monde, 1: L'Europe occidentale*, eds. Mohammed Arkoun, Rémy Leveau and Bassin el-Jisr (Beyrouth: Centre Culturel Hariri, 1994), contains more detailed studies. *The Integration of Muslims and Hindus in Western Europe*, eds. W.A.R. Shadid and P.S. van Koningsveld (Kampen: Pharos, 1991) focuses on some specific problems. Islam and social issues are discussed in *Muslims in Europe: Social Change in Western Europe*, eds. Bernhard Lewis and Dominique Schnapper (London: Pinter Publishers, 1994). Overviews as well as more specialised studies are published by the Centre for the Study of Islam and Christian–Muslim Relations at Selly Oak Colleges, Birmingham (England), in the series *CSIC Papers: Europe* (before 1990 called *Research Papers: Muslims in Europe*

1979–1989). Views on Islam and how the Islamic presence in North America and Europe influences the West are discussed in Claus Eggewie's *Alhambra – Der Islam im Westen* (Reinbeck bei Hamburg: Rowolth, 1993). Muslim missionary endeavours and conversions are focused on in Larry Poston's book *Islamic Dawah in the West: Muslim Missionary Activity and the Dynamics of Conversion to Islam* (Oxford: Oxford University Press, 1992).

A valuable introduction to Islam in North America is *The Muslims of America*, ed. Yvonne Y. Haddad (Oxford: Oxford University Press, 1991). Garbi Schmidt's recent book *American Medina: A Study of the Sunni Muslim Immigrant Communities in Chicago*, Lund Studies in History of Religions, 8 (Stockholm: Almgvist & Wiksell International, 1998), provides an in-depth view of the situation in an important city. Interesting essays on Islam in, among other countries, Brazil and Trinidad are found in *The Oxford Encyclopedia of the Modern Islamic World*, ed. John L. Esposito, 4 vols. (New York and Oxford: Oxford University Press, 1995).

Part One

Africa

Chapter One

Somalia

Bernhard Helander

At the beginning of 1985 I had a conversation with an elderly man residing in the Somali interior. Our discussion on this, and numerous other occasions, evolved around the issue of my own confessional standing. The man argued that if I would only open my heart and embrace Islam (what he really said was that I should 'surrender', *iska Islaam*), not only would the doors of paradise unlock for me, but it would also facilitate my work at the time, collecting material for my doctoral thesis. I retorted by asking if he really meant that I should convert just for the sake of making my field work easier. He then partially withdrew his statement and ventured into a long discourse, the point of which was that as a non-Somali I would not be a good Muslim anyway. In a sense the man was right; Islam constitutes a fundamental cornerstone in Somali social and cultural life. There is hardly any daily event that does not to some extent involve or invoke Islam. Even in circles of urban and secularised intellectuals, Islam makes itself remembered through expressions uttered or customs that have to be observed. A Somali atheist will, just as anyone else, utter an astonished *Bismillahi!* (in the name of God) to express his or her surprise.

More than seven years of brutal civil war and the total collapse of the Somali state has left Somalis with few solid ties – outside those of clan and subclan membership – apart from those provided by Islam. While certainly at times also divisive, Islam in Somalia has always been able to suggest solutions where secular institutions have failed. For many Somalis, Islam also provides a means of positioning themselves in the world and in history; the different peoples of the world and the different religions are sometimes presented as the descendants of the different prophets. By some, Muslim eschatology can also at times be drawn upon to explain the relative poverty of their own continent as well as a consoling promise that, for believers, compensation for mundane imperfections awaits in the 'next world'.

Background

Somalia is situated on the very tip of the Horn of Africa and is estimated to have a population of about 8 million. At least two-thirds of these live in the rural areas where they engage in various forms of nomadic animal husbandry and settled agriculture. Animal produce from camels, cows, goats and sheep, constitutes both core subsistence items and valued export articles. Widespread cultivation of sorghum, maize and vegetables exists in both rain-fed and riverine communities and banana plantations have also been established in the south. The rapidly growing urban areas have a long tradition in overseas and internal trade. Family-based handicraft enterprises are also an important part of the subsistence activities in urban areas.

Before the advent of European colonialists towards the end of the nineteenth century, Somalia did not exist as a political entity. The area was made up of different clan-based sultanates of varying size and length of reign. The southern coastal strip held strategically located freshwater sources attracting Arabian and other traders on their way from East Africa to the Arab peninsula and beyond. For a time the area was colonised by the Oman sultanate. Southern Somalia was purchased by Italy from the Omani sultan and remained an Italian colony until 1943, while northern Somalia came under British control. Following the Second World War and a period of UN trusteeship, the two former colonies were united in 1960 and granted full independence. The 1960s was a decade of chaotic experimentation in parliamentary democracy that came to an abrupt end in 1969 in a coup d'état staged by a group of army officers led by Mohamed Siyad Barre. Barre's regime developed into a brutal East-bloc dictatorship, drawing inspiration and support from, *inter alia*, Kim Il Sung of North Korea and Ceauşescu of Romania. From 1979, Barre was able to obtain support from the United States, Italy and other Western governments. He was overthrown by a coalition of clan-based militias in early 1991 and Somalia has remained without a central government since then. In 1992 large-scale militia battles led to famine in the southern interior. Difficulties in delivering relief aid eventually resulted in an armed intervention by international peace keepers from December 1992 until March 1995.

From an ethnic point of view Somalia has mostly been described as relatively homogeneous. The country is almost exclusively populated by members of the same ethnic group, the Somali. Before the civil war, larger urban centres contained sizeable settlements of Arab, Pakistani, Indian and Italian traders. Somali is a nationwide language understood and spoken in all parts of the country. However, in the so-called inter-river area in the south a dialect known as Af-May exists. The language and ethnic homogeneity have played crucial roles in the articulation of nationalist feelings throughout the latter half of the twentieth century. The ambition to found a nation-state for all Somali speakers – including those in the neighbouring countries Djibouti, Ethiopia and Kenya – came to colour much of the post-colonial politics. However, after the collapse of the state and the ensuing civil war this ambition has frequently been questioned.

Islam has a long history in Somalia. Excavations in the capital Mogadishu have revealed remnants of a mosque that is one of the oldest on the entire continent. Early inscriptions also confirm the early arrival of Islam in the coastal cities, and burial remains in the interior indicate a comparably early spread of Muslim funerary practices. By the end of the eleventh century most people in what is today Somalia had at least been in touch with Islam. It is generally assumed that prior to Islam, the Somalis shared another religion with other Cushitic language speakers such as the Oromo of Ethiopia and the Afar of Djibouti and Eritrea. Traces of this 'Cushitic religion' can still be found in certain practices and in some religious terminology. One example is the name of the Cushitic sky god, *Waaq*, which is still used as one of the names for God in modern Somali.

Somalis are almost exclusively Sunni Muslims and follow the Shafii school of law. In later years, some followers of the Wahhabi (Hanbali) school of law have also emerged as well as some Shia influences. To what extent these forms of Islam are gaining ground is hard to assess due to the civil war. Non-Muslim Somalis are relatively few. There are Christians who went to schools organised by either Italian Catholics or North American Mennonites. However, Christian missionary movements in general have never gained any greater foothold in the country.

The Somali social system

The traditional social system in Somalia ties together all people in a wide-branching system of clans. By calculating descent along paternal lines, every Somali can position himself or herself in one particular clan. The clan, or a sub-group of it, is what has traditionally served as a social security system, judicial system and unit of solidarity in times of warfare. Since the collapse of the state in 1991, clans form the only viable organisation to shoulder these functions in many areas of Somalia.

Somalis divide themselves in six larger clusters of clans. Daarood live in the northeast and in the far south. They are also found in eastern Ethiopia and in northern Kenya. Isaaq live in the central northern Somalia. Hawiye inhabit the central parts of the country and the fertile stretches along the river Shabeele. They are also found in the southern coastal cities. This southern zone moreover comprises members of the different Dir clans, the majority of whom, however, live in the northwest and in Djibouti. In the area between the two southern rivers, Jubba and Shabeele, live the Digil and Merifle groups of clans, collectively known as Reewin or Rahanweyn. Each one of these six clusters is divided into clans (*qoolo* or *qabiil*). It is only on that level of division that kinship assumes concrete social and political significance. The basis for the division in clans is the Somali descent system according to which each person belongs to the same descent group as his or her father, grandfather, great-grandfather, etc. The size of clans can vary considerably; some may comprise just a few thousand members while others number some 100,000 members. In the latter case it is the subdivisions within the clan that function as the politically significant groups.

From a Western point of view, a clan's internal organisation may appear chaotic. Decisions taken by councils of elders and other bodies are valid, in principle, only among those participating in the decision. In some clans it is possible to have verdicts pronounced by one group of elders retried by yet other assemblies of elders. The clanship's most tangible function is the handling of blood compensation (*diya*), that is, the fines exacted for breeches of customary rules. When someone is sentenced to pay such fines, it is seen as the collective responsibility of that person's descent group. Similarly, if one stands to receive compensation from someone else, this should be distributed within one's sphere of patrilineal kin. There are no self-evident boundaries for this form of solidarity but it is decided in different clans according to a principle called *heer*, a kind of contract specifying the range of solidarity as well as the size of fines to be paid for different types of infractions. Clan elders also have the option of organising large-scale raids in defence of the clan or in revenge of acts committed against it.

In this strongly decentralised political system, religion often assumes the role of a uniting force. Religious leaders are expected to intervene where secular leaders have failed and religion also plays a role in the recurrent nationalist movements, comprising all Somalis. However, despite this pivotal position of Islam, it is only rarely that secular leaders seek to validate their own power in religious terms, and ordinary people often perceive a great divide between the secular and religious leadership. Traditionally it is impossible to gain both worldly and religious repute as every man is either a *waranleh* (spear bearer), someone engaged in the well-being of his clan, or a *wadaad* which is the Somali term for religious leaders or *shaykhs*. The dualism between profane and religious leadership implies that Somalis sometimes, but not always, regard with scepticism political leaders seeking to legitimise their power in religious terms. For instance, when, shortly before his downfall, the overthrown president Mohamed Siyad Barre tried to establish himself as a religious national leader by giving religiously inspired public addresses, these events were generally ridiculed by the public. Similarly, those who today are against the increasing presence of Islamist groups, often argue that it is really politics masked as religion.

The cornerstone of the social system are the genealogies comprising one's ancestors that all Somalis are taught by heart at an early age. A genealogy (*abtiris*, 'counting ancestors') may comprise more than twenty generations of relatives. By comparing one's genealogy with others it is possible to assess exactly how closely related one is to other persons. Such proximity may be expressed by the counting of ancestors; one can hear it said that 'we

A Somali member of the Qadiriyya demonstrates her religious genealogy which unites her with her *shaykh* and ancestors all the way back to the Prophet Muhammad. This tablet is more than three yards long and includes thousands of names (photo: Bernhard Helander).

count eight ancestors', meaning that the genealogies of the two persons merge eight generations back. Although genealogies play this crucial role in shaping both personal identity and patterns of social interaction one should not be tempted to regard them as authentic historical documents. The further back in time one gets along the lines of names that are recited, the larger the amount of purely fictional elements. On a high genealogical level many Somalis regard themselves as descendants of the Prophet Muhammad's lineage Quraysh, usually mediated by the Prophet's uncle Abu Talib. This implies the possibility of arguing that Somalis are of Arab descent, a topic that remains disputed among many Somalis. When Somalia joined the Arab League in 1974 as the only non-Arabic speaking country, it was partly motivated by rhetorical statements according to which 'Somalis are Arabs'. The strong and widespread Somali commitment to Islam is another fact often brought forth by those arguing for an Arab ancestry.

There are some Somali clans which are believed to descend from the Prophet more directly than others. These include, for instance, the Asheraf clan, members of which enjoy a great amount of respect and are frequently called upon as mediators in disputes. Their ability to assume this and other functions is based both upon the fact that their ancestry is seen as lying outside that of the Somali genealogical grid and the religious grace (*baraka*) they are held to possess.

Somali custom and Islamic law allow a man to have four wives simultaneously. The different wives of a man form their own independent households and it is also common for the children of a particular wife to take on specific roles in the larger family economy. While conflicts between siblings and half siblings are not uncommon, the family as a whole is a relatively tightly organised social unit. The fact that all members of a family function together as one economic unit contributes to this. The authority of the parental generation is strong and to some extent based on the ability of elderly people to pronounce blessings (*duco*) or curses (*inkaar*). The fear of parental curses is widespread, even among highly educated young people.

The organisation of Somali Islam

During the latter part of the nineteenth and the early twentieth centuries a number of Muslim revitalisation movements spread in the Somali interior. These movements were Sufi orders of which four still exist in the country and formally organise nearly all Somalis. The three largest orders are the Qadiriyya, Ahmadiyya and Salihiyya. The Rifai order has also been represented among the population of Arab origin that lived in the southern coastal cities before the war. To be a member of a Sufi order implies that one counts as a spiritual disciple of the founder of the order. Through his grace, *baraka*, and teachings, members are able to lead lives that enable them to be in touch with God. An order is often referred to as 'a way', *dariiqa* (Ar. *tariqa*), in a religious sense. While it is not uncommon to find people who change their membership of one order for another, the specifics of order membership begin in Quranic schools. Among the more conspicuous differences between the orders are the religious celebrations that each order manifests, beyond those common to all Muslims. Normally these are commemorative rites in celebration of previous local leaders of the order. Deceased leaders and other prominent order members can sometimes be elevated to saintly status and the shrines erected for them become sites for country-wide pilgrimage during festive periods. Pilgrimages to the shrines of saints are in many orders seen as actions mediating contact with the founder of the order, the Prophet Muhammad and, ultimately, with God. There are also minor liturgical differences between the different orders, such as distinct songs of worship and texts that are regarded as order-specific. The success of Sufi orders in Somalia must to some extent be seen in relation to their capacity to institute social unity in religious terms. More than once in Somali history, Islam has been able to provide more inclusive identities than those provided through the tracing of patrilineal descent in the system of clanship. The ability to bridge clan differences by offering a more basic form of unity has also been in line with the nationalist sentiments that swept across the country for decades – at least before the civil war. While mentioning these unifying tendencies in Somali Islam, it should also be borne in mind that the different orders have occasionally fought harsh battles against one another.

The Qadiriyya, named after its twelfth century Iraqi founder Abd al-Qadir al-Jilani, is probably the largest order in Somalia and it was also the first one to reach the country. The support it enjoys in the country is a result of a cleverly conducted campaign by Shaykh Uways Muhammad Baraawe (1847–1913) during the decades around the turn of the century. Shaykh Uways, who was descended from a family of former slaves in the city of Baraawe, returned after studies in Baghdad to become the leader of a local branch of the Qadiri order, nowadays often named 'Uwaysiyya' – a term at times extended to mean the entire Somali Qadiri movement. During extensive travels in Somalia and neighbouring areas, Shaykh Uways and his disciples spread poetry and religious songs – composed into local dialects – that skilfully combined insights into local political affairs with the teachings of the Qadiri order.

The Ahmadi order was founded in Mecca by Sayyid Ahmad ibn Idris al-Fasi (1760–1837). This reform movement was spread in Somalia by Shaykh Ali Maye Durogba (d. 1917). The latter part of the nineteenth century saw intense competition between the Ahmadiyya and Qadiriyya. The Ahmadiyya opposed local practices, such as tobacco chewing, on the grounds that these were not in keeping with Islam. There are still Somalis who argue that the Ahmadiyya teachings are more strictly in adherence with Islam than are those of the Qadiriyya.

The Salihi order is originally an offshoot from the Ahmadiyya and was founded in Mecca by Sayyid Mohamed Salih (1853–1917). Under the leadership of Sayyid Mohamed Abdulle Hassan (1864–1920) this order was developed into a militant movement that for twenty years maintained an armed struggle against the presence of British and Ethiopian troops on Somali soil. The British press dubbed him 'the Mad Mullah', but he remains known as simply *Sacidka*, 'the Sayyid', a term reserved for those who, in a spiritual or real sense, are thought of as direct descendants of the Prophet Muhammad. The followers of Sayyid Mohamed – known as 'the dervishes' – at times pursued large-scale armed raids against their opponents. They saw the Qadiri movement as their particular enemy. Shaykh Uways, the leader of the Qadiriyya, was killed by dervishes in Biyoole in southern Somalia in 1913.

The more devout members of an order frequently form their own settlement (*jamea*). There is a large number of such settlements scattered across the interior of southern Somalia. The members of a *jamea* are originally disciples of a *shaykh* who gradually also start to attract other settlers to join them. Formally, such settlements are fully governed and controlled by the *shaykh*. They draw historical inspiration from the many small sultanates that existed in northern Somalia and Ethiopia between the fifteenth and seventeenth centuries. The best-known of these, Adal (or Ifat), had its centre in the town of Zeyla and was, like the present-day *jamea*, populated by a mixture of people from different clans and social strata. Members of such settlements may choose to abandon or downplay the significance of their secular social ties. Genealogies linking them to their clans of origin are replaced by a religious genealogy (*silsilad*, Ar. *silsila*, 'chain') consisting of *shaykhs* within the order. In such a chain the leader of the settlement is the first name, followed by the name of the person who was his teacher and so on until the chain reaches the Prophet Muhammad and, sometimes, even beyond him to earlier prophets. The generation links suggested by this practice are of a spiritual, inspirational kind. While they have little to do with real genealogies, these documents (they are frequently committed to writing) are by most people seen as a replacement for their ordinary genealogies. Consequently, members of a *jamea* often speak of the leader of the settlement as their father, not just in a spiritual sense (*aaw*), but also in a real sense (*aabe*). This custom of replacing real (or socially assigned) ancestors with religious teachers and leaders is probably one important factor in explaining why even Somali secular genealogies ultimately posit descent from the Prophet's lineage of Quraysh. In a similar way, many Somalis argue that Christians are descended from Nabi Isa, the prophet Jesus, while Jews are believed to count descent to their prophet, Moses.

The religious settlements have often served as safe havens for people in difficulties. The growth and establishment of many of them seem to be connected to times of social upheaval. A wave of settlements was established shortly after the large manumissions of slaves in the mid 1920s. Another peak in settlement activities occurred shortly after the Second World War. Again, in the 1970s, many of the ethnic Somalis who had fled from Ethiopia found sanctuary in the religious communities. During the 1980s many of the religious settlements were engaged in social and economic experiments. New types of houses and huts were developed and new crops and growing techniques introduced. While these efforts took place largely without any form of outside support, development projects as well as government organised cooperatives displayed a high degree of interest in the settlements. Some religious settlements were forced to label themselves 'cooperatives' to help boost the record of the otherwise meagre results of the cooperative movement.

During the current civil war members of 'fundamentalist' movements have founded several large settlements that, in terms of organisation, bear a strong resemblance to the more traditional *jamea*. One of the better-known of these is situated in the town of Luuq along the Jubba river in the southwest of the country. While the settlement was attacked by Ethiopian airforce and army contingents in 1996 and 1997 on the grounds that it served as a basis for terrorist activities in neighbouring Ethiopia, many reports also point to the calm and relative affluence that has been created there in the midst of the civil war.

The so-called fundamentalist or Islamist movements in Somalia have gained strength and attracted followers during the civil war. In the course of the escalating resistance against the former regime during the 1980s, a group popularly known as Akhiwaan Muslimen – the Muslim Brotherhood – grew. Originating among Somali students at the Islamic university Al-Azhar in Cairo and elsewhere, the movement was influenced by the more militant Egyptian movement of the same name. The Akhiwaan in Somalia were initially engaged in a moral critique of the corruption in government circles. Religiously, this and other movements draw direct inspiration from the Wahhabis, who are prominent in, for instance, Saudi Arabia. Since the autumn of 1990, the Islamist movements have changed shape and have become a force in the struggles for political power. Intermittently, various groups of the movement have received armaments from Iran, Libya and the Sudan. In 1992 an Islamist group calling themselves Al-Ittihad Al-Islami, 'The Islamic Struggle', attacked the northern port city of Bosaaso. This led to a series of armed clashes with local militia called the Somali Salvation Democratic Front (SSDF) which has its power base among the Majerteen clans in that area. In 1994 the Islamist group said that they would continue their struggle for power by peaceful means. While they have not sought to gain seats in any of the political bodies that have been established in the north-east, their influence remains visibly strong in, for instance, dress code, hospitals, schools and mosques.

It is not established to what extent the northern Al-Ittihad movement is organisationally connected with the southern movement of the same name. In the south, too, the actions of the Islamist groups have been a part of the clan war and their support for one of the major factions, the Somali National Alliance (SNA), is of great importance in the over-all political balance. In the eyes of the factions opposed to SNA, the Islamist support is seen as threatening, and the Ethiopian attacks on Al-Ittihad settlements mentioned above have been supplemented by attacks from neighbouring militias. Some reports suggest that there exist close links of co-operation between the Al-Ittihad and three other Islamist groups that operate in the country: Harakat Al-Aslah, Mujuma Al-Uluma and Wahdat Al-Shabab Al-Islami.

Many Somalis are openly opposed to the growth of the Islamist movement. It is often regarded as too alien in comparison with the traditional Somali Islam, often known as the Islam of the *ulama* (the religious scholars). The mixture of political ambitions and religious teachings represented by the Islamists is one factor that directly opposes the traditional Somali tendency to keep separate religious and secular power. In contrast to the leaders of the Islamist movements, traditional

Somali religious leaders have in a number of cases acted as peace negotiators. It deserves to be pointed out, also, that there are tendencies in Somali society that may be misread as heightening Islamist power, while in fact they only are effects of the increasing significance attributed to religion generally. Many Somalis argue that this significance ultimately may be traced back to the absence of a government. One should also be cautious not to give the impression that the only form of religious innovation in the country is that represented by militant Islamist groups. On the contrary, the traditional brotherhoods are very active and new groups based on traditional Somali Islamic beliefs continue to appear. One of the most recent examples of such groups is called Timo Weyne ('big hairs'), which has established a number of settlements in the northeast. They are followers of Shaykh Muhammad Rabi (b. 1920) and frequently engage in open dispute with Islamist groups over matters such as the control of mosques.

Everyday Islam

The life of a Somali person is surrounded by religious events. One of the first things done when a child is born is to lean towards its ear and recite the call for prayers. The Quran is also one of last things a person will hear as it is customary to recite the *sura Yaasiin* for a dying person. Verses from the Quran are among the first things a child learns to write, usually already at three or four years of age. For a vast number of Somalis, Quranic schools remain the only form of education establishment they enter. To become a Quranic school teacher or perhaps a *shaykh* is the only form of intellectual career available in the interior of the country. For most Somalis, the only foreign travel they ever engage in is the pilgrimage to Mecca. Although it is often modestly designed, even the remotest village frequently has a mosque of its own. Islam also functions as more than just a collection of articles of faith. Diseases among humans and animals are treated with Quranic verses and there are probably very few Somalis who have never worn a leather amulet stuffed with Quranic citations around their neck.

Despite these important roles played by Islam on both national and individual levels, the dominant approach to religious matters is light-hearted. Conventionally Somali women have never worn veils, but revealed both arms and shoulders wearing their colourful traditional dress (*guntiino*). The transparent silk dress (*dira*) worn by many urban women can even be regarded as slightly coquette. However, from the late 1980s, women's dress code began to change with the introduction of Saudi-inspired attires, often supplemented by a veil. This dress, known in Somali as *shuko*, covers the entire body with the exception of feet and hands. While this form of dress initially spread primarily among women within the Islamist groups, it has lately also inspired women of a more secularised orientation.

The Islamic law, *sharia*, has never been rigorously implemented in Somalia. Media reports on, for instance, mutilations and stoning, remain isolated exceptions to this more general trend. The growing number of so-called *sharia* courts that exist across the country are mainly concerned with civil cases and the settling of compensation disputes. Where criminal cases are brought to court, the Somali penal code of 1962 (written in Italian) remains the principal legal instrument. This is due to the fact that judges in *sharia* courts have the ability to pronounce a case to be *taasir*, i.e. a less serious crime, in which case there may be a choice of which code to apply. Where traditional courts of clan elders are involved in legal proceedings there may sometimes emerge discussions about whether Somali customary law or the *sharia* should be used in determining the size of the fine to be paid by the respondent. The only implication of this, however, is that the fines suggested by the use of Islamic law often are regarded as higher. In cases of homicide, execution of the culprit is generally carried out swiftly. However, the bereaved party have the right to waive their claim, pardon the culprit and settle with only the blood compensation for their murdered relative. Somali customary law and Islamic law have a uniform view on a number of important issues. This is the case, for instance, in matters of inheritance. When, in 1975, the former regime introduced a legislation that gave women the right to inherit on an equal basis to men, it led to country-wide demonstrations. The wave of protests was halted only after the public execution of ten leading *shaykhs* and opponents to the new law. In practice the new inheritance law was never implemented, but women continue to inherit half the amount their brothers inherit.

A normal day in a Somali home features a number of religiously inspired events. Even before dawn, many people leave their homes to visit the mosque. The late 1980s saw an increasing attendance in mosques, but it is still mainly men who pray outside their homes. While the husband and, perhaps, some of the older sons visit the mosque, the wife lights incense in the house. This is done twice a day in most Somali homes – at sunrise and sunset, or as the expression goes: 'at the two red lights'. Regarded as brief moments during which 'blessings are accepted' the custom may be inspired by the belief in Muslim eschatology that the sky will be coloured red shortly before the day of judgement. It is also said that 'the angels bear one's prayers to God'. Others point to the way in which the incense helps to ward off the *jinns* and other lingering spirits of the night.

Early in the morning the younger children leave for Quranic school. The number of years spent in this form of schooling varies greatly. In general, boys attend for longer than girls although families differ in this respect. Quranic schools aim at teaching their students large parts of the Quran by heart. Depending on the skills of the teacher the education may also feature explanatory lectures. There is a surprisingly high number of Somalis who are able to recite the entire Quran. The fact that Somalis on several occasions have won international contests in Quranic recitations is a matter of national pride.

On Fridays many families call a *shaykh* to their home to perform a weekly blessing. He will be seated with a cup of water in front of his mouth and while he silently recites, he will spit over the water which then may preserve to use for curing ailments of household members during the coming week or simply sprinkle in different rooms as a blessing. The spitting, common in many forms of blessings, is probably of pre-Islamic origin. The water is called *tahaliil* and may be used for a variety of different purposes, such as blessing the fields before the season of cultivation. Fridays are also the days when beggars will appear in front of houses. In the dualism between religious and secular power that Somalis maintain in many contexts, the poor and destitute are often seen as possessing mystical forces that may be harmful if their demand for alms is rejected. These potentially dangerous forces are something a compensation for what they may lack in terms of worldly goods.

Household members usually eat together, both women and men. Previously it was common for women to eat separately from men, a practice that still is in effect when entertaining guests and when eating in restaurants and cafés. In the latter one rarely encounters women at all, unless separate rooms are provided for them. Before eating it is customary for the oldest male to grab a bit of the food and say *Bismillahi Arahmani Arahim*, 'in the name of God, the Omnipotent, the Merciful'. This way of blessing the food is so fundamental that the very expression 'begin to eat' is 'go ahead and say *Bismillahi*'. To initiate something in the name of God is not restricted to meals but occurs in a wide variety of contexts. When entering a bus, when starting a car, when getting out of bed or going to sleep and in a large number of other settings, many Somalis mouth a silent *Bismillahi* or some related expression.

After the midday prayer – in Somalia usually coinciding with lunch and the afternoon rest – people may pull out a rosary (*tusbah*) and remain seated on their carpets. On such occasions they perform particular tasks (*awraad*) and recitations normally suggested by some *shaykh* who has been consulted. Among the least complicated tasks are to keep repeating a specific phrase a couple of hundred times, carefully counting them on the beads of the rosary. The reasons for such additional tasks are manifold, ranging from seeking to restore personal health to more theologically inspired aims. Among the ordinary prayers, the late afternoon prayer, *assar*, is generally regarded as hard to say. For people, like herders, who have spent the entire day in the sun, the time for prayer comes as the animals begin to seek shade, giving the herders a first chance to rest. For urban dwellers this prayer usually interrupts the midday nap.

During the month of fasting, Ramadan (in Somali known simply as *soon* 'fast'), many daily routines change. Somalis, like many other Muslim peoples, prepare particular dishes served only during the night meals of this month. Everyone above the age of fifteen should fast, except for those who are ill. Most Somalis often start the fast with the intention of maintaining it to the end of the month. However, it is not uncommon to find people resuming normal eating after a week or so. The general level of poor health in the country is probably a major contributing factor in this. The date of the commencement of the fast is a topic widely debated across the country, as well as in the many exiled Somali communities. Somalis view with suspicion those who let the dates for the holy month be ruled by calendars, relying themselves solely on lunar observations. On the night marking the beginning of the month, a thin crescent should be visible at sunset. As the new moon has been sighted the observation is rapidly broadcast on short wave radio to the entire country. It is reported that cloudy weather once forced Somalia to commence Ramadan a few days after that the rest of the Muslim world had started. Similarly, on local community level, it is often observation of the sunset that determines the appropriate time for the daily breaking of the fast (*af-furow*, 'open the mouth'). National radio calls to break the fast are ignored if they contradict observations at the local mosque.

Most Somalis wish to carry out the *hajj*, the pilgrimage to Mecca, at least once in their life. In the past this was something that relatively few people were able to find the means to do. In the 1940s and 1950s there was considerable prestige attached to being able to return to one's home village or town adding the title of *haji* (for men) or *hajiya* (for women) to one's name. Today, a considerable number of Somalis perform the *hajj*, some even several times in their lives. The traditional male sign of having done the pilgrimage, a small cap called *kofiyad*, can today be worn by anyone.

Within the Qadiri order there are groups who maintain a local alternative to the Mecca pilgrimage. Travelling to the mountain Bur Heybe in central south Somalia for seven consecutive years and participating in the rites staged there every year, counts as equal to one 'real' pilgrimage. On the top of this mountain are some remarkable rock formations that are said by some to be the graves of Adam and Eve.

Funerals are religious events of major importance in Somali Islam. Even the most ordinary funeral contains crucial social symbolism in which the members of a village or neighbourhood reconfirm their mutual relations as friends and neighbours. While graves themselves remain little-decorated and may even become nearly invisible after a few years, they are always meticulously dug in the same fashion. A deep trench is dug so that one of the long sides faces Mecca. Inside the grave, a small chamber is carved out in the long side and in it the corpse is placed. Even with the mass burials during the famine 1992, it was attempted to design each grave in this way.

The religious landscape

The world of beliefs of a Somali Muslim is constructed from a number of fundamental assumptions provided by Islam, Somali tradition and, to a lesser extent, influences from pre-Islamic religion. However, even the most basic Islamic beliefs often have specifically Somali connotations generated by the local tradition of interpretations. In this final section I shall point to some of the particular qualities of Somali Islam and seek to outline how the 'religious landscape' appears from a Somali point of view.

Even secondary school leavers often host doubts concerning what physics classes have taught them about the nature of the universe. It is a widely held view that the idea of the earth revolving around the sun is something the Soviets forced Somalis into believing during the 1970s at which time Somalia was something of an African Cuba. The moon landings are also dismissed as pure propaganda; space flights are held to be possible only in the lower spheres where communication satellites are stationed. I have met Somalis who argue that there are American movies (for instance 'Capricorn One') that show how the bluff of the Apollo satellites was staged.

The evolutionary theory of the human species' gradual development from monkey-like ancestors is firmly rejected. There is an interesting Somali variation on this theme that reverses the sequence of events entirely. There are large numbers of monkeys, both in the interior and in the cities, and Somalis admit that these do display some very human traits, both in features and in behaviour. It is said that the monkeys once were humans who were transformed into monkeys as the result of a curse. Another – and slightly more moral – version of this tale has it that the cursed ones were insubordinate pupils of a Quranic school teacher and the curse pronounced as a punishment for their insubordination.

The earth is seen as populated not only by humans but also by invisible spiritual beings, *jinns*. These spirits are seen as harmless and are believed to establish their settlements in places where humans will not disturb them. Nevertheless, it may happen that humans accidentally stumble over and hurt *jinns* who, in revenge, will inflict sickness or death. For Somalis there is no evil power in the cosmos that challenges the might of God. The term *shaydaan*, Satan, is in Somali just a synonym name for the relatively harmless *jinns*. Apart from the *jinns*, the existence of which is described in the Quran, many Somalis also believe in other forms of spirits which are thought to be able to possess people, causing them great harm. Unless the wishes of these spirits are obeyed, the possessed person will never be freed from the affliction. However, given proper attention, the spirit possession may even become advantageous. Throughout Somalia there is a wide variety of different spirit possession cults that seek to cater for the demands of particular types of spirits. Members of such cults, all presumed to be possessed by the same type of spirit, meet regularly to perform spectacular rites featuring ecstatic behaviour and attempts to communicate with the spirits – often in foreign languages. It should be mentioned that there is a considerable number of people who view these cults with scepticism and argue that they are contrary to Islamic faith. Members of the cults deny this and regard instead the possession cults as ordinary Sufi orders. Many cults, for instance the so-called *Boraane* of Shaykh Hussein, do bear indisputable traces of copied symbolic traits from the large Sufi orders. Since many spirit possession cults recruit their members among politically and socially peripheral categories, it has been argued that the cults could be seen as a form of social protest.

Somali Islam provides a number of specific explanations for the different character of the peoples of the earth. A distinction is often made between 'history' and 'origin'. While secular political leaders and clan elders are held to be knowledgeable about the former, the religious experts possess expertise on the latter. According to the religious experts, Africans' dark complexion is due to their descent from the cursed son of the prophet Noah, Ham. The descendants of the other son, Sam, have remained light-skinned. Similar types of explanation are also frequent in seeking to explain the relative status of different clans. When remote villages were reached by relief food drops during the famine of 1992, there were those who regarded this as a sign of the moral superiority of the light-skinned relief workers.

Somali Sufism also contains a mystical orientation. The differences between the different orders are considerable in this respect (and are also one of the reasons for their historical disagreements). However, the basic tenet is that everything in the universe is seen as related to everything else. The name and personality of a person, the celestial bodies and the different prophets, the seasons of the year and the genders are but a few of the phenomena whose mutual relations can be ascertained and analysed by the knowledgeable. However, knowledge of the full extent of this system of cosmic correspondences is not regarded as possible for humans, as it forms part of the way in which God created the world. At the same time it is also seen as signs left in the creation by God for the faithful to discover through devout studies. By mastering at least parts of this system, *shaykhs* are believed to be able to perform useful services – and sometimes miracles – for the laity. Most religious experts are regularly consulted for a variety of purposes: to cure sickness as well as finding missing objects or livestock. One of the more conspicuous cases of such religious expertise that I have encountered was in 1988 when a *shaykh* was arrested and threatened with execution for having helped deserting soldiers from the government army to turn invisible.

One could argue that a basic idea of both practice and theory of Somali Sufism is that the truth is hidden in reality; that things are not what they appear to be but that pious study may reveal fragments of their true nature. On an even deeper level, human beings must also discover that 'this world' (*adduunyo*), that is our existence on this side of judgement day, is but an imperfect replica of what awaits in 'the next world' (*aakhiro*) where the righteous will have their reward in paradise. Perhaps it is this insight in the extreme consequence of eschatological teachings that is behind the warning so often exchanged between Somalis: *Ilaahi ka abso*, 'fear God'.

In view of the importance of Islam in Somali social life, and given the proximity to matters of faith in everyday routines, it is hardly surprising that the civil war has fostered hopes that Islam in some way should provide a bridge across the chasms that have torn through previous state. Even among highly secularised intellectuals one finds the expressed opinion that Muslim morality – within the framework of the Somali tradition of interpretation – should be made the guide for how to reconcile the nation. Among the more than 1 million Somali who now live in exile, Islam has partially assumed new functions. While Somalis abroad previously proudly presented themselves as Somalis, the destruction of this identity brought about by the civil war now occasionally has people presenting themselves simply as 'Muslims'. It is not only for such persons that Islam provides a social identity; in every conceivable future Somali state or federation, Islam is likely to play a far greater role than was the case during the previous regime. Exactly what shape this influence will assume is hard to discern. On the one hand the support for hard-line militant forms of Islamism may grow, on the other hand there is reason to assume that the broad popular support for the traditional form of *ulama* Islam may serve to revitalise the Sufi orders.

Literature

The writings of Ioan M. Lewis provide the best introduction to Somali social life as well as Islam in Somalia. *A Modern History of Somalia: Nation and State in the Horn of Africa* (Boulder: Westview, 1988) devotes considerable space to Islam. *Religion in Context: Cults and Charisma* (Cambridge: Cambridge University Press, 1986) offers a good overview of recent research on spirit possession. Lewis' recent book *Saints and Somalis: Popular Islam in a Clan-based Society* (Lawrenceville, NJ: Red Sea Press, 1998) contains both classic essays on Somali Islam and newly written material.

Bradford G. Martin's *Muslim Brotherhoods in Nineteenth-Century Africa* (Cambridge: Cambridge University Press, 1976) and J.S. Trimingham's *Islam in Ethiopia* (Oxford: Oxford University Press, 1952) are helpful in placing Somali Islam in a regional and historical perspective. Mohamed Mohamed-Abdi's *Histoire des croyances en Somalie: Religions traditionelles et religions du Livre* (Besançon: Annales littéraires de l'Université de Besançon, 1992) provides some interesting insights into Sufi traditions and the history of Islam in Somalia. Said S. Samatar's *Oral Poetry and Somali Nationalism: The Case of Sayyid Mohamed Abdille*

Hasan (Cambridge: Cambridge University Press, 1986) is a detailed study of the foremost leader of the Sahlihiyya order in Somalia, while the rich volume *In the Shadow of Conquest: Islam in Colonial Northeast Africa* (Trenton: Red Sea Press, 1992), ed. Said S. Samatar, presents Somali Islamic history in a political context. Mohamed Haji Mukhtar's essay 'Islam in Somali History: Fact and Fiction', included in the otherwise disappointing volume *The Invention of Somalia* (Lawrenceville, NJ: Red Sea Press, 1995), ed. Ali Jimale Ahmed, provides a brilliant reassessment of crucial aspects of conditions promoting Islam's spread in Somalia.

Chapter Two

Nigeria

Christopher Steed and David Westerlund

The Federal Republic of Nigeria, which was granted independence from Britain in 1960, is often referred to as the 'giant' of sub-Saharan Africa. Trisected by two wide rivers, the Niger and the Benue, Nigeria contains diverse geographical environments. This tropical country has a population of over 90 million, and contains a vast diversity of ethnic backgrounds, encompassing over 400 languages and cultures. Two-thirds of the population, however, come from the three largest ethnic groups: the Hausa-Fulani in the north, the Yoruba in the southwest and the Igbo in the southeast. The use of English, as the official language, is one of the chief factors unifying the nation. In the northern half of the country the Hausa language is also used as a *lingua franca* amongst many ethnic minorities. With half the population under twenty years of age, migration to the towns and cities is one of the dominant characteristics of modern Nigerian life.

It is estimated that about 50 per cent of the population is Muslim. The Christians are possibly somewhat fewer. The question of which of these two religions has most followers is a perennial subject of controversy, and no recent census has officially recorded figures for religious affiliation. Islam in Nigeria predates sustained Christian contact with the country by many centuries. Muslims entered Nigeria from the interior of the continent, from across the West African savannahs and the Saharan desert to the north, while Christianity spread along the West African coast, via the Atlantic ocean to the south. Roughly speaking, this has meant that Christianity is mostly located along the southern coast, and in the rain forests and plains (populated by the Igbo, Efik and Tiv, among others), whereas the savannahs and Sahel of northern Nigeria (chiefly inhabited by the Hausa, Fulani and Kanuri peoples) are seen as the Islamic 'heartland' of the nation.

Two areas of the country are religiously mixed, having both strong Muslim and Christian identifies. Firstly, the west with its dense network of towns and cities (including the former capital city of Lagos), is the home of the Yoruba-speaking peoples, whose cultural identity has been able to embrace Christianity as well as Islam. Secondly, the so-called Middle Belt across the median of the country, an area of riverine grasslands, plateaux and mountains occupied by scores, if not hundreds of ethnic groups, is an expanse where there is intense rivalry between the two world religions.

Historical background

From the eleventh century onwards, when the king of Takrur in Senegambia became a Muslim, Islam in West Africa was closely connected with the development of states such as ancient Ghana, Mali and Songhay. Initially introduced to West Africa by Berbers and Arabs from the Sahara to the north, Islam gained many converts among local trading communities. West African societies fused elements of the new Muslim religion to their own traditional beliefs, creating a form of 'mixed' Islam. Islam came to northern Nigeria from two directions: in the eleventh century from the northeast, via Arab and Berber merchants from North Africa and the Sahara, to the kingdom of Kanem-Borno; and from the west in the late fourteenth and early fifteenth centuries, through the influence of Wangarawa-Dyula traders, to the city kingdoms of Hausaland.

The first Muslims came to Nigeria via the trade routes from Tripoli in North Africa, through the Lake Chad region, to the Kanem-Borno kingdom. Some of these traders probably belonged to the Ibadiyya, a branch of the Kharijite movement, and they may have entered this corner of Nigeria, along with Shuwa Arabs, sometime during the eighth century. In the eleventh century, a Muslim by the name of Hummay established the Muslim dynasty of the Saifawa, which was to rule the Kanem-Borno state for the next 700 years until 1846, when it was replaced by the present al-Kanemi dynasty. By the late fifteenth century Islam was well established at Gazargamu, the new capital of Kanem-Borno, with the *ulama* (sing. *alim*, religious scholar) holding eminent positions in government. By this time Quranic education was well developed and Borno had extensive ties with other leading intellectual centres in the Islamic world. Borno's prestigious heritage of calligraphy and Quranic expertise is still significant.

There seems to have been a Muslim group of traders from other parts of West Africa in the great northern Nigerian Hausa city of Kano by the middle of the fourteenth century, though it was not until a century later that the first king of Kano converted to Islam. Before the sixteenth century Islam in northern Nigeria was very much mixed with local Hausa religion. Until this time Islam was chiefly the religion of the towns and the trading classes. Quranic schools were opened, and literacy in Hausa or Fulfulde, using the Arabic script, was gradually incorporated into the governmental structure of the main Hausa kingdoms of Kano, Katsina and, later, Zaria. From the fifteenth century on, these Hausa city states grew rich and powerful. Regional trading networks led to the establishment of Hausa mercantile colonies throughout West Africa, and the Hausa traders soon perceived the commercial and social advantages of conversion to Islam. This trading

The new central mosque in the old city of Kano (photo: Roman Loimeier, 1987).

diaspora brought back a wealth of knowledge about Islam to the Hausa heartland and facilitated the gradual acceptance of the new religion in the Hausa kingdoms.

Hausa chiefs and kings began to rely on Muslim literati, the expanding group of *ulama*, for the governance of their kingdoms, and Islamic jurisprudence was gradually accreted to traditional legal customs. By the sixteenth century a written form of Hausa, known as *ajami*, had evolved from a modified Arabic script. By 1700 Islam began to generate substantial support amongst all levels of Hausa society. The *ulama* were divided in their response to the mixed form of Islam that continued to develop in the Hausa kingdoms. Some believed in a long-term evolution towards Islamic orthodoxy, while others pleaded strongly for reform and a cleansing of Islam of local polytheistic customs. By 1800 Islam was well established in the savannahs of West Africa, from Senegambia in the west to Lake Chad in the east. In this region a number of reform movements, all more or less characterised by militancy, were launched during the nineteenth century. The motivation for these *jihads* ('holy wars') was to purify Islam. The *jihad* movement in West Africa had connections with the Islamist Wahhabi movement and the foundation of the Tijani Sufi brotherhood in the Maghreb. The West African leaders of the reform movements all had the similar aim of creating a theocratic state based on the Islamic law, *sharia*.

Shehu (*shaykh*) Usuman dan Fodio, the celebrated Fulani scholar led the *jihad*, beginning in 1804, and within six years all the major towns of the Hausa kingdoms were ruled by Fulani Muslim emirs. Usuman dan Fodio had studied under a North African Muslim *alim*, and he was aware of Muslim reformist ideas in the wider world. The *jihad* resulted in a 'federal' theocratic state, with extensive autonomy for emirates, recognising the spiritual authority of the caliph or sultan of Sokoto. The Islamic character of the caliphate, at least in the early years, was reinforced by a close partnership and identification between the religious scholars, the *ulama*, and the new military and political rulers. By 1810 most of the emirates, such as Kano, Katsina and Zaria, were established, while others, for example Ilorin and Nupe, were created later. In all, over thirty major emirates were formed throughout the course of the nineteenth century. Shehu Usuman dan Fodio retired in 1812 from politics and returned to scholarship, and his son Muhammad Bello succeeded to the caliphate with the Shehu's death in 1817. From the time of the Shehu, there were twelve *Sarkin Musulmi* ('commanders of the faithful'), or caliphs, until the British conquest of the caliphate at the beginning of the twentieth century.

The expansion of the caliphate through military conquest, especially to the south, into the so-called Middle Belt region, led to the forceful incorporation of numerous ethnic minorities and non-Muslims into the emirates of the Islamic polity. By a series of military outposts and frontier fortresses, the caliphate perceived itself as the 'territory of Islam' (*dar al-islam*), confronting the 'territory of the infidel' (*dar al-kufr*). Non-Muslims could be enslaved in order to work on the Hausa-Fulani aristocracy's plantations around the great northern cities, or to be exported to the slave markets of the Middle East. The demand for slaves was a major reason for the caliphate's expansion into non-Muslim areas to the south. It has been estimated that slaves comprised between a quarter and a half of the population of the emirates. The *jihad* was essentially a reform movement to purify an already semi-Islamised society rather than forcibly convert non-Muslims. This can also be illustrated by the fact that there continued to exist large groups of non-Muslim Hausa, known as Magazawa, living in sparsely populated areas of a number of emirates. The imposition of *sharia* law provided a unity to socio-economic life in Northern Nigeria. Islamic education and literature in Arabic, Fulfulde and Hausa languages developed quickly. One of the most distinguished literary personalities in the caliphate was the daughter of Shehu Usuman dan Fodio, Nana Asma'u (1793–1865). Not only an accomplished poet, she devoted herself to the cause of education for Muslim women. Her contribution was of wide significance and she continues to be a source of inspiration to the present day.

Islam in Yorubaland before the 1804 *jihad* has been little researched, with only the barest outlines known. From the beginning of the seventeenth century southwestern Nigeria was dominated by the Oyo empire. In exchange for firearms the kingdom sold war captives as slaves for the Atlantic trade. Through its strategic commercial position, the Oyo kingdom was also in contact with Hausa Muslims to the north. Slaves were sold to Muslim traders in exchange for horses, which were used to increase its military strength. Muslim traders lived in distinct wards in the city of Oyo, and their worship attracted in particular Yoruba traders to Islam. Towards the end of the eighteenth century the Oyo empire reached its greatest strength but soon after began to weaken. In 1817 pastoral Fulani, Hausa slaves and Muslim Yoruba converts began to revolt in the northern part of the Oyo kingdom, around the major town of Ilorin, which was proclaimed a new emirate of the Sokoto caliphate. This Muslim-supported rebellion sounded the death-knell for the Oyo empire, which had finally disintegrated by 1836, plunging Yorubaland into a series of internecine civil wars which lasted intermittently until nearly 1900.

There was much hostility towards Islam in the southeastern part of Nigeria, caused by the Sokoto caliphate's annexation of Ilorin and northern Yorubaland. However, Muslim traders gradually began to re-establish themselves in the commercial world of Yoruba cities, and this led to the development of Yoruba Islam, integrated into traditional society. Islamic education, divination, healing and open-air preaching were some of the methods that Muslims used to gain converts. The expansion of Islam amongst the Yoruba reached a high point around 1900, by which time, for example, half the population of Lagos were Muslims. Islam became well integrated in the Yoruba peoples' traditional culture and has maintained a special character which in many ways is different from Islam in Northern Nigeria. Yoruba Muslim women are, for instance, very independent and *sharia* does not have nearly the same strong position that it has in the north. The widespread adherence to local Yoruba culture has subsumed modern religious affiliation to Islam and Christianity.

When British colonial rule was established, Muslims in Nigeria did not develop any co-ordinated response to defend themselves. Some Muslims in Northern Nigeria responded by using the traditional Islamic *hijra* ('emigration') tactic, in the same way that the Prophet Muhammad did when he left Mecca and went to Medina. There were also armed revolts, many inspired by Mahdist and millenarian expectations. Other Muslims decided on cultural and spiritual *hijra*, in other words a policy of non-involvement with Europeans, the colonial administration and Western education. The Bamidele movement in Ibadan during the 1930s is an example of this kind of opposition. Many Muslims saw Christianity as the underlying fabric of both the Western and secular culture that the British colonialists introduced, and felt it to be incumbent upon themselves to resist this foreign encroachment. On the whole, however, most Muslims accepted the colonial take-over and the majority of Muslim leaders co-operated with the new authorities who, in turn, recognised the traditional emirate leadership. Once conquest had been achieved and apprehension of the 'Islamic peril' of Mahdism had subsided, the colonial powers were faced with the problem of reaching an accommodation with their new Muslim subjects. There was little evidence of a well thought through colonial policy towards Islam, and consequently, imperial responses were often based on the expediency of each situation. Essentially based on pragmatism, the British established a system of 'indirect rule'. There were too few colonial administrators proportionately to the numbers of Northern Nigerians for Britain to govern single-handedly.

The nineteenth-century emirate structure was utilised by the British colonial administration and became the main African example of the policy of 'indirect rule'. The Muslim emirs established a close working understanding with the British administration and were allowed to keep most of their local power. Many emirs were suspicious of Christian missions and banned them in their own emirates. These decisions were in most cases accepted by the colonial administration. This colonial *modus vivendi* gave Islam significant prestige. The ethnic minorities of Northern Nigeria and the Middle Belt gained social and economic benefits by converting to Islam, and this was especially so for those communities who lived in peripheral areas near Muslim centres. What the Sokoto caliphate failed to achieve by conquest in the nineteenth century, in converting Middle Belt societies to Islam, was accomplished during the colonial period.

European predictions over the decline of Islam were widely off the mark. Under European colonialism Islam progressed more quickly than in pre-colonial times. It has been estimated that the number of Muslims in tropical Africa doubled during colonial rule. There are many reasons for this expansion. Urbanisation and the greater social and geographic mobility facilitated the expansion of Islam. The building up of an infrastructure helped, for example, Hausa traders to extend the range of their commercial networks. Migrants from Hausa communities travelled south to Yoruba towns and established 'strangers' quarters', which contributed to the expansion of Islam. Seasonal migrant labour was another cause of this expansion, as foremen and plantation overseers were often Muslim. However, backwardness in Western education meant that Muslims were ill-equipped for direct involvement in the apparatus of the colonial state and its successor, independent Nigeria. In this respect the Christians with their mission schools had the advantage. The social and economic conservatism as a characteristic of Nigerian Islam is reflected in the Muslim reactions to the early nationalist movement, which became dominated by Christian Nigerians from Southern Nigeria. The emirs and their courts were afraid to loose their privileges. In conclusion, the absence of a comprehensive system of Western education in large parts of Muslim Nigeria meant that Christian Nigerians held the initiative in the development of popular nationalism.

Sufi orders

The influential orthodox tradition has certainly helped make Nigerian Islam of particular importance in Black Africa, but there is a wide range of Islamic groups and identities in Nigeria. This diversity has been most clearly illustrated by the Sufi orders or brotherhoods. The most important brotherhoods in Nigeria are the Qadiriyya and the Tijaniyya. The authority of *shaykhs* has traditionally been immense, and adherents regularly give them notable presents. Pilgrimages to the shrines of saints and praise singing to the Prophet Muhammad are other controversial attributes of the orders. The margin between Sufism and orthodoxy is however not necessarily clear-cut. In the Qadiri order in particular there are many Muslims who have great regard for the *sharia* and who strive for an 'unadulterated' Islam. Shehu Usuman dan Fodio, whose *jihad* led to the establishment of the *sharia*-based Sokoto caliphate, belonged to the Qadiriyya.

The British suspected the Tijaniyya in particular of having revolutionary tendencies and estimated the Qadiriyya to be a somewhat less serious threat to colonial rule. The colonial government was always extremely suspicious of Sufi *shaykhs* or *marabouts* and of the activities of Sufi teachers. As many of these were ambulatory, it was difficult to control their influence. For much of their history there has been tension and rivalry between the Qadiriyya and the Tijaniyya. During recent decades, however, many of the differences between them have been set aside and they have begun instead to cooperate. This has largely arisen from the need to maintain a united front in order to face the challenge from new Islamist groups. Even before the advance of the modern Islamist groups in the 1970s, Ahmadu Bello, Premier of Northern Nigeria 1954–66, had created a religious movement called Usmaniyya and one of its purposes was to bring together the two large Sufi orders. After Bello's death – he was murdered in 1966 – divisions between the two main Sufi brotherhoods resurfaced.

A schism occurred within the Tijaniyya in the 1920s, when Ibrahim Niass (d. 1975), from Kaolack in Senegal, established his own branch of the order, sometimes known as the Reformed Tijaniyya, eventually resulting in major repercussions in Nigeria. Ibrahim Niass gained a large following across the breadth of the West Africa region, and many think of him as the single most important personality in twentieth-century West African Islam. He maintained extensive international contacts and more than anybody else strengthened ties between West African Muslims and the wider Islamic world, at a time when colonial governments were attempting to reduce such contacts. In Nigeria Ibrahim Niass and his anti-colonial and socialist ideas were opposed not only by the colonial authorities but also by the Sokoto caliphate. Tijaniyya attempts to recruit potential followers from the Qadiriyya caused much resentment and tension. In Zaria, Katsina and Kano the Tijaniyya successfully gained new followers at the expense of the Qadiriyya. By the late 1950s this rivalry resulted in riots which entailed some loss of life. Today the Tijaniyya have more adherents than the Qadiriyya in Northern Nigeria, particularly in the countryside. However, the Tijanis are also more divided among themselves.

Education

The twentieth century has seen progressively large numbers of Nigerian Muslim students coming to study in the universities and religious centres of North Africa and the Middle East. Particularly attractive has been the University of al-Azhar in Cairo. During the colonial period the British tried to control the influx of Islamic ideas, often by screening Arabic and Islamic books and papers. Nigerian students in Islamic countries sometimes changed their religious perceptions of Islam, and when they returned home they were dismayed by the lack of orthodoxy in the Islam of their own communities. For example, the puritan Wahhabiyya revival movement reached Nigeria and other parts of West Africa in the 1930s through Muslims returning home after pilgrimage to Mecca. The Wahhabis condemned moral laxity, Sufi brotherhoods and Muslim magical practices, which were often disseminated by West African *marabouts*.

The challenge of Western education and the response of Muslims to new educational opportunities is arguably one of the most important issues that have faced Muslim communities during the twentieth century. It was even more of a critical subject with regard to the education of Muslim women. In Northern Nigeria, with its own Islamic scholarly tradition, new forms of Western education were not popular and there were difficulties when the colonial administration attempted to apply Western educational norms to Islamic teaching traditions. The main problem for Muslims, quite understandably, was the perceived link between Western education and Christianity. Most modern schools were run by Christian missions, who expected their pupils to be open to the Christian message. As indicated above, emirs requested the colonial government to prevent Christian missions from proselytising to the Muslim population of Northern Nigeria. The British accedence to this request was based on the policy and practice of 'indirect rule'. When the Anglican Church Missionary Society (CMS) was allowed into Kano city in 1929, this was conditional on its concentrating its work on the Christian groups who had come from the south of the country. By the end of the colonial period there were very few Muslims in Northern Nigeria who had basic competence in English.

It was a deliberate policy by the British administration and the emirates to prohibit Christian evangelisation in Muslim areas. Because of this there was a very slow development of Western education in Northern Nigeria. Many colonial administrators thought that an orderly, if slow, development of Islamic culture was more suitable than access to modern education and Christianity. British officials developed their administration in Muslim areas in conjunction with established rulers, such as the emirs and the *ulama*. Muslims educated in the traditional Quranic schools were employed as clerks, policemen and district village heads. The British also accepted Islamic law, which was recognised over wide areas as it was easier to administer than the various local laws and customs.

In southwestern Nigeria, Muslims were better informed about the education provided by Christian mission schools and were, in many cases, attracted by Western education. The colonial government in Lagos gave a measure of assistance to modern Muslim education, but the support was hardly on the scale needed in order to satisfy demand. Instead Yoruba Muslims formed various societies whose task was to provide Muslims with a modern education which did not conflict with Islamic values. The most famous of these Muslim educational organisations, the Ansar-Ud-Deen Society, founded in 1923, had by 1960 over 50,000 members and ran numerous training colleges and secondary schools, as well as over 200 primary schools. Linked with this expansion and integration of Western and Islamic education was the development in southwestern Nigeria of a modern Islamic culture. The first Muslim printing press was established in Abeokuta in 1933, and by 1952 the town had a total of sixteen Muslim presses. These ventures by Southern Nigerian Muslims illustrate the need that many felt for a modern expression of Islam. Partly in order to improve their educational opportunities, Yoruba Muslims appealed for assistance to the Ahmadiyya movement in Pakistan. The Ahmadis, viewed with scepticism by many other Muslims, responded by sending their first missionary, Abd-ur-Rahim Nayyar, to West Africa in 1921. The Ahmadi involvement in Nigeria was, and remains, controversial.

By the time of independence, many Northern Nigerian Muslims were hampered from participating in the technological development of the country by their hesitant response to Western education as well as by lack of opportunities for such modern education. This imbalance in educational attainment between the south and the north of the country has contributed to the serious regional tensions that the federal republic has experienced. Most Nigerian Muslims have realised that they cannot afford to ignore modern education, unless they wish to put themselves at a permanent disadvantage in relation to Nigerian Christians.

A girls' class in a modern Qadiri school in Kano (photo: Roman Loimeier, 1987).

Islam and politics

With the creation and development of political parties, there soon occurred a clear division of loyalty and support from each of the three administrative regions of the colonial government of Nigeria. Simply put, the Western Region was the home of the Action Group (AG) and backed by the Yoruba people, and the Eastern Region and its largest ethnic group, the Igbo, supported the National Council of Nigeria and the Cameroons (NCNC). The large Northern Region was geographically, religiously and politically divided between the dominant Northern Peoples' Congress (NPC), the Nigerian Elements Progressive Union (NEPU) and the United Middle Belt Congress (UMBC).

It was particularly in the extensive Northern Region that religion became a matter of political importance and tension. Within the northern Muslim population, the traditional establishment controlled the NPC, while Muslim reformers, radicals and those generally at odds with the élite of the emirates chose to support the NEPU under the leadership of Aminu Kano (1920–83), one of the greatest Muslim scholar-politicians of twentieth-century Nigeria. Divisions between traditional and radical groups of Muslims not only affected the political parties and doctrines, but also contributed to an increase in antagonism between the Qadiriyya and Tijaniyya. Ahmadu Bello, the Premier of the Northern Region, led the NPC and sought to consolidate the authority of the traditional Muslim establishment in the north of the country. For a number of years he went on pilgrimage to Mecca twice a year and frequently travelled in West Africa and Arab countries, particularly Egypt and Saudi Arabia; he developed close contacts with the Muslim world and in 1963 became the vice-president of the Muslim World League.

Within Nigeria Ahmadu Bello sought to reform and unite the Sufi orders, and tried to extend the frontiers of Islam to non-Muslim areas. For both purposes he instigated in 1962 the founding of the Jamaatu Nasril Islam (Society for the Victory of Islam), and the following year set up an Advisory Committee on Islamic Affairs, whose forty-six members were recruited from leading Northern Nigerian Muslim teachers (*mallams*). Ahmadu Bello contributed to the revival of interest in the great nineteenth-century *jihad* leaders, Shehu Usuman dan Fodio and Muhammad Bello. As Premier of the Northern Region he attempted to use Islam as a unifying force in the enormous region. In the 1960s he led a number of conversion campaigns, particularly among ethnic communities in the Middle Belt area. The mainly southern-based Nigerian press depicted these campaigns as Ahmadu Bello's own *jihad*, while the northern Christian churches were alarmed by the use of political power to achieve conversion to Islam.

In connection with the *coup d'état* in January 1966 many political leaders were murdered, including Ahmadu Bello and the Federal Prime Minister Tafawa Balewa, and Nigeria had its first military government. After the second coup of July 1966, the country was ruled by General Yakubu Gowon, until his overthrow in 1975. The new military government's most difficult problem was the secession of the Igbo-dominated Eastern Region of the country, which proclaimed itself the new country of Biafra. This attempt at secession caused the Nigerian civil war between 1967 and 1970, which ended with victory for the federal government in Lagos and the safeguarding of the federation. A crucial contributory factor of the civil war was the massacre of thousands of Igbo Christians living in the northern half of the country, and the exodus of more than 1 million Igbo back to their crowded home areas in Eastern Nigeria. To many, the massacres were seen as the beginning of a *jihad* waged by Islam on Christianity, and this perception of events was adopted by Biafran secessionist propaganda. To the Biafrans, the civil war was also a religious war against the perceived threat of Islam. Even though half or a majority of the federal army were Christian, Biafran propaganda sought to portray the federal forces as Muslim oppressors who were determined to Islamise the entire country. Following the defeat of Biafra, Gowon's policy of reconciliation between the Igbo and other Nigerians was widely admired.

In 1963 the federal republic was composed of four regions. In 1967 the Gowon government split up these regions and instead created twelve states.

The number of states has been successively enlarged by later military administrations, and currently (1998) there are thirty-six states, as well as the new federal capital territory of Abuja. This division has adversely affected the authority and power of the traditional Muslim establishment to rule the former Northern Region, itself based on the nineteenth-century Sokoto caliphate. Today, the northern half of the country is divided into nineteen states plus the Abuja capital territory. The murder of Ahmadu Bello did not mean the end of attempts to maintain the Muslim élite's traditional political influence. Some of the younger Muslims who will preserve the legacy of Ahmadu Bello have come together to create an informal network of modernising aristocrats, technocrats and other professionals and politicians. Members of this network are popularly known as the Kaduna Mafia, although this does not imply a criminality. One of the leading members of this group, Ibrahim Dasuki, was appointed in 1988 to be the eighteenth Sultan of Sokoto, until he was deposed in 1996 by the then military ruler of Nigeria, General Sani Abacha. However, since Ahmadu Bello's death it has been hard to maintain an Islam-based traditional political unity for the northern half of the country. Structural administrative changes notwithstanding, a major reason has been the rapid growth of Christianity amongst many of the peoples of the Middle Belt area in the southern half of the old Northern Region.

Between 1978 and 1985 many Northern Nigerian towns and cities were shaken by the armed insurrections led by Mohammed Marwa Maitatsine and his Yan Tatsine movement. He had a long history of fomenting Islamic unrest in Northern Nigeria, and in 1962 he was deported from Kano to his native Cameroon. His followers, numbering a few thousand, mainly came from semi-Islamised areas of the Middle Belt or were foreigners from Niger, Cameroon and Chad. To a large extent they were indigent migrants to Nigerian urban centres, alienated from the mainstream of Nigerian life through poverty and relegated to a marginal status as refugee foreigners. After the return of Maitatsine to Nigeria and under his leadership, this marginal group waged a *jihad* against the Muslim majority who did not accept their teachings. Perhaps inspired by the 1979 siege of the Kaba mosque in Mecca, in 1980 the Yan Tatsine group attempted to capture the Kano central mosque, leading to the loss of at least 4,000 lives including innocent civilians, Maitatsine and other insurrectionists. After his death, groups of Maitatsine followers who had escaped from the Kano bloodbath attempted various smaller uprisings in other cities: the most serious incidents causing widespread loss of life occurred in or near Maiduguri (1982), Yola (1984) and Gombe (1985).

It is perhaps no coincidence that the unrest started in 1978 (in Maiduguri) and culminated in the 1980 Kano uprising, as this period corresponded with the beginning of a new century according the Muslim calendar – the fifteenth century AH (after *hijra*). There is a widespread belief, especially in Sufi Islam, that a *mujaddid* (reformer or renewer) will arise each century to purify and revitalise the faith. This belief no doubt inspired Maitatsine to regard himself as the *mujaddid* of the century beginning AH 1400. Extreme deviation from normal everyday activities and societal norms are millenarian characteristics. Millenarian movements have arisen a number of times before in Northern Nigeria. As late as 1965, for example, Abubakar Bawanke from Toranke near Sokoto proclaimed himself to be the Mahdi and spiritual heir of the Prophet Muhammad, which led to violent disturbances with the Nigerian police. However, the type of Islam that Maitatsine preached was a very special mixture of traditional Muslim conceptions and local African elements. There is enough proof to believe that Maitatsine relied on various 'pagan' beliefs in his teachings. Some of the movement's victims, for example, were murdered because it was thought that their organs would give Maitatsine's followers certain 'magical' powers. To describe Yan Tatsine as a 'fundamentalist' Islamic movement, a common description in the Nigerian mass media, is consequently misleading.

Since 1983 to the present (1998) Nigeria has been ruled by military government under a succession of army generals. In 1993 there was an attempt to return the country to civilian rule. General Ibrahim Babangida, who led Nigeria 1985–93, allowed two political parties to contest civilian elections held in 1992–93. The effect of this was that one party was viewed as being controlled by the powerful Muslim northern élite, while the other was seen as representing predominantly 'southern' and Christian interests. Although both candidates for president were Muslim, these elections were thought to have been won by Chief Moshood Abiola, a Yoruba millionaire businessman, from the Social Democratic Party, widely thought to be the 'southern' party. However, this election result was annulled by the Babangida military government, and since 1994 Chief Abiola has been held in detention without trial. The reason commonly given for this aborted return to civilian rule was that the 'Kaduna Mafia' and other influential northern Muslim military and civilian groups could not countenance the passing of political power from the North to the South and into the hands of such a strong leader as Abiola.

Islamist groups

The Islamist movement has grown stronger in Nigeria than in other countries of Black Africa. This is partly due to the fact that Sufism is not as strong in Nigeria, as for example it is in Senegal and Somalia. Moreover, Nigeria has its own theocratic heritage dating from the time of the Sokoto caliphate, a source of deep inspiration for the country's Islamists. Pan-Islamic consciousness is common, and many Nigerian Islamists have widespread international contacts. This Islamist network has contributed extensively to the building and running of many new mosques and other Islamic institutions, such as schools, hospitals, clinics, pharmacies and banks, that have been established in Nigeria during the last few decades of the twentieth century.

There are today a large number of Islamist organisations in Nigeria, most locally based but some organised nationally. Of particular significance are the Muslim Students' Society (MSS) and Izala. The MSS was founded already in 1954 but only later did it become radicalised. Today the society has branches mainly at hundreds of universities and colleges, and it is very active in organising Islamic activities at educational institutions. The MSS also actively propagates through producing radio and television programmes and the dissemination of Islamic literature. The society cooperates with numerous international Islamic organisations and has drawn inspiration from developments in Iran after the 1979 revolution. In some cases militant action, for example physical attacks on non-Muslim students and against Muslim students accused of drinking alcohol, has lead to the temporary closure of a number of universities.

In 1986 a new organisation, the Council of Ulama (CU), was created by present and past members of the MSS and their sympathisers. Many CU members are university teachers, such as Ibrahim Sulaiman at Ahmadu Bello University at Zaria, one of the foremost proponents of Islamisation in Nigeria. Sulaiman is one of a number of Islamists who have undertaken intensive research on the Sokoto caliphate. Many members of the MSS and CU are sharply critical of Jamaatu Nasril Islam, which is held to be both an 'official' and an 'irrelevant' organisation which has betrayed the heritage of Usuman dan Fodio and the Sokoto caliphate. A smaller and more radically Islamist group is the Islamic Movement of Nigeria, lead by Ibrahim al-Zakzaky, who has repeatedly been imprisoned. Since the members of this movement are strongly inspired by the Iranian revolution, Nigerian mass media [erroneously] refer to them as 'Shiites'.

Izala was created in 1978, and its full name, Jamaatu Izalat al-Bida wa Iqamat al-Sunna, announces that its members reject innovation and instead work for the preservation of the Sunna. Until his death in 1992, the leading representative of Izala was Abubakar Gumi, who had been born in a small village in Sokoto province in 1924. Gumi received a good Islamic education and became a very successful and respected religious scholar (*alim*), which made him influential in prominent Muslim circles in Northern Nigeria. He developed good contacts with Ahmadu Bello and in 1960 became his adviser on religious questions. Two years later Gumi was appointed Grand Kadi (judge), the highest Islamic legal position in Northern Nigeria. After Bello was assassinated in 1966, Gumi lost his protector but gained a greater freedom to articulate his own Islamist viewpoint. Gumi's most important concern was to try to unite Muslims politically. In his view, the 'sectarianism' of the Sufi brotherhoods was the greatest hindrance to the longed for co-religionist unity. In 1972 he published a large didactic work on orthodox Islam and its foundation in the *sharia*; however, as this tome was published in Arabic, its Nigerian readership was limited to religious scholars. To spread his ideas wider, Gumi published in 1978 a small book in Hausa, *Musulunci da abinda ke rushe shi* (Islam and the things that lead to its corruption or destruction). After the book's publication the conflict between Gumi and the brotherhood leaders widened and even degenerated into violent confrontation among ordinary Muslims in the towns and villages of Northern Nigeria.

Yan Izala, as Izala members are called, powerfully attack those religious elements in Sufism that they feel are contrary to the Quran and the Sunna. As important is their criticism of the Sufi social system. Young Muslims in particular have supported Izala's hostility to the fees paid to the *shaykhs* and against the high cost of bridewealth. As an alternative to the *shaykhs'* Quranic schools, Izala has established a large network of modern schools. The disruption and schisms that have been caused by Izala's uncompromising attitude and actions, have led to a more acute conflict than the earlier disharmony between the Qadiriyya and Tijaniyya. Izala has started or has led a process where the young are in conflict with the old, women against men and the poor against the well-established. For the weaker groups, the young, women and the poor, Izala offers a new way of life and a new conception and legitimacy of leadership. This opposition to the dominance of the Sufi *shaykhs* and traditional ways of life is interpreted as a struggle against non-Islamic forces.

The Sufi leaders of the Qadiriyya and Tijaniyya have vigorously rejected these attacks and, putting to one side disputes among themselves, they have formed a common front in their counterattack against Izala and other Islamist forces. The Sufis have denounced Gumi and his followers on many accounts: for interpreting the Quran too independently; for inciting children and youth to rebel against their parents; for encouraging women to disobey their husbands; for ridiculing the emirs; for falsifying the Sunna; and for trying to control the mass media for evil purposes. One of the leading Sufi strategists in this struggle against Izala, the Tijani *shaykh* Ibrahim Saleh, developed close relations with General Ibrahim Babangida, Nigeria's military ruler and president between 1986 and 1993, and Saleh was widely held to be the president's personal *marabout*.

The Tijani *shaykhs* have been the target for Izala criticism, more than their Qadiri colleagues. This difference can be explained partly because the former are geographically more widely spread than the latter, and partly because the Qadiriyya had historic links with the Sokoto caliphate, which Izala members and other Islamists respect even though Usuman dan Fodio and his closest followers belonged to the Qadiriyya. Gumi in fact claimed, without providing clear evidence, that Fodio had left the Qadiriyya before he died; this assertion has hardly been believed, and the tremendous

Nasiru Kabara (1925–96), leader of the Qadiriyya in Nigeria, leaving his house in the old city of Kano to celebrate the birthday of the founder of this brotherhood (photo: Roman Loimeier, 1987).

influence of the famous *jihad* leader among Nigerian Muslims is so widespread that too great an attack on his order would be counter-productive. The Izala struggle against the Tijaniyya has had a greater effect, partly because this order is split into different competing factions and partly because they have more controversial teachings than the Qadiriyya. Because of the disputes with Izala large numbers of Tijanis in certain areas, for example in Kaduna, have left the order. In some areas Tijani activities have practically ceased, and many of the order's mosques have either been abandoned or taken over by the Yan Izala. However, defectors from the Qadiriyya have been much more limited in number.

With the death of Abubakar Gumi in 1992, Izala lost its natural and charismatic leader, and the unity of the movement was weakened. This background of dissension among Muslims and divisions between Islamic associations has made it easier for Christians to win many elections for local government during the last few years. This has led to efforts to reduce conflict between different Islamists and the Sufis. For example, leading representatives from the Council of Ulama, a much broader organisation than Izala, have been engaged in reconciliation efforts.

Issues of conflict

One of the immediate reasons for the creation of the Council of Ulama was the national turbulence caused by Nigeria's entry into the Organisation of the Islamic Conference (OIC) in 1986. The Babangida government's decision to join the OIC, as well as the secrecy surrounding it, brought about a wave of sharp protests from Christian leaders, churches and other organisations. Before such united criticism from Christians, Muslims were acutely aware of the importance of unity. President Babangida pleaded the economic advantages of OIC membership, but Christians accused him of religious favouritism and pointed out that one of the OIC's aims was to work for Islamic solidarity between member states. Many critics argued that membership conflicted with Nigeria's constitution, which stated that no religion shall be given official status. Babangida replied that the country's entry into the OIC did not mean that Nigeria would become an Islamic state. He pointed out that Nigeria was not the only 'secular' OIC member. In the aftermath of the OIC dispute and the resultant acrimonious tension between Muslims and Christians, the president created a committee of mediation, the Advisory Council on Religious Affairs, with both Christian and Muslim members appointed by the president. The committee's commission was to forward dialogue, consultation and increased understanding between the different religious groups. The members however found it difficult to agree on their work, even though militant Islamists and Christian fundamentalist groups were not represented on the committee.

In the middle of the 1980s the question of the *hajj*, the pilgrimage to Mecca, was also a burning subject of debate. Many Muslims were dissatisfied with the restrictions and the control exercised by the state, while Christians perceived the *hajj* as yet another example of the state favouring Islam. Certain restrictions on the numbers of pilgrims had already been drawn up during the 1960s, but they were not rigorously implemented, and the numbers quickly increased to over 100,000 in 1977. The government demanded that this number should be halved, and the federal state governments were apportioned different maximum numbers of those allowed to perform the pilgrimage. In 1975 the military government had created the Nigerian Pilgrim's Board with the aim of managing the practical and logistical problems involved in pilgrimage. Earlier, for example, transport and lodging had been up to individual initiative, but the *hajj* became increasingly under official control. At the beginning of the 1980s a special 'presidential allowance' for additional places was introduced, and the numbers began again to rapidly increase until the middle of the 1980s when President Muhammed Buhari drastically reduced the numbers permitted. Critics felt that the quota of reserved places for the president was used by political favourites. By becoming an *Alhaji* (male pilgrim) or an *Alhaja* (female pilgrim) a Muslim could gain great prestige. It could even enhance an individual's employment possibilities. Because of the prestige that a pilgrim's title could give, even Christians in the 1980s who had returned from pilgrimage to Rome or Jerusalem designated themselves respectively as RP or JP.

Part of the official argument for limiting the numbers of pilgrims was economic. Significant sums of public money were spent on federal, state and local government levels for pilgrimage administration, and enormous sums of foreign exchange were taken out of the country each year because of the *hajj*. Some Nigerian pilgrims have also been accused of involvement in international drug smuggling and other criminal activities, which has resulted in them being imprisoned in Saudi Arabia. An important reason for government control of the pilgrimage, albeit not publicly acknowledged in Nigeria or in other African states, is the fear that the Islamist 'contagion' will further invade the country. Islamists from all over the world meet together at Mecca and important international contacts and networks are established. Some pilgrims also return with Wahhabi literature which they distribute in Nigeria. It is hardly surprising that in particular it has been Islamists in Nigeria who have criticised the government's intervention in pilgrimage affairs. The Islamists stress that it is every faithful Muslim's duty to perform the pilgrimage to Mecca at least once in a lifetime, provided that there is no reasonable obstacle, such as inadequate economic resources. They feel that secular authorities such as the Nigerian government have no right to limit or hinder individuals from following the precept of their religion. Some critics think that there should be an international Muslim organisation, Universal Hajj Council, with representatives from across the world, which should manage and facilitate the performance of pilgrimage.

One of the most important questions of conflict during the recent decades has been about the position which should be accorded to the *sharia*. During the colonial period Islamic law covered all parts of the law in Northern Nigeria, including criminal justice, even if punishments such as amputation and stoning were forbidden. With only a few exceptions, the British did not change the legal heritage derived from the Sokoto caliphate. During most of the two first decades of independence there was no major legal change in Northern Nigeria. It was only after 1979 that some important changes were implemented. The question of Islamic law on a federal level came into focus. Islamists who wish to turn Nigeria into an Islamic state feel that the *sharia* should be practised on a federal level. The Council of Ulama's deputy chairman, Ibrahim Saleh, declared that there was no doubt that Nigeria would one day become an Islamic state based on the *sharia*. Ibrahim Sulaiman has sharply criticised those Muslim leaders who are prepared to compromise over the issue of the position of Islamic law.

Before the inauguration of the Second Republic there was a long and stormy debate on *sharia*. The constituent assembly in 1976 had proposed that there should be a *sharia* federal court of appeal under the leadership of a chief *mufti* (scholar learned in Islamic jurisprudence) and that every state that wished should have a Islamic court of appeal at state level. Lateef Adegbite, the first president of the Muslim Students' Society, was one of the prominent Muslims from Southern Nigeria who supported this proposal and who stated that Southern Nigerian Muslims had for too long been denied the right to have their affairs judged according to Islamic law. However, there were many Southern Muslims, particularly from Yoruba-land, who pleaded for a compromise to solve this intractable conflict between Muslims. There was also a small group of Northern Muslims who were in favour of a compromise, partly because they feared that Abubakar Gumi would be appointed Chief Mufti if the original proposal was accepted. The end result was a compromise which allowed for the creation of a special bench with Muslim jurists in the High Court, whose task would be to scrutinise those cases sent from the state court of appeal. The controversial question of the status of *sharia* arose again at the end of the 1980s when plans for a new constitution for the expected Third Republic were discussed. This time too, those Muslims who wished to see the creation of a federal Islamic court of appeal did not succeed in getting a majority in favour of the proposal. In both debates, at the end of the 1970s and ten years later, the military authorities were very active in making sure that the religious divisions did not go out of control.

Only from the 1940s were Christian missions able, in theory, to operate throughout Northern Nigeria. This evangelistic expansion to a large extent corresponded with the migration of Christian southerners to work in northern towns and cities, and these educated migrants ran much of the modern governmental, commercial and communication administrations. Before the 1966 massacres it was particularly the Igbo who dominated church life in the northern cities. After the civil war there developed a more localised Christianity, mainly by northern Christians from the Middle Belt. The increase in the numbers of Christians from among the many Middle Belt ethnic communities has been exceedingly fast since the 1960s. In the last few decades a number of riots and disturbances have flared up between Christians and Muslims. This antagonism is naturally not just based on religious rivalry but also involves economic, ethnic and political issues. However, the violent disturbances in Kaduna State in 1987 and in Kano 1991 have primarily been based on religious confrontation. The 1987 outbreak resulted in the burning of seventy-five churches and the death of at least twenty-five people. In the 1991 Kano uproar it was reported that over 300 people were killed after demonstrations against the arrival of a 'fundamentalist' Christian preacher. The city and state of Bauchi experienced two outbreaks of riots, in 1991 and 1992, between Christians and Muslims, and both conflicts were rooted in local ethnic animosity. During the 1980s and 1990s religious antagonism between Christian and Muslim students has also arisen in a number of Nigerian university and college campus cities such as Ibadan, Sokoto and Zaria. These confrontations in part reflect the anxiety caused by the increase in contact between Muslims and Christians. Neither Christianity nor Islam are now confined to particular areas of the country. Religious tension has a clear connection with the growth of uncompromising Muslim and Christian activism. It has been suggested that there has recently occurred an 'Islamisation' of Christianity in Northern Nigeria, with Christians demanding equal funding for Christian pilgrimages and the incorporation of Christian canon law into the constitution, as the counterpart to state Muslim pilgrimage organisations and the importance of *sharia* in the country.

Literature

A broad and stimulating introduction to Nigeria's past, that discusses the role of Islam, is Elizabeth Isichei's *A History of Nigeria* (London: Longman, 1983). The significance of Sokoto in the Fulani empire is expertly recounted in Murray Last's *The Sokoto Caliphate* (London: Longman, 1967). Mervyn Hiskett's *The Sword of Truth: The Life and Times of the Shehu Usuman Dan Fodio* (2nd edition, Evanston: Northwestern University Press, 1994) is an excellent biography of the outstanding leader of the Fulani *jihad*, and information on Usuman dan Fodio's significance for Nigerian Muslims today can be obtained, for example, from the two books by Ibrahim Sulaiman, *A Revolution in History: The Jihad of Usman Dan Fodio* (London: Mansell, 1986), and *The Islamic State and the Challenge of History: Ideals, Policies and Operation of the Sokoto Caliphate* (London: Mansell, 1987). Islam's development in the southwest of Nigeria is the subject of T.G.O. Gbadamosi's *The Growth of Islam among the Yoruba 1841–1908* (London: Longman, 1978). For understanding the background of Tijani Sufism, see Jamil M. Abun-Nasr, *The Tijaniyya* (London: Oxford University Press, 1965). An exceptionally good local study on the politics of Islam and Sufi adherence is that by John N. Paden, *Religion and Political Culture in Kano* (Berkeley: University of California Press, 1973). The position of women in Muslim society is the subject of Barbara J. Callaway's

Muslim Hausa Women in Nigeria: Tradition and Change (Syracuse: Syracuse University Press, 1987). In Jean Boyd's book, *The Caliph's Sister: Nana Asma'u 1793–1865: Teacher, Poet and Islamic Leader* (London: Frank Cass, 1989), the life and work of a daughter of Usuman dan Fodio is presented. The growth of modern Islamist groups is given by Peter B. Clarke and Ian Linden in their *Islam in Modern Nigeria: A Study of a Muslim Community in a Post-Independence State* (Mainz: Grünewald, 1984). Klaus Hock's *Der Islam-Komplex: Zur christlichen Wahrnehmung des Islams und der christlich-islamischen Beziehungen in Nordnigeria während der Militärherrschaft Babangidas* (Hamburg: Lit Verlag, 1996) is a fine and detailed study of Christian–Muslim relations. A thorough and expert account of Islamism and the conflict with the Sufi orders is provided in Roman Loimeier's recent book, *Islamic Reform and Political Change in Northern Nigeria* (Evanston: Northwestern University Press, 1997).

Chapter Three

Senegal

Eva Evers Rosander and David Westerlund

Senegal has a reputation in the West for being a democracy and one of the most politically stable countries in Africa. It was the first African country to liberalise its political life by, for instance, legalising political parties and allowing a free press. Senegal's good reputation has earned it a great deal of development aid from Europe and the United States. In recent decades Arab countries have also offered money and other gifts for the building of, among other things, mosques, hospitals and schools. During this time, moreover, Islamist donors have pleaded for a pure and unified religion in Senegal and opposed the Sufi orders' more popular or syncretistic forms of Islam. Yet, in the otherwise turbulent African continent, Senegal stands out as a politically and religiously relatively quiet country, where a secular state co-exists with powerful Sufi orders, small groups of Islamists and a minority of Christians who to a certain extent collaborate with the Muslim majority.

What kind of democracy do we actually find in Senegal? While some critics argue that it is still in practice a one-party system, others seem to find its specific pattern of interaction of religion and politics intriguing and puzzling. Many conclude that the old and predominant Parti Socialiste (Socialist Party), which competes with a few other parties until now left without a fair chance in elections, is not manifesting a fully acceptable model of democracy. Nevertheless, the country is exceptional because of the elaboration of a peculiarly effective institutional network for the assertion of an authentic statehood over most of the national territory, which involves rural masses as well as élites, through the intermediary auspices of the Sufi brotherhoods or orders (Ar. *turuq*, sing. *tariqa*). Sufism in Senegal is a bewildering mixture of piety, commercialism and politics. Particularly in discussions about democracy, it is important to draw attention to the Sufi leaders, or *marabouts*, and their crucial position between the state and society. This link is semi-covert or informal and therefore very difficult for outsiders to grasp. The Sufi orders constitute what amounts to a religiously-based civil society, the social foundation of the Senegalese state. The *marabouts* co-exist with the state and the Islamic movements in Senegal. This relatively peaceful co-existence of the secular state and the Sufi orders may continue as long as the Senegalese state maintains its economic capability to hand out allowances to *marabouts* and some other Islamic leaders and is able to keep them integrated in the political game. The sustainability of the orders is, moreover, wholly dependent on the organisation of succession. Thus, there are certain weak points which in the future may affect the apparently stable current situation.

In Senegal more than 90 per cent of the population of about 7 million is (Sunni) Muslim. Approximately half a million are Christians, and other religious minorities are mainly adherents of indigenous African religions. The Christians, mostly Catholics, remain largely influenced by the French culture and way of life. Many of them have studied in France or in French schools in Senegal. They live in cities like Dakar, Thies and St Louis as well as in the Casamance Province in the southwestern part of the country. The main ethnic groups are the Wolof, Fulbe and Serer. Other, less numerous peoples, are the Toucouleur and Djola. Wolof is the dominating language, even among other ethnic groups, and the Wolof constitute more than one third of the Senegalese population. Thus, their influence over religion and culture is considerable.

Historical background

From the eleventh century onwards, Islam was spread along the shores of the Senegal river by Muslim traders. The Toucouleur in particular were early influenced by Islamic culture and traditions. Through this trade, and the missionary activities which Arabs and Berbers who came to the region were involved in, other ethnic groups also became influenced by Islamic beliefs and customs. Many Arab and Berber men married African women of the region that today constitutes Senegal. Conquests and political treaties were other reasons for the spread of Islam. Some local political leaders converted to the new religion, but only rarely did their subjects follow their example. During the seventeenth and eighteenth centuries several Islamic reform movements contributed to an increased Muslim influence in Senegal. However, such movements were urban and therefore attracted only small numbers of participants. They almost entirely lacked support from the rural masses. One of the best known reform leaders of the seventeenth century, Nasir al-Din from Mauretania, was defeated by Wolof kings after a long struggle. Nonetheless, the reform efforts resulted in the establishment of enduring institutions such as Islamic schools. At the same time they caused divisions which in turn facilitated the French colonisation of the region.

In the seventeenth century the first French settlements were established, and the French initially competed with the British for control over the coastal areas. The real colonising occurred during the nineteenth century, when the French made massive efforts to penetrate the interior parts of

Senegal. This was the time of several fairly important reform or *jihad* (effort, 'holy war') movements. One famous leader was Umar al-Futi, who had studied religion in Arab countries and made the *hajj*, the pilgrimage to Mecca. Umar al-Futi was a member of the Tijaniyya and claimed he had *istikhara* (mystical knowledge). He championed *ijtihad* (new interpretation of the Quran and Sunna) and had a profound interest and belief in the promotion of the worldwide Muslim community (*umma*). When, according to al-Futi, preaching was not sufficient to purify Islam and to unify the believers, he took to the *jihad* of the sword. His attacks were directed against Muslims who 'mixed' Islam with indigenous African religions as well as against the French colonisers.

Umar al-Futi was one of several *jihad* leaders who claimed to be the *mahdi* (divinely guided leader, 'Messiah'). Most of the Mahdi revolts were sporadic and short-lived. The different initiatives of the reformists were not well coordinated and local leaders resisted them forcefully. Besides, the French punished revolters very severely. Yet, even if the effects of the *jihad* movements were limited, they left a heritage of ideas about the universal Islamic community and an increasing respect for the Sunna. As they were not only military but also intellectual movements, they promoted literacy. To a great extent they contributed to the spread of Sufism, which soon became the predominant form of Islam in this geographical area. The expansion of the Sufi orders was to a certain degree a reaction to colonialism and represented an Islamisation with strong nationalistic features.

In the late nineteenth and early twentieth centuries the French openly manifested an aggressive attitude to Islam. Gradually, however, they adopted a more pragmatic view and showed an increased willingness to make compromises. The French colonial regime conceived of 'Arab Islam' as fanatic, intolerant and aggressive and preferred more Africanised forms of Islam – 'l'islam negrifié'. French scholars such as P. Marty and V. Monteil wrote several books about this 'black' or 'African' Islam; and during some periods the French colonialists forbid pilgrimages to Mecca in order to protect Senegalese Muslims from becoming 'contaminated' by the Arabo–Islamic 'infection'. For similar purposes a special corpse of French officers, specialising in Muslim affairs, was founded at the beginning of the twentieth century. These officers collected detailed information about religious practice, and on each important *marabout* they had a dossier. The French supported those *marabouts* who were prepared to collaborate, and they realised that Senegal could not be controlled and reigned without the help of the *marabouts*. The leaders of the main Sufi orders – the Tijaniyya, the Mouridiyya and the Qadiriyya – were particularly privileged. They participated at important colonial receptions and ceremonies. Furthermore, the French colonial administration offered them great material privileges in the form of land concessions and financial resources as gifts or loans. Religious leaders who had a benevolent attitude to the French could even get the costs for the pilgrimage to Mecca paid by the colonisers as well as receive contributions for the construction of mosques.

The French motive for this interest in Senegalese Sufism and its leaders at the beginning of the twentieth century was related to agricultural changes of great significance. More than any other Sufi leaders in Senegal, the *marabouts* of the Mouridiyya concentrated their efforts on peanut production, and the production of peanuts was a top priority for the French. It is true that the colonial process of modernisation was initiated mainly in the cities, but through the peanut cultivation the rural regions also became affected by the modern capitalistic economy. With the help of their disciples, *talibés*, the *marabouts* dedicated themselves energetically to the production of peanuts, benefitting from the favours of the French administration. The acquisition of new areas for cultivation attracted numerous disciples and increased the income of the *marabouts*. The disciples worked without any claims for payment or regulated working hours, and the French exported the peanuts to Europe, where they made considerable profits. As a result of the collaboration between the French and the *marabouts*, the latter supported the French rather than the Muslim Turks when the First World War started in 1914. They publicly prayed for a French victory and served the French by helping them to find Senegalese soldiers to recruit. However, French ambitions to promote an assimilation policy in Senegal was neither consistent nor successful. Even though a small number of 'assimilated' Senegalese were offered limited political rights – in 1914 Senegal sent its first representative to the deputy chamber in Paris – the great majority of the people was deprived of any participation in political life, and the few *marabouts* who officially were politically active had no clear profile.

When, after the end of the Second World War, the Catholic Léopold Senghor started organising a political movement, he successfully looked for support among leading *marabouts*. Consequently, he encouraged the French to continue their financial support for the construction of mosques and Islamic schools. The *marabouts* preferred moderate political leaders like Senghor rather than more radical intellectuals with a French university education who disapproved of the conservatism of the *marabouts*. A third political force, opposed to Sufi *shaykhs* as well as to radical French-educated intellectuals, was represented by some staunchly anti-colonial reformist Muslims who in 1953 formed the organisation Union Culturelle Musulmane. In criticism of these forces who were critical of the *marabouts'* collaborative tendencies, and in order to strengthen their own political influence, the *marabouts* organised themselves in different associations such as the Conseil superieur des chefs religieux (Superior Council of Religious Leaders).

The character of Sufi Islam

Since the great majority of the Senegalese Muslims are members of Sufi orders, this essay will concentrate on the characteristics of Sufism. Due to the interest shown by numerous Western and Senegalese scholars, especially from political science, the best-documented order is the Mouridiyya, which will also be in particular focus here. According to the American political scientist Lucey Creevey, the number of Mouridiyya disciples is around 2 million, while the members of the Tijaniyya may be in the region of 3 million. The most important of the smaller orders in Senegal are the Qadiriyya and the Layenne. Sufi piety is largely charismatic and emotional. Religious doctrines lack systematisation and are seldom codified. In particular the greatest leaders, who are called caliphs (*khalifs*) and are found at the top of the more or less hiearchically organised systems, have a special blessing or spiritual power called *baraka* in Arabic (*barke* in Wolof), which contributes to giving them a mediating role between God and humans. *Baraka* is a hereditary and predominantly male resource, although exceptions can easily be found, as will be shown later in this essay. There exists a chain of *baraka* which connects the different generations of *marabouts* with their disciples. Ideally, the disciples are ranked socially as well as religiously in terms of religious merits. However, not only pious and ritual acts but also economic achievements in the form of financial contributions to the *marabouts* and caliphs are meritorious.

In Senegal, as elsewhere, Sufism is largely mixed with local beliefs and practices. Belief in *jinns* (spirits mentioned in the Quran) is combined with belief in the existence of local spirits. Regional cults of saints, usually male *marabouts*, and faith in miracles characterise the orders, whose attitude towards regional variations and local beliefs has been extremely flexible and tolerant in Senegal. The great success of Sufism can partly be interpreted as a need to 'popularise' the message of Islam. As will be shown in the sections on Mouridism, the relations between the *marabouts* and their disciples are of great importance not only for religious but also for social and economic reasons.

Originally the Sufi orders had their stronghold in the rural areas. Even if this may still be so, the rapidly growing cities and the increasing migration to urban areas have caused significant changes. Thus, *marabouts* are nowadays found in great numbers in the cities as well as in the countryside. Often they have one home in a rural village, which is also the sacred space and goal for the annual pilgrimage of the *marabout's* disciples, and one home in cities like Touba, Dakar, Kaolack or Thiès. The top leaders of the orders, the caliphs, are chosen among the male family members. Succession fights are not unusual and reveal splits within the orders. Normally, however, these splits are concealed from the disciples. As leaders for huge groups of believers, the caliphs have a politically important position, and

81

their relation to the state officials is characterised by a mutual interdependence.

While the institutions of the state reach a limited group of people, mainly in urban areas, the *marabouts* are found in virtually all parts of the country. Good relations with the *marabouts* are, therefore, of great importance for the politicians. The *shaykhs* can, for example, contribute to increasing the efficiency of the payment of taxes without actually participating in it. The religious leaders can also legitimise the representatives of power, while simultaneously avoiding becoming too closely allied with the leading politicians. After independence (1960) the ministers of the government and persons close to them have, just like earlier colonial officials, contributed financially and in other ways to the building of mosques and to the *marabouts'* and their sons' studies abroad. Now, as earlier, gifts of land from the state to the *marabouts* are also of great significance. In the post-colonial period the *shaykhs'* great support for the dominating Socialist Party has had a decisive significance for the political development of Senegal. The French political scientist Christian Coulon underlines the *marabouts'* role as a stabilising factor promoting continuity in Senegalese politics. In the battle between Senghor and his radically socialist prime minister Mamadou Dia in the early 1960s, most Sufi leaders, and particularly the Mouridiyya Khalif Falilou Mbacké, supported the Catholic Senghor rather than Dia, who was a Muslim. Dia had his best support from Tijani *marabouts*. The competition with Dia did not last long, however. In 1962 he was arrested, accused of having organised a *coup*.

The relationship between Muslims and Christians has been relatively peaceful and harmonious. The strength and influence of Sufism are probably the main reasons behind the continued good relations. Lately some deterioration has been noticed, however. This is due partly to new Islamist tendencies and partly to the political conflicts in the Casamance region. Some Senegalese Christians have criticised the membership of Senegal in the Organisation of the Islamic Conference. In recent years not only adherents of the indigenous African religions but also the Senegalese Christians have in increasing numbers converted to Islam as a result of Muslim missionary efforts.

More than the other Sufi orders, the Tijaniyya assert the importance of education. The principle of *ijtihad* is stressed, and the order presents itself as rational. A great number of Quranic schools for boys and girls as well as higher educational institutions have been established. As early as at the beginning of the twentieth century, Malik Sy (d. 1922) developed in Tivaouane, in western Senegal, something like a folk university. Sy is one of two particularly important families within the Tijani order of today. The other family is Niass, and its centre is in Kaolack, southeast of the Sy centre, Tivaouane. Compared to the Mouridiyya, the Tijani order is less hierarchical. An ideal of equality is promoted, and social progress is

The tomb of Limamou Laye, the founder of the Layenne brotherhood, in Yoff, Senegal (photo: Roman Loimeier, 1991).

legitimised by religion. Through Ibrahim Niass' efforts a radically socialist branch of the Tijaniyya developed. Inspired by Gamal Abdel Nasser, and maintaining close contacts with Ghana's President Kwame Nkrumah, Niass (d. 1975) travelled widely and recruited followers in other African countries, such as Nigeria, too.

The Qadiri order in Senegal has to a large extent been lead by Moorish rather than black African families. Many of the Qadiri *marabouts* are Mauretanian and frequently reside in Mauretania, which limits their influence with the Senegalese state. Furthermore, the order is divided into various factions and not very vigorous. Yet some Qadiri *shaykhs* have become famous as outstanding healers. The Layenne order was founded in the nineteenth century by Seydina L. Laye, a healer who was perceived of as a Mahdi by his followers. For that reason he was fought by the French in spite of the fact that he abstained from all forms of violence. The Layenne is a small and ethnically quite exclusive order, whose members are mainly Lébou, a small group of Wolof-speaking people who live on the Cap Verde peninsula and south of it. The kind of Islam which the members of the Layenne practise is heavily influenced by the traditional Lébou religion. Laye did not know Arabic and, like the Mourids, the Layenne Muslims do not sing their religious songs in Arabic.

A wood-painting in Dakar depicting a meeting between Amadou Bamba, the founder of the Mouridiyya, and the French (photo: Roman Loimeier, 1991).

The Mouridiyya

This order was founded by Shaykh Amadou Bamba (1850–1927), who, from 1889, was actually a member of the Qadiriyya. According to various accounts, he received many revelations from God, urging him to build a big mosque in Touba. As a charismatic religious leader with a clear anti-colonialist message he was repeatedly forced into exile by the French. In 1907, in his Mauritanian exile, he started to recite a new litany of prayers *(wird)*. This year is regarded as the foundation year of Mouridism – now the most rapidly expanding *tariqa* in Senegal.

No-one knows exactly how to define the spheres of power and influence within which the Mourids act and negotiate. Their contacts with the government and the financial leaders who control the main capital flows in Senegal are mostly informal and hidden from direct insight. The order demands obedience, subjection, discipline and hard work from its members. Central moral values for a member are to be not only good, peaceful and generous but also industrious. This means that the leaders can mobilise their disciples in a moral idiom for their purposes, be it in the interest of the leaders themselves and their disciples or to the benefit of the goverment or some other central power. When a *marabout* gives an order *(ndigeul)*, it is an almost sacred duty for the disciple to obey. *Njebbel,* or *njebbelu,* is the vow of obedience and subjection to the *marabout* that the male disciple pronounces as a sort of initiation ritual. Without this vow, one cannot be considered as a proper disciple. No women are supposed to pronounce the *njebbel,* although there are a few exceptions. The exceptional female cases usually concern women of maraboutic families.

The *shaykh* expects total submission and obedience from his disciple. The relation between the *marabout* and his disciple is hierarchical and yet, as mentioned earlier, in a sense reciprocal. The disciple is actually waiting for and, as it seems, longing for occasions to manifest his obedience to his *marabout.* The *ndigeul,* the maraboutic order, to his disciple offers this opportunity for the latter to make a public manifestation of his unquestioned obedience. It may be a demand to clear up a forest by cutting down the remaining trees and bushes to prepare land for peanut cultivation. It can also be an order from the supreme leader, the *khalif général,* to vote in the elections for a particular politician, whom the leader wants to support. The majority of the *shaykhs* have disciples in the Senegalese countryside as well as in the cities. They all contribute in different ways to the *marabout's* commercial activities, providing him with capital through their work in his fields, through gifts of money or through their trading activities under his guidance in other countries around the world. Today, when the modern sectors of the economy seem to have failed to expand in African countries, this informal religio–economic sector, closely associated with international migration, prospers. It can perhaps be seen as a contemporary extension of the old trans-saharian trade.

Maraboutic prosperity has a divine dimension for the disciples. A *shaykh* with much money has much *baraka* – he is blessed by God. A wealthy and powerful *marabout* also has much to share with his followers, both in terms of material support and spiritual power. The *marabout's* white Mercedes and his driver confirm this belief in the mind of his disciples. The disciple contributes to this prosperity through his work and donations of money. Yet he does not work for paradise in the Weberian sense of a 'Protestant' ethic. He does it for his *shaykh,* who channels *baraka* to the disciple.

Within the Mouridiyya there exists a subdivision, Bai Fall, whose profile differs somewhat from Mouridism in general. The model of the male members is Shaykh Ibra Fall, Shaykh Amadou Bamba's first and most famous disciple. He was always completely loyal to his master, whom he saw as his task to watch over and to defend with arms if necessary. Ibra Fall's charismatic personality attracted many followers who became a kind of holy soldiers in the development of the Mouridiyya in the early decades of the twentieth century. The religious meetings of the Bai Fall can be very intense and emotional, as the participants enter into *djeul* (trance). The Bai Fall *marabouts* are known for their polygynous marriages. Through marriage strategies they form influencial networks. This is the case with many *shaykhs*, but the Bai Fall in particular are famous for having many wives.

Shaykh Ibra Fall formed a 'school' of his own, characterised by a very particular life style. The young Bai Fall disciples live together in small groups; they owe nothing and survive through begging money and food in the streets, sharing everything they get between themselves. Their only 'payment' is prayers. As they are supposed to do the heaviest physical work, including the defense of their leaders with the use of arms if need be, and are in charge of the preparation and transportation of food for the big feasts, they neither have to fast during the month of Ramadan, nor to pray five times a day. This is not well-viewed among the members of the other brotherhoods, nor among the Islamists, who consider such exceptions from the pillars of Islam as heretical.

Gender relations

From a male point of view, Mourid women are comparatively invisible in the religious practice and not considered to be disciples in a strict sense. They are not allowed to declare their vow of obedience to their *marabouts* nor to sing the *qasaids*, the holy songs based on the Quran and written by Amadou Bamba. Ideally, a woman should relate to her husband as the man to his religious leader in terms of subjection and obedience. The women's main task in the countryside is to provide food for the men who work in the maraboutic fields and to help prepare food for the main religious feasts. They also pay annual visits to shrines and attend the main pilgrimages. Whatever they do in a Mouridiyya context – work for and give money to the *marabouts*, pray, learn about holy men and women, go on a pilgrimage or visit a shrine – they confirm and strengthen their identity as female Mourids.

Some women are also formally, and in the eyes of the men, highly esteemed and significant, worthy of respect and adoration. These women are called *sokhnas* and are the daughters and wives of great *marabouts*. The female title *sokhna* corresponds to *serigne*, the term for a leading male *shaykh*. Just like their male counterparts, some of the *sokhnas* may have disciples and give vows of obedience to the caliph. This is, however, most unusual. One example is Sokhna Muslimatou, well-known in the 1960s for her distinguished position as sister of the caliph of that time, Falilou Mbacké, the son of Shaykh Amadou Bamba. She lived on her estate in Diourbel and had her own disciples, who were both male and female. Today Sokhna Magat Diop in Thiès holds a similar position. She inherited her *baraka* from her father Serigne Abdulaye Niakhep, an eminent Bai Fall *marabout*. Sokhna Magat's father chose her to take over after him as a religious leader, because he had no sons. She is in close contact with the caliph in Touba and pronounced her vow of obedience to him. Like Sokhna Muslimatou she has her own disciples, some of whom live on her estate.

Others visit her annually to show her their deference and to give her the *addiyya*, the money collected for her by her disciples. However, on those occasions she does not speak publicly. Her son talks to the disciples who have come to the house to see her.

The female *marabouts* or *sokhnas* receive young girls whose parents have left them to grow up in a certain *sokhna's* household, to be educated by her and to work for her. All the girls carry the same name as the *sokhna* and stay with her until they reach marriageable age. It is the female *marabout* who chooses the husbands for the girls and helps them to arrange and finance the weddings. The *sokhna*s sometimes act as teachers of religion and Arabic, or they trade or engage themselves in agricultural production, all depending on their family background, where they live and on their own personal interests. One wife of a well-known *marabout* not far from Touba cultivated the land that she had inherited with the help of her disciples, but she was also the owner of a few public telephone kiosks, a mill for the pounding of millet in Touba and two lorries that she hired out on demand. All this property was managed and made profitable by her disciples who carried out her orders. They did not receive any determined wages for their services and work. The disciples' payment is said to be spiritual and material at the same time, and this is the same for both men and women. Ideally, they work for paradise when working for the *marabout*, who also sees to it that the disciples do not suffer materially.

The *Magal*

The pilgrimage to Touba, the *magal*, is the greatest and most important manifestation of the Mouridiyya. In addition to its central religious role, it has a considerable political significance. It is celebrated each year on the eighteenth of Zafar (the second month of the Islamic year), the date when Shaykh Amadou Bamba was exiled from Senegal by the French. During the *magal* the pilgrims visit the main mosque, the tomb of the founder of their order and the houses of the supreme *marabouts*, who belong to the Mbacké family and constitute the core group of the Mouridiyya. All the pilgrims try to get a glance of the current *khalif général*. The disciples leave their gift of money with the *shaykh* to whom they 'belong' and stay there overnight, eating and resting, praying and listening to religious songs for one or two days.

A new organisation of young Mourids called Hizbut Tarkhiyya (Le partie de l'élévation spirituelle, association for spiritual elevation) has a key role in connection with the *magal*. This association was formed in the mid 1970s by Atou Diagne, who lives in Touba with his four wives, one of whom is the daughter of Abdou Lahad Mbacké, the former caliph. In several ways the members of Hizbut Tarkhiya have modernised Touba. For instance, they have built a library and they have their own radio station,

A *car rapide*, full of protective 'magic', in Touba, the centre of the Mouridiyya (photo: Roman Loimeier, 1991).

which they use during the *magal*. It is a very powerful organisation with considerable economic resources, and Atou Diagne has become one of the most influential men in Touba. The members are well educated disciples. In addition to those who are still students, there are, for example, medical doctors, engineers, technicians, computer specialists and traders. Their mission, like that of other disciples, is to obey the orders of the caliph and to serve him. Although they are modern and well educated, they essentially defend the same values as did Shaykh Amadou Bamba. Among other things, they are opposed to the system of secular schools inherited from the colonialists, and they regard Serigne Touba (i.e., Shaykh Amadou Bamba) as 'a gift from God'. Their main task is to organise the *magal*, which in their view is the *raison d'être* of the Mouridiyya. The members of the association are in charge of all the food preparations for the visitors. In 1997 they prepared, among other things, about 3,000 chickens, 300 oxen, 1,500 goats, three camels and many tons of rice and vegetables. 'Nothing is big enough to honour Shaykh Amadou Bamba', said Atou Diagne.

In West Africa, Islam and economic activities are traditionally closely linked. Today the tendency among the *marabouts* is to change from local groundnut cultivation to national and international import and export. From the rural areas to the city of Dakar, as well as further to European countries and more distant continents, these trading *shaykhs* travel and activate their disciples' networks, celebrating improvised *magals* and creating new business contacts. The local Mouridiyya entrepreneurs are investing in sectors of low capital intensity, such as small trade, and, in the case of the entrepreneurs with access to more capital, trade particularly in electronic household utensils, real estate and transport.

Dara and *daira*

From the very beginning of Mouridism it has been possible to replace religious education for the rural disciples with agricultural work. In this respect Mouridism differs considerably from the more education-oriented Tijani brotherhood. Mouridism was, and largely still is, associated with the rural areas of Senegal and with the Wolof people. The language of the Mourids is Wolof, and most of their *marabouts* in the countryside do not know French, the language of the former colonialists and the new urban élite.

Dara is the term for a religious school for the sons of the disciples of a certain *marabout* as well as for a rural place where the boys live and work for the *shaykh* in his fields of groundnuts and millet. The Mourid farmers, who live in villages 'owned' or controlled by the *shaykhs*, certainly have a social pressure on them to send their sons to the *daras*, as well as to contribute with their own labour once a week in the maraboutic 'Wednesday field'. The farmers are linked to the *marabout* in several ways: many have come to the village as landless peasants, receiving their field from the hands of their *shaykh*; others were offered their land by the *shaykh* or by his father after having spent some years themselves as young boys in the *dara*. The boys usually work and study in the *daras* between the ages of 7 or 8 to between 12 and 15. The daughters stay at home or live in the households of the *sokhnas*. Life in the *dara* is tough – the *imam* who teaches often uses harsh educational methods, and the agricultural labour is heavy. Also, the sanitary conditions are very poor. Clothing and food provided by the *marabouts* are sometimes deficient, and the general standard of living is low. The hardships are thought of as a way to prepare the young boys for future material shortcomings compensated for by a religious conviction, a firm belief in Mouridism and obedience to their spiritual leaders. The *marabout* decides when a boy can leave the *dara* and return home. Later in life the *marabout* will find a wife for the boy and pay his wedding costs, including the bridewealth, and provide him with a field for his own cultivation. If the boy emigrates, he will still remain in contact with his *shaykh*. The *marabouts* put pressure on the Senegalese state in order to obtain access to new land – mostly protected or classified forests – for cash crop cultivation and distribution to their disciples. As a result of these demands, large areas have become deforested. Soil erosion and a lowered level of the subsoil water are other consequences of the ruthless exploitation of land.

Dairas are primarily associated with urban forms of Mouridism. Nowadays, however, not only *daras* and 'Wednesday fields' but also *dairas* are found in the countryside. The *dairas*, which are religious associations devoted to a certain *marabout* or to the caliph himself, have an important function in urban political as well as religious life. Members of the *dairas* are mostly grown-up children and grandchildren of urban migrants. The members of an association are divided according to age group and sometimes according to sex. Many *dairas* are based on profession, others on vicinity, while some may be associated with a certain handicap such as blindness. Yet others may have nothing else in common except the *marabout*. Thus, people from different ethnic and social groups as well as migrants from various regions of Senegal can be found among the members of one and the same *daira* in a town. In a rural village, by contrast, all the *daira* members come from the same section of the village, obeying the same *marabout*, who usually lives nearby. The urban *daira* is a place to meet and an association to join for the disciples who cannot work regularly for their *marabout* in his fields. They contribute weekly or monthly sums of money (*addiyya*) as a gift to their *shaykh* or to the caliph. Occasionally, these urban dwellers are also mobilised to work for a short period on the maraboutic fields through the pronouncement of an *ndigeul*, the maraboutic order.

In the weekly meetings religious songs are sung, issues related to the *daira* and its *marabout* are discussed and sums of money are collected. The two leading persons of the *daira*, the president and the treasurer, are often the only representatives of the *daira* who have any contact with the *marabout* except for the visit during the *magal*. Their *shaykh* knows their names and receives them in his house in the countryside or in Touba. The *marabout* has no lists of the members, however, who may vary over time, since the urban population is highly mobile, always in search of jobs wherever they can be found.

The international Mouridiyya network

The social scientist Victoria Ebin has studied what she calls the informal sector of the Mouridiyya-controlled market place of Sandaga in Dakar. She states that a key reason for the success of the commercial activities of the Mouridiyya in Dakar is the network they have created and maintain with the emigrant communities of Senegalese disciples. She refers to the disciples who live in large international urban centres and who trade 'en grosse' in cosmetics, shoes, gold, electronic household utensils and other items. Emigration from Senegal has taken the Mourids around the world, to cities like New York, Atlanta, Los Angeles, Torino, Milan, Rome, Paris, Toulouse, Lyon, Hong Kong, Berlin, London, Madrid and Yaoundé. In the 1970s most Senegalese emigrants went to France, while in the 1980s Italy and the United States, especially New York, became centres for Senegalese Mourid migration. In France the stereotype of a Senegalese migrant used to be that of a blue collar man, usually doing unskilled work. In Italy and the United States he was, and still normally is, a street vendor. Even today many migrants begin their careers in the new country by selling cheap goods in the streets. Most of the emigrants are men, but recently women have started to go abroad to earn more money. The disciples who migrate to cities, where well-organised Mouridiyya communities exist, will normally be taken good care of and are helped to start in some of their established enterprises.

The emigrants live very closely together. They organise weekly meetings in their *dairas*. Some of them have jointly started their commercial careers by pooling their resources to be able to buy wholesale goods for retailing. For the merchants who remain in Dakar the migrant communities in the United States and Europe are a great asset. In New York a group of traders expanded their activities and formed an organisation called The Senegalese Murid Community of Khadimul Rasul Society (Khadimul Rasul is another name for Amadou Bamba). In various ways the *marabouts* adapt to the prevalent financial situation, and they have markets and disciples in Senegalese rural and urban areas as well as abroad. The development from *dara* to *daira*, and further to national and international markets, is smooth and efficient, since the Mouridiyya institutions actually co-exist and cooperate. Wherever they live, the disciples seek security, work and a religious framework for their endeavours.

Islamist tendencies

Since the 1970s Islamist organisations have appeared in Senegal which oppose the Sufi forms of Islam and favour the establishment of an Islamic state with *sharia*, the universal Islamic law, as its basis. The Islamist revival manifests itself not only in political demands. Meetings for praying and singing, conferences, new publications as well as substantial educational efforts are all important aspects of this revival. As in other Muslim countries, a great proportion of the members of the new Islamist associations are young people, among whom students and other intellectuals are well represented. However, not only Islamists but also other reform-minded intellectuals, some of whom belong to the Sufi orders, are critical of certain aspects of Sufi Islam. They criticise the *marabouts* and their misuse of power and money. In the eyes of Islamists and other critics, the *shaykhs* have become degenerated and corrupt.

The previously mentioned reformist organisation Union Culturelle Muselmane (UCM) has recently become somewhat more radical. Its principal leader, Shaykh Touré, has on different occasions expressed the need for an Islamic state in Senegal. Like other Muslim radicals, Touré criticises not only Sufism but also Western secularism. The UCM wants to promote and introduce Islamic education in public schools. Currently, the teaching is in French, and Islamic, and other religious teaching is normally lacking. The UCM has been fairly successful in terms of recruiting female members, particularly from the middle class. Despite its Islamist tendencies some of this organisation's leaders, for example Ahmed Lyane Thiam, have had good contacts with, and in some cases also been members of, the leading Socialist Party.

In 1979 a militant Islamist organisation was created by the so-called Ayatollah from Kaolack, Ahmed Khalifa Niass. In his view, obeying an authority other than God was *shirk*, polytheism, and to separate religion from politics was against Islam. Niass' Party of God, Hizboulahi, was however forbidden since political parties based on religion are not allowed in Senegal. The government's repressive actions against Niass and his supporters, who had close contacts with Libya, showed that even in Senegal Islam is a politically sensitive issue. Other Islamist associations, which have been formed during recent decades, are Al-Fallah, or Harakat al-Fallah (The Salvation Movement), and Jamaatou Ibadou Arrahman, or Jamaat Ibad ar-Rahman (the Community of God's Servants). Associations such as these oppose the secular character of the Senegalese state and plead for the creation of an Islamic republic. One of the sources of inspiration for, among others, the members of Al-Fallah is Wahhabism, the Arab reform movement which has influenced many current Islamist groups in the Muslim world. Jamaatou Ibadou Arrahman was formed by UCM-supporters who wanted a more radically Islamist alternative.

Dahiratoul Moustarchidina wal Moustarchidati (Association for Male and Female Students) is a religious organisation created by the Tijani *marabout* Moustapha Sy. Although it is mainly oriented towards the Senegalese youth, it has the character of a political movement which attracts people from all parts of the country and is a good example of the blending of Islamism and Sufism. It has borrowed from Islamist groups both in terms of contents and rhetoric, but it has emerged as a mass movement by using its base as a Tijani movement. It is a maraboutic movement influenced by modern reformism, or Islamism, rather than the reverse.

The new religious associations in Senegal publish many periodicals and other publications as well as produce cassettes and programmes in the broadcasting media. *Le Réveil Islamique* is the name of a UCM journal, and *Etudes Islamiques* is another well-established and quite prestigious journal, which was started in 1979 by Shaykh Touré. In 1983 two other Islamist periodicals, *Wal Fadjri* and *Djamra*, appeared for the first time. *Wal Fadjri* is published by Muslims who are influenced by Ahmed Khalifa Niass. Niass' own journal, *Allah Akbar,* was outlawed shortly after its first issue had been published in 1978. *Djamra* is published by an organisation with the same name and is concerned primarily with moral and educational issues. Thus, themes like prostitution, alcoholism, drug problems and homosexuality, which are interpreted as the result of secularism and decadent Western influences, are often discussed in *Djamra.*

Islamist groups in general have a great interest in education, and they support Quranic schools in the countryside, the introduction of religious classes in public schools and urban institutes for higher teaching and research. One example of the latter is the Institut Islamique, situated close to the main mosque in Dakar, which was inaugurated in 1979. However, not only Islamists but also *marabouts* have dedicated themselves to the spread of religious education and language training centres, and more new schools are opened by them than by Islamists. Even though Sufis and Islamists normally oppose each other, there are also examples of cooperation. In particular, the *marabouts* sometimes need to recruit Islamist-inspired teachers to their schools, as they themselves often lack sufficient educational qualifications.

With regard to gender issues, leading Islamists like Shaykh Touré have attacked both Western liberal endeavours to achieve gender equality and the conservative attitudes of the Sufi leaders. Touré argues that equality between the sexes is a basic idea within Islam. People should neither be valued on the basis of sex nor because of 'secular' achievements but according to their moral behaviour. In criticism of the *marabouts'* religious legitimation of polygyny, which is associated with the idea that the more wives a *marabout* has, the more descendants will inherit his *baraka*, Touré stresses monogamy as the 'truly' Islamic ideal. In 1972 a new family law, *Code de la famille*, was introduced in Senegal with the purpose of improving women's position and creating a more homogeneous legal system. The law was bitterly criticised by the *marabouts.* However, all the important Muslim leaders and organisations agreed in condemning the new family law because of its several deviations from Islamic law (*sharia*). The new family law stipulated, among other things, that men could no longer divorce their wives simply by pronouncing the Muslim divorce formula (*talak*). Each divorce case had to be tried in court. Since the law improved the status of women in several respects, Muslim critics called it the 'Code de la femme' (the woman's law), and the Catholic President Senghor was accused of forcing secular and Western ideas upon the Senegalese people. As a result of the vehement criticism, however, people were allowed to choose which legal code they wished to follow, the new one or the *sharia*. Since it is normally the men who make the choice, the effects of the *Code de la famille* in terms of gender equality have been relatively limited. While the Islamists have continued to argue that the new law should be abolished, the *marabouts* nowadays mostly seem to ignore it.

The continued support of the Senegalese government for the great *marabouts* shows that the representatives of the state still regard Sufism as an ally in their endeavour to counteract the Islamist 'politisation' of Islam. Simultaneously, the government tries to 'disarm' leading Islamists by offering them attractive and well-paid administrative posts. Several Islamists have, for example, become ambassadors in Arab states. To a limited extent, measures have also been taken to satisfy the Islamists' demand for teaching time for the Arabic language and Islam in public schools. However, Islamism seems to be a very marginal threat to the current political and religious system in Senegal. Sufism still constitutes by far the strongest Muslim force. The Islamists are somewhat alienated from the popular culture and cannot, unlike the *marabouts*, provide a whole social and religious 'welfare system' for their followers and sympathisers. In that respect, neither the Islamists nor the state can be compared to the *marabouts* who continue to wield their considerable influence over the majority of the Senegalese people. Concerning the present relationship between the Sufis and the state, Donal Cruise O'Brien in a recent review article entitled 'The Senegalese Exception' (1996) concludes that:

> The viability of the state still rests above all on the Sufi brotherhoods, extending government authority to the countryside. Sufi Muslim hierarchy thus underpins secular democracy in Senegal, and that hierarchy has been effective because it includes its own (concealed) democratic component. It is this relatively intricate mechanism which provides the Senegalese exception in terms of statehood, the logic of the 'Wolof model' of brotherhood intermediation with the state. The intermediary power of the *marabouts*, Montesquieu style, has protected zones of autonomy, and relative liberty, for the Sufi clienteles. Hierarchy has protected liberty, in twentieth-century Senegal as it did in *ancien régime* France.

O'Brien sees the hierarchical system represented by the *marabouts* as a mechanism for doing business with the state, for learning to live with it. The more the pressure for democracy, the more this hierarchical model will be threatened. Yet if the younger disciples reject the maraboutic orders as far as politics is concerned and ignore instructions to vote for the governing Socialist Party, then the *marabouts* will certainly lose weight in dealing with the government. In this case what O'Brien calls 'real democracy in Africa, as distinct from the democracy of Western sermons addressed to Africa' will appear and may lead to an urban anarchy of drugs and violence which can provoke demands for renewed authoritarianism. Still the grip of Sufism over both the Senegalese people and its government prevents such tendencies to spread unrestrainedly.

Literature

There are a great deal of good scholarly publications on Islam and Muslims in Senegal, written particularly by political scientists. A classic work is Christian Coulon's book *Le marabout et le prince (Islam et pouvoir au Sénégal)*, Institut d'Etudes Politiques de Bourdeaux, Centre d'Etude d'Afrique Noire, Série Afrique Noire II (Paris: Editions A. Pedone, 1981). On the historical role of *marabouts*, see also *Le temps des marabouts: Itinéraires et stratégies islamiques en Afrique occidentalde française v. 1880–1960*, eds. David Robinson and Jean-Louis Triaud, Hommes et sociétés, 46 (Paris: Karthala, 1997). The role of women is discussed in Christian Coulon's essay 'Women, Islam and *Baraka*', pp. 113–33 in *Charisma and Brotherhood in Africa*, eds. Donal Cruise O'Brien and Christian Coulon (Oxford: Clarendon and New York: Oxford University Press, 1988) and in Eva Evers Rosander's 'Women and Muridism in Senegal', pp. 147–77 in *Women and Islamization*, eds. Karin Ask and Marit Tjomsland (Oxford: Berg, 1998). A fine classical study of the Tijani brotherhood is Jamil Abun-Nasr, *The Tijaniyya: A Sufi Order in the Modern World* (London: Oxford University Press, 1965). Some valuable books about the Mouridiyya are Tidiane Sy's *La confrérie sénégalaise des mourides: Un essai sur l'islam au Sénégal* (Paris: Présence Africaine, 1969), Donal Cruise O'Brien's *The Mourides of Senegal: The Political and Economic Organisation of an Islamic Brotherhood* (Oxford: Clarendon Press, 1971) and Jean Copans' *Les marabouts de l'arachide: La confrérie mouride et les paysans du Sénégal* (Paris: L'Harmattan, 1988). An interesting article about the commercial strategies of the Mouridiyya is Victoria Ebin's 'A la recherche de nouveaux "poissons" – stratégies commerciales mourides par temps de crise', *Politique Africaine*, 45 (1992), pp. 86–101. The expansion of Sufism into urban areas is treated, for example, in Donal Cruise O'Brien's essay 'Charisma Comes to Town', pp. 135–55 in *Charisma and Brotherhood in African Islam*, eds. Donal Cruise O'Brien and Christian Coulon (Oxford: Clarendon and New York: Oxford University Press, 1988).

An overview of Islam in contemporary Senegal, which includes, among other things, a discussion of Islamist groups, is Moriba Magassouba's book *L'islam au Sénégal: Demain les mollahs?* (Paris: Karthala, 1985), and a more recent presentation of the Islamist opposition to secularism is found in Roman Loimeier's essay 'The Secular State and Islam in Senegal', pp. 183–97 in *Questioning the Secular State: The Worldwide Resurgence of Religion in Politics*, ed. David Westerlund (London: Hurst and New

York: St Martin's Press, 1996). In *Islamic Society and State Power in Senegal: Disciples and Citizens in Fatick* (Cambridge: Cambridge University Press, 1995), Leonardo A. Villalon provides a detailed analysis of the situation in one town. This study, and some other new books on Senegal, are discussed by Donal Cruise O'Brien in the review article 'The Senegalese Exception', *Africa*, 66:3 (1996), pp. 458–64.

Chapter Four

Tanzania

Abdulaziz Y. Lodhi and David Westerlund

Tanzania had more than 30 million inhabitants in 1995. Although the population growth is high, the country is – like most countries in Africa – sparsely populated. The population consists of a large number of ethnic groups. The great majority of these are speakers of Bantu languages. The largest ethnic group is the Sukuma, spread south of Lake Victoria. South of the Sukuma live the Nyamwezi who, culturally and linguistically, are closely related to their northern neighbours. Tanganyika became independent in 1961 and three years later formed a union with Zanzibar called Tanzania. The official language of the Union is Swahili, a Bantu language with a large number of Arabic loan words. The traditional speakers of Swahili have also been influenced linguistically and culturally by Persians and Indians. The old colonial language English is still very important in trade, commerce and higher learning.

It is difficult to estimate the total number of Muslims in the country. According to the 1967 population census, about one third of the population was Muslim, one third Christian and most of the remaining third were followers of traditional religions. The reliability of the statistics has, for good reason, been questioned and there are no up-to-date statistics at hand. The question of the percentage of Muslims and Christians is a politically sensitive issue in Tanzania, as in many other African countries. The statistics provided by Christian and Muslim organisations are biased and notoriously unreliable. It is apparent that the number of Muslims and Christians has been increasing at a high rate during the past decades, but it is hard to determine which of the two religions has increased more rapidly.

Historical background

The earliest concrete evidence of Muslim presence in East Africa is the foundation of a mosque in Shanga on Pate Island where gold, silver and copper coins dated 830 were found during an excavation in the 1980s. The oldest intact building in East Africa is a functioning mosque at Kizimkazi in southern Zanzibar dated 1007. It appears that Islam was widespread in the Indian Ocean area by the fourteenth century. When Ibn Battuta from

The sultan's palace in Zanzibar (photo: David Westerlund, 1977).

Maghreb visited the East African littoral in 1332 he reported that he felt at home because of Islam in the area. The coastal population was largely Muslim, and Arabic was the language of literature and trade. The whole of the Indian Ocean seemed to be a 'Muslim sea'. Muslims controlled the trade and established coastal settlements in South East Asia, India and East Africa.

Islam was spread mainly through trade activities along the East African coast, not through conquest and territorial expansion as was partly the case in West Africa, but remained an urban littoral phenomenon for a long time. When the violent Portugese intrusions in the coastal areas occurred in the sixteeenth century, Islam was already well-established there and almost all the ruling families had ties of kinship with Arabia, Persia, India and even South East Asia owing to their maritime contacts and political connections with the northern and eastern parts of the Indian Ocean. At the end of the seventeenth and beginning of the eighteenth centuries the coastal Muslims managed to oust the Portugese with the help of Omani Arabs. These Arabs gradually increased their political influence until the end of the nineteenth century when European conquerors arrived on the coast of East Africa.

During the time when the Omanis dominated the coast politically, the spread of Islam intensified in the interior of East Africa also. Trade contacts with peoples in the interior, especially the Nyamwezi, increased in importance and places like Tabora in Nyamwezi territory and Ujiji at

Lake Tanganyika became important entrepôts in the ever-increasing trade in slaves and ivory. Many chiefs, even in parts of Uganda, converted to Islam and cooperated with the coastal Muslims. Trade served to spread not only Islam, but also the language and culture we call Swahili. Before the establishment of German East Africa in the 1880s the influence of the Swahilis or coastal people was mainly limited to the areas along the caravan routes and around their destinations.

The great expansion of Islam in the interior of Tanganyika began during the German colonial era. After having conquered the coastal area the Germans began hiring coastal Swahilis as civil servants, thus creating a cadre of literate people who accompanied the Germans into the interior. These subordinate administrators, *akida*, and Muslim soldiers are an important feature in explaining why Islam spread so much faster in the areas controlled by the Germans than in territories occupied by the British (Kenya and Uganda). The Germans established a government school system along the coast with Swahili as the language of instruction, in contrast to the missionary schools in the interior which used the vernaculars.

Even if many Muslims cooperated with the Germans, there were also large groups who did not benefit from colonial rule and who were more or less openly opposed to it. These groups were primarily found in the poorer sections of the rural population and were attracted to the activities of the Sufi orders. Several orders were active during and after the German era, the most important being the Qadiriyya and Shadhiliyya. Many Sufis played an influential role in the Maji Maji uprising (1905–07) against the Germans. The name Maji Maji refers to powerful water (Sw. *maji*, water) which was thought to give protection against the German weapons. The traditional African ideas of Kinjikitile, the leader of the uprising, were to an extent intertwined with Sufi ideas. Though our knowledge of Sufi expansion in German East Africa is limited, the fact remains that Sufi influence was an important factor in the expansion of Islam.

After World War I, when the British took control of Tanganyika, the growth of Islam decreased somewhat. The British system of local government, 'indirect rule', favoured local chiefs rather than Muslims from the coast. Ever-increasing missionary activities as well as the establishment of Christian schools promoted the employment of Christians. Muslims were gradually alienated from the administration and the political scene. From around the time of World War II the influence of reformist and anti-colonial movements increased, and during the 1950s Pakistani Muslim preachers regularly visited eastern and southern Africa to promote Muslim renewal and to revive political consciousness among Muslims. This was a reaction to colonial oppression and the increased Christian influence in society. Muslims thus exerted great influence over the independence movements. When the Tanganyika African National Union (TANU) was founded in Dar es Salaam in 1954, coastal Muslims played an important role. Even in spheres where Islam played a minor part Muslims were able to hold strategic positions in TANU. The Christian reactions to the independence movement were mixed; many local and Western church leaders discouraged their followers from joining the movement.

Islamic denominations

The great majority of the Muslims in Tanzania are Sunni. Most of them follow the Shafii judiciary tradition, though the Sunni of Indo–Pakistani origin are generally Hanafi, and some of them are loosely organised into a branch of the Qadiri order introduced by the 'Bawa', alias Shaykh Ahmad-shah Qadiri Bukhari of Cutch, India, who has been regularly visiting East Africa since 1958. Small groups of Yemeni origin belong to the Maliki and Hanbali schools. The Shiite minority, mostly of Asian origin, are Imamites, Ismailis who follow the Aga Khan, and the Bohra. The latter are also known as Mustali Ismailis and have their seat in Bombay. The Muslims of Omani origin constitute a special case, most of them being Ibadiyya, a moderate branch of the Khariji movement. A small but active Ahmadiyya group is also present in the country. Some researchers claim that three-quarters of Tanzania's Muslims are Sufi. Even if it is impossible to get the exact figure, the fact remains that several scholars, such as J.S. Trimingham, have failed to appreciate the importance of Sufism in this part of Africa.

The variation of beliefs and religious practices among the Sufis is considerable. Not only in the interior but also along the coast, Islam shows many local African characteristics. Local practices and beliefs are often very obvious. In the interior it is sometimes hard to distinguish the dividing line between Islam and the indigenous religions. Prayers, the fasting month of Ramadan and other principles of official Islam are seldom strictly adhered to. The knowledge of Arabic is very limited. Both religiously and culturally the Muslims of Tanzania have a strong local African identity. What is known as 'African Islam' is characteristic of these people as well of Muslims in other parts of East Africa.

The Shiite Muslims of Asian origin constitute an exception. Many Shiites came to East Africa during the colonial era and many of them are relatively well-to-do and live in a somewhat secluded way. The Ismaili followers of Aga Khan in particular have concentrated on establishing schools, hospitals, libraries, building societies and guest houses as well as engaging in industrial development. Before the radicalisation of socialist politics in Tanzania following the Arusha Declaration in 1967, large amounts were invested in Aga Khan Industrial Promotion Services and Ismaili Holding Companies. It is difficult to estimate the number of Shiites in Tanzania, but they constitute a small minority living mainly in the larger towns and cities. A large number have emigrated to North America and Western Europe during recent decades. As opposed to the Ismailis, the Imamites have, through the Bilal Mission, been active among black Africans but with little success in terms of conversions. Like the followers of Ahmadiyya, Imamites and other Shiites have issued or distributed a considerable number of publications. Due to economic and other reasons most of the Sunnis have encountered difficulties in this respect.

Sufism is represented by several orders, but their work and organisation remain largely unknown. The largest brotherhood in Tanzania is the Qadiriyya which is divided into many independent branches. The origin of this order in this part of the Muslim world is connected to the Somali Shaykh Uways bin Muhammed who, having been invited by the sultan, arrived in Zanzibar in the 1880s. Shehu Awesu, as Shaykh Uways is called in Swahili, paid several lengthy visits to Zanzibar and initiated many disciples into his order, who afterwards spread it to the mainland as far as the Congo area. One of the most renowned leaders of the Uwaysiyya branch of the Qadiriyya was Shaykh Zahur bin Muhammed who lived in Tabora between 1894 and 1908 where he laid the foundations of the brotherhood by teaching newly converted Muslims the typical Sufi 'chanting' feature which in Swahili is called *dhikiri* (Ar. *dhikr*, remembrance). His successors then officially established the brotherhood in Tabora and began initiating new disciples. Further east in Bagamoyo, north of Dar es Salaam, the Qadiri order started its activities in 1905. Under the leadership of Yahya bin Abdallah, of slave origin and generally known as Shaykh Ramiya, this brotherhood expanded in the area around Bagamoyo and Tanga and further north. In the west Ramiya's influence was felt as far afield as Ujiji at Lake Tanganyika.

The Shadhili brotherhood, which came to East Africa from the Comoros, did not start expanding until the end of the German colonial period. It was chiefly through the efforts of Husayn bin Mahmud from Kilwa that Shadhiliyya spread throughout East Africa. He exerted great influence and Shadhiliyya, unlike Qadiriyya, did not divide into different branches. The number of Shadhiliyya disciples is, however, smaller than Qadiriyya. The only order founded in East Africa is Askariyya, established around 1930 in Dar es Salaam by Shaykh Idris bin Saad. Like Shaykh Husayn his first contacts were with Qadiriyya. The Askari order is represented in cities like Dar es Salaam, Morogoro in eastern Tanzania and further south in Songea, among other places, but the number of members is presumably rather low. Its doctrines are kept secret from outsiders.

The fact that the position of a Sufi Muslim is not primarily based on book-learning but on personal piety has attracted the masses to Sufism. In Tanzania there are numerous examples of *shaykhs* who have volunteered to live their lives in poverty and to share in the simple day-to-day activities of their disciples. They also take part in *dhikiri*-gatherings and the celebration of the birth of Muhammad (Sw. *maulidi*, Ar. *mawlid*), which is particularly important to Sufi Muslims. The birth of Muhammad is celebrated as a

101

national holiday in Tanzania. Another illustration of Sufi egalitarianism is that their leaders to a great extent have been black Africans, unlike the erudite urban *ulama* (scholars), traditionally of Arab origin. Many Sufi *shaykhs* can be strikingly learned like the *ulama* and highly valued because of their erudition, but they first and foremost possess a divine quality called *baraka*. Through their charisma they can bring about wonders, heal the diseased and act as intermediaries between God and men.

One may claim that it was above all through Sufism that Islam was Africanised and 'nationalised'. Its non-dogmatic standpoint and openness towards indigenous African beliefs and practices encouraged local adaptation. In comparison with the more alien and bureaucratic Zanzibar sultanate the orders were able to establish more informal and local structures. Through the Sufi *shaykhs* was provided a 'close centre' as well as personal relationship with the leaders. The African character of the orders and their extensive organisation also furthered the growth of the nationalist movements. Many Sufi *shaykhs* became 'natural' advocates in TANU, and after the collapse of colonial rule in 1961 Sufi Muslims continued to a large degree to support the socialist policies in Tanzania.

Islam in society

Mainly on account of the leading role of the Catholic president Julius Nyerere several Western researchers have underestimated the importance of the Muslims in shaping Tanzanian socialism in the 1960s. Because of the Christians having better access to higher education they became over-represented in the administration. However, Muslims constituted a majority in TANU, called CCM (Chama cha Mapinduzi means the Revolutionary Party) after the 1977 merger with its sister party ASP (Afro–Shirazi Party) on Zanzibar. After the introduction of the one-party system, CCM was the major political factor in societal change. The socialism of Tanzania bears many similarities to Islamic socialism, and Nasserism in particular influenced many Muslims in Tanzania.

The few Muslims who turned against the socialist politics were mostly of Asian origin. Some of the Muslim resistance was initially channelled through the East African Muslim Welfare Society (EAMWS), which was founded in Mombasa in 1945 by the then Aga Khan with the aim of promoting Islam and raising the standard of living for East African Muslims. Asian Shiites, especially Ismailis, dominated and financed the organisation, but Aga Khan recommended that all Muslims regard this welfare society as an organisation with pan-Islamic ambitions. When its headquarters were moved from Mombasa to Dar es Salaam in 1961, the Nyamwezi chief and TANU opponent Abdallah Fundikira, regarded as Nyerere's principal political rival in the 1960s, became the president of the organisation. EAMWS concentrated on building schools and mosques, providing scholarships and spreading literature. There were also plans for founding an Islamic university in Zanzibar or Mombasa, but these were never realised. However, the Muslim Academy founded in Zanzibar in the early 1950s continued to exist as a training college for teachers of Arabic and Islamic education until it was closed down by the autonomous Revolutionary Government of Zanzibar in 1966. In regard to this it is interesting to note that several times since January 1993 Zanzibar had announced plans for a separate Islamic University, which has now been founded. There are plans also for high schools connected to the University of Dar es Salaam; and since the middle of the 1970s the Muslim Academy has been reopened, a new Muslim secondary school has been built and Arabic has been adopted as the third official language of Zanzibar.

Because of the pan-Islamic tendencies and the capitalist-oriented leadership of EAMWS, pro-TANU Muslims opposed it. The organisation, it was claimed, constituted a threat to the ruling party. The antagonism culminated in 1968, when the organisation was declared illegal in Tanzania. Other Muslim organisations were also dissolved. Instead the pro-TANU Muslims, with several leading Qadiriyya *shaykhs* playing important roles, formed with the support of TANU the new national organisation Baraza Kuu la Waislam wa Tanzania (Tanzania Supreme Islamic Council), Bakwata, whose constitution was in large part a copy of the TANU constitution. Because of its close connections with the ruling party and many leading Muslim politicians' interference in Bakwata's activities, the role of the organisation has been controversial. Its achievements have been limited due to poor finances. Criticism of Bakwata increased during the 1980s, when opposition to the socialist politics of Tanzania grew and liberalisation began. Under internal Muslim pressure and international Islamic tendencies, Bakwata has recently become some-what more defined. The organisation has arranged lectures on Islam in different parts of the country, and in 1987 it called on the government to reinstall the system of courts that existed in colonial and post-colonial times. With this clearer profile international Islamic contacts are on the increase. Some Arab countries have financed new mosques, schools, scholarships, dispensaries and provided teachers for the newly established schools.

For a long time the question of schools and Islamic education has been Tanzanian Muslims' main concern. They had few equivalents to the mission schools whose activities not only spread Christianity but also led to a higher educational level among Christians. The decision by the TANU government to nationalise the schools in 1969 was therefore warmly welcomed by Muslims. The Islamic schools which have been founded lately in a political climate more favourable to private initiatives, for example Kunduchi Islamic High School in Dar es Salaam, seem to have an uneven standard but constitute an interesting development for the Muslims of Tanzania.

The proposal to reinstate separate Muslim courts is very controversial. Under the slogan 'Don't mix religion with politics!' the governments of Tanzania have endeavoured to 'privatise' Islam or marginalise the effects of Islamic law. An example of religious conflicts involving legal matters is the discussions about a government proposal to introduce a new marriage law which was presented in 1967. The implementation of the law in 1971 was preceded by two years of intense discussions. In particular the position of *sharia* in the judicial system of the country was debated. Before 1971 Muslims, as well as Christians and Hindus, followed their own marriage and divorce laws. Traditional judiciary systems of the different ethnic groups practising customary law were also in force. In addition, one could marry monogamously in a civil marriage. To counteract religious and ethnic exclusivism in favour of increased national consciousness, the government presented its aim in its 1969 White Book to create more uniformity in the sphere of family law. The other important aim was to improve the position of women. One of the tangible proposals was that the minimum marital age for boys was to be eighteen and for girls fifteen. The fifteen-year limit for girls was presented with reference to UN recommendations. According to *sharia*, puberty decides when a girl is marriageable.

The proposal that caused the most serious debate was the idea that a man who wanted to marry a second wife had to get permission from his first wife. The proposal that would forbid men to punish their wives corporally was also met with some resistance as well as the installation of an obligatory reconciliation agency for couples on the verge of divorce. If the agency failed to reconcile the parties concerned the husband in a Muslim marriage would legally be able to pronounce the divorce formula *talaka* (Ar. *talaq*). Many Muslims who took part in the discussions opposed the idea of creating a more unified marriage law, especially where the proposed marriage law was in conflict with *sharia*. Since family law is a central part of the Islamic law, any change which does not conform to it is particularly sensitive and controversial. Despite the criticism from the Muslims the government's proposed law was passed in 1971 with only minor changes.

The proposals of Bakwata in 1987 to reinstate separate Islamic courts is only one example which demonstrates that the question of the position of *sharia* in Tanzania is still a burning issue. In 1988 Sofia Kawawa, leader of the Tanzania Women's Union, UWT (Umoja wa Wanawake wa Tanzania, closely affiliated to CCM), came under fire after having publicly criticised Islamic rules that she felt were oppressive to women. According to Sofia Kawawa, polygyny should be forbidden and women should have the same rights of inheritance as men. Her statements caused protest and some riots. A group of young Muslims wrote an open letter which demanded that the secular regime refrain from interfering with religious matters. In Zanzibar two men died in the riots against the leader of the UWT. The

Muslim president Ali Hassan Mwinyi, who a few years earlier had succeeded the Catholic Nyerere, hurriedly explained that Kawawa had expressed her personal views and not the views of CCM or the government. Mwinyi saw no need to change the law, while Kawawa and other Muslim women continued to argue against certain Islamic laws. In some of her statements in 1990 Kawawa claimed that polygyny helped to spread AIDS.

In questions concerning for example polygyny, Muslim critics such as Kawawa have gained some support from the Christian quarter. Christian criticism to some degree is, however, part of a wider propaganda campaign against Islam. It may be noted that many Christian men, especially outside the circles of leadership, actually have defended polygyny, albeit with reference to traditional African cultures rather than to Christian belief. This was especially obvious during the parliamentary debates preceding the legal changes in 1971. Many Christian men and women also support female circumcision which is practised rather widely, even by fourth or fifth generation Christians, although it is forbidden by law. Female circumcision does not exist among Tanzanian Muslims other than those of Somali origin, and a mild form of it is practised among the few Asian Shia Bohra.

The relationship between Muslims and Christians has by and large been harmonious in Tanzania. A certain tension has certainly existed under the surface, but it has seldom led to open conflict. In his valedictory address in 1985, Nyerere stressed the fact that the risk of religious conflict in Tanzania has been greater than ethnic strife. According to him large religious conflicts have been avoided not least because most Muslims have placed national interests ahead of religious concerns. Lately however, a tendency toward increasing conflict between Muslims and Christians has been discerned in Tanzania. One of the reasons for this is growing Christian fundamentalism. To many fundamentalist Christians, Islam is considered the arch-enemy, particularly since communism is no longer perceived as a threat.

New organisations and tendencies

New Islamic organisations have also added to the increased polarisation between Christians and Muslims. Few of these organisations are officially registered. More rigid Islamist groups spreading propaganda for the surrection of an Islamic government in Tanzania are few and small, but less far-reaching signs of revitalisation of Islam are evident. Zanzibar constitutes a special problem with its deeply rooted Islam, and some Muslims who emphasise the importance of Islam want to see the Union dissolved. This is also desired by some Christian fundamentalists on the mainland, particularly the unregistered Democratic Party led by the Rev. Mtikila.

One of the Islamic congregations which has more or less openly criticised the 'official' Bakwata is Warsha ya Waandishi wa Kiislam (Islamic Writers' Workshop). Warsha was founded in 1975 as a unit within Bakwata, its main concern being educational issues. The unit had many young and well-educated members, some of whom were Shiites. This radical group was supported by the Bakwata secretary general, Shaykh Muhammed Ali, and demanded Islamic education alongside secular subjects in the Islamic secondary schools run by the organisation. Muslims faithful to the regime argued that this went against the secular foundation of the state, and after some conflict the Warsha group was excluded from Bakwata in 1982 and its members were forbidden to work at Bakwata institutions. The young Warsha members have however continued to strive for their goal. In their simple headquarters at Dar es Salaam's Quba mosque, courses are arranged and literature is published. One of the Swahili publications, *Uchumi katika Uislamu* (economy in Islam) has attracted attention due to its severe criticism of the Tanzanian socialist system *ujamaa*, which they consider communist. Most of the publications, however, deal with the Pillars of Islam, for example *Sala* with the official prayer (Ar. *salat*) and *Falsafa ya Funga ya Ramdhani* with fasting during Ramadan. Warsha is also trying to reform the old and mosque-based Quranic schools where education still consists largely of memorising parts of the Quran.

Another organisation is Baraza la Uendelezaji Koran Tanzania (Tanzania Quranic Council), Balukta, whose 1987 constitution states that its main aim is to promote the reading of the Quran and the spreading of Islam through financial and material support to Muslim schools. The organisation is also making an effort to establish and run Islamic centres and institutes for Islamic higher education. Other constitutional aims within the educational field are, for instance, publishing and conferences. Business projects like hotels and restaurants have also been announced. Holders of positions of trust are expected to have a sound knowledge of Islam. Compared to Warsha, characterised by its young members, Balukta seems somewhat old-fashioned. In April 1993 some Balukta members under the leadership of its president, Shaykh Yahya Hussein, were involved in attacks against butcheries selling pork in Dar es Salaam. Three slaughterhouses were destroyed and some thirty people, including Hussein himself, were arrested. The background to this is that the rearing and slaughtering of pigs has become common in religiously mixed areas and some Muslims have reacted strongly.

The Dar es Salaam University Muslim Trusteeship is another organisation which strives to protect Muslim interests in higher education. It has produced statistics which point to the much publicised under-representation of Muslims at the universities and in the administration. A parliamentary commission of inquiry has also come to a similar conclusion, followed by a report of the Roman Catholic Church of Tanzania in 1992 which confirms

The mosque at the university of Dar es Salaam (photo: David Westerlund, 1977).

the political and educational imbalance between Christians and Muslims. A book in 1994 by Aboud Jumbe, a former president of Zanzibar, further describes the dominance of the Christians and the underprivileged position of the Muslims in the country. The members of the Trusteeship try to promote a better understanding of Islam as a way of life. Another organisation, Baraza Kuu la Jumuia na Taasisi za Kiislam (Supreme Council of Islamic Organisations), founded in 1992, has a strikingly large number of university employees among its membership. This new council is trying to take over the leading role of Bakwata as a unifying organisation for all Muslims in the country, and its activities are closely monitored by the government.

Islamic renewal in Tanzania has been supported by organisations abroad. The World Council of Mosques, with its headquarters in Jeddah, has opened an office in Dar es Salaam to facilitate its work in Tanzania. It is claimed by some Christian groups that some foreign organisations have supported minor domestic Islamic movements which aim to change the country into an Islamic state. The Iranian revolution has inspired some Tanzanian Muslims, among others Khamis Muhammed, who is the editor of the Islamic magazine *Mizani*. In a 1990 interview he said that the Islamic Revolution should be followed by all Muslims in the world. Khamis Muhammed has also been influenced by, and has written about,

Wahhabism. Embassies of some Islamic countries have in different ways tried to support the radicalisation of the Muslim forces in Tanzania. Some Muslim heads of state have also supported the Muslim aspirations. Through the embassies, means have been provided for the building or renovation of several mosques, Muslim secondary schools, hospitals and clinics. Favourable loans have been given through these channels to Muslims engaged in commercial activities. However, the activities of the embassies has caused divisions among Muslim groups within the country. Nonetheless, personnel and financial contributions from the Middle East and Asia to Muslim activities in Tanzania remain much less than those from Christian organisations from Western countries involved in church and missionary activities.

In connection with a visit by the Anglican Archbishop of Canterbury in 1993, President Mwinyi, adhering to the secular stance towards religious issues of his predecessor Nyerere, complained about some extremely religious individuals abusing freedom of speech to create chaos in the country. Archbishop Carey talked about the fundamentalist threat. Zanzibar's becoming a member of the Organisation of Islamic Conference (OIC) was heavily criticised by Christian leaders, who argued that this contravened the secular constitution of Tanzania. The sharp criticism and the risk of a dissolution of the Union resulted in the Zanzibari government's decision to leave OIC. On some occasions, as in connection with the government crisis in Zanzibar in 1988, the year when the demonstrations against Sofia Kawawa, took place Mwinyi and other representatives of the regime have pointed to Muslim groups in Zanzibar and in exile who, despite the great autonomy of the island state, dispute the Union. One of the controversial groups is the Pemba-based Bismillahi who want a referendum on the Union between Zanzibar and mainland Tanzania. A visitor to Zanzibar soon realises that Islam is not only a private matter, although the authorities nowadays are less concerned with, for example, public eating and drinking during Ramadan, which have become more common because of the influx of tourists and Westerners.

For many years, elements critical of the regime, among others Warsha and the magazine *Mizani*, issued propaganda for a multi-party system. However, when Tanzania introduced multi-partyism in 1992, it was understood that all parties should have a national profile and that religion and ethnicity must not constitute the basis for new parties. Muslims in particular were warned not to use the multi-party system for religious purposes. Apart from the usually limited political demands, Muslim revival in Tanzania, as in other parts of Africa, has been noticeable in the growing number of mosque-goers and in the increased popularity of Islamic-style clothing. In the propaganda activities some Christian influences are discernible. Public Muslim sermons are being held in streets and squares. The practice of inviting foreign 'revivalists', spreading tracts and pamphlets, as well as putting stickers on vehicles and distributing cassettes and videos has become more common among Muslims.

Literature

A classical study of Islam in Tanzania and other parts of East Africa, albeit somewhat out-of-date, is J. Spencer Trimingham's *Islam in East Africa* (Oxford: Oxford University Press, 1964). The historical development of Islam on the East African littoral is well described in Randall L. Pouwel's *Horn and Crescent: Cultural Change and Traditional Islam in the East African Coast, 800–1900*, Africa Studies Series, 53 (Cambridge: Cambridge University Press, 1987). An outline of the history of Islam in the coastal areas is found in some of the chapters of Lena Eile's thesis *Jando: The Rite of Circumcision and Initiation in East African Islam*, Lund Studies in African and Asian Religions, 5 (Lund: Plus Ultra, 1990). The status of Muslims at the beginning of this decade is described by Abdulaziz Y. Lodhi in his article 'Muslims in Eastern Africa – their past and present', *Nordic Journal of African Studies*, 3:1 (1994), pp. 88–99, and by Aboud Jumbe in his controversial book *The Partner-ship: Tanganyika-Zanzibar Union – 30 Turbulent Years* (Dar es Salaam, 1994).

The question of Arab influence in Zanzibar is treated in A.Y. Lodhi's article 'The Arabs in Zanzibar from the Sultanate to the People's Republic', *Journal: Institute of Muslim Minority Affairs*, 7:2 (1986), pp. 404–18. Sufism is briefly described in François Constantin's essay 'Le saint et le prince: Sur les fondements de la dynamique confrérique en Afrique centrale', pp. 85–109 in *Les voies de l'islam en Afrique orientale*, ed. François Constantin (Paris: Karthala, 1987), and more thoroughly treated in August H. Nimtz's book *Islam and Politics in East Africa: The Sufi Order in Tanzania* (Minneapolis: University of Minnesota Press, 1980) whose main focus is on the political importance of the Qadiri order. A broader account of the political importance of Islam and other religions is found in David Westerlund's *Ujamaa na Dini: A Study of Some Aspects of Society and Religion in Tanzania, 1961–1977*, Stockholm Studies in Comparative Religion, 18 (Stockholm: Almqvist and Wiksell International, 1980). The political role of Islam is also described in Imtiyaz Yusuf's more recent thesis *Islam and African Socialism: A Study of the Interactions between Islam and Ujamaa Socialism in Tanzania* (Temple University, 1990). Although Frieder Ludwig's monograph *Das Modell Tanzania: Zum Verhältnis zwischen Kirche und Staat während der Ära Nyerere mit einem Ausblick auf die Entwicklung bis 1994* (Berlin: Dietrich Reimer, 1994) focuses on church–state relations, it also contains much information on the role of Muslims in Tanzanian politics.

The relationship between Muslims and Christians in Tanzania (and northern Nigeria) is discussed in Lissi Rasmussen's *Christian–Muslim*

Relations in Africa: The Cases of Northern Nigeria and Tanzania Compared (London: British Academic Press, 1993) and, with special focus on the political aspects of this relationship, in Frieder Ludwig's essay 'After Ujamaa: Is religious Revivalism a Threat to Tanzania's Stability?', pp. 216–36 in *Questioning the Secular State: The Worldwide Resurgence of Religion in Politics*, ed. David Westerlund (London: Hurst, and New York: St Martin's Press, 1996).

Chapter Five

Southern Africa

Abdulkader Tayob

Until recently, observers were generally unaware of the Islamic presence in southern Africa. It was assumed that Islam in its southern spread stopped somewhere around Lake Malawi, and little was known about the arrival of Muslims in the slave hulls of colonialism and during nineteenth-century international trade in sugar, gold and British-manufactured goods. This obscurity changed dramatically when groups of Muslims joined anti-apartheid demonstrations in the 1980s, which the international media beamed across the world. Since then, Islam has taken its small but influential place in the media mosaic of southern Africa. Sometimes Muslims are important social and political leaders in the region, sometimes they emerge as champions of dramatic campaigns. This chapter is an attempt to delineate the features of Islam in southern Africa, with a special focus on South Africa. It begins with a brief historical outline of Islam in the different countries, followed by a more extensive treatment of the contemporary religious map and challenges facing Muslims in South Africa.

Islam in southern Africa consists of a number of communities which together constitute a broad Islamic presence in the region. In spite of the 'universal nature' of Islam, a nature which Muslims espouse and experience, plural identities are deeply inscribed in religious institutions and rituals. Muslims in the south African region are a cosmopolitan group consisting of a variety of ethnicities, language groups and social classes. These were formed by a combination of willing and unwilling immigrants during various periods of colonial rule and apartheid, and more recently, indigenous peoples who converted to Islam. Produced in the history of the region, these identities are historically unequal. The economic support by Indians of mosques, in alliance with a particular religious outlook, dominates Islam in southern Africa, but other identities continue to thrive. Ironically, the particular history of South Africa, especially its apartheid conundrum, gave concrete shape to an Islamic universalism with two broad tendencies. One supported the nation-building exercise of the new South Africa, the other espoused an exclusivist Islamic position. Both, in one way or another, placed relationships among local communities, the nation and the international Muslim *umma* (community of Muslims) under the spotlight.

111

South Africa

Muslims first arrived on the southern tip of Africa in 1658 from the Indonesian archipelago. For the next 150 years, a steady stream of political exiles, convicts and slaves from the islands of South East Asia and some parts of India established the foundations of what came to be called the Cape Malays. Shaykh Yusuf, a political exile banished to the Cape in 1694, has become a founding symbol for this first Muslim community in South Africa. Muslims were only allowed to establish mosques and schools during the nineteenth century. Since then, however, they have become one of the most significant groups in Cape Town. A second distinct group of Muslims arrived from India from 1860 onwards as British-indentured labour on sugar plantations, and a little later as independent traders, merchants and hawkers. The latter contributed to the building of mosques, schools and cemeteries, and have since lived mainly but not exclusively in the northern and eastern regions of South Africa. Muslims from further north, particularly Malawi but also Zanzibar, form the third component of Islam in South Africa. Although less influential than either the Malays or Indians, they have also contributed to the particular ethos of Islam in southern Africa. Finally, conversion has formed another distinct group within South African Islam. During the nineteenth century, the Cape Town region witnessed significant conversions which were assimilated into the Cape Malay community. Missionary activity since the 1950s has led to a more distinctive and notable presence of African indigenous Muslims in the townships of South Africa. They constitute the fourth visible group within the heterogeneous Muslim presence in South Africa.

South African Muslims represent only 0.2 per cent of the total population. While Muslims themselves put their numbers at close to 1 million, the last government statistics, published in 1991, record only 324,400. Nevertheless, Muslims in South Africa are a highly visible urban group concentrated in the major cities of Cape Town, Durban and Johannesburg. They are now well represented in government, and professions such as medicine, accountancy and law. The economic base in the past was business and trade among Indians, and building and craftsmanship among the Cape Malays. They have come a long way from being slaves, indentured labourers and hawkers. Muslims from Malawi have been economically less successful as labourers in factories, farms and forestry. In 1922, the Jamiatul Ulama Transvaal was formed to represent the aspirations of *imams* and religious scholars. Since then, similar associations have followed, representing different regions and religious orientations. These have played a significant role in promoting Islam. A number of welfare and youth groups also serve the community and express a variety of orientations among Muslims. Sometimes, they represent particular political approaches, for instance the Claremont Muslim Youth Association of 1957 or the Call of Islam of 1983.

The role and position of Muslim women in South Africa needs to be mentioned separately. In the Western Cape, they contribute significantly to the economic well-being of the household. This was also the case in Durban and Johannesburg, but most often in the context of family businesses in which women's contributions were not clearly reflected and acknowledged. Most Muslim homes do not strictly define gender spheres, but men and women gravitate respectively around living rooms and kitchens. The religious sector does not reflect this more liberal social space, however. Women experts in religious sciences are rare. Some leaders like Mawlana Yunus Patel in Durban have recently established finishing schools for young girls. Presented as a bulwark against the moral decay of society, fathers are encouraged to remove girls from government schools and enrol them in these special religious establishments. The schools ensure the social reproduction of the subservient Muslim woman. In the western Cape, there exists a more egalitarian understanding of women's rights within Islam. Women play a large role in religious organisations including anchor persons in community radio stations, women's movements and more traditional Mawlud (*mawlid*, the birthday of Prophet Muhammad) organisations. However, under the tutelage of the powerful mosque *imams* and the dominant interpretations of Islam, a more egalitarian approach to women's position in South African Islam is severely limited. The overwhelming majority of religious leaders have resisted any explicit change for what women may do inside Islam, even as Muslim women make progress outside the mosques.

Botswana

A small group of Indians constituted the first Islamic presence in Botswana in 1890, but were restricted by colonial authorities to urban areas. As the history of Botswana moved from one urban centre to another, the Muslims created successive Islamic centres out of them. Now the capital city of Gaborone represents the centre of Islam in Botswana, and a magnificent mosque built in 1982 exemplifies and celebrates this fact. Malawian Muslims first made their appearance in Franciston in the 1950s from where South African mining companies recruited labour from the rest of Africa. Many Malawians have settled permanently in the country and continue the Malawian traditions. There were not many conversions to Islam until the 1970s when Libya employed Shaykh Ali Mustapha of Guyana with the specific purpose of attracting converts in prisons and townships. Botswana Muslims now represent 0.3 per cent of the total population.

Zimbabwe

Islam in Zimbabwe also illustrates the dominance of Indian institutions, but Ephraim Mandivenga reminds us in his book that the Varemba were

A shop in Ramotswa, Botswana, which was used for Muslim festival celebrations such as *Id al-Adha* from about 1900 to 1966 (photo: James Amanze, 1998).

probably the first Muslims in the country. They are the descendants of long-established contact between Africans of the interior and Swahili Muslims on the east coast of Africa. In the Zimbabwe region, this presence dates back to the seventeenth century. The Varemba still adhere to clearly identifiable practices like circumcision and abstention from pork as well as the use of a number of Arabic personal names. This people came to the attention of the Muslims in the 1960s, who initiated a successful conversion campaign thereafter. One of the most prominent of the religious leaders, Shaykh Adam Makda, founded the Zimbabwe Islamic Mission in 1977, with assistance from Saudi Arabia. Malawian Muslims arrived in the country from 1890 onwards as farm- and mine-workers, and have tried to maintain their identity against considerable odds. While most of their mosques were funded by Indian support, mosques within mines were built with monthly subscriptions. Moreover, the Zimbabwe Council of Imaams (established 1975) represents religious leaders of mosques serving mainly Malawian Muslims. These fledgling Malawian associations mentioned briefly by Mandivenga are unusual for southern Africa. In Zimbabwe,

Indians arrived at the beginning of the twentieth century. In addition to their support for missionary work, they built mosques and prayer halls and determined the major ethos of Islam through their religious leaders. In 1945 the Pakistan Muslim Youth Club was the first among many other modern organisations which expressed the social and political aspirations of students and youth and followed, more or less, the pattern of South African organisations.

Swaziland

Islam in Swaziland began in 1963 with the first Malawian workers in asbestos mines. The Malawian practice of Islam attracted followers, and soon Malawi–Swazi communities took shape in a few small towns. Islam was recognised by the Swazi king as a religion in 1972, and Muslims have since joined the national Good Friday celebrations to pray for him. Islam in the major cities of Mbabane and Ezulwini was mainly the preserve of South African and Indian immigrants. The Ezulwini Islamic Institute outside Mbabane was built in 1981; other urban institutions have since complemented and unfortunately overshadowed the humble beginnings of Islam in this small country.

Lesotho

Not much is known about Muslims in the mountain kingdom of Lesotho. However, one of the pioneers of Islam in Durban, the great Soofie Saheb (d. 1910), established a mosque in the country at the turn of the century which has given rise to a unique Muslim community in Butha Buthe. This is an African community which is Muslim but speaks an Indian language. Unfortunately, no study exists on this community.

The Texture of Islam

Islam in the religion is thus represented by a number of ethnic and linguistic groups. What is, however, even more interesting is how these divisions are reflected and maintained by symbolic systems within Islam. I turn first to the Indian hegemony which dominates the region. This domination is financial in principle, but articulated in the organisation of the mosques, and the dominance of a particular religious outlook. From the early nineteenth century, Indian traders contributed enormously to the building of mosques in almost every town. In Indian neighbourhoods, in particular, no cost was spared in materials and luxury, and committees consisting usually of influential traders manage the mosques. In the 1960s, mosque-building in South Africa was accompanied by an upsurge in daily religious observance, often preceded by the call to prayer from a powerful public address system. The motivation for this particular religiosity may partly be explained by the pressures placed by the apartheid system on communities facing mass removals. However, seen from within the Muslim community, it is important to note the role played by religious leaders who promoted and shaped the particular ethos in the mosques. Thus, in the Gauteng region of Johannesburg, the Jamiatul Ulama Transvaal guided the believers towards a strict Hanafi Deobandism, in reference to the founder of one of the Sunni law schools, and its revival in India in the nineteenth century. In addition to daily prayer, the observance of Islamic dress, for both men and women, became more prominent. The religious scholars, however, not only relied on their preaching and teaching to promote Islamic observance. Another Indian-inspired mass movement, the Jamaat al-Tabligh, popularised the authority of the scholars and their particular interpretation of Islam.

The ethnic orientation of the scholars and the mosques was unmistakable. In the name of the *sunna* (normative practice or exemplary behaviour) of the Prophet, the dominance of Indian culture, from the Urdu language, and to a certain extent Gujarati, to clothing and cuisine, dominated the mosque ethos. The overt message was a universal Islam, but the ethos was unmistakably Indian. The scholars and mass movement together provided a coherent worldview within which Indian ethnicity and culture was nurtured and legitimated. During the height of the apartheid era, it provided a self-evident manner in which to be an Indian Muslim in Transvaal and Natal. This very peculiar reading of Islam, including both financial support and religious orthodoxy, also became a package for export and propagation. It prevailed upon and threatened other interpretations of Islam. For example, the Mawlud celebration of Malawians (commemorating the Prophet's birth) was devalued, and the Afrikaans used by Cape Muslims was peppered with Urdu and Gujarati phrases. The Hanafi Deobandism of the middle-class traders and religious scholars was countered in Kwazulu-Natal by the Barelwi tradition, also originating in India. In South Africa, in particular, the Barelwi tradition celebrated the great Sufi saints who lived in the past, and built Islamic practices and identities around them. The most prominent of these saints in South Africa were Badsha Peer (d. 1885) and Soofie Saheb (d. 1910) who was buried in magnificent tombs in Durban. In contrast to the Deobandi Hanafis, the Barelwi tradition legitimated different class and ethnic groups among Indians.

Like the Indian ethos, even if not as influential, other interpretations of Islam also defined and constructed identities through deep, idiosyncratic perceptions and ritual practices. The examples of mosque-building and leadership models in the Cape become clear in relation to contrasting Indian and Malawian traditions. Support for mosque construction among Indians took the form of donations, often in the conviction that one would benefit directly from every person performing worship in a mosque one has

The shrine of Shaykh Yusuf in Faure outside Cape Town (photo: Abdulkader Tayob, 1997).

helped to build; or, that building a mosque on earth would be rewarded with a house in heaven. In the Cape, this specific religious motivation was rarely used for soliciting donations. Monies were accumulated over a longer period of time through a variety of fund-raising activities such as dinners and community fairs. Furthermore, artisans from the community usually provided their services during weekends at minimal or no cost. Both communities built mosques, but the social actors, traders on the one hand and fund-raisers and builders on the other, defined a different social and symbolic space in the making of a mosque. Such differences inscribed subtle and explicit boundaries among Muslims in South Africa. In spite of any religious teaching to the contrary, an Indian Muslim could not really become part of a Cape Malay mosque and *vice versa*.

Conceptions of authority also defined boundaries within Islam in South Africa. For example, Cape religious leaders were trained either in the city or in the Arab world. Moreover, when they assumed leadership in the mosques, they constructed and reinforced that authority on the basis of educational and ritual services to the community. In addition to the usual leadership during prayer times, *imams* would also be expected to organise religious classes, preside at the naming of a new-born child and perform the final rites at a burial. In contrast, Malawian Muslim leaders were trained in

Malawi itself or in Zanzibar, and played a very prominent role in leading their communities at the head of celebrations for the birthday of the Prophet, or sometimes as herbal or spiritual healers. Malawian communities in South Africa were scattered throughout the country, and the *imams* could not establish models of authority around daily worship or regular education. In contrast to the Cape tradition, thus, Malawian leaders maintained leadership through the annual celebrations in an Islamic calendar, or at the service of individual needs. Both Cape Malay and Malawian Muslims were led by highly visible religious leaders. In each case, the leaders were constituted through different patterns of authority, thus producing different Muslim moral subjects.

Clearly, the Muslim *umma* of southern Africa was a rich tapestry of local communities defined and reinforced by rituals and symbols. This pluralist nature of Islam has been noted in a number of other contexts as well, most notably by Michael M. Fisher and Mehdi Abedi in their seminal work on the discourse of Iranian Islam (*Debating Muslims*, 1990). The celebration of local discourses of Islam should not preclude an appreciation of a universal Islamic discourse. Often, the two stand in tense relationship to each other. In South Africa, in fact, such a universal discourse of Islam emerged within the context of apartheid. When apartheid emphasised the geographical origins of the various Muslim communities, their ethnicities and language preferences, some Muslims found shelter in the religious forms of these identities. Youth in Cape Town and Durban, and to a lesser extent Johannesburg, however, appealed to the supra-national character of Islam against the classification of apartheid ideology. The notion of an international race-less Muslim identity was posited against the classification of 'Malay', 'Indian' or 'African' in the context of a South African obsession with race. Not all Muslims were persuaded by this religio–political rhetoric, but youth groups at universities adopted Islam as an identity, and later also as an ideology with which to resist apartheid. The emergence of a cross-cultural, united Islamic discourse in such a specific context is particularly instructive for illustrating the tensions between Islamic pluralism and universalism.

In South Africa, they help us to understand the challenges facing Muslims in relation to the local, national and international Islamic senses. Here, the supra-national discourse of Islam gave rise to two trends, not clearly distinguishable when first espoused. Firstly, it created an Islamist discourse in South Africa which held tenaciously to the uniqueness of Islam as a culture, civilisation and ideology. This tendency, most eloquently advocated by Achmat Cassiem in the Cape, has decried democratic developments in South Africa from an Islamic ideological point of view. Cassiem consistently opposed apartheid, and spent many years either banned or in jail. Since the success of the Islamic revolution in Iran, moreover, he couched that resistance to apartheid, and now the new democracy, in Islamic terms. Moreover, he now heads an Islamic Unity Convention (established 1994) which represents a number of organisations and bodies, particularly in the Western Cape. His discourse shares a basic affinity in style and form with international Islamist rhetoric in many other parts of the Islamic world. However, his has taken shape in the political praxis of South Africa. Cassiem has inherited an international Islamism which was first articulated and developed in response to South African politics. The parochialism of the international discourse was inscribed in its geographical location, and in its political character.

The prospects for Islamist rhetoric in post-apartheid South Africa have been illustrated in the emergence of the anti-crime campaign called People against Gangsterism and Drugs (PAGAD). Hurtled onto world media when it attacked and killed a well-known drug lord in Cape Town in August 1996, PAGAD used the Islamic symbols of unity, martyrdom and retribution to gain support for an anti-crime and anti-drug campaign. Desperation against rampant crime guaranteed them instant support from all South Africans. Their insistence on brandishing only Islamic symbols and their promise to solve the problems 'with Islam', however, naturally restricted their support. The intractable and difficult problems of drug distribution, demand, territory and rehabilitation could not be solved with promises and slogans. For over six months, however, Muslims were engulfed in a drama in which they thought Islam was going to solve the problems of crime in South Africa. The rise of PAGAD illustrates the possibility of mobilising Muslims on social and political issues around universal Islamic symbols. PAGAD, however, also showed the serious limitations of such exclusive Islamic symbols both in their restriction to Muslim peoples, as well as in their inability to deal effectively with the problems thus identified.

Cassiem and PAGAD have not been the only inheritors of the discourse of Islam against apartheid. The Call of Islam (founded 1984) and the Muslim Youth Movement (established 1970) also opposed apartheid, but wholeheartedly supported the new nation. For these groups, Islamic identity did not mean that they had to reject South African patriotism, nor did it mean that they could not identify with international Islamic issues. However, their commitment to the new nation was explicit and unconditional, and articulated in religious terms. In South Africa, the writer's own work *Islamic Resurgence in South Africa* (1995) has analysed the historical roots of this trend, while Farid Esack's *Quran, Liberation and Pluralism* (1996) sets forth its particular hermeneutical trajectories. Esack argues that Islamic teachings of the universal *umma* and teachings on relations with other religions must be interpreted contextually. The different history and experience of Muslims in the modern world demands that the received notions of non-disbelievers, women and the struggle for justice be revisited.

This attitude to the nation was also present in other southern African countries, like the Swazi celebration of the king on Good Friday, and the support and participation of key Botswana Muslim leaders in national politics. In these countries, however, a national Islamic discourse has not been articulated. This unarticulated acceptance of the nation was also present among most Muslims in South Africa, who participated enthusiastically in the democratic elections, and have since entered government service in greater numbers than ever before. They articulated neither an International Islam nor a South African one like Cassiem or the Call of Islam respectively. Often, they paid homage to the former and thanked God for the latter.

National politics has not been the only source for international Islamic consciousness. In the past twenty years or so, other world events have also contributed to the emergence of an international Islamic discourse. A few examples will suffice to illustrate its importance for South African Muslims. Since the oil boom in the Middle East made it possible for Saudi Arabia to build an extensive infrastructure for pilgrimage, a greater number of South Africans have made this trip than ever before. During apartheid, in fact, special arrangements were made for South Africans to participate in this event in spite of South Africa's isolation. In 1979, the Islamic revolution in Iran contributed in no small measure to a greater awareness among Muslims of Islam's international breadth. The media's coverage of Muslim communities, particularly crises such as the war in Bosnia and Somalia, and the natural disasters in Bangladesh, has also led to greater awareness of the predicament of the *umma*. South Africans have responded to these crises by offering humanitarian aid and supplies. By acting together in support of a world crisis, or going together as South Africans on pilgrimage, Muslims have become aware of, and involved in, an international community.

The international consciousness of Islam has, mirror-like, contributed to a greater awareness of a South African Muslim community. Going together on pilgrimage or contributing to the alleviation of crises created a South African awareness. The Bosnian example, which exemplified international *umma* consciousness to a great extent, also revealed a South African Muslim consciousness and its place in the greater South African nation. When South African Muslims supported Bosnia and sent a mobile hospital to Bosnians in the throes of a genocide, some Muslims criticised this dramatic gesture. In particular, they decried the fact that Muslims had a similar obligation towards poverty and disease at home. The relief effort for Bosnia was highly successful, however, but it did not completely ignore the criticism. A project of similar hospitals in the rural areas of Kwazulu-Natal also received the support of Muslims. During the past ten years, the boundaries of a national Muslim consciousness have started to be shaped in other ritual acts as well. Muslims have begun to adopt a national strategy for sighting the new moon for announcing the end of Ramadan and the beginning of the month of pilgrimage. Various other attempts, not least the deeply Islamist Islamic Unity Convention, focused on the national consciousness of being Muslims in South Africa.

There are basically two interrelated challenges facing Muslims with regard to the nation. Firstly, the nation as an entity is only affirmed unconsciously or in terms of ritual practice. Hence, the practice of celebrating an *Id* festival on a single day signifies the national character of such a process. Similarly, the organisation of *hajj* (pilgrimage) facilities in Mecca for South Africans emphasises the national boundaries of Muslims. In either case, however, the nation has no place in contemporary Islamic discourse. In fact, it is often discredited in the name of an international discourse of unity. The challenge for Muslims lies in reconciling practice and theory, as well as reconciling national being with a supra-national Islamic consciousness. The second challenge arises as a result of the first. In the absence of a recognition of national boundaries in Islamic discourse, it is difficult to propose structures and mechanisms to deal with national issues. As a result, acts of national significance and importance are often taken as extensions of local power hegemonies or ritual preferences. Hence, for example, when traders offer to help build mosques in townships, they manifest Islamic national unity as well as Indian religious hegemony by insisting on a particular religious ethos. Even the national sighting of the moon revealed key anomalies. Its acceptance by the general community was a measure of how Muslims regarded themselves as being part of one community. However, for the *Id al-Adha* (festival of sacrifice) about fourteen mosques in Cape Town insisted on celebrating the occasion in terms of ritual procedures in Mecca. Consequently, national issues were forced to follow discourses of Islamic law and their representatives in specific mosques. In the absence of the nation in the discourse, the parochial hegemonies set the terms of the national agenda for Islam.

The conundrum of southern African Islam is reflected in a number of other social and political issues and events as well. South Africa's new constitution makes provision for a pluralist legal regime. The new constitution recognised the injustice perpetrated against marginalised legal cultures, and adopted legal pluralism in matters of personal law. For Muslims, this represented the recognition of Islamic practices after years of denial and rejection of their marriages, testamentary wishes and obligations to their progeny. However, the new constitution also demanded that all laws be evaluated in terms of the Bill of Rights. Conservative religious scholars welcomed the recognition of Islamic law but refused to accept the provision of the Bill of Rights. Faithful to a literal interpretation of Islamic law, they pointed out possibilities in the new constitution by insisting that the provision of freedom of religion overruled the provision of gender equality in the Bill of Rights. In 1998, nevertheless, it appears that these leaders are prepared to accept the demands of the constitution and the Bill

Two *imams* in Cape Town (photo: Muhaymin Bassier, 1991).

of Rights. Without this national category imposed by the state, Muslim discourse was not able to propose models for how Islam would relate to issues of national significance.

In recent years, the popularity of Sufism across the variety of Muslim identities added another dimension to Islamic life. Sufi orders and teachers have emerged across the divisions and begun to attract many followers. The teachers and the orders are the familiar ones like the Qadiris and Chistis from India, but also the Ba Alawiyya and Alawiyya of Mecca and Algeria respectively, and the Maryamiyya of the European convert Frithjof Schuon. Texts on Sufi healing, *dhikr* ('remembrance', Sufi worship) and contemplation have become extremely popular. In one sense, such a turn towards an order or a teacher confirmed the need to belong, adding to the existing Islamic identities rooted in ethnic, *sharia* (Islamic law) and class identities. On the other hand, the turn towards Sufism was also a turn of the individual towards his or her personal experience. The importance of personal experience may provide a re-orientation for many individuals frustrated with the challenges in post-apartheid South Africa, once performed by ethnically restricted religious institutions. The inner dimension of Sufism would appear as a legitimate alternative to the ethnic and linguistic boundaries drawn by legal and political structures and entities.

Symbols of identity pervaded Islamic life in South and southern Africa. Whether they were rituals inscribing ethnic identity, laws preserving the Muslim subject, or women bearing the burden of a pure Islamic past, identity seemed to be a major factor in the Islamic presence in this part of Africa. Over the past 350 years, identities took shape in the patterns of religious authority and rituals, inscribing the historical experience of diverse groups. These religious practices have had a definite impact on people's sense of the world. At the same time, however, the rituals and symbols were themselves subject to change. In modern southern Africa as elsewhere, Muslims were not simply the objects of ritual adherence. In the context of apartheid and liberation, a universal Islamic identity became a powerful counter-force to race and ethnicity. This encounter engendered a challenge to existing identities and gave rise to political mobilisation during and after apartheid.

As Muslims approach the end of the twentieth century, it is clear that the context of the new South Africa with its progressive constitution is already forcing Muslims to respond anew. In the absence of a nation-centred discourse, the powerful institutions (mosques, *ulama* bodies and conventions) are likely to approach the challenges from the angle of the particular interests they represent. Hanafi, Shafii, African, Iranian, or progressive, these approaches were developed in the context of apartheid. Some of these were conservative, preserving the existence of the community, while others were iconoclastic, challenging the political philosophy of South Africans. Either they were intensively conservative and inward-looking, or they were extremely combative. Both were the products of apartheid and resistance to apartheid. It seems that Muslims need a bold orientation towards the new state and the new democracy in the country. Such an approach will give greater meaning and integrity to the fact that most Muslims participated and voted in the new elections. It will also help Muslims to approach their institutions, their relations with the state and the outside world, with greater integrity, creativity and dignity. With the rise of Sufism and militant Islamic discourse, Muslims are being offered the more familiar and convenient options of marginalisation, rhetoric and inner development. Given the rich history of Islam in Africa in general, and South Africa in particular, it is comforting to note that these will not be the only alternatives.

Literature

Achmat Davids, *The Mosques of Bo-Kaap: A Social History of Islam at the Cape* (Cape Town: The SA Institute of Arabic and Islamic Research, 1980) is a pioneering study of the first mosques established in Cape Town, South Africa. The study focuses on the establishment of these mosques and their leadership structures. In the book *Qur'an, Liberation and Pluralism: Towards an Islamic Perspective of Inter-Religious Solidarity against Oppression* (Oxford: Oneworld Publications, 1997), Farid Esack has explored the unique interpretation of the Quran within the struggle of apartheid. His work reflects some of the notions developed particularly within the Call of Islam and the Muslim Youth Movement. M. Shamiel Jeppie's 'Historical Process and the Constitution of Subjects: I.D. Du Plessis and the Re-invention of the "Malay"' (Honours Paper, University of Cape Town, 1987), exposes the construction of the Malay identity by Afrikaner ideologists. It is a study which unpacks the notions of race and religion in apartheid and anti-apartheid discourse. *Islamic Resurgence in South Africa: The Muslim Youth Movement* (Cape Town: UCT Press, 1995), by Abdulkader I. Tayob, is a monograph on the Muslim Youth Movement which traces the emergence and development of a new paradigm of Islamic thought and practice among Muslim youth in South Africa. This study locates Islamic political thought in the context of religious leadership.

The following are some of the few studies of the position of Islam in the countries around South Africa, which contain useful information and contexts of the arrival of Muslims and the establishment of institutions: Peter Kasenene, *Religion in Swaziland* (Braamfontein: Skotaville, 1993); Saroj N. Parratt, 'Muslims in Botswana', *Journal of African Studies*, 48:1 (1989), pp. 71–81; Ephraim Mandivenga, *Islam in Zimbabwe* (Gweru: Mambo Press, 1983); J.N. Amanze, *Islam in Botwana: Past and Present 1882–1995* (unpublished manuscript, 1995).

Part Two

Asia
and
Oceania

Chapter Six

Turkey

Svante Cornell and Ingvar Svanberg

The events from 1994 to the present day have accentuated the inherent difficulties of the Turkish state's relationship with religion. First of all, religion has re-emerged in the open in society in a way unseen since the republic was proclaimed in 1923. The tension between secularists and Islamists in the political sphere has increased, and polarisation seems on the increase throughout society. Deeper in society, the sectarian fragmentation of Islam is possibly growing, and certainly more publicised than ever. The Turkish public, which on the whole – this is especially true for the secular establishment – has a poor knowledge of Islam both generally and in Turkey, is suddenly exposed to extensive media coverage of the activities of Islamist groups. Moreover, the existence of a non-Sunni minority of Alevis which may compose up to one third of the population of the country was news to many Turks, not to mention foreigners. As mainly foreign observers are warning of an Islamic revolt or a development of the Algerian type, Turks are quick to explain that Turkey is not Algeria. However, there is a very poor awareness of Islam in Turkey, as well as in Europe, although scholarly interest is increasing. In Turkey, this ignorance has led to the spontaneous support for the military-led efforts to suppress religious radicals and conservatives, which many secularists adopt without questioning its virtues and drawbacks.

Historical background

Since 1923, Turkey has been a heavily Western-orientated secular republic. The role of Islam in society has varied with the political leadership of the state. However, in general it can be said that the main tendency has been a constant pressure from large parts of the population to lend more importance to Islam, whereas this has been resisted by the secular élite, a policy warranted by the strongly secularist army. In terms of history, Turkey's relation to Islam can be called a U-turn. Turkey is the main successor state of the Ottoman Empire, which was based not on an ethnic identity but on the religious identity of Islam. The sultan of the empire was also the caliph, the spiritual leader of all Muslims in the world. By contrast, the republic founded by Mustafa Kemal Atatürk in 1923 was based on the concept of Turkish ethnicity and staunchly rejective of religion.

However, the transition from the Ottoman Empire to the Turkish Republic cannot be termed a 'U-turn' of the 1920s. The Westernisation of the Ottoman Empire began in the middle of the nineteenth century. Throughout the century, the empire had suffered an increasingly rapid disintegration, with not only its European parts but also subsequently its Middle Eastern provinces rising up in nationalist rebellions, eagerly supported by its numerous enemies; and nationalism was a concept the Ottoman Empire was particularly ill-fit to tackle. It recognised minorities – but only religious minorities – through the *millet* system, whereby the religious minorities had a significant level of autonomy. As an answer to these developments, an awareness grew in the empire that it had lagged behind the West. An urge for modernisation emerged, as the empire was seen to be in rapid decay. This urge for modernisation was paralleled by a movement which saw reform as necessary not only in regard to the state and military but also to the entire society. A national project was necessary to prevent the total dissolution of the empire. Among the military élite, a movement known as the 'young Ottomans', or later 'young Turks', emerged, which sought a thorough transformation of the society and state. Ziya Gökalp, the author of *Türkçülügün Esaslari* (The Essence of Turkism), is often credited as one of the earliest and most influential theorists of Turkish nationalism. His motto was 'Turkify, Islamise and Modernise', a blueprint for a modern Turkish identity, still heavily coloured by Islam. However, inspired by European practices, Gökalp also promoted the separation of Islam from the state. This illustrates the fact that modernisation in Turkey since the times of the Ottoman Empire has been equated with Westernisation.

The second half of the nineteenth century was a period of confusion, where the social structure of the empire was challenged by refugee flows and a generally chaotic external environment. As nationalist, separatist forces among minorities were strengthened, Islamic militancy increased among the Muslim population; and as tensions between religious groups grew, Russia, France and Great Britain claimed a role as protectors of religious minorites in the empire – a notable humiliation for the sultan. Furthermore, with the dismantling of the European parts of the empire, large refugee flows of Muslims from these areas were migrating to the Anatolian heartland, which increased the Islamic demographic character of Anatolia, which until then had been largely multi-cultural. The official Islam of the empire was Hanafi Sunni. The religious hierarchy was strict and represented a normative Sunnism, which guided education and the judiciary. Sufi orders were viewed with suspicion and resisted by the state. Nevertheless, their strength increased during the last decades of the empire. This was particularly true for the Naqshbandi, Qadiri, Bektashi and Rifai orders.

Kurdish-speaking Muslims in a Central Anatolian village (photo: Ingvar Svanberg, 1990).

Mustafa Kemal Atatürk was heavily influenced by the young Turk movement, but he differed from it, and from Ziya Gökalp, in one decisive respect – he saw Islam as one of the main obstacles in Turkey's Westernisation and modernisation – leaving 'modernisation' and 'Turkification' from Gökalp's motto, two paths on which Atatürk capitalised. The Ottoman empire was thus transformed into a modern, secular nation-state: the Turkish republic. With the proclamation of the republic, the sultanate was abolished, and so was the caliphate in March 1924. The educational system was immediately affected, and religious education was successively abolished in the country. Atatürk was also very suspicious of Sufi orders, which he saw as potentially subversive, and prohibited them from operating. This was unsuccessful, however, largely due to the secret and underground nature of these associations. Hence the orders hibernated and have recently seen a resurgence. Atatürk's reforms have often been interpreted as an attempt to eradicate Islam from Turkish society, which is far from the truth. Even more far-fetched are comparisons with Albania's Enver Hoxha period or Stalinist Soviet Union.

Turkey under Atatürk was not an atheist regime. As Ilber Ortayli has rightly observed, Turkish leaders have always been buried with religious funerals, as opposed to the leaders of the French revolution or Bolshevik Soviet Union. Religious holidays were always observed, and mosques have always existed. Atatürk's objective, though, was clear: to prevent religion from being used for political purposes. To this end, the Directorate for Religious Affairs, Diyanet Işleri Başkanligi, was founded with the aim of ensuring a state monopoly and control over religious affairs, and to subordinate the mosques to the state, thereby pre-empting anti-state propaganda. Similarly, theological faculties were introduced at universities. Atatürk's brand of Turkish nationalism was in retrospect a masterpiece of nation-building. It was not based on ethnicity as such, but was inclusive of all nationalities and minorities residing within the territorial boundaries of the republic. According to the parole *Ne mutlu Türküm diyene*, 'happy he who calls himself a Turk', whoever was willing to take part in the nation-building process was welcome to do so. To a remarkable extent, considering the ethnic and cultural melting pot that Anatolia was, Atatürk succeeded in his endeavour. The one and only exception was the 'feudal' Kurdish society in the southeast which remained unintegrated, whereas Kurds all over Turkey were assimilated into a Turkish identity. The official history-writing sought to stress the link to Central Asian nomadic tribes, and to minimise the historical links to the Islamic world as well as the Byzantine heritage. As a corollary, the centre of gravity of the Islamic world moved from Istanbul towards the Arab heartlands of the Middle East, which was going through a re-Islamisation. Hence Kemalism sought to give primacy to nationalism over religion, and Turkish identity came to be associated with language and territory instead of religion. This necessitated a gigantic effort in terms of popular education. As Anatolia was heterogeneous in terms of language and culture, the 'second army' of teachers would socialise the young into a strong Turkish national identity. However, this task proved to be more difficult than expected. The country became increasingly divided between a secular élite and a conservative rural mass. Social change proved distinctively slower than political change.

Hence, as multi-party democracy was permitted in 1946, the first free elections led to the victory of the Democratic Party which eased the harsh restrictions on religious life. This amounted to an Islamic revival. In the 1970s a religious party emerged in parliament, and reached the government through coalitions, which extended Islamic influence in the state. During the 1980s, Özal's liberal policies toward religion led to the building of

Slaughtering a sheep in connection with the *Id al-Adha* festival in a suburb of Istanbul (photo: Ingvar Svanberg, 1979).

thousands of mosques and religious schools (*Imam-Hatip*). Finally, the 1990s saw the dramatic increase in popularity and power of the Welfare Party (Refah Partisi), which culminated in it becoming the senior partner in a coalition goverment in the summer of 1996. Before moving to the role of religion in Turkish politics today, however, it is necessary to see the structure of Islam in the country.

Religion and political culture in Turkey

Despite the clearly secular character of Turkish society, this image is blurred in certain respects. To the foreign observer, a striking relationship between the concepts of 'Turk' and 'Muslim' is present. In this context, it is interesting to note than when confronted with a foreign practitioner of another religion, Turks, including Islamists, have no prejudice but are only interested in learning about foreign religious practices. On the other hand, Turkish converts to Christianity, especially, are viewed as traitors and persecuted to an extent which has forced most of them to leave the country, according to the observations of several Catholic and Protestant priests. This circumstance seems to fit badly with the generally secular and tolerant character of the Turkish society, particuarly as it is not paralleled in many Muslim societies. Indeed, many states with Muslim majority have no difficulty harbouring linguistically similar but religiously differing minorities. Examples are the Christians in Indonesia or in Palestine, or the Hindus and Christians in Bangladesh. In Turkey, however, there seems to be a reigning paradigm that a 'Turk' is by necessity a 'Muslim' – and indeed, 99 per cent of the population are nominally Muslims. Non-Muslims are not viewed as Turks, even if they are Turkish citizens.

This attitude is interesting in historical view as the Ottoman Empire never was a fully Islamic state, but rather a flexible system able to respond to the needs of a multi-religious empire. As Ilter Turan has noted, 'Turk' designates an ethno-linguistic characteristic of the political community. Further, he notes that the concept of 'Muslim' is not related to whether the person is a believer or not, but to an Islamic ancestry, hence a cultural tradition. Even with the creation of the secular republic, perhaps even strengthened by it, the religious appartenance was a necessary condition for membership of the political community. This factor is one which should be recalled when analysing the Islamisation of Turkish society. Indeed, although it might seem paradoxical in view of recent events, this tendency was strengthened and given official sanction by the military coup in 1980. As the military were determined to crush left-wing extremism and weaken right-wing nationalism, it encouraged the moderate increase of Islamic observance. This has been called a 'Turkish–Islamic synthesis'.

Sufism

Sunni Islam is the majority form of Islam in Turkey, thought to be the belief of 70 to 80 per cent of the population. The bulk of the remaining 20–30 per cent is made up of by the Alevis. Smaller religious minorities are, in particular, Greek Orthodox (2,500), Armenians (40,000), Assyrian Christians (10,000) and Jews (19,000–26,000). Within the majority religion, Hanafi Sunni Islam, the importance of Sufi orders is not to be underestimated, notably not in politics. The main Sufi order is the Naqshbandi, in Turkish Nakshibendi. The Naqshbandi order posed from the early years of the republic a direct threat to the state. In fact, Sufi orders were banned largely due to the identification of the Shaykh Said rebellion of 1925 with the Naqshbandiyya.

The Naqshbandi order differs from many other Sufi orders in its relative lack of mysticism. Rather, it is characterised by sobriety and discipline. It is known for an 'inward-looking attitude' which differs significantly from smaller groups like the Aczmenci, whose *zikr* (Ar. *dhikr*) forms of prayer are characterised by a significant level of mysticism. Simultaneously, as far as activism is concerned, the Naqshbandis are more active than other Sufis. This is the case precisely because other Sufi brotherhoods are largely interested in achieving closeness to, or even unity with, God by mystical means on an individual level. The Naqshibandis, on the other hand, follow the teachings of the Prophet more strictly and are more susceptible to politicisation. As the sociologist Şerif Mardin argues, 'the Naqshibandiya order has always been alert for opportunities to use power for what is considered the higher interests of Muslims'. It has also always had elaborate instruments for political mobilisation. The Naqshbandi order, moreover, is not a homogeneous unit. It is split into several wings, and this fragmentation is not totally counteracted even by its leaders. Rather, initiative by local leaders is encouraged and is one of the strengths of the order. The main sections of the order, believed to be followed by 2.5 million people, are the reportedly statist and nationalist Mensil (the aim), which is active in western Turkey; Çarsamba (Wednesday), active mainly in Istanbul and in organising religious education; and Iskender Pasha, reportedly critical of Erbakan, in central and western Turkey, which aims to infiltrate the administration in order to Islamise it.

During the twentieth century the Naqshbandi order in Turkey has been represented by two main figures. One was Mehmet Zahid Kotku, a follower of the powerful nineteenth century Shaykh Ziyaeddin Gümüshanevi. Kotku's circle in the 1960s included a number of key figures in Turkish society of later decades, including the Islamist leader Necmettin Erbakan and president Turgut Özal's brother Korkut Özal, as well as Hasan Aksay and Fehmi Adak. Kotku died in 1980 and was succeeded by Esat Çosan, a high-ranking professor of theology. The second main figure was Bediüzzaman Said Nursi (1874–1960), who established relations with the Young Turks during the early part of the century. Nursi was, thus, very politicised to begin with, a circumstance which changed later, as he abandoned politics, believing that in any case religious mobilisation would have direct political consequences. Nursi was a travelling preacher, who realised that traditional theology was not relevant enough. He developed an interest in science and capitalised on education as the key to his movement. Said Nursi interpreted the Quran in the light of modernity in his *Risale-i-Nur* (the Epistle of Light). Through this work, which is also disseminated through audio tapes, his teachings are spread. Associating with modernity, however, did not mean accepting the secular republic. In fact, Rainer Herrmann illustrates the Turkish contradiction between Atatürk, the seculariser and Westerniser of the country, and Nursi, the representative of 'the believing countryside'. Nursi was, then, the founder of the Nurcu, and a constant source of unease for the secular state, which led the government to send him into years of internal exile. The Nurcu has today developed into a brotherhood of its own, separate from the Naqshbandiyya. One main difference lies in the perception of modernity and science. In fact, the Nurcu has become known as an order advocating the union of Islam with modernity. This does not prevent it from being anti-capitalist, promoting Islamic social justice in its place.

The so-called Fethullahis, founded and led by Fethullah Gülen, is the clearest focus within the Nurcu movement. Fethullah Gülen, as Rainer Herrmann states, one of the most powerful figures in the Turkish society, is a person whose photograph did not appear in the media until 1994. He is widely known as Hojaefendi in Turkey. Gülen's understanding of Islam, inherited from Said Nursi but altered, preaches allegiance to the state and support for democracy, modernisation and even closer relations with Europe. Allegiance to the state, however, does not necessarily mean allegiance to all principles of Kemalism. Further, Gülen's Islam is different from that of the Naqshbandiyya by being nationalistic, explicitly advocating a Turkish Islam. It should also be noted that Gülen implicitly claims descent from the Prophet himself, although he prefers not to address the issue openly. Gülen publicly proposes a more liberal version of Islam, emphasising rather the need for societal consensus. Hence he displays no enmity towards Alevis, and regards the issue of women's wearing of headscarves as 'peripheral'. For Gülen, Islam is not static, but rather a religion in evolution.

In 1971 Gülen was apprehended and put on trial for his activities. In his biography, he expresses surprise that he, who had always preached obedience to the state, was tried along with subversive extremists. Politically, Gülen has traditionally supported the largest party on the centre-right, except for a short period in the 1970s when he lent support to the National Salvation Party (Milli Selamet Partisi) of Erbakan. During the military coup of 1980 and its aftermath, Gülen continued his preacher travels throughout the country, although he was officially wanted by the authorities. From 1983 onwards, he had increasingly close relations with Turgut Özal and his Motherland Party (MP). During Özal's time as prime minister, Gülen opened innumerable schools and study centres all over Turkey, also investing in the media, to a degree that he today commands, among other things, one of the largest-selling newspapers in the country, *Zaman*, and a private television channel, Samanyolu TV. With the death of Özal, Gülen moved closer to the True Path Party/Dogru Yol Partisi (DYP) of Tansu Çiller. Çiller, concerned over the increasing popularity of Erbakan's Welfare Party, wanted to ensure Gülen's support for her party.

1995 was the year Gülen chose to go public. He hit the headlines of most major newspapers, gave interviews, appeared on state television and met with all major political leaders, including those on the left. The military, nevertheless, remained wary of Gülen. In the 1980s the army was purged of 'Fethullahis' and the military warned of the strength of his followers, estimated then at 4 million. In 1995 he was again investigated by the state security court. The military suspects Gülen of planning to establish an Islamic state, based on *sharia* (Islamic law), but for the time being applying *taqiyya* (concealment), the primarily Shiite practice of dissimulation in a hostile environment, an accusation that has also been directed against Erbakan whenever he has pledged allegiance to the republic.

What, then, are Gülen's aims? What kind of a society does he want for Turkey? If one is to trust his own words, and those of most secular observers, Fethullah Gülen wants a modern, pluralist society open to the West but which does not suppress or ignore 'Anatolian' traditions, where a modern, Turkish Islam is dominant. Naturally, once in a dominant position, Gülen might change his rhetoric, but on the ideological level, the Nurcu form of Islam is distinctively more apt for a conciliation with the secular state than is the Naqshbandi. However, in practice, Naqshbandiyya elements have infiltrated the state to such a degree that a glorified president and at least one prime minister have been known to be very close to the order. Nevertheless the Islamisation of the state has been kept in controllable proportions.

Other brotherhoods and movements

Besides the two major currents, less important Sufi orders exist, most of them with uneasy to conflictive relations with the state. A strictly radical and militant order active mainly in the 1950s was the Tijaniyya (Ticani), which earned fame by destroying Atatürk's statues all over Central Anatolia. This order found its supporters among the urban lower class as well as the rural population which saw Kemalist reforms as atheistic and corrupt. However, the order's leader, the lawyer Kemal Pivaloglu, was subsequently apprehended and incarcerated, after which the Tijanis seem to have totally disappeared from public life.

Another, more important group is the Süleymanli movement. Founded by Süleyman Hilmi Tunahan (1888–1959), a son of a Naqshbandi *shaykh* who immigrated from Silistria in Rumania in the 1930s. The Süleymanli movement is profoundly radical and comes close to the original meaning of the term 'fundamentalist'. It accepts no other writings or norms than the Quran and the Sunna, and hence seeks to reinstate *sharia*. The Süleymanli movement is seen in Turkey as extremely anti-intellectual and opposed to science, as it is in outright opposition to public schools, including the religious education given by the Directorate for Religious Affairs, and seeks to forbid civil weddings, to replace the Latin alphabet with the Arabic, and to consider Turkey a country of *jihad* ('holy war'). Moreover, the order is profoundly suspicious of other Islamic organisations (particularly the Nurcu), seeing them as non-Muslim. This suspicion towards outsiders, the rumour goes, leads members to change the formulation of the greeting from *selam aleyküm* (peace be upon you) to *sam aleyküm* (curse be upon you). The Süleymanli movement spreads through an organisational system on a par with the Naqshbandiyya or Nurcu. The founder, Tunahan, instructed every disciple to open a Quranic school wherever he settled in the country, and to ensure that five further were opened. This has led to the order growing enormously not only in Turkey but also, for instance, in Germany, Sweden, Denmark, Norway, France, Belgium and the Netherlands. Since Tunahan's death, the order has been led by his son-in-law, Kemal Kaçar, a former parliamentary deputy.

Another, less-known order is Isikçilar (followers of the light, or the enlightened). Like the Süleymanli, Isikçilar emanated from the Naqshbandiyya, and polemises against secularism. Moreover, its founder Abdülhakim Arvasi paid special attention to strict Sunni belief and therefore polemises against Shiism, Wahhabism and reformist tendencies within Islam.

Istanbul is the centre for another order, the Khalwatiyya Jerrahi (Halveti Cerrahi) order which attracts many Western converts. Musafer Özak travelled all over Europe and in the United States and founded Khalwati circles. Traditionally, the Khalwati order has been very influencial on the Balkan peninsula and during the twentieth century many members have been initiated into the order in *tekke*s (convents) located in Macedonia. Most famous are the whirling *dervishes* of the Mevleviyya, which have their *tekke* in Konya.

In the last few years, a hitherto unknown group which has surfaced publicly is the Aczmenci. The Aczmenci are originally a part of the Nurcu, but in comparison to the Fethullahis they are distinctively more radical. Like many other orders, the Aczmenci drew their main support from eastern Turkey. It has been militantly opposed to Turkey's relations with the United States and has been accused of the murder of secularists. The order gained fame during 1995–96 very much due to the televised apprehension of their leader, Müslüm Gündüz, undressed with a young woman. Gündüz and an associate, Ali Kalkanci, who later was found to be a fraud, were blatantly exposed in national television. The young woman in case, Fadime Sahin, explained in a live broadcast how youngsters like herself were attracted to the order, and fooled into believing that having sexual intercourse with leaders 'would bring them closer to God'. As this scandal was unveiled, the Aczmenci mystical forms of worship, including collective head-shaking, one form of the *zikr* rites which aim at causing a state of trance, were shown on video recordings of those rites. Furthermore, connections between senior members of the Welfare Party such as the Istanbul mayor Recep Tayip

Erdogan and the parliamentary group leader Temel Karamollaoglu and the Aczmenci *shaykhs* were discovered, as both Kalkanci and Gündüz were arrested for rape and antisecularism respectively.

As Turkey watched with confusion, the overwhelming majority of the citizens were surprised, not to say shocked, by the very existence of these groups and their 'alien' form of worship. The representatives of official Islam such as the head of Diyanet, Mehmet Yilmaz, in a genuine reaction discarded the Aczmenci rites as being non-Islamic. A debate subsequently emerged around the question of 'what is and is not Islam?', while the Aczmencis, dressed in long robes, turbans and equipped with walking sticks and occasionally swords, increasingly showed themselves in public. The issue has somewhat been shoved aside in the shadow of other political developments, but its impact on Turkey was great. Not only did Turks get exposed to an unknown variant of Islam, they also understood how little they knew about Islam in general.

In sum, religious orders play a role in modern Turkish society which is far greater than has been generally known both in the West and in Turkey itself. As we shall see later, these sectarian divisions have entered politics and directly affected the situation of the country.

The Alevis

The term 'Alevi' is thought to refer to *Ali evi* or 'the house of Ali', the son-in-law of the Prophet Muhammad and the founder of Shia Islam. The belief of the Alevis is related to that of the Alawites in Syria – the main difference being cultural, as the Alawites are an Arab phenomenon and the Alevis distinctively Anatolian. However, it has to be noted that the Alevi belief is far from traditional Shia Islam, so far that the question is often raised as to whether the Alevis are in fact Muslims at all. As has already been mentioned, the Alevis are by far the largest religious minority in Turkey, possibly numbering some 20 million. This is a fact that is surprisingly unknown, as Turkey is known as a country with a homogeneous Sunni structure. The Alevis have historically been found mainly among the rural Central Anatolian population. Among these are outcaste groups like the Abdals, the itinerant Tahtaci in the south who specialise as lumberjacks, and a group of shepherds known as Karapapah or Terekeme in northeastern Turkey. It is notable that there are both Kurdish- and Arabic-speaking Alevis, the former mainly in the province of Tunceli but also in Bingöl.

The religious origin of the Alevis is disputed and the discussion about the place of Alevism in Islam has led to a large variety of interpretations. The most extreme views are those which see Alevism as the belief of Anatolian Turks who adopted Sunni Islam in an insufficient and incorrect manner, and those which see Alevism as an extreme form of Shia where Ali is seen as God. Ismail Engin divides the interpretations primarily between those that treat Alevism under Islam and those that do not. Among the former, one finds views that see Alevism as

a) the true form of Islam, the other forms originating in the Umayyad dynasty being untrue and divisive, a view taken by certain Alevi religious leaders;
b) a form of Islam separate from Sunnism, either as a Turkish religion based on Islam or as a 'Turkified' belief (these views emphasise the difference towards Sunnism);
c) a form of belief uniting Islam with Turkish identity;
d) a part of Sunni Islam, either as 'a Turkmen form' of Sunni, or as a Sufi order within Sunnism;
e) a heretic belief which can and must be brought back to the original belief;
f) an Anatolian cultural synthesis which comes close to the core of Islam;
g) a form of Islam different from Sunnism or Shiism, although with its roots in the latter, but with increasing differences since the sixteenth century;
h) a syncretistic belief with its origin in Islam;
i) a non-Islamic belief created by Jews to divide Islam;
j) a Kurdish philosophy rather than religion; and
k) an Anatolian religion in its own right.

From the outline above, it seems clear that defining Alevism is a difficult task, far beyond the scope of this chapter. However, it is safe to say that there are strong arguments for its inclusion within Islam. The Alevis accept the basic Islamic creed: 'There is no god but God, and Muhammad is his Messenger'. At the same time, many elements of Alevism are alien both to Sunni and Shia Islam. For example, Alevis have no mosques but community houses, *cemevi*; do not pray five times a day but only when they feel the urge or need; do not practise the pilgrimage to Mecca; do not fast during Ramadan; women do not bear veils; worship and prayer are carried out by men and women together; initiation rites contain alcohol, similar to the Christian communion; do not apply *sharia*; do not seem to view the Quran as God's word. The Alevi perception of the *sharia* is particularly interesting. In principle, *sharia* is the law to be followed by everyone. However, through initiation the individual Alevi can reach a higher Sufi religiosity, whereby the dogmatic elements of *sharia* do not have to be obeyed to the letter. Mystics can reach two higher levels, *marifet* and *haqiqat* (truth), which imply union with God.

Closer studies indeed give the impression that Alevism is a syncretistic belief proper to Anatolia with elements of both Islam and Christianity but also of Zoroastrianism and Central Asian Shamanistic traditions. Due to their dubious identity and suspected heresy against Islam, the Alevis have faced and still face many difficulties in the Turkish society. The 'Alevi problem' surfaced in the spring of 1995, for example, after violent riots in the Istanbul district of Gaziosmanpasha. However, the same publicity had not been given to previous suppression of, or violence against, the Alevis. A recent example was the hotel arson in July 1993 which resulted in the death of thirty-seven leftist intellectuals, mainly Alevis, in Sivas in Central Anatolia. The main target of the Islamists who organised the fire was the late Aziz Nesin, a then 78-year-old writer who has allegedly translated excerpts of Rushdie's *The Satanic Verses* into Turkish. Nesin miraculously survived the fire, but an aggravating factor was that the local mayor, a Welfare Party member, did not act to prevent the demonstration which led to the arson, nor was the fire brigade sent in immediately. In the late 1970s, amid the general violence throughout Turkey, hundreds of Alevis were killed in riots in Kahramanmarash and Çorum.

However, the suppression of the Alevis is a centuries-old phenomenon. As early as the sixteenth century, an Alevi mystic, Pir Sultan Abdal, led a rebellion against the Ottoman state and was executed. He is still seen as a central figure, and a statue of his was to be raised in Sivas the day after the 1993 arson. In fact, the Alevis were blamed for supporting the Shiite Persian empire against the Ottomans, and were unwillingly incorporated into the Ottoman Empire in 1514. During republican times, the Alevis wholeheartedly supported Atatürk's reforms and may have been the most loyal population group on which Atatürk could count. Since then, they have mainly supported the Republican People's Party, which Atatürk founded. In the 1950s, as the Democratic Party opened the gates of Sunni renewal, the Alevis felt threatened and rallied around the Republican People's Party, which they perceived as a guarantor of their rights. With the polarisation of Turkish society in the 1960s, and particularly in the 1970s, the Alevis came to be identified with the left, and as the main basis for extreme-leftist organisations. Alevis can be thought to have been attracted to communist ideas partly because of their historical opposition to the state as such, as well as their quest for an identity among Alevis that had recently moved to the urban areas and lost contact with their community. The military were ambivalent in the confrontation between leftist, pro-Soviet, Alevi recruited groups and extreme-rightist Sunni groups with a heavy religious influence. In the end, fear of the Soviet Union led to a crack-down concentrated on destroying the leftists, while the rightist groups were allowed to continue. This fear of communism also prompted the coup makers to create the 'Turkish–Islamic' synthesis, including obligatory religious education in schools, which was intended to prevent communism from spreading in the young generation.

The religious revival sponsored by the state had no place for the Alevis, however. The Directorate for Religious Affairs, which has been the financial sponsor of, among other things, new mosques and *imams*, although not theoretically designed only for the Sunni majority, has not profited the

Alevis. On the contrary, mosques have been built in Alevi villages whereas Alevi community houses and religous leaders are not supported by the state. Religious life, then, especially since the 1980 coup, has been monopolised by the Sunni majority. This has led to a situation where the Alevis, who traditionally have not been prone to mobilisation around their religious community, are becoming increasingly frustrated, in particular as the state's negligent and occasionally hostile attitude showed no tendency to change until recently. Alevi frustration reached a peak when, in conjunction with the trial of the perpetrators of the Sivas arson, the state security prosecutor charged Aziz Nesin with having acted in a provocative manner, an accusation which set a precedent both legally and socially, and was utterly explosive. The situation seemed to improve in the middle of 1997, however, with the coalition led by Prime Minister Mesut Yilmaz openly stating that one of its aims was to ameliorate the situation of the Alevis, including the financing of study centres and university activities related to Alevism.

One can only become an Alevi by birth, a fact which distinguishes the faith from most others. However, the Bektashi order is closely related to Alevism and a gateway for non-Alevis who share their beliefs. The Bektashis have been termed the intellectual superstructure of the Alevis, and were also active during Ottoman times. In particular, the Bektashi order was responsible for the religious education of the Christian-born children raised to serve in the Ottoman bureacracy through the *devshirme* ('blood tax') system. In the Hatay province along the border to Syria, and in the provinces of Adana and İçel, there is an Arabic-speaking population of Nusayrites, calling themselves Alawites. Their number is estimated at around 200,000. They regard themselves as separated from the Alevis of Turkey by better knowledge of the doctrines and an emphasis on the divine aspects of Ali. There are several orders within the Nusayri group. Most important are the Haydariyya and Kilaziyya.

Islam in Turkish politics

Islam can be said to have disappeared from the political sphere with Atatürk's consolidation of power. However, it staged a come-back in 1950. After the Second World War, Turkey's firm Western connection encouraged it to democratise society. Hence Celal Bayar, a former prime minister, broke out of the ruling Republican People's Party and formed the Democratic Party. As this party appealed to rural interests and traditional values, it captured power by a landslide in the first free election in 1950. As a result, Ismet Inönü resigned from presidency and was succeeded by Celal Bayar, who named Adnan Menderes as prime minister. The one-party regime of the Republican People's Party between 1946 and 1950 occurred immediately after the Second World War, which, although Turkey had not participated, had inflicted additional hardships on the population, in the form of rationing and taxation. The regime further attempted to fulfil Atatürk's ideals and embarked on a process of transferring the functions of religious communities and leaders to new, civilian institutions. The overwhelming effect of the aftershock of the U-turn, or to use a term from another context, the great leap forward, of Turkish society also led to a reaction and an increasing distance between ruler and ruled.

Centre-right parties have been in power in Turkey for the better part of a half-century of multi-party democracy. During this time, they have managed to transform the role of religion in society. The Democratic Party government had a mixed record. Its popularity increased due to its easing of restrictions regarding Islam, but huge agricultural subventions and other economic policies led to an economic debacle. As the regime's popularity started dwindling compared to that of the Republican People's Party, the government tried to resort to authoritarian measures, making even the fatal mistake of asking the military to help suppress the Republican People's Party. The response was a coup in May 1960 staged among others by Alparslan Türkes, a coup which has been called the Colonels' coup in contrast to the 1980 Generals' coup. The military intervention was based mainly on defence of the secular state, against the far-reaching religious reforms initiated by the Democratic Party, but also against the emerging authoritarian attitude of the civilian leaders. The military felt the need to set an example, executing Menderes and two other ministers, but not Bayar who was spared due to old age.

The 1960 constitution, enacted to replace the 1923 one, was significantly more liberal and democratic than its predecessor – or for that matter, than its successor. In fact the 1960 constitution was the most democratic blueprint for social structure Turkey has ever had. The question is whether Turkish society was prepared for it. In retrospect, it would appear that it was not. After 1960, politics continued to polarise between 'left' and 'right'. Notably, the rise of the left led to a reaction from the right, and instability in the political sphere translated into violence throughout society. In the end this led to the 1971 military ultimatum and a slight revision of the constitution. The 1970s only meant a worsening situation, with chronic political instability, where the smaller parties, religious and nationalist, had a disproportionate influence as neither of the two larger parties in parliament, the centre-left Republican People's Party and the centre-right Justice Party (Adalet Partisi, the continuation of the Democratic Party) ever achieved a majority. Hence the extremist parties were necessary for coalition building, and consequently all governments of the 1970s had a rightist element, which was pro to the religious revival.

The first outright religious party was founded in 1967 by a group of Islamically oriented politicians within the Justice Party, the latter already under the leadership of Süleyman Demirel. In 1969, Necmettin Erbakan, one of the students of Kotku, was thrown out of the chairmanship of the chamber of commerce, perceived as a political threat by Demirel. In spite of this, Erbakan applied for membership of the Justice Party and wanted to run for parliamentary elections the same year. As Demirel vetoed Erbakan's candidature, the latter stood as an independent and was easily elected. This was a great victory for Kotku, who had been looking to establish an Islamic party and had capitalised on believers' disappointment in Demirel. As an informal section of the Justice Party centred around religious figures had formed in 1967, a good number of parliamentarians were in favour of Kotku's plans. In January 1970, Erbakan and seventeen colleagues founded the National Order Party (Milli Nizam Partisi), which claimed to be founded on the heritage of the Ottoman Empire and of Atatürk's war of liberation as well as on the just order preached by Islam.

However, the military ultimatum of 1971 led to the closure of the recently founded National Order Party. Erbakan fled to Switzerland, fearing a fate similar to that of Menderes, but was asked to return by the military, mainly as he was useful as an instrument in weakening Demirel's standing in the right. Hence in October 1972 the National Salvation Party (Milli Selamet Partisi) was founded, although Erbakan did not assume the role of leader until the 1973 elections. These elections can be termed the breakthrough of political Islam, as the National Salvation Party received over 11 per cent of the votes. Still, the rise of the Islamists was not among the principal factors in Turkish politics of the time. Rather, it remained a peripheral factor as the country was hit by an economic and social crisis in the aftermath of the invasion of Cyprus in 1974, which was executed by a coalition government led by Bülent Ecevit. Ecevit, chairman of the Republican People's Party, had staged an electoral success by re-orienting the left to a more standard social democratic rhetoric, gaining 33 per cent of the votes. However, Ecevit lacked a majority in parliament and could not form a government until the beginning of 1974 – with Necmettin Erbakan as his coalition partner. This coalition was one of necessity, and as the political scientist Elisabeth Özdalga quotes an Islamic writer of the time, it resembled a dish made out of honey and garlic, original but not particularly tasteful.

The economic and social crisis of the country only deepened with the loss of foreign aid and the increasing political and social instability. Erbakan managed to enter a new coalition in 1977 with Demirel and the nationalists, but his influence remained limited. The real struggle in Turkey was that between the extreme left and the extreme right. This controversy spilled over into street violence throughout the country which in its heyday claimed over twenty lives a day. The political instability with short-lived governments meant that the state power necessary to keep order was absent. This led to the military intervention of 1980, which was greeted with relief by the population. As mentioned above, the military administration saw the extreme left as the most dangerous threat to the republic, and to counteract the rise of leftist forces hoped that a moderate revival of religion would counterbalance this tendency. Hence religious education was made obligatory in schools and the 'Turkish–Islamic synthesis' was born.

The man to carry it into practice turned out to be Turgut Özal. He was an engineer and economist of Kurdish origin who had been a candidate for the National Salvation Party in the 1970s. Özal managed to win the trust of the military authorities and was allowed to found an independent party, the Motherland Party (Anavatan Partisi) in time for the first free elections of 1983. In contrast, the Welfare Party, the continuation of the National Salvation Party, was not allowed to appear, and many of its supporters took a Motherland Party ticket instead. Özal engineered the Turkish economic boom of the 1980s, and was known as a taboo-breaker in all fields except one: religion. Coming from a family close to the Naqshbandiyya, Özal paid considerable attention to religious issues and, not unlike Menderes in his time, sponsored the Islamic revival of the 1980s. Unlike Menderes, however, Özal worked wonders with the economy, which might be one reason for the military toleration of his overtly pro-Islamic activities.

The representation of Islamic interests within the Motherland Party led to difficulties for the Islamists in organiseing themselves into a separate party. Hence the Welfare Party received less than 5 per cent in the municipal elections of 1984. Another reason, naturally, was that Erbakan was banned from politics like all major political leaders, including Demirel and Ecevit. This ban was only lifted by a referendum in 1987, and immediately the Welfare Party won over 7 per cent of the votes in that year's parliamentary election – but did not gain representation in parliament, as a 10 per cent threshold had been adopted in order to prevent small parties from playing the role they had played in the late 1970s. By now, the strategy of the party had changed. Both the National Order Party and the National Salvation Party had used a clearly religious discourse, which was still defended by traditionalists within the Welfare Party. However, this discourse was not particularly attractive to new voters, and was too abstractly ideological to bring the party beyond an electoral support of 10–12 per cent.

In the 1980s, however, the Islamist leaders started to deal increasingly with worldly issues, such as administration and economics. At the same time, the party created a country-wide organisation which was neither challenged nor parallelled by any other party. Moreover, the party adopted a political agenda based on the concept of just order, *adil düzen*. On closer scrutiny, the concept of an Islamic social justice shows clear socialist undertones, notably in its criticism of the society created by the secular parties. The aim of this new image was clear: to create a popular movement, not an élite party with an ideological base. This process has proven fruitful, but has also blurred the identity of the party, and come under criticism from the traditionalists. Hence the party has won tremendous support from the urban poor, a support which it has earned by truly humanitarian actions, which in turn have been made possible by its

'Unwarranted influence'. According to this drawing in an Islamist journal, the United States has used satellites in order to spread its anti-Islamic propaganda in Turkey.

continuous flood of money from abroad, in particular Saudi Arabia. However, the party has also lost some of its most traditional, *sharia*-orientated electorate. Nevertheless, in political terms the gain is many times larger than the loss and represents a slide which is difficult to depict in right–left-terms. In fact it brought the Welfare Party ideology closer to the left, but not to the centre-right.

The 1990s brought the boom of the Welfare Party. In the 1991 election, it engaged in an electoral alliance with the extreme-nationalist National Labour Party under the legendary Alparslan Türkeş, in order to overcome the 10 per cent threshold. Eventually the alliance obtained 17 per cent of the vote and sixty-one seats in parliament. The breakthrough was the 1994 municipal elections, in which the Welfare Party unexpectedly came to power in the municipal administrations of, among other cities, Ankara, Istanbul, Konya and Adana. This success showed with great clarity how the Welfare Party's popularity was based on the urban poor. Interestingly, the urban poor, especially recent migrants from the countryside, had historically been ardent supporters of the left and had been the cornerstone of Ecevit's success in the 1970s. The transformation and division of the centre-left can thus be seen as a primary reason for the Welfare Party's popularity. Indeed, the left has increasingly assumed the urban *avant-garde* identity, Kemalist and modern, but not in conjunction with the interests of the urban poor, who would be the most logical supporters of social democracy. Furthermore the competition between three centre-left parties in the early 1990s, now 'only' two, has increased the disillusionment of the electorate with the left. However, the result of this development is, in a sense, that the Welfare Party, as Ersin Kalaycioglu and Ilter Turan have remarked, can be termed a party of the 'new left'.

The 1995 elections can be viewed in this light: a further loss of strength for the left and a leap forward for the Welfare Party. The two centre-left parties captured approximately 25 per cent, the Welfare Party over 21 per cent, and the two centre-right parties 40 per cent. In comparison with the late 1970s, it becomes clear that the Islamic growth has not occurred at the expense of the centre-right, as might be thought – the latter, as throughout republican history, commands about 40 per cent of the electorate – but the centre-left, whose support has hovered around 35 per cent, is now down to ten percentiles. This amounts exactly to the increase in support of the Islamic current: about ten percentile units.

The left in Turkey can be thought to have drawn its support from three main groups: first, the intellectual left, whose number must be relatively small though increasing as the middle class grows; second, the Alevi population which remains loyal mainly to Ecevit, including rural as well as urban, wealthy as well as worse-off elements; third, the (mainly) urban poor of Sunni denomination. This last group of former sympathisers of the left have clearly been the nucleus of the electoral success of the Welfare Party. This fact is corroborated by an opinion poll among Welfare Party voters:

Political Self-Identification of Welfare Party Voters, 1997

Political self-identification	Percentage
Muslim	51.5
Muslim Democrat	28.2
Democrat	7.8
Nationalist	4.9
Liberal Democrat	1.0

Source: *Cumhuriyet*, 24 October 1997.

The table above suggests that half of the Welfare Party sympathisers clearly defined their political identity as Muslim. This corroborates the accepted view that the core Islamist support group hovered around 10 per cent of the population. However, it is the other half, those who describe themselves as Muslim Democrats (a term which deliberately parallels West European Christian democracy), that brought the Welfare Party to its position as the largest party in parliament and to power in the summer of 1996.

Once in power, the Welfare Party dropped most of its professed ambitions to revolutionise the state. Erbakan did sign several military agreements with Israel, probably in order not to alienate the military at an early stage, although before the elections Welfare Party officials had harshly criticised cooperation with Israel. However, once in power, the Islamisation of the state started. This had already occurred in the municipal administrations under Welfare Party control after the 1994 elections and had led to widespread protests from the secular establishment. As the level of Welfare Party domination in the coalition government, which was formed with the True Path Party (Dogru Yol Partisi, the heir to Demirel's Justice Party) led by Tansu Çiller, increased, the military took up its role as watch-dog of the secular republic. In February 1997, after a pro-*sharia* demonstration in the Ankara suburb of Sincan, growing resistance to the Islamist-led government led to a mass movement orchestrated from military headquarters and supported by the secular establishment to oust the Welfare Party from power. In a remarkably well-planned flow of events during the spring of 1997, the government was finally forced to resign in August. Furthermore, the Welfare Party was banned by the constitutional court in January 1998 for agitation against the secular republic. Apparently, Kemalist forces have now secured their hegemony in Turkish politics.

However, the question is what will become of the genuinely popular movement that was the Welfare Party? The Welfare Party has indeed been abolished, but this does not mean that political Islam has been defeated in Turkey. The Islamic renaissance remains a fact, and some voices fear that the Islamist quest for power will be transferred from the parliament to the streets, and that Turkey would see a new era of near civil war as in the late 1970s. Others maintain that the Welfare Party will be resuscitated under a new name with a more centrist perspective, and will become a true Muslim democratic party like the Christian democratic parties of Western Europe. As this would lead to the alienation of extremist elements in the party, it would mean that the problem of religious extremism would persist or perhaps even increase. However, if this were to be the case, the extremist elements would be more of an irritation in society than a direct threat to the republic as the National Salvation Party and Welfare Party were perceived to be.

From another perspective, the Naqshbandi variant of political Islam can be said to have failed to consolidate its position in Turkish politics. During

Özal's era it acquired a significant position behind the scenes; and during Erbakan's time it achieved this position in the open, but through its impatience it failed to sustain its position and experienced a substantial setback. Meanwhile the Nurcu movement is growing in strength and can be expected to profit from the failure of the Welfare Party, as Gülen's model constantly has been to seek accommodation with the secular state, not to act against it either openly or subversively. If the military is interested in perpetuating the Turkish–Islamic synthesis, it would seem logical for it to use Gülen as a partner. Perhaps this can be the solution to the severe troubles regarding Islam's place in Turkish society and politics. Yet some observers doubt Fethullahis' real aims. Is the rhetoric of accommodation with secularism only a case of *taqiyya*? Is it, in other words, a tactic of dissimulation which will be reversed once the movement's power has increased? The answer to this question falls beyond the scope of this chapter, but the problem remains that Turkey has to find a way of reconciling the secular identity of the state with the Islamic traditions espoused by substantial sectors of its population. A perhaps simplistic approach, which nevertheless makes a great deal of sense in the conceptual sphere, was proposed by the political scientist Bassam Tibi: 'In Turkey there is a contradiction between Secularism and Islamism. If you manage to remove the "isms" from the two terms, you may have come a long way in solving the contradiction'.

Literature

For a general introduction to the political, cultural and social development of Turkey, see *Türkei*, ed. Klaus-Detlev Grothusen (Göttingen: Vandenhoeck, 1985). The ethnic diversity is discussed in *Ethnic Groups in the Republic of Turkey*, ed. Peter A. Andrews (Wiesbaden: Ludwig Reichert, 1989); Ingvar Svanberg, *Kazak Refugees in Turkey: A Study of Social and Cultural Persistence,* Studia Multiethnica Upsaliensia, 8 (Uppsala: Almqvist and Wiksell International, 1989); and *Denying Human Rights & Ethnic Identity: The Case of Turkey* (New York: Human Rights Watch, 1992). The role of Islam in contemporary Turkey is dealt with in *Islam und Politik in der Türkei*, eds. Jochen Blaschke and Martin van Bruinessen (Berlin: Express, 1985); Binnaz Toprak, *Islam and Political Development in Turkey* (Leiden: Brill, 1981); *Islam in Modern Turkey*, ed. Richard Tapper (London: I.B. Tauris, 1991); Sencer Ayata, 'Patronage, Politics, and the State: The Politicization of Islam in Turkey', *The Middle East Journal*, 50:1 (Winter 1996), pp. 26–37; Eli Karmon, 'Radical Islamic Political Groups in Turkey', *Middle East Review of International Affairs*, 4 (January 1998); Rainer Herrmann. 'Die Drei Versionen des Politischen Islam in der Türkei', *Orient*, 37:1 (1996) pp. 35–86; and Rainer Herrmann, 'Fethullah Gülen – Eine muslimische Alternative zur Refah-Partei?', *Orient*, 37:4 (1996), pp. 619–30.

In recent decades the interest in the Alevis has increased considerably. Some anthropologists have studied Alevi segments of the Anatolian society, while others have focused on their ideology and impact on contemporary society. See Krisztina Kehl-Bodrogi, *Vom Revolutionären Klassenkampf zum "Wahren" Islam: Transformationsprozesse im Alevitentum der Türkei nach 1980* (Berlin: Das Arabische Buch, 1992); *Alevism in Turkey and Comparable Syncretistic Religious Communities in the Near East in the Past and Present*, ed. Krisztina Kehl-Bodrogi (Leiden: Brill, 1997); and Ilhan Ataseven, *The Alevi Bektaşi Legacy: Problems of Acquisition and Explanation*, Lund Studies in History of Religions, 7 (Lund: Almqvist and Wiksell International, 1997).

Sufi Orders are presented in Şerif Mardin, 'The Nakşibendi Order in Turkish History', in *Islam in Modern Turkey*, ed. Richard Tapper (London: I.B. Tauris, 1991) and *The Dervish Lodge: Architecture, Art, and Sufism in Ottoman Turkey*, ed. Raymond Litches (Berkeley: University of California Press, 1992). The Nurculuk movement is described by Ursula Spuler, 'Zur Organisationsstruktur der Nurculuk-Bewegung', pp. 423–42 in *Studien zur Geschichte und Kultur des Vorderen Orients: Festschrift für Bertold Spuler zum siebzigsten Geburtstag*, eds. Hans Roemer and Albrecht Not (Leiden: Brill, 1981); Paul Dumont, 'Disciples of the Light: The Nurju Movement in Turkey', *Central Asian Survey*, 5 (1986), pp. 33–60; and Şerif Mardin, *Religion and Social Change in Modern Turkey: The Case of Bediüzzaman Said Nursi* (New York: State University of New York Press, 1989). No systematic study of the Süleymanli movement exists. Most information is still fragmentary and anecdotal. A brief but useful account is found in Altan Gökalp, 'Les fruits de l'arbre plutôt que ces racines: Le Suleymanisme', pp. 423–35 in *Naqshbandis: Cheminements et situation actuelle d'un ordre mystique musulman*, eds. Marc Gaborieau, Aleksandre Popović and Thierry Zarcone, Varia Turcica, XVIII (Istanbul and Paris: Institut Français d'Etudes Anatoliennes d'Istanbul, 1990).

Chapter Seven

Turkic Central Asia

Roberta Micallef and Ingvar Svanberg

Until 1991 the region which comprises the five now independent republics Kazakstan, Kirghizstan (Kyrgyzstan), Uzbekistan, Turkmenistan and Tajikistan was known as Soviet Central Asia. Since independence the Central Asians have had to find new ways of thinking of their relationship to their own nationals and to one another as well as to the world at large. Consequently Central Asian interest in the region's history and culture is flourishing. The focus of this chapter is Islam in the Turkic republics of Kazakstan, Kirghizstan, Turkmenistan and Uzbekistan.

Kazakstan, which according to the traditional Soviet classification system did not belong to Central Asia, was formally declared to be part of that geographic region in the 1993 Central Asia Summit. The Kazak president, Nursultan Nazarbayev, actively fought for the maintenance of some form of the Soviet Union, but after Russia, Ukraine and Belarus established the Commonwealth of Independent States (CIS) on December 8, 1991 Kazakstan had no choice but to declare its independence, which it did on December 16, 1991. Shortly thereafter, on December 21, 1991, Kazakstan joined the United Nations. President Nazarbayev still (1998) remains in power. Independent Kazakstan is the largest Central Asian Republic with an area of roughly 3 million square kilometres. Largely made up of steppe-lands with mountains to the east and to the south, Kazakstan also has pasture lands to the north which, in the twentieth century, have been cultivated mostly by Russian and Ukrainian farmers. Kazakstan is an important producer of cereals and has a major mining industry. As it straddles China and Russia, it is of considerable geopolitical significance. To the south, Kazakstan borders Turkmenistan, Uzbekistan and Kirghizstan and to the east the Caspian Sea. The Kazak capital was until the autumn of 1997 Almaty (Alma Ata) when it was replaced by Aqmola in the northern part of the country. The republic has severe environmental problems and the health situation is alarming in many areas. The Kazakstani population of 17 million is far from homogeneous. According to the 1989 census it was made up of 39.7 per cent Kazaks and 37.8 per cent Russians. This vast number of Russians as well as proximity to Russia have made the repatriation of Kazakstan into a larger Russia a recurring theme for the

149

ultra-nationalist factions in Russian political circles. Also Germans, Ukrainians, Uzbeks, Tatars, Belarussians and other peoples live within the borders of Kazakstan, although as many ethnic Germans are immigrating to Germany, their number is on the decrease. Due to the Sino–Soviet conflict at the beginning of the 1960s, Kazakstan took in a large number of Uighur and Kazak refugees from China, thereby increasing the Muslim population. Finally there are also some smaller ethnic groups, such as Caucasians, Crimean Tatars, Koreans and Kurds, who are the descendants of those exiled to Kazakstan during Stalin's reign in the 1930s and 1940s.

Kirghizstan, a mountainous republic dominated by the mountain chain Tian Shan, borders China to the east, Tajikistan to the south, Uzbekistan to the west and Kazakstan to the north. Kirghizstan was a Soviet Socialist Republic from 1936 until 1991. The smallest of the five Central Asian republics with 198,500 square kilometres, Kirghizstan has a population of 4.3 million. Ethnic Kirghiz comprise 48 per cent of the population, Russians 26 per cent, Uzbeks 12 per cent and Tatars 2 per cent. Koreans, Germans, Dungans, Uighurs and a few other minorities also reside in the republic. The capital of Kirghizstan is Bishkek, which has a population of 570,000. The Kirghiz speak a Turkic language related to Kazak and Uzbek. However, the Kirghiz élite, like many of the Central Asian élites, is heavily concentrated in the cities and Russified.

Uzbekistan is a composite of different parts of the former governate of Turkestan, the Emirate of Bukhara and the Khanate of Khiva. The country became a Soviet Socialist Republic in October, 1924 and remained so until August 31, 1991 when it declared its independence. Uzbekistan borders all of the Central Asian states of the former Soviet Union as well as Afghanistan. To the west and north it borders Kazakstan, to the east Kirghizstan and Tajikistan, to the south Afghanistan and to the southwest Turkmenistan. Its capital is Tashkent and other major cities are Samarqand, Bukhara, Andijon and Namangan. The country boasts the largest army and internal security force in Central Asia.

Uzbekistan is rich in natural resources, but it is for the most part 'white gold', cotton, which is the basis of Uzbekistan's fortune and misery. Cotton production has caused much environmental damage. Several ecological catastrophes have occurred lately, including the shrinking of the Aral Sea by one third which has resulted in severe changes in the climate and serious health problems. Most tragic are the developments in Karakalpakstan which lies in the delta of the Amu Darya and has been an autonomous republic within the boundaries of Uzbekistan since 1936. The environmental damage to the Aral Sea has had a devastating impact on the local fishing and agricultural industries. The dimensions of the environmental catastrophe are made obvious by the rates of child mortality and longevity which are as high and low respectively as the worst cases among Third World countries.

Uzbek girls in Samarkand (photo: Ingvar Svanberg, 1990).

Islam Karimov, the president of Uzbekistan, made his career within the old Communist Party. Since independence it calls itself a socialist party. Opposition parties such as Birlik (Unity), Erk (Independence) and the Islamic Renaissance Party, which came into being before independence, have been banned or effectively silenced. In a referendum held on March 26, 1995 the Uzbeks approved a three-year extension of Karimov's presidency to the year 2000 in order to synchronise future parliament and presidential elections. According to Uzbek sources 99.6 per cent of the voters participated in the referendum which was arranged in the old Soviet style. Since Karimov was the only candidate, the voters' sole alternative was to protest against him by crossing out his name. The majority of Uzbekistan's nearly 20 million inhabitants are Uzbeks, but there are also 1.6 million Russians, 1 million Tajiks, 800,000 Kazaks and 500,000 Tatars as well as other peoples who are descendants of peoples exiled by Stalin in the 1930s and 1940s. The relations between the Turkic Uzbeks and Persian Tajiks are complicated, especially in the two important southern cities of Samarqand and Bukhara where the population has traditionally been bilingual and often identified itself as Tajik. Uzbekistan has an old and relatively large Jewish population. Currently, however, many Jews are emigrating to Israel and the United States.

With an area of 488,000 square kilometres, Turkmenistan borders Iran to the south, Afghanistan to the southwest, Uzbekistan to the north and west, Kazakstan to the north and the Caspian Sea to the east. Its population of approximately 4 million includes over 400,000 Uzbeks, about 400,000 Russians, 250,000 Kazaks and finally about 50,000 Azeris and Armenians respectively. Across the borders in Iran and Afghanistan lives a population of some 2 million Turkmens. Three-quarters of the Turkmen lands are deserts. In agricultural zones, however, Turkmenistan produces rice and cotton. Like Uzbekistan, Turkmenistan relies on the Aral Sea for irrigation and has contributed to the ecological damage wreaked on the Aral Sea. Once one of the poorest republics of the Soviet Union, Turkmenistan is now on its way to becoming prosperous thanks to the discovery of natural gas and petroleum reserves. Since independence it has had the fastest developing economy among the Central Asian republics. Turkmenistan celebrates its independence on October 21. Its capital is Ashgabad and President Saparmurat Niyazov Turkmenbashi, who originated from the ranks of the Communist Party. On December 16, 1991 the former Communist Party was renamed the Democratic Party of Turkmenistan and on May 18, 1992 a new constitution with increased presidential powers was passed. This constitution seems somewhat contradictory in its description of citizens' rights. For example, opposition parties cannot be registered because they might damage 'the health and morals of the people'. On June 21, 1992 Niyazov – the sole candidate – was re-elected for a period of 10 years with 99.5 per cent of the votes.

Central Asia's first encounter with Islam occurred as early as the seventh century when the Umayyad Arabs conquered this region. Islam rapidly superseded other religions, and Islamic customary law took firm root. Although many traditions of pre-Islamic Turkic culture were preserved, most of the Central Asian Turkic peoples became Muslims during the eleventh and twelfth centuries. Over the centuries Central Asia was conquered by many different rulers such as the Mongols under the leadership of Genghis Khan in the thirteenth century and Tamarlane in the fourteenth century who more or less managed to control the entire region.

Sufism and Jadidism

An alternative approach to social organisation and a locus of resistance to foreign hegemony, Sufism has played an important role in Central Asian history. It was via Sufi missionaries in the fifteenth century that Islam was first introduced among the Kazaks and Kirghiz. Moreover, Sufism played an important role in the resistance to the Russians during both the Tsarist and the Soviet eras. The most influencial Sufi brotherhoods in Central Asia are the Yasavi and the Naqshbandi, which also have branches throughout the Muslim world. The Yasavi order was founded in the mid-twelfth century by Ahmad Yasavi, who is regarded as the first Turkic mystic. He is credited with popularising, spreading and implanting Islam in Central Asia. The founder of the Naqshbandiyya is Baha al-Din Muhammed al-Buhari (1318–89) from present-day Bukhara in Uzbekistan. The followers of this brotherhood praised God with mental or spoken recitations of litanies, worked on their relationship with God as individuals and their ability to concentrate on God whether they were in a crowd or alone. Sufism left several doors open for modernisation in the nineteenth century. Thus, many of the members of the Jadid or modernisation movement were Sufis.

By 1890 Russia had completed its conquest of Central Asia. At that time the Russian empire stretched from Poland in the west to the Pacific Ocean in the east, reaching the Black Sea and the borders of Turkey and Afghanistan in the south. Since it was just emerging from feudalism, Russia was seen not only as a great power but also as a backward country. Russia was only just beginning to become industrialised. As part of the Russian empire, at the turn of the century Central Asians saw the changes taking place both in Russia and in Europe, encountering European economic, political and cultural ideas. Perhaps more importantly they also came into contact with other Muslim subjects of the empire, such as the Crimeans and Caucasians. Questions such as whether they should accept Russian ways or not became important, as did the issue of whether or not they should follow the reform movements that had started in the Ottoman empire and the Jadid or reform movement that was begun in the Caucasus in the 1880s by Ismail Bey Gasparali, known as Gasprinskii in Russian and most Western sources.

Gasparali (1851–1914), a Crimean Tatar who had been educated in Europe and had worked in Istanbul and Paris, began to publish a newspaper, *Terjuman*, in 1883. For him Islam was a cultural and political entity, a defence against the West. At the same time, he advocated the adoption of Western institutions such as secular education, women's emancipation, and commercial and industrial enterprises. The movement, which initially was an effort to improve the education standards of the Muslim subjects of the Russian empire, spread rapidly. Gasparali opened the first *usul-u Jadid* (new method) school in 1884. His aim was to increase the standard of education of teachers and to create a literary language that could be understood by every Turk, from those living 'along the shores of the Bosphorus to those living in Kashgar'. Gasparali argued also that Muslims must borrow from the West to revitalise their intellectual and social lives. While Islam could remain a philosophical and theological system, Muslim peoples had to become part of the modern technologically oriented civilisation. He visited Central Asia to spread his ideas, and by the 1890s *usul-u Jadid* schools were being opened in Central Asia and Uzbekistan. Many of the Central Asians who had been active in promoting reform in the education system joined his movement becoming the Central Asian Jadids. Jadidism became a political movement, even though the Jadids did not all share the same political views. Besides, the Jadids faced opposition from the *qadims* (supporters of the old methods) who were often supported by the *ulama*, the religious scholars.

Initially the Jadids and the Russian revolutionaries found that they could help one another. The Bolsheviks felt that they had found their allies in this small group of local intelligentsia who were receptive to the idea of modern technology to improve the lot of their people. The Jadids' opposition to the low status of women, and their efforts to modernise the education system at first seemed to afford ground for collaboration with the Soviet regime. However, when the Jadids realised that the communist aim was to destroy Islamic beliefs, and the Bolsheviks discovered that the Jadids were interested in nationalism rather than class war, discord became inevitable.

Islam in the Soviet era

In the early days of the Soviet era many of the Central Asian intelligentsia cooperated with the Soviet Communist Party, aiming at ethnic equality and independence. Sultan Galiev was one of the most important Muslim leaders who chose to cooperate with the communist leaders on these grounds. He presented a secular Muslim socialism which suggested that a national revolution must precede class war. The Russian Communist Party resisted any attempt at organising a Muslim national identity while at the same time attempting to cooperate with the Muslims in order to gain their support. Sultan Galiev became a trouble spot for the Communist Party which was striving for a homogenous Soviet Communist Party and preferred that any revolution begin in Europe rather than Asia. Thus Galiev was thrown out of the party in 1923 and sent to a labour camp in 1928, after which he 'disappeared'. For Central Asians, socialism was a tool rather than the end goal. It provided the élite with a technique for underground activism, mass action, a way of gaining foreign support and a possibility of equality even if independence could not be achieved. They realised how mistaken they had been in their assumptions shortly after integration in the Soviet Union

In 1924, when the Soviet government carved out the five republics that form contemporary Central Asia, the regime also instituted a campaign of secular education in local indigenous languages. In 1927 Central Asian communist organisations, under the supervision of two party members from Moscow, launched the *khujum* (attack) movement which aimed at counteracting traditions linked to Islam and in particular to 'liberate' Muslim women.

In the 1920s feminist activists in Russia were attacking traditional customs relating to marriage and the status of women. Couples could marry or divorce by sending in registration cards. Children born out of wedlock were granted the same rights as offspring of married parents, and abortion was legalised. On paper these laws became effective throughout the country, making traditions sanctioned by Islam such as polygyny and child marriage 'crimes based on custom'. Mosques were closed or converted to sports arenas or depots and *waqfs* (religious foundations) were liquidated. Although fluctuations did take place in tolerance toward Islam in general, religion was only permitted under the strict supervision of the authorities.

Between 1937 and 1939 most of the leading Central Asian Jadids and intellectuals lost their lives in the Stalinist purges. Islam in general and the Sufi brotherhoods in particular were not spared Stalinist attacks. They were assaulted in the name of the new ideology, atheism. Consequently the Sufi brotherhoods developed a new field of interest, 'saving Islam from Marxist pollution'. The Soviets attacked Sufi shrines which were places of pilgrimage. The regime discouraged pilgrimages and established anti-religious museums on holy sites. It took several years, however, before the Sufi opposition could be stymied. However, by 1936 even the two strongholds in the Caucasus and the Ferghana Valley of Turkestan had been crushed, although in many cases the population kept Sufi traditions alive as a type of parallel Islam co-existing with the official Islam which was open to manipulation by the regime. During the Stalinist era the Qadiri brotherhood emerged in Central Asia. This brotherhood came with the Chechen and Ingush who were deported by Stalin to the area during World War II. Women have sometimes reached leadership positions in Sufi groups, and this is especially true in some branches of the Qadiriyya. This old brotherhood gained a foothold in Kazakstan and has continued to grow since 1945.

With the Twentieth Party Congress in 1956, the Soviet Union entered a new historical period. This party congress, the first one after the death of Stalin, closed a three-year interim period of successional struggle and marked the onset of Khrushchev's predominance. Khrushchev delineated Stalin's crimes against the Communist Party and Russian national interest at this congress. In his speech, Khrushchev, then first secretary, emphasised that Stalin and the cult of the individual had been wrong. While Khrushchev's policies were assimilationist, his relations with the national-ities in the Soviet states were again marked by ambiguity and contra-dictions. During his years as president, concessions were made to the Muslims and other non-Russian minorities, especially in the areas of linguistic policy and historiography. However, a strong anti-religious campaign was carried out from 1954 to the end of Khrushchev's reign in

1964, involving the deregistration of religious leaders and the destruction of mosques.

By 1968 the Brezhnev group had tightened its control within Russia. Stalin's image was refurbished and a centralised planning system emphasised the military and heavy investment. Intellectuals were arrested, deported or declared insane when they questioned governmental policies. However, Brezhnev did allow the nationalities to delve into their own cultures in ways that would not have been possible even in Khrushchev's time. The late 1960s were characterised by a wave of de-Russification in such areas as language, cadres and history. Native historians and artists re-emphasised the ancient roots of their communities and their cultural debt to traditional Islamic, especially Arabic and Persian, influence, while downgrading the Russian contribution. In much literature the individual Soviet republic replaced the Soviet Union as the object of patriotic loyalty.

Muslim national identity

Gorbachev's policies of *glasnost* and *perestroika* in the late 1980s had a dramatic impact in reviving Central Asian Islam or rather bringing Islamic practices into the open. Underground groups and private prayer circles emerged and began to build mosques and criticise the established Muslim hierarchy. For the most part, from the Russian era to the end of the Gorbachev era, the structure of official Islam had remained the same. The Muslims of Central Asia were divided under four spiritual boards led by a *mufti* of Central Asia and Kazakstan in Tashkent, considered the biggest jurisdiction and established on October 20, 1943. The Muslims of European Russia and Siberia were to turn to the Muslim Spiritual Board in Ufa, Bashkiria for guidance. The third spiritual board was in charge of the Muslims of northern Caucasia and Daghestan and located in Machatj-Qala in Daghestan. While the first two spiritual boards followed the Hanafi tradition, the Daghestan board was Shafi. The fourth was the Muslim Board of Baku which guided the Muslims of Transcaucasia who were Shiites of the Jafari tradition as well as Sunni Muslims of Abkhazia. The spiritual boards directed the activities of the few existing mosques, made decisions in questions concerning theology and ritual and printed religious material and journals. Religious organisations were not supported by the state but rather financed by gifts, donations, book sales and fees for various activities.

While the state could control official Islam it could not control what came to be known as unofficial Islam, the Sufi brotherhoods and the beliefs of people. Muslim rituals were regularly practised, perhaps most obviously those surrounding funerals. Even party members and 'atheists' were buried according to Muslim rites. Interestingly, in many cities throughout the Soviet period there continued to be separate burial places for Muslims,

From the interior of the Telyashayakh mosque in Tashkent (photo: David Thurfjell, 1998).

Christians and Jews. In 1989 the only Muslim religious institutions functioning officially were a *madrasa* (seminary) in Bukhara, a religious academy in Tashkent and a small number of registered mosques. By 1990, however, dramatic changes had taken place. Muslims now printed previously banned Islamic literature and simple pamphlets that described how to pray. Saudi Arabia sent 1 million Qurans to Central Asia, and there was a boom in Quran publishing as the holy book was translated into local languages. In February 1990 Muslims demanded the resignation of the *mufti* Shamsuddin Khan Babakhan, the chairman of the Muslim Board for Central Asia in Tashkent. They accused him of womanising and deviations from Islam. He was forced to step down. At the same time the *qadi* (Islamic judge) of Alma Ata, Radbek Nishanbai, had himself elected grand *mufti* of Kazakstan, thus creating a separate Kazak Muslim Board. The other Central Asian republics followed suit, and now each Central Asian republic has established a religious council, a *muftiyat* or *kaziyet*, which manages or supervises the religious life of the Muslim citizens of the nation.

Furthermore, a boom in the building of new mosques has taken place since independence. By October 1990 there were a total of fifty new mosques in Kirghizstan compared to fifteen in 1989, thirty in Turkmenistan

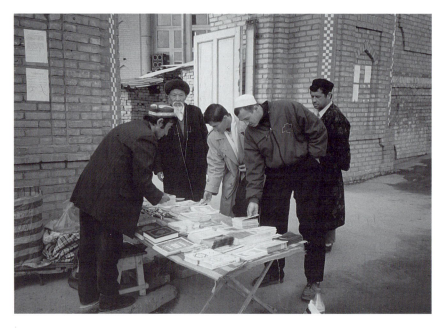

Islamic literature for sale outside the Barak Khan *madrasa* (Islamic college) in Tashkent (photo: David Thurfjell, 1998).

compared to five before, forty in Tajikistan compared to seventeen before and ninety in Kazakstan compared to thirty-seven before. In Tashkent city there were thirty new mosques compared to just two in 1989. While in 1987 there were only 260 mosques in the region, by 1992 the number had grown to roughly 5,000. Since independence from Moscow over 10,000 pilgrims from Uzbekistan have made the *hajj* (pilgrimage to Mecca), a substantial increase when seen in the light of those twenty who made the annual pilgrimage during the Soviet period. In 1997, around 3,000 Uzbek pilgrims were expected in Mecca. However, fearing 'Islamic fundamentalism', the Uzbek government shut down two Tashkent *madrasas* in February 1997, thus eliminating all openly functioning religious schools in the capital. In December 1997, the Uzbek government charged so-called Wahhabis with the murder of four militia men in the city of Namangan in eastern Uzbekistan. The Wahhabi is one of many religious groups who appeared to spread their word after the collapse of the Soviet Union. Wahhabis are also active in other Central Asian states. The Uzbek government responded to the murders by arresting hundreds of people, mostly those involved in or interested in the Wahhabi movement. However, the murders seem more consistent with local mafia activities then with the actions of Wahhabi sympathisers.

The new nationalism could sometimes be manifested in the contemporary Islamic culture of Central Asia. In the town of Turkistan in Kazakstan, a new mosque was opened in 1996 and named after the old Communist Party leader Dinmukhamad Kunaev, who had been removed from office by Gorbachev in December 1986. In the Gök Tepe fortress, forty kilometres to the west of the capital Ashgabad in Turkmenistan, the Saparmurat Haji mosque, named after the current autocratic Turkmen president, was completed on independence day in October 1997. It is the largest mosque in Central Asia, and it stands together with a memorial to the memory of the Turkmens who were killed fighting Russian troops in the late nineteenth century. Since the final Gorbachev years, mausoleums have been restored and continue to attract increasing numbers of pilgrims, and since independence Central Asians have been celebrating and exploring their Sufi heritage. On September 17, 1997, celebrations were held to commemorate the 675th anniversary of the birth of Bahauddin Naqshband, the medieval Sufi teacher who now has followers across the Muslim world. The manifestation was supported by the *mufti* of Tashkent and the Uzbek government, both of which understand the importance of such events that transcend political views and ethnic differences. The mosque complex just outside Bukhara, which was the site of the celebrations, functioned as a 'museum of atheism' during the Soviet years and was renamed a shrine in 1989. It was well attended by members of the international Muslim community. A second such event was the declaration of 1993 as the 'Yasavi year' for the entire Turkic world. The founder of the Yasaviyya, Ahmad Yasavi, is buried in Turkistan, and the declaration of 1993 followed the signing of a protocol between Turkey and Kazakstan regarding the restoration of the saint's mausoleum in Turkistan. Moreover, a Turkish–Kazak university, named after Yasavi, has been established in Turkistan. At a meeting with six of the university trustees, the Turkish minister Namik Kemal Zeybek stated that this university had 17,000 Anatolian Turkish and Kazak students. They have access to modern technology and the university may well be the best equipped in the Turkic world.

On an individual level three surveys commissioned by the United States Information Office conducted in Kazakstan, Kirghizstan and Uzbekistan in 1992 and 1993 found that the Central Asians' response to Islam was multifaceted. While half of the Kazaks and Uzbeks and four-fifths of the Kirghiz claimed faith in Islam, only one in five Uzbeks and Kirghiz acknowledged participating in religious services at a mosque or prayer house every month. However, of the surveyed about half the Kazaks and seven-tenths of the Kirghiz agreed that Islam should play a larger role in their countries. But the proportion of those who agree completely with this proposal is much less, approximately one-fifth of the Kazaks to about two-fifths of the Uzbeks.

Naqshbandi students in Samarkand (photo: David Thurfjell, 1998).

Islamic revival?

Islam has emerged as one of the most important elements of national identity formation in Central Asia. It is also hoped that Islam will act to counterbalance the national–ethnic tendencies in the region. However, it is most likely that religion will be a component of a national identity rather than a force to unify Central Asia under the banner of Pan-Islam. How this interest and pride in an Islamic heritage will manifest itself in the future is a complicated question. In a sense, it would be inaccurate to describe the current interest in Islam in Central Asia as Islamic revival since Islam in Central Asia never died out. While official Islamic institutions may not have been able to function during the Soviet period, David Tyson demonstrates, in a well-documented article based on field work, the important role played by shrines and shrine pilgrimage in Turkmenistan in sustaining popular Islam. Pilgrimages to shrines play an important role in many Muslim societies with large rural populations. The pilgrimage tradition generally remains outside the control of the government, and traditional Islamic shrine worship and pilgrimages provided and continue to provide a space for popular discussion that is difficult to monitor.

Another aspect of informal Islam which survived Soviet attempts at combating Islam even if in weakened form, are the *otins*, or the female

160

Muslim dignitaries who oversaw the daily basis of the lives of other women believers. The *otins* were traditionally in charge of teaching women the Quran. In the newly formed women's *madrasas* in Kokand and Bukhara, *otins* have been called upon to supervise female students while they teach Chagatay Turkish, the former written language of Central Asia, and the rudiments of Quranic exegesis, the actual teaching of the Quran remains in men's hands for the moment. A new group of *otins* who have travelled to Mecca and received special religious training have emerged and hope to re-Islamicise the female population. As their work takes place not just in the classroom but also in the neighbourhood and in the home, this group is another one that is difficult to supervise and control.

Just as in the Soviet period, official Islam is now strictly controlled by the government. Religious political parties have been banned in all Turkic Central Asian republics. Although the president of each of these republics proclaims himself as a faithful Muslim, each one of them has also proclaimed his intention of maintaining a secular system of government. Karimov, for example, opens parliament sessions with prayers, peppers his speeches with quotes from the Quran and has been on the pilgrimage to Mecca. He has also enlisted Uzbekistan in the Organisation of the Islamic Conference. Yet he has stated that Uzbekistan, like Turkey, will not tolerate 'Islamic fundamentalism'. To emphasise the secular nature of the government, in June 1995 Karimov passed a resolution granting more money to the Russian Orthodox Church in Uzbekistan. Kazakstan has actively attempted to avoid religious conflicts and substantiate its secular nature. For example in October 1995, the Kazak president Nazarbayev stated that Islam and Christianity are the two flanks of Kazak spirituality. The Kirghiz have also embraced Islam but in a cautious and limited way. In late 1992 the Kirghiz president Akayev promoted the inclusion of this statement in the new constitution's preamble: 'The people of Kirghizstan, while adopting the constitution . . . proclaim their adherence to universal moral principles, national traditions, and the spiritual values of Islam and other religions.' By 1994 the Kirghiz government nevertheless felt it necessary to curtail Islamic activity. Niyazov, the president of Turkmenistan, has also pursued similar strategies regarding Islam. On the one hand he has actively promoted Islam as part of the cultural and moral heritage of Turkmenistan, while actively curtailing political activity based on Islamic tenets or ideology on the other. By 1993 the Turkmen government was totally in control of the official religious establishment.

Foreign policy

All Central Asian republics have established relations with Arab and other Muslim states but not exclusively with such states. They are very interested in developing contacts with Europe and the United States and there have been many joint cultural projects with Turkey. All republics discussed in this chapter have chosen to switch their alphabet to the Latin script rather than maintaining Cyrillic or changing to Arabic. Israel has established contacts with all the new republics and is participating in several agricultural and environmental projects. The Kirghiz president Akayev caused confusion in January 1993, when he claimed to support the Palestinian demand for an independent state and at the same time agreed to open up diplomatic representation in Jerusalem after being offered a suitable property. Eventually Akayev stated that he would open an embassy in Israel only after the conflict in the Middle East had been resolved.

Good relations with neighbouring states has been a foreign policy priority for all the Central Asian states. Kazakstan, which shares a 1,700-kilometre border with China, has made a special effort to foster cooperation with that country. In May 1994 Nazarbayev visited China and signed an agreement concerning transborder railroads. More significantly, for the first time China agreed to formalise a border with a neighbour officially acknowledging the Chinese–Kazak border. Kirghizstan, which shares a 1,000-kilometre border with China, aims to sign a similar agreement. Turkmenistan, which shares a border with Iran and Afghanistan, but is also very rich in natural resources, is concerned with keeping 'fundamentalism' in check while exploiting its resources.

Whether they actually share a border with Russia or not, all Central Asian states have been very concerned with maintaining good relations with this country, while preventing Russian intervention in their internal affairs. They have cooperated in CIS agreements and institutions which, however, have not produced any concrete results. Nazarbayev, the president of Kazakstan, is quoted as having lamented 'participating in nine CIS meetings, at which we signed over 100 documents that nobody intends to implement'. Kazakstan and Kirghizstan have chosen to participate in a customs union with Russia, while Uzbekistan is considering membership of the union. However, few real steps have been taken to lower tariffs on imports. Kazakstan, which has a considerable Russian minority, has been wary of the extreme right-wing Russian talk concerning the colonising of Kazakstan. In 1993 Turkmenistan became the first Central Asian state to sign an agreement with Russia allowing the local Russians dual citizenship. Russia would like to see such an agreement signed with all the Central Asian states.

Some effort at promoting cooperation within Central Asia has also taken place. After 1991 there were plans to open the 'Great Silk Road' and to act as a bridge between Europe and Asia, but these plans are yet to be fulfilled. Kirghizstan, Kazakstan and Uzbekistan founded a Central Asian Union in 1994 to strengthen their political, economic and cultural ties. The presidents of the three states, Askar Akayev, Islam Karimov and Nursultan Nazarbayev met in July 1997 to discuss security in the light of the fighting in Afghanistan and to find ways for increased cooperation.

Political parties

In 1993 there were six political parties in Kazakstan, but for the most part they supported Nazarbayev's policies and only differed in minor details. While Nazarbayev does not have a political party, the Kazak Peoples' Unity Party has accepted him as their leader and they are seen as a centrist party. Of the parties to the left and right of KPUP the significant ones are the Kazak Peoples' Congress Party led by the international anti-nuclear activist and poet Olzhas Suleymanov. The Socialist Party established from the remnants of the old Communist Party is seen as a centre-left party. While there are some Kazak nationalist parties, a Russian nationalist party called Edintsvo, established in 1991, was banned in 1992. In Kirghizstan by 1994 there were seven official political parties. They represent centre-left, left, radical nationalist and mildly nationalist views.

At the time of its independence Uzbekistan had an interesting political arena with openly active opposition parties. Since then any meaningful, organised political opposition has been banned, although the Uzbek constitution which was accepted in 1992 includes many democratic principles. In 1991 the Democratic People's Party replaced the old Communist Party and although for the most part opposition was suppressed, Erk (Freedom), under the leadership of Muhammed Salih was allowed to participate in the elections but only received about 12 per cent of the votes. Erk was banned on December 9, 1992 and it now functions in exile. The most important political opposition came from Birlik (Unity), which was established in May 1989 by intellectuals. Its platform was nationalist, secular but still religious and based on language law reform. However, Karimov was able to co-opt much of Birlik's platform and its members were defined as a social movement in 1991. Another important political party is the Islamic Party which was promptly banned. A legal opposition party with no members in the parliament is the Vatan Taraqqiot Partiyasi (Fatherland Progress Party), which was established in May 1992.

For many centuries, Central Asia was the centre of Islamic philosophy, art, science and religious interpretation. During the Soviet period religion was combated and any religious observation or activity that was allowed was strictly controlled. However, on an individual level as well as on an unofficial level, people maintained their religious traditions and rituals, especially when it came to events such as births, circumcisions, marriages and burials. Today each Central Asian state has claimed Islam as part of its national heritage and for the most part its national identity, even though the leadership of each state is strictly committed to secularism and the separation of state and religion. In fact, since 1991 all religious parties have been banned in Central Asia. In contemporary Central Asia official Islam continues to be under strict government supervision, and when any Islamic movement is perceived as a threat or a locus of opposition, the leadership does not hesitate to suppress it. Nevertheless, Sufism and the unofficial elements such as shrine pilgrimages largely continue to elude government control.

Literature

For a general introduction to the history of Central Asia, see *Central Asia: 130 Years of Russian Dominance*, ed. Edward Allworth (New York: Columbia University Press, 1995); *Det nya Centralasien: Fem forna sovjetrepubliker i omvandling*, eds. Bo Petersson and Ingvar Svanberg (Lund: Studentlitteratur, 1995); and Ahmed Rashid, *The Resurgence of Central Asia: Islam or Nationalism?* (London: Zed Books, 1994). The development of national identity in contemporary Kazakstan is dealt with in Ingvar Svanberg, 'Kazakhstan and the Kazakhs', pp. 318–33 in *The Nationalities Question in the Post-Soviet States*, ed. Graham Smith (London: Longman Inc., 1996) and Ingvar Svanberg, 'In Search of a Kazakhstani Identity', *Journal of Area Studies*, 1994:4, pp. 113–23, while the situation of Uzbekistan is discussed in Gregory Gleason, 'Uzbekistan: From Statehood to Nationhood?', pp. 331–60 in *Nations and Politics in the Soviet Successor States*, eds. Ian Bremmer and Ray Taras (Cambridge: Cambridge University Press, 1993) and Cassandra Cavanaugh, 'Historiography in Independent Uzbekistan: The Search for National Identity', *Central Asia Monitor*, 1994:1, pp. 30–32. The situation of Kirghizstan is described in Gene Huskey, 'Kyrgyzstan: The Politics of Demographic and Economic Frustration', pp. 398–418 in *Nations and Politics in the Soviet Successor States*, eds. Ian Bremmer and Ray Taras (Cambridge: Cambridge University Press, 1993).

Edward J. Lazzerini discusses the Jadid movement in 'Beyond Renewal: The Djadid Responce to Pressure for Change in the Modern World', pp. 151–66 in *Muslims in Central Asia: Expressions of Identity and Change*, ed. Jo-Ann Gross (Durham, NC: Duke University Press, 1992). See also Sergei Poliakov, *Everyday Islam: Religion and Tradition in Rural Central Asia* (Armonk, NY: M.E. Sharpe, 1992). A very useful overview on Islam in the Soviet Union is given in Aleksandre Bennigsen and S. Enders Wimbush, *Muslims of the Soviet Empire: A Guide* (London: Hurst, 1985).

Official Islam is discussed in Bhavna Dave, 'Inventing Islam and an Islamic Threat in Kazakhstan', *Transition*, 18–24 (October, 1995), pp. 22–25; Arthur Bonner, 'Islam and the state in Central Asia: A Comparative Essay', *Central Asia Monitor*, 1995:6, pp. 27–36; and Alma Sultangalieva, 'Religion in Transition: The Kazakstani Experience', *Central Asia Monitor*, 1996:6, pp. 28–31. Aspects of folk religion in Kazakstan are dealt with in *Contemporary Kazaks: Cultural and Social Aspects*, ed. Ingvar Svanberg (London: Curzon Press, 1999); Richard Dobson, 'Islam in Central Asia:

Findings from National Surveys', *Central Asia Monitor*, 1994:2, pp. 17–22; David Tyson, 'Shrine Pilgrimage in Turkmenistan as a Means to Understand Islam among the Turkmen', *Central Asia Monitor* 1997:1, pp. 15–32; and Habiba Fatih, 'Otines: The Unknown Women Clerics of Central Asian Islam', *Central Asian Survey*, 16:1 (1997), pp. 27–43.

Chapter Eight

Iran, Afghanistan and Tajikistan

Bo Utas

The three republics Iran, Afghanistan and Tajikistan have much in common. All three are dominated by speakers of Iranian languages, mainly variants of Persian, and they share much of a long history, having belonged more often than not to the same state. The modern Islamic Republic of Iran is the largest of the three republics, covering about 1,648,000 square kilometres, followed by Afghanistan with 650,000 and Tajikistan with 143,000. The populations are proportionate to the areas with around 65 million in Iran, possibly around 20 million in Afghanistan and about 5.5 million in Tajikistan. The population growth in Iran and Tajikistan was until recently as high as above 3 per cent a year, among the highest in the world. After almost twenty years of war and interior chaos the population situation in Afghanistan is quite difficult to survey. Millions of the inhabitants of that country probably still remain in exile, especially in Pakistan and Iran.

Common to the three countries is a considerable ethnic fragmentation, with many ethnic groups represented in two or all three of the countries. For Iran and Afghanistan there are no reliable numbers regarding the various ethnic groups, but for Tajikistan there are quite detailed and fairly accurate census reports from the Soviet era, the last from 1989, recording linguistic and ethnic belonging. The table below gives a general overview of the supposed ethnic composition, based on linguistic criteria, of the three countries (situation of 1992). The figures for Iran and Afghanistan are based on very rough estimates by this author, and in the case of Tajikistan, the figures are from the last Soviet census of 1989.

The religious situation is also common to Iran, Afghanistan and Tajikistan, insofar as they are completely dominated by Islam. In Iran and Afghanistan close to 100 per cent of the inhabitants would regard themselves as Muslims, whereas the Central Asian areas that today include Tajikistan were homogeneously Muslim until the last century. At present the great majority of the Tajiks, Uzbeks, Tatars, Kirghiz, Turkmens and Kazaks that live in Tajikistan, that is close to 90 per cent of the population, would regard themselves as Muslims. Islam has a very long history in all the Iranian cultural areas, which include the three republics under discussion

166

Iran

Persians (centre, south, east; all cities)	45%	28 million
Azeri- and Qashqa'i Turks (northwest; cities)	30%	18 million
Kurds (west, northwest)	13%	8 million
Arabs (southwest)	5%	3 million
Baluchs (southeast)	4%	2.5 million
Turkmens (east of the Caspian See)	2%	1.4 million
Others (Armenians, Assyrians, Jews etc.)	1%	0.6 million

Afghanistan

Pashtuns (east, south, partly north; cities)	45%	8 million
Persians ('dari-speaking': Farsiwan, Tajiks, Hazaras etc.; west, centre, north; cities)	40%	7 million
Uzbeks (north)	11%	2 million
Turkmens (northwest)	2%	0.4 million
Baluchs (southwest)	1%	0.2 million
Others (Nuristanis, Kirghiz, Pamiris, Hindus)	1%	0.2 million

Tajikistan

Tajiks (south, centre; all cities)	62%	3.4 million
Uzbeks (north, southwest)	24%	1.3 million
Russians (cities)	6%	0.3 million
Tatars	1%	0.05 million
Kirghiz	1%	0.05 million
Ukrainians	1%	0.05 million
Others (Germans, Turkmens, Koreans, Kazaks, Jews, Pamiris etc.)	5%	0.3 million

here, and the present religious situation in many ways reflects this long and complicated course of history.

Common history

Having defeated the Sasanian Great King at Qadisiya (in present Iraq) in 637 and at Nihavand (Western Iran) in 642, the Arabs had already conquered the greater part of Iran by the middle of the seventh century. They pressed on towards the east and northeast, and the greater part of the area we are discussing here had been conquered by them before 750, when the Abbasids succeeded the Umayyads as leaders of the Caliphate. In 751 the Arabs, with the help of Turkish troops, also defeated the Chinese at Talas (north of Tashkent), opening up the whole of Central Asia for Islamic penetration. Only the eastern and unaccessible central parts of Afghanistan could hold out against the Caliphate for a couple more centuries.

Real Islamisation, however, was much slower. During the first 100 years the Arab conquerors were generally not interested in making proselytes for their new religion, but from the beginning of the Abbasid reign a conversion of broad bands of people started. The Sasanian state religion, Zoroastrianism, which had dominated most of the region, seems to have been in a state of decay during this period. Our sources depict it as a rigorous system of legal regulations with a religious superstructure that had petrified into bigotry. Zoroastrianism seemed to have had comparatively weak power of resistance to Islam, but many other religions were represented in the region, especially various Eastern Christian denominations, such as Nestorians and Monophysites, as well as Manichaeans and, in the eastern parts, Buddhists. Even if this is little studied and difficult to prove, it is probable that elements from those pre-Islamic religions live on as substrates in local forms of Islam. Thus Islamic, and perhaps especially Shiite, law seems to be influenced by Zoroastrian regulations and conceptions of purity, and Sufism, the Islamic form of mysticism, by Manichaean and Buddhist monasticism.

In Central Asia, the Turks soon became zealous champions of Sunni Islam. Especially in areas bordering with non-Islamic peoples they developed the militant tradition of *ghazi*, fighter for the religion, which accompanied them on their way to Asia Minor, where such Turkish *ghazi*s were to lead the attacks on the remnants of Christian Byzantium. As early as in the tenth century the Turks emerged as a leading force within the Eastern Caliphate. They first entered Iranian territories as nomads and traders but soon attained special importance as soldiers, initially as slaves and mercenaries but soon rising in rank to generals, governors and even monarchs. The last genuinely Iranian or Persian dynasty in Eastern Iran (including present-day Afghanistan and Tajikistan) was the Samanids, who from their capitals, Samarkand and Bukhara, ruled over an east-Iranian state which the Tajikistan of today likes to see as its own forerunner. Around the year 1000 CE, the Samanids were replaced by the Turkic Ghaznavid dynasty, which made Ghazna (in present southeastern Afghanistan) their capital, and from there Sunni Islam was brought into India.

From the Ghaznavid era up to our own century almost all the ruling dynasties of this region were of Turkic origin, the most important exception being the Mongolian Il-Khans who conquered Baghdad in 1258 and put an end to the original Sunni caliphate. The Turkic dynasties were generally militantly Sunni, while their Iranian-speaking subjects often professed themselves adherents of various forms of Shiism, both the now dominant Twelver school and denominations of Seven-Imam Shia, especially Ismailiyya. The conflict between these two doctrines runs like a red thread, at times visible, at times invisible, through the religious history of this region. There was, however, one religious manifestation in which the difference between Sunni and Shia played only a minor role – that was Sufism. This form of mysticism had its roots in the original, Arabic Islam, but it was in Eastern Iranian Khorasan and Mavaraonnahr (Transoxania, that is the land between the rivers Oxus and Jaxartes) that, in the tenth century, it started to crystalise into specific 'orders' or brotherhoods. During the turbulent centuries that followed, these Sufi orders developed rapidly, and their leaders, called *murshid, shaykh, pir, eshan* etc., attracted huge numbers of adherents from all social classes and at times also acquired great political influence. An excellent example of this is the Naqshbandi *shaykh* Khvaja Ahrar (d. 1490), who became one of Central Asia's most powerful men during the rather weak reigns of the Timurid ruler Abu Said and his sons.

A decisive development in both the religious and political history of the whole region was the rise to power in Iran of the Safavid dynasty around the year 1500. This originally Sunni family of Sufi *shaykhs* in Ardabil (close to the Caspian Sea) allied itself with some militant Turkmen tribes in northwestern Iran, the so-called Qizilbash ('redheads'). In contrast to most other Turks, these Qizilbash were Shiites. The Safavid *shaykh* Ismail linked up with their militant and very special form of Shiism, and when with their help he came to power in Iran, he made Twelver Shiism the state religion. A veritable Shiisation of Iran was harshly enforced. The power of the Sunni Sufi orders was broken, and Iran was brought to a state of confrontation with its Sunni neighbours in the west, the Ottoman empire, as well as in the northeast, the Uzbek Shaibanid state, and the southeast, the empire of the Great Moghuls in India. Sanguinary border wars were carried on, especially against the Ottomans and the Uzbeks. This was the beginning of the final split of Perso–Turkic Muslim culture. Iran, in the sense that it has today, chiselled out for itself a separate identity as the first Shiite state after that of the rather short-lived Fatimids in Egypt (969–1171). It was not a 'national state', in its proper sense, but rather a centralised structure that has formed the basis of modern Iran. At the same time the open communications along the age-old trade routes in what used to be the Eastern Caliphate were cut. Central Asia and the border region that was to become Afghanistan were isolated.

Towards the end of the Safavid era, the pronounced cultural, economic and political decline that has been characteristic of the whole of this region up until the twentieth century began to manifest itself. For Central Asia the isolation had disastrous consequences. The successors of the Shaibanid state, the Khanates of Bukhara, Khiva and Kokand, remained like relics from a time gone by and became easy prey for expanding Russian imperialism. From a religious point of view this meant that the brilliant learned traditions from the time when Bukhara and Samarkand were veritable cultural capitals of the Caliphate shrank to the mere ability to maintain only the most fundamental ritual and legal functions. Even the Afghanistan that was created by Afghan (i.e. Pashtun) tribes, after the final liquidation of the Safavid state through one of those very tribes in 1722, remained relatively isolated. Its communications ran more towards India than Iran, and its special position as a buffer zone between the expanding Russian and British empires kept it screened off from the outer world.

When we enter the twentieth century, Iran and Afghanistan thus exist as reasonably independent entities, but Iran is in a deep political and economic crisis and is effectively divided into a Russian and a British zone of interest. Due to its inaccessible position, Afghanistan in its internal structure remained relatively unaffected by the colonial powers, but Great Britain kept its formal control over Afghan foreign policy until 1917. The borders of both Iran and Afghanistan had been drawn by those same colonial powers with due regard to their own strategic interests. Tajikistan entered the twentieth century as a backward province of the ossified Emirate of Bukhara, which in its turn stood under Russian control, although it was not formally dissolved until after the October Revolution. After various reorganisations, a Soviet Tajik Autonomous Republic was set up in 1924. It is obvious that the difficult political, cultural and social situation in which the three countries found themselves at the beginning of the twentieth century has been formative for the development of Islam there in later decades.

Iran

In the sixteenth and seventeenth centuries, Twelver Shiism thus became the dominant form of religion in Iran. Today about 80 per cent of the population embrace this creed. It is above all Kurds, Baluchs and Turkmens who profess themselves adherents of Sunni Islam, while Persians, Azeri Turks and Arabs are generally Shiites. According to very uncertain estimates some 65 per cent of the Iranian Kurds are Shafii Sunnites, while 80 per cent of the Baluchs and 95 per cent of the Turkmens are Hanafi Sunnites. The rest are Shiites, apart from some quite small Kurdish groups that belong to very special sects, like Ahl-i Haqq (Kakayi) and similar extreme Alid groups. To this a number of small non-Islamic groups should be added: Armenian and Syrian ('Assyrian') Christians, Zoroastrians, Jews and believers of the Bahai religion which developed out of Islam in the end of the nineteenth century. Due to the political sensitivity of the matter there are no reliable estimates of the number of Bahais in Iran, but at least up until the Islamic Revolution in 1979 they must have been quite numerous.

On the ritual level, the difference between the Shiites and Sunnites of Iran is relatively small. There are some minor divergences in the call to prayer and the praying postures. In religious law, that is the interpretation of *sharia*, the differences are greater. The Shiites follow their own legal school, nowadays called the Jafari rite after the sixth Imam, Jafar al-Sadiq. It differs from the various Sunni schools, for example the Shafii and Hanafi, *inter alia* in family law. This concerns, for instance, regulations governing inheritance and marriage (e.g. the special Shiite rules for temporary marriage, so-called *muta* or, in Persian, *sighe)*. A more important difference is, however, found in the structure of the religious leadership. The Sunni groups in Iran are comparatively small and dispersed and lack a structured leadership. Their theologians (*ulama*) and religious functionaries (*mullas*) have only a local influence. There is no national hierarchy.

Twelver Shiism, on the other hand, as early as in the sixteenth century developed a complicated hierarchic system of religious leadership. Following the example of the actual founder of the dynasty, Shah Ismail, the Safavid Shahs had very exclusive pretensions. The original role of the family as leaders of a Sufi order based in Ardabil, at the southwest corner of the Caspian Sea, was developed into a charismatic leadership first of all over the Qizilbash, but soon extending to all Shiites. This was based on an alleged kinship with the family of the Prophet through the first Imam, that is Ali. The aspirations of the Safavid Shahs to a nearly divine status necessarily clashed with the conceptions and interests of the Shiite theologians. At the time of the reshaping of Iran by Shah Ismail, these theologians had to a considerable extent been called in from abroad (especially from Bahrain and Lebanon), since Iran at that time had no developed Shiite theologian traditions of its own. From the outset they were thus dependent upon the Safavid rulers, but as their position in Iranian society was strengthened, they were able to turn against the role of the Shahs as the supreme leader of the religion.

The Shiite theologians of Iran at an early stage became divided into two schools, one called *akhbari* ('the traditionalists') and one *usuli* ('the fundamentalists'). The former maintained that the theology should be founded on all the material that theologians and jurisprudents had worked out through centuries, while the latter school wanted to go back to the *usul*, that is 'foundations, principles', of Islam, taken as the Quran and the examples of the Prophet and the Shiite Imams. During the eighteenth and nineteenth centuries the *usuli* theologians gained the upper hand. They attached greater importance than did the others to the so-called *ijtihad*, that is authoritative reinterpretation of the law through the leading jurisprudents (*mujtahids*). In principle they refused to acknowledge the legitimacy of secular power, which means that they represented a more radical political attitude than the traditionalists. Towards the end of the nineteenth century, leading *usuli* theologians joined forces with liberal and secular groups in resistance to the corrupt and powerless Qajar rule with its increasing dependence on foreign powers. The Iranian 'awakening' which gained momentum around the turn of the century thus had both Islamist and secular instigators, two groups with widely differing aims. The liberals published journals, generally in exile, while the theologians made use of the religious law and the deep-rooted Islamic sentiments of the population. The latter fought Qajar power with legal decisions (*fatwas*), as for instance the opposition to a British concession for the trading of tobacco, which led to the so-called tobacco boycott, forcing the Shah to retreat and cancel the concession.

The alliance between radical theologians and secular liberals finally, in 1906, compelled Muzaffar ud-din Shah to accept a constitution and the election of a parliament (*majlis*). However, the political euphoria proved shortlived. With active support from the colonial powers, Great Britain and Russia, the Qajar regime was soon able to quench the budding democracy. An American economist, Morgan Shuster, adequately termed this process *The Strangling of Persia* in the title of a book he wrote about his frustrating experiences as financial adviser to the state. After the failure of this democratic experiment the radical theologians went their own way. Many of them emigrated and settled at the Shiite shrines in Iraq, especially in Najaf. Among the theologians active there we find Muhammad Husain Naini (d. 1936), who elaborated an advanced theory for an Islamic system of government. When Khomeini was exiled in 1963, he came, after a short stay in Turkey, to Najaf where he held his famous series of lectures on 'Islamic government' (*hukumat-i islami*). Naini and Khomeini both base their arguments on the strict Shiite conception that religious as well as secular leadership of the Islamic community, the *umma*, belongs to the twelve Imams, who in their esoteric tradition have kept the full knowledge of God's intentions towards man. After the twelfth and last Imam, Muhammad al-Mahdi, in 941 had entered the 'greater occultation', only the most prominent of the jurisprudents of each epoch are capable of leading the society, including leadership in its secular aspects, in the way foreseen by God. This is what Khomeini termed *vilayat-i faqih*, 'the government of the jurisprudent'.

The specific hierarchical order which prevails in Twelver Shiism stipulates how these 'most prominent jurisprudents' are elected. In principle they are found among the *mujtahid*s who have reached the rank of a *marja-i taqlid*, 'object of emulation' (i.e. an absolute spiritual authority whom all believers are obliged to follow). They receive the title of Ayatollah, properly *ayatullah al-uzma*, 'the greatest sign of God'. Such a *marja* reaches his position through an informal process, in which he is spontaneously chosen as spiritual leader by an adequate number of adherents. These theologians traditionally have their base in the city of Qum, 150 kilometres south of Tehran. There they run their respective theological seminars (*hauze*), which are not only centres for theological education but also for administration of the considerable economic resources that are put at the disposal of each *marja* through the religious dues (*khums*, 'fifth', i.e. of income above what is necessary for the subsistence of one's own family) given to him by his adherents for distribution for altruistic purposes. A *marja* may reside also in some other important Iranian city, as for instance Mashhad (place for pilgrimage through the shrine of the eighth Imam, *Astan-i Quds-i Razavi*) or the theological centre of the Shiites in Iraq, Najaf (there are always means of sending collected funds across the borders).

The principle of 'the guidance of the jurisprudent' is regulated in the following way in Article 5 of the Islamic constitution that was approved by an overwhelming majority of the population in a referendum in December 1979:

> During the occultation of His Holiness the Ruler of the Age (may God the High, expedite his return) in the Islamic Republic of Iran the supervision of the government and the leadership of the community are incumbent upon a just and pious jurisprudent, abreast with the time, courageous, energetic and judicious, the leadership of whom has been acknowledged and accepted by a majority of the people, and in case no jurisprudent can attain such a majority, these tasks are entrusted to a leader or a leadership council composed of jurisprudents who meet with the above-mentioned conditions, according to Article 107.

Articles 1 and 107 of the constitution point to Khomeini, mentioned by name, as this leader. The expression 'Ruler of the Age' refers to the hidden twelfth Imam, al-Mahdi, and here the milleniaristic undercurrent that characterises Shiism becomes visible. The return of the hidden Imam is the ultimate guarantee for the final victory of the good. In popular consciousness, in particular, the return of al-Mahdi is taken to be near, since the world just before this return is supposed to sustain its most severe trials, and trials are rarely absent. All through the history of Islam, both in and outside Iran, many an alleged al-Mahdi has appeared, and with the, from a popular point of view, wonderful victory that Khomeini won over the Shah and his heathen helpers (especially the United States) it was easy to see him as the returning Imam. Such claims were never expressly made by Khomeini or the theologians surrounding him, but the politico-religious propaganda still had a strong undercurrent of Mahdism, as for instance in the common song of homage to Khomeini: *Ai imam-i ma!*, 'O, our Imam!' Conveniently, *imam* also means any leader of a Muslim community, especially the leader of the Friday prayer.

Another characteristic property of Iranian Islam is the mystery of suffering which is symbolised by the grief for the martyrdom of Imam Husayn and his intimates at Karbala in 680. These traumatic events are recreated every year in the so-called Passion of Muharram, that is a series of mourning ceremonies, recitations, dramas (*taziye*) and processions that culminate on the tenth of Muharram, the anniversary of the tragedy at Karbala. The mourning processions on the tenth of Muharram may, in particular, develop into violent and sanguinary mass scenes with ecstatic mourners lashing and cutting themselves and shouting religious slogans in mighty chorus. This collective grief is a powerful expression of the traditional view of the Shiites of themselves as perpetually persecuted and

Symbolic scourging during the Ashura celebration in Isfahan (photo: Franz Wennberg, 1994).

suppressed. This is combined with a strong distrust of worldly power and a devotion to the religious leaders that give the latter a far stronger position than that of the Sunni *ulama*.

Since Muharram, like the fasting month Ramadan, is a month of the Islamic lunar year, which is eleven days shorter than a solar year, the Muharram Passion moves over the solar calendar. In 1978 the tenth of Muharram fell on the eleventh of December. That day millions of people marched through the streets of Tehran shouting out their grief over the martyrdom of Husain together with their hatred against Yazid, the Umayyad caliph who had given the order for the massacre of Husayn and his troop. In politico–religious propaganda, the Shah had already been identified as the Yazid of our time, and the processions thus turned into a gigantic political demonstration. The Shah, who watched the processions from a helicopter, obviously lost the last of his courage and left Iran one month later, on January 11, 1979.

When Khomeini and his followers landed at the airport of Tehran on the first of February the same year and were met by huge masses of people, he was presented with the task of putting into practice the Shiite *usuli* theories about an Islamic system of government. A revolution which had been brought about above all through a mobilisation of broad strata of the people by exploiting the traditional Shiite hatred of all worldly supremacy was to be transformed into a system of government, in which the religious leaders themselves had also to represent the secular power. It can be maintained that neither Khomeini nor his successors actually succeeded in bringing about this reversion of the ideological poles.

The non-Shiite religious groups in Iran were naturally little-attracted by this politicised Shiism. The new constitution is expressly based on Twelver Shiism, although its Article 12 also guarantees a broader religious liberty:

> The official religion of Iran is Islam, and its law school is the Jafari tradition of *Ithna ashari* [Twelver] Shiism. This principle is eternal and unalterable. The other law schools of Islam, among them Hanafi, Shafii, Maliki, Hanbali and Zaidi, are regarded with full respect, and the followers of these law schools are free to exercise their religious rites in accordance with their own religious legal system. The law schools are officially recognised for teaching and education and for personal affairs (marriage, divorce, inheritance and framing of wills) and legal cases with reference to these in the courts of law; and in each region where the followers of any of these law schools form a majority, regional regulations within the areas of competence of the councils shall be formulated according to that law school with preservation of the rights of the followers of other law schools.

In spite of this reassurance there was much unrest among Sunni Kurds, Baluchs and Turkmens when this constitution had been approved, and Khomeini felt obliged to promise improvements in the protection of the rights of religious minorities. However, such changes were never brought about. In this context it should be noticed that the constitution also guarantees Zoroastrians, Jews and (Eastern) Christians the liberty 'within the jurisdiction of the law to perform their religious services and act according to their cannon as far as their personal status and religious teachings are concerned' (Article 13).

Even within the Shiites of Iran there are antagonisms which find their expression in religious terms. The large Azarbaijan–Turkish minority, which not only dominates the northwestern provinces but also constitutes a considerable part of the population of Tehran, to a great extent regarded Ayatollah Kazim Shariat-Madari, the main competitor of Khomeini, as their *marja*. In December 1979 and January 1980 severe disturbances broke out in Tabriz, the capital of Iranian Azarbaijan, whereafter the leaders of the politically dominant Islamic Republican Party succeeded in having the Republican Party of the Muslim People of the Azarbaijanis banned. Later on Shariat-Madari lost all real influence, when he had to make a televised public apology for contacts with the dismissed and later executed foreign minister Qutbzade. Similarly, the Tehran regime neutralised the leader of the Shiite Khuzistan Arabs, Shaykh Khaqani, by taking him to Qum and isolating him there.

175

The interior of the Khomeini mausoleum still under construction south of Tehran (photo: Franz Wennberg, 1994).

It is still far from clear what influence the present Islamic regime of Iran will have on long-term religious development. The politicisation of the official religion seems to lead to quite disparate reactions in various social classes. The poor, in towns as well as in villages, and especially those who in the propaganda are called *mustazafin*, 'the destitute', and those who send their sons to serve in the Revolutionary Guards (*pasdaran*), have every reason to feel solidarity with both the religious and the political aspects of the new order, but a large part of the middle class and those of the upper class who have not emigrated are probably taken aback by what they regard as a hypocritical use of religion. Although the society appears to have become vigorously Islamised, as seen for instance in the fields of law and education, in the lively participation in the congregational Friday Prayers, rather strict compliance with to the rules for public dress of women, prohibition of alcohol, of eating and smoking in the daytime during the fasting month and so on, it remains uncertain how far this really means a religious activation on a deeper level of Iranian life. Paradoxically, it is possible that the new order rather contributes to a modernisation and, in the long run, perhaps also secularisation of Iran, and this more effectively than the Shah's many Westernisation programmes.

Afghanistan

More than 99 per cent of the population of Afghanistan are Muslims. The proportions of Sunnites and Shiites are the reverse of that in Iran. Close to 80 per cent of Afghans are estimated to be Hanafi Sunnites, while about 18 per cent are considered to be adherents of Twelver Shiism and somewhat less than 2 per cent Seven-Imam Shiites, that is Ismailis. It is often difficult to distinguish between Sunnites and Shiites, because the latter have traditionally been able to resort to so-called *taqiyya*, that is simulated adherence to the dominating creed for the sake of personal safety. While in Iran the group that defines the country is Shiite Persians, it is the strongly Sunni Pashtuns (the 'Afghans' in a narrow sense) that have upheld the political system of Afghanistan since its appearance as an independent state at the end of the eighteenth century. More than 98 per cent of the Pashtuns are Sunnites. Only a couple of small tribes (Turi and Bangash) on the border to Pakistan are Twelver Shiites. On the other hand, about half of the Persian-speaking part of the population (Farsiwans, Tajiks, Hazaras and Aimaks), who live in the west, central and north provinces and in the capital, Kabul, are Twelver Shiites. About 5 per cent of the Persian-speakers living in the central mountains north of Bamiyan and in the mountainous province Badakhshan in the northeast, are Ismailites, as are the small groups in the extreme northeast who speak Pamiri languages. The Uzbeks, one of the largest groups in the northern provinces, and the smaller groups of Turkmens (in the northwest), Baluchs (in the south) and the Kirghiz (in the northeast) are probably more or less completely Sunni. In the towns there are also small groups of Hindus, Sikhs and Jews, although most of the latter seem to have left the country in recent years. The eastern province of Nuristan was Islamised as late as the end of the nineteenth century. Earlier the Nuristanis had an indigenous religion and were called Kafirs ('infidels') by their Muslim neighbours.

Sunnism appears in Afghanistan in a quite traditional form. Especially among the Pashtuns it has a strong admixture of tribal customs, that may differ rather much from what is actually stipulated in Islam but still is regarded as true Islam. Segregation between men and women is strongly prescribed. Only for a few decades before the coup d'état of 1978 and among the upper classes (and to some extent among nomads and farmers) unveiled women could be seen. The Afghan veil (*purda*) is heavier than the type common in Iran (*chadur*), completely covering the body, with only a grid in front of the eyes. Local religious functionaries (*mullas* or *maulavis*) take care of the ceremonies that regulate private life according to traditional customs. A secularisation of the teaching and the legal systems had started before the coup d'état in April 1978. The new, Marxist leaders wanted to accelerate these programmes, but since their policies quickly led to immediate and widespread opposition and soon to civil war, which in its turn led to the Soviet invasion and more unrest, war and confusion, the trend towards secularisation has probably been reversed in most places, insofar as any organised social activity has been at all possible.

The Sunnite theologians (*ulama*) of Afghanistan have never held a position that could compete with that of the Shiite leaders in Iran. Sunni Islam has no counterpart to the Shiite hierarchy with a *marja* at the head. Throughout the history of Islam, Sunni theologians as a rule have been content to confirm the legitimacy of the secular power, as long as the continued existence of Islam was not threatened. This has also been the case in Afghanistan. The rough-handed unifier of the state, Amir Abdurrahman (reigned 1880–1901), personally controlled both the theologians and central dogmatic matters. He exploited this systematically in his attempts at unifying the country. For the same purpose Nader Shah in 1932 formed an Association of Theologians (Jamiyat-i ulama) which has, since then, supported every new ruler, including the more or less Marxist regimes of Nur Muhammad Taraki, Hafizollah Amin, Babrak Karmal and Najib.

During the civil war and the Soviet invasion much of this traditional order was overthrown. It is true that there were always theologians around who were prepared to support the regime in power, but many others went into exile and joined the various resistance movements. A prominent example of this is Burhanuddin Rabbani, a professor of theology at Kabul University who became the leader of the resistance organisation Jamiyat-i islami-yi Afghanistan (The Islamic Association of Afghanistan), later to become the interim president of the country after the fall of the communist regime. His colleague Abdurrasul Sayyaf became the leader of the organisation Ittihad-i islami, which was especially favoured by Saudi-Arabia. In spite of this, such traditional theologians did not play a major role in the religiously motivated mobilisation of the greater part of the Afghan population for the war against the communists and their Soviet backers. Instead, at the beginning of the war there was another type of Islamic intellectual who took the lead, young people who had received a semi-westernised education. Some of them were, for instance, technicians who had studied at the polytechnic high school in Kabul, which was founded by the Russians. Typical representatives of this new type of Islamist politicians are Gulbuddin Hikmatyar, leader of the radically Islamic Hizb-i islami (The Islamic Party), later prime minister in the attempt at forming a post-communist coalition government, and Shah Masud, the almost legendary resistance leader in the Panjshir region northeast of Kabul. In principle Shah Masud always belonged to the party of Rabbani, but he has been quite independent in his political activities. In the coalition government he was first minister of war but was forced to retire and return to his base in Panjshir.

Among the Sunnites of Afghanistan the Sufi orders have had a considerable influence for hundreds of years. They are led by more or less charismatic leaders, affiliated to one of the main orders, Naqshbandiyya, Qadiriyya, Chistiyya or Suhravardiyya. These *shaykhs* have a broad register of functions stretching from the teaching of advanced esoteric ideas and meditation practices to aspects of popular religion centred around saint worship, shrines and healing. At least until the end of the 1970s the vast majority of the population had some kind of relationship to such a *pir* or *shaykh*. The inner circle of an order, the proper Sufis, take part in the ceremonial meditation exercise which is called *zikr* (Ar. *dhikr*) which through rhythmical movements, special techniques of deep inhalation and continuous repetition of certain holy phrases may lead to states of ecstasy. The activities are centred in the residence of the *pir*, called *khanaqah*, which also houses the venerated tombs of his ancestors and to which his adherents come at least once a year in order to show their allegiance. Traditionally the more important *pirs* ran Quranic schools, perhaps the most important popular teaching institutions before the introduction of a Western type of secular school system in the middle of the twentieth century. Before the coup d'état of 1978 these Quranic schools had lost most of their importance, but it is not impossible that they have received a new relevance in some of the provinces during the chaotic years that followed.

The influence of a Sufi *pir* on his followers is similar to that of a Shiite *marja*. He is an example to follow, and his authority may in many instances be absolute. During the heyday of Sufism in Iran and Central Asia, for instance under the Timurids in the fifteenth century, the leading *pirs* also wielded great political influence. In Iran these potential centres of power were crushed by the Safavids, leading to the near extinction of the orders in the areas where they had full control. Only in Kurdistan in the west and the areas that later became Afghanistan and Tajikistan in the east did the traditional Sufi orders remain undisturbed. In Afghanistan they have continued to play an important political role up to the present day. The leading Naqshbandi and Qadiri families were allied to the royal family through strategic marriages, and consequently they were harshly persecuted after the coup d'état of 1978.

The leading *shaykhs* of the Mujaddidi family, who belong to the Naqshbandi order, were executed soon after the coup, but one of the surviving members of that family, Sibghatullah Mujaddidi, founded one of the resistance organisations based in Peshawar: Jabha-yi najat-i milli-yi Afghanistan (The National Liberation Front of Afghanistan). A member of the Qadiri Gailani family, Sayyid Ahmad, also founded a resistance organisation: Shuray-i inqilab-i islami va milli-yi Afghanistan (The Islamic and National Revolutionary Council of Afghanistan). However, neither Sibghatullah Mujaddidi nor Ahmad Gailani was an active Sufi leader before the coup. Mujaddidi, who was regarded a supporter of the Muslim Brotherhood, was the leader (Imam) of the Islamic community in Copenhagen and Gailani was a businessman in Kabul. Still both could

The Mazar-e-Sharif mosque in northern Afghanistan, where the caliph Ali is said to have been buried, surrounded by holy doves (photo: Bo Utas, 1978).

count on a certain amount of support from the traditional adherents of their respective families. The active *pirs* who survived the persecutions and stayed on in the country were often able to assist local guerilla groups. In a few cases they even seem to have been active as guerilla leaders themselves, but the Sufi orders above all acted as flexible and well-ramified informal organisations that could inspire people to fight against foreign invaders and against a political order that was seen as a deadly threat to all traditional values, in short what was regarded as 'true Islam'.

The Shiites were also active in the fight against the regime in Kabul. The Shiites of the central mountain region, the Hazaras, at an early stage made themselves independent under their traditional secular and religious leaders. However, this leadership was soon challenged by radical groups that were supported by Iran and wanted to start an Islamic revolution against a system that they regarded as feudal. In time, and probably depending on shifts in Iranian Afghanistan policy, these antagonisms were smoothed out and during later years this region, Hazarajat, has upheld a reasonably united independence. The Shiite resistance movements in central and western Afghanistan were thus to a great extent dependent on Iranian support while the Sunnite resistance, with its five major exile organisations in Peshawar, depended primarily on Pakistan and through it on help from the United States, Saudi-Arabia etc. This heavy foreign involvement in the politics of Afghanistan has also contributed to the fragmentation of the country and the difficulties in establishing some kind of stability after the fall of the last communist government, that of Najib, in 1992.

The relatively small Ismaili minority has generally isolated itself from its Muslim brethren, especially as these often do not regard the Ismailis as genuine Muslims. Little is known about their religious life and ceremonies. For instance, they do not have mosques but congregational meeting places (*jama'at-khana*). Historically they belong to the Nizari group, but they have in recent times joined the Khojas, the Ismaili faction that regards the Aga Khan as its spiritual leader. During the civil war they achieved a certain political weight, since the strategically important roads which run from Kabul to the north and the Soviet borders pass through their territory. Consequently they were treated well by the communist regime, and the militia they organised was regarded as its ally until it, in a crucial phase close to the fall of Najib, joined the troops of Shah Masud together with the Uzbek militia of Dostam Khan.

The state of Afghanistan has few cohesive elements and rather weak historical traditions on which to base a feeling of national identity. The ethnic group that dominates the state politically, the Pashtuns (the true 'Afghans'), have a strong ethnic identity of their own which they have tried to transfer to the country they have chiselled out: Afghanistan, the land of the Afghans. However, half of the Pashtuns (the 'Pathans') live in the northwestern province of Pakistan, outside the state of Afghanistan, and the more than 50 per cent of the inhabitants of the country that belong to other ethnic groups have not been eager to call themselves Afghans. Therefore Islam is of great importance in the attempts at creating a national feeling of belonging. Through the political development during the last centuries the dominant form of very traditional, Sunnite Islam has come to demarcate Afghanistan quite clearly from its neighbours: from Shiite Iran in the west, from British India, ruled by 'Kafirs' (infidels), in the east and south, and from the equally 'Kafir' Russian or Soviet Central Asia in the north.

This national identity, based on a traditional form of Islam, was probably the greatest spiritual asset of Afghanistan during the long war against the Soviet invaders and the regime that was supported by them. The Islamic identity has certainly been strengthened by war and hardships, but at the same time the ideas about what Islam is or should be have changed in ways that are not easy to grasp even for the believers themselves. At the beginning of the 1970s Afghanistan was still a relatively isolated buffer-state, when it was thrown open to influences from the whole world. A new generation of leaders introduced political interpretations of Islam inspired by the Muslim Brothers, the Wahhabis, Mawdudi and Khomeini and others, that despite all pressures from the outside may remain alien to a majority of the population. This has provided an avenue for new and desperate attempts to formulate the true Islamic identity of Afghanistan, for a time lighting a star of hope, as in the first enthusiasm that met the advancing Taliban, but in the end adding confusion to confusion. It would be a fair guess that most Afghans remain uncertain about the true character of the religion they have fought so hard for twenty years to protect.

Tajikistan

About 90 per cent of the population of Tajikistan consists of what is often termed 'ethnic Muslims', that is peoples that before the Russian conquests in the nineteenth century were homogeneously Islamic and that in their private lives have upheld Muslim customs. These are people that speak Iranian (Tajik and various Pamir languages) or Turkic languages (Uzbek, Kirghiz, Turkmen, Kazak, Tatar etc.). Their percentage of the population is rising quickly, partly because of their high birth rate, partly through the emigration of citizens of European origin, mainly Russians, Ukrainians and Germans. In 1989 the population growth rate of Tajikistan was as high as 3.22 per cent, the highest figure in all of what was then the Soviet Union. The proportion of Russians in the population has decreased continuously from 13.3 per cent in 1959 to about 6 per cent today.

Insofar as they are at all aware of their religious identity, the majority of these ethnic Muslims would regard themselves as Hanafi Sunnites. A smaller group, consisting mainly of the Pamir peoples in the uppermost valleys of the river Oxus, are Ismailites, that is adherents of Seven-Imam Shiism. The census of 1989 also registered around 15,000 Jews, some of them so-called Chala, Jews that were converted to Islam by the rulers of Bukhara at the end of the eighteenth and the beginning of the nineteenth centuries. The Jewish colonies of Central Asia have a long history. Jews have probably lived there since pre-Islamic times. During recent years they have, however, emigrated in great numbers.

When, after the October Revolution, the Emirate of Bukhara was finally liquidated and the Autonomous Tajik Republic was erected in its eastern parts in 1924, the borders were drawn in such a way that the Persian-speaking Tajiks were separated from their old capitals, Samarkand and Bukhara. These cities were incorporated in the Uzbek Soviet Republic, and their importance as political, cultural and religious centres was systematically reduced. On the whole, the Soviet authorities treated the Muslims of Central Asia quite high-handedly, and a lengthy rebellion broke out which was not finally crushed until the middle of the 1930s. The insurgents, whom the Russians called 'basmachi', a Turkish word for robber, were to a great extent recruited among the adherents of the Sufi orders, and they were strongly motivated by Islam in their fight against the atheistic Soviet system which they regarded as a threat to their traditional way of living. They

Tajik pilgrims in Samarkand (photo: Ingvar Svanberg, 1990).

found shelter in the inaccessible mountainous regions of Tajikistan, but in the long run they could, of course, not keep up their isolated struggle against the well-equipped Soviet army. Due to the Sovietisation of Central Asia and the Basmachi rebellion considerable numbers of people, especially Uzbeks and Turkmens, fled to Afghanistan where they still live and are known as *muhajirin*, 'refugees'.

The new administration of Tajikistan, which was completely dominated by Russians, systematically repressed all official expressions of Islam. However, the Soviet power did set up a nominal Islamic organisation, which for Tajikistan meant that it came under the so-called Spiritual Directorate in Tashkent. This directorate was led by a *mufti* chosen and controlled by the central power, and under him Tajikistan had a similarly officially appointed Islamic judge (*qazi*, Ar. *qadi*), but this official religious organisation was rudimentary. There were hardly more than ten official mosques in the country and not a single school for training religious functionaries. For the whole of Soviet Central Asia there were only two theological seminars, one in Bukhara and one in Tashkent. Religious literature, and especially the Quran, was not made available to believers but only to limited scholarly circles.

The Naqshbandiyya and the Yasaviyya (Yesevi) are the indigenous orders of Central Asia. The latter was founded by a Turk from Yasi (nowadays called Turkistan, a town in south Kazakstan) known as Ahmad Yasavi (d. 1166), and it achieved a vast influence especially among the Central Asian Turks. The Naqshbandi order, on the other hand, had its original centre in Bukhara and was, from the outset, particularly active among the Persian-speaking urban population. This order was first known as Khajagan, but in the fourteenth century it was reformed by Baha al-Din Naqshband (d. 1389) and became known as Naqshbandiyya all over the Muslim world, where it has become extremely widespread. Into the twentieth century this order has also played an important political role in many countries, for instance through the branch called Khalidiyya in Kurdistan. The Qadiri order, too, has been active in Central Asia.

These old Sufi orders were integrated in networks that were spread right across the Muslim world. They were often dynamic organisations that played a leading role in the local cultures. When, from the eighteenth century onwards, Central Asia was cut off and isolated, these international networks broke up and the local orders stagnated. They lived on under the leadership of *pirs* (in Central Asia often called *eshan*) who were gradually removed from their learned traditions and whose activities became dominated by a type of popular religion that centred on the veneration of holy places and tombs of saints, so called shrines (*mazar* or *ziyarat*). In Tajikistan, without access to religious literature and subject to persecution from the Soviet authorities, the Sufi and Islamic educational traditions became extremely impoverished. The Sufi orders and their *eshans* constituted the mainstay of religion among wide bands of the population. This obviously meant a serious lack of reliable knowledge about Islam, something which became obvious when around 1990 the religious practice was set free.

In the Soviet invasion of Afghanistan around Christmas of 1979, many of the soldiers that were used in the first round were of Central Asian origin, among them many Tajiks. This was necessary for logistic reasons, but it is likely that the Soviet leaders also had assumed that these 'ethnic Muslims' would be more acceptable to their brethren south of the Oxus river than European soldiers. The result rather turned out to be that the experiences of the Central Asian soldiers in Afghanistan strengthened a budding tendency to reject the Soviet system. The contacts with a more living and struggling

From the Nouruz (new year) celebrations in Dushanbe (photo: David
Thurfjell, 1998).

Islam inspired a revival of this religion in Central Asia also. Qurans and
other religious books in the banned Arabic writing were smuggled into the
Soviet Union on a huge scale. In official Soviet media, reports of problems
with the so-called atheistic propaganda became increasingly common.

In October 1980 the Tajik party newspaper *Kommunist Tadzhikistana*
reported on the inefficiency of the anti-religious propaganda in the province
of Kurgan-Tappa and complained that not even lectures, film-shows and the
activities of the Kolkhoz clubs had succeeded in turning the interests of the
Tajiks away from Islamic family rituals (including the paying of bridewealth), shrines, *mullas* and *eshans*. From other regions there were reports
that even intellectuals and party members continued to run their family
affairs according to Islamic rite and that public funds were embezzled to be
used for the upkeep of shrines and other holy places. It became clear that the
masses of the people, despite more than sixty years of atheist propaganda,
regarded Islam as a main constituent of their national or ethnic identity.

Together with Islam, the native language, Tajik (a variety of Persian),
and the literature which had been written in that language for more than
1,000 years was seen as a mainstay of Tajik identity. In this context the
writing system also had an important symbolic value. After the Tajik–
Persian literature had been written with the Arabic alphabet for 1,000

years, the Soviet authorities in 1927 introduced a new alphabet based on Latin orthography. In 1940 it was forcibly substituted with a writing system based on the Russian (Cyrillic) alphabet. Although the divisive language policy that the Soviet authorities pursued in Central Asia checked a threatening Uzbekisation of the Tajik language and Tajik culture, the new writing reform meant that the living connections with the indigenous cultural heritage were cut.

When the nationalistic movements gained momentum with the beginning disintegration of the Soviet state at the end of the 1980s, language questions acquired a considerable symbolic importance. After lively discussions, the Supreme Soviet of the Tajik Soviet Republic in 1989 passed a language law which gave the Tajik language (in the text also called *farsi*, i.e. Persian) the status of the only state language. Not only the Russian population reacted against this but also large parts of the Tajik bureaucracy, 'nomenklatura', which saw the language law as a threat against their interests. From then on, Russians also had to learn Tajik in order to pursue their interests in the republic. The religiously minded regarded this as a first victory, but from their point of view an important step remained to be taken, the reintroduction of Arabic writing. It was not difficult to find support for this idea, since at least among the less well-educated the Arabic alphabet is supposed to be an almost magic symbol of Islam. 'Arabic [that is, the script] is our religion', is one symptomatic saying. The pressure from religious groups finally became so strong that the parliament made a declaration of principle favouring the transition to Arabic script. However, no serious steps were taken in that direction.

In 1989 the nationalistic forces formed themselves into a popular movement called Rastokhez ('Resurrection'), which was registered as a political party in 1990. The activists of this party belonged to progressive circles within the intelligentsia and were mainly of a secular bent. The struggle between the Communist Party and the opposition groups escalated and in February 1990 serious disturbances broke out in the capital, Dushanbe. Demonstrations were dispersed by the military and an unknown number of people were killed. Martial law was declared, and under these circumstances, under strong government control, a new Supreme Soviet (that is parliament) was elected which became dominated by the communists. At the same time the Islamic activists founded a party of their own, but this was banned by the Supreme Soviet.

The unrest continued and Islamic groups became increasingly prominent in political demonstrations, especially against the previous Communist Party Secretary Rahmon Nabiev who was elected president by the new parliament. As a result Nabiev was soon forced to resign. When it became clear that the Moscow coup d'état of August 1991 had failed, Tajikistan declared itself independent under the name of the Republic of Tajikistan. In October of the same year, the Islamic Party was legalised under the designation the Islamic Revival Party. This party included a broad spectre of political tendencies, from liberal democrats to Islamists who advocated the establishment of an Islamic Republic. Its programme was, however, only mildly Islamist, speaking for a change of the constitution in accordance with the rules of the Holy law (*sharia*) and for a strengthened role of Islam in culture and education.

There were presidential elections in November 1991, but the opposition to the old party establishment proved to be divided, not only between secularists and Islamic activists but also between groups from various geographical regions. The old party organisation won an easy victory and Nabiev was re-elected president. Islamic circles started violent demonstrations and Nabiev was once again forced to resign in September 1992. An alliance of Islamic and so-called democratic troops took control of the capital, but Russian troops were sent in (in order to protect the Russian population it was said) and have since then been the guarantors of the Tajik regime. The pro-communist Imonali Rahmonov was reinstated as president and an uncertain peace was established. This situation has perpetuated itself: a semi-independent nomenklatura type of government in Dushanbe, propped up by Russian troops, and continual unrest in rural areas, especially in the east (for instance in Garm), generally based on a religiously motivated mobilisation. The main religious leaders, among them the once official Soviet Qazi (*qadi*) of Tajikistan, Turojonzoda, have generally been in exile (especially in Iran). Negotiations have led to various peace agreements, but a real national reconciliation is hardly within sight.

The political development that has been summarily sketched above depends on many components, social, economic, geographic, religious etc. Not having any real historical state tradition of its own to fall back on when the Soviet system collapsed, Tajikistan is suffering from strong disintegrating tendencies. Leaders and party factions from the various regions compete with all means at their disposal. This is often depicted as a competition between 'northern Tajiks' (from the Khojand area) and 'southern Tajiks' (from the province of Badakhshan), but as a matter of fact there are many more regional factions, such as the Kurgan-Tappa group against the Kulobis. The Islamic and Islamist formations also have various regional connections, but they are, moreover, influenced from abroad. In part they are connected with the various parties and groups that are engaged in the power struggle in Afghanistan and who at times probably assist their fellow-believers in the north with military support. In part it is a question of other Islamic states eagerly competing with each other for influence over the development of Tajikistan. In particular Saudi Arabia and Iran seem to continue there the indirect confrontation they started in Afghanistan. Propagandists of Saudi-Arabia, so-called Wahhabis, stress the Sunni character of their message to the rather unknowing

Sunnites of Tajikistan, while partisans of Iran hold that country up as a brother in language and historical culture and a unique example of a radically Islamic state. The two competitors have probably given considerable economic support to various Islamic Tajik formations. A great number of mosques, schools and seminaries have been built with the assistance of those foreign interests.

The potential for Tajik Muslims to orient themselves in the new world which has opened up to them must be rather limited. All organised forms of Islam were suppressed over more than seventy years, and prior to that indigenous religious traditions were isolated and impoverished. Tajikistan thus lacks both theological competence and real lay knowledge about Islam. The unofficial proponents for Islam from the Soviet era, probably often associated with the Sufi orders, may easily lose their position in competition with new populist leaders and propagandists financed from abroad. Both the Wahhabi and Shia–Iranian ideologies have quite a negative attitude to the Sufi orders. In the present labile position of Afghanistan, Islamic and pro-Iranian agitation could potentially be quite successful. Unfortunately it has been witnessed in many instances that it is easier to stir up and exploit religiously based nationalistic feelings than to control them and form them into constructive politics.

Literature

There is a rich, if not always reliable, literature on religion and politics in Iran, particularly after the revolution of 1979. An interesting account of the history of Iran is Fred Halliday's *Iran: Dictatorship and Development* (Harmondsworth: Penguin, 1979). Iranian Shiism is well presented in Yann Richard's *Le shiisme en Iran: Imam et révolution* (Paris: Maisonneuve, 1980) and *L'islam chi'ite: Croyances et idéologies* (Paris: Fayard, 1991). Roy Mottahedeh, *The Mantle of the Prophet: Religion and Politics in Iran* (New York: Simon and Schuster, 1985) provides a good background to the recent developments in Iran, while Amir Taheri, *The Spirit of Allah: Khomeini and the Islamic Revolution* (London: Hutchinson, 1985) is a well-informed but somewhat biased account of the life of Khomeini. A more recent work on the Islamic republic is Ervand Abrahamian, *Khomeinism: Essays on the Islamic Republic* (Berkeley, CA: University of California Press, 1993).

There are many studies of the recent political development in Afghanistan, but fewer on religious issues. Louis Dupree's *Afghanistan* (Princeton: Princeton University Press, 2nd edition, 1980) is a general introduction to the country. A political overview is found in Anthony Hyman, *Afghanistan under Soviet Domination, 1964–91* (London: Macmillan, 3rd edition, 1992). *Islam and Resistance in Afghanistan* (Cambridge: Cambridge University Press, 1990) is a translation of Olivier

Roy's study of the role of Islam in recent political development, *L'Afghanistan: Islam et modernité politique* (Paris: Seuil, 1985). A more recent work in this field is Asta Olesen's *Islam and Politics in Afghanistan* (London: Curzon Press, 1995). Bo Utas' article 'Notes on Afghan Sufi orders and khanaqahs', *Afghanistan Journal*, 7:2 (1980), pp. 60–67, provides information on Sufi orders that is otherwise hard to find.

There is not much literature specifically on Tajikistan. However, Muriel Atkin's *The Subtle Battle: Islam in Soviet Tajikistan* (Philadelphia: Foreign Policy Research Institute, 1990) is a comprehensive study on Muslims in this country. Some valuable information on Islam in Tajikistan can also be found in books on Muslims in the Soviet Union, such as Shirin Akiner, *Islamic Peoples of the Soviet Union* (London: Routledge and Kegan Paul, 1986); Alexandre Bennigsen and Chantal Lemercier-Quequejay, *Les musulmans oubliés: L'islam en Union soviétique* (Paris: F. Maspero, 1981); and Alexandre Bennigsen and S. Enders Wimbush, *Mystics and Commissars: Sufism in the Soviet Union* (London: Hurst, 1985). A recent broad work on Tajikistan is *Tajikistan: The Trials of Independence*, eds. Mohammad-Reza Djalili, Frédéric Grare and Shirin Akiner (London: Curzon Press, 1998).

Chapter Nine

China

Justin Ben-Adam

Since the early 1980s, China has followed a liberal and pragmatic approach to religious and cultural affairs among its over 18 million Muslim peoples in the hope of encouraging stability and undermining nationalist movements. With the fall of eastern European communism in 1989–90, however, such stability has declined in the face of escalating Muslim ethnic nationalism. In 1989, China's Muslims took to the streets of Beijing and other major cities calling for the death of Salman Rushdie and protests were conducted against the book *Xing Fengsu* (sexual customs), written by a Han author who slanders the Islamic faith. In response the government halted mosque construction and closed many Islamic schools. In April 1990, Turkic Muslim Uighurs and Kirghiz in Xinjiang rioted to protest these anti-Islamic actions and over birth control policies causing the government to airlift troops to intervene for the first time since the Tiananmen protests in Beijing in 1989.

China's disaffected Muslims have increasingly resorted to violence and rioting. In 1992 and 1993, a bus bombing in Urumchi and a bomb blast in Kashgar claimed nine lives; and in 1995, Uighur worshippers rioted in Khotan against police mistreatment. The government in 1996 extended its 'Strike Hard' anti-crime campaign by cracking down on Muslim 'national splittist' (separatist) groups which resulted in a grave series of protests in Ili during 1997 (one protest involved upwards of 5,000 people), where over 30 Muslim protesters were killed when police opened fire. Some Uighurs responded by derailing a train filled with ethnic Hans, then bombed three buses, killing twenty-three people, in the capital Urumchi to coincide with the state funeral of Chinese leader Deng Xiaoping. Some days later, Uighurs in a daring move struck Beijing by bombing a city bus in the capital's busiest shopping district. Muslim terror had struck China's leadership in their own nest. By 1998, the Muslims of China, and particularly the Turkic Muslims of Xinjiang, had become China's greatest security concern, surpassing even Tibet.

This chapter focuses on China's two largest Muslim minorities, the Turkic Muslim Uighurs of Xinjiang and the Huis (Tungans or Chinese Muslims) found throughout China. While these two ethnic groups are religiously and

190

culturally distinct, their lives within the Chinese state are remarkably similar. Both ethnic minorities did not exist before the emergence of modern China and are in fact creations of the modern Chinese state. Yet, they trace their contact with, and history in, China to about the same time, the seventh to ninth centuries. Both have been influenced by contacts with cultures beyond China's borders and both show tremendous diversity if not divisions within their present identities. The Huis and Uighurs have a history of interaction which has defined, and continues to shape, notions of who they are as Muslim peoples. Today, both share the same distinction of causing the Chinese government tremendous concern.

The majority of the over 18 million Muslims of China live in Xinjiang and are speakers of Turkic dialects that are mutually intelligible to one degree or another. The 7.2 million Uighurs are the majority population of Xinjiang, China's northwesternmost province. The Huis, also known as Tungans, a non-Turkic people, are the largest of China's Muslim nationalities who number 8.6 million throughout China and 682,900 in Xinjiang, according to the 1990 census. The Huis, who trace their ancestry to Arab Muslims but who are seen by most Turkic Muslims as Han converts to Islam, are found in nearly every county in all of China's provinces. The Huis have moved into Xinjiang in large numbers since the nineteenth century and have formed an intermediary position between the Hans, whose population in Xinjiang has grown from 250,000 to over 6 million since 1949, and the Uighurs. In Xinjiang, many Huis are bilingual and live in close proximity to the Uighurs.

The over 1.1 million nomadic Kazaks, whose kin live across the Xinjiang border in Central Asia's largest country Kazakstan, also play a strong political role in Xinjiang. The other Muslim nationalities of China are relatively small. In Xinjiang, the nomadic Kirghiz (141,900) who have kin in Central Asia's most democratic country Kirghizstan, are culturally and linguistically related to the Kazaks. The small number of Uzbeks (14,500) in Xinjiang, whose kin live in Central Asia's most politically powerful country Uzbekistan, are most culturally and linguistically similar to the Uighurs as they are sedentary agriculturists who are heavily involved in trade. The other minor Muslim ethnic groups of Xinjiang include the Tatars (4,900), a Turkic people, and the Tajiks (33,500) who are Persian speaking and distantly related to those in Tajikistan. Three other groups found primarily in the northwest province of Gansu are Turkic peoples who speak a combination of Turkic, Mongolian and Han Chinese dialects and include the Bao'ans (12,200), Salars (87,700) and Dongxiangs (373,900).

Making Islamic nations in China

Although neither the Huis nor the Uighurs existed as nationalities prior to the twentieth century, it is ironic that it was the Huis who were intimately involved in the definition of the Uighur people in this century. Although the Huis and the Uighurs are Muslims, there is a long history of animosity between them because the Chinese historically utilised Hui troops and officials to maintain their rule in Xinjiang. The Turkic Muslims viewed the Huis as allies of the Han Chinese administration and thus as the enemies of the Turkic Muslim peoples. Although this enmity and opposition helped the Turkic Muslims envisage themselves as a single group, the Chinese government gave this group its name, the Uighurs.

While scholars consistently trace the ethnic origin of the Uighurs to the Uighur Empire (745–840) located in northwestern Mongolia, it was not until the mid-1930s that the Chinese government, from the top down, defined the modern Uighurs as oasis-dwelling Muslims of Xinjiang. Prior to 1935, the name Uighur was not associated with Islam. Moreover, during the 500 years between 1450–1935, the name Uighur ceased to be used as an ethnic label. The identity became an historical undercurrent, part of a symbolic repertoire that was redefined when the occasion presented itself in 1931. At that time ethnic violence, caused by government disaffection, plunged Xinjiang into profound ethnic turmoil. Hui armies from neighbouring Gansu province invaded, and the rebellion against the Chinese government spread to the southern rim of the Tarim Basin. The violence set the local Turkic population in opposition to the Han Chinese and to the Huis. By the end of 1933, Chinese authority in the region had virtually collapsed.

Chinese government officials, with the aid of Soviet advisors, defused the tense inter-ethnic climate by applying the ethnic classification system used in Soviet Central Asia. The Chinese defined the oasis dwellers of Xinjiang as Uighurs under this process and the other significant ethnic groups were defined as Kazaks, Tungans (Huis), and Hans. The Chinese government's classification effectively drew a map within which the Uighurs already saw themselves living. However, the use of the term 'Uighur' veiled over a whole host of internal differences among the oases of the Tarim Basin.

In history, the large distances separating the individual Uighur oases effectively held them in isolation from one another. Thus, Uighur oases maintained separate and strong local identities despite their common religion, language and culture. For example, Kashgar, historically the most Islamically volatile oasis, came under the strong Islamic influence of Samarkand and Bukhara to the west. The southern oasis of Khotan came under the Buddhist influence of India. The highly secular northwest steppe oasis of Ili was oriented toward Russia and has been a political threat to Chinese control, and the Turpan oasis in the east has been focused towards China throughout its history. This Turpan region for five centuries prior to 1450 was called Uighuristan and provided scholars, scribes, administrators and advisors to Genghis Khan.

The definition of the Huis is as much or even more of a puzzle than that of the Uighurs. The Huis have been defined by a process of elimination, one that left them as the most numerous of the Muslim minorities of China. This was not an accident. Sun Yat-sen, the father of modern China, delineated five peoples of China including the Han people, who make up 91 per cent of China's population today – the Tibetans, the Manchus, the Mongols and the Muslims (Huis). This Hui grouping did not distinguish between the ten Muslim minorities of China today. Under the communists, Turkic nationalities and other mixed linguistic peoples such as the Dongxiangs, Bao'ans or Salars were defined as non-Hui peoples. By default the remaining peoples, those Muslims who were a minority within their own majority, peoples such as Muslim Tibetans, Muslim Hans and Muslim Mongols were defined as Huis. While many Huis claim descent from Arab Muslims who lived in China over 1,000 years ago, Turkic Muslims perhaps more accurately view them simply as Hans who converted to Islam and who feel closer to their fellow Chinese-speaking Han people than they do to their Muslim brothers. It has indeed been in China's best interest to define the Huis, China's closest ally among the Muslim minorities and who are most culturally and linguistically similar to the Hans, in a way that makes them the most numerous of China's Muslim peoples.

The Huis are not considered an ethnic nationality anywhere in the overseas Chinese communities outside China. In the Republic of China on Taiwan, Huis are considered Hans who practice Islam. What then explains the communist's definition of the Hui? It is clearly Han orientalism. The Huis, as believers in a foreign religion, are exotic members of the Chinese society. This is not the case for Chinese Buddhists because although Buddhism is also a foreign religion, it became an intrinsic part of China's identity. It must be asked why then are the Huis defined as a separate people and the Chinese Jews or Chinese Christians are not separate nationalities in modern China. In fact, Chinese Jews, distinguished for wearing blue skull-caps, were once defined in terms of their traditional white skull-cap wearing Muslim brothers as *lan-mao Huihui*, meaning 'the Muslims who wear blue hats'.

The answer to this question lies in the meaning of the word Hui itself. Historians relate the word Hui to 'Huihui', the Chinese name used over 1,000 years ago for the ancient Uighur people. It should be clarified that in Central Asia, including Xinjiang, the Huis are known as Tungans (Dungans) because the Russian word Hui refers to a sexual organ. Nevertheless, the Chinese character for Hui, which in the modern Chinese language means 'to return', is a key to our understanding. The character for Hui is a box within a box. The box symbolises a nation, and thus the character for Hui indicates a nation within a nation. The character is most suitable for the Huis because for the most part those who convert or become Muslims in China do not separate themselves from Chinese society. Instead they occupy a niche within society. The character 'Hui' may also symbolise the internal quest to find the kingdom of God within oneself.

The decorated prayer hall of the mosque at Ox Street (Niu Jie) in Beijing, where Arabic calligraphy is combined with traditional Chinese chrysanthemum patterns (photo: Ingvar Svanberg, 1986).

The Huis almost always resemble the society within which they live, be it Han, Tibetan, Mongol. They are like the Niujie mosque in Beijing, which is Chinese in form on the outside and Islamic on the inside. It is important to note that, likewise, the Huis, particularly the majority that resemble the Hans, do not view themselves as opposed to Chinese cultural values as do the Uighurs. Instead the Huis maintain a different internal life by rejecting pork and alcohol consumption, and by practicing Islam. For this Han exterior and Muslim internal practices they have also faced mistrust, not only by the greater Han society, but by other Muslims such as Turkic and Arab peoples. In the terminology of the Chinese Muslims, those that mistrust the Huis view them as *bugou qingzhen*, not sufficiently pure and true.

The term *qingzhen*, literally 'pure and true', is akin to *halal* or *kosher* in the sense that it refers to those aspects that contribute to a spiritually whole Muslim life. Food, restaurants and lifestyle are all referred to as *qingzhen*. Some scholars see the term *qingzhen* turning the tables on Confucian society by claiming that Islam is the pure and true faith, not Confucianism. However, *qingzhen* is more correctly viewed as a justification to Confucians, one that attempts to make the faith acceptable to the Confucian élite. Similarly, the Chinese Jews justified their faith to Chinese society in completely Confucian terms. *Qingzhen* is also an assertion to Arab and other Muslims that the Chinese Muslims are true believers. Such an assertion still must be frequently made when Huis go on *hajj* (pilgrimage) to Mecca. Uighurs claim that during the *hajj* the Huis are seen as *bugou qingzhen* by their co-religionists.

The anthropologist Dru Gladney, an authority on the Huis, has used *qingzhen* as an analytical trope to understand the purity (*qing*) of Hui belief and the truth (*zhen*) of their ancestry. But the reverse is more appropriate. Precisely, the Huis are concerned with the purity (*qing*) of their ancestral lines and the truth (*zhen*) of the faith that one holds within. Ancestries, peoples that maintain genealogies know, are constructed and manipulated by each generation. So the 'truth' of one's ancestry is not as important as maintaining the 'purity' of one's relations, that is Muslims *versus* Hans. *Qingzhen* can also have different interpretations. The word *qing* can be read as 'clear', so it could also mean 'one must see through the outside of the person, the Han-like exterior, to see the truth of a Hui's heart and convictions'. The term *qingzhen* is most likely a product of the zealotry of the Han convert to Islam. It is a fervent assertion to Chinese society and to Muslims around the world that though they may look *bugou qingzhen* on the outside, internally their ancestry is pure and their belief is true.

Muslim identities behind the veil

The modern definitions of the Uighurs and Huis veil the great diversity within the societies of these two Muslim peoples. Within the Huis, communities vary from those religiously observant to those that are considered Huis simply because they do not use pork in the ritual worship of their ancestors or because the Chinese traditional genealogies they maintain reveal their distant Muslim backgrounds. For the Uighurs, traditional aspects of Uighur society that have existed since 840 go unrecognised by the current definition of the Uighurs, for example it does not account for strong local oasis identities. Most importantly, both the Uighur and Hui identities obscure the very different strategies that each locality historically employed to respond to political, social, economic and geographical forces.

Historically, contacts across the borders of Xinjiang were much more frequent and important than those between the oases themselves. In the past, people covered the distances between oases so slowly that the oases populations remained isolated from one another. This historical legacy of oasis division carries over into local conceptions of Uighur identity today; Uighurs identify themselves according to the oasis in which they live. In the modern period, the Chinese government weakened the relations between individual oases and the peoples and cultures lying outside today's borders by radically turning Xinjiang's focus inward. The most important changes after 1949 were communist China's policy of cutting Xinjiang's cross-border ties, linking Xinjiang's economic development with China, and sending millions of Hans to Xinjiang to help in that development. For the first time in their history, the inhabitants of the Xinjiang oases were completely isolated from their historical, religious, kin and economic ties. The imposed internal focus became a crucial factor in the coalescing of the modern Uighur identity.

The opening of the borders in 1985 reversed the focus of the oases, once again turning their economic, political, social and cultural ties from Urumchi and China to their neighbours across the borders. When China opened Xinjiang's borders in 1985, foreign business, trade and tourism began to develop along traditional oasis lines. In the 1930s many Uighurs from Hami (Qomul), Turpan and Khotan fled to India and settled in Pakistan. Many are now re-establishing trade relationships with their cross-border kin there. Uighurs from Soviet Central Asia visit relatives and a small number of Pakistani merchants conduct business in Kashgar. Japanese tourists flock to Turpan to see the Silk Road and make Buddhist pilgrimages to religious sites. Many young Uighur donkey-cart drivers who take Japanese tourists on bumpy rides to historical sites startle their guests by speaking to them in near-fluent Japanese.

Delegations from Turkey now visit Xinjiang, inspiring pan-Turkist aspirations and the growing Islamic movement in Xinjiang. Uighur officials who appear on television seemingly are able to discuss issues with their Turkish counterparts without the aid of interpreters. In 1992, a railroad from Xinjiang was connected to the Kazakstan border and Aeroflot flies from Urumchi's airport. There have been numerous trade, technical and cultural exchanges from the Central Asian republics. In Xinjiang department stores, western Central Asians stare, wide-mouthed and in disbelief at the teeming shelves. Xinjiang is helping Central Asian republics build light industries that are in short supply there. Uighurs in Urumchi are studying Russian intensively to take advantage of better ties with Russia and the Central Asian republics. Han Chinese, on the other hand, think it best to study English because they see little hope for Russia and hope to go to the West instead.

In a comprehensive study on the Huis, Dru Gladney describes the tremendous diversity of the Huis by concentrating on four specific communities. According to the Hui charter of origin, they are descendants of foreign Muslim merchants, militia and officials. However, it is ironic that only those Huis who live along the southern coast of China, who no longer practise Islam and are the most assimilated, maintain lineage records that preserve their families' distant origins. The most religious Huis who live in the predominantly Muslim Gansu and Ningxia provinces that lie near Xinjiang, do not maintain genealogies and thus cannot prove deep Islamic roots. Such differences are not surprising when one considers the influence of geography and cultural interaction which historically has had a profound effect on the communities now defined as Hui.

Ancestry written in stone

In the city of Quanzhou in Fujian lives a Hui community that is so assimilated into the local Han culture that they do not practice Islam but claim Hui ethnicity because they can trace their foreign Islamic ancestry through 1,300-year-old tombstones. Lineage records also preserve this historical connection. Because of their non-Islamic practice, the government first classified them as Hans, but reclassified them in 1979 as Huis because of their historical ethnic claims. Most Huis do not maintain genealogies, as this is more commonly a southern Han practice. Thus, the assimilation to Fujian Han culture saved the memory of Muslim ancestry for the Huis there. The same is true for the 5,000 Uighurs who live in Mao Zedong's Hunan province. Their founding ancestor, an Uighur military commander from Turpan stationed in Beijing, was sent to Hunan in the mid-1300s, with the collapse of the Mongol-led Yuan Dynasty. Though they do not resemble the Uighur Turks nor practice Islam, the genealogies they maintained following Han custom preserved their identity for over 600 years.

Of all of China's minority ethnic groups, the Huis are the most urbanised. In cities such as Beijing, where Huis live among Hans who are nearly identical to them culturally and linguistically, they focus on what can be called a *qingzhen* lifestyle, which differentiates them from the Hans. Food, namely pork abstention, is what most separates the Huis from the Hans. The Hui have a profound revulsion of pork, the principal meat consumed by Hans, and pork, as opposed to alcohol or cigarettes, is the main taboo for the urban-dwelling Huis. Urban homes of the Hui have little to distinguish them from Han homes except perhaps for an Islamic calendar. As urban Huis and Hans are indistinguishable in dress, Han beggar children frequently besiege foreign visitors to Beijing's mosques, who assume them to be Muslims. Mosque caretakers frighten these children away and accuse the Han children of exploiting Muslim charity.

Very little historical documentation is presented of Hans embracing Islam to become a non-Han people. Perhaps this is because those that embraced the Islamic faith were considered Hans who worshipped Islam and not a people apart. The historical records of the Uighur embrace of Islam, however, is extremely well documented; it took nearly 500 years for most to become Muslims. The first Uighur embraced the faith in Kashgar around 950, and the last holdouts were the Uighurs in Turpan as late as 1450. In contrast, it is likely that there was a blurring between the boundaries separating Hans and Chinese Muslims especially over the past 1,300 years of contact in urban areas. Today in China it appears that a Hui who ceases to be a believer is still a Hui and not a Han, but this might not have been the case before the communist take-over. We do not know whether non-practicing Huis will become Hans after several generations, especially among those who intermarry or who do not maintain genealogies. There are Hans who do marry into Hui families in order to gain power and trade connections among entrepreneurial families. Some Han men find it easier to embrace Islam in urban areas such as Beijing since most urban Hui men do not practice Islam with much devotion if at all.

Outside urban locales where Huis live in the midst of Hans, in rural areas Huis have created for themselves isolated ethnic enclaves making what could be called '*qingzhen* islands in a pork infested sea'. Such enclaves replicate the nation within a nation symbolised by the Chinese character for Hui. Some of these communities have been designated as 'Hui autonomous villages' where Huis maintain their identity through intra-enclave endogamy, an extremely unusual practice among Chinese Muslims who prefer to increase their kinship, social and economic networks through outmarriage. Unlike the southern communities, Muslim families in Hui villages outside Beijing are unable to trace their ancestral origins prior to four or five generations ago. However, to maintain the belief that their community has had an uninterrupted descent from Hui ancestry, they engage in endogamy by not marrying daughters to non-Hui. Most surprisingly, they do marry with others of the same surname, a practice taboo in Han society. These Huis prefer close marriage with their relations though they prohibit intermarriage with anyone that is a close relative within five generations.

Islamism and Sufism

The region of China where Islamic 'fundamentalism' is on the rise is the northwestern provinces of Ningxia and Gansu, where geography has been a strong force in determining Islamic identity. In these communities there is very little record of foreign Muslim ancestry, but their Hui identity is fervently expressed in Islamic practice. Thus, these Huis principally interacted for many hundreds of years with Turkic Muslims who maintained that the Huis were not sufficiently Muslim. Thus these Huis have needed to demonstrate their Islamic piety to outside Muslims through fervent practice. Some consider the Hui religious conservatism here to be the result of Han conversion to Islam and attribute the Islamism they display to the zealotry that converts typically exhibit.

Such communities have also been greatly influenced by Sufi orders from areas west of Xinjiang. When various Sufi teachings spread from the Middle East through Central Asia, Muslims in the northwest accepted various schools of teaching as a strategy to identify with Muslims from outside China and thus increase their Islamic prestige in comparison with Turkic Muslims in Xinjiang. Though these Muslims could not trace their family ancestry to foreign Muslims, they could trace the lineage of their Sufi practices to the Islamic heartland of the Middle East. These communities are now also conceiving of themselves in more international religious terms by soliciting closer ties with foreign Muslim countries to secure loans for economic development projects. The Chinese government also exploits these more religious Huis by sending them as representatives to Muslim nations to help improve Chinese relations with the Muslim world.

The Sufi orders spread from Central Asia into Xinjiang in the early fifteenth century. Sufism's influence only arrived to the Hui communities in China in the late seventeenth century. Sufi institutions or *menhuan*, which are economic, social, religious and political in nature, were built around the descent groups of early Sufi leaders, those who achieved saintly status. Tombs of Sufi saints were treated as shrines, centres of religious veneration and activity. The strongest of the Sufi paths emphasising the veneration of saints that influenced both the Uighurs and the Huis was the Naqshbandi order, founded in Central Asia in the fourteenth century. After gaining ascendancy in Xinjiang among the Uighurs in the fifteenth century, this order spread among the Hui communities in Gansu through the influence of Kashgar leader Appaq Khoja (d. 1694). The Qadiri order was one of the earliest to appeal to the Hui communities of China. This brotherhood combined ascetic mysticism with non-institutionalised worship. Its focus on the tombs of saints rather than on mosques, emphasised self-cultivation through the paths of meditation, poverty and celibacy to achieve a mystical experience of the oneness of Allah within each believer. As such this de-emphasised the five pillars of traditional Islam that called for fasting, pilgrimage to Mecca, alms and recitation of the *shahada* (creed) in favour of a mystical inner search.

The Naqshbandi order was committed to social reform through political action leading them into conflict with Manchu-ruled China. The Jahriyya branch of the Naqshbandiyya, which utilised vocal meditation in their *dhikr* ('remembrance', worship), particularly resisted Qing rule advocating Islamic militarism and organising armed uprisings against them. Jahriyya rebellions against the Qing led to the Yakub Beg rebellion 1864–77 which expelled the Chinese government from Xinjiang. The Khufiyya branch, which found its greatest influence in Ningxia, utilised silent meditation in their *dhikr* and bodily swaying during voiced chanting. It emphasised the veneration of saints and active participation in society rather than ascetic retreat.

Throughout their history, members of the various Sufi orders have worn distinctive attire to differentiate themselves. They do so either through wearing specific skull caps or by shaving the sides of their beards. Those that join a particular Sufi order will remain highly loyal to that order. Sufi orders, with their high degree of organisation and extensive networks, have provided unity and a strong collective response when faced with social crises. It can be argued that Sufi orders have, in fact, allowed for the economic and political survival of Huis and Uighurs throughout China.

Islam communist style – the Xinjiang example

As part of the Chinese communists' desire to improve relations with Muslim countries, the government actually encourages Muslim party officials to participate in religious events, justifying its policy by asserting that such events are part of ethnic 'tradition' and separate from religious beliefs that contradict communist doctrine. As part of this policy, the government even provides financial support for members of the Muslim party élite so that they may be able to make the *hajj* to Mecca, considered by intellectuals to be linked more to ethnic cultural tradition than to religion, and thereby increase their prestige and influence at local level. The Chinese government has dramatically reversed its earlier attempts at cultural subversion. The communists have concluded that a controlled 'revival' of cultural and religious affairs would encourage stability and economic development among Muslims and at the same time undermine Muslim nationalist movements and anti-government protests. Religious freedoms have brought about the reopening of mosques and a flurry of mosque construction. Religious leaders again officiate at Islamic weddings, and the Quran and other Islamic texts are once again sold openly.

In Xinjiang, Islam permeates all realms of Uighur life – political, social and economic. In fact, the term Muslim (*Musulman*) is not only a reference for a religious person, but is used to refer to all native Central Asians. Thus, to call oneself an Uighur is also to accept Islam. Even Uighur intellectuals who are against Islamic traditionalism and its resurgence consider themselves Muslim and take part in Islamic cultural practices. Here there is a clear symbiosis between national and religious identity. Although Islam separates the Uighurs and Hans, both religiously and ideologically, Chinese liberalisation policies related to religion have fostered positive sentiments toward the Chinese government among Turpan Uighurs. This reaction contrasts markedly with that of Uighurs in Kashgar who, over time, have tenaciously held to anti-Chinese sentiments. Kashgar Uighurs have less land for grape and cotton cultivation and have therefore not experienced the same economic growth. Although the Chinese government plays up the Islamic threat in Xinjiang, there is only one volatile Islamic centre that historically incited many rebellions against Chinese rule. This is the oasis of Kashgar. Even today anti-Han sentiment is still stronger in Kashgar than in any other Uighur oasis mainly as a result of its religious tradition.

In general, Islamic life in the south, particularly in Kashgar, is more conservative. Women, for example, are completely veiled in brown cloth, in contrast to women in Turpan, who wear only head-scarves. In addition, precisely because of the strong anti-Chinese sentiment in Kashgar, the

اَيَاتُهَا (٧٥) سُورَةُ الْقِيَمَةِ مَكِّيَّةٌ رُكُوعَاتُهَا

第七五章　复　活

(给亚马)

共四〇节，分二段

(一)释名：本章得名于第一节。早期麦加章节。

(二)释义：本章一方面说明复活的真象，同时也间接说明阿拉伯人及其他的人在接受伊斯兰之后，可以在精神上复活。

第一段　复活的真象

本段说明真宰的大能，能使死者复活，而人却不信。同时也指出在复活日，人将亲见他所做过的一切。

奉大仁大慈安拉尊名

بِسْمِ اللهِ الرَّحْمٰنِ الرَّحِيمِ

1. 不，我叫(人)见证复活日。

2. 不，我也叫(人)见证自责人[1]。

3. 人可是以为我不能把他的骨骼凑合起来吗？

4. 是的，我有能力完全恢复他的手指骨骼。

5. 但是人总是要否认他眼前的。

6. 他问道："复活日在什么时候？"

7. (那是)当人们眼花缭乱时，

8. 月光黯淡时，

9. 和太阳与月亮联合在一起时。

10. 那天，世人会说："往哪里逃呀？"

11. 没有！没有避难的地方！

12. 在那天(只有)与你的主同在，才是安全的[1]。

13. 在那天人将被告诉他已经做过的和留下未做的。

14. 事实上，人才是自身的见证，

15. 即使他提出种种藉口。

16. 你不要用你的舌头去搬动(天启)的字句，以便你可以匆匆地读(完)它。

The resurrection *sura* from a Chinese translation of the Quran, published in 1981.

Chinese government has regulated religious education and mosque construction more strictly. In contrast, the Chinese view Turpan citizens as more trustworthy than those of oases to the south. Chinese officials appear to believe that the growth of Islam in Turpan, a historically quiet region, is less likely to produce anti-Chinese disturbances than in the western oases.

Muslim rituals influence all realms of Uighur life. The most powerful ritual for Uighur males is circumcision, which takes place at the age of seven, when children are old enough to understand at least some of the religious significance of the ritual. The Islamic ritual calendar also reinforces a strong Islamic identity at the local level. By and large, the older Uighur generation is more devout, observing all the events and requirements of the Islamic ritual calendar. In contrast, a number of younger Uighurs, those under forty, do not observe the month-long fast during Ramadan, but their numbers are diminishing as Islam gains in popularity. As a result of Islam's growth, the influence of the more conservative elders at the village level has also grown. Increasingly, Uighurs decorate their homes and restaurants with posters depicting religious rather than political themes. Religious posters, such as those depicting Mecca, are sold only in Urumchi and Kashgar, since Urumchi is central to all Muslim minorities in Xinjiang and Kashgar is the Uighur Mecca. The posters reinforce consciousness of the Muslim symbols and spur their mission to multiply the followers of the faith.

The strong local oasis identities in Xinjiang, so characteristic of the region prior to the 1930s, have puzzled Central Asian scholars. It is clear, however, that the geographic isolation of the oases from one another has caused them to develop their own internal oasis culture based on the unique ways they celebrate different occasions and rituals within Uighur culture and Islamic and folk religious practice. In Turpan, there is a resurgence and strengthening of Islam resulting in the increase in power of *mullas*, the local religious leaders. *Mullas*, in new positions of influence, have taken the opportunity to voice their fervent opposition to certain Uighur social practices that have gained popularity in the villages, particularly the drinking of alcoholic beverages and mixed-couple dancing to waltzes and fox-trots. *Mullas* have threatened to refuse Islamic burials for those who allow such 'un-Islamic' behaviour.

Islamic education in Turpan has increased and, consequently, so has the prestige of local *mullas*. Outside the mosques, Qurans and other Islamic books and pamphlets of various complexity are sold. Some of the pamphlets use illustrations to teach people how to wash and pray, others list all the saints and holy people mentioned in the Hebrew Bible, the New Testament and the Quran. In general, there are materials sufficient to educate and reinforce the understanding of the followers of Islam in China. Before many Uighur children enter elementary school they receive instruction on saying Islamic prayers. If a child is educated for only five years in secular schools, he or she will normally be sent to schools run in the home of a religious leader for an additional three years of Quranic instruction.

Although the government has laws against the Islamic education of minors, which includes those under eighteen years, children between ages thirteen and eighteen attend small Quranic schools. Uighur officials look the other way at these violations, reluctant to be viewed negatively by fellow Uighurs, and Han officials do not want to enforce unpopular laws in a region that has been historically calm and stable. A large factor influencing the growth of Islamic education is the cost of secular education. Students throughout Xinjiang who attend secular colleges now have to pay tuition. Furthermore, since the government no longer places all graduates, students are no longer guaranteed employment. Thus, Uighur peasants do not consider secular education, specifically college education, a viable option for their children, further contributing to the rise in prestige of Islamic education.

Folk religious practice

While the traditional Islamic practices differ to a slight degree among the oases of Xinjiang, the degree, type and frequency of folk religious practices vary tremendously. Such practices are widely conducted among the Uighurs and serve to foster a strong and unique religious identity. Outside of orthodox Islamic ritual, these folk practices permeate most Uighur rituals. They deal mainly with warding off *jinn* (evil spirits). In Uighur villages it is common to see pouches wrapped in coloured thread hanging from branches. These are called *qonchaq* and are used to ward off *jinns*. *Mullas* instruct people who suffer from illness or bodily pain to place *qonchaq* in trees. Uighurs believe that misfortune is caused by spirits of people who have died, sometimes at a young age because of a *jinn*-caused illness. The most orthodox religious leaders are opposed to *qonchaq* and other amulets, called *tömar* and *köz mönchaq*, that protect against the evil eye. *Tömar* are triangular leather pouches with Islamic prayers written on paper inside. *Köz mönchaq* are round black plastic balls, the size of cherry pits, with white dots all over them. They are worn by children and sewn into women's garments to ward off the evil eye.

Uighurs today also use fire to ward off *jinns*. Fire is used in childhood rites, wedding ceremonies and cemeteries. During the *büshük toy*, the swaddling ceremony of a newborn infant, a religious leader waves a flaming stick above the baby to purify it and to ward off *jinns*. Some Uighur families place an unsheathed knife in the crib of their baby for the same purpose. Fire is also used during the wedding ceremony. When the bride is brought from her parent's home to the groom's home a fire burns in the road and the vehicle carrying her drives over the fire. In some ceremonies, when the bride is transported by a horse-drawn cart, the cart is led around the fire seven times, seven being a holy Muslim number. A fire is also placed in a ladle inside the entrance to the groom's home, and the bride steps over this upon her arrival.

The incorporation of folk religious practices in Uighur life-transition rituals is seen clearly during death and birth rituals. In cemeteries, jars of paper and medicine are burned on top of, or near, tombs in Uighur cemeteries to appease the spirit of the dead. Jars of medicines ineffective in treating patients before they died are used indicating familial intentions to have tried to their best ability to bring health to the deceased when he or she was still alive and, once dead, to restore health to the spirit of the deceased in the afterlife. After a child's birth, parents bury the newborn's afterbirth in the mud wall of the house but never tell the child where. Uighurs in Turpan believe that if the afterbirth is simply disposed of or buried in the ground, the child's eyes will always be cast down. Likewise, if the afterbirth is buried too high in the wall, the child will constantly look upwards. Thus, it is buried at adult eye-level and, because of Turpan's arid environment, the afterbirths dry and do not rot. The afterbirth is called *hämra*, meaning companion, and is seen as the constant companion of an individual through life. Hans were surprised and considered such a practice a waste since they know it to have a health benefit and so make the afterbirth into medicine or simply eat it.

Ethnic Borders

The home, mosque and to some extent food establishments are ethnic borders that are rarely crossed by Hans, Uighurs and Huis. These social borders may appear invisible from the outside, but they become salient in structuring inter-ethnic social, religious and commercial interactions. Hans and Uighurs rarely mix socially at each other's homes. Because Hans eat pork, Uighurs will not eat in their homes. Hans feel uncomfortable being in Uighur homes as they feel their lack of knowledge of Uighur social customs may offend their hosts. Furthermore, Hans in general do not like the taste of mutton which is the staple meat eaten by the Uighurs. Hans rarely eat at Uighur food restaurants, believing that the Uighur restaurants are not as clean as Hui ones. While Uighurs will eat at Hui restaurants, they never buy meat from a Hui butcher, mistrusting its purity. In fact, mistrust of Hui religious observance gave rise to teacher protests in Turpan in 1989. Two Huis were hired by Han officials to manage the Muslim dining hall at the Turpan Teachers Training Academy, but Uighur teachers refused to eat, mistrusting the purity of the food.

While marriages between Uighurs and Huis are rare, marriages between Hans and Uighurs are almost unheard of. In Turpan, Uighurs hold weddings on Sundays and Huis hold weddings on Saturdays, enabling each to attend the other's weddings. Hans only attend Uighur and Hui weddings in the capacity of work supervisors. Their visits are generally short, obligatory appearances. The rare instances of marriage between Hans and Uighurs have occurred mostly among students who had gone to China proper for their education. These Uighurs are invariably disowned or told not to return to Xinjiang. Children of mixed Han and Uighur parentage, known in Mandarin as *erzhuanzi*, and in Uighur as *piryotki* (from Russian) are stigmatised; they are not allowed to attend Uighur funerals, have difficulty finding marriage partners, and are confronted with mistrust throughout their lives.

The Huis have been an integral part of the political map of Xinjiang since the mid-nineteenth century. Although the Uighurs and Huis are both

Muslim, there is a surprising separation in their religious practices. Huis pray in separate mosques and maintain separate Islamic schools. Furthermore, they revere different Islamic saints. While the chief Islamic festival for Huis is *Roza Heyt*, the end of the Ramadan fast, the *hajj* pilgrimage festival *Qurban Heyt* remains the chief festival for the Uighurs. Huis have lived in Turpan in large numbers for over seven generations and have been the central vehicle for fostering positive Uighur sentiments toward the Hans.

Sharing Islam with the Uighurs and the Mandarin language with the Hans, the Huis are the ideal cultural intermediaries between the two. For the most part, relations in Turpan between Huis and Uighurs have been good. Huis show respect for Uighur customs and society. Huis also serve as intermediaries for Uighurs and Hans in Mandarin language instruction at Uighur schools. Both Hui and Uighur school teachers serve to ameliorate inter-ethnic tensions in their roles as agents of acculturation for the Chinese state. Hui teachers in Uighur schools stress the importance of being a good student of the Chinese nationality, emphasising citizenship in the Chinese state.

The intermediate status of the Huis in Han–Uighur relations sometimes results in ethnic tensions. It is not unusual for Huis, Hans and Uighurs to have difficulty distinguishing themselves from one another. This is especially so whenever Uighurs encounter Huis and assume they are Hans. Although the Hans and Huis often speak the same language, some Hans feel that Huis are dishonest and fear that because Huis are Muslims they might turn on Hans. Uighurs, on the other hand, express this same view but in reverse: they fear that the Huis will side with the Hans with whom they share both language and culture. Uighurs use the expression *tawuz* (watermelon) to refer to the Huis because they wobble between siding with the Uighurs on one issue and with the Hans on another. Some Uighurs even claim that the Huis are actually half Han and thus impure in their Muslim observance, as Hans do not practice the Islamic faith.

The increasing economic opportunities in Turpan have resulted in positive sentiments of the Uighur peasantry toward the Chinese government and Han Chinese in general. Peasants are relatively pleased with the religious, economic and cultural changes introduced by the government and are optimistic about the future. This attitude is a stark change from years past caused by the heavy influx of Han Chinese to the region beginning in the early 1960s. The majority of Hans in Xinjiang settled outside Uighur areas, and the ensuing division of towns into Uighur and non-Uighur areas exacerbated misunderstandings. Hans claim this settlement pattern allowed the Uighurs to continue their way of life without Han interference. To many Uighurs, however, this pattern was perceived as an encirclement. Uighurs increasingly saw the Han Chinese as their opponents.

An Uighur anti-drugs poster.

Uighur perceptions of Han Chinese as the oppressor who are always in dominant positions over the Uighurs changed since 1987 as an estimated 250,000 'self-drifter' Hans have poured into Xinjiang each year to look for work. Han 'self-drifters' enter Xinjiang on their own without official government permission in search of economic opportunity and many are hired as day workers by Uighurs. The traditional Han perception of Xinjiang as a bitter and cruel place has changed dramatically. Hans in China proper perceive Xinjiang as the land of plenty and opportunity. They believe there is much money to be made there. In general, Uighur peasants in Turpan do not harbour the strong resentment toward Hans found among Uighurs in other oases. Instead, they see themselves on the same socio-economic level or on even a higher level. Some of the new Han immigrant 'self-drifters' are so impoverished that they roam Uighur villages collecting animal bones and old shoes to recycle. This dramatic change has inspired Uighur ethnic pride and the sight of large numbers of Han Chinese doing menial tasks for Uighur peasants has transformed Uighur–Han relations.

Islamic resistance to Chinese rule

The practice of Islam is a symbolic means of confronting the Chinese state. By embracing Islam, Uighurs reject the atheism of Chinese communism as well as its goals of modernisation and social liberation. The growth of Islamic tradition at the local level also encourages resistance to Chinese acculturation. Because Islamic culture separates Uighurs from Chinese society and cultural influence, Islam becomes reinforced. It is this relationship that the Chinese seem not to understand in their attempts to limit or control Islam. Government religious reforms were intended to quell Uighur disaffection with Chinese rule and cause Uighurs to develop more harmonious sentiments for their fellow Hans. However, although Uighurs felt more oppressed when the communists suppressed Islam and Uighur culture, by allowing the controlled development of Islam, the Chinese have actually caused the Uighurs to feel a greater sense of separation. The Chinese are caught in a dilemma. If they suppress Islam, Uighurs feel oppressed and oppose the government; if they allow or encourage it, Uighurs become more content with the government but feel more separated from Chinese society.

The emergence of a young Uighur student called Urkesh (Wuerkaixi) as a leader at the forefront of the Beijing Tiananmen student protests in 1989 was an extremely significant event in the development of Uighur separatist feelings. Uighur intellectuals feel considerable pride that of all the millions of people involved in the demonstrations, it was an Uighur who led the movement. Most Uighurs believe that Urkesh, by attaining world recognition, put the Uighurs on the map. In the aftermath of Tiananmen, many Uighur boys were named Urkesh. When peasants spoke of their heroes, invariably, all would speak of Urkesh. One intellectual simply stated: 'Urkesh is our only hero'. Uighur intellectuals will often praise an Uighur cultural hero as a 'second Adolf Hitler' (*ikkinchi Getlär*). This expression was frequently used to describe Urkesh.

Admiration for Hitler's power and charisma is prevalent throughout all levels of Uighur society – peasant, merchant, and intellectual. Uighurs are impressed by the great power and discipline that the Nazis represent. The Uighur peasantry, filled with admiration for Hitler, has absorbed the Nazi salute into their cultural repertoire. Uighurs sometimes greet people dressed in military uniforms, such as police and soldiers, with a smiling 'Heil Hitler', while giving the Nazi salute. Foreigners are also called out to in this manner. William Shirer's book *The Rise and Fall of the Third Reich*, translated into Uighur in 1988 and 1989, was a best seller in the region. This fascination with Hitler does not appear related to Uighur anti-Semitism. Many Uighurs, like most people throughout China, view Jewish people in a positive light and admire Albert Einstein, Karl Marx and Henry Kissinger. Though Uighurs may express admiration for Jews, considering them the 'sons of Israel' (*bäni Israil*), or disdain, viewing them as the 'enemies of God' (*Hudaning düshmäni*), few Uighurs are aware of the atrocities the Nazis committed against Jews and other groups including gypsies and homosexuals.

Uighur intellectuals have created various historiographies of their people and for this region, some of which have proven to be popular while some have not. The Uighurs are manipulating history to create Uighur ethnic identity and unity. In attempts to claim a grand past, they use elements from myths and legends, treating these as historical facts. Some Uighurs have redefined their history through the adoption of collective myths which tell of Uighur superiority over Hans. Symbolic formulations and mythologies of origin and descent are socially constructed ideologies by which the Uighurs confront the Chinese state. Some of these myths, involving the early origin of the Uighurs, maintain that they settled in the Tarim Basin before it became a desert over 8,000 years ago. In these stories, ancestors of the Uighurs moved to the northwest Mongolian steppe when the Tarim Basin became desiccated and then returned to the oases with the fall of the Uighur Empire in 840 CE. Such Uighurs claim to have a civilisation that is 3,000 years older than China's which gives them the rightful claim to their own independent homeland.

Kashgar intellectuals have attempted to stir the nationalistic sentiments of Uighurs by disseminating information about ancient historical figures from Kashgar such as Mähmud Qäshqari, the eleventh-century scholar, and Satuq Bughra Khan, who in the tenth century became the first Xinjiang Turkic leader to embrace the Islamic faith. But it was found that neither figure became a symbol strong enough to embody the nationalist spirit of Kashgar. A different approach was developed by Kashgarlik Turghun Almas in his 1990 book *Uighurlar* (The Uighurs). Turghun Almas' book claimed a 6,000-year history for the Uighurs and had a stylised wolf motif on its cover, a blatant pan-Turkic symbol. One week after the book reached the book stores in February 1990 it was banned and removed. Turghun remains under virtual house arrest in a weary and broken condition. The book's popularity soared as it passed secretly from reader to reader. The government reacted by distributing a pamphlet, entitled 'The One Hundred Mistakes of Turghun Almas' Uighurlar', throughout Xinjiang. However, the government's efforts achieved the opposite of their intended one. Many more Uighurs were exposed to Turghun Almas' ideas than could have been possible by obtaining copies of the original banned book and many Uighurs, Huis and even Hans found Turghun's historical account very compelling.

Dancing Uighurs in Xinjiang (photo: Justin Ben-Adam, 1989).

Such constructions of mythologies and ideologies like the Uighur fascination with Hitler are best understood as passive forms of resistance and as symbolic means of confrontation. Uighurs feel powerless in Xinjiang. Though the Xinjiang province is officially called the Xinjiang Uighur Autonomous Region, Uighur autonomy is questionable. Given the immigration of millions of Han Chinese, Uighurs are quickly becoming a minority nationality within their own province. While there are periodic riots and fist fights between Uighurs and Hans, resistance against Chinese government control generally is passive, often taking the form of verbal attacks, such as jokes and curses, against the government and Hans. One Uighur denigrated the significance of Han Chinese culture for the Uighurs by pointing to the example of the Great Wall: 'The Chinese take immense pride in the Great Wall. But think of it. It was built to keep us Uighurs out.'

Besides passive verbal attacks, few other means of protest have been viable for the Muslims in China. Written protests lead to arrests, marches are broken up, riots are swiftly cracked down upon and can result in deaths. Some have found that the use of bombs in Xinjiang and in Beijing are an effective means of letting others become aware of, if not share, their pain. Perhaps such terrorist tactics will drive the communist leadership into the more peaceful arms of the much abused Tibetans and their spiritual leader, the Dalai Lama, who preaches compassion in exile. But as Uighur separatists resort to bus bombings of daring and lethal proportions, the Chinese government may realise that even more liberal policies for its Muslim peoples, including symbolic confrontations and the changes they bring, are preferable to a reign of Muslim terror.

Literature

For a bibliographical survey, see Raphael Israel, *Islam in China: A Critical Bibliography* (Westport, Connecticut: Greenwood Press, 1994). A classical study of Chinese Muslims is Marshall Broomhall, *Islam in China: A Neglected Problem* (London: Morgan and Scott, 1910). See also Donald Daniel Leslie, *Islam in Traditional China* (Belconnen, ACT: Canberra College of Advanced Studies, 1986) and Barbara L.K. Pillsbury, 'The 1300-Year Chronology of Muslim History in China', *Journal: Institute of Muslim Minority Affairs*, 3:2 (1981), pp. 19–29. Cultural perspectives of Muslim ethnic identies are discussed in Dru C. Gladney, *Muslim Chinese: Ethnic Nationalism in the People's Republic of China* (Cambridge, MA: Harvard University Press, 1991); Wang Jianping, *Concord and Conflict: the Hui Communities of Yunnan Society* (Stockholm: Almqvist and Wiksell International, 1996); Justin Jon Rudelson (Ben-Adam), *Oasis Identities: Uyghur Nationalism along China's Silk Road* (New York: Columbia University Press, 1998); and Linda Benson and Ingvar Svanberg, *China's Last Nomads: Culture and History of China's Kazaks* (Armonk, NY: M.E. Sharpe, 1998). Dru Gladney has recently also published *Dislocating China: Muslims, Minorities and Other Sub-altern Subjects* (London: Hurst, 1997). See further Dru Gladney, 'The Ethnogenesis of the Uighur', *Central Asian Survey*, 9:1 (1990), pp. 1–28, and Justin Rudelson, 'Uighur Historiography and Uighur Ethnic Nationalism', pp. 63–82 in *Ethnicity, Minorities, and Cultural Encounters*, ed. Ingvar Svanberg (Uppsala: Centre for Multiethnic Studies, 1992). Muslim and non-Muslim relations in China are dealt with in Raphael Israeli, *Muslims in China: A Study in Cultural Confrontation* (London: Curzon, 1980); Barbara Pillsbury, *Cohesion and Cleavage in a Chinese Muslim Minority* (PhD thesis, Columbia University, 1973); Linda Benson, *The Ili Rebellion: The Moslem Challenge to Chinese Authority in Xinjiang 1944–49* (Armonk, NY: M.E. Sharpe, 1990); and Jonathan Lipman, 'Hans and Huis in Gansu, 1781–1929', in *Violence in China:*

Essays in Culture and Counterculture, eds. Jonathan N. Lipman and Stevan Harrell (Albany: State University of New York Press, 1991). Sufism and minor Muslim groups are discussed briefly in Raphael Israeli, 'The Naqshbandiyya and Factionalism in Chinese Islam', pp. 575–87 in *Naqshbandis: Cheminements et situation actuelle d'un ordre mystique musulman*, eds. Marc Gaborieau, Aleksandre Popović and Thierry Zarcone, Varia Turcica, XVIII (Istanbul and Paris: Institut Français d'Etudes Anatoliennes d'Istanbul, 1990); Françoise Aubin, 'La Chine', pp. 261–67 in *Les voies d'Allah: Les ordres mystiques dans l'islam dès origines à aujourd'hui*, eds. Alexandre Popović and Gilles Veinstein (Paris: Fayard, 1996); and Raphael Israel, 'Is there Shi'a in Chinese Islam', *Journal: Institute of Muslim Minority Affairs*, 9:2 (1988), pp. 49–66.

Chapter Ten

South Asia

Ishtiaq Ahmed

South Asia covers more than 4 million square kilometres, consisting mostly of the land mass of the Indian subcontinent and some islands in the Indian ocean. Currently there are five states on the mainland. These are Pakistan, India, Bangladesh, Nepal and Bhutan. The island states of Sri Lanka and the tiny Maldives also belong to South Asia in an ethno-cultural and geographical sense.

Although Muslims are to be found in all parts of South Asia, most of them are concentrated in its northwestern (Pakistan) and northeastern (Bangladesh) zones. Out of an estimated total population of 1,274 million, Muslims make up some 360 million. The overwhelming majority are Sunnis who can be distinguished between, on the one hand, the preponderate Hanafi school of orthodox rites which entered South Asia in the wake of successful invasions launched from the northwest by Muslim armies and, on the other hand, the almost imperceptible growth of the Shafii school along the Malabar coast in southern India and in Sri Lanka. Its origins can be traced to small colonies established by Arab traders and sailors who spread their faith among local people and intermarried with them. It also established itself in the Maldives. A significant Shia minority is also to be found, dispersed mainly in the northern and northwestern parts of the subcontinent. The Sunni are divided into several subgroups. Sunni–Shia hostility has been a regular feature of South Asian history, but even among Sunni subgroups considerable doctrinal disagreements exist. Such conflicts can at times result in violent confrontations between zealots of the various organisations. There are also religious entities such as the Ahmadiyya and Zikris which in recent years have been attacked by the orthodox *ulama* (Muslim scholars) for holding views allegedly outside the pale of Islam altogether, notwithstanding their own claim to being Muslims.

South Asian Islam presents a variegated and complex structure, formed and tempered in the context of the historical process. It possesses typical features of the core Arabic–Islamic ethos as well as specific South Asian peculiarities and innovations. The echo of the contemporary worldwide Islamic revival has indeed reverberated throughout South Asia. Common to such a revival is greater conformity to Islamic practices, rites and rituals

212

among the younger generation. An overall radicalism seems to have been taking place since the 1980s. However, since the Muslims in the region live in different states they have to relate to the Islamic revival in the light of their own concrete sociopolitical conditions. Furthermore, given the class, ethnic, linguistic and religious subdivisions that obtain among them the Islamic revival carries quite different implications for these subgroups and strata. No uniform or standard social and political objectives can therefore be assigned to the Islamic revival, notwithstanding its manifest salience among the Muslims of South Asia.

Historical background

Well before the advent of Islam in the Arabian peninsula in the early seventh century, Arab traders and sailors had been in contact with India. Such contacts however remained peripheral, occasional and undramatic. The second pious caliph, Umar bin Khattab (ruled 634–44), is reported to have emphasised the importance of spreading Islam in India. The first Muslim armed incursion into India, however, took place half a century later during the Umayyad period (660–750). An Arab army arrived on the western coast of India near present-day Karachi in 711 with the intention of chastising the Hindu ruler of Sindh, Raja Dahir, who allegedly had been harassing Arab merchant vessels returning with their cargoes from Sri Lanka and beyond in the East. Dahir was defeated and many of his subjects embraced Islam. Sindh and southern Punjab were conquered by the Arabs and remained attached to the caliphate based in Damascus and later Baghdad. However, it was the Turco–Afghans who, from the eleventh century onwards, launched successive waves of invasions on the sub-continent from the mountain passes in the northwest. By the early thirteenth century the important city of Delhi had fallen to the Muslims. Thereafter for the next 650 years Muslim dynasties dominated the Indian subcontinent, particularly in the northern, northwestern and northeastern regions. The last Muslim dynasty to rule northern India was the fabled Mughul empire (1526–1857).

The Muslim community that evolved in South Asia comprised both local converts and the continuous stream of migrants who abandoned their homes in Central and Western Asia and headed for India either as a part of invading armies or as fugitives from wars and famines. A Muslim ruling élite known as the *ashraf* evolved in the process which included largely Turkic-speaking central Asians, Afghans, Persians and a body of people considered holy because of alleged descent from the Prophet Muhammad and his companions, the *Sahaba*. Upper-caste Hindus who became Muslims were accorded respectable status and in due course assimilated into the *ashraf*. Most of the conversions to Islam, however, came from the lower castes and peripheral tribes. Such conversion did improve the social standing of these lower strata in comparison to their inferior and degraded status within the caste system, but the *ashraf* also kept their social distance from these converts. Muslims of India were thus divided into the so-called *ashraf* and ordinary Muslims called *aam log*. It is important to note that despite the conversion of many indigenous peoples to Islam it remained a minority religion in South Asia. For example, on the subcontinent, only one in four Indians was a Muslim by the time the British established their rule. Although more than 80 per cent are converts from Indian stock, those claiming to be of a distant foreign descent number many more.

In the precolonial period, the *sharia* was invariably the formal basis of public law, although most rulers were despots who could exercise considerable arbitrary powers. The stronghold of orthodox Islam were the *ulama*, who acted as custodians of the *sharia* and public morals. However, the enforcement of *sharia* was limited largely to urban centres as the precolonial state lacked the structural capability to govern the whole society in an integrated or totalitarian sense. In northern India, typically, a segmentary, decentralised socio-political order with a Muslim ruler at the apex and a loose descending power hierarchy constituted of lesser Hindu and Muslim princes, chiefs, caste leaders and tribal headmen presided over the mass of peasants, craftsmen, artisans and other categories of working people. The Muslim upper classes considered themselves as the proper representatives of chaste Islamic culture. They spoke Turkish, Persian or, later, vintage Urdu, in contrast to the vernacular languages used by ordinary Muslims. The vast majority of the converts to Islam continued to practise many of their earlier beliefs and customs alongside a popular version of Islam. Customary law based on caste and tribal traditions was observed locally by the peasant-converts in their internal affairs. The state rarely interfered with such practice.

Sufi orders are believed to have played a significant role in the propagation of Islam in South Asia. It is not uncommon to come across tribes and castes who trace their conversion to Islam in a distant past at the hands of some Sufi saint (usually called *shaykh* or *pir*). Four main Sufi orders, originating in the heartland of Islamic mysticism – the region between Iraq and Central Asia – have been active in the Indian subcontinent. Among them the most successful was the Chisti order (founded by Muin al-Din Chisti who died at Ajmer in 1236). The other three were the Qadiriyya (founded in Baghdad by Abd al-Qadir Jilani who died in 1166), the Suhravardiyya (founded in Baghdad by Umar al-Suhravardi who died in 1234), and the Naqshbandiyya (founded in Turkestan by Baha al-Din, called Naqshband, the painter, who died in 1389). There are also to be found indigenous orders and movements.

Usually conquest and consolidation of political power by Muslims in a territory preceded the missionary work of the Sufis. Some Sufi orders, such as the Chishtiyya, introduced quite novel methods of expressing their message which mainstream *ulama* and the nobility usually looked down upon – dance, music and ecstatic physical gestures and movements. Pantheistic ideas, more in tune with the ancient Indian philosophical tradition and local mystical cults, also entered into Sufi literature and practice. Some individual Sufis became openly non-conformist and a few defied the will of the state. However, such deviations from orthodox dogma were not the main form of Sufism. The more normal relationship between Sufis and the state was one of mutual support and interdependence. The established Sufis received substantial support, including liberal donations in land and money, from rulers. The Suhravardiyya in particular were known for working in close association with the state and combined worldly riches with their proselytising activities. The Naqshbandiyya were strict followers of the *sharia*, while the Qadiriyya were more liberal. Each order had its own hierarchy of masters and saints. The disciples, called *murids*, were taught skills purported to cleanse the soul of temptations and base desires and to prepare it for higher spiritual attainments. The various members constituted a network. South Asian orders were linked to networks and movements obtaining in other parts of the Muslim world. Although mainstream Sufism remained doctrinally a part of the Sunni creed, Shia ideas were incorporated by some tendencies and movements.

The Sufi tradition retained its vitality during the heyday of Muslim civilisation in South Asia. Later, when the European powers wrested power away from the Muslim ruling class the decline and pessimism which beset Muslim society in general also affected the Sufi orders. In its degenerate form Sufism became simply a trade in charms, talismans and other magical formulae.

The majority of South Asian Shias belong to the Ithna Ashari (the Twelvers). The coming to power of the Safavids in Persia at the beginning of the sixteenth century greatly enhanced Shia influence in the Indian subcontinent. From that time onwards, rivalry between the Shia Persian nobles and the more numerous Sunni Turkish and Afghan nobles was a recurring feature of court intrigues and conspiracies. Some Shias also succeeded in establishing their own states in different parts of the subcontinent. However, nowhere did the Shias form a majority; only one in thirteen Muslims was a Shia during the British period. Minor Shia subgroups such as the Ismailis and Bohras also won converts, mainly among the trading Hindu castes of the western coast. In Sri Lanka and the Maldives there was virtually no Shia presence.

Several mystical movements emanated within South Asian Sufism which acquired heterodox features and characteristics. Among them the Mahdawi movement founded by Sayyid Muhammad Jaunpuri (1443–1504), a prominent Sufi mystic, was the most significant during the precolonial period. In 1499 Jaunpuri proclaimed himself as the Mahdi (the idea of the Saviour, called Mahdi, is a cardinal doctrinal belief of the Ithna Ashari, but the idea has also existed in Sunni societies and from time to time some individual has come forward claiming to be the Mahdi). He travelled to various parts of the subcontinent to preach his mission. He extolled a life of hard work and austerity and criticised the pompous lifestyle of the Muslim upper classes. People mostly from the lower ranks were attracted to his charismatic personality and radical ideas. Subsequently the Mahdawis came into conflict with the Mughul state which ordered severe action against them. Some of them sought refuge in faraway Sindh and Baluchistan. The present-day Zikri community in Baluchistan is an off-shoot of the Mahdawi movement.

In the precolonial period, whenever the state in Muslim societies has been perceived to have deviated from its Islamic character some form of censure has sooner or later ensued from the orthodox establishment. Despotic sultans, who in personal conduct might have violated *sharia*, were nevertheless constrained to demonstrate their adherence to it in public. Rarely did a ruler defy such strictures. Thus the Mughul Emperor Akbar (ruled 1556–1605) tried to consolidate his vast empire on a composite Indian basis rather than on an exclusive Islamic one. He abolished the poll-tax, *jizya*, in 1564; Hindus of the warrior Rajput caste were encouraged to join the imperial army; Rajput princes were placed in positions of command; he himself married Rajput princesses; and to crown it all he founded a new composite religion called Din-i-Ilahi (Divine Faith). These drastic measures greatly perturbed the orthodox establishment. Later, Shia influence at the Court of Emperor Jahangir (ruled 1605–27), increased significantly.

Under these circumstances, Shaykh Ahmed Sirhindi (1564–1626) of the puritanical Naqshbandiyya began a campaign against the declining Islamic standards of the Mughuls. He also condemned the prevalent practices of many Sufis which he alleged were borrowed from Hinduism. Such activities led to his incarceration on the orders of Jahangir. Sirhindi's warnings found reception in the policies of Emperor Aurangzeb (ruled 1658–1707). The Sunni establishment regained its influence at the court. In 1679 the *jizya* was reimposed and Shia cultural practices were curbed. However, Aurangzeb came to power at a time when the Mughul empire was in a state of overall decay and exhaustion. The restoration of orthodoxy at the centre only provoked rebellions and breakaway attempts in the peripheral regions of the empire. Aurangzeb's protracted military engagements against the Sikhs in Punjab, Hindu Marathas in the Deccan and the Shia states of Bijapur and Golcanda in the south occupied most of his long reign. His death hastened the disintegration of the empire.

Shah Waliullah (1702–63) emerged as an outstanding reformer at a time when Muslim power seemed to be on the wane irreversibly. After completing his education in the classical Islamic sciences of jurisprudence and theology, Waliullah travelled to the Hijaz, the Islamic holy land, where the cities of Mecca and Medina are located. During his sojourn he came into contact with the contemporaneous reformist movements prevalent in Arabia. After spending fourteen months there he returned to India and started predicating a return to the original purity of Islam. Deeply distressed by the growing power of the Hindu Marathas and Jats, Waliullah began to search for a Muslim prince or warlord who could revive Muslim power. He failed to find one close at hand. He therefore decided to invite the Afghan Ahmad Shah Abdali to invade India. Abdali launched several invasions on India between 1747–69. His raids, however, showed little regard for Muslim solidarity. Instead, looting, plundering and killing both Muslims and non-Muslims remained his main concern. The Mughul state was meted severe blows. Waliullah's hopes for a revival of Muslim power were therefore dashed completely.

It was in the religio-cultural sphere that Waliullah achieved profound influence. He translated the Quran into Persian – a rather radical act at that time. He advocated egalitarian economic reforms, because he believed that without economic justice the social purpose of Islam could not be fulfilled. He rejected the traditional position that the Islamic legal system was complete and therefore fresh *ijtihad* (application of independent judgement in interpreting the Quran and *Sunna*) was not required. He decried the contemporary *ulama* for their elaborate rites and rituals which he denounced as un-Islamic accretions. However, like so many other earlier reformers in Muslim history, Waliullah was haunted by an idealised version of the pious caliphate, the *salaf* tradition as some have called it. The principle of back-to-the-book or rather back-to-the-pious-caliphate put him in the class of restorers rather than innovators. More interesting is the political legacy he bequeathed to future generations of Indian Muslims. On the one hand, he continued to preach, in the tradition of Sirhindi, exclusiveness of the Muslim community from the Hindu majority, but on the other hand, he deviated from it by adopting a more conciliatory attitude towards Shias. The peculiar type of communalism which he prescribed sanctioned separatism from Hindus but co-operation with Shias.

The period of British colonialism

Shah Waliullah expended most of his energies and intellectual prowess on looking for ways and means of halting the decline of Muslim power in general and of the Mughul state in particular. He could not, however, anticipate the true magnitude of the emerging challenge posed by the various European powers which were gradually expanding their influence in the distant coastal areas of western, southern and eastern India. This task was left to radical *ulama* of the later period. The British East India Company was able to drive out other European competitors from the subcontinent by the early nineteenth century. In 1757 the British had defeated the Mughul governor of Bengal, Siraj-ud-Daula. Thereafter nothing could stop their further expansion. It took, however, another 100 years before the whole of the mainland was conquered.

The early nineteenth century was a period when the British were rapidly expanding their power in northern India. Sayyid Ahmed of Rai Bareli (1786–1831) emerged as a militant Islamist who aspired to establish an Islamic polity, based on the model of the pious caliphate, throughout the length and breadth of India. He was joined by Waliullah's son Shah Abdul Aziz, who was a leading scholar of Islam in his own right. Earlier, Aziz had issued a *fatwa* (ruling of a leading Muslim scholar on a point of law or doctrine) that India had become a *dar al-harb* (enemy territory; lands outside the jurisdiction of Islam) under British domination.

Ahmed visited Mecca and Medina in 1822. It left him deeply impressed by the Wahhabi movement on the Arabian peninsula, both in terms of its fiercely monotheistic ideology and emphasis on armed struggle. However, he never categorically called himself a Wahhabi. Rather he retained his formal Hanafi affiliations, but sought to advance puritanical monotheism within such a framework. The appellation Wahhabi was attached to his teachings by his critics. The established traditional *ulama* strongly disapproved of his iconoclastic approach to contemporaneous Islamic practices and beliefs steeped in saint-worship and elaborate rites and rituals, many of which were adaptations of local and regional folk culture. Upon his return, Ahmed started recruiting men for the impending *jihad* (struggle in the way of God; striving for justice; holy war, in this case purported to liberate Muslim territories). The call to *jihad* was heeded by many Muslims from different parts of the subcontinent who flocked to his sermons and joined his army. Patna in northeastern India became the headquarter of his activities. His preparatory campaign was largely secretive. Much of it was conducted in areas controlled by the British. However, Ahmed took the controversial decision of launching *jihad* (effort, 'holy war') against the Sikhs of Punjab rather than the British. He justified it on the grounds that whereas the Sikhs were allegedly suppressing the Islamic religion and persecuting Muslims, the British did not interfere with their religious affairs. This rather peculiar doctrinal argument was severely criticised by the traditional *ulama*. Some of them even suggested that Ahmed was a British agent, because the British authorities did not try to stop his soldiers from passing through territories under their control on their way to northwestern India and Punjab. No solid conclusive proof of Sayyid Ahmed's complicity with the British has ever been furnished by his detractors, but the controversy continues to figure in doctrinal debates.

In any case, Sayyid Ahmed launched his *jihad* against the Sikhs in 1826. He travelled to the north where Pukhtun tribes joined him. Several battles took place between the Sikhs and the Islamist militants, but the former could not be defeated. In 1831 Sayyid Ahmed and many of his close associates were slain at Balakot; hence the title Shaheed (martyr) was added to his name by his followers. Ahmed's death proved to be a major setback to the movement, but Islamic militancy persisted for a long time. In Bengal, especially, peasant uprisings against oppressive landlords took puritan Islamic overtones reflective of Wahhabistic monotheism. The British maintained strict surveillance over the 'Wahhabis' in all parts of the subcontinent.

Haji Nisar Ali, alias Titu Mir (1772–1831), is believed to have met Sayyid Ahmed either at Calcutta or in the Hijaz. He became a disciple of the latter and began to preach puritanical Islam to Muslim peasants in his district, many of whom had only nominal allegiance to Islam. Along with an Islamic consciousness the peasants learnt to organise themselves against oppressive landlords who ruthlessly exploited them. Among the landlords were also British Indigo planters. Gradually, armed confrontations began to take place between Titu Mir's followers and the landlords. Some initial success scored by the peasants made the movement popular on an expanding basis until thousands had joined it. Some Hindu lower castes also joined the struggle. Amid the threat of a growing peasant insurrection the British sent an armed contingent equipped with heavy weaponry such as field canons. In the battle which ensued the poorly-equipped peasant army of Titu Mir was defeated. He, along with fifty of his followers, fell fighting on the battlefield.

In the early nineteenth century, another returnee from Hijaz, Haji Shariatullah, initiated a parallel reform movement in another district of Bengal. This movement came to be known by the name of Faraizi which was derived from *farz* which means obligatory duty. It implied strict literalist observance of the Quranic injunctions. The social goal of the Faraizi movement was equity and justice and it encouraged the predominantly Muslim peasantry to resist their oppressive landlords, most of whom were Hindus. Upon Shariatullah's death his son, Muhsinuddin, popularly known as Dudhu Miyan (1819–60), continued to lead the Faraizis. He preached the radical doctrine that, in Islam, land belonged to God and therefore no one could claim private ownership of land. Dudhu Miyan also managed to organise an army of several thousand peasant militants which presented tough resistance to the landlords and the British Indigo planters. The British authorities deployed armed police to quell the rebellion. Both Muslim and Hindu landlords supported the British. Dudhu Miyan and sixty-five of his poorly armed followers were overwhelmed and arrested and the movement disintegrated under severe repression. In their long-drawn struggle the Faraizis had established their own courts and devised novel methods of non-cooperation and civil disobedience against the British.

The decline of the Mughul empire was indicative also of a general intellectual decay and stagnation which beset the Muslim community. The traditionalist *ulama* practised a type of Islam which was based heavily on reverence for past authority. Saint-worship, both of dead masters and living *pirs*, was a prominent feature of the anti-intellectual implications of traditionalism. The rise of 'Wahhabi extremism' and later the emergence of the puritanical, but moderate, Deoband school were perceived of as serious threats by the traditionalists. Largely in reaction the traditionalists also embarked upon a process of greater doctrinal and organisational consolidation. This task was undertaken by Ahmed Raza Khan (1856–1921) born in the northern Indian town of Bareli; hence the popular designation of Barelwis, deriving from his town of birth, acquired by his followers. Ahmed Raza Khan did not agree with the radical *ulama* that India under British suzerainty had become a *dar al-harb*. He had a positive attitude to the tolerant religious policy of the British and suggested that India remained a *dar al-islam* (abode of peace, where Islamic law prevailed and Islamic faith was not suppressed). The Barelwis remained largely passive during the freedom struggle. They were supported by the landlords and *pirs* who generally sided with the British. Until just before the end of the colonial period, the Muslim League mobilised them for the campaign for Pakistan. As the group with the largest following among Muslims the Barelwis proved an invaluable asset to the separatist project of the modern-educated Muslim élite.

In 1857 a popular uprising broke out among the Indian soldiers of the British East India Company. Many Hindu and Muslim princes with grievances against the colonialists also joined the popular movement. The old Mughul Emperor, Bahadur Shah Zafar, long since reduced to a figurehead, was proclaimed leader of the struggle. The *ulama* reiterated the ruling that India was a *dar al-harb* and gave the uprising the status of *jihad*. However, many native rulers remained loyal to the British. The participation of the people was sporadic and disorganised. Consequently the British were able to crush the insurrection. The general feeling among the British was that Muslims were the main culprits. The old Muslim aristocracy of northern India had to pay dearly in terms of loss of life, material possessions and influence.

On the other hand, popular participation in the uprising convinced the British that fundamental reforms had to be introduced to assuage Indian opinion. In this regard, a drastic change of policy occurred because the rule of the Company was abolished and India was placed directly under the Crown. Further, it was decided to associate more Indians in the managing of the huge empire. Modern education, including the learning of English and other liberal and scientific subjects, was to be made available to the upper classes. Unlike the Muslim aristocracy which had suffered considerable repression at the hands of the British and was therefore negatively disposed towards them, many sections of the Hindu upper castes took advantage of the new opportunities.

Rapprochement between the British and Muslim upper classes was delayed for several decades after the 1857 confrontation. While most *ulama* remained hostile, Sir Sayyid Ahmed Khan (1817–98), a scion of the old Muslim aristocracy of northern India, who had worked in the Company's judicial services and saved many British lives during the uprising, worked indefatigably to win over British sympathies towards the Muslims. He realised that Muslims had a bleak future ahead of them in India if they did not acquire a modern education. For doing that, good relations had to be cultivated with the new rulers. With the British he argued that Muslims were not the main culprits in the uprising and that British policy had also played a role in bringing about estrangement between them. Also, he pointed out that it was important for the British to extend their favours to Muslims who were an important community in India. With the Muslims Sir Sayyid pleaded that India under British rule was not a *dar al-harb*, because the colonial state did not interfere with the religious affairs of Muslims. His efforts led to a thaw in the otherwise cold and unfriendly relations between them. In 1886 Sir Sayyid established the Muslim Educational Conference. It was followed by the founding of a college at Aligarh where Muslim students, mostly from upper-middle-class backgrounds, came to receive modern education based on the Cambridge University system.

Sir Sayyid's most ambitious attempt at reform was one aimed at reconciling Islam with modern science and reason. He argued that Islam was a faith based on reason. Therefore there could not be any conflict between the laws of nature and Islamic faith. This audacious standpoint was rejected by the *ulama*. Some even accused him of heresy. Surprisingly none of his followers maintained this radical stance on religion. It therefore failed to serve as a complete modernist reform of Islamic theology and faith. Politically, Sir Sayyid continued to argue in the separatist mould of Shah Waliullah. He warned Muslims to keep away from the Indian National Congress (1885) which he dubbed as a Hindu organisation. On the other hand, his rationalistic approach to Islam encouraged Sunni and Shia modernists to relegate dogma to the background and instead emphasise a communal identity based on Islamic culture and past grandeur.

In 1867, an orthodox Sunni seat of learning was established at Deoband in northern India. The Deobandi *ulama* adhered to rationalism but one deriving from classical scholasticism which had prospered during the great days of the Abbasid caliphate (750–1258). They sought neither complete rupture with the traditional-historical Islam that the Wahhabis stood for nor complete, unflinching conformity to it as was the case with the Barelwis. Politically the Deobandis conformed to the anti-British approach of the radical *ulama*, and many of them were involved in clandestine anti-British movements. Consequently, the Deobandis held in contempt the pro-British policies of Sir Sayyid and his followers. They argued that patriotism was not inimical to Islam. Rather defence of *watan* (homeland) was a higher calling for Muslims. Later, when the freedom struggle led by the Indian National Congress (1885) assumed a mass character, the Jamiyat-i-Ulama-i-Hind (Party of the Islamic Scholars of India), formed by leading Deobandi *ulama,* preferred cooperation with the Congress in the struggle for the liberation of India. They rejected the separatist movement which the modern-educated followers of Sir Sayyid, organised in the Muslim League (1906), launched in the 1940s.

South Asian Muslims have always retained a keen interest in the larger Muslim world, especially in the affairs of Western Asia and other parts of the Middle East. The dismemberment of Ottoman Turkey after the First World War at the hands of the European allies created great consternation among Indian Muslims. They formed the Khilafat Committee in 1919 (an organisation for the preservation of the Ottoman caliphate) to plead the case of Turkey with the British government. Anti-imperialist Hindus also extended the support to the Khilafatists. Mahatma Gandhi was elected as one of the leaders of the Khilafat Committee. It was a time when radical *ulama* of various schools of thought joined ranks and took part in a major manifestation of the anti-colonial feelings of all the communities of India. Many disturbances took place and a delegation was sent to England to plead the case of Turkey, but the British government remained unmoved.

Some Muslims despaired at British insensitivity and apathy, and started propagating that since India was a *dar al-harb,* Muslims should undertake *hijra* (emigration) to *dar al-islam.* Several thousand people responded to the call. They sold their properties and other belongings and embarked upon a journey to neighbouring Afghanistan in 1920. Although initially the Afghan government showed sympathy for the Muslim refugees, it could not offer economic and other facilities on such a large scale. It also feared further influx from India. It became clear that most of the refugees were not wanted by the Afghans in their country. In these circumstances, most of them had no choice but to return to India. They came back heart-broken and disillusioned. Some young men crossed into Soviet Central Asia and later became pioneers of the communist movement in India.

The abolition of the caliphate by the Turks themselves in 1924 rendered the Khilafat issue obsolete and left the Indian activists confused and perplexed. In political terms, the Khilafat and Hijrat movements provided avenues for radical *ulama* to enter the era of mass politics in the modern period. It is interesting to note that the modern-educated Muslim élite showed little enthusiasm for these movements. The future leader of the Pakistan movement, Mohamed Ali Jinnah, even expressed disapproval of religious radicalism.

The Muslim upper classes were wary of the Indian National Congress's claim that it alone represented all Indians irrespective of their religious faiths and cultural affiliations. The Muslim League (founded 1906) was, therefore, established by Muslim professionals of landowning and bourgeois backgrounds as a reaction to the growing power and influence of Congress in national politics and the growing economic power of the Hindu middle classes. The Muslims were encouraged by the British to organise on a communal basis. Until the end of the 1930s, the Muslim League remained a party of the gentry which concerned itself mainly with questions about a share in employment and representation in government services and legislative bodies for Muslims. It was only in the early 1940s that the Muslim League started campaigning earnestly for a separate Muslim state. In order to achieve such an end it had to mobilise mass support among Muslims.

The ideologue of a separate Muslim national state was the scholastic poet-philosopher, Allama Iqbal (1878–1938). He studied at Cambridge, was called to the Bar in that country and acquired a doctorate from Germany in Persian metaphysics. He was an ardent supporter of *ijtihad* which he believed each generation of Muslims was entitled to exercise to deal with their contemporaneous problems. However, Iqbal subscribed to the traditional standpoint that religion and state were inseparable in Islam. Also, despite a strong sympathy for social and economic justice, Iqbal remained somewhat unconcerned about women's rights and emancipation. As regards the idea of a separate Muslim state, he wanted the Muslim majority areas of northwest India (he did not mention the Muslim majority areas of East Bengal in his scheme) to be organised into either a separate independent state or in some loose union with the rest of India. He was convinced that development of the *sharia* in the light of modern ideas could serve as the ideological and legal basis for egalitarian change in Muslim society.

In the 1937 provincial elections the Muslim League did not campaign for a separate Muslim state. It only asked the Muslims for a mandate to represent them at the centre. At that time, the regional parties in the Muslim-majority provinces were able to win most of the seats. On an overall basis, however, Congress emerged as the triumphant party. The Muslim League was completely routed. In March 1940 it proclaimed the creation of a Muslim state in the Muslim majority regions of the subcontinent. That decision was to prove a turning point in its fortunes. In 1942 Congress launched the Quit-India Movement with the aim of winning independence immediately. The British acted swiftly and sternly by imprisoning Congress leaders and activists. On the other hand, Jinnah and the Muslim League extended a hand of cooperation in the war effort, which concretely required helping the government recruit soldiers into the army in areas where it enjoyed influence. Thereafter the British facilitated the growth and expansion of the Muslim League, which from 1944 onwards rapidly established itself in the Muslim majority provinces where previously regional parties had held sway. From such a vantage point, and while Congress was practically absent from the political scene, it began propagating the idea of Pakistan. The vision which was projected of a future Pakistan was one based on Islamic values of justice and equality. These proved very attractive to the Muslim intelligentsia who went about soliciting support for the Pakistan demand.

Already in 1942 Britain had committed itself to a withdrawal from South Asia once the Second World War was over. Therefore when, in the winter of 1945–46, elections were held, the Muslim League contested the elections from a platform demanding the creation of Pakistan while Congress contested from the opposite platform of keeping India united as a single state. The Muslim League conducted a patently communal campaign. It could mobilise also important dissenting voices in the otherwise pro-Congress Deobandi camp, such as Ashraf Ali Thanvi and Shabbir Ahmed Usmani, to its cause. It was able to mobilise Barelwi *ulama*, *pirs* and young students in their thousands to propagate the idea of Pakistan. A patently communal propaganda was conducted. Not only Hindus and Sikhs were demonised but also Muslims who were opposed to the Pakistan scheme were condemned as renegades and traitors to Islam. *Fatwas* were obtained which made support for Pakistan a religious duty for Muslims. Some *fatwas* went so far as to prohibit proper Islamic burial for Muslims who did not support the Pakistan demand.

Such tactics proved immensely effective. The Muslim voters gave a clear verdict in favour of Pakistan. British India was partitioned in mid-August 1947 into the two independent states of India and Pakistan. It is important to point out that the provinces of Bengal and Punjab were also divided on a religious basis: the eastern portions of Bengal and the western portions of Punjab had Muslim majorities and were therefore separated and allotted to Pakistan. The partition was attended by communal massacres in which Muslims, Hindus and Sikhs suffered great loss of life and property. While most of the Hindus and Sikhs left their ancestral homes in West Pakistan, in East Bengal more than one-fifth of the population continued to consist of Hindus, while more than 30 million Muslims continued to live on in India.

Pakistan

On August 14, 1947 Pakistan became an independent Muslim state. It consisted of the Muslim-majority zones in the northwestern and north-eastern regions of the subcontinent, which came to be called West and East Pakistan. They were separated from each other by more than 1,500 kilometres of Indian territory. In December 1971 Pakistan broke up after many months of civil war between the Pakistani army and the Awami League-led resistance movement of the people of East Pakistan. Henceforth East Pakistan became Bangladesh. Pakistan was left only with her territories in the western part.

Punjabi Muslims in Lahore (photo: Ishtiaq Ahmed, 1982).

The current population of Pakistan is estimated at 132 million. There are four provinces: Baluchistan, North West Frontier Province (NWFP), Punjab and Sindh. According to official statistics, Muslims make up more than 96 per cent of the total population. Although figures are not available regarding the divisions among Muslims, Sunnis of various subgroups are estimated to be between 80–85 per cent, while the Shias, including the main Ithna Ashari and the minor Ismaili and Bohra groups make up 15–20 per cent of the Muslim population. The Christians (largely to be found in Punjab and Karachi) and Hindus (almost all to be found in Sindh province) together make up slightly over 3 per cent, while the Ahmadiyya (who describe themselves as Muslims but are officially classified as non-Muslims since 1974) are given as less than 200,000 (the Ahmadiyya themselves claim to number many more).

The areas comprising present-day Pakistan were the first to be conquered by the Muslims entering the subcontinent from the northwestern mountain passes and sea routes. Except for a brief Sikh interlude when Ranjit Singh (1799–1839) established the Kingdom of Lahore, it was unbroken Muslim rule which obtained in this region until the British annexed it. Baluchistan and the NWFP, being adjacent to Western and Central Asia, have always had closer cultural and ethnic affinity with those regions. However, much of Punjab and Sindh belong more properly to the South Asian ethno-cultural sphere. Before partition in 1947, Hindus and Sikhs were found in large numbers in these provinces. The Muslims of Punjab and Sindh are mostly of Hindu extraction and consequently many Hindu customs and traditions are observed by Pakistani Muslims, albeit with modified Islamic trappings. It is not, however, uncommon for many ethnic groups, tribes and castes in Punjab and Sindh whose exact place in the Hindu social order is undefined or obscure to claim some foreign origin. Claims to Turkish or Mughul ancestry are quite common, but tracing an Arab origin, especially back to the Prophet and his tribe, has always held an attraction in South Asian Muslim society. Such fiction seems to serve a need for improved self-esteem and a sense of authenticity to people wanting to identify with Islam rather than a Hindu origin.

The Hanafi school prevails throughout Pakistan. The social order in Baluchistan is predominantly tribal. All-powerful tribal chiefs command great influence and power in their domains, although in recent years the *ulama* have been trying to increase their influence. In NWFP also tribal chiefs are quite powerful. In Sindh particularly, but also in many parts of rural Punjab and NWFP, influential *pirs* are often major landowners too. Many of these *pirs* claim descent from Muhammad. From the beginning of this century, a tendency among many of them has been to incorporate elements from the cult of Ali and other Shia practices into their religious ceremonies. Many are no longer practising Sufis. Rather they exploit their traditional prestige in the furtherance of mundane interests. As a parasitical landowning class they are notorious for employing quite tyrannical methods of exploiting poor peasant and artisan sections of society. The mainstream Chishtiyya, Qadiriyya, Naqshbandiyya and Suhravardiyya networks are to be found throughout the country and among Pakistani immigrants settled abroad.

The *pirs* and the vast majority of *ulama* subscribe to the Barelwi school. Most mosques in Pakistan are under Barelwi control. Deobandi and the Ahl-i-Hadith, that is followers of the Prophetic Sayings, the name preferred for themselves by puritanical Muslims who are generally called Wahhabis by others, also have their following in all parts of Pakistan. So do the Ithna Ashari Shias. Small communities of Ismaili and Bohra Shias are to be found in Sindh. Significant Ismaili and Ithna Ashari communities exist in the mountainous areas of Hunza and Chitral in NWFP. The Ahmadiyya have followers in all parts of the country too, although they are mainly concentrated in Punjab and Karachi. In Baluchistan is to be found the obscure Zikri community. The Zikris (with their antecedents in the heterodox Mahdawi Sufi movement of the fifteenth to sixteenth centuries) were, until recently, little known outside Baluchistan. For some years now the orthodox *ulama* have been campaigning for restrictions on some of the Zikri customs and practices which are allegedly contrary to Islam. Clashes between the Zikris and Sunnis have occurred in recent years.

The modernists who led the movement for Pakistan had argued that Indian Muslims formed a separate nation and that Islam prescribed a distinct way of life. This ideology of Muslim nationalism was put forth to justify the demand for an independent state of Muslims. In the 1945–46 election campaign anyone who declared that he or she was a Muslim and had been so entered in the census records was admitted into the Muslim League. Thus support for Pakistan was sought from Sunnis, Shias and also the controversial Ahmadiyya community.

Once in power, the modernists had to define the relationship between Islam and the state. They were ill-prepared for such a task. The supreme leader of the Pakistan movement, Mohamed Ali Jinnah, who had played the pivotal role in ascribing credibility and legitimacy to the religious basis of nationhood and on that basis brought about the division of India, made an unexpected speech on August 11, 1947, i.e. three days before independence, to members of the Pakistan Constituent Assembly in which he proclaimed that Pakistan should be a secular democratic state. He never again repeated such a commitment although he lived for another year. After his death on September 11, 1948, secularism and Jinnah's speech became the slogan of marginal elements – liberal and left-leaning politicians, academics and oppressed minorities – hoping in vain to give the ruling élite a bad conscience for its drift towards greater theocratisation of state and society.

The second position was put forth on March 7, 1949, by Prime Minister Liaqat Ali Khan in the Objectives Resolution. It proclaimed that sovereignty over the entire universe belonged to God. The authority of the chosen representatives of the people of Pakistan was to be limited by God's will. Democracy was to be practised within Islamic limits. The rights of minorities were also to be defined in the light of Islamic injunctions. The resolution was couched in populist terminology which could appease a broad spectrum of opinion. Most importantly, definite constitutional supremacy was accorded to God's sovereignty with all the various implications and vagaries inherent in the concept. The modernists could not agree upon a formula for power sharing. Consequently, there were frequent changes of government. It meant also that constitutional developments were slow and unstable. The Objectives Resolution, with minor changes, has been the preamble of the 1956, 1962 and 1973 constitutions. During the Zia period it was made an integral part of the constitution.

The 1956 constitution declared Pakistan an Islamic republic and the president was required to be a Muslim. The government was to appoint a commission which was to advise the government on bringing the laws of Pakistan into line with the Quran and Sunna. On the other hand a bill of fundamental rights was also included which assured protection of all the usual fundamental rights upheld by liberal theory, including the freedom of belief and conscience, to the people of Pakistan. The 1962 Constitution deleted the appellation 'Islamic' and declared Pakistan simply as a republic. However, the *ulama* protested against such a change and in 1963 Pakistan was renamed as an Islamic republic. An Islamic Advisory Council and an Islamic Research Institute were to be established to assist the government in making existing laws conform with the Quran and Sunna. The president was required to be a Muslim. The 1973 constitution adopted during the period of Zulfikar Ali Bhutto went even further in terms of Islamisation. Not only the president but also the prime minister had to be Muslims. Their oath of office required an explicit declaration that they believed in the finality of the prophethood of Muhammad. Such a requirement meant that only qualified Sunnis and Shias could contest and hold such positions.

Pakistan was created under heavy debt to Islam. The modernist formulae of Islamic democracy failed to satisfy the more theocratic aspirations of the *ulama*. Consequently the *ulama* of the various Sunni subgroups began clamouring for the creation of a true Islamic polity. The Shias, being a minority, showed less enthusiasm for such an idea because it implied hegemony of Sunni interpretations of the Islamic state. Most centrally the *ulama* insisted that only male Muslim citizens should have full political rights in Pakistan. Further, they held that any version of Islamic democracy put forward by the modernist leadership of the Muslim League was unacceptable if it did not acknowledge the supremacy of the *sharia*. Restrictions on the participation of women in public life and in politics were also demanded.

Abul Ala Mawdudi and the Jamaat-i-Islami

The main architect of the Islamic state model in Pakistan has been the leader of the Jamaat-i-Islami (Party of Islam), Abul Ala Mawdudi (1903–79), who wrote over the course of half a century, beginning as a journalist and distinguishing himself as a skilful essayist on Islam. Mawdudi was born at Aurangabad in the Deccan in southern India, but it was from Pathankot in present-day Indian East Punjab that in 1941 he launched an organised political movement and founded the Jamaat-i-Islami. Mawdudi opposed the nationalist movement led by the Congress. He was equally dismissive of the Muslim League's scheme of a Muslim homeland, asserting that Muslims could not get involved in a freedom struggle which was based on secular nationalism. However, upon the creation of Pakistan, Mawdudi moved to Lahore in the Pakistani West Punjab and set up his headquarters. His most successful early achievement was the compilation in 1951 of a twenty-two–point programme about Islamisation of Pakistan. The leading *ulama* of all the different Sunni subgroups and the Ithna Ashari Shias were signatories of the programme. Such unusual consensus was meant to demonstrate that, notwithstanding doctrinal differences, a common programme of Islamisation was acceptable to all schools of thought.

Mawdudi theorised in the typical restorative tradition of so many earlier Islamist purists: the pious caliphate model of state and society had to be resurrected in both spirit and action if a just order were to prevail on earth. His sympathies for puritanical Sunni Islam were well known. Many considered him to lean heavily towards Wahhabism and Deobandi ideas, but Mawdudi remained an eclectic scholar within the broad Hanafi framework. On approach to doctrine, Mawdudi inherited the mantle of Waliullah and preached *ijtihad* in, what he described were, unoccupied areas (i.e. issues on which the *sharia* was silent). However, on questions of economic and social justice, Mawdudi did not share Waliullah's radical views. Rather he supported the traditionalist position that no limits could be set on private property if it had been acquired through proper means; this applied also to agricultural land.

Mawdudi advanced a totalitarian vision of the Islamic state. Through the agency of such a state all sectors of life were to be brought into conformity with the *sharia*. Western democracy, female equality and a territorial basis of citizenship were to be rejected. Only deserving Muslim male adults were to be assigned key positions in the state machinery. On the other hand, there were to be no special privileges for any caste, class or race. All senior officers, including the head of state, were to be answerable for their conduct to the Muslim electorate and could be tried in a court of law for misconduct. Women were to be allowed limited participation in political life. On female matters they were to be consulted in law-making. Non-Muslims were to be provided with protection for their life and property on equal terms with the Muslims. They could be represented in the legislature, but on the basis of separate electorates.

Mawdudi has been one of the most influential ideologues of the Islamic state in recent times. His prolific writings have been translated into Arabic and several other languages and his influence in popularising the doctrinal Islamic state model in the Muslim world, including the volatile Middle East, has been huge. His authority as a *bona fide* Sunni theorist makes him far more acceptable than Ayatollah Khomeini to the predominantly Sunni societies, even though the latter uniquely effected the current worldwide Islamic revival by successfully demonstrating in Iran that an Islamic state can be installed through mass agitations and revolutionary struggle.

Not only did Mawdudi write extensively, but also established under his leadership the best-organised political party in Pakistan, the Jamaat-i-Islami. Based on restrictive, hierarchical membership the Jamaat confers full membership only on its most devoted and consistent supporters. The interesting thing to note is that its performance in elections has been extremely poor. It has never won more than four seats in the national parliament, but has exercised a powerful ideological influence over the Pakistani state. One explanation for this great imbalance between lack of popular support but considerable influence on the state can be found in the peculiar position it has enjoyed in Pakistani politics. Regarding its limited appeal, it can be asserted, that since, on the one hand, all mainstream political parties in Pakistan, even moderate ones such as the Muslim League, have been sectarian or communal parties, the Jamaat-i-Islami is one among many other parties claiming to work for the Muslim or Islamic good. On the other hand, its puritanism is not accompanied by a radical position on socio-economic issues. Therefore Mawdudism holds an attraction only for narrow sections of the population such as the moderately educated intelligentsia, middle-range landowners and upwardly mobile peasant–proprietors–sections most susceptible to puritan morals as well as acquisition of material goods.

As for its considerable influence on the state a number of internal and external factors combined to place it in such a position. Since Pakistan was officially committed through its various constitutional commitments to creating conditions for a full realisation of the Islamic way of life, Mawdudi always held the initiative in pointing out in a learned and consistent manner what Islam prescribed for the concretisation of such a commitment. From the mid 1960s onwards, class struggles and regional conflicts sharpened in Pakistan. The rise of Islamic socialism under the leadership of Zulfikar Ali Bhutto in West Pakistan and regionalism under Shaykh Mujibur Rahman in East Pakistan greatly perturbed the Pakistani ruling circles and the *ulama*. At that time, Maoist ideas were fast gaining ground in many parts of the Third World. In South Asia, militant peasant movements inspired by Maoist ideas and led by revolutionary Marxists emerged in different countries. Pakistan itself was fast coming under the sway of Bhutto's radical rhetoric. There was also a visible increase in peasant- and working-class actions and disturbances. Under such circumstances, Mawdudi's version of an Islamic state appeared as the most formidable ideological weapon which the ruling circles could wield against the radical forces. Therefore some of his fundamental ideas were incorporated into official ideological proclamations. Thus an ordinance issued by the military government of General Yaha Khan in 1969 declared Islam exclusively as the Ideology of Pakistan. With the coming to power of General Muhammad Zia ul-Haq in 1977 Pakistan had a person in power who shared Mawdudi's vision of Islam.

Mawdudi died in 1979. With his departure the most able exponent of the Islamic state theory in Pakistan was gone, but his influence continues to be considerable on subsequent ideological debates. As for the Jamaat-i-Islami, it went through a period of internal leadership struggle. Nobody could command the same authority and prestige in the party as Mawdudi. Moreover, disagreements over strategy and policy led to some amount of factionalism among various regional and ethnic cliques present in the party. Although somewhat weakened it continues to function as an influential political party in Pakistan.

Recent Islamisation policies in Pakistan

The government of Z.A. Bhutto (1972–77) was toppled by General Zia ul-Haq (1977–88). Zia declared unequivocally his intention to Islamise Pakistan. He visualised a social order in which all sectors of life including administration, judiciary, banking, trade, education, agriculture, industry and foreign affairs were regulated in accordance with Islamic principles. In 1979 the Zia government announced the imposition of the Hudud Ordinance, i.e. punishments laid down in Quran and Sunna for the offences of adultery (death by stoning); fornication (100 lashes); false accusation of adultery (80 lashes); drinking alcohol (80 lashes); theft (cutting off the right hand); highway robbery (when the offence is only robbery, cutting off hands and feet; for robbery with murder, death either by the sword or crucifixion). Interestingly enough apostasy, which traditionally had been part of Hudud law, was not included in the Hudud ordinance. In 1984 a new Law of Evidence was adopted which reduced the worth of the evidence of a female witness to half that of a male witness in a court of law. In 1985, two members of the Jamaat-i-Islami moved a so-called Shariat Bill which sought to establish the supremacy of the Quran and Sunna in a substantial manner in the constitutional and legal systems of Pakistan. Sunni–Hanafi interpretations of the Deobandi variety were to be the standard norm and practice. Most central to the bill was the creation of Shariat courts. Hudud offences were to be placed within the exclusive jurisdiction of such courts. Against judgments of Shariat courts there could be no appeal in a higher court. The bill was adopted in a revised form in 1986. Economic and fiscal matters were originally exempted from the competence of the Shariat courts, but some judges have rejected such limitations. The Shias and Barelwis expressed strong reservations against the Deobandi bias present in the formulations of the Bill.

In the economic field, banking reforms were introduced which ostensibly eliminated 'interest' but replaced it with 'profit'. *Zakat* (an annual alms tax of 2.5 per cent levied on wealth) was imposed on the Muslim citizens. However, the Shias refused to pay *zakat* to the government of General Zia ul-Haq as it was Sunni in its orientation and therefore could not claim *zakat* from them. The government initially dismissed the Shia demand. It resulted in widespread agitation by the Shias. Finally they were exempted from paying *zakat*.

The ideology of Muslim nationalism contained immanently a confessional bias. Constitutional theocratisation of the state proceeded gradually. Islamisation under Zia became more comprehensive and tangible. For women, minority groups and non-Muslims such developments have carried many disadvantages. Although Sir Sayyid pioneered the cause of Muslim modernism and established educational centres for such a purpose, it was mostly upper-middle-class men who could benefit from his reforms. Thus it was only a very small number of Muslim women who had attended college or university prior to independence. The various governments that came to power in Pakistan before the Zia regime had gradually expanded educational facilities for women. Consequently some had started working as doctors, nurses, teachers and in various other capacities. Among legal measures purporting to improve the situation of married women was the promulgation of the Muslim Family Law Ordinance of 1961 which made polygamy difficult. Under General Zia, however, several measures were undertaken to impose an Islamic behaviour pattern on women. In 1980 a circular was issued to all government offices which prescribed a proper Muslim dress for female employees. Wearing of a *chadur* (a loose cloth worn to cover the head) was made obligatory. A campaign to eliminate obscenity and pornography was also announced, but it assumed more the form of a campaign against the general emancipation and equal rights of women. Leading Muslim theologians known for their antipathy to female emancipation were brought on the national television to justify various restrictions on women.

As the general situation of women deteriorated some of the educated women of the larger cities of Lahore, Karachi and Islamabad brought out demonstrations demanding a stop to the anti-women campaign. The elections of Benazir Bhutto as prime minister in 1988 despite rabid opposition by many *ulama* exposed the hollowness of sterile Islamisation campaigns. However, neither Benazir Bhutto (1988–90) nor the succeeding present government of Nawaz Sharif has removed the laws and other social restrictions imposed during the Zia era against women. The general climate has undoubtedly hardened for women in Pakistan.

The Shias of India were wary of the idea of Pakistan as it portended domination by the Sunni majority. However, Mohamed Ali Jinnah and many other leading members of the Muslim League were Shias. They were able to placate Shia fears with promises of basing Pakistan on non-sectarian Islam. In contemporary Pakistan, Shias are dispersed in society at all levels and in all regions. Among major landowners, industrialists, bankers and the civil and military apparatuses, Shias are prominently represented. Recruitment from some Shia localities in Punjab is quite substantial in the army. Moreover, on the élite level there is considerable assimilation among Sunnis and Shias. On the mass level Sunni–Shia theological differences have always tended to rupture into ugly brawls and violence. This problem has worsened in recent years.

After General Zia ul-Haq came to power, Pakistan acquired clearly Islamist Sunni overtones. On the other hand, the Shias were emboldened by the coming into power of Khomeini in neighbouring Iran in early 1979. Thus assertive and at times provocative Shia behaviour in Pakistan could be noted. The power politics of the Gulf region also impinged upon the intra-

Muslim tension in Pakistan. For several decades now, Shia Iran and her Sunni Arab rivals have been involved in a power struggle to establish hegemony in the Gulf region. The Iranian revolution added an ideological dimension to the power game. Most notably it meant fierce competition between Iran and Saudi Arabia to try to lead the Muslim world. However, both Iran and Saudi Arabia – Islamist and very rich – nevertheless represent two opposite and mutually hostile types of doctrine: Shiism is heterodox while Wahhabism is vehemently critical of the veneration of saints prevalent among traditional Sunni societies.

At any rate, more than 1 million Pakistanis work in the Gulf region, and the Pakistani armed forces have been involved in the defence and security arrangements of Saudi Arabia and several other minor Arab emirates. Both Iran and Saudi Arabia have considered it important to cultivate support in Pakistan. The Iraqi regime, notwithstanding its secular pretensions, has also sought to cultivate a lobby among Sunni *ulama*. In the 1980s, on the one hand, the Iranian–Saudi ideological and power competition and, on the other hand, the Iraq–Iran war, intensified the efforts of these actors to seek greater support in Pakistani society. Consequently in the late 1980s large sums of money, leaflets, books, audio and video cassette-tapes poured into Pakistan, projecting one or the other point of view. Such propaganda offensives have been backed by the influx of weapons of a quite sophisticated nature. The result has been the formation of militias bearing such belligerent names as the Sipah-i-Sahaba (the militia devoted to the Companions of the Prophet, a Sunni outfit) and the Sipah-i-ahl al-bayt (militia devoted to the Family of the Prophet, a Shia outfit) later renamed Sipah-i-Muhammad (the militia devoted to Prophet Muhammad). These and several other extremist outfits indulge frequently in terrorist attacks against one another. Pakistan is currently serving as the battle ground for Middle Eastern proxy wars, albeit so far on a small scale.

The notion of a separate homeland for Muslims in Muslim-majority areas of British India contained inherently the likelihood of non-Muslims being treated as second-rate citizens of the Pakistani state. The founder of Pakistan, Mohamed Ali Jinnah, denied such a possibility. His early successors also believed that non-Muslims could be accorded almost all political and civil rights available to the Muslim citizens. However, the Ahmadiyya controversy clearly showed that people considered as non-Muslims by the state could not be proper citizens of Pakistan. As mentioned earlier, the belief in the promised or awaited Imam has held a popular attraction in all Muslim societies. A claimant to such an office was Mirza Ghulam Ahmad (1835–1908), born at Qadian in the Punjab. Although Mirza began his religious career as a keen Sunni debater who confronted both Christian missionaries and Hindu reformers with clever doctrinal arguments, he later staked a claim to being a prophet and made several other controversial pronouncements which were not easily reconcilable with mainstream Sunni doctrines. He made unambiguously pro-British statements, especially ruling out *jihad,* in the form of armed struggle, as a legitimate means of opposing the colonial power. In his various communications with the colonial authorities Mirza resorted to sycophancy and appeasement. The *ulama* accused him of being an impostor and a British stooge.

Mirza won converts mainly in Punjab. After his death, the Ahmadiyya movement went through a period of internal rift and conflict. It culminated in a split and two groups emerged: the main group, with its headquarters currently at Rabwa, regarded Mirza as a prophet, and the minor Lahori group acknowledged him only as a reformer. The pro-British policy was continued by the Ahmadiyya. Classically this was illustrated during the First World War by the distribution of sweets by the Ahmadiyya at Qadian in 1918 to celebrate the defeat of the Ottoman Turks at Baghdad and the fall of that city into British hands. In return the Ahmadiyya received government protection and patronage. Many were recruited into the army, including the higher level commissioned services. The influence of the Ahmadiyya elsewhere in South Asia was marginal.

It should be pointed out that the Ahmadiyya were not alone in adopting a pro-British position. Almost the whole Muslim landowning class of Punjab and elsewhere, which included powerful *pirs*, rendered many services to the British during peace time and during both World Wars. These included active help in getting soldiers recruited into the imperial army from areas in which they had influence. The Ahmadiyya probably earned the wrath of the *ulama* because of fundamental doctrinal deviations from orthodox doctrines. Additionally the Rabwa group pursued an active and disciplined missionary policy both in South Asia and abroad. Such activities were perceived as threats to Islam by the *ulama*.

Some prominent Ahmadiyya of the Rabwa faction, among whom Sir Muhammad Zafrulla Khan was the best-known, played a leading role in the struggle for the creation of Pakistan. Sir Zafrulla had subsequently been made the first foreign minister of Pakistan by Jinnah. In the early 1950s the Ahmadiyya controversy again cropped up. The *ulama* alleged that the Ahmadiyya were misusing their official positions to spread their faith among Muslims. Statements by the head of the Rabwa-based Ahmadiyya Mission, Mirza Bashiruddin, indeed suggested that he gave orders to Ahmadiyya officers to spread their faith in Pakistan, particularly in Baluchistan. The *ulama* demanded that the government declare the Ahmadiyya non-Muslims and, in accordance with the ideological requirements of an Islamic state, remove Ahmadiyya from important positions. Most concretely it was demanded that Sir Zafrulla should be removed from the post of foreign minister. In 1953 a violent disturbance broke out in Punjab against the Ahmadiyya. Not only the *ulama* but also cadres and officials of the provincial Muslim League government were guilty of fomenting riots in which Ahmadiyya property was looted, their homes burnt and many were killed. The central government imposed martial law and the trouble was crushed. The Ahmadiyya issue receded into the background for some years, but in 1974 Zulfikar Ali Bhutto, hoping to wrest away a popular issue in Punjab from the *ulama*, took the initiative in getting a bill passed by the National Assembly of Pakistan declaring the Ahmadiyya non-Muslims. During the 1980s many restrictions were placed on their religious freedoms and there was a new wave of violent attacks on them. They are today a persecuted group in Pakistan.

Conversions to Christianity took place in the areas which comprise present-day Pakistan largely after the British had annexed Punjab and Sindh in the 1840s. Most conversions took place from among the poorer sections of society, particularly from among the untouchable Hindu castes. A number from middle-class and élite families also embraced Christianity. At the time of the partition of India, Christians who belonged to the Pakistani areas accepted the new state as their homeland. In fact some of their local leaders in Punjab cooperated with the Muslim League during the campaign for Pakistan, because Jinnah and other modernist Muslim League leaders had in their public utterances dissociated themselves from traditional theocratic ideas of the *ulama*. The policy of nationalisation of important sectors of the economy begun by Bhutto in the early 1970s also included the takeover of some of the missionary-owned educational institutions in Punjab. However, as these schools and colleges were practically the only places where Christians could find employment they opposed such nationalisation. Demonstrations and protest marches were organised against the takeovers. The protesters were beaten up and fired upon by police and some casualties occurred. Staff were forcibly evicted from their homes and property owned by the missions was confiscated.

Thereafter the Christians were not heard of again in mainstream politics until General Zia ul-Haq embarked upon his Islamisation policy. In 1985 the system of separate electorates was reintroduced in Pakistan (it had been inherited from the colonial period and was formally abolished in 1956 when the first constitution came into force). General Zia, in compliance with traditional Islamic law, wanted to separate the primary Muslim–Pakistani nation (that is a nation entitled to equal rights) from the non-Muslims. This reform was welcomed by some Christian leaders and the Catholic Church as it assured the minorities representation while in the general electorates they tended to be ignored. However, the more radical sections of the Catholic and Protestant communities expressed their opposition to it, alleging that separate electorates excluded them from the Pakistani nation and gave constitutional sanction for discrimination and segregation.The apprehensions of the Christian radicals seem to have been borne out by subsequent experience. In the late 1980s several acts of violence were carried out by fanatical sections of Muslim society against Christians. At least one murder and many cases of burning of churches and Christian property were reported in the early 1990s. Under the Blasphemy Ordinance of 1986 a Christian, Gul Masih, was sentenced to death by a Pakistani lower court in October 1992 for allegedly having made derogatory remarks about the Prophet Muhammad.

In Sindh some half a million Hindus remained after partition. Very few Hindus were to be found elsewhere in West Pakistan. After the riots in the earliest years after independence Sindhi Hindus preferred to lie low and avoid attracting political attention as their religious links with India place them in a vulnerable position in Pakistan. Communal attacks against Hindus began to occur in the mid 1980s as the overall ethnic situation in Sindh deteriorated. Following the destruction of the Babri Mosque at Ayodhya and the brutal killings of Muslims which accompanied it, a fierce reaction took place in Pakistan. Destruction of property and temples took place all over Pakistan, and Hindus were killed and injured in their hundreds, mainly in Sindh but also in Baluchistan. Although the government officially urged the people to exercise restraint, some ministers were responsible for whipping up mass hysteria through crass demagogy and other such devices. Mobs of angry protesters marched on to Hindu temples and destroyed them. Ironically most temples in Punjab were no longer in use as places of worship simply because there were no Hindus around to use them. Impoverished, homeless Muslim refugee families from 1947 had been residing in some of them. The net result of the mob fury was that these people were left without a roof over their head.

As regards the minor religious minorities such as the Parsees, Sikhs and Buddhists, they have also been adversely affected by the increasing theocratisation of Pakistan. In the Gilgit and Chitral regions are to be found Ithna Ashari Shias, Ismaili Shias and Sunnis. Here the competition to win converts between Iran, the Ismaili mission headed by Prince Karim Agha Khan (based in Europe), and the Zia government backed by the Saudis, led to several clashes in the 1980s. The tiny community of some 4,000 of the Kalash Kafirs of the Chitral Valley were in particular subjected to aggressive conversion onslaughts during the Zia regime. Some *ulama* demanded that all non-Muslims should be declared *dhimmis* and made to pay *jizya* (poll tax). Such a drastic demand has not received serious attention from the state thus far.

Notwithstanding the considerable differences between the modernist and the *ulama*'s visions of the Islamic state, what all notions of an Islamic polity contain inescapably is a logical link between membership in the Islamic community and citizenship rights in the state: the true believer has to be differentiated from the hypocrite, the heretic and the non-believer. Such an in-built bias imposes several disabling limitations upon Pakistan's prospects of becoming a democratic state and society.

Muslim pilgrims gathering in prayer and remembrance outside the tomb of the Sufi saint Muin al-Din Chisti in Ajmer, hoping for blessings and intercession (photo: Ron Geaves, 1998).

India

India is constitutionally a secular, democratic state. The total population of India is estimated at 967 million. Some 82.6 per cent of the population consists of Hindus including the high castes, the low castes, and casteless and tribal peoples. The Indian Muslim population is some 127 million or 12 per cent of the total. However, except for the State of Jammu and Kashmir, where Muslims make up more than 66 per cent of the population, they are a minority in all other Indian states. The greatest concentration of Muslims is in the Kashmir Valley, where they constitute more than 94 per cent of the population, and in a district of Mallapuram in Kerala in southern India where they form a majority. In some towns and cities of the largest and politically most important State of Uttar Pradesh (UP) Muslims form a significant part of the population. There is an urban bias in the composition of the Muslim population: 30 per cent are town-dwellers as compared to their overall proportion of 12 per cent of the total Indian population. The overwhelming majority of Indian Muslims are Sunnis (85–90 per cent). The Barelwi group is the largest, although the Deobandis have enjoyed greater prestige with the Indian government because of the support

237

they gave to the Congress movement during the freedom struggle against the British. The Ahl-i-Hadith denomination is also to be found as small groupings among orthodox Muslims. The followers of the Shafii school are to be found along the Malabar coast. The Ithna Ashari Shias are found in all parts of northern and northwestern India, but are concentrated mostly in the Lucknow district of UP. Smaller Shia communities consisting of Ismailis and Bohras are located on the west coast, mainly around Bombay.

The creation of Pakistan as a separate Muslim state was a devastating blow to the overall position of Muslims who stayed behind in India. It greatly angered the Hindus for whom the whole subcontinent was an indivisible cultural whole wherein were located their ancient roots. Moreover, Muslim entrepreneurs and the intelligentsia of northern India migrated to Pakistan leaving a largely poor and uneducated Muslim population behind. Consequently Muslims were severely handicapped in competing for the opportunities that development brought about. At the beginning of 1981, out of a total of 3,883 Indian Administrative Service Officers only 116 were Muslims. In the Indian Police Service there were fifty Muslims out of a total of 1753. In other lower-grade services the same under-representation was to be found. Employment in the private sector was much worse. Such under-representation does not make sense in terms of Muslim incompetence alone; discrimination in practice surely exacerbates the overall inability of Muslims to find employment. Muslim ownership in the production sector is limited to small-scale production. Since the mid 1970s many Muslim craftsmen have been able to make substantial gains from business and employment opportunities in the Arab countries. It has been suggested that increasing anti-Muslim violence in the 1980s has been concentrated in those towns and cities which have undergone economic development and where Muslims have fared well. The police sent to control the situation are known to have joined the attacks on Muslims.

In recent years Hindu nationalists have sought to highlight the alleged wrongs done against the Hindu community and its religion by the Muslims between the thirteenth and nineteenth centuries. The classic allegation is that in 1528 the founder of the Mughul empire, Zahiruddin Babur, had a mosque built at Ayodhya in northern India on the exact spot where the god Rama is believed to have been born thousands of year ago. Such a claim has been rejected by more serious Indian historians. Some even doubt the historical existence of Rama. At any rate, a campaign to dismantle the mosque began in real earnest in 1986. On the other hand Muslims organised themselves to defend the Babri mosque. Prime Minister Rajiv Gandhi tried to placate the inflamed feelings on both sides by, on the one hand, allowing the Hindus to pray inside the mosque, and on the other, by recognising Urdu as the second official language of UP.

The Hindu nationalists, however, intensified their campaign for the destruction of the mosque. It culminated in hundreds of thousands of extremists from different parts of the country coming to Ayodhya in early December 1992. They easily overpowered the small police force, climbed onto the mosque and demolished it in a few hours. Brutal mob attacks on Muslims occurred all over India. Suddenly India was in the midst of perhaps the most serious communal conflict between Hindus and Muslims since the partition. The Hindu fundamentalists intend to destroy some 3,000 other such mosques built allegedly on Hindu temples and holy places.

Indian Muslims have generally supported secular parties, and until the mid 1970s they formed a vote bank for the Congress Party. Thereafter the Muslim vote split because Congress was no longer perceived as a consistent protector of minorities. Communal riots against Muslims intensified during the 1980s. It was not simply the cumulative effect of communal conflicts which adversely affected the position of Indian Muslims. The peculiar working of the Indian political system has inadvertently enhanced their isolation. Given the strong sense of group affiliations, especially in the rural areas, most people relate to the political process not as individuals but as part of socio-cultural blocs and groups. Caste, religion, sect, ethnic group, all serve as rallying points for aggregating group interests and making demands on the political system. Important in this connection are local community leaders who bargain the support of their group with different political parties in return for promises of specific facilities and concessions to their group. For religious minorities such group bargaining only strengthens communal isolation.

The pro-Congress Deobandi *ulama* of the Jamiyat-i-Ulama-i-Hind extracted significant concessions on Muslim issues from the Congress-led post-independence government of Prime Minister Jawahar Lal Nehru, which in the longer run tended to hinder the integration of the Muslims in a larger modern Indian citizenry. Among them the most crucial was the preservation of the Muslim Personal Law in its traditional form. Thus while the Indian government made some radical modernist changes in the Hindu religious affairs, such as conferring the right on the so-called Untouchables to enter Hindu temples, passage of the Hindu Marriage Act, and so on, the Muslims were permitted to practise their own traditional personal law which upholds the superior position of men in family matters.

In 1985 the problem of Muslim personal law for modern society and equal citizenship rights was highlighted when Shah Bano, a middle-aged Muslim woman, who had been divorced by her husband, M.A. Khan, sought economic support from her former husband. According to Indian law, as a citizen of India, she was entitled to financial support in case she had no economic means of her own. She filed a petition in the Madhya Pradesh High Court which ruled in her favour. But her ex-spouse took the plea that in Islam no such permanent financial responsibility devolved upon the man beyond the limited period of *idat* (period of probation of three months following divorce so as to establish if pregnancy had occurred prior to dissolution of marriage). Khan appealed in the Indian Supreme Court against the judgment, but his pleas were rejected. Meanwhile, the case assumed great political significance as the Muslim community led by the *ulama* and other conservative leaders including Sayyid Shahabuddin, president of the influential All-India Muslim Majlis-i-Mushawarat (Muslim consultative assembly), took to the streets and protested vehemently against the alleged intrusion into the internal domain of Muslim social life by the Indian state.

Many modern Muslims including academics, lawyers, jurists, members of parliament, women activists and political workers came out boldly in favour of the judgment. Arguments were put forth by both sides of Muslim opinion, but the conservative forces greatly outnumbered the modernists. The whole episode turned into a great manifestation of Islamic traditionalism. Unwilling to antagonise the large Muslim vote bank Prime Minister Rajiv Gandhi went along with the traditional standpoint, and a special law exempting Muslims from the general divorce law was passed.

Given the exposed and vulnerable nature of the Indian Muslim community, any apparent sign of Muslim strength can antagonise Hindu nationalists. There is a widespread belief in India that the Muslim population is increasing more rapidly than others because of early marriage. Indian Muslims have also had some advantage in finding employment in the Gulf region. Both Iran and Saudi Arabia have taken a keen interest in the affairs of the Muslim community in India. Substantial economic aid is given to Muslim religious organisations for the building of study centres, Quran schools and the upkeep of mosques. Such aid, given mainly to *ulama* and groups supportive of these countries, has helped bolster the position of conservative Muslims *vis-à-vis* modernist Muslims. These changes have been perceived as threats by Hindu parties. Even the national press has from time to time commented negatively on the growing Islamic assertiveness among Indian Muslims.

In this context, the question of conversions to Islam are of particular significance. In the past, the Hindu social order, sharply divided into two virtually separate social categories, on the one hand, the so-called twice-born upper three castes and, on the other, the unclean low castes and Untouchables, functioned more or less as two separate societies. Historically conversions to Islam, Sikhism and Christianity had come largely from the lower ranks. This had not been seen by caste Hindus as a major loss. However, the growing religious nationalism of the early twentieth century and the post-independence need for votes in the democratic process rendered the question of numbers and numerical strength crucial for politics. Upper caste Hindu nationalists have therefore been confronted by a dilemma. On the one hand, they resent the upward mobility of the lower castes, which has been facilitated through the system of fixed quotas introduced soon after independence by the Nehru

A placard on the island of Diu exhorting national unity instead of religious disintegration (photo: Christer Lagvik, 1992).

government and later expanded; on the other, if the low castes show a willingness to embrace another religion it creates panic among the Hindu nationalists because it means a loss in terms of numbers. Embracing another religion by the low castes has not only been viewed with dismay by Hindu nationalists, but even the secular sections of society have reacted with concern and bewilderment. This problem became forcefully manifest when some Dalits (the so-called Untouchables, also called Harijans) embraced Islam in the southern state of Tamil Nadu in 1981. Several Hindu nationalist parties and organisations demanded that a law be imposed which would prohibit provision of economic benefits and other alluring promises by foreign missionaries (Christian, Muslim and others) to

Indians with a view to converting them to their faith. Some state governments have enacted such restrictions, but thus far such a law has not been adopted by the central Indian parliament.

In the late 1980s a powerful separatist movement emerged in Kashmir among the Muslims. It led to a major confrontation involving violence and terrorism on a large scale between Indian police and paramilitary forces and Kashmiri separatists. The situation has been aggravated by covert Pakistani backing of the Kashmiri militants. In retaliation Hindu extremists have intensified anti-Muslim propaganda in other parts of India.

Bangladesh

Bangladesh emerged as an independent state on December 16, 1971. The founders of the new state initially declared it to be a secular democratic state. Gradually, Islamic features have been added, but constitutionally it continues to be a democracy. The current population of Bangladesh is estimated at 125 million. Of these 85.3 per cent are Muslims, almost entirely Sunnis. Upper caste Hindus constitute 6.8 per cent, and 6.6 per cent belong to the low-caste and casteless categories. Buddhists, Christians and others make up the rest of the population. Ever since the sixteenth century the eastern region of Bengal was called Vanga and the western called Gauda. The eastern region was predominantly of Mongoloid extraction whereas West Bengalis were largely of mixed Aryan stock. Although for more than 500 years both regions were under Muslim rule, conversions to Islam took place largely in East Bengal where Buddhism had a large following.

In 1204 a Turkish adventurer, Ikhtyaruddin Bakhtyar, led the first Muslim incursion into Bengal. He founded a kingdom which included portions of western and northern Bengal. It was however not until the last decade of the thirteenth century that eastern and southern Bengal were penetrated by a Muslim power. It took another 200 years before the whole of Bengal was conquered. In the long drawn-out struggles for expansion different Turkish and Afghan factions competed with one another besides fighting the Hindu rulers in the region. Later the Mughuls defeated all other powers and annexed Bengal to their empire.

In much of Bengal the caste system was practised with great rigidity by the Hindu upper castes. The lower castes and the large Buddhist peasantry were therefore subjected to various cruel and oppressive forms of degradation. Sufism entered Bengal as a liberating force. Many early Sufis active in Bengal promoted social reform. Their monasteries provided sanctuary where ideas of human equality and solidarity were encouraged. Consequently many oppressed Hindus and Buddhists eagerly entered the fold of Islam. All the major Sufi orders were active in Bengal. Typically the more innovative Sufis tried to blend their teachings with local cultural traditions. However, Bengali Muslim society was typically marked by the division between *ashraf* and *am log*. The *ashraf* spoke Persian and wrote in Persian or Arabic. Common Muslim converts spoke Bengali in everyday life. Although it was predominantly Sunni Islam which spread in Bengal, old Hindu customs and traditions continued to be observed by the masses. During the seventeenth century some Shia influence also appeared when fearful Shias sought refuge in Bengal from the growing Sunni orthodoxy at the court of Aurangzeb. Few significant local conversions to Shiism took place, however.

The reformist-militant movements of Titu Mir and the Faraizis in the early nineteenth century imparted a strong sense of Islamic identity to significant sections of the Bengali Muslim peasantry. In the peculiar class structure of Bengal, Muslims were generally the poorer community while landlords were often upper caste Hindus. The first partition of Bengal took place in 1905 when Lord Curzon divided it into West Bengal (predominantly Hindu) and East Bengal (predominantly Muslim). The Hindus lamented it, but Muslims soon realised that there were some advantages in it for them. The Bengali nationalists, who were almost entirely Hindus, began a massive campaign against the partition. It included terrorist attacks upon the British and the Muslims. In 1911 the government annulled the partition under pressure from the Hindus and the Congress Party. The ghost of the 1905–11 confrontation continued to haunt the two communities. In the 1945–46 elections the Bengali Muslims voted in favour of separating from West Bengal and joining Pakistan.

Much to the chagrin of the Bengalis, in March 1948 Governor-General Mohamed Ali Jinnah declared in a public speech at Dhaka that Bengali shall be the sole national language of Pakistan. Now, Bengali was not only the mother-tongue of more than 55 per cent of united Pakistan's population, but also a highly developed language which had been in official usage for a long time. Jinnah's speech provoked angry demonstrations by Bengali students. The language question was to become the centrepiece of emergent Bengali nationalism. In the economic sphere also, Bengali grievances began to mount. The flight of Hindus to India did provide opportunities for the Bengali Muslims to advance into lower- and medium-range professions and economic activities. However, the top positions in the bureaucracy and army remained in the hands of West Pakistanis. Similarly, big business and industry located in East Pakistan was owned by the West Pakistan bourgeoisie. The period 1955–65 saw Pakistan make impressive strides in industrial development, mostly in light consumer production. However, East Pakistan's share in the economic wealth was much less than its contribution to it. The Awami League led by Shaykh Mujibur Rahman appeared as the main representative of Bengali separatism in the late 1960s. Thus when in 1970 the first general elections were held in Pakistan the Awami League made a clean sweep of the polls and won 160 out of 162 seats for East Pakistan in the 300-member Pakistan National Assembly. It was therefore entitled to form the government at the centre. However, President Yahya Khan refused to hand over power to Mujib. This brought forth massive strikes and disturbances in East Pakistan. On the evening of March 25, 1971 the army launched a military operation against perceived targets of a growing insurgence. Thereafter followed several months of bloodshed and debauchery at the hands of the army. Hindus, students and trade union activists were particular targets of the army. Several million Bengalis fled to India. Thousands came back trained to fight the army. They wreaked their vengeance with equal barbarity. Thousands of West Pakistani armed and civilian personnel, their families and Bengali and Bihari collaborators were killed. On December 3, the Indian army intervened in support of the Bengali resistance. By December 17, 1971 the Pakistan army had been defeated.

Although Bangladesh has the usual subdivisions of the Hanafi school of orthodox law and rites, and traditionalist *ulama* of the Barelwi brand and *pirs* abound in large numbers, this does not mean that they enjoy the same degree of prestige as in Pakistan. There are several reasons for this: population growth in one of the most densely population countries in the world has resulted in fragmentation of landholdings; the continuing influence of the reformist movements of the last century created a stronger social base for puritanical and egalitarian Islam; dispossession of the major Hindu landlord class who fled to India in 1947 and land reforms after independence resulted in the liquidation of large-scale landlordism. Consequently the conservative social order upon which typically the *pir*-cum-landlord structure thrives had been effectively undermined. Moreover, the overall prestige and influence of the *ulama* had seriously been undermined during the liberation struggle against Pakistan. The East Pakistan branch of the Jamaat-i-Islami and some other *ulama* supported the Pakistan army. They had therefore been thoroughly discredited in the new state.

Notwithstanding the initial declaration of Bangladesh as a secular-democratic people's republic, the influence of Islam in politics has gradually been growing. There are various reasons for this. Relations between Bangladesh and India became strained after the assassination of the founder of Bangladesh, Shaykh Mujibur Rahman, in 1975. Disputes arose between the two countries on several economic and political issues, but the most serious was one about proper sharing of river waters. Consequently the religious perspective on politics found a revival in Bangladeshi politics. The government of General Ziaur Rahman (1975–81) began emphasising the Islamic cultural identity of the state. In 1977 the constitution was amended and instead of the commitment to secularism it was stated that trust and faith in the Almighty Allah alone was to be the basis of all actions. In 1988 Islam was declared the state religion. These changes facilitated cultivation of good relations with Saudi Arabia and the Emirates. Bangladesh began to receive economic aid and Bangladeshi workers were permitted in substantial numbers to seek work in Saudi Arabia and the Gulf region. The governments of General Ershad (1982–90), and Mrs Khalida Zia (1991–96) continued to emphasise the Islamic identity. Gradually relations with Pakistan were also normalised.

Bangladeshi Muslim women have traditionally not been observing the *purdah* (seclusion of women) as strictly as is common in many other parts of South Asia. Most wear the sari or a flowing skirt covering the legs. Although the rate of literacy is very low among women an increasing number are now receiving a modern education. The Muslim Family Laws Ordinance of 1961, adopted during the Pakistan period, still applies, making polygamy difficult and conditional. However, the general Islamic revival has also hit Bangladesh and its typical concerns have been questions about Islamic morality and piety, which in turn have meant calls for making the female population conform more strictly to traditional Islamic requirements of segregation. The state has not thus far gone along with such demands.

Bengali Hindus constitute the main religious minority of Bangladesh. They are dispersed throughout the country both in the rural and urban areas. In 1947 Hindus made up some 23 per cent of the population of East Pakistan. In 1951 the Hindu percentage had dropped to 22 per cent. By 1961 it declined to 18 per cent. Hindus kept migrating to India because of an increasing sense of insecurity resulting from recurrent communal riots. During the 1971 civil war, the Pakistan army particularly targeted the Hindus in its cleansing operations. This resulted in a massive flight to India. The delayed census held in 1974 (that for 1971 could not be held because of the civil war) reported the Hindu population as only 13.5 per cent. Thus a decrease of almost 5 per cent occurred because of the civil war. The 1981 census gives the Hindu population as 12.1 per cent. Therefore the trend of Hindus migrating to India has continued. Attacks on Hindus increased dramatically after the 1992 Babri Mosque incident at Ayodhya in India. Retaliatory attacks resulting in destruction of Hindu temples, and acts of arson, looting, rape and killing against Hindus took place in Bangladesh. It led to a new wave of migration of Hindus to India.

As regards Christians and other minorities dispersed in the society, very little is known. The tiny Buddhist tribal communities of the Chittagong Hill Tracts have many grievances, largely of economic nature, against the state and the Bengali majority. They especially resent the encroachment on their forest habitats by Bengali plains-people and through various government developmental schemes. Additionally, the attempts of the Bangladesh government to propagate Islam in their area with the help of Saudi funds is perceived as a serious threat to their cultural autonomy and identity. An armed conflict between the Bangladesh government and the tribal people resulted in thousands of deaths during the 1970s and 1980s. Nothing much has been heard during the 1990s, but a final peace accord has not yet been agreed.

Sri Lanka

Sri Lanka is a democracy which acknowledges a special relationship between Buddhism and the island. The total population of Sri Lanka is estimated in excess of 18 million. The largest ethnic group in Sri Lanka is the Sinhalese who make up 74 per cent of the total population. Sinhalese are overwhelmingly Buddhists. The second group is the Tamils. They are classified as two distinct groups: Sri Lankan Tamils who have been on the island since time immemorial and the so-called Indian Tamils who were brought from southern India to work as indentured labour on the plantations in the nineteenth century. Together the Tamil population constitutes 18.2 per cent of the total population. The Tamils are predominantly Hindus. There are significant Protestant and Catholic minorities among both Sinhalese and Tamils. Muslims constitute some 1.3 million or 7.4 per cent of Sri Lankan population. Known as the Moors, Sri Lankan Muslims traditionally trace their presence to the settlements established by Muslim traders and emigrés in the very early period of Islam. These settlements were located on the northeast, north and western coasts of Sri Lanka. Currently significant Muslim minorities are to be found all over the country, but are concentrated in the eastern districts of Amaparai (41.5 per cent), Trincomalee (28.9 per cent), Batticalo (23.9 per cent) and Mannar (26.6 per cent) in the north. All these are Tamil-dominated areas. There are also some Indian and Malay Muslims settled on the island. Sri Lankan Muslims subscribe to the Sunni-Shafii branch of orthodox Islam. Their mother tongue is almost invariably Tamil. A Muslim élite consisting mostly of gem merchants is concentrated in the capital Colombo.

A violent ethnic conflict has been raging since the late 1950s in Sri Lanka between the Sinhalese and mainly Sri Lankan Tamils. During the 1980s, the level of violence escalated drastically. While the Sinhalese insist upon keeping Sri Lanka a unitary state the Tamil extremists have gone beyond demands for regional autonomy and declared the creation of a separate Tamil homeland as their goal. Inevitably the various other communities on the island have been affected by the violence around them.

The strategic location of Sri Lanka in the Indian Ocean rendered it an important element in inter-coastal trade between Europe and the Far East. Arabs were already engaged in such trade in the pre-Islamic period. After the rise of Islam the sea-trade in the region came to be dominated by Arabs who established permanent trading posts on Sri Lanka. Those early Arabs maintained close contacts with the Arab world until the fall of the Abbasid caliphate in 1258. Thereafter they turned towards the Muslims living along the Malabar coast of southern India. Their numbers grew naturally, as well as through an influx of Muslims from India and conversions of the local population to Islam. Although some petty Muslim chiefdoms existed during the mediaeval period, Muslims have not historically displayed any ambition to establish an Islamic state. On the whole, Muslims benefited from the religious tolerance of the Sinhalese kings and the local population of pre-colonial times. Some Muslims have prospered as gem merchants, but most work as subsistence farmers.

The arrival of the Portuguese in 1505 greatly worsened the position of the Moors in Sri Lanka. The Portuguese were not only trade rivals of the Arabs, but entertained a profound hatred for the Islamic faith. As they expanded and consolidated their hold over the island they made every effort to destroy the flourishing trade of the Muslims and used force to convert them to Christianity. In response the Muslims sided with those local princes who resisted the Portuguese. Notwithstanding considerable hardship the Muslim population resisted successfully the proselytising zeal of the Portuguese. The loss in material terms was considerable, however. The Dutch who succeeded the Portuguese in 1658 were also hostile towards the Muslims, although the latter had sided with them against the Portuguese. The Dutch tried to drive away Muslims both from international trade as well as from the internal retail trade sector. Also restrictions were imposed on certain social and religious ceremonies of the Muslims, and Muslim merchants from India were denied residence rights on Sri Lanka.

Consequently when the British sought to establish their power on Sri Lanka the Muslims supported them. The new colonial power did not hurt the interests of the Muslims. However, when the English introduced modern education in the new colony, the Sri Lankan Tamils especially but also Sinhalese took advantage of the new opportunities offered by the missionary schools. The Muslims stayed away fearing that education in such schools might endanger their children's faith in Islam. On the other hand, a more active and positive interest was taken in the economic opportunities offered by the British. Consequently Muslims entered the plantation economy, the communication and transport sector, and the packing and fishing industries as contractors and middle-men. It was however in the gem industry that the Moors continued to hold a leading position.

The apathy towards modern, English-medium education shown by the Muslims inevitably affected them adversely in terms of communication and political influence in relation to the colonial government. The traditional Quran schools known as the *maktabs* and *madrasas* imparted a basic knowledge of traditional Islam and helped maintain a sense of separate religious identity, but it enhanced the isolation of the Muslim community from the rest of society. In the late nineteenth century some leading Muslims such as M.C. Siddi Lebbe, Arabi Pasha (an exile from Egypt), I.L.M. Abdul Azeez and Wapichi Marikar joined forces to rectify the situation. In their view, the acquisition of modern education was imperative for Muslims to keep pace with the changes underway and to partake effectively in the economic and political spheres. At first Muslims paid little heed to these initiatives, but the modernisers persisted with their efforts. Eventually attitudes changed and a modern-educated intelligentsia among Muslims also began to evolve. By the turn of the century a modern-educated political élite emerged among the Moors which demanded representation in the Legislative Council.

Earlier in 1888 a controversy raged between Tamil and Muslim leaders over the question of the exact ethnic origin of the Muslims. Sir Ponnambalam Ramannathan, a Tamil leader, asserted that the Muslims of Sri Lanka were merely Tamils converted to Islam. The implication of such an assertion was that Muslims should assimilate into Tamil society and give up claims to special identity. This position was challenged by I.L.M. Abdul Azeez who stressed the Arab ancestry of the Muslims. Beginning in 1889, Muslims were nominated to represent their group in the Legislative Assembly. Later, separate electorates were introduced for the minorities and Muslims were elected on that basis in the expanded Legislative Assembly. On the other hand, the fairly peaceful relations between Muslims and Sinhalese suffered a setback at the beginning of the twentieth century when rising Sinhalese nationalism began to blame non-Sinhalese and non-Buddhists for the ills of Sinhalese society. In 1915 anti-Muslim riots were instigated by Sinhalese nationalists, especially against the coastal Moors who were recent arrivals from South India.

The Donoughmore Commission (1927–28) arrived from Britain to study the problems of communal representation and to suggest changes. It recommended universal adult franchise, but rejected the principle of communal representation. Universal suffrage was instituted in 1931, but because the Muslim community was dispersed in society it was a loser under the new system of joint electorates. Only one Muslim candidate was elected under the new system to the first assembly, and in the elections to the second assembly none was elected. Meanwhile the British had been preparing Sri Lanka for self-rule. In 1944 Lord Soulbury arrived as the head of a new constitutional commission whose task was to prepare the framework for an eventually self-governing Sri Lanka. Leaders of the Sri Lankan Tamils pleaded before the Soulbury Commission for a 50–50 share in power between the Sinhalese and the rest of the minorities. Muslim leaders did not support such a demand and instead sought to align themselves with the Sinhalese in national politics. On the other hand they demanded separate electorates. The Soulbury Commission rejected such a demand. It prescribed a unitary form of government based on the Westminster model. Although it expressly forbade discrimination against minorities a bill of rights clearly defining the rights of individuals and minorities was not included. The constitution was adopted and enforced in 1947.

The Colombo-based Muslim leadership continued in the post-independence period to align itself with the Sinhalese. The Sinhalese responded by including some Muslim ministers in the government. Amid the intensified ethno-nationalist hostilities of the 1980s between the Sinhalese and Tamils the Muslims also reviewed their Islamic identity. Partly such identity was a reflection of the exposure of many Sri Lankan Muslims to Arab culture. From the 1970s onwards Sri Lankan Muslims had been seeking employment in the Gulf region in large numbers. Those who stayed there a few years returned home groomed in Islamic culture and practices. Alienated from the growing Sinhalese–Tamil polarisation, and frequently exposed to brutal attacks from both sides, Muslim youths were easily attracted to the Islamic discourse of the returnees from the Arab countries. Consequently, congregational offering of prayers became more widespread, and the Friday prayers in particular were attended in large numbers. Organisations such as the Moors Islamic Cultural Home and the Islamic Secretariat have been trying to propagate chaste Islamic habits among the young. Such developments have led to discussions about communal solidarity. In this regard the wealthy Muslims have been severely criticised in community discussions for neglecting welfare obligations towards the poor. Particularly evading the alms tax, *zakat,* has been made a major issue in the discussions.

The escalation of ethnic conflict between Sinhalese and Tamils inevitably dragged the Muslim community into its sphere. The policy of Sinhalese colonisation in the east and north also hurt the Muslim population living there. Consequently, as Muslims became politicised, both Sinhalese and Tamil extremists intensified their terrorist activities against them. In response the Muslims established their own militias and began to organise defence committees. However, as most of them were settled among Tamils the main confrontation took place between them and the Tamils. The policy of ethnic cleansing which the Tamil separatists have been pursuing since 1988 in the north and east led to considerable loss of Muslim life and property. Therefore Muslims have been demanding the creation of a Muslim province or council in the east and north.

Prior to the colonial intervention Sri Lankan Muslims practised the *sharia* in their communal matters. The Portuguese period was one of general suppression of Muslims and this applied to their laws too. The Dutch compiled a code of Muslim Law, which was then approved by Muslim headmen and recognised by the Dutch judicial system. The Code covered inheritance, succession, marriage and divorce. The British recognised the Code and later undertook a revision of it in 1806. The revised code was applied under an Ordinance of 1852. The present-day Muslims continue to be governed by the Code of Muslim Law, although some reforms such as compulsory registration of marriages and divorce were subsequently added to reduce the abuse of traditional law by men. On the whole, Sri Lankan Muslim women are freer than their counterparts on the subcontinent. Because of the strong Tamil element in the Muslim community and the absence of a sovereign political power among Muslims, the pressures towards conformity to orthodox *purdah* are less effective. Education among Muslim women is limited although a few Muslim girls' colleges and training institutions do exist.

Maldives

The tiny Maldives republic in the Indian Ocean consists of more than 1,000 coral islands which together make up only 298 square kilometres of dry land. It is, however, a very densely populated state. Its population of 260,000 is predominantly of Sinhalese and Tamil extraction with some intermixing with Arab settlers. Until the middle of the twelfth century, Buddhism was the main religion of the people. In 1153 the king converted to Islam and made his followers embrace the new faith. It is believed that a Moroccan traveller, Abu Barakaat Yusuf al-Barbary was responsible for this conversion. He introduced the Maliki branch of Sunni Islam. Another version credits Sheikh Yusuf Shamsuddin of Täbriz, a renowned scholar, for the conversion of Maldivians to Islam. At any rate, the Shafii branch had prevailed in the Maldives for a long time. The language spoken by the people is Devehi, an Indo–European language related to Sinhala. Although Maldives is a traditional Muslim society its cultural ethos bears a heavy imprint of Sri Lankan culture.

Since the arrival of the Portuguese in the sixteenth century to the Maldives, European influence has existed – not continuously but intermittently – on the islands. In 1887 the Maldives became a British protectorate but retained internal self-government under a sultan. In 1965 Maldives became independent and in 1968 a republic. Under the 1968 constitution the president is elected by popular vote for a five-year period. The legislative assembly, the Majlis, consists of forty-eight members and serves also for five years. Forty of its members are elected and eight are nominated by the president. In recent years the president, Mamoon Abdul Gayoon, has assumed rather absolute powers notwithstanding the elective nature of his position. In doing so he has been flirting with Islamic symbolism to legitimise authoritarian modifications in his approach to politics.

Literature

For a general historical account of mainland South Asian Muslims prior to independence, see Mohammad Mujeeb, *The Indian Muslims* (London: George Allen and Unwin, 1967). See also Ram Gopal, *Indian Muslims: A Political History (1858–1947)* (Lahore: Book Traders, 1976) and *Muslim Self-Statement in India and Pakistan 1857–1968*, eds. Aziz Ahmad and G.E. von Grunebaum (Wiesbaden: O. Harassowitz, 1970). For the recent period before independence, see Wilfred C. Smith, *Modern Islam in India* (Lahore: Sh. Muhammad Ashraf, 1963). See also Peter Hardy, *The Muslims of British India* (Cambridge: Cambridge University Press, 1972). For a historical account of the role of the *ulama* in northern Indian politics, see Ishtiaq Husain Qureshi, *Ulema in Politics* (Karachi: Mareef, 1974). See also Ziya-ul-Hasan Faruqi, *The Deoband School and the Demand for Pakistan* (Lahore: Progressive Books, 1980). Contemporary Muslim communities in South Asia are described in *Muslim Communities of South Asia: Culture, Society and Power*, ed. Triloki Nath Madan (New Delhi: Manohar, 1995). Sufism in the Indian subcontinent is discussed in Shuja Alhaq, *A Forgotten Vision: A Study of Human Spirituality in the Light of the Islamic Tradition* (London: Minerva Press, 1996). For a statement of the modernist approach to Islam, see Sir Muhammad Iqbal, *The Reconstruction of Religious Thought in Islam* (Lahore: Sh. Muhammad Ashraf, 1960) and for a statement of the Islamist (fundamentalist) approach to Islam, see Abul Ala Mawdudi, *The Islamic Law and Constitution* (Lahore: Islamic Publications, 1980).

An introduction to Islam in contemporary South Asia is given in *Islam in Asia: Pakistan, India, Bangladesh, Sri Lanka, Indonesia, Philippines, Malaya*, ed. Asghar A. Engineer (Lahore: Vanguard, 1986), pp. 113–226; André Wink (ed.), *Islam, Politics and Society in South Asia* (Delhi: Manohar, 1990); and Katherine P. Ewing, *Shariat and Ambiguity in South Asian Islam* (Delhi: Oxford University Press, 1988). The role of Islam in ethnic politics and separatism of South Asian Muslims is discussed in Ishtiaq Ahmed, *State, Nation and Ethnicity in Contemporary South Asia* (London and New York: Pinter, 1996). For an analysis of the discussion on the Islamic State in Pakistan, see Ishtiaq Ahmed, *The Concept of An Islamic State: An Analysis of the Ideological Controversy in Pakistan* (New York: St. Martin's Press, 1987). See also Leonard Binder, *Religion and Politics in Pakistan* (Berkeley: University of California Press, 1961); *Report of the Court of Inquiry Constituted under Punjab Act II to Enquire into the Punjab Disturbances of 1953* (Lahore: Government Printing Press, 1954); Kalim Bahadur, *The Jamaat-i-Islami of Pakistan* (Lahore: Progressive Books, 1978); and David Gilmartin, *Empire and Islam: Punjab and the Making of Pakistan* (Delhi: Oxford University Press, 1989). For the Islamisation of law in Pakistan, see *The Application of Islamic Law in a Modern State,* ed. Anita M. Weiss (Syracuse: Syracuse University Press, 1986). Khawar Mumtaz and Farida Shaheed, *Women of Pakistan* (Lahore: Vanguard, 1987), discusses the women question in Pakistan.

A study of the post-independence situation of Indian Muslims is found in Mushirul Hasan, *Legacy of a Divided Nation: India's Muslims since Independence* (London: Hurst and Company, 1997) and Balmukand R. Agarwala, *The Shah Bano Case* (New Delhi: Arnold-Heinemann, 1986). For a general discussion on religion and politics in India, see *Religion, State and*

Politics in India, ed. Moin Shakir (Delhi: Ajanta Books, 1989). On Islam in Bangladesh, see Rafiuddin Ahmed, *The Bengali Muslims, 1871–1906: A Quest for Identity* (Delhi: Oxford University Press, 1981). See also *Islam in Bangladesh: Society, Culture and Politics*, ed. Rafiuddin Ahmed (Dacca: Itihas Samiti, 1983) and Richard M. Eaton, *The Rise of Islam and the Bengal Frontier, 1204–1760* (Berkeley: University of California Press, 1996).

Chapter Eleven

Indonesia and Malaysia

Sven Cederroth

In both Indonesia and Malaysia, two Southeast Asian countries with almost the same official language and a similar Malay culture, Islam is the predominant religion. In Indonesia, which has more Muslims than any other country and where more than 90 per cent of the population are Muslims, Islam has no official position. In principle all recognised religions are equal. In *pancasila*, the five principles which make up the constitution of the Indonesian republic, the first point refers in general terms to belief in God, without mentioning any specific religion by name. With reference to *pancasila*, the Partai Persatuan Pembangunan (PPP), the political party that is seen as the Muslim alternative in Indonesian politics, was some years ago even forbidden to use the *kaba*, the sacred black stone of Mecca, as its symbol. In Malaysia, where only somewhat more than 50 per cent of the population are Muslims, Islam is paradoxically the official state religion; and by being classified as *bumiputra*, sons of the earth, the native population, that is the Muslim Malays, have all kinds of privileges. Under the influence of a large number of orthodox mission groups, known as the *dawa*-movement, the position of Islam in Malaysian society has steadily become strengthened during the last two centuries. The two dominant Malay parties, the United Malays National Organisation (UMNO) and the Persatuan Islam se-Malaysia (PAS), Pan Malayan Islamic Party, almost seem to compete to satisfy Islamic demands. Nowadays, Muslims who are caught drinking alcoholic beverages or who neglect to fast during Ramadan, the Muslim fasting month, may be punished. In Kelantan, one of the states of the Malaysian federation, PAS attempted a few years ago to introduce *hudud*, the Muslim penal code.

What are the reasons for Islam in these two culturally and linguistically closely affiliated countries assuming such radically different roles in social and political life? Is Islam understood in the same way in both countries or could it be the case that the religious forms of expression, despite the common designation, look quite different? To be able to answer these questions, it is necessary to take a closer look at the social role of Islam in the two countries.

The Indonesian archipelago

Whenever Indonesia is discussed it is necessary to remember that this is a large and heterogeneous country. The archipelago that stretches from the Asian continent in the north to Australia in the south consists of more than 12,000 large and small islands. Of these, some 300 are inhabited by an ethnically, linguistically and culturally heterogeneous population of some 200 million people. Almost two-thirds of the total population live on the island of Java, which, however, only occupies some 8 per cent of the total land area. This means that while the Javanese are crowded together on their extremely densely populated island, the remaining third of the population is thinly spread across many almost empty islands. This demographical imbalance is only one of many easily visible paradoxes in this divided country. The number of languages, for instance, is high and it is not uncommon to encounter several different languages on one and the same island. On the small East Indonesian island of Alor, for example, there are no less than eight clearly distinguishable languages and some seventy dialects. Across the entire archipelago there are at least 250 languages and a great number of dialects.

From a cultural point of view, similar conditions persist too. With its more than 360 different ethnic groups, Indonesia is one of the world's ethnically most divided countries. In the jungles of the inner parts of the larger islands we still come across nomadic hunters and gatherers. Among these, some groups such as Kubu on Sumatra and Punan on Kalimantan belong to the Veddic race and represent the scattered remains of the oldest inhabitants of the islands who are believed to have migrated into the archipelago some 8–10,000 years ago. In the Javanese sultanates we find an old, culturally complex civilisation, with elegant forms of artistic expression, which began to flourish more than 1,000 years ago and which has produced several large empires. Between these two extremes there is a world of cultures so rich and varied that it is hardly imaginable. Over the course of millennia all the main world religions have at one time or another taken root and flourished. Beneath, however, there has always been an original Indonesian, animistic cosmology according to which every living being has a soul and which postulates the existence of a large number of spirits that affect human beings. All these various belief systems have influenced each other in many different ways and created a great number of original forms of religion, many of which are still alive and flourishing.

In many cases, what is formally called Islam is a far cry from more orthodox religious doctrines and shows varyingly strong influences, not only from the original animistic beliefs but also from Buddhism and Hinduism. During recent decades a stricter version of Islam has grown, especially among sectors of the urban population, although it is still a minority that adheres strictly to more orthodox religious tenets. On the island of Bali, Hinduism still flourishes, and in many of the outer Islands, such as Flores, Sumba and North Sulawesi, Christianity has strong footholds. In general, Indonesians show a great degree of tolerance towards other forms of belief, and, as already indicated, the *pancasila* constitution gives all the officially recognised religions (Islam, Buddhism, Christianity – Catholicism and Protestantism – and, Hinduism) an equal position. What is not accepted, however, is atheism which is here equated with communism, the ideology of which has been banned ever since the traumatic experiences connected with the coup d'état of 1965.

The western parts of the archipelago, above all Sumatra and Java, early came under the influence of the Indic cultural sphere. Over the course of the centuries, a number of more or less powerful and long-lived Hindu-Buddhist kingdoms emerged. The mightiest of these, the legendary Majapahit, succeeded, during the thirteenth and fourteenth centuries, for the first time ever in uniting large parts of the archipelago. The Majapahit empire slowly dissolved during the latter part of the fourteenth century, and about that time Islam began to make its presence felt, first in the northwestern parts of the archipelago and then spreading slowly from there. The new religion entered the region by way of the coastal trading centres and penetrated the interior in a process that lasted a couple of hundred years. Thus, the old Hindu–Buddhist civilisation of the interior was able to withstand the advance of Islam for a long time and even after formal conversions, many of the earlier forms of belief continued to be practised. As a result of the many centuries of Hindu–Buddhist dominance during which various forms of mystical speculation had played a prominent role, pre-Islamic elements also found a fertile ground in Islam, especially in the interior kingdoms, whereas in the coastal areas a more pietistic, pure form of Islam became dominant. In the old Hindu–Buddhist core areas, Islam therefore took on a syncretistic character in which elements from different religious traditions were mixed and fertilised each other. As a result of such fertilisation a new and uniquely Javanese religion, the Agami Jawi, developed. The cleavage thus created between a more purely Islamic coastal population and syncretistic groups in the interior still persists today.

Ever since the naval route to India was discovered, the East Indian archipelago has played an important role as a source of raw materials to European merchants. At first, it was mainly all kinds of exotic spices that proved to be attractive, but later, various plantation crops such as coffee, tea and sugar were also included. As a result of its fabulous riches, the archipelago soon turned into a battlefield between a number of potential colonial powers. The Dutch finally emerged victorious from these battles, and up until the end of the Second World War Indonesia, then known as the Dutch East Indies, remained their colony. However, during the latter part of the nineteenth century and the early part of the twentieth century a

Ceremonial rice-pounding during the celebration of the Prophet Muhammad's birthday on the island of Lombok (photo: Sven Cederroth, 1987).

nationalistic resistance movement developed in Indonesia. In this resistance, the Muslims played an important role and the first nationalistic mass movement, the Sarekat Islam (SI) that was founded in 1911, had a Muslim character. During the first decade, the SI grew quickly until it comprised several million members and became the core of the anti-colonial resistance movement. The rapid growth, however, also led to divisions within the movement, and in 1921 it was split into two parts, one pan-Islamic, the other socialistic. After the division, the SI rapidly declined, and from the remnants of its two wings two political parties emerged, one a nationalist party under the leadership of later on President Sukarno and, the other, a communist party.

After the decline of the SI, the Muslim wing of the resistance movement was represented mainly by two groups, the Muhammadiyah and the Nahdatul Ulama (NU). The former group can be characterised as pietistic and modernistic. It strives to reform Indonesian Islam in such a way that while the teachings are those of the Quran, they are interpreted in a modern way. In contrast to SI, the Muhammadiyah has never become a true mass movement, but has always had its primary basis among the urban middle classes and among intellectuals. The NU, on the other hand, finds most of its support among conservative farmers in the rural areas. In its ideology, the NU departs from the Islamic tradition, as it has developed on Java, and it can therefore be described as pietistic and tradionalistic. The movement has harshly criticised Muhammadiyah because of its lack of understanding for specifically Javanese traditions. Both movements still exist and are important forces in contemporary Indonesian society.

At independence, the Muslim forces worked hard to reach their goal of having the new nation proclaimed an Islamic state. The nationalists around Sukarno realised, however, that such a declaration would cause rifts that might be impossible for the young nation to overcome. As an alternative the above-mentioned, vaguely worded, *pancasila* doctrine was therefore introduced. The, until now, only completely free elections that have been held in Indonesia took place in 1955, and it was widely expected that the Muslim parties would win a majority. However, the Islamic parties gained less than half of the votes. The results of this election are also interesting because it represents the first, and so far the only time, that we have seen an official indication of the strength of the different tendencies within Indonesian Islam. The result was that the parties representing a Javanised Islam, mainly the NU, together gained somewhat more votes than the more orthodox Muslim parties.

After the 1955 election, the influence of the orthodox Muslims diminished radically, while the strength of the Communist Party grew rapidly. During the first half of the 1960s, the party challenged president Sukarno and the nationalists in an intense power struggle. This period, now known as *Orde Lama*, the Old Order, ended with the coup d'état on October 1, 1965 and the subsequent massacres on known communists and their sympathisers. To a large extent it was the youth organisations of the Muslim parties who, together with the army, bore the main responsibility for the bloody pogroms. With the Communist Party now eliminated, there were great expectations among many orthodox Muslims that there would be a renaissance for Islam in Indonesian politics. It soon turned out, however, that the new president, Suharto, was also eager to restrict the influence of the Muslim forces. During the long rule of President Suharto – he remained in power more than thirty two years after the events that put him there – Islam has all but disappeared as a political alternative in Indonesia. The elections that have been held have been free and universal, but only three strictly controlled parties have been allowed to contest. Among these, the government-controlled party, Golkar, has always won a comfortable majority, while the other two parties have played the role of a democratic hostage. They are not allowed to work freely, and, as mentioned above, the Muslim party is not even allowed to appear in its true form. After the fall of Suharto in May 1998, the party system has been reformed, and many old and new parties now appear ready to contest in the upcoming elections scheduled to be held in 1999.

Currents in Indonesian Islam

In order to understand the situation that has been outlined above, it is necessary to take a somewhat closer look at the various currents of Indonesian Islam. In doing so, let us begin with the old Islamic syncretism, the Agami Jawi.

When Islam replaced Hindu–Buddhism as the official religion, it was as a pawn in the power struggle between various petty kingdoms. Before the arrival of Islam, mystical speculation had played a prominent part in the courts, and the acceptance of Islam did not abolish this practice – it just meant that it took on an Islamic character. To justify the king's position as a divine ruler, the royal genealogies during the Hindu time had usually been constructed so as to show a god, usually Shiva, as the founder of the dynasty. When Islam took over as the official religion, Shiva was replaced with Nabi Mohammed, the Prophet Muhammad, in the royal genealogies. However, that was about as far as it went and *adat*, the old customary law, rather than *sharia*, the Islamic law, continued to determine relations between people and regulate right versus wrong.

In an attempt to characterise the central elements of this court culture, on Java known as *priyai*, it may be appropriate to start with some words about emotions. In the *priyai* philosophy one finds a conviction that harmony with oneself as well as with the surrounding world is the primary thing for which everyone must strive. In order to achieve this harmony, the individual must first of all learn to control his or her feelings. A Javanese who aims at some refinement may never show any lack of self-restraint. Not only are bursts of fury a mortal sin, but also spontaneous manifestations of joy and other public expressions of an inner emotional life are looked upon with great displeasure. To hide all emotions and show a calm face is therefore the ideal, and white lies are fully accepted as long as they contribute to the achievement of harmonious relations. It is only when this has been achieved that the prerequisites for living a happy life have been reached. To obtain this desired harmony, the *priyai* culture allows the individual two roads, an inner and an outer.

The inner road consists of mystical practice. On Java many books about mysticism which teach different procedures have been published. These

Mourners at a funeral in the village Bayan on the island of Lombok (photo: Sven Cederroth, 1985).

books are widely read, especially among *priyai* intellectuals. The most important purpose with all Javanese mysticism seems to be to train the individual to accept the unavoidable with patience and without being upset. Thus, happiness and unhappiness are considered to be inseparably connected to each other and when one has accepted unhappiness and learnt to live with it, it is no longer a problem. The individual may disconnect his or her inner emotions from the shattering events of the outer world and create the conditions necessary to reach the final goal – *rasa*. This concept is not easy to define exactly but refers to a feeling of direct and total affinity with the universe and the forces controlling it.

The second, outer road to the kind of harmony that is a prerequisite for reaching *rasa* can be seen as complementary to the inner road. Its purpose is to prevent shattering emotions by building a protective wall around everything that is potentially upsetting. This state of things is reached by formalising social life in such a way that it is easy to anticipate – that is, all human relations have to be regulated by a strict etiquette. The Javanese are intensely status conscious, and the social distance between two persons is very clearly indicated, not only through the etiquette but also in the language spoken. A person of lower rank humbles herself or himself when she or he socialises with someone from the élite and when addressing that person, she or he does it with utmost politeness, using a careful, wrapped up and indirect language. The Javanese language can be spoken in several different ways varying from a simple and rough everyday language to a refined, ritualised way of talking. Which of the different language levels is chosen depends partly on the situation but mainly on the relative position of the two actors in the status hierarchy. Especially when two persons whose positions are more or less equal meet, a very careful and subtle searching takes place with the intention of determining the status of the other person *vis-à-vis* one's own. It is only when this has been done that it becomes possible to determine an adequate language level for communication with the other person. Tightly linked to this persistent striving for inner and outer harmony there also exists a refined form of art which, with a subtle symbolism, dramatises and enhances the basic values of the *priyai* culture. It is above all in the popular shadow-play theatre with its eternal struggle between good and bad that these values are clearly expressed. In these plays the syncretistic vein of the Javanese is also clearly visible since the legends recited are taken entirely from the classical Indian Hindu eposes Mahabarata and Ramayana.

The kind of syncretism that has been briefly described above is part of the culture of the élite and belongs to the so-called large tradition. This old court culture is still alive, and it is probably no exaggeration to say that it has had a decisive influence on the shaping of the modern Indonesian state. Many of the leading statesmen, including President Suharto himself, have a *priyai* background, which has heavily influenced his style of leadership. However, also among ordinary Javanese, such as the farmers in the thousands of villages, we come across another form of syncretistic tradition. This 'little tradition', on Java known as *abangan*, consists of a balanced integration of animistic and Hindu elements which have been thinly coated with a varnish of Islamic beliefs. It would be a mistake, however, to view the syncretistic religion of the Javanese farmers merely as a somewhat diluted and coarsened image of the large tradition. Rather, it contains many unique elements, one of the most apparent being animistic beliefs about the world as animated and inhabited by a large number of spirits of various kinds. These may influence the lives of men for good as well as for bad, and it is therefore important to be able to control the spirits and protect oneself against the evil ones. For the syncretistic Javanese, the spirit realm is an absolute reality which often and in many different ways influences people's daily lives. By referring to the spirit world, answers can be provided to unexpected, shocking or otherwise inexplicable events.

In the Javanese villages there is a category of diviners known as *dukun*. These are ordinary villagers who, by different means, are able to communicate with the spirit world. Some of them are said to possess supernatural powers which they have acquired by means of fasting and meditation. In trance such persons can communicate with the spirits and induce them to assist themselves and their friends or attack and destroy enemies. Diviners are often employed to find out the underlying reasons for

Mosque for *wetu telu* (syncretistic Muslims) in Bayan (photo: Sven Cederoth, 1985).

a sickness and to assist in curing it. Thus, most often diviners attempt to aid their fellow beings, but there are also evil ones who specialise in 'black magic' and use their magical powers to harm instead of help. Depending on how deeply a *dukun* has penetrated into the supernatural world, he or she may possess different degrees of knowledge and magical ability. A diviner may employ his ability to fight another diviner, whereby the one with superior magical knowledge and power will defeat the other. Such battles are not physical but are fought entirely by spiritual means. If a sick person believes that his or her illness is caused by a spirit which is controlled by an evil *dukun*, he may turn to another diviner and request him to fight against the first mentioned *dukun*. If the latter defeats the adversary, the person who has employed him will recover.

A central element in the syncretism of the little tradition is found in the communal meal, known as *slametan*. Generally speaking, farmers are less attracted by mystical speculation and by the subtle symbolism of the shadow plays, which are both essential elements of the large tradition. However, within the little tradition the communal meal fulfils a similar function of focusing and organising essential values by controlling emotions and behaviour. A *slametan* can be arranged for almost any conceivable purpose but is perhaps most frequent in connection with life crises of some kind. Basically, a *slametan* consists of a joint meal accompanied by a prayer, but it can be more or less elaborated depending on the wish of the person sponsoring the ceremony.

Many syncretistic Javanese, *priyai* as well as *abangan*, have experienced a great threat from more orthodox Muslims who criticise their behaviour and try to induce them to adopt other, more properly Islamic customs. It was in particular during a period for some years following the coup d'etat in 1965 that this threat was specifically acute. As a part of the fight against a perceived communist threat, a decree was issued in 1966 which stated that all Indonesians must practice an approved religion. Since Agami Jawi, the Javanese syncretism, was not among the approved religions, orthodox Muslims saw this as an opportunity to attack the Islamic syncretists. Faced with this threat, many syncretists have felt the necessity to join forces in more solid organisational forms. The various mysticist groups have therefore joined together and hold yearly congresses in which thousands of people participate. In 1984, the number of registered mystical groups amounted to no less than 353. The exact number of adherents is not known, but one of the groups, Sapta Darma, claims to have 10 million members.

Syncretist Islam on Java can be seen as an example of how earlier patterns of belief and local customs have been woven together with Islamic beliefs and practices into a uniquely Javanese interpretation of Islam. A close examination of Islamic documents will show, however, that this form of Javanese Islam deviates quite considerably from what has been prescribed by the Quran, the Sunna and the *sharia*, the Islamic law. Ever since Islam was first introduced on Java there have been persons who have reacted against local traditions influencing Islamic practice and who have adhered to a more pietistic lifestyle. But it was not until the end of the nineteenth century that such persons were able to influence the development of Indonesian Islam in a more significant way.

This gradual change of the religious climate was caused, above all, by two factors. Firstly, about 100 years ago communications with the Arab world started improving, which made it possible for a growing number of Indonesians to undertake the pilgrimage to Mecca. There they met with Muslims from other parts of the globe and were exposed to more orthodox interpretations of the religion. This exposure to the surrounding world went hand in hand with the growth of a new social class, mainly consisting of merchants in the cities. This new class was neither *priyai*-aristocrats nor peasants but represented an entirely new stratum in Javanese society. For the merchants, syncretistic Islam was identified with obsolete feudal conditions and was therefore seen as a threat against their activities. Pietistic Islam with its emphasis on individual responsibility was a suitable alternative, and the merchants proved themselves to be highly susceptible to the pietistic dogmas and practices.

Not all pilgrims came from the new emerging social classes, however. Even in the rural areas, pietistic Islam gained new adherents, above all among the leading land owners. This group was less radical and more bound to traditional modes of life than were the merchants. The two tendencies within orthodox Islam became organised in two movements, Muhammadiyah and Nahdatul Ulama. The former, which is mainly urban-based, was established in 1912 in Yogyakarta by Haji Ahmed Dahlan, the son of a batik merchant. In 1890, Dahlan went to Mecca where he studied for several years, and after returning to Yogyakarta he founded Muhammadiyah. The stated aim of the organisation was to improve educational standards, above all in religious education. The organisation also aimed at spreading its modernistic ideas to the population by publishing books and pamphlets. The basic philosophy of Muhammadiyah is that the character of the individual can be improved through education. According to Muhammadiyah, each individual can determine his or her own fate, and the organisation therefore stresses the importance of diligence and hard work as a means for the individual to improve her or his chances in life. Throughout its existence Muhammadiyah has striven for a high quality education and modern pedagogical methods. In the schools of Muhammadiyah the students are taught not only religion but also other subjects, and the curriculum is quite similar to that of the public schools.

Muhammadiyah strives for the achievement of a personal religious experience, in contrast to the routinised religion which, according to Muhammadiyah, is characteristic of Nahdatul Ulama. As already mentioned, NU has its strongest footing in the Javanese countryside, and in contrast to Muhammadiyah, this movement cares for specifically Javanese traditions. This has given rise to many conflicts between the two organisations. An example is the Javanese custom to visit the graves of one's ancestors, decorate these with flowers and burn incense. This is a syncretistic custom that is accepted by NU but which has been condemned by Muhammadiyah as representing a Hindu survival which has no place in Islam. Moreover, in contrast to Muhammadiyah, the NU maintains that the destiny of each individual is predetermined by Allah and cannot be influenced by human endeavours.

Patterns of cleavage in contemporary Indonesian Islam

Today, NU has some 25–30 million members and is thereby by far the largest religious organisation in the country. During most of its existence, from 1926–84, the NU was organised as a political party. Even though the movement never succeeded in achieving all its goals, it has nevertheless influenced the development of the country in many ways. During the entire Sukarno era, the NU took a very cautious line, by and large supporting government policies. In exchange for this support, the NU achieved many advantages, such as control of the Ministry of Religious Affairs. After the shift in power, which brought Suharto to power and established the New Order regime, the NU expected new advantages in exchange for its active assistance in the nationwide fight against communism. Suharto, however, had other ideas, and he neither supported nor cooperated with NU. This forced the party to ally itself with other Muslim groups in a new united Muslim party, Partai Persatuan Pembangunan (PPP), the United Development Party. Until today this party has never won more than some 25–30 per cent of the votes and has thus failed to establish itself as a forceful opposition to Golkar, the governing party.

After devastating internal conflicts, the NU finally, in 1984, decided to withdraw from PPP. Instead it has now established itself as a social movement and pressure group. Its role is very similar to the contemporary role played by Muhammadiyah. The decision to withdraw from PPP coincided with a shift of power within the organisation, whereby a liberal 'progressive' faction under the leadership of Abdurrahman Wahid took over. Wahid is convinced that a prerequisite for Islam to retain its attraction is a contextual interpretation of the religion, that is, it must adapt itself to changes in the surrounding society and be responsive to modern methods, techniques and knowledge. During the years following his election, Wahid established himself as a forceful critic of the Suharto regime and its lack of democratic disposition. Among other things, he criticised Suharto for having made too many concessions to militant Islamic modernists. For instance when the regime supported the establishment of Indonesia's first Islamic bank, Wahid protested and instead he led the NU into a cooperation with Summa bank, which is owned by a Christian Chinese. Wahid fears that the Muhammadiyah modernists are gaining too much influence which will eventually lead to grave conflicts with other Muslim currents as well as with adherents of other religions.

In October 1990, the weekly magazine *Monitor* published the results of a popularity survey, which placed the Prophet Muhammad in an unimpressive eleventh position. This angered many Muslims, and there were large demonstrations outside the office of *Monitor*. The government submitted to the pressure, banned the magazine and jailed the publisher who was subsequently sentenced to a five-year prison term for blasphemy. Alone among influential Muslim leaders, Wahid condemned this attack against the freedom of the press. In an interview he said that the incident clearly showed that democracy had very shallow roots in Indonesia. Partly as a reaction against these events, Wahid, together with a group of likeminded, later established the organisation Democratic Forum. This pressure group has been regarded with great suspicion by the authorities which have tried to thwart its activities. In March 1992, just before the election, Wahid called upon NU members to demonstrate their support for *pancasila* and for Islam as a democratic social power. More than 2 million participants had been expected, but due to harassments from the government a mere 200,000 joined the demonstration. The following day Wahid wrote a letter to President Suharto in which he warned about the consequences of the current development. If it continues like this, Wahid wrote, the present state will be replaced by an Islamic state.

Islam in Malaysia

Compared with neighbouring Indonesia, Malaysia is a small country with a population of some 17 million people. The present nation-state consists of two separate parts, West and East Malaysia. The former part of the country, which is politically as well as economically dominant, consists of a peninsula, the southernmost part of the Asian mainland. East Malaysia, which is poorer and less developed, is made up of the northwestern part of the island of Borneo.

Before the arrival of Islam, the Malay population had a cosmology very similar to the one prevalent in the archipelago and which can be characterised as a mixture of animism and Hinduism. The daily life was regulated by a set of rules known as *adat*. This customary law has very deep roots in Malay society and controls virtually all human relations, from private life to political conditions. There is a Malay proverb that is widely known and which reads as follows: *biar mati anak, jangan mati adat* – 'never mind if the child dies, as long as the *adat* lives on'. The Malay *adat* rules gave the feudal rulers an enormous power and a means to crush all attempts to revolt. Even after the formal acceptance of Islam, the Malays continued to adhere to their *adat*. In many fields, although far from all, the *adat* and the Islamic law collide with each other. Over a long period of time, and to a certain extent still today, pre-Islamic norms and values had a bigger influence on the development of the Malay culture than had Islam. The result was a syncretistic mixture of Islamic as well as non-Islamic practices which until quite recently was dominant in Malay Islam.

There are a number of different theories about when and from where Islam first came to Malaya. Most researchers seem to agree that this happened somewhere around the thirteenth century and that later on the fifteenth century Malacca sultanate was of central importance for the spread of Islam in the region. This sultanate was strategically situated at the straits of Malacca, whereby it was able to control trading in the whole region. At this time, Malacca had only one serious rival, the Javanese Majapahit empire, with which there was competition for power and influence. In Malacca, where Islam was accepted around 1450, Sufi teachers held prominent positions and from Malacca Sufi ideas and practices spread widely.

The Portuguese, who dominated Malacca for more than 100 years after 1530, followed a strictly anti-Islamic policy and did whatever they could to prevent further spread of the Muslim religion. When, in 1641, the Dutch succeeded in defeating the Portuguese, they chose a more tolerant policy of religion and attempted to cooperate with the Islamic Malay sultanates. About 150 years later there was a new shift of power in Malaya, when the British became the new colonial masters. In an agreement made between the sultans and the British, the latter promised not to interfere in matters pertaining to Malay customs and religion. Later practice would show, however, that the British nevertheless intervened in several areas which affected both the Malay culture and Islam. It was mainly in three important fields that the British policy proved to be of decisive importance for the future development. Firstly, and above all, since the Malay labour reserve was insufficient to cover the needs of the British, many foreign labourers, principally Chinese but also Indians, were imported to work as coolies in the tin mines and on the plantations. These immigrants lived in separate communities and were never integrated into the Malay society. A census carried out in 1921 showed that the Malays had now become a minority in their own country. Secondly, the British offered only a very limited group of Malays – mainly the aristocracy – admittance to higher secular education, while ordinary Malays only had access to elementary religious education. Thirdly, the British introduced their own administration of justice in Malaya with the result that the domestic Muslim legal system, based on the *sharia*, was relegated to a secondary place.

During the colonial period a large number of radical changes took place which resulted in new economic conditions, immigration, urbanisation, the establishment of a modern administration and a secular education policy. These new conditions contributed to the fact that the Malays now began to see themselves as a separate ethnic group in relation to other such groups. Thereby the insight grew that the Malays, as a group, had been treated unfairly, and now occupied a backward position in many respects. Towards the end of the nineteenth century, a movement rose among engaged, educated Muslims with the aim of correcting these bad conditions. This was a predecessor to what would later be known in Malaya as Islamic reformism, a movement which shows close affinity with the Indonesian modernists in the Muhammadiyah movement. The reformers were inspired mainly by the Arab world. Many Malay Muslims had studied in Mecca, Medina or Cairo where they had been influenced by reformistic ideas which they later brought with them back home to Malaya.

Just like the Indonesian modernists, the Malaysian reformers maintained that it was important to adapt Islam to the demands of the modern world. To achieve this it was necessary to return to the sources, particularly the Quran and Sunna, and gain new insights and strengths from a study of these. The Muslims had to be educated and taught to understand their own religion and the demands it put on their lifestyle. First of all it was necessary for the Malays to stop a number of non-Muslim activities such as the consumption of alcohol and dancing. According to the reformers, it was above all the Malay concern with their *adat* which had previously corrupted Islamic practices. Ideas such as these were propagated and spread among the Malays, mainly through a number of influential newspapers and journals. During the period before independence, and especially during the 1920s and 1930s, Islamic reformism was an active and important force in the transformation of Malay society. During these years an influential reformist group named Kaum Muda (the young group) was active. Their leaders were mainly non-Malay Muslims from the Arab world, India and Indonesia. The explicit aim of the young group was to purify Malay Islam by removing all Hindu-influenced remains and to fight against the feudal elements in Malay society, particularly the almost unlimited power of the sultans.

The impact of Kaum Muda as well as other reformers was restricted, however, by a number of factors. Most important among these was the fact that the battle for independence came to be fought more with ethnical than with religious overtones. Many Malays also reacted against the fact that there were mostly non-Malays among the leaders of the Kaum Muda reformers. In opposition to the Kaum Muda and their radical demands, native Malays created the Kaum Tua (the old group). They stressed ethnicity, and formed a category of 'pure Malays' (*Melayu jati*), in contrast to the immigrants, irrespective of whether these were Muslims or not. As a consequence of this attitude, the overriding demand in the fight for freedom centred on arguments about the land of the Malays, which should not be lost to non-Malays, rather than on abstract Islamic, universalistic and humanistic principles. Much of what the Islamic reformers had fought for during the first half of the twentieth century now disappeared, or was at least suppressed, when Malay leaders with strong ethnical and nationalistic inclinations took over the leadership of the independence movement.

In 1946 the United Malays National Organisation (UMNO) was created and their policy can be summarised in the catchphrase *Hidup Melayu!* (long live the Malays). Thus, UMNO's main political demands lay in the satisfaction of Malay ethnic interests, to work for a betterment of their economic, social and cultural position in society and to make sure that Malays would come to dominate in the political life of the nation. Thus, it was the Malay ethnic and nationalistic forces, in collaboration with the ruling élite, the sultans and conservative Kaum Tua members who at the time of independence opposed the growth of an Islamic political alternative.

Political parties

When Malaya reached its independence in 1957, UMNO was the leading political power. Its ethnic-nationalistic policies meant that Islam was not

A *sharia* court in Kuching (photo: Ingvar Svanberg, 1995).

given a prominent place in the constitution of the new nation. The policy of UMNO was directed towards the building of a nation rather than on the building of Islamic institutions. Although Islam was declared the official religion of the state its role was mainly ceremonial, not political. Islamic legislation was the responsibility of the sultans in each of the states of the federation. At the same time it was clearly stated in the constitution that all legislation that went against the federal law was automatically invalid. In practice this meant that if any of the states tried to implement a more far-reaching *sharia*-based legislation this was immediately invalidated by the federal constitution. Nevertheless, the sultans held a very powerful position and they also stood above the law. Thus, whatever they did they could not be taken to court. *Sharia*-based laws were applied only in the sphere of family law and were restricted to laws determining conditions for marriage and divorce. In all other cases the civil law had precedence.

As a reaction against the limited place given to Islam in the policy of UMNO, the Pan-Malayan Islamic Party, PMIP, later renamed as Persatuan Islam se-Malaysia, PAS, was created in 1951. This party has a Malay-nationalistic basis too, but with a greater emphasis on Islam as an important element of Malay identity. Most of its adherents come from the conservative rural population, and the party has concentrated on questions which are of importance for the rural Malays, such as the question about religious versus secular education. PAS often accuses UMNO of being too devoted to worldly and materialistic goals. As a consequence of this profile it is no wonder that PAS has been most successful in states such as Kelantan and Trengganu, where rural Malays constitute a large majority. Impressed by the successes of the *dawa* movement over the past two decades, PAS has now strengthened its Islamic identity even further at the expense of Malay nationalism. In this endeavour catchphrases such as *semangat keislaman mengatasi semangat nasionalisme*, 'the power of Islam will defeat the nationalism', have been used. With regard to the unlimited power of the sultans, PAS has kept a low profile, but carefully, and in indirect terms, the party has criticised non-Islamic habits such as exaggerated materialism, gambling and liquor consumption.

After independence in 1957, UMNO continued a very nationalistic policy. The first major crisis caused by this policy concerned the relations with Chinese-dominated Singapore which, to begin with, was part of the Malaysian federation. Within UMNO as well as PAS there had been great scepticism about the incorporation of Singapore since there were fears in both parties that it would weaken the position of the Malays in the new nation. Therefore, when the Singapore leader Lee Kuan Yew questioned the clause in the constitution which regulated the special rights of the Malays, Singapore was asked to leave the federation. After the withdrawal of Singapore the ethnic conflicts increased rapidly in Malaysia. The Chinese reacted with great bitterness against Malay demands for special treatment and all kinds of privileges. After an election in May 1969 the antagonism had grown to such an extent that it resulted in a wave of violence in which many people were killed or wounded, above all among the Chinese. As a result of these riots, the Malays became even more persistent in their demands for economic equality. As a response the government introduced a policy of reconciliation, known as the New Economic Policy. The aim was to increase the Malay share of the economy to at least 30 per cent within a twenty-year period. To reach this goal, the *bumiputra* (sons of the earth), the native Malays, were given exclusive rights and advantages in many economic fields, while admission for Chinese and Indians was severely restricted.

This new policy, however, did not lead to the results that the government had expected. The many privileges given to the Malays, and especially to rural Malays, in the fields of economy as well as education, not only served to increase their economic welfare but also gave rise to an Islamic recovery. In order to meet the increasing Islamist challenges against their policy, UMNO successively took a more and more benevolent attitude towards their demands. During the first five years following the riots UMNO mainly limited itself to supporting demands which strengthened Islam as an institution promoting a Malay identity. Government regulations such as the introduction of fines for Malays who were caught drinking liquor in public places or neglected to fast during the month of Ramadan all contributed to a strengthening of the identification between Islam and Malays. However, towards the middle of the 1970s a new power began to emerge on the political scene in Malaysia. This was the so-called *dawa* movement which in a very forceful way has succeeded in building upon and making use of this Malay–Muslim identification.

The dawa movement

The concept of *dawa* means to propagate for Islam, to do missionary work and make converts. However, as the concept has been used in Malaysia, it refers to movements which primarily aim at fellow Muslims, demanding that they take their religion more seriously and practice the religious norms in their daily life. The Malaysian *dawa* movement is not uniform. On the contrary, it consists of many quite disparate groups. Among these there are three main movements that have become well-known on a wider, national scale and which therefore are selected here as representative of the entire phenomenon. The three are Darul Arqam (the house of Arqam), named after a friend and protector of the Prophet Muhammad, 'the mission organisation' Jemaat Tabligh (Jamaat al-Tabligh) and, finally, the Angkatan Belia Islam Malaysia (ABIM), the Malaysian Islamic Youth Movement.

The first mentioned of the three movements, the Darul Arqam, is also the most radical. Thus, it has most uncompromisingly challenged the religious and political establishment. The founder and leader of the movement, Ustaz Ashaari Muhammad, is a well-educated and very charismatic person, who comes from a religious family. He is a forceful and popular orator who has written many books and pamphlets. Ustaz Ashaari Muhammad demands absolute obedience towards Allah and his Prophet, wants to strengthen the brotherhood of all Muslims, emphasises the importance of a Muslim education and finds it essential that the Muslims gain economic independence. He has also shown tendencies towards a kind of Sufi mysticism, manifested for instance in Mahdi expectations. It has even been maintained that Ustaz Ashaari considers himself to be the Mahdi and that he is trying to create for himself a position similar to that of Ayatollah Khomeini in Iran.

To be able to realise their ideals, the members of Darul Arqam have established a large number of communes all over Malaysia in which the members live and work. In these communes, the movement has established its own ideal society built entirely upon the founding fathers' ideas on how an Islamic social system should be organised. The movement strives to establish an egalitarian society where all property is jointly owned. Ustaz Ashaari Muhammad calls upon his followers to reject all Western material luxury and to live an ascetic life in the spirit of the Prophet. In the Darul Arqam communes, polygamy is the rule rather than an exception. The surrounding world is seen as hostile, and the communes are therefore characterised by a negative attitude towards outsiders. To avoid being dependent on the surrounding society, the members of the communes try to become self-supporting, producing themselves everything they need for their survival. In August 1995, the government finally cracked down on the Darul Arqam movement, placing Ustaz Ashaari Muhammad under a kind of house arrest, and attempted to dissolve the communes.

The second of the three movements, the Jemaat Tabligh, is not a native Malaysian organisation. It was established in 1925 in India, where its headquarters is still situated. In contrast to the strict organisation which characterises Darul Arqam, Jemaat Tabligh is very loosely organised. The aim of the movement is to revive the Islamic spirit, and it makes use of a large network of voluntary missionaries who work in a completely idealistic way and often far away from home. They visit people in their homes and try to convince them to devote their lives to Islam. The missionaries, who are always men, work in pairs, and when they arrive in a new place they first of all try to establish a base in a neighbourhood mosque, after which they walk from house to house inviting men to participate in their meetings in the mosque. Jemaat Tabligh has a very low social profile and does not publish any literature. It is therefore difficult to determine exactly the ideology of the movement. Individual members seem to have varying opinions on most questions. In line with this liberal attitude it is maintained that theirs is the most democratic of all *dawa* movements; there is no formal hierarchy and no official leadership. Because of its low socio-political profile, Jemaat Tabligh is not seen as a threat either by the government or by traditional religious leaders.

The third *dawa* movement, ABIM, is the largest and best-known of the three. It began in 1971 as a student organisation and recruited its first leader, Anwar Ibrahim, directly from the University of Malaya. It soon became clear that he, just like Ustaz Ashaari Muhammad, was an inspiring orator, with an ability to adapt his message to his listeners and easily attract their attention. Today there are ABIM groups in all the Malaysian states, but the organisation still has its strongest base in the universities and among the urban middle class. ABIM attempts to convince the Malays that Islam is a superior alternative to Western materialism. To spread its message, ABIM publishes a number of journals, and the organisation has established a number of schools in which an alternative higher education is provided. The curriculum of these schools contains all the ordinary 'secular' subjects but, in addition, there are also a couple of specifically Islamic subjects. According to the ABIM view, science is part of the legitimate Islamic tradition, at least as long as it does not conflict directly with religious values.

In its official declarations, ABIM has appeared as the least Malay-nationalistic of all the *dawa* organisations. In a 1979 speech which

Aids information, condemned by West Malaysian *ulama*, in Kota Kinabalu, East Malaysia (photo: Ingvar Svanberg, 1995).

attracted much attention, Anwar Ibrahim asserted that racism and colonialism are unknown to Islam, and the fact that these were nonetheless present in Malaysia was due to Western influences. In a much publicised incident in the same year, a group of ABIM students in England claimed that the New Economic Policy was incompatible with the development of a harmonious multi-ethnic society in Malaysia. However, this official ABIM policy is not always in harmony with the actions of its members. Many of the ABIM student groups, for instance, are openly anti-Chinese in their proclamations as well as in their actions. With regard to the question of an Islamic state, ABIM has taken a very cautious stand. In principle, the organisation is in favour of the establishment of such a state. In practice, however, the ideals have never been translated into official policy, and the movement has carefully avoided any indication of how such a society could be established and what it should actually look like.

As already mentioned, ABIM has often criticised the government. In 1981, members proclaimed, for instance, that the government was 'un-Islamic' and that corruption was a serious problem among the political élite. The government has taken this criticism seriously and has often counterattacked. For some time, public sale of ABIM's journals was, for instance, forbidden. However, when Dr Mahathir bin Mohamad became prime minister in 1981, he decided to try another tactics. Within a short time he had succeeded in convincing Anwar Ibrahim to join UMNO and accept a ministerial post in the government, where he has now advanced to become deputy prime minister. In defence of his new political career, Anwar has claimed that he will thereby have a position which makes it possible for him to push Islamic questions, work against corruption and defend Malay interests more effectively. For some time it seemed as if his defection would cause a split within ABIM since PAS sympathisers threatened to withdraw. In September 1998, Anwar was dismissed by Mahathir and was accused of, among other things, corruption and homosexual activities. The arrest of Anwar and the subsequent trial have lead to a severe political crisis in Malaysia.

Within the Malay society there is a sharp dividing-line between the conservative rural population and the more radical urban masses. It is above all among the latter that the *dawa* movement has made deep inroads. The urban Malays, who are in most cases first – and in other cases not more than second – generation immigrants from the rural areas, have been exposed to radical changes in the form of a rapid industrialisation and a penetrating Western influence. Thereby, many people have lost the footing they had in their traditional religiosity. In such a situation, the *dawa* groups offer an attractive alternative by providing the confused town-dweller, or student, a set of values which can give her or his life a new meaning. In the rural areas the changes have, so far at least, not been as thorough; here the population has, by and large, accepted their traditional *ulama* and continued to give their political support to UMNO or PAS. In many Malay villages, thus, there still exists a traditional, syncretistic Islam with magical and mystical overtones. The question now is whether the *dawa* groups will be able to spread their message more effectively among the rural population as well.

Patterns of cleavage in contemporary Malaysian Islam

In sum, it can be concluded that Malay society is caught in a cleavage between two currents, both of which can be traced back to colonial times. The deepest cleavage is found with regard to the view of power and its legitimacy and the role of Islam in social life. Somewhat simplified, we have a first current, represented by the UMNO, which stands for a secularised apparatus of power and supports the sultans and the originally feudal power structure represented by them. The advocates of this current are usually labelled *bumi*-Malays, that is, persons who support the nationalistic *bumiputra* policy, the aim of which is to give many advantages to these 'sons of the earth' in order to achieve economic equality with the Chinese. A *bumi*-Malay is willing to cooperate, politically as well as economically, with non-Malays and non-Muslims but always aims at using these alliances to favour Malay interests. Within this broad category there are several different groupings. One is represented by the technocrats who support the use of Western capitalism and technological development as long as it is in the interest of the Malays. Another current within the category of *bumi*-Malays is represented by the conservative royalists.

The second current, which is opposed to the above-mentioned pragmatic view, is represented by PAS. The PAS supporters demand a strengthened religious leadership and want to isolate the Malays from the other ethnic groups. They are also Malay nationalists but are not prepared to cooperate pragmatically with other groups as a means of achieving their goals. Their ultimate goal is the establishment of an Islamic state. In this context it is important to point out that what has been said here in no way implies that the *bumi*-Malays are antireligious. On the contrary, UMNO and its leadership frequently make use of Islamic symbols and programmes. To a certain extent this Islamic 'bumiputerism' is a strategically conditioned response to the criticism from PAS and the *dawa* movement, but it certainly also represents an honest opinion. Thus, both currents primarily aim at satisfying nationalistic Malay interests, and for this purpose they both make use of Islam, albeit with different emphases. In Malaysia religion is largely used politically, and paradoxically the Malays are both united and divided by their common religion.

The Islamic advance since the 1970s, represented primarily by the *dawa* movement, must be seen in the light of the prolonged cleavage between the two main currents in the Malay society. The questions that have been raised by the *dawa* movement touch upon a number of basic, and still unresolved, questions about the role of secular power and authority as well as about Malay relations with other ethnic groups in a multi-ethnic society. By raising these questions the *dawa* movement has challenged the *bumi*-Malays and thereby also the entire political establishment. In the cultural field, the *dawa* movement has again brought to the fore the old debate about the relationship between Islam and *adat*.

Islam in Indonesia and Malaysia: a brief comparison

The above description clearly shows that the position of Islam in the two countries of Indonesia and Malaysia differs quite considerably. In Malaysia, Islam has been identified with the Malays and with Malay culture to such an extent that when a non-Muslim converts, he or she also at the same time becomes a Malay (*masuk Islam/masuk Melayu*), irrespective of any earlier ethnic attachment. As a result of this close identification with the politically, although not economically, dominant ethnic group, Islam – rather than other components such as language or customs – has been used as the primary instrument for creating a Malay identity. In Malaysia, the ethnic

274

cleavages deeply divide the society, and they are now expressed primarily in terms of religious affiliation. Instead of being a universalistic power, Islam in Malaysia has been utilised as a means of legitimating ethnic particularism. Both the main Malay parties, UMNO as well as PAS, refer to Islam as a way of legitimating their claims to power. The only difference between them is found in the balance between special treatment for the Malays, on the one hand, and the emphasis on the creation of Islamic social institutions, on the other.

Thus, in the political power struggle between ethnic groups in Malaysia, Islam has become a contributing factor in the creation of deep and seemingly unbridgeable gulfs in the society. In Indonesia, the development has been quite different. Here, Islam and politics have effectively been kept separate by reference to the *pancasila* constitution. Its first principle, belief in God, is so general and unspecified that no ethnic group can oppose it. A permanent argument in favour of the Indonesian so-called *pancasila* democracy, with its emphasis on religious tolerance, harmony and consensus, has been the necessity of creating and maintaining good relations between the various ethnic groups. Critics have seen this as nothing but manipulation by centrally placed and powerful Javanese interests as a means of maintaining Javanese dominance over the other ethnic groups. Seen from the viewpoint of the critics, it is not an unreasonable argument, but given all the latent tensions that exist in Indonesia, the country would most probably have been torn apart long ago if the religio-political development had been allowed to follow the same course as in Malaysia.

In contrast to the Malaysian situation, Indonesian Islam has therefore, at least for the time being, almost no political role. Due to the doctrine about the dual function (*dwifungsi*), the military has a great influence. By playing the two groups, the military and the orthodox Muslims, against each other President Suharto succeeded throughout his long reign in neutralising both groups. As discussed above, there are now signs indicating that the proponents of more orthodox Islam are gaining a larger influence at the expense of the other groups. In March 1998, Suharto was re-elected as president for another five-year term and his present flirtation with orthodox Muslims has been interpreted as nothing but another manoeuvre in the continuing power struggle aimed primarily at neutralizing some of the military influence. Only two months later, Suharto was forced to resign and in the present period of reforms, orthodox forms of Islam have gained a new vitality. It must also be remembered that in Indonesia, syncretistic Islam, in its classical *priyai* form as well as in the form of more recent mystical organisations, is infinitely stronger and better-organised than is the case in Malaysia. As long as Suharto, himself a *priyai* aristocrat and former general, remained in power, there were no decisive changes in the balance of power. If, in the future, the modernists will gain greater political influence, not only Christians and Hindus, but also representatives of the syncretistic currents, will forcefully oppose all attempts to introduce an Islamic state in Indonesia.

The question may be asked why Islamic modernism has had such a relatively limited influence in Indonesia as compared to Malaysia. A decisive reason is probably found in the fact that in Malaysia Islam has been identified with an ethnic group which has been forced to vie with other strong groups for political and economic influence. In such a situation Islam offers a ready-made cultural and political alternative which is perfectly suitable as a means of demarcating one's own group and strengthening its morale against other groups. On Java, on the other hand, the position of Islam has been completely undisputed. Furthermore, the influential Javanese aristocracy has to a large extent been heavily influenced by syncretistic beliefs and practices. In the absence of a political role for Islam, Indonesians have been free to devote their energies to mystical speculation about the relation of humans to God and their place in the universe.

Literature

A broad and general introduction to Javanese culture and religion can be found in Koentjaraningrat, *Javanese Culture* (Singapore, Oxford and New York: Oxford University Press, 1985). A thorough, albeit quite disputed presentation of the different forms of Javanese Islam, is Clifford Geertz' *The Religion of Java* (Glencoe, IL: Free Press, 1960). The Muhammadiyah movement has been described by Mitsuo Nakamura, *The Crescent Arises Over the Banyan Tree* (Yogyakarta: Gadjah Mada University, 1983) and by James Peacock, *Purifying the Faith: The Muhammadijah Movement in Indonesian Islam* (Menlo Park, CA: Benjamin/Cummings Pub., 1978). See also H.M. Federspiel, 'The Muhammadijah: A Study of an Orthodox Islamic Movement in Indonesia', *Indonesia*, 10 (1970), pp. 57–79. A discussion about Nahdatul Ulama and its role is found in an article by its present leader Abdulrahman Wahid, 'The Nahdatul Ulama and Islam in Present Day Indonesia', in *Islam and Society in Southeast Asia* eds. T. Abdullah and S. Siddique (Singapore: Institute of Southeast Asian Studies, 1986) and in S. Jones, 'The Contraction and Expansion of the "Umat" and the Role of Nahdatul Ulama in Indonesia', *Indonesia*, 38 (1984). Javanese mysticism is presented by Niels Mulder, *Mysticism and Everyday Life in Contemporary Java* (Singapore: Singapore University Press, 1978) and by Harun Hadiwijono, *Man in the Present Javanese Mysticism* (Baarn: Bosch and Keuning, 1967). See also Antoon Geels, *Subud and the Javanese Mystical Tradition* (London: Curzon Press, 1997). On the relationship between Islam and *adat*, see the article by Roy Ellen, 'Social Theory, Ethnography and the Understanding of Practical Islam in South-East Asia', pp. 50–91 in *Islam in South-East Asia*, ed. M.B. Hooker (Leiden: E.J. Brill,

1983). On the political role of Indonesian Islam, see Ruth McVey, 'Faith as the Outsider: Islam in Indonesian Politics', pp. 199–225 in *Islam in the Political Process*, ed. J.P. Piscatori, (Cambridge, MA.: Cambridge University Press, 1983). See also Robert Hefner, 'Islamizing Java? Religion and Politics in Rural East Java', *Journal of Asian Studies*, 46:3 (1987), pp. 533–54.

There is a lack of a really good introduction to Islam in Malaysia, but much has been published on the subject of Islam and ethnicity. Two works that can be recommended are Hussin Mutalib, *Islam and Ethnicity in Malay Politics* (Singapore, Oxford and New York: Oxford University Press, 1990) and Raymond Lee, 'The Ethnic Implications of Contemporary Religious Movements and Organisations in Malaysia', *Contemporary Southeast Asia*, 8:1 (1986), pp. 70–87. A thorough work describing the political role of Islam in one of the Malaysian states is Clive Kessler, *Islam and Politics in a Malay State: Kelantan 1838–1969* (Ithaca, NY: Cornell University Press, 1978). A more general volume on the same theme is John Funston, *Malay Politics in Malaysia: UMNO and PAS* (Kuala Lumpur: Heinemann Educational Press, 1980). Some implications of the *dawa* movement are discussed in Judith Nagata, *The Reflowering of Malaysian Islam* (Vancouver: University of British Columbia Press, 1984) and in Chandra Muzaffar, *Islamic Resurgence in Malaysia* (Petaling Jaya: Fajar Bakti, 1987). On this subject, see also Zainah Anwar, *Islamic Revivalism in Malaysia: Dakwah Among the Students* (Petaling Jaya: Pelanduk Publications, 1987).

Chapter Twelve

Australia and New Zealand

Michael Humphrey and William Shepard

The stories of both Australia and New Zealand and of their Muslim communities are stories of immigrants. Indeed, they represent the furthest geographical reaches of both European and Muslim emigration. British settlement began with a penal colony in Australia in 1788 and today all but the 1–2 per cent who are Aboriginal Australians are descended from immigrants. British settlement began in New Zealand in the 1820s and 1830s but even previous inhabitants, the Maoris (now about 13 per cent of the population), came from elsewhere some centuries ago according to their traditions. The Muslims came later in both countries and form only a small proportion of the population, about 0.83 per cent in Australia and only 0.37 per cent in New Zealand. Thus they have faced the problems of being cultural minorities, benefiting from the multi-culturalism that has developed in recent years, especially in Australia, and suffering from the backlashes, again particularly in Australia.

Australia

Muslims first arrived in Australia during the mid nineteenth century as part of the colonial transmigration of labour in the development of the British Imperial system. The early Muslim migrants were from southwest Asia and were recruited to assist in the development of the vast arid Australian interior to serve in transportation as camel train drivers. While usually collectively referred to as 'Afghans' their actual ethnic and tribal origins were more diverse, coming from the North West Frontier, Baluchistan and Punjab regions of contemporary Pakistan. No permanent community survived from these early migrants although traces of their presence can be found in religious and community culture. The oldest mosque in Australia, a corrugated iron building in the mining town of Broken Hill dating from 1891, is a material expression of their presence as is the railway train called 'The Ghan', a reference to the term used to describe the caravanserai they inhabited on the outskirts of outback towns.

The establishment of more permanent Muslim communities dates only from the 1950s. This coincides with the major period of mass migration to

Australia and the diversification of the origins of Australian people. The post-1947 migration programme had originally sought to increase the population by 1 per cent annually from the British Isles, in keeping with the policy established at Federation to preserve Australia as a 'White' (European) society. However, these immigration targets could not be met from Britain alone and recruitment quickly expanded to include the entire Mediterranean. Post-war Muslim migration was a product of the diversification of immigration sources. The most rapid increase in Muslim migration occurred after 1970 and produced a distinct geographical concentration of Muslim settlement in Australia's two largest cities, in Sydney (50 per cent) and Melbourne (23 per cent).

The expansion of immigration intake to include the Mediterranean produced a distinctive pattern of migration often referred to as 'chain migration'. Family and community ties were the basis for the recruitment of new migrants as well as social support in the process of settlement on arrival. Chain migration consequently helped produce a very family- and community-centred social life. Village associations have been a ubiquitous expression of settlement amongst Mediterranean migrant communities.

Muslim migration and settlement after the 1950s followed the same pattern of recruitment and settlement from the Mediterranean. The first of these large 'community' migrations were the Turkish Cypriots in the 1950s and 1960s. They were followed by Turkish immigrants between 1968 and 1972. The largest Muslim community, the Lebanese, established itself principally after 1970 and especially after the outbreak of civil war in 1975. According to the 1991 Census the Turkish and Lebanese Muslim communities represent the largest communities with 14.5 per cent and 17.4 per cent respectively out of a total population of around 146,600. More recently the number of Indonesian (3.2 per cent) and Malaysian (1.4 per cent) Muslims as well as Bosnian Muslims (3.5 per cent) has also grown. The heavy concentrations of Muslim immigrants in New South Wales and Victoria reinforce this picture of concentrated communal settlement.

Distribution of Muslims by State

New South Wales	77,825	(52%)
Victoria	49,617	(34%)
Western Australia	8,227	(6%)
Queensland	5,605	(4%)
South Australia	3,092	(2%)
Australian Capital Territory	1,862	(1%)
Tasmania	1,623	(1%)

Source: 1991 Population Census

Many of the much smaller communities such as those from Fiji and South Africa also re-established communal life based on separate national or ethnic associations and mosques. This formation of the Muslim community through diverse sources of migration and with strong attachment to family and community has created a very multi-cultural Islam focused on distinct ethnic/national groupings. Australian Muslims have their origins in every continent and from many ethnic and racial backgrounds constituting a truly international community of believers.

The multi-cultural character of Australian Islam is evident in the membership of the peak Islamic organisation in Australia, the Australian Federation of Islamic Councils (AFIC), a federal organisation comprised of national and state committees. To be eligible for representation on the state committees, societies and organisations must have a minimum membership of 100 and be registered as a charitable organisation. AFIC was established as the peak Islamic organisation in 1964 and was built from the top down largely through the efforts of mainly Muslim professionals from diverse origins – Pakistan, India, Burma, China, Egypt. The multi-cultural diversity of AFIC becomes most apparent at state level where community associations and Islamic societies constitute the representational basis for membership. Given their strong ethnic, sect and national origins it is here that the tension between an Australian Muslim identity and ethnic identities are played out. State councils have explicitly tried to eliminate sectarian and national names from the constitutions and societies; for example, Lebanese Muslim Association, Sydney Turkish Islamic Society, Pakistan Islamic and Urdu Society. While never ethnically exclusive, language and ethnic culture certainly continue to shape the character and congregation of most mosques and community associations.

The ethnic diversity of Australian Islam is matched by its sectarian diversity. Most minority Islamic religious denominations have a presence in Australia. Given the relatively small size of the Muslim community (150,000) this diversity is notable. The most numerous are the Sunnis followed by the Shias. Smaller communities include Alawites, Druse, Ahmadiyya and Ismailis.

The range of activities AFIC undertakes also points to its distinctive immigrant origins and character. These include representations to overseas governments, organisations and individuals on behalf of Australian Muslims, assistance with the immigration of religious leaders, nomination of Muslim marriage celebrants to the Federal Attorney General's Department, administration of Islamic schools, religious instruction for Muslim youth, publications, subsidies for the salaries of some religious leaders and the certification of *halal* meat slaughtering in Australian abattoirs for meat exporters to international markets in Muslim countries. These activities draw it into liaison with a range of government departments involved with national as well as international affairs.

280

At state level AFIC councils have become more directly involved in the everyday spiritual and material needs of Muslim communities. For example, the Islamic Council of NSW advertises on its Internet website that it provides services in the areas of education, employment and training, community development, youth and recreation, information and community liaison and housing. Many of these services are provided as adjuncts to state government programmes or as special services in part supported by government grants for the delivery of migrant services. For example the 'Islamic Religious Programme' organises religious education classes for Muslim pupils in government schools and the Islamic Council of NSW Employment and Training Centre case-manages long-term unemployed Muslim migrants in conjunction with state government employment programmes such as the 'Jobskills Programme'. Similar specialised services linked to state government agencies are conducted in areas such as health, counselling, welfare assistance and immigration matters. It was also at the level of the state councils of AFIC that matters such as the right to bury the dead according to Muslim rites was negotiated. The Islamic Council of NSW, for example, had to negotiate with the Funeral and Allied Industries Union of NSW to be allowed to bury their dead without a coffin.

While AFIC has established itself as the national coordinating body, the actual organisation of religious life has largely been founded in local community life. Paralleling the experience of many minority immigrant communities, religious organisation and practice has emerged out of the everyday spiritual and ritual needs of individual believers. The impetus for the development of religious life has grown out of the spiritual as well as social needs of local communities linked by ties of origin rather than being the product of bureaucratic or state organisational initiatives.

Requirements for ritual life as well as basic immigrant needs such as housing, work and information about state welfare services and benefits were the social context in which religious life re-established its communal focus. Migrant settlement was a major concern of mosque associations as it had been for many minority immigrant churches. Mosques, as congregational centres, provided a focus for the dissemination of information and services. For Muslims this has particularly been the case since the 1980s. Government agencies came to see the mosque as an important point of connection with new communities they neither understood nor had access to. Consequently Australian politicians and bureaucrats supported the establishment of specialised welfare and educational services around them. In the case of the Lebanese Muslims, government agencies saw the mosque as an organisational focal point which transcended the rivalry between proliferating village, social and political organisations, all of which sought government recognition on the basis of their claims to represent specific ethnic constituencies.

The establishment of mosques was generally an indication of the consolidation of community organisation and development. Mosque-building marked a stage in the development of social and religious life. Communities would organise themselves in social and cultural associations based on their communities of origin – for instance village or town associations – which subsequently expanded to serve as *ad hoc* mosques. This transition from associational to congregational use at times led to conflicts over mosque building in the suburbs. What from the perspective of community members appeared to be a natural step of social and cultural consolidation was regularly regarded by non-Muslim residents as a sign of the infiltration of an alien religious culture into suburban life and a disregard for the normal local government procedures for urban development applications.

Suburban controversies over mosque building have highlighted the locally based character of Muslim religious organisations. It has been local associations and not AFIC national and state bodies which have initiated mosque building developments. It is local Muslim communities which have done battle with Municipal Councils and the Land and Environment Court to establish the right to have a place for religious congregation. Each community has had to establish itself in its own suburban environment. With this strong communal focus and the solidarity engendered by the struggles to build mosques it is not surprising that many associations have been reluctant to drop distinctive national/ethnic markers from their names as a condition of membership in AFIC.

However, the local character of religious organisation has sometimes contributed to instability in religious leadership. The associational basis of Muslim communities has meant that the appointment and dismissal of *imams* has largely remained in the hands of the mosque community itself. This is in direct contrast to minority churches where communities are sent clerics by a central administrative body. This has occasionally led to the politicisation of the position of *imam* in some of the larger ethnic communities. The most notable case was the contest over mosque leadership at the Lakemba Mosque in Sydney. From its establishment in 1976 until the late 1980s the spiritual leadership at the Imam Ali Mosque was also a contested position. The first two *imams* were successively challenged and ousted by *imams* introduced from overseas by different sections of the Lebanese Muslim community. The contest was intensified by the political backdrop of the Lebanese civil war and the emergence of more Islamist Sunni and Shiite movements in Lebanon. These struggles over local mosque leadership were transformed into contests to secure international sponsorship and financing of mosque building to maintain influence and support in local immigrant communities.

The principal exception to this pattern of locally grown organisations is the case of the Turkish immigrant mosques which have remained closely tied to the Turkish government religious ministry which provides salaried *imams* (*hojas*) and funds for mosque building. The pattern amongst Turkish communities has been to recruit a *hoja* from the Turkish Diyanet İşleri, the department overseeing religious affairs in Turkey. However, the involvement of the Turkish state in appointing a *hoja* in the community has not altogether avoided politicising immigrant religious leadership. Turkish mosque communities divided along factional lines based on their identification with different political movements in Turkey.

Another feature of immigrant life which has tended to reinforce the local community character of immigrant Islam is the legal capacity of *imams* in matters of marriage and divorce. *Imams* have emerged as an important link between two distinct legal traditions, the Islamic and the Australian civil law. Their Islamic legal credentials derive from their knowledge of *sharia* (Islamic law) and, in some cases, their recognised legal capacities under national legal systems. Their legal capacity in Australian civil law derives from their official recognition as Australian marriage celebrants by the Federal Attorney General's Department.

Community perception of the legal capacity of *imams* is largely determined by the status of Islamic law *vis-à-vis* civil law in their countries of origin. In a case like Lebanon, where religious law held exclusive jurisdiction in matters of marriage, divorce and inheritance, the immigrant community often assumed *imams* could fulfill the same religio-judicial role in Australia. Thus if an *imam* was able to marry according to Islamic law (and conduct a parallel marriage ceremony under Australian civil law) then surely he could also witness a divorce or even effect a valid judicial separation. If an *imam* can draw up a pre-nuptial agreement which specifies an amount of bridewealth (*mahr*) then surely he can ensure its enforcement if the marriage breaks down.

This dual legal capacity can place *imams* in a difficult position balancing a limited judicial capacity with respect to marriage under Australian law with community expectations of having broader legal capacities under Islamic law. Conflicts of legal expectations occur over the minimum age of marriage, the capacity of an *imam* to effect a religious divorce and the capacity to enforce bridewealth (*mahr*) agreements.

In the interplay between these religious and secular legal traditions there is a mutual reinforcement of legal authority. The state ensures marriage is registered according to its laws by making *imams* civil celebrants and *imams* become celebrants to bolster their religious and legal authority in turn. The Australian secular state helps affirm the claims to religious authority through the recognition of *imams* as marriage celebrants. To be legally empowered to conduct and register a valid Islamic and Australian marriage at the same time affirms the religious authority of the *imam* in the community. In fact the state can actually be used to enhance a claim to religious authority by conferring the status of marriage celebrant. In the

Muslim immigrant community there is not just one route to be recognised as having religious authority. One can either be recognised as learned in religious matters because of qualifications or be attributed religious authority through piety and selfless dedication to the needs of Muslim migrants – having an open door to individuals or families with problems. A recent controversy over conflicts in the role of the *imam*/celebrant and the legal tangles which can result was recently highlighted in the case of an Alawi celebrant in Sydney.

An *imam* then must not only be knowledgable in religious matters but have the capacity to resolve the difficulties of immigrants operating between different cultural and legal worlds. His reputation as a 'trouble-shooter' in the practical problems of everyday immigrant life is often as important as respect for his religious learning. The ability to manage the crises of family life – marital conflict, divorce and death – with respect to the law, as a counsellor and the practical matters of welfare services and support is an essential part of gaining community respect. This makes the position of *imam* a demanding and difficult one as he must negotiate the transition of Muslim immigrants moving between very different cultural and political worlds.

Mosque communities have also become an important arena for negotiating the changing status of Muslim immigrant women. The new demands on women as mothers, workers, and community members have seen the development of special organisations and services catering to the needs of women. These include representative organisations such as The Muslim Women's Association as well as crisis centres such as Islamic women's refuges where women involved in serious domestic conflicts can go for support and assistance. The refuges were established to provide Muslim women alternatives to the mainstream women's refuges which were often regarded as culturally compromising, and beyond the reach of the usual family, community and religious networks to intervene. In the Islamic women's refuges the space for negotiation and cooling off was at least possible, with greater prospects that the *imam* might be able to preserve the marriage.

Women's organisations have become the focus of education and health campaigns originating from mainstream government agencies. In one notable case a Shia Muslim women's organisation in Sydney – Al Zahra Muslim Women's Association – became the focus for an education and poster campaign about HIV/AIDS awareness. The campaign broached issues about sexuality and health traditionally difficult to raise in public. The participation of these women's associations in such pressing public issues represents innovative social responses to the demands placed on individuals and cultures in migration.

The question of women's status and behaviour remains a very important area of domestic and community regulation. In many ways Muslim women

An HIV/AIDS Muslim poster designed by a group of women in Sydney (courtesy of the Multicultural HIV/AIDS Education and Support Service, Camperdown, New South Wales, 1997).

in Australia confront the problem of being made cultural icons by their own communities with all the burdens that this implies. In a social environment which strongly advocates the equality of opportunity and rights of all Australian women, Muslim communities are constantly under the scrutiny, if not criticism, of the dominant society over their alleged attitudes towards women. The dominant culture uses the image of Muslim women as oppressed to criticise Muslim culture and make them a focus for intervention, a practice which dates back to the nineteenth-century colonial enterprise of cultural devaluation and justification for intervention. A Muslim woman in *hijab* (head scarf) is the emblematic image for

285

representation of Muslim values in migration by both conservative Muslim representatives and the dominant society. In fact no media representation of Muslims would be complete in fulfiling popular stereotypes if an image of a woman in *hijab* were not included, along with that of an overcrowded mosque spilling out into the street.

One issue which more than any other has been put forward as the cultural oppression of Muslim women in Australia is clitoridectomy – so-called female circumcision. Although the practice has not been widespread, it is regarded by the dominant culture, and many Muslims, as a repugnant cultural practice, and allegation of child abuse led in 1996 to specific legislation against it being recommended by the Family Law Council of Australia.

The influence of local mosque communities and *imams* as distinct from national Islamic organisations has also been enhanced by the wider politics of multi-culturalism in Australian society. With ethnic identity being the basis for claims of disadvantage and cultural rights in the wider society, the mosque itself has tended to become a representative organisation, a voice in the context of multi-cultural identities. This has placed the *imam* in the dual position of spiritual as well as community leader, one who defends the interests and good name of Muslims in the wider society.

This defense of Islam and cultural identity by community leaders is linked to a broader problem of prejudice against Muslim immigrants. The contemporary international cultural identity of Islam as politically turbulent and inspired by religious fundamentalism has served to reinforce the general suspicion towards all Muslim immigrants in Australia. The international image only reinforces tendencies towards distrusting Muslim immigrants and their willingness to become 'Australians'. Indices of social disadvantage – high unemployment and welfare reliance – are turned, through prejudice, into judgements about cultural worth. Thus the chronic high levels of unemployment experienced by Turkish- and Lebanese-born populations since the early 1980s has made them ready targets for discrimination. As one prominent public figure commenting on Australian immigration policies and immigration intake levels observed in the late 1980s: 'We can't keep bringing in Lebanese who have been told, "You don't have to go to paradise, there's a place called Australia where you don't have to work and the Government will pay you"'.

Muslim religious and cultural practices have also received regular and prominent public attention in the media. These have included complaints about sheep slaughtering in backyards, opposition to mosque building in suburban areas, controversy about Muslim burial rites, under-age marriage, plural marriage, and accusations that clitorodectomy is a continuing practice. A wide range of government departments and regulatory bodies have become involved in order to establish procedures to either accommodate or facilitate Islamic practices and to make illegal practices regarded as oppressive – for instance specific legislation against the practice of clitorodectomy.

The live sheep and cattle shipping trade to the Middle East which caters for Muslim Arab consumer taste for freshly slaughtered *halal* meat has even contributed to reinforce negative images of Muslims. Animal rights campaigners have severely criticised this trade on the grounds of cruelty caused by overcrowding or by the rejection of livestock cargoes on health grounds and the subsequent suffering caused to these shipbound animals.

The need to deal with government regulatory bodies over particular religious needs and permission to carry out traditional rites as well as the attention such practices receive in the media have contributed to shaping a sense of Australian Muslim identity. Muslim spokespeople are frequently called upon to explain these rites, to clarify what is and what is not 'Islamic' practice and belief. Challenging Muslim stereotypes in the press has become the focus of many organisations. One organisation, the Australian Arabic Council, has made monitoring the press its primary concern. It rewards fair and informed reporting on Arab and Muslim communities through an annual media award.

The experience of discrimination as immigrants has engendered a greater consciousness of being part of a global Islamic culture. Fear in the West of Islamic radicalism and the impact of events such as the Salman Rushdie affair, the kidnapping of Western hostages in Lebanon and the Gulf War frequently expresses itself as fear of Muslims at home. The tendency to blame Muslims living in Australia for events overseas reminds Muslims that they are part of a global religious culture; that despite all their efforts to be good Australian citizens and their right to be treated equally and without prejudice, fear of Islam projected from very different worlds and political environments can jeopardise their best efforts and intentions.

New Zealand

The Muslim community in New Zealand is much smaller than that in Australia, both in absolute terms and as a proportion of the total population. It is, nevertheless, a vigorous and growing community which has more than doubled numerically in the last five years. The past twenty years have seen an almost ten-fold increase and striking organisational progress. According to the 1996 census there were 13,545 Muslims resident in New Zealand, representing 0.37 per cent of the total population of about 3.6 million. By comparison, the 1991 census counted 5,772 Muslims, representing 0.15 per cent of the New Zealand population. The majority live in Auckland, New Zealand's largest city, but there are also organised communities in at least five other cities and Muslim student associations at most of the universities.

Fijian Indians, that is, descendants of Indians who migrated to Fiji to work in the late nineteenth and early twentieth centuries, constitute the largest ethnic group among New Zealand Muslims. Between 1879 and 1916 over 60,000 Indians came to Fiji as indentured labourers to work on the plantations. About 12.6 per cent of these were Muslims. The indentures were cancelled in 1920, and while Muslim community organisation soon developed politically, Muslims were identified as Indians and after independence in 1970 were associated with the Indian political party. Although the Indians make up about half of the population of Fiji, the independence settlement assured the political dominance of the ethnic Fijians. When a predominantly Indian party came to power by election in 1987 it was immediately ousted by a coup d'état led by a Fijian military officer. In the aftermath of this a number of Indians emigrated from Fiji. There is a strong Ahmadiyya presence among Muslims in Fiji, but there is little evidence of Ahmadi activity in New Zealand. Fijian Indians, along with other South Asians (Indian, Pakistani, Bangladeshi), probably account for over half the community although other ethnic groups have certainly increased in proportion in the most recent years. Only about one fifth of the Muslims in New Zealand have been born in the country according to the 1996 census. There are also perhaps 1,000 overseas university students at any one time, some of whom come with their families and make significant contributions to local groups while they are in the country, and a small but active group of Western converts.

The roots of the present community go back to a handful of Gujarati men who arrived after 1906 and opened shops but mostly did not bring their families until after the Second World War. While a few Muslim families came from Turkey and the Balkans after the Second World War, these seem to have made less effort to maintain their ethnic and religious identities. Significant Muslim growth began in the late 1960s. A period of liberalised immigration about this time made it possible for a small number of professional and white collar workers, mainly South Asians and Fijian Indians, to come, although the majority of Muslim wage earners are probably 'blue collar' workers or shopkeepers, especially in Auckland. As of 1991, the median income of New Zealand Muslims was only slightly below the average for the country. The 'chain migration' phenomenon appears evident in New Zealand as in Australia, but New Zealand has never encouraged mass immigration in the manner that Australia did just after the Second World War.

The recent dramatic rise in numbers has resulted partly from political events elsewhere. The 1987 coup in Fiji caused a considerable influx and more recently around 1,000 refugees from Somalia have been admitted to the country, with more expected. Some have also come from Bosnia. The Somalis currently are the largest Muslim ethnic group in two centres, Christchurch and Hamilton. The other major factor is that changes to the

288

immigration regulations in 1992 have again allowed a number of professional people to enter, especially from the Middle East. Unfortunately, these most recent immigrants have faced considerable difficulty finding employment. Many professionals have found that their qualifications are not recognised in New Zealand and that it is very difficult to obtain local qualification. The Somalis, composed of a large number of women and children, have often been traumatised in their own country and face a greater cultural gap than most. As a result the 1996 census reports a median Muslim income considerably lower than the New Zealand average.

In addition to employment problems, Muslim immigrants have faced the usual problems of adapting to the local climate and customs and learning English. There has been some discrimination, probably more negative stereotyping, occasional racial violence and some conflict between Muslim customs and local ways, such as difficulty arranging time and place for *salat* (official prayer) at work or school, insensitivity of health agencies and schools to Muslim concerns (such as suitable school uniforms for girls), and legal problems with marriage and divorce. Partly because of the small numbers and low profile of the community, these problems do not seem to be unduly serious. On the whole, recent immigrants seem to see New Zealand as a tolerant place though they are concerned about maintaining their Muslim identity and raising their children in a society whose standards on such matters as sexual morality and parental authority seem unduly lax. Health authorities have had some concern about clitorodectomy among the newly arrived Somalis, but their actions have been low-key and there has been little discussion in the media, although female genital mutilation was made a criminal offence at the beginning of 1996.

While the Muslim community as a whole is now firmly established in New Zealand, there is considerable individual transiency. Students eventually return to their home countries and those who cannot find suitable work here may move on. Many have extended families partly living elsewhere and are more committed to these families than to their country of residence. As a result, some of the smaller communities experience extremely high turnover, and continuity of organisational leadership becomes a problem.

The first formal Muslim organisation, the New Zealand Muslim Association, was established in Auckland in 1950 and continues to the present day. Initially its membership was mainly Gujerati, with Fijian Indians and others coming in later on. An association was formed in Wellington, the capital, in 1966 and took the acronym IMAN (International Muslim Association of New Zealand). Initially based on university students, its core is now permanent residents. As the name suggests, its leaders have been particularly concerned to stress the multi-ethnic nature of Islam. Other associations were founded in Hamilton, Palmerston North and Christchurch between 1977 and 1980, and in 1989 in Dunedin. An

From the ceremony for laying the foundation stone of a new mosque in Hamilton (photo: Anisur Rahman, 1997).

association has also begun in Hastings but its current status is uncertain. In 1989, due to the growth and spread of the Auckland Muslim community, the South Auckland Muslim Association was founded and since then two or three other semi-independent centres have developed in other parts of the city. There are three purpose-built mosques in New Zealand and construction of a fourth has just begun. Other groups have converted facilities at this stage.

Depending on numbers and resources, the associations provide for the main religious services, including *salat*, prayers and activities for Ramadan and the main festivals, as well as basic religious teaching, Arabic instruction and various social activities. Some organise the provision of *halal* food. Most or all of the associations have marriage celebrants and burial space in a local cemetery. Some have separate women's groups and organise youth activities, including sports. Many have 'usrah' groups, informal small groups usually meeting in homes. The associations in Auckland and Wellington have full time paid teachers (*imams*), but policy control is largely in the hands of 'lay' leaders in these associations as well as in the others. Outside financial assistance, from sources in such countries as Saudi Arabia, has been necessary both for the buildings and for paying *imams*. In recent years the Auckland community has established two day schools, one at elementary and one at middle level.

The associations make some effort to publicise Islam in the larger community and in several centres have had a variety of more or less formal contacts with churches. Steps are currently being taken in Auckland to form a Christian–Muslim Council along the lines of the existing Jewish–Christian Council. When some people objected to the plans to build a mosque in Hamilton, both Church groups and Maori groups gave crucial support in the debate that took place in the pages of the local newspaper.

Very important for some New Zealand Muslims is the activity connected with the Tabligh movement, Jamaat al-Tabligh, which was begun by Muhammad Ilyas in India in the 1920s and has since spread around the world. Its primary concern is to encourage regular practice of the very basic religious obligations and it relies heavily on trained 'lay' volunteers who travel about, both within the country and internationally, meeting with local Muslims and preaching their message. Organisation is quite loose, but there is usually an *amir* (leader) for a given area or group of activities. Since 1979 there has been an annual national gathering. While some criticise it as being a conservative force and too associated with Indian ethnicity, its informality, use of 'lay' leadership and emphasis on the basics make it well-suited to the New Zealand situation, where there are few trained teachers and basic identity is still a concern.

The world-wide Islamic resurgence has influenced New Zealand in various ways. For some it has increased their Islamic identity in comparison to their ethnic one. There is a greater concern about such matters as segregation of the sexes and increased use of *hijab* by women. There is also an increased desire to manage affairs by the Islamic method of *shura* ('consultation') rather than by Western-style majority rule and balloting, which many feel encourage disruption and disunity. *Shura* as interpreted here seems to involve something like concensus decision-making and a strong role for the leader.

Among issues that have arisen within the community recently have been the propriety of celebrating Mulid al-Nabi (*mawlid*, the Prophet's birthday) and the acceptability of drinking Kava, a Fijian drink which is evidently considered by Muslim authorities in Fiji to be intoxicating and thus forbidden. The *imam* in Wellington has spoken out against both; other leaders appear to agree with him on Kava but not necessarily on the Mulid. Other on-going debates relate to the need, felt by some, to develop a distinctly New Zealand approach to Islam. Some, for example, feel the mosques and centres should be constructed mainly as places for prayer and other specifically Islamic activities while others would prefer to see buildings that suggest greater openness to the surrounding community. Some have criticised the dominance of ethnic customs at Muslim functions, as is illustrated by an exchange that took place some years ago on the pages of the newsletter of the Wellington association. One writer, a Western convert, stated: 'Becoming a Muslim does not mean that you have to sit on the floor and eat rice and curry'. Another, a Pakistani, responded: 'Becoming a Muslim does not mean that you have to sit on the floor and eat rice and curry, I am not so sure. However, what I am sure of is that to sit on the floor like a Muslim and eat rice and curry is better than biting (as dogs do) ham sandwiches or standing or drinking and driving and smashing everything that comes in the way including one's self'. This sort of exchange would be less likely today, but it illustrates the fact that one cannot easily draw the line between cultural and moral concerns.

New Zealand associations are not divided along ethnic or sectarian lines, mainly because of the small number of Muslims generally, and the extremely small number of non-Sunnis. Ethnic feelings are not absent, however, and may manifest themselves in the internal politics of the associations and in issues concerning certain celebrations and customs (members of one ethnic group will sometimes say that those of another group confuse their ethnic customs with Islam). Although some have felt a stronger Islamic identity in recent years, as noted above, there is evidence that ethnic sensibility has also been increasing, mainly because of the increasing numbers of people from different groups. So far, the leaders have been able to contain the potential tensions involved; what the future holds remains to be seen.

In 1979 a national organisation, the Federation of Islamic Associations of New Zealand (FIANZ), was formed to help coordinate the activities of the local associations and also to coordinate financial requests and other dealings overseas. FIANZ has assisted in fund raising for the local mosques and centres and in coordinating relations with overseas organisations such as the Muslim World League, the World Association of Muslim Youth, and the Regional Islamic Dawah Council of South East Asia and the Pacific (RISEAP). It also selects candidates to attend overseas conferences and meetings, holds Quran recitation competitions, distributes books, videos and other literature and arranges visits by overseas speakers. Particularly important has been its *halal* certification service. New Zealand began sending meat to the Middle East in 1975 and increased its sales dramatically when the revolutionary government in Iran began to accept sizeable shipments. In the process, a considerable number of New Zealand abbatoirs shifted to *halal* slaughter. Sales to Iran have decreased in recent years but have been replaced by sales to other Muslim countries. FIANZ is one of two certifying agencies in New Zealand and sole certifier for the United Arab Emirates, Saudi Arabia and Kuwait. In 1993 FIANZ set up a consultancy company, AMANA, to be its business arm. One of its goals is to make New Zealand Muslims less dependent on donations from overseas for major projects.

Of the nineteen seats on the FIANZ executive council, two are reserved for women (other women are sometimes chosen as representatives of local associations). Since about 1991 there has been a very active women's group at the national level, the Islamic Women's Council of New Zealand, which holds an annual conference and sponsors youth camps for girls.

Neither FIANZ nor the local associations have taken a prominent role in relation to the economic, social and legal problems faced by immigrants, preferring to let such matters be handled in a low-key and informal matter. The writers believe that one or two cases relating to time-off for *salat* have been taken to the government's Human Rights Commission, but do not know that the associations have been formally involved. Neither have they formally sponsored immigrants, although they have offered advice to sponsoring organisations and have given help to immigrant families after their arrival. They have been more active in some cases of negative publicity and hostility arising out of events overseas such as the Rushdie Affair and the Gulf War. On at least three occasions FIANZ has taken legal action against the media and it sponsored or participated in several public forums on the Rushdie Affair. Members of IMAN, in Wellington, have intervened in some cases where material deemed derogatory to Muslims was being used in the state schools.

In the early 1980s a leader of one of the recently formed associations said that its main purpose was 'to keep them Muslim'. This will always be a concern, given the small proportion of Muslims in New Zealand, but both institutionally and otherwise the community has grown beyond merely this concern and its leaders generally express optimism for the future. A few years ago some in New Zealand expressed the hope that the community would shift from being 'Muslims in New Zealand', that is an immigrant community surviving in an alien environment, to being 'Muslims of New Zealand', that is developing forms of Islamic expression appropriate to the local society and interacting significantly with that society. In the case of New Zealand the community is still very much in the mode of 'Muslims in New Zealand', probably more so than five years ago, given the size of the recent influx in relation to the size of the community and the problems they face. It will take time and suitable circumstances to become 'Muslims of New Zealand', but significant steps have been taken and the institutional basis has been laid. The same issue may be raised for Australia. There, too, the Muslims appear to be mainly 'Muslims in Australia' but because of their larger relative and absolute numbers, their more developed institutions and their higher profile, both positive and negative, they have probably moved further along the path toward becoming 'Muslims of Australia'.

Literature

Much of the information in this essay is based on personal communications and the authors wish to express their appreciation to the members of the Muslim communities of both countries, and others, who have taken the trouble to provide information. Islam in Australia is dealt with in Gary

Bauma, *Mosques and Muslim Settlement in Australia, Bureau of Immigration and Population Research* (Canberra: AGPS, 1994); Michael Humphrey, 'Religion, Law and Family Disputes in Lebanese Muslim Communities in Sydney', pp. 183–98 in *Ethnicity, Class and Gender in Australia*, eds. Gillian Bottomley and Marie de Lepervanche (Melbourne: George Allen and Unwin, 1984); Michael Humphrey, 'Community, Mosque and Ethnic Politics', *Australian and New Zealand Journal of Sociology*, 23 (1988), pp. 233–45; and Michael Humphrey, 'Is this a Mosque Free Zone? Islam and the State in Australia', *Migration Monitor*, 12:3 (1989), pp. 12–17.

Middle East Research and Information Association (MERIA) has published *Islamic Communities in NSW* (Sydney: TAFE, 1984). Other studies of Australian Islam are Laura Nader, 'Orientalism, Occidentalism and the Control of Women', *Cultural Dynamics*, 2:3 (1989), pp. 323–55; Wa'el Sabri, 'A Model of Community Development within the Arabic Muslim Community in Sydney', unpublished MA essay in sociology at University of New South Wales, 1997; and Greg Sheridan, 'The FitzGerald philosophy', *The Weekend Australian*, June 4–5, 1988, p. 21.

Not much has been written on Islam in New Zealand. Census figures from 1991 are available in *New Zealand Now: Asian New Zealanders* (Wellington: Statistics New Zealand, 1995). For a historical survey and details concerning the various communities within New Zealand as of about 1991, see William Shepard, 'Muslims in New Zealand', *Journal: Institute of Muslim Minority Affairs*, 16: 2 (1996), pp. 211–32, and Christopher Van der Krogt, 'Islam', pp. 181–213 in *Religions of new Zealanders*, ed. Peter Donovan (Palmerston North: Dunmore Press, 1990). Useful information and a helpful perspective is presented by Qamer Rahman, 'Muslim Women in New Zealand: Problems and Prospects', *Al-Nahdah*, 16:1–2 (January–June, 1996), pp. 34–35. For an overview of Islam on the Fiji Islands, see Ali Ahmad, 'Muslims in Fiji: A Brief Survey', *Journal: Institute of Muslim Minority Affairs*, 3 (1981), pp. 174–82.

Part Three

Europe and the Americas

Chapter Thirteen

Bosnia and Herzegovina

Kjell Magnusson

Before the war in Bosnia, few Westerners were aware of the existence of an indigenous Muslim population in southeastern Europe. Islam was usually regarded as a problem associated with migration or political relations between the West and the Middle East. In fact, about 10 million inhabitants of the Balkans are of Muslim origin. The largest group is to be found in former Yugoslavia, where about 5 million, or one fifth of the population, are Muslims. Others are living in Albania, 3.5 million (70 per cent of the population), Bulgaria, 1.4 million (10–15 per cent), Greece (150,000) and Rumania (50,000). The figures are not exact and do not necessarily refer to actual religious identification.

If Balkan Muslims are ranked according to ethnic origin the following picture emerges: Albanians (5–6 million), Bosnian Muslims (2.3 million), Turks (1.5 million), Roma/Gypsies (500,000), Bulgarian-speaking Pomaks (180,000), Macedonian-speaking Torbeshi (100,000–200,000) as well as smaller groups of Slavic- and Greek-speaking Muslims. In terms of territorial dominance, the largest concentrations of Muslims are found in Kosovo (90 per cent), Albania (70 per cent), the Sandžak province in Serbia and Montenegro (50 per cent), Bosnia and Herzegovina (45 per cent) and Macedonia (30 per cent).

The Islamic presence in southeastern Europe is the result of five centuries of Ottoman rule, beginning towards the end of the fourteenth century and lasting until 1913. Balkan Muslims are Sunni of the Hanafi school of law, although an important role has been played by Sufi orders, notably the Bektashiyya. In Albania it is estimated that 20–25 per cent of the Muslims are Bektashis, and in Kosovo and Macedonia, as well as in Bosnia, the Bektashiyya and other orders still have followers. Ottoman rule was to have far-reaching effects on the history of the Balkans. First, a social and political system developed which differed radically from feudal society in Western Europe. Second, a specific Balkan culture evolved, partly isolated from major currents in European thought, and generating an ambivalent attitude towards 'Europe'. Third, and as a consequence of these factors, the process of nation-building among both Christians and Muslims was affected.

Bosnian Muslims

The Muslims of Bosnia illustrate perhaps more clearly than other ethnic groups the unusual complexity of nation-building among the southern Slavs. Although Serbs, Croats, Montenegrins and Bosnian Muslims speak the same language, religious and cultural differences were sufficiently important to serve as a basis for the formation of distinct national identities. This was to a large extent due to political circumstances during the nineteenth century, but is ultimately a result of prolonged foreign domination and the characteristics of social and cultural processes in the Hapsburg and Ottoman Empires.

In the Ottoman Empire, citizens were categorised according to religious affiliation. From the point of view of the Turks, society was made up of Muslims, Jews and Orthodox, Catholic or Armenian Christians. This principle of classification was a consequence of an Islamic world-view and the lack of a Western concept of religion. There was no clear distinction between a religious and a secular sphere, between state and religion, but society–culture–religion was understood as a unified whole, subject to the Islamic law, *sharia*. As *sharia* could not be universally applied, since a majority of the inhabitants of the Balkans were not Muslims, the Turks' solution was to allow the conquered peoples a considerable degree of autonomy. They retained their own legal system and were represented politically by their religious leaders.

This social order, which is usually referred to as the *millet* system, meant that different socio-religious groups, or *millet*, lived together, or rather side by side, and gave rise to a specific multi-ethnic culture where the cities became meeting grounds of Christians, Muslims and Jews. Every group lived in its own residential area or *mahala*, where it preserved its language and lifestyle. People prayed to their God in Hebrew, Arabic, Church Slavonic or Byzantine Greek, but met in the market place and the streets of artisans. In Balkan towns and cities, Turkish, Greek, Judezmo, Albanian or Slavic dialects were spoken, and, irrespective of ethnic origin, many people were multilingual.

As a rule the Turks did not actively engage in missionary activities and therefore a majority of Greeks and southern Slavs maintained their original culture and religion. A notable exception is Bosnia, where a large part of the population converted to Islam, according to one theory because of their Bogomil heritage, according to another primarily for social and economic reasons. Whatever the case may be, the Muslims in Bosnia and Herzegovina are descendants of these Serbo-Croatian-speaking converts. During Ottoman rule they were regarded by themselves and others as 'Turks' or, rather, people of 'Turkish Faith'.

Westernisation

The occupation of Bosnia and Herzegovina by Austria–Hungary in 1878 was a turning point for the Muslims. They were confronted with the lifestyles of modern European society, and the question of their ethnic identity was suddenly brought to the fore. As long as the Ottoman Empire and the *millet* system prevailed they had no reason to identify themselves as anything but Muslims. However, the rise of Serb and Croat varieties of modern nationalism during the nineteenth century made the identity of the Muslims a complex and pressing issue. As in other similar situations several alternative options were initially available. Muslims belonging to the modern segments of society often identified themselves as Serbs but more often as Croats, as both Croatia and Bosnia were parts of the same political framework, and Zagreb was a major cultural centre.

Between 1878 and 1918 the Austrian authorities consciously tried to popularise the idea of a Bosniac nation and a Bosniac language. This policy was, however, not very successful, as Serbian and Croatian identities were already available to Orthodox and Catholic Bosnians, while for a majority of the Muslims the traditional adherence to Islam was still the primary identification. In addition, since the characteristic feature of Bosnia was its Islamic heritage, the term Bosniac practically referred only to Muslims, especially as the oriental aspects of Bosnian culture were perceived as alien by nationally conscious Serbs or Croats.

The Austrian occupation initiated a process of dramatic cultural and political change. The Muslims lost their privileged position, and Islam was reduced to a minority religion in a predominantly Christian state. The Austrians interfered even in purely religious matters, for example by introducing a new hierarchical and church-like organisation, and creating the position of *reis-ul-ulema* as the religious head of Bosnian Muslims. The state also took control of the important religious foundations, the *vakuf* (Ar. *waqf*). These policies, as well as insensitive missionary activities of the Catholic Church, gave rise to strong opposition and the decades around the turn of the century were dominated by a Muslim struggle for religious and cultural autonomy, which was finally achieved in 1909.

As a consequence of the political changes, a great number of Muslims left Bosnia and Herzegovina and moved to areas still controlled by the Ottoman Empire. According to some estimates, about 150,000 Bosnians emigrated to Turkey between 1878 and 1914, which resulted in a significant change of the ethnic structure in Bosnia. The census of 1879 reported a Muslim population of 448,613 or 38.7 per cent of the inhabitants. In 1910 there were 612,137 Muslims, but their share of the population was only 32.3 per cent.

Yugoslavia: Religion and Nation

In the Kingdom of Yugoslavia only Serbs, Croats and Slovenes were recognised as founding nations of the new South Slavic state, and the position of the Bosnian Muslims was initially quite difficult. Immediately after the First World War there were cases of harassment and persecution, and the agrarian reform particularly affected the Muslims, since practically all landowners in Bosnia and Herzegovina were Muslims, and the Muslim farmers were discriminated against. The most drastic change, however, was that Bosnia and Herzegovina no longer existed as a political and administrative unit. The Muslims concentrated their efforts on preserving Islam and the religious institutions, while trying to obtain some degree of autonomy. Their political party, Jugoslovenska Muslimanska Organizacija (the Yugoslav Muslim Organisation, JMO), under the competent leadership of Mehmet Spaho, skilfully used the rivalry between Serbs and Croats to improve the position of the Muslims.

In 1930 the government established the Islamic Religious Community, abolished the religious-cultural autonomy of 1909, and, like the Austrian authorities, took control of the *vakuf* foundations. Another important step was to move the function of *reis-ul-ulema* to Belgrade. However, due to the key position of JMO in Yugoslav politics, in 1936 the Islamic Religious Community managed to inaugurate a new constitution, which re-established religious autonomy. The community regained its control of the *vakuf* foundations, *reis-ul-ulema* moved back to Sarajevo, and the Muslims were allowed to keep considerable parts of the *sharia*-based family law. There were also Islamic educational institutions both on secondary school and university level, in addition to several hundred Quranic primary schools.

During World War II, Bosnia and Herzegovina was annexed by the Croatian Ustasha state. Muslims were officially regarded as 'the flower of the Croat nation' and a monumental mosque was established in the centre of Zagreb. Parts of the Muslim population sympathised with the fascist regime and a Muslim SS-unit, the Handžar division, was organised. It should be pointed out, however, that Islamic religious leaders at a very early stage publically condemned the Ustasha atrocities and genocidal policies against the Serbs. There were also strong sympathies among the Muslims with the communist-led partisan movement. Bosnia and Herzegovina became the central battle ground in a cruel civil war between Serbs, Croats and Muslims. Nowhere else were people killed on a such a scale or in such a shocking manner. At the same time Bosnia symbolised the possibility of a life together. Under the slogan Brotherhood and Unity the partisans managed to mobilise Bosnians of all ethnic groups, and it was logical that the post-war Yugoslav federation should be proclaimed in the town of Jajce in 1943.

In Tito's Yugoslavia the Muslims of Bosnia in many respects occupied a specific position. At first, Islam as a religious community was seriously affected by the antireligious policies of the socialist regime. The Muslim infrastructure, in which the *vakuf* foundations played a key role, providing education and welfare, was dismantled. Land and buildings were confiscated, the Quranic schools and higher institutions of learning were closed, the Muslim press was silenced, *sharia* abolished and the veil forbidden. When the resistance was broken, the Islamic Religious Community, due to its relatively weak organisational structure, became the most tightly controlled of all religious institutions.

After Yugoslavia's break with the Soviet Union in 1948 and the creation of a specific brand of self-management socialism during the 1960s, the position of the religious communities improved substantially. Because of Tito's aspirations to become a leader of the non-aligned movement, the Muslim population, as well as the institutions of Islam, were given a special role in foreign policy. Yugoslav ambassadors in Muslim countries were generally recruited among Turks, Albanians, Macedonian or Bosnian Muslims, and the mosques of Sarajevo were always visited by prominent guests from the Islamic world. Taking advantage of these developments, the Islamic Religious Community gradually consolidated its position. More than 600 mosques were built or reconstructed all over Bosnia and Herzegovina, mostly financed by the believers themselves. The *medrese* (Ar. *madrasa*), religious secondary schools, started to function again and a Muslim theological faculty was solemnly opened in 1977. In addition, a great number of Bosnian Muslims studied at Islamic universities, such as the famous Al-Azhar in Cairo. As a result, the Islamic Community was strengthened by a new cadre of well-educated *imams* and other syllabification functionaries. A case in point is the famous Bosnian politician Haris Silajdžić.

Nation-Building and Secular Nationalism

Bosnia differed from other Yugoslav republics in one very important respect. There was no *Staatsvolk* constituting a majority of the inhabitants and making its imprint on society and culture. Instead three ethnic groups, Serbs, Croats and Muslims, were supposed to share political power. Immediately after the war several options, including partition, were in fact considered, but the communists chose to create the Republic of Bosnia and Herzegovina, partly because of the strong Muslim segment, partly in order to curb Croat and Serb rivalry and territorial aspirations. Between the two World Wars the Yugoslav Communist Party – on Comintern's order – had advocated the dissolution of Yugoslavia and issued statements that might indicate that the Bosnian Muslims at least potentially were a distinct people or nation. The dominant view within the party, however, was that the Muslims of Bosnia constituted a religious group, which due to specific historical circumstances possessed certain characteristics of an ethnic group. It was generally expected that they would finally assimilate.

However, it was very difficult even for a secularised Muslim to become a Serb or a Croat, as these identities were ultimately based on religious boundaries. Moreover, from a Serb or Croat perspective, Bosnian Muslims were, and to a considerable extent still are, a kind of traitor, who adopted the religion and culture of the invading Turks and were on the wrong side during the glorious wars of liberation which constitute the national myths of Serbs and Croats. Thus, at the same time as Croats and Serbs claimed that the Muslims were actually part of their own national corpus, they despised them. This meant that the process of assimilation which began in the late nineteenth century involved only a minority, and in the absence of a secular identity the only viable option for many Muslims who left the Islamic tradition was to become 'Yugoslavs'.

In the Arab- or Turkish-speaking Muslim world it is possible to construct a national identity based on language and perhaps pan-Arabic or pan-Turkish ideologies. This alternative was not available in Bosnia, as the high culture of Serbocroatian-speaking Muslims during the Ottoman period was not indigenous, but part of a universal Islamic civilisation. While the Slavic dialect was used in everyday life, the literary languages of educated Muslims were Arabic, Persian and Turkish. Bosnian culture before the Ottoman conquest, on the other hand, was Christian, and a matter of dispute between Croats and Serbs. The ambiguous status of Bosnian Muslims was reflected in the post-war censuses. In 1948 it was possible to declare oneself as 'Serbian Muslim', 'Croatian Muslim' or 'Nationally Undecided Muslim'. A majority, almost 800,000 individuals, or 90 per cent, chose the latter alternative. In 1953 there was another option: 'Undecided Yugoslav', and in 1961: 'Muslim - Ethnic Affiliation'. When Yugoslavia during the 1960s had given up any plans to establish a common Yugoslav (ethnic) identity, and was transformed into a highly decentralised federation, Bosnian Muslims were finally, in 1969, recognised as a state-building people, or nation, on the same level as Serbs, Croats, Slovenes, Macedonians and Montenegrins. This was confirmed by the constitutional changes in 1974, but as early as in the census of 1971, the category 'Muslims' (in a national sense) was introduced.

The Bosnian Communist Party was controlled by a coalition of Muslims, Serbs and Croats, where an important role was played by certain Muslim families or 'clans'. These secularised Muslims within the party actively pushed for a recognition of the Bosnian Muslims. The new nation was given the name *Muslimani*, i.e. Muslims, and the recognition started a process of nation-building where the history and culture of Bosnian Muslims was strongly emphasised. As the communists wanted to downplay the religious dimension as much as possible, there was a clear tendency to stress the (possible) Bogomil origin of the Muslims, which at least indirectly implied that the Muslims were actually the dominant nation of Bosnia and Herzegovina. The communists might have expected that by chosing the term Muslim, they would neutralise the socio-cultural and political role of Islam, but the effect was rather the reverse. In Serbo-Croatian the only way to distinguish between Muslims in an ethnic and religious sense was to use capital 'M'. As ethnic identity in this case would be inconceivable without a religious basis, it more or less automatically followed that those who did practice Islam were, after all, more genuine Muslims than others. This was further accentuated as cultural institutions, which in other parts of Yugoslavia had a strong national and symbolic function, in Bosnia and Herzegovina were supposed to be the common property of three nations. However, while Serbs and Croats had 'their' academies of sciences and cultural foundations in Zagreb and Belgrade, the only Muslim analogy were the Islamic institutions. Moreover, in the Islamic world it was impossible to apply the distinction between religion and nation, and it is hardly a coincidence that the Islamic Religious Community in 1969 changed its name to the Islamic Community.

The new attitude towards the Muslims coincided with a general modernisation of Bosnian society, which acquainted a growing number of Muslims with an industralised and urban environment, as well as higher education. Their share of the membership in the Bosnian Communist Party rose dramatically during the 1970s, and they were increasingly employed in the state apparatus and other power structures. Between 1971 and 1981 the number of Muslim communists grew three times, which meant that in the 1980s they were represented according to their share of the population. In addition, due to rapid population growth and extensive Croat and Serb migrations, the Muslims finally became the largest ethnic group in Bosnia. After World War II they constituted 30.8 per cent of the population, the Serbs 40.5 per cent and the Croats 22.2 per cent. In 1991 the situation was completely different. Now, 43.7 per cent of the population was Muslim, 31.3 per cent Serbian, and 17.5 per cent Croatian, and a Muslim majority was a likely prospect.

The demographic changes, and the political and religious mobilisation of the Muslims, worried both Croats and Serbs, in particular the latter. Serb intellectuals started to refer to a Stalinist-type 'Islamic socialism' which had allegedly conquered Bosnia, and many well-known personalities left Sarajevo. The accusation was partly correct, in the sense that the Bosnian regime was one of the most conservative and dogmatic in Yugoslavia. Using the delicate balance between religious and ethnic groups as a pretext, the Republican Communist Party reacted severely against anything that might be labelled ethnic hatred or nationalism. Statements or activities which in Croatia or Serbia were hardly controversial, might lead to imprisonment in Bosnia. This, however, affected all religious communities, especially Islam.

The Sarajevo Trial

After the revolution in Iran the Bosnian leadership grew visibly nervous and started a campaign against 'clero-nationalist' tendencies in all religious communities. The offensive culminated in 1983 with the infamous trial of thirteen Muslim intellectuals in Sarajevo. They were accused of having conspired against the socialist order with the purpose of creating an Islamic state ('Islamistan') in Bosnia. Among the prosecuted were engineers, economists, lawyers, teachers and religious scholars, including two women. The main suspect, Alija Izetbegović, the current president of Bosnia and Herzegovina, was sentenced to fourteen years in prison, of which he served almost six. The accusations focused on the Islamic Declaration, a treatise written by Izetbegović in 1970, and published in Arabic, Turkish and English, but not (until 1990) in Serbo-Croatian. Inspired by the declaration, the offenders had allegedly formed a secret organisation, which tried to spread its message during seminars at the Faculty of Islamic Theology, as well as in certain mosques. The group had also been in touch with foreign governments (Iran).

The trial, which rested on a weak legal foundation, was a traditional political performance of the communist type. Harmless circumstances or events were treated as stages in a conspiracy; discussions with relatives or friends were interpreted as enemy propaganda, and meetings in private homes were defined as the creation of a secret organisation. In his defence, Izetbegović argued that Bosnia or Yugoslavia were not even mentioned in his essay, and that he explicitly declares that an Islamic state can only be established in a country where Muslims constitute a majority of the population.

A large number of people were interrogated or arrested, and those involved later said that it was more or less chance that decided whether one would be prosecuted or called as a witness. The sentences, which were unusually severe, were widely criticised, both in Yugoslavia and abroad, and relations with Muslim countries seriously deteriorated.

The Islamic Declaration

In terms of genre, the Islamic Declaration is a religious and moral-political essay which, in a broad sociological perspective, passionately discusses the predicament of Islam and Muslims in the contemporary world. The general point of departure is that Muslim peoples live in a situation of moral decay and humiliating stagnation. In order to change these conditions a return to Islam and the Quran is necessary. However, a renewal is blocked by two forces: the 'clerics' and the 'modernists'. *Ulama*, the class of learned scholars, represents a degenerate Islam, which has turned religion into form without content, while modernist intellectuals try to popularise a Westernised culture which is foreign to Islam and the intimate feelings of the broad masses. The Muslim masses, therefore, lack the leaders and ideas which would awaken them from their lethargy, and there is a tragic distance between the intelligentsia and ordinary people. What is needed is a new brand of Muslim intellectuals, reborn in the spirit of their own tradition.

The ultimate aim of the spiritual revival is to establish an Islamic order, which according to Izetbegović encompasses two dimensions or elements: society and state. Without a society where people practice Islam, there can be no Islamic state. An Islamic state which does not rest on a living faith would be a hypocrisy, and could not exist without violence. This means that a mere political usurpation of power would only be a continuation of a situation which has led to the present crisis. On the other hand, says Izetbegović, the Islamic society must be protected by an Islamic state. Islamic renewal does not mean a denial of the rational aspects of modern society. Science and technology cannot and should not be ignored, but must be used in a proper way. Contrary to other religious and philosophical systems Islam offers a comprehensive vision of history and the world, which will overcome the contradictions of modern society.

For Izetbegović the Islamic order represents a more profound type of democracy. It is an expression of authentic freedom, because individual actions and society as a whole correspond to the essential character of the people, i.e. Islam. A true Islamic society can therefore never be coercive, although on the surface it might be different from the ideals of Western democracy. A society based on a genuine understanding of the Quran and an Islamic education will have certain consequences, though. Alcoholism, prostitution or pornography cannot be allowed. Neither can one accept that cultural norms and lifestyles opposed to the spirit of Islam are openly propagated. There must, says Izetbegović, be a 'congruence' between the message of media and mosque. An important issue concerns the position of non-Muslim minorities in an Islamic society. Their rights must be respected, to the extent that they do not harm Islam, and the declaration stresses that this is a consequence of the traditional tolerance towards Christians and Jews, which existed in the Ottoman empire.

The Young Muslims

It is sometimes argued that one should not dwell too much on the Islamic Declaration, since it was written some twenty-five years ago, and Izetbegović today has adopted a different position. This overlooks both recent statements by the president and the fact that there is a continuity in Izetbegović's views which goes back to his youth and involvement in the association of Young Muslims, a movement which has hardly been noticed in the West.

This organisation was formed shortly before the outbreak of the Second World War, as a reaction against the general conditions of Muslims in the Kingdom of Yugoslavia. The Young Muslims strived for a renewal of Islam and were convinced that a religious renaissance was essential to the integrity and independence of Bosnian Muslims. To achieve this it was necessary to form a movement of dedicated young people who would initiate a process of re-education and serve as examples of true Muslims. During the war they were active within the El Hidaje, the association of *imams*, or the humanitarian organisation Merhamet. On ideological grounds they were against both the Ustasha state and the communist partisans. In particular, they opposed the partition of Bosnia, which was a consequence of the formation of an autonomous Croatia in 1939.

After the war the Young Muslims continued their activities, and unsuccessfully tried to infiltrate Preporod, an organisation loyal to the regime. In 1947 ten Young Muslims were brought to trial and sentenced to long prison terms, accused of having conspired against the socialist order. One of the leaders of the movement was Alija Izetbegović, who was sentenced to three years imprisonment by a military court. After this serious set-back, the resistance was radicalised and the organisation started to function as a highly conspirative network. For some time the Young Muslims succeeded in keeping their activities secret, but in 1949 the authorities finally managed to uncover the organisation. At a second trial four leaders were sentenced to death for allegedly having planned terrorist activities. It is estimated that several thousand followers were affected by repression in some way or another, which means that the Young Muslims represented the most widespread ideological protest against the Yugoslav communist regime.

Religion and Politics in Bosnia

The Legacy of the Young Muslims is in many respects noticeable in today's Bosnia. When the Party of Democratic Action, SDA, was formed in March 1990, the nucleus consisted of former Young Muslims, their relatives, or persons who had supported Izetbegović in the 1970s and had been involved in the trial and persecutions of 1983. Although SDA had a neutral name and political programme, it was nevertheless a strictly Muslim party with an unmistakable religious orientation. In a very short time it grew into an impressive movement among Serbocroatian-speaking Muslims, not only in Bosnia and the Sandzak region, but also in Kosovo and Macedonia. The meetings during the Bosnian election campaign in 1990, with prayers, religious music, green flags and participants in oriental dress, were powerful manifestations of the religious and cultural identity of Bosnian Muslims.

Although religion played an important role during the election campaign, and SDA definitely was the 'most religious' of all major political parties in former Yugoslavia, it should be stressed that Izetbegović repeatedly denied any plans to form an Islamic state. He even rejected a (secular) Muslim national state. Throughout the political crisis in 1990 and 1991 he advocated a 'civic state' and a 'multi-ethnic society'. The latter

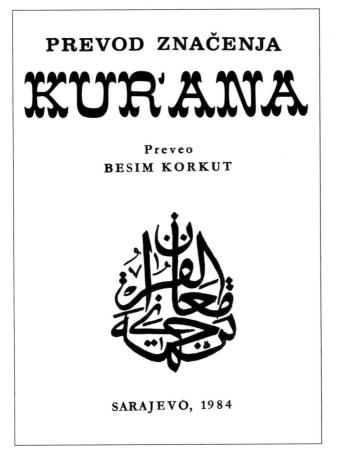

PREVOD ZNAČENJA

KUR'ANA

Preveo
BESIM KORKUT

SARAJEVO, 1984

The cover of a Kroatian translation of the Quran.

concept has caused some confusion among Western observers, who have tended to interpret it within their own frames of reference. It should be made quite clear that when Izetbegović and his political associates are referring to a multi-ethnic society, they do not mean a society where ethnicity – or religion – would be unimportant. On the contrary, a multi-ethnic Bosnia was – given the circumstances – the only way to guarantee the preservation and further development of a Bosnian–Muslim identity. For precisely this reason Izetbegović tried to prevent the dissolution of Yugoslavia right to the very end.

Developments during the war illustrate this very clearly. Whatever Croats or Serbs might think, the war has finally completed the process of nation-building among Bosnian Muslims, who are now officially defined as

Bosniacs. Moreover, 'Bosniac' is increasingly becoming synonymous with 'Bosnian', and political leaders often refer to the Muslims as 'the majority nation' of Bosnia. As far as religion is concerned, Izetbegović has stated very clearly that in the future, Bosnia will be a society where Islam naturally plays an important role. For him a Bosnian identity without Islam is unthinkable, which does not mean that Islam has to become a state religion, or that other world views or religions should be banned.

Religious Beliefs and Practices

It has generally been taken for granted that the role of religion in Bosnian society is negligible. A common remark is that the Bosniacs are European Muslims who do not have much in common with Islamic 'fundamentalists'. It is certainly true that Bosnian Muslims live in Europe, and that Serb and Croat propaganda about 'fundamentalist' conspiracies is exaggerated. On the other hand, it seems that the constant insistence on the idea of a highly secularised Bosnia says more about Western ambivalence towards Islam than about actual conditions in Bosnia. Albeit on a different scale, Muslims in Bosnia are faced with the same basic issues that confront all Muslim societies: How to formulate an ethnic identity different from religious identification, or how to distinguish between religion and politics in an environment where this was traditionally not being done? This has been the dilemma of Muslims in Bosnia over the past 100 years.

The question about the influence of Islam in Bosnian society cannot be answered unequivocally, as there is a lack of detailed and reliable surveys, of the kind available in, for example, Slovenia and Croatia, where sociologists of religion since the 1960s have investigated religious attitudes and practice. However, data from empirical research, as well as other sources, seem to indicate that Islam does play a significant role in Bosnian society. In the Yugoslav census of 1953, citizens were able to state their religious affiliation or to identify as non-believers. In Yugoslavia as a whole about 12 per cent of the population classified themselves as atheists, but regional and other variations were considerable. The percentage of atheists was larger among groups belonging to Orthodox Christian culture (Montenegrins 39.5 per cent, Serbs 15.8 per cent, Macedonians 15.8 per cent), than among those with a Catholic background (Slovenes 10.3 per cent, Croats 10 per cent). The decidedly lowest number of non-believers were to found, however, among the categories 'Yugoslavs' (mainly Bosnian Muslims), 4 per cent, and 'non-Slavs' (most of whom were Albanians), 3.3 per cent. A decade later (1964) a comparative sociological investigation was undertaken in all Yugoslav republics and autonomous areas. The percentage of believers was greatest in Kosovo (91 per cent) and Bosnia and Herzegovina (83.8 per cent), i.e. areas with a large Muslim population.

Unfortunately there are few recent studies on a Yugoslav level. To the extent that they exist they are often questionable from a statistical point of view. One example is a survey from 1990 according to which the proportion of believers would be 28 per cent in Bosnia, compared to 67 per cent in Kosovo. It turns out, on closer inspection, that Muslims constitute only 28 per cent, and party members more than 50 per cent of those interviewed, which in both cases drastically differs from the actual situation, and thus influences the results. If one compares religiosity and confessional background, according to the same survey 62 per cent of the Catholics, 60 per cent of the Muslims and 39 per cent of the Orthodox regard themselves as believers.

According to a sociological survey conducted by the University of Stockholm in the summer of 1996 on a sample of 3,200 inhabitants of Bosnia and Herzegovina, almost 90 per cent of the Muslim respondents identified themselves as members of the Islamic community. More than 80 per cent said they believe in God, whereas 27 per cent attended mosque every week, and another 9 per cent at least once a month. It is true that participation in religious activities is higher among Catholics (46 per cent attend mass every week), but this investigation shows that religion was more important among Muslims than is usually assumed. Moreover, due to the overrepresentation of people with higher education, the religiosity of Muslims is probably underestimated.

A common feature of Yugoslav investigations is the substantial variation in religious attitudes and practice according to educational background, or between rural and urban areas. The Bosnian sociologist Esad Cimić, who in the beginning of the 1960s reported an average of 60 per cent believers among Muslims in Herzegovina, found that such variations are particularly high among the Muslims. In his well-known study of village and market places in Western Bosnia, the American ethnologist William Lockwood refers to a situation where practically all Muslim villagers practice Islam. Perhaps, they do not pray the obligatory five times, but at least three, and Ramadan is generally observed. His field studies were undertaken in the 1970s, and it is interesting to note that the Norwegian ethnologist Tone Bringa in her recent book on a Muslim village near Sarajevo gives a similar account. While there are variations in religious practice, most people's identity is firmly grounded in Islam. Children are sent to the *mekteb* (Quranic school), Ramadan is observed, people visit the mosque, and of special importance are practices related to Sufism and Sufi orders.

Figures on intermarriage offer indirect evidence of the importance of religion. Reports about the Bosnian conflict have almost unanimously emphasised the presumably high percentage of people marrying outside their own ethnic group. While it is true that there is a fairly high degree of mixed marriages in urban areas, or in higher social strata, in general the rate of intermarriage is surprisingly low. In Yugoslavia as a whole, during

A Muslim boy in Macedonia dressed up for a circumcision ceremony
(photo: Ingvar Svanberg, 1984).

the post-war period there was an increase from 8.6 to 13 per cent. In Bosnia
the proportion was lower, about 12 per cent. Moreover, intermarriage was
more common between Croats and Serbs, than between Muslims and Serbs
or Muslims and Croats. That is, in Bosnia, as well as in Macedonia or
Kosovo, people of Muslim origin were less prepared to cross the cultural–
religious border. In other words, regardless of personal religiosity, religious
background acts as a powerful boundary mechanism.

Islamic Renaissance?

What is the role of Islam after the political changes in 1990, and, in
particular, after a devastating war, which has not only led to human losses
and ethnic cleansing, but to massive destruction of the religious and cultural
infrastructure? It is obvious that Islam is present in public life to an extent
which radically differs from conditions in socialist Yugoslavia. Religious
leaders usually attend official occasions, they frequently appear in the
media, and are generally treated with reverence. Another feature is that
religious holidays increasingly tend to acquire a semi-official character. In
this respect the situation is similar to that of Serbia or Croatia, where the
Catholic and Orthodox churches play a prominent role. In Bosnia this

tendency is particularly strong, due to the character of Islam as a socio-religious system and the close relations between religious institutions and the major political party. After all, the Bosnian president is a believer who actively practices Islam, and in 1994 fulfilled the obligation of *hajj*, accompanied by wounded war veterans on his pilgrimage to Mecca.

On the other hand, the religious renaissance might be understood as a natural return to positions which Islam lost artificially and by force when the communists took over in 1945. Therefore, the higher societal presence of religion does not necessarily mean that the influence of Islam is increasing on a more profound level. Fairly large parts of the middle strata of Muslim society in Bosnia are certainly secularised, partly because they were members of the Communist Party. This is confirmed by Alija Izetbegović himself, who makes the sociologically plausible comment that Islam is stronger in villages and larger cities and that peasants and intellectuals are religious, whereas the middle classes are not. Therefore, recent changes are probably alien to a substantial part of the urban population, something which is reflected in the frequent disputes between secular media and the Islamic press. In any case, official Islam has strengthened its position as an institution. In 1993 the Bosnian Muslims formed their own independent Islamic Community when Mustafa efendija Cerić was elected *reis-ul-ulema* and leader of the Bosnian *rijaset* (Islamic authority). During the war Cerić has emerged as a strong popular leader who has stressed the social and political dimensions of Islam. Especially during the tragic events of Srebrenica in the summer of 1995 he played a very important role.

In spite of the war the Islamic Community has created a more vigorous organisation and has also tried to improve education on all levels. Apart from the theological faculty and the *medrese* in Sarajevo, there are four new Islamic institutions of higher learning, the *medrese* in Tuzla, Cazin, Gračanica near Visoko, and Travnik. Important changes have also occurred as far as religious education of children and youth is concerned. In 1994 religion was introduced as a subject in Bosnian schools. It is confessional and voluntary, but there seems to be a strong psychological pressure to participate and according to news reports about 80–90 per cent of Muslim children are enrolled. Islam is thus more noticeable in the media, and has, moreover, media of its own. Besides the official organs of the Community (*Preporod, Islamska Misao, Mualim*) the most important Islamic paper is the weekly *Ljiljan*. Its former editor-in-chief, Džemaludin Latić, was sentenced to prison at the Sarajevo trial in 1983. The magazine is a successor of *Muslimanski Glas*, which was the official organ of the SDA, and although *Ljiljan* is independent it is no doubt very close to the ruling party. It is here that Alija Izetbegović and other politicians give their most important interviews. A specific feature of *Ljiljan* is its professionalism. In journalistic terms it is simply of high quality. The general outlook is modern, without the typical inward and traditionalist tone characteristic of the religious press in (former) Yugoslavia. Besides, it is advocating a vigorous national line, stressing the Bosniac cultural heritage and, above all, religion. The general frame of reference is that of Izetbegović: without Islam there is no Bosniac identity. Another expression of these developments is the publication of books, not only belonging to the corpus of Bosnian national literature, or dealing with Bosnian history, but also purely Islamic works, both in translation and by Bosnian authors. Recently a new exclusive edition of the Quran was published.

An interesting aspect is the tendency to reaffirm the Sufi traditions in Bosnian Islam. Already during the late socialist period Sufism played an important role in the official magazine *Preporod*. This is even more so today. The Sufi orders are being revived and traditional meetings, *mevlud* (Ar. *mawlid*) are given wide publicity. It has even been said that officers and commanders of the Bosnian army are not only influenced by Sufi traditions, but are themselves, in some cases, *shaykhs*. In general there is a strong religious presence in the army. *Imams* constitute a natural element in the organisation, an equivalent to the political commissars in the former Yugoslav Peoples Army, and many *imams* have participated – and died – as soldiers or officers. Certain units make a point of cultivating Islam, such as the 7th Army Corps, which at the parade after the victories in Western Bosnia in 1995 greeted the president with 'Alahu ekber' (Ar. *Allahu akbar*, God is greater). In fact, the Bosnian government has been criticised for neglecting professional skills and giving too much importance to religious and political (SDA) loyalty when appointing military commanders.

Within the framework of the Bosnian army there have also been volunteers from Islamic countries, the well-known *mujahidin*. They consisted of some 3,000 soldiers concentrated in the Zenica area, expressing a strong Islamist position. Together with these soldiers, various Islamist religious and humanitarian organisations worked in Bosnia during the war. This sometimes caused problems not only in relation to the United States or secularised segments of the population, but also led to clashes with representatives of official Islam.

The dominant circles of the ruling party display a distinct Islamic orientation. Several leading personalities, including the *reis-ul-ulema* and sometimes the president, have expressed worries regarding moral issues, such as women's clothes, mixed marriages, birth rates, the educational system, or the marketing of pork meat in Sarajevo. A much-debated incident involved the character of the celebration of New Year's Eve 1996 on Sarajevo television, which prompted President Izetbegović to write a public letter denouncing behaviour alien to the Bosnian–Muslim tradition.

Foreign journalists who initially described Bosnia as a secular society have noted that, as the war continued, the social presence of Islam became stronger. A common explanation is the war as such, that is in a situation when people are labelled as Muslims and killed because of their ethno-religious affiliation, when mosques are being destroyed and graveyards flattened, they will identify as Muslims out of sheer self-preservation. At the same time it is pointed out that refugees from Eastern Bosnia to a large extent are behind the changes in Sarajevo. This actually shows that there was a basis, that Islam did constitute a living reality among large segments of the Muslim population. Without this basis Islam would hardly grow in importance. The natural alternative would instead be secular nationalism, which, incidentally, does exist.

It is very difficult to say anything definite about the degree to which Islamist ideas are effective within the population at large. That they do exist is clear, but we have no detailed knowledge about popular attitudes or organisational structures. It seems as if such tendencies, at least until now, have been channelled within the official Islamic Community, as well as the Party of Democratic Action and its affiliated organisations. In an interesting study of sermons during the Ramadan of 1992, Xavier Bougarel analyses a variety of currents along the dimensions political/non-political and conservative/revivalist Islam. He concludes that a political, revivalist version of Islam seems to have been strengthened during the war. In her book *Being Muslim the Bosnian Way*, Tone Bringa makes the important point that these developments have largely been influential in urban areas.

It seems unlikely that extreme Islamist tendencies will become dominant in the Bosnian context. There have been tensions within the ruling party, and when Prime Minister Silajdžić left the government and SDA in 1996, this was generally interpreted as a clash between 'fundamentalists' and 'Westerners'. It is doubtful whether this assessment is correct. The conflict was primarily political, rather than religious, and concerned issues like the role of the Bosnian army, the character of the Bosnian state and relations with Croatia. It is, nevertheless, of considerable interest that SDA, with its religious–national message, won an overwhelming victory in the first post-war elections of 1996, while Silajdžić's new party, generally expected to be popular among the urban and modern strata of Bosnian society, made a rather poor performance.

The war in Bosnia was brought to an end by the Dayton Agreement in November 1995. The major points of the agreement have not yet (1997) been implemented, and the prospect of a unified, multiethnic Bosnia and Herzegovina is uncertain. It is interesting to observe that Džemaludin Latić, writing in *Ljiljan* on several occasions, has a vision of the future which seems to be a restoration of the Ottoman *millet* system. He advocates selective use of modern technology and a return to authentic Islam, and suggests that the major ethnic groups should live together, side by side, governed by their own religious traditions. In his view, Bosnian believers of all major religions have a common interest in defending moral and spiritual values against the onslaught of a materialist and godless culture.

Literature

For a general introduction to the history of Muslims in Bosnia, see Noel Malcolm, *Bosnia: A Short History* (London: Macmillan, 1994); *The Muslims of Bosnia-Hercegovina: Their Historic Development from the Middle Ages to the Dissolution of Yugoslavia*, ed. Mark Pinson (Cambridge, MA: Harvard University Press, 1994); Robert J. Donia and John V.A. Fine Jr, *Bosnia and Hercegovina: A Tradition Betrayed* (London: Hurst, 1994); and Francine Friedman, *The Bosnian Muslims: Denial of a Nation* (Boulder, Co: Westview Press, 1996).

National and political currents among Bosnian Muslims during Austrian rule are discussed by Robert J. Donia in *Islam under the Double Eagle: The Muslims of Bosnia and Hercegovina, 1878–1914*, East European Monographs, 78 (Boulder, Co: East European Quarterly, 1981). A standard work on socio-cultural change and Muslim identity in post-war Yugoslavia is William Lockwood, *European Moslems: Ethnicity and Economy in Western Bosnia* (New York: Academic Press, 1975). On the religious situation, see Tone Bringa, *Being Muslim the Bosnian Way: Identity and Community in a Central Bosnian Village* (Princeton, NJ: Princeton University Press, 1995); Michael Selss, *The Bridge Betrayed: Religion and Genocide in Bosnia* (Berkeley: University of California Press, 1996); and Xavier Bougarel, 'Ramadan During a Civil War as Reflected in a Series of Sermons', *Islam and Christian-Muslim Relations*, 6:1 (1995), pp. 79–103. For an extensive survey of literature on Islam and the Balkans, see Alexandre Popović, *L'Islam Balkanique: Les musulmans du sud-est européen dans la période post-ottomane*, Balkanologische Veröffentlichungen, 11 (Berlin: Osteuropa-Institut an der Freien Universität Berlin, 1986). Comprehensive data on religious and cultural affairs are also found in Smail Balic, *Das unbekannte Bosnien: Europas Brücke zur islamischen Welt* (Köln: Böhlau Verlag, 1992). See also, from the perspective of political science, Andreas Kappeler, Gerhard Simon and Georg Brunner, *Muslim Communities Re-emerge: Historical Perspectives on Nationality, Politics, and Opposition in the Former Soviet Union and Yugoslavia* (Durham, NC: Duke University Press, 1994). For data on religion, political attitudes and ethnic identity, see Kjell Magnusson, *Attitudes and Values in Bosnia and Herzegovina: A Sociological Investigation* (Stockholm: Centrum för invandrarforskning, 1996).

Chapter Fourteen

Germany and Austria

Franz Kogelmann

In the spring of 1995, the German Booksellers' Trade Association nominated the internationally renowned Oriental Studies specialist Annemarie Schimmel for its annual peace prize. The Association cited Schimmel's work as 'furthering the understanding and knowledge of Islam', seeing its award as a 'symbol for the encounter rather than confrontation of cultures, a symbol for patience, poetry and global culture that respects difference'. The political power of such an award was dramatically demonstrated after the prize-winner indicated in a TV interview a degree of understanding for the occasionally vehement reactions within the Islamic world to Salman Rushdie's *Satanic Verses*. Over the following few weeks, Schimmel found herself at the centre of a heated public debate regarding her entitlement to the award.

The affair polarised the intellectual, artistic and political worlds alike. Although it was not possible to define any clear lines of demarcation, the political right in German public life tended to support the awarding committee's decision without reserve. On the other hand, several left or left of centre intellectuals, politicians, women's rights activists and publishers attempted to defame Schimmel and stop the award being presented. As far as they were concerned, Schimmel's comments on the injured feelings of Muslims put her under suspicion of being an advocate of Islamic fundamentalism, and her pronouncements seemed to chip away at the foundations of Western society and the universality of human rights. Over and above this, the left had the impression that the winner of the German Booksellers' Association Peace Prize was herself an Islamic fundamentalist who supported the spread throughout Europe of a militant religion whose goal was world revolution against the achievements of Western civilisation – 'the Fifth Column on the march', as it was expressed by the leftist politician and publicist Rolf Stolz.

The award of the peace prize to Annemarie Schimmel was, however, not halted by these suspicions and accusations. The narrow view of a dynamic world religion as mediaeval and threatening, and as the antithesis to Western enlightenment and modernism, does seem to be common in society at large. This was clearly acknowledged by the president of Germany, Roman Herzog, in his eulogy at the award ceremony:

> It is no sweeping statement when I say that the associations conjured up by many in connection with the word 'Islam' are things such as 'inhumane punishment', 'religious intolerance', 'oppression of women' and 'aggressive fundamentalism'. But this is tunnel vision, and we must correct it.

It is not only events such as the conferral of a cultural award on a renowned Oriental Studies expert that can provoke public debate on the relationship between Islam and the West – religious symbols have the same potential. When the president of the Islamic community in Austria in 1995 instructed Muslim schoolgirls to wear a head-scarf during Islamic religion lessons, it ignited a debate over domestic policy. Although the Education Ministry's position was clear – namely, that religious education is the internal concern of each of the officially recognised faiths – representatives from each of the political parties grasped the opportunity to proclaim their attitude towards Islam and Muslims in Austria in the full glare of the media spotlight. Aside from careful and considered statements regarding the integration of Muslims into society and remarks drawing attention to the right to religious freedom, there were also voices that openly set a choice before Muslims: assimilate or be excluded. It was above all the conservative, Germanic-nationalist element in Austrian politics that tended to make the connection between the Muslim minority and religious fanaticism.

There can be no doubt that the last twenty years have seen political developments in some Muslim countries which have lead to a less than rosy image of Islam in the West. A bestseller such as Betty Mahmoudy's *Not Without My Daughter* perhaps owes its impressive success in Germany and Austria to certain latent prejudices in these societies regarding the Islamic world, and after the Iraqi invasion of Kuwait which led to the Gulf War in 1991 it was even easier for military strategists to find a new threat to Western interests. The disintegration of the Warsaw Pact at the end of the 1980s had taken away the threat to world peace and the search for a new concrete enemy by influential political advisors and strategists such as Samuel Huntington resulted in the prediction that future conflicts would develop out of a *clash of civilizations* and, in particular, the Islamic 'threat'.

The Mediterranean regions, shaped as they are by both Islam and Christianity, are steeped in centuries of common history which is remarkable not just for its succession of wars and rulers but also for the vast richness of its cultural achievements. This community of history – insofar as it is present in the collective consciousness of the people – has, however, not helped either the breaking down of prejudice or the creation of tolerance of cultural and religious differences. As a result, Central Europe is dominated by fixed, simplistic conceptions of the Islamic world in which national, ethnic and confessional differentiation is largely unknown. Islam is generally equated with certain political Islamic movements, and the word 'Islam' is all too easily used as a synonym for fanaticism. The danger is that such simplistic and discriminatory preconceptions will be transferred onto the millions of Muslims living throughout Europe, thus leading inevitably to the exclusion of a religious minority from society at large.

Historical Background

In contrast to the main colonial powers of the nineteenth century, England and France, both Germany and Austria have relatively little experience of contact with the Islamic world or colonial rule over a Muslim society. The smallness of the German states until their unification in 1871 prevented any intensive contact with Islam. The Turkish Wars in the sixteenth and seventeenth centuries brought perhaps a few thousand Muslim prisoners of war, the so-called *Beutetürken* (booty Turks), under German control, and the expanding military power Prussia was able to raise at least some units of Muslim cavalry in the nineteenth century. These early contacts between Germany and the Islamic world were in themselves of little or no significance for the history of Islam at large or, indeed, the history of Islam in Germany, and the short period of colonial rule over a few Islamic areas in East and West Africa had no consequences in that sense either. When the Ottoman empire joined the German and Austro–Hungarian side in the First World War, the Islamic question became important, however, at least for the propaganda machinery of the military planners. German strategists attempted to use the fact that the formal head of Sunnite Muslims, the Ottoman Sultan-Caliph, was on their side to exercise some influence over the Muslims serving under the Western Allies. However, the propaganda campaign to portray the war as a holy Islamic war (*jihad*) was not aimed simply at the front or only at Muslims serving with the British, French and Russian forces; German authorities also attempted to indoctrinate Muslim prisoners of war in specially created camps, in order to use them themselves. This '*jihad* made in Germany' was not particularly successful in the final analysis, but some 15,000 Muslims came to Germany initially and a rudimentary Islamic infrastructure grew up under the auspices of the propaganda campaign, consisting of a mosque and the appointment of *imams*. It barely impinged on ordinary daily life in Germany, however.

Austrian contact with the Islamic world developed along rather different lines, caused by the proximity of the Ottoman empire. Although there were early cultural and economic contacts between scattered Muslims around the Danube and present-day Austria in the Middle Ages, the history of Austro–Islamic relations is dominated by episodes of a war-like nature. Traces of the horrific experiences of Austrians in the Turkish Wars can still be found today in numerous folk tales. Inhabitants of Austria who lived close to the border were faced with attacks by Turks from the fifteenth century onwards, and the threat to the Habsburg dynasty was at its greatest with the second siege of Vienna in 1683. The defeat of the Turks before the gates of Vienna was a turning point for both the Austrian monarchy and the Sublime Porte itself. The Ottoman expansion into Europe ended with this defeat and from this point onwards the empire was increasingly on the defensive against Christian Europe. The complete conquest of Hungary by the Holy Alliance, formed by Austria, Poland and Venice, among others, brought the dual Austro–Hungarian throne to the Habsburg dynasty and eventually its rise to the top European stage. The Islamic threat to the Christian Occident was thus repelled.

The Congress of Berlin in 1878 gave Austria rights to the occupation and administration of the Ottoman provinces of Bosnia and Herzegovina, and so the Habsburgs came into possession of a colony containing about 60,000 Muslims. The two provinces were annexed in 1908 before becoming part of the Kingdom of Yugoslavia after the collapse of the Austro–Hungarian Empire in 1918. The forty years under Austrian rule created a new situation for those Muslims who had chosen not to emigrate to the Ottoman empire. Before this time, Muslims under their caliphs had been in a privileged position compared to the Catholic and Orthodox Christians. Now they found themselves subjects of a Christian power.

It is difficult to assess what concrete effects the Habsburg reforms of religious infrastructure, education or economy had on the lives and national awareness of Muslims in Bosnia and Herzegovina, but the Austro–Hungarian state was confronted with the new situation of having to come to terms with the phenomenon of Islam. The administration of an area settled by Muslims, the recruitment of Muslim soldiers and the presence of Muslims in the heart of Austria necessitated a social and legal mechanism. For the Muslims living in the multi-national Habsburg empire, the biggest impact was that made by the Islam Law (*Islamgesetz*). Based on laws dating from 1867 and 1874, which guaranteed individual religious freedom and formalised legal recognition of religious groups and their relationship with the state, the Islam Law was passed in 1912. This law referred to Muslims of the Hanafi school of law within the Austrian half of the empire, placing Muslims *de jure* on the same footing as the followers of other religions and giving the teachings of Islam, as long as they were not contrary to it, legal protection. This creation of religious equality did not, however, go hand in hand with the creation of an Islamic community in Austria; it was only in the second half of the twentieth century that the time was ripe for such a step.

There was little contact between Germans or Austrians and Muslims until the restructuring of Europe after World War I, and what contacts there were had a clearly defined power structure. The strict conditions of the Versailles Peace Treaty hindered any development of diplomatic relations between the Weimar Republic or the first Austrian Republic and Muslim countries, most of which were under French or British colonial, protectorate or mandate rule. In addition, at that time only a small number of Muslims had settled in either Austria or Germany, although some Islamic groups were found in Berlin and Vienna, partially as a result of the activities of German and Austrian converts. These groups had a wide range of goals, from the simple cultivation of Islamic culture to the creation of an international network in the fight against the imperial powers that governed the homelands. After coming to power, the Nazis either remoulded Islamic groups so that they were acceptable to their own aims, or banned them outright.

After the outbreak of World War II, both the Wehrmacht and the SS (*Schutzstaffel*) made attempts to continue the rather unsuccessful First World War policy on Islam. The primary goal was, of course, to muster and indoctrinate Muslim fighting units, especially the SS, in both the Soviet and Yugoslav theatres of war, but the Nazi propaganda machine also made use of prominent Muslims who were opposed to Britain and France, and this lead to the *mufti* of Jerusalem, Amin al-Husaini, being in Germany from late 1941 onwards. The *Abwehr* (secret service) agent, the Hungarian Count Lászlo E. Almásy – the central character in the film *The English Patient* (1997) – even saw Amin al-Husaini as the future Caliph. Shakib Arslan, a Druse leader, mentor of various nationalist movements in the Arab world and a prominent enemy of France, was even given the dubious honour of being elevated to the rank of honorary Aryan. But surely the most absurd step taken in the name of the policy on Islam was the SS's order to find places in the Quran that could be used in propaganda to indicate that Hitler was the executor of Muhammad's prophecies.

The Arrival of the *Gastarbeiter*

The reconstructed industrial societies in Central and Western Europe which grew up out of the rubble of the Second World War proved to be a powerful attraction for people in the economically disadvantaged regions of Europe, Asia and Africa and, because the requirements for cheap labour caused by the booming economies could not be fulfilled from the native workforce from the 1960s onwards, several European governments attempted to use agreements and treaties to direct the stream of immigrants into specific channels. Workers, hired by both government and private organisations, looked for ways of earning a living in the rich north. As of the 1980s, however, wars and political or economic crises played the greater role in shaping international population movements and these became difficult to channel.

The overwhelming majority of migrants to Germany and Austria came from the Mediterranean basin. Neither country had any significant numbers of aliens within its borders at the beginning of the 1950s – except the allied occupation troops and other experts assisting in the creation of new administrative structures, but the proportion grew sharply after 1960. Germany signed an employment treaty with Italy as early as 1955 and Greece, Spain, Turkey, Morocco, Portugal, Tunisia and finally Yugoslavia followed between 1960 and 1968. The Austrian recruitment of foreign workers began in 1962 after initial resistance from the unions. Today, shortly before the new millennium, the total number of legal and statistically recognisable aliens living in both states constitutes about 9 per cent of the total population. The regional distribution of aliens is uneven and concentrated chiefly on the conurbations. Unlike the United States, Canada or Australia, neither Germany nor Austria see themselves as immigrant countries; the immigration of foreign labour was originally seen as temporally limited. The workers were intended to return to their native soil after only a few years and make room for others to take their places according to demand. They were not immigrants in the true sense of the word but rather, subject as they were to the laws of supply and demand, *Gastarbeiter* (guest workers).

In view of the native countries of the *Gastarbeiter*, a high proportion of them were Muslims, although a direct link between nationality and religion can be made in only a few cases; and even if the workers are nominally Muslim, this tells us nothing about the degree of religiosity or the role that Islam plays in their daily life. It can be said with relative safety that all the roughly 28,000 Tunisians, 80,000 Moroccans and 35,000 Pakistanis currently living in Germany are Muslim. Among the Turkish nationals, by far the largest group of aliens, most, but by no means all, are Muslim. Ethnic and religious minorities in particular have shown a willingness to leave Turkey and there are, apart from Turkish Christians, a disproportionately high number of Turkish Alevites in Germany and Austria. Little concrete is known about this Shiite group or the contents of its doctrine and there are only vague estimates that the proportion of the Turkish population made up by them is between 15 and 25 per cent. Just as the Sunnite Turks cannot be identified with any particular ethnic group, so the Alevites are to be found among ethnic Turks as well as Turkish nationals of Kurd or Arab origin. According to their own figures, there are about 600,000 Alevites out of a total of slightly more than 2 million Turkish nationals living in Germany. It is even more difficult to identify *Gastarbeiter* from modern Yugoslavia (Serbia and Montenegro) with particular ethnic or religious groups. However, despite the ethnic cleansing, the repressive measures aimed at Muslims in Kosovo and the Sandzhak, Islam is still the third strongest religion in the Federal Republic of Yugoslavia, comprising about 12 per cent of the population and, as such, it is certainly not a small percentage of the approximately 750,000 Yugoslav *Gastarbeiter* currently working in Germany who are Muslim. There are even some members of the

A Turkish restaurant in Berlin (photo: Ingvar Svanberg, 1980).

Greek Muslim minority among the some 350,000 Greeks living in Germany.

The 1980s and 1990s saw different reasons for the immigration of Muslims. Wars or social and economic problems caused hundreds of thousands of Muslims to leave their homes and stream towards Central Europe not as officially recruited *Gastarbeiter* but looking for protection. Thus a large proportion of the 60,000 Afghans, 110,000 Iranians and 55,000 Lebanese, not all of whom are Muslim, came to Germany as asylum-seekers. The debate on domestic politics that raged in the Federal Republic at the end of the 1980s, dominated as it was by fears of being taken over by foreigners, riots directed against foreigners and wholesale pre-judgements of asylum-seekers as frauds or economic refugees, led to a drastic tightening of the asylum regulations. The stream of supplicants was reduced to not much more than a trickle but, since the causes of such migrations remain, thousands still hope to find a better life in Central Europe, be it as asylum-seekers or as illegal immigrants risking life and limb. After the outbreak of the civil war in Bosnia–Herzegovina in 1992, around 340,000 Bosnian refugees, mostly Muslim, were taken in by Germany and about 70,000 by Austria. Aside from the *Gastarbeiter*, who were the advance guard, ever more Muslim students, academics and diplomats are settling in both countries. However, even though there are several thousand Muslim students at German and Austrian universities, numerous international organisations have opened branches in the cities of the two countries and most Muslim countries have diplomatic contacts with both, the largest group of Muslims is still formed by workers. The ethnic, national and confessional make-up of the alien Muslim community in Germany is generally comparable to that in Austria. In both countries, the Muslims constitute an estimated 2.5 to 3.5 per cent of the total population. This means that there are in Germany between 2 and 2.7 million Muslims, in Austria 200,000–300,000. Turkish nationals form the largest group by far, followed by Muslims from the Balkans. Arabic- and Berber-speakers from the Near East or the Maghreb are minority groups, as are Iranians, Afghans and Muslims from the Indian subcontinent and black Africa. The majority of all Muslims are Sunnites but there are minority confessions such as the above-mentioned Alevites from Turkey, Shiites from Iran and even a small minority who belong to the two – by many Muslims seen as heretical – Ahmadiyya movements, Ahmadiyya Movement in Islam (Qadian) and Ahmadiyya Anjuman Ishaat-i Islam (Lahore). Thus multilingualism, multi-culturalism and religious pluralism has become both reality and the norm in Germany and Austria.

Few detailed facts can be given about the former German Democratic Republic. It is certain that hardly any foreign nationals settled in East Germany, either before or after the reunification. Naturally enough, what economic, political and cultural contacts East Germany had with the Islamic world were with the so-called socialist brother states. Training and education programmes in both military and civil spheres necessitated short- or long-term stays by Muslims from Syria, Iraq, South Yemen, Algeria and the former Spanish West Sahara. However, they cannot have amounted to more than a few thousand officers and specialists. Similar numbers of students from the Near East and North Africa also came from countries such as South Yemen, Libya and Algeria. The Palestine Liberation Organisation (PLO), and other liberation movements, received generous educational aid beside humanitarian and military support.

Societal and organisational issues

The dispersion of Muslims throughout Europe raises some fundamental political, social and cultural questions which cannot be answered by either the religious and social traditions of Islam or those of the European nations themselves. On the one hand, European history is full of discrimination against ethnic and religious minorities, including the physical extermination of minority groups. On the other hand, there have been changes in the relationship between Muslims and Europeans since the end of European colonialism. Whereas a European minority previously ruled over a Muslim majority in the colonies, nowadays a Muslim minority lives within a

European majority. The Islamic legal tradition has developed a model regarding Muslims and non-Muslims living together in one society. However, this model assumes that the Muslims are in the majority and are the ruling power, framing the laws and ensuring that jurisdiction proceeds according to Islamic law. Of course, this situation does not exist in Germany and Austria, where Muslims form a minority whose influence on society's decision-making is small. It is possible that this situation could make them uncertain about their legal position from an Islamic point of view, but it seems that the majority of Muslim migrants have no difficulty in disregarding the traditional regulations, which shows that many of the Muslims living here no longer feel bound by Islamic law.

Western governments followed the economic impulses of the job market throughout the 1960s and gave little thought to the social, cultural and political effects for all concerned. The oil crisis in 1973 and the resultant economic recession caused the German government to take steps to reduce the immigration of foreign labour. Bonn called a halt to the recruitment of labour from outside the European Economic Community (EEC), but this failed singularly to achieve its aim of reducing the number of *Gastarbeiter*. In fact, the numbers of Turkish nationals, the largest group of Muslims, increased drastically from 900,000 to more than 1.3 million in the period between 1973 and 1980. The main reason for this growth was the desire among many of the Turkish *Gastarbeiter* not to be separated from their families for a long time. Whereas the 1960s had seen mostly men alone leaving home to try their luck in foreign lands for a limited period only, it became clear in the 1970s that for many reasons the stay in those foreign lands would be of longer duration than originally planned. The German government reacted to the huge numbers of immigrants, mostly Turkish women and children, with a more restrictive foreign policy. However, measures such as financial support for workers from outside the EEC to return home were effective only in the short term, and even reintegration plans developed in Turkey and subsidised by Germany enjoyed only limited success. The numbers of Muslims living in Germany and Austria continued to rise, and today the third generation of 'children with a foreign passport' – the official German designation – is growing up in both countries, largely alienated from their ancestral homeland.

Turkish nationals, in particular, tend to view the country in which they have worked for several decades, where their children and grandchildren have grown up and now live, as the focal point in their lives. According to a survey made by the Centre for Turkish Studies in Essen in 1992, 83 per cent of the Turkish nationals living in Germany said they did not wish to return to Turkey. Germany and Austria have become *de facto* immigrant countries. A migrant who decides to settle for a longer period in Germany or Austria must face a number of drawbacks. Foreigners must reckon with numerous disadvantages on the housing and job markets and, even though all are protected by laws, these laws allow nationals from the European Union (EU) far more freedom than nationals from outside the EU. The restrictive norms of the laws governing aliens in Germany and Austria are thus applicable to Muslims, most of whom come from non-EU countries, the thinking behind this legal framework being the fear of an uncontrolled flood of immigrants.

Austria started to allow migration only within set quotas in 1992, and five years later the Austrian parliament passed the so-called *Fremdenrecht* (Rights for Aliens). Apart from a very limited immigration based on a quota system and linked to economic demand, these Rights are essentially concerned with the integration of aliens already living in Austria. This means, among other things, a permanent right of residence after eight years of legal residence and assured residency for second generation aliens who have grown up in Austria. The most effective method of integrating foreign nationals into society is, of course, to naturalise them, with all the rights and obligations that entails, but both Austria and Germany define nationality according to extraction (*jus sanguinis*), i.e., nationality is decided by place of birth, as long as one of the parents possesses the citizenship of the country in question. Whereas Austrian law permits naturalisation after ten years of legal residency – and the resignation of previous citizenship – German citizenship is harder to obtain. Until 1993, an applicant had an automatic legal right to naturalisation only if married to a German national, all other cases being decided by the authorities. German law has offered a simplified form of naturalisation since 1991 which applies principally to young foreign nationals and aliens who have been resident in Germany for many years. It is only since 1993 that this latter group has had the right to naturalisation.

Naturalisation generally requires the resignation of original citizenship to avoid cases of dual citizenship. However, the German authorities may accept dual citizenship, for example if the renouncing of the original citizenship is difficult or impossible. The surrender of citizenship sometimes brings the loss of certain rights; in some states, only full citizens may purchase property or inherit property or family rights. However, emotional factors also play a certain role. The surrender of the original citizenship is often felt as a loss of cultural identity and ultimately means the breaking of all ties with home, and the willingness of non-EU aliens to surrender their citizenship is accordingly low. Instead they try to obtain dual citizenship. Although the German authorities do frequently accept this solution, there are relatively few Turkish nationals who are willing to take this step. For example, only 1.5 per cent of Turkish nationals became naturalised Germans in 1995.

Apart from the legal issues, Muslims also have other problems concerning their integration. Unlike Christian immigrants from southern Europe, the majority of the Muslims were faced not only with social and cultural but also with religious alienation. The lack – at least initially – of a religious infrastructure in the form of mosques and other Islamic institutions only reinforced the feeling of religious and cultural deracination. The first Muslim *Gastarbeiter* who came to Germany and Austria in the 1960s were mostly single men who were housed by the companies that employed them. They had little chance of coming into contact with the population of their host country, housed as they were in men's hostels and isolated by linguistic and cultural barriers. Just as the greater part of their private lives was spent behind closed doors, so did little of their religious practices become known to the world outside. Thus the native population had little or no chance to find out about these practices and the details of the faith of this minority. Certainly there was also little interest in doing so, and Islam as a consequence – if it was recognised at all – in the 1960s came to be seen in Germany as a *Gastarbeiter* religion, stigmatised by the low social status of its practitioners. As the *Gastarbeiter* were not expected to stay long, there was no need to delve any deeper into this virtually invisible religion.

As far as Muslim *Gastarbeiter* are concerned, the mosque is more than a place for fulfilling one's religious duty; it is also a place of community and preservation of identity, a piece of home in a foreign land. Apart from two mosques founded in the 1950s by the Qadian branch of the missionary Ahmadiyya movement in Hamburg and Frankfurt-am-Main, for a long time there were hardly any sacred Islamic buildings in post-war Germany that would have been regarded as such by the population at large. There are a few representative buildings in the Islamic style in cities such as Munich, Hamburg, Mannheim and Aachen which have developed into centres of Islamic culture, but the majority of Muslim religious life takes place in private apartments rented for this purpose, garages, old factory halls or basements. The construction of a mosque or the conversion of another building into one, is generally regarded with suspicion by the local population and there is often a massive civil protest against projects of this kind.

In Germany and Austria religious communities have three different possibilities for organising themselves in a legal way. Most Muslim religious groups in these countries are organised as registered societies (*eingetragene Vereine, e.V.*). Aside from the status of a foundation (*Stiftung*), taken only by a few large Islamic cultural centres, the law also offers religious communities the possibility of recognition as institutions under public law (*Körperschaften des öffentlichen Rechts*). Until now, however, only Christianity and Judaism are recognised in this form in Germany because Islam fails to fulfil a fundamental prerequisite for recognition as a public body, namely the existence of a representative umbrella organisation. Despite several attempts, no organisation has yet managed to convince the authorities that it represents all Muslims in Germany. Reflecting as they do the national, ethnic and confessional interests of their members, the differences between the various Islamic groups are too great for them to be somehow covered by one umbrella organisation. In Austria, by contrast, the Islamic community has been recognised as a public body since 1979. The Islam Law of 1912 formed the legal basis of this recognition, and the efforts of the *Moslemische Sozial Dienst* (Muslim Social Service), supported by sympathetic political and church circles, were instrumental in driving the recognition claim through. As a result of the recognition of the Islamic community as a public body, certain special rights and obligations arise. Among the latter is the obligation to make all institutions and statutes public, while the former include numerous tax advantages and the right to air-time in the public media. The Islamic community in Austria also possesses a range of legal organs, for example, on a national level, the Shura Council, which functions as the highest organ in the community. As an executive organ of the Shura Council, the Council of Elders deals with all the important concerns of the community, such as the appointment of *imams*. The foundation of an officially recognised umbrella organisation could not, however, prevent the creation of a multiplicity of occasionally competing Islamic associations in Austria.

Muslim Organisations

Stranded at the end of the Second World War, a number of Muslim refugees settled in Germany immediately after the cessation of hostilities, primarily in the south of the country, and – long before the first wave of Muslim workers reached German shores – one of the best-organised Muslim societies, the Geistliche Verwaltung der Muslimflüchtlinge (Muslim Refugees' Spiritual Organisation), grew up in their midst. This organisation has now taken on numerous humanitarian tasks as a result of the civil war in Bosnia–Herzegovina, as have several other organisations recently founded with the purpose of representing Muslims in the Balkans. With few exceptions, the majority of Muslim organisations have been formed only within the past twenty years.

The Persian Shiites in Germany are relatively poorly organised on a religious level, with the exception of the prestigious Islamic Centre in Hamburg, which is funded by Iran, while the Alevites have an umbrella organisation, the Vereinigung der Alewiten Gemeinden (Association of Alevite Communities), with its headquarters in Cologne since 1994. In the 1990s there has been a dynamic development in Alevite organisations in Germany as a result of confrontations between Sunnite and Alevite Muslims in Turkey, the pressure Alevites feel is put on them by Sunnites in Germany to assimilate and the general uncertainty among young Alevites about their own religion. Afghan organisations have been largely preoccupied with refugees. The broad spectrum of Islamic movements found in the Near East and the Maghreb is only reflected to a small degree in Germany primarily due to the low numbers of people from these parts of the Islamic world. However, a number of influential Islamic organisations from the Near East are represented in Germany, such as the Islamisches Zentrum Aachen (Islamic Centre in Aachen), affiliated to the Syrian Muslim Brotherhood, and the Islamisches Zentrum München (Islamic Centre in Munich), linked to the Egyptian Muslim Brotherhood. Both of these organisations have been, or are, subject to political persecution at home and, although they attempt to influence the ideological direction of Islam in Germany, their priorities lie more in their homelands. Members of the Algerian Islamic Salvation Front (FIS) have very recently received asylum in Germany as political refugees.

The numerous Turkish Muslim groups that are active in Germany – most have their European offices in Cologne – are not concerned with the problems of Turkish migrants to Germany alone but are also active in the cause of political change in Turkey. The main object of many groups' activities is to oppose the principle of secularism that is enshrined in the Turkish constitution. Although there are many close contacts with Turkish political parties, the Turkish organisations in Germany are at some pains to present themselves as religious rather than political associations. There is a low degree of organisation amongst Turkish, as well as other, Muslims living in Germany and Austria. Only between 10 and 15 per cent of all Muslims are members of an Islamic organisation, and most practise their religion in private although they use the religious infrastructure provided by the associations. The first Turkish–Islamic organisation to try to organise various locally set-up mosques under a nationwide umbrella association was the Verband der Islamischen Kulturzentren (VIKZ, Union of the Islamic Cultural Centres). The activities of the VIKZ started at the end of the 1960s, and by 1990 the organisation had over 250 branches throughout Germany. The religious principles of the organisation are generally considered to be connected with the Süleymanli movement. This reformist association began in Germany in the 1960s with Quran courses in which its strongly mystical principles were propagated among Turkish *Gastarbeiter*. In the 1970s and 1980s it often made the news as a determined opponent of Muslims integrating themselves in Germany, but recently it has become more open and signalled a readiness to talk with other Islamic associations as well with the Christian churches and the state.

The Nurculuk movement (Islamische Gemeinschaft Jamaat un-Nur) has likewise been active in Germany since the 1960s. It is a mystical reformist movement that began in Turkey in the twentieth century. The members attempt to reconcile the achievements of the modern age with Islam and, as opposed to members of other Turkish–Islamic associations, they run no mosques but only Islamic education centres (*madrasas*) in which readings from the writings of the movement's founder Said Nursi play the central role. The movement now has about thirty *madrasas* in Germany. With its missionary activities, which include the production of numerous publications in the German language, it appeals principally to an intellectual circle.

Among the best-known and most successful Turkish–Islamic associations in Germany today is without doubt the Islamische Gemeinschaft Milli Görüş (IGMG). This influential organisation is also known under its former official Turkish name Avrupa Milli Görüş Teskilatlari (AMGT). It arose in 1975 out of a union of different mosque associations, the Türkische/Islamische Union Europa (Turkish/Islamic Union of Europe), and is held to work closely with the Islamic Welfare Party (Refah Partisi) (banned since January 1998) of Necmettin Erbakan, prime minister of Turkey from 1996–97. Officials deny any close links between the two organisations, but members of the Erbakan family sit in the executive committee of IGMG. According to Milli Görüş itself, some 539 mosques in Germany were associated with this organisation in 1994, but other sources put the number at 220. The umbrella organisation of IGMG as well as the regional and local organisational bodies are divided into numerous subgroups with the result that, for example, the especially well-developed women's section has not only organisations for women and girls but also one for German female Muslims. There were close contacts between IGMG and the Muslim Brotherhood-controlled Islamisches Zentrum Köln until the middle of the 1980s, and ideologically there is a great deal in common between the two organisations. However, the political demands of IGMG are directed towards Turkey, and it rejects the Turkish constitutional principle of secularism, propagating instead the idea of an Islamic state. In publications for its members, IGMG opposes the political system in Germany although – such radical statements notwithstanding – the leadership does in fact seek contact with political and church representatives and declares itself open to dialogue.

There was a split in the organisation in 1984 when Cemalettin Kaplan, who had originally been sent from Turkey to ideologically strengthen the Islamic Union of Europe, left that organisation and founded the Föderation der Islamischen Gemeinden und Gemeinschaften (Federation of Islamic Communities and Associations). Kaplan's uncompromisingly antidemocratic and radically Islamic attitude was directed at Turkey and his followers there were persecuted. The Federation controls about fifty mosques in Germany, and after Kaplan had declared himself head of state and caliph of the thus far fictive Islamic Republic of Turkey in 1992, his model apparently being the Islamic Republic in Iran, he became known in Germany as 'the Khomeini of Cologne'. The introspective leadership of Kaplan's Federation has little official contact with other Islamic associations and rejects any sort of integration of Muslims in Germany and, as a result, cooperation with the German state becomes superfluous. Since Kaplan's death in 1995, there have increasingly been signs of a power struggle within the leadership which has, according to police reports, even included the murder of dissidents.

Popularly known as *Graue Wölfe* (grey wolves), the Föderation der Türkisch-Demokratischen Idealistenvereine in Europa (Federation of European Turkish-democratic Idealists' Associations) is primarily an ultra-nationalistic political organisation founded in 1978 which only started to use Islam for its own purposes during the 1980s. According to its own figures, it controls 180 associations, but suffered a blow when the Union der Türkisch–Islamischer Kulturvereine in Europa (Union of European Turkish–Islamic Cultural Associations) separated from it in 1978 for personal and ideological reasons. The Union controls some 120 associations. Both organisations advocate a synthesis of Turkish nationalism and Islam, but the Union stresses the Islamic element more. The goal of both is to maintain the religious and cultural identity of the generation of young Turkish people who are growing up in Germany and are thus threatened by assimilation.

The Turkish–Islamic Union for Religious Affairs (Türkisch–Islamische Union der Anstalt für Religion), better known under the abbreviation of the official Turkish name DITIB (Diyanet Işleri Türk–Islam Birligi), came relatively late onto the Turkish–Islamic scene in Germany. It is an offshoot of the uppermost religious authority in Turkey, the Diyanet Işleri Başkanligi (Directorate of Religious Affairs), which is under the direct control of the prime minister. When the DITIB was founded in 1984 it manifested a reaction by the Turkish government to the continuing success of Turkish–Islamic associations in Germany. The DITIB sees itself as the official representative of Turkish Muslims in Germany and, consequently, as the most important dialogue partner for all church and state authorities. With some 740 associations, it has become the largest Turkish–Islamic organisation in Germany, and its activities are coordinated by the religious attachés of the diplomatic mission. All the *imams* in the DITIB-controlled mosques are employees of the Turkish state, sent to Germany and paid by Ankara. There were rumours at the beginning of the 1980s that these *imams* were paid by the Saudi Arabia-based Islamic World League (Rabitat al-Alam al-Islami), which was thus able to influence the authorities concerned with the organisation of Islam in Turkey and also the Islamic infrastructure in Germany. The DITIB *imams* come to Germany as a sort of *Gastarbeiter* for a five-year period, usually unprepared for the problems faced by the Turkish minority and with a patchy knowledge of German, and their task is to educate the Turkish Muslims living in Germany in the official Islamic doctrine of the Turkish state. However, the dependency of the uppermost Turkish religious authority on the majority in the Turkish parliament has an effect on the work of DITIB in Germany. During Necmettin Erbakan's one-year prime ministership in 1996–97, there was thus an undeniable congruity between DITIB and Erbakan's German power base, the Milli Görüş.

Apart from the Islamic associations which were founded by and for Turkish Muslims, Germany is home to a number of other organisations. Two of these claim to represent the majority of Muslims to the German state, church and other institutions. The Islamrat der Bundesrepublik Deutschland (Islamic Council of the Federal Republic of Germany), founded in 1986, contains more than twenty independent Islamic associations and groupings of Islamic associations, and its goal is to coordinate the different views of these groups regarding the integration of Muslims into German society and thus to present the German authorities with a largely unified and consistent picture of Islam in Germany. The same effort is made by the Islamischer Arbeitskreis (Islamic Working Group), founded in 1986. Since 1994 the name of this organisation is Zentralrat der Muslime in Deutschland (Central Council of Muslims in Germany).

Sufism

The doctrines represented by the Union of Islamic Cultural Centres, the Nurculuk movement and the Alevites do indeed contain certain mystical elements and their roots go back to Sufi brotherhoods (*tariqa*, pl. *turuq*). They should, however, not be confused with them. The Sufi brotherhoods apparently have not as yet played a significant role among the Muslim immigrants in Germany and Austria. Naturally, members of a brotherhood feel themselves tied to their *tariqa* even when abroad and maintain, as far as circumstances allow, contact with fellow members in their countries of origin. Little is known about Sufi brotherhoods and their influence upon Muslims in Germany and Austria, but it is certain that they have managed to establish Sufi centres in a few large cities, some founded and frequented by immigrants, others founded by Europeans and recruiting European members.

Inayat Khan, a famous musician of Indian origin and spiritual guide (*pir* or *murshid*) of a branch of the Chishtiyya *tariqa*, was the first successful Sufi master in the modern Western world. During a stopover on his way to the United States in 1910 he was able to recruit at least a few followers in Germany. Another Sufi brotherhood which gained some influence in Germay before the First World War was the Bektashi *tariqa*. This Turkish brotherhood also seems to have been introduced in Germany in 1910. Its German mentor was the Baron von Sebottendorf who also founded the occultistic and secret Thule Society, whose members were early supporters of Nazism.

Sufi leaders have recognised and used the opportunities offered by the increased interest in the esoteric in the Western world since the 1960s, and above all since the 1980s, to spread their knowledge outside their habitual spheres. Nowadays nearly every bookstore offers in its department for esoteric literature Sufi-inspired books written by Sufi leaders like Titus

Burckhardt, Frithjof Schuon, Idries Shah or Reshad Feild. One of the pioneers was the German Sufi *shaykh* Abdullah Khalis Dornbrach. He was initiated to the Turkish Mevlevi *tariqa*, better known in Europe as the order of the 'whirling dervishes' of Konya. Together with Dornbrach and his first German disciple, Hussein Abdul Fattah, the Egyptian Sufi master Mohammed Salah Eid founded in 1979 the Institute for Sufi Research in Berlin. Eid himself was initiated into the Burhani, Rifai and Naqshbandi brotherhoods. His clientele were not only Arab or Turkish Muslims, but also German psychologists and psychotherapists interested in the Sufi way of knowledge.

The 'Haus Schnede', a Sufi centre in Northern Germany, inaugurated in 1981, was managed by Abdul Fattah. With lectures and seminars on topics related to Sufism 'Haus Schnede' in a short time became quite popular. The Maktab Tarighat Oveyssi Shahmaghsoudi School of Islamic Sufism runs three centres in Germany and one in Austria. This *tariqa* is, just like the Nimatullahi Sufi brotherhood, of Iranian origin. Under their present master Javad Nurbakhsh, a former professor of psychiatry in Tehran, the Nimatullahi *tariqa* has flourished in- as well as outside Iran. In Germany it manages at least one centre. However, the most successful Sufi brotherhood in Germany and Austria seems to be the Naqshbandiyya. The so-called Golden Sufi Centres in the United States and Europe belong to the Mujaddidi branch of this brotherhood. Their leader Llewellyn Vaughan-Lee, who holds a doctorate in psychology and lives in California, regularly visits his German disciples, who are organised in meditation groups. The Golden Sufi Centre offers lectures, seminars and retreats to an interested public.

Through two main centres in Germany and one in Austria, the Haqqani Foundation controls a number of smaller groups in most major cities. The head of the Haqqani foundation is the *mufti* of Cyprus, Shaykh Muhammad Nazim al-Haqqani, who belongs to the Khalidi branch of the Naqshbandiyya. As for most Sufi *shaykhs*, conversion to Islam is not a prerequisite for attendance; most activities of the Sufi brotherhoods are open to everybody interested in new spiritual inspiration. Thus, it is impossible to give any reliable statement about the increase in the number of converts. However, some of the Sufi brotherhoods have been very successful in imparting new dimensions to the consciousness of their predominantly middle- and upper-class clientele in the search for meaning.

The role of converts

The numbers of Muslims of German or Austrian nationality are difficult to ascertain statistically, but estimates for Germany put the figure at between 50,000 and 100,000. These figures include both naturalised Muslims and German converts. Usually the conversion is the result of marriage to a

Muslim partner, but ever more Germans are finding their way to Islam not because of marriage but for other, wideranging motives. While most Christian churches for a long time have been bemoaning shrinking congregations, Islamic associations have seen a constant – if modest in absolute terms – growth in the number of German members. Since many of the converts are academics, their educational standards are above average. Thus, they represent not only a quantitative, but also a qualitative gain for the Islamic community. Best-known to the German public of the converts to Islam is the former ambassador to Morocco, Murad Wilfried Hofmann. His fame is not, however, based mainly on his Islamic articles and books but on a television interview in which he made some comments on the flogging of wives in Islam. After that interview, he was promptly denounced in the media as an Islamic fundamentalist, and there was talk of 'Allah's Fifth Column'.

Despite being only a small minority within the Muslim community, the importance of the German converts should not to be underestimated. They were active in founding Islamic associations in Germany and Austria in the 1930s, and today they have taken over important roles within the Muslim community as mediators between cultures. For instance, the current deputy director of the Islamic Centre in Munich is the German convert Ahmad von Denffer who, as the author of numerous books and pamphlets, tries to disseminate Islamic ideas in German society and is a keen participant at many international conferences throughout the Islamic world. Because of their connections in German or Austrian society, the converts are ideally suited to articulate Muslim demands and desires. A number of these converts have joined Islamic associations, and since 1976 there have been regular meetings for German-speaking Muslims. The educational system is seen by Muslims as inadequate for their children and, therefore, German converts are actively involved in the opening of German–Islamic kindergartens and schools as well as in the planning of curricula for an Islamic religious education or even a general German–Islamic education.

German Muslim women frequently do not fit the stereotype of the faithful and submissive wife who stays at home to look after their husbands and children. Veiled or not, they are very active in Islamic associations and do stand up for their rights. Of course, not all associations offer women the opportunity to turn their conceptions of religion into reality but some, especially the reformist movements, have realised that a great deal of influence can be exercised on society by careful support of the women's cause. Female Muslims, both German converts and those born into Islam, with very different cultural backgrounds and images of the Islamic way of life, meet each other, and the result seems to be far less a *clash of civilizations* than the beginning of a process which bears fruit for both sides involved. Their participation in Islamic associations gives Muslim women the impression that there is also in

Europe an Islamic route to emancipation, and it is not difficult to expose the constitutionally enshrined equality of rights for men and women as a fiction in European society.

Relations to non-Muslims

The last twenty years have seen the religious infrastructure of Muslims in Germany undergo great changes. The Turkish–Islamic associations have proved particularly successful in terms of meeting the needs of Muslims through their close-knit network of mosques, and the development of such organisations clearly shows that Muslims are able to adapt themselves to their host country in the long term. Apart from religious instruction, the associations offer pastoral support, assistance in the fulfilment of religious duties such as the pilgrimage to Mecca, financial aid for the transportation of the body in cases of death and many other temporal services. The organisations appeal to a wide range of society through their education programmes for adults, which include courses in German and computing, and leisure activities for young people, ranging from summer camps to martial arts courses. The associations are sometimes blooming economic concerns which offer their clientele ritually pure foods from their own farms or slaughterhouses in shops attached to the mosque, and their range of services includes insurance and holdings in Islamic trading companies. In addition to these economic activities, members' contributions and donations as well as money from abroad help these Islamic associations to be financially self-supporting. Moreover, Islamic associations try to counteract the public's negative image of Islam in the face of growing xenophobia, and many mosques have regular open days or give interested outsiders an insight into Muslim life via guided tours. Some associations publish information leaflets for the general public in addition to those for their own members, and an important function of these associations continues to be the representation of the Muslim community's demands and desires to the authorities of the host country in question.

Since the majority of Muslims have settled permanently in their host country, it is obvious that a social infrastructure needs to be built up in addition to the religious one. Previously most immigrants envisaged at least their burial in their homeland, but now, as the third generation of Muslims grows up in Germany and Austria and their contact with the land of their ancestors becomes increasingly tenuous, growing numbers of Islamic associations are actively campaigning for the expansion of existing, or the dedication of new, Muslim cemeteries. Indeed, the care of the elderly will become a particular challenge for the associations as well as for the host country itself. German kindergartens are largely under the control of church authorities which try to influence the children in a Christian way and refuse to employ non-Christian teachers. Thus, the Muslims' fears that kindergartens have an insidious missionary function are strengthened. For some time now the Muslim associations have been particularly active in campaigning for an Islamic religious education in German state schools. There is no doubt that the state school system is an important instrument for the integration of Muslims into German and Austrian societies. Religion is the only subject that the German constitution makes compulsory (i.e., religion must be offered in all schools). However, only bodies recognised under public law may determine the confessional content of the teaching and, as we have seen, the Muslim community is not recognised under public law. Individual federal states have occasionally offered religious instruction for Muslims in what is called 'native tongue additional lessons', but these voluntary lessons are generally only for Turkish pupils.

The decision-makers in the various state education ministries quickly realised that they could not influence this kind of religious instruction in any way. A curriculum for an Islamic religious instruction has been developed in North-Rhine Westphalia, which has been taken as a model by other federal states and is now being used in some schools. There is, however, a shortage of teachers able to teach the Islamic religion. The most obvious solution would be to use Turkish teachers, but other, non-Turkish-speaking Muslims are understandably against the lessons being in Turkish. In addition, Turkish views of Islamic history differ from Arabic views, and there may be differences between Sunnites and Shiites. The confessional, as well as the linguistic and ethnic, variety within the Islamic community in Germany itself, together with divisions within Islamic organisations over the contents of the curriculum, form an obstacle to the creation of a universal Islamic religious instruction.

The Islamic community in Austria has taken advantage of the fact that religious instruction is the right of recognised churches and religious communities and has conducted religious education since 1980. The Islamic teachers are paid by the Austrian state and the pupils are provided with appropriate materials; the lessons are held in German on account of the different linguistic backgrounds of the children. This form of Islamic religious education, based on a curriculum designed by the Islamic community itself and approved by the state, guarantees the state that Islamic religious instruction will not take place outside the school and undermine the state school system.

The office responsible for defending the constitution in Germany (Verfassungsschutz) has been watching the activities of Islamic organisations for a number of years. Until the mid 1990s, it considered the danger posed by them to the constitution to be relatively small, but since 1997 it has become obvious that the office has been taking the conceived threat from such organisations as Milli Görüş or the Federation of Islamic Communities and Associations ever more seriously, and it speaks of Islam as a challenge for the twenty-first century. It cannot be denied that the influence of political and religious associations on Muslims living in Europe has increased since the 1980s. Work-related migration necessarily results in mature social structures being given up and identity-giving traditions being lost. As both ethnic and religious minorities, Muslims occupy a distinct social place in their host countries, and their identity is frequently questioned. Religio-political associations plunge into this cultural disloca-tion felt by Muslims in Europe and support their members both materially and with wide-ranging social services. The new associations serve as replacements for lost social contacts and they create a new identity. Yet, even if religio-political associations have grown in influence in the European Muslim community very recently and even if militant Islamic groups have received abstract and material support, the majority of Muslims do not dispute the secular organisation of European societies. Rather, their understanding of Islam seems to be influenced by it and corresponds to their fundamental desire for acceptance and integration. However, their wishes also include the retention of their own religious and cultural identity. A complete assimilation seems to them as Muslims and immigrants to be neither desirable nor possible. What they demand is equality within a pluralistic society and a framework that guarantees this equality, placing their community on the same footing as the Christian and Jewish communities. Above all, they want the populations of their host countries to recognise that Islam is a religion in the same way the others are.

Literature

For general introductions to the situation of Islam and Muslims in Germany, see Yasemin Karakasoglu and Gerd Nonneman, 'Muslims in Germany, with Special Reference to the Turkish–Islamic Community', pp. 241–67 in *Muslim Communities in the New Europe*, eds. Gerd Nonneman, Tim Niblock and Bogdan Szajkowski (Reading: Ithaca Press, 1997); and Ursula Spuler-Stegemann, *Muslime in Deutschland: Nebenein-ander oder Miteinander* (Freiburg: Herder, 1998). Concerning the situation of Muslims in Berlin, see Hanns Thomä-Venske, 'The Religious Life of Muslims in Berlin', pp. 78–87 in *The New Islamic Presence in Western Europe*, eds. Tomas Gerholm and Yngve Georg Lithman (London: Mansell, 1988). For an account of the history of Islam in Germany, see Muhammad Salim Abdullah, *Geschichte des Islams in Deutschland* (Graz, Wien and Köln: Styria, 1981). On Austria, see Anna Strobl, *Islam in Österreich* (Frankfurt/Main: Peter Lang, 1997). For a study of interreligious dialogue in Austria, see M. Kristin Arat, 'L'Islam en Autriche et le dialogue', *Islamochristiana*, 18 (1992), pp. 127–73. A very sophisticated introduction to the problem of Islam and state relations, with special reference to the diaspora situation of Muslims in Europe, is offered by Baber Johansen's 'Staat, Recht und Religion im sunnitischen Islam – können Muslime einen religionsneutralen Staat akzeptieren?', pp. 12–81 in *Essener Gespräche zum Thema Staat und Kirche,* eds. Heiner Marré and Johannes Stüting (Münster: Aschendorff, 1986).

On the situation of Turks in Germany, see Czarina Wilpert, 'Religion and Ethnicity: Orientation, Perceptions and Strategies among Turkish Alevi and Sunni Migrants in Berlin', pp. 88–106 in *The New Islamic Presence in Western Europe,* eds. Tomas Gerholm and Yngve Georg Lithman (London: Mansell, 1988) and Valérie Amiraux, 'Les transformations de l'identité islamique turque en Allemagne', pp. 146–58 in *Exils et Royaumes: Les appartenances au monde arabo-musulman aujourd'hui,* ed. Gilles Kepel (Paris: Presses de la Fondation nationale des Sciences politiques, 1994). Christoph Elsass focuses his interest on education, 'Turkish Islamic Ideals of Education: Their Possible Function for Islamic Identity and Integration in Europe', pp. 174–86 in *The Integration of Islam and Hinduism in Western Europe,* eds. W.A.R. Shadid and P.S. van Koningsveld (Kampen: Kok Pharos, 1991). Islamic and/or Turkish organisations are discussed by Hans Vöcking, 'Organisations as Attempts at Integration of Muslims in Germany', pp. 100–11 in *Muslims and Christians in Europe: Breaking New Ground,* eds. Gé Speelman, Jan van Lin and Dick Mulder (Kampen: Uitgeverij Kok, 1993); see also Metin Gür, *Türkisch–islamische Vereinigungen in der Bundesrepublik Deutschland* (Frankfurt-am-Main: Brandes and Apsel, 1993); and Bahman Nirumand, *Im Namen Allahs: Islamische Gruppen und der Fundamentalismus in der Bundesrepublik Deutschland* (Köln: Dreisam-Verlag, 1990). For the political and religious attitudes of the Turkish youth in Germany, see Wilhelm Heitmeyer, Joachim Müller and Helmut Schröder, *Verlockender Fundamentalismus: Türkische Jugendliche in Deutschland* (Frankfurt-am-Main: Suhrkamp Verlag, 1997).

Chapter Fifteen

France

Neal Robinson

'In 732, Charles Martel defeated the Arabs at Poitiers.' This snippet of information, dutifully memorised by generations of French schoolchildren, does justice neither to the extent nor to the duration of the Arab–Muslim occupation of the territory which is now known as France. There were in fact three separate waves of immigration in the course of the eighth, ninth and tenth centuries. The first wave began in 716 when North African troops, led by officers from Arabia, entered France via Spain. The invaders took Narbonne in 719, making it a protectorate and converting the atrium of the Christian basilica into a mosque. They rapidly overran the whole of the southeast, pressing northwards well beyond Lyon into Burgundy, and penetrating as far west as the outskirts of Toulouse. Reinforcements, who arrived from Pamplona in 731, took Bordeaux and pillaged much of the southwest. Charles Martel defeated them at Poitiers the following year and went on to drive the Muslims out of Lyon, but Narbonne remained a Muslim stronghold until 759.

The second wave of immigration began in 793, the invaders again arriving overland from Spain. Narbonne was besieged and some of the towns in the southeast were briefly reoccupied. However, Charlemagne retaliated by invading Spain, and the emir of Cordoba made a truce with him in 810. The third wave differed from the others in three respects: it lacked their religious motivation, it affected Provence, and the invaders were sea-borne. Around 850, Arab pirates, who had raided the Provençal coast repeatedly during the previous half century, settled in the Camargue and built a port which was to serve them as a base for twenty years. A decade after it was destroyed, the pirates constructed a second port much further east in La Garde Freinet. From there, they raided Fréjus, Toulon, Antibes, Marseille, Aix-en-Provence and Villefranche-sur-Mer. They also established two small forts inland from the mountainous region between Toulon and Fréjus, which still bears the name Massif des Maures ('the Moors' Massif'), and used them as staging posts for expeditions to pillage the wealthy monasteries in the Alps. In 972, they kidnapped Mayeul, the Abbot of Cluny, and held him to ransom. The incident was swiftly avenged by the combined forces of Provence, Italy and Byzantium, who subdued the whole of the Massif.

There were further maritime raids against Narbonne in 1019–20, but they did not result in settlements. Nevertheless, throughout the Middle Ages there was a Muslim presence in the south of France. It consisted of isolated individuals, most of whom were traders but some of whom were slaves. There was, however, a fourth wave of immigration in 1610. This time the Muslims came not as conquerors but as refugees. They were *moriscos*, the descendants of Spanish Muslims who had accepted baptism in the wake of the *Reconquista*, but who had continued to practise Islam in secret. The Inquisition discovered their existence and Philip III gave them twenty days to leave the country. Although the majority fled to North Africa, 120,000 settled in Languedoc-Roussillon and the Basque country, principally in Narbonne and Béarn.

Between July 1095 and September 1096, Urban II, the aged French pope, toured the south of France canvassing support for a crusade to liberate Jerusalem from the Saracens. The First Crusade was officially launched by him at the Council of Clermont, in the Massif Central, on November 27, 1095. It is beyond the scope of this chapter to give a detailed account of subsequent events. Suffice it to note that many French cities have historic links with the crusades and those who led them. The crusader Kingdom of Jerusalem was ruled successively by Godfrey of Bouillon, Baldwin of Boulogne and Fulk of Anjou; the theological justification for the crusades was provided by St Bernard of Clairvaux; in 1190, King Philip II of France set off from Vézelay on the Third Crusade; and in 1270, another French king, Louis IX, better known as St Louis, died in Tunisia on his way to the Holy Land for the second time.

France's modern encroachment on the Muslim world began in 1637, when she established a trading post in West Africa at the mouth of River Senegal. That the town was given the name St Louis is an indication that the crusading spirit was still alive. Between 1798 and 1801, Napoleon Bonaparte occupied Egypt. Although the occupation was shortlived, it resulted in a systematic survey of the country's historic monuments. Moreover, the French initiated administrative reforms which set Egypt on the path of modernity. French troops conquered Algeria between 1830 and 1857; Tunisia was made a French protectorate in 1881; and French West Africa was colonised between the early 1880s and 1912, the year in which Morocco was also made a protectorate. During the First World War, France was an ally of Russia and Britain in the conflict with the Ottoman Empire and Germany. In 1916, she secretly signed the Sykes–Picot Agreement with Britain, laying detailed plans for dividing the post-Ottoman Middle East into French and British spheres of influence. In accordance with this agreement, in 1920 the League of Nations gave her a mandate to rule Syria and the Lebanon. The Lebanon gained independence from France in 1941; Syria in 1946; Tunisia and Morocco in 1956; Mali and Senegal in 1960; and Algeria in 1962.

Wherever the French went, they attempted to implant their language and culture. The extent of their influence varied, however, from country to country. In West Africa it was relatively superficial, but in Algeria it was profound. During the fourth and fifth centuries, the area which now forms the Algerian coast had been a stronghold of Latin Christianity, the home of no less a figure than St Augustine of Hippo. Thus, when Algiers was taken in 1830, the bells of Notre Dame Cathedral in Paris rang out to celebrate the triumph of Christendom. Although the southern part of Algeria long remained something of a Wild West, the north soon came to be regarded as an overseas extension of France. It was divided into three *départements* populated with European colonists who had full French citizenship; it depended on the Ministry of the Interior rather than on the Ministry of Colonies; and by the end of the nineteenth century it had its own elected assembly and budgetary independence. The indigenous Muslims were not, however, granted French citizenship unless they were prepared to relinquish the *sharia*. The majority formed an underclass with 'Quranic status', which meant that in civil matters they were subject to Islamic law administered by *gadis* (Muslim judges). Not that the French wished in any way to foster Islam. The study of Arabic was discouraged and participation in the annual pilgrimage to Mecca was subject to stringent conditions for fear that the pilgrims might come under harmful external influences. In 1962, when Algeria became independent after eight years of conflict, only a few thousand French colonists opted to remain and become Algerian citizens – three-quarters of a million hastily moved to France. Many of these so-called *pieds-noirs* ('black feet') experienced difficulties integrating in French society and have continued to be hostile towards Muslim immigrants.

Immigration from Muslim Countries in Modern Times

Early in the nineteenth century, a few of Napoleon's Muslim soldiers settled in the Rhône Valley. Subsequently, around 1870, itinerant salesmen known as *turcos* arrived in France from Algeria. Towards the end of the century, there were about 800 Muslims living in Paris, most of them students. The influx of Algerian workers began in 1900, and was followed a few years later by that of Moroccans. In 1914, on the eve of the First World War, there were about 30,000 North Africans in France. The war led to a massive increase: 132,000, mostly Algerians, were recruited to work on French farms and in factories, while a further 175,000 served in the army. Some 25,000 died in action. After the war the majority of the survivors returned home, with the result that there were only 100,000 North Africans left in France in 1919. The number began to increase again the following year, reaching 120,000 in 1924 and remaining relatively stable until the 1930s, when the recession led many to depart. After the Second World War,

Muslim immigrants in Toulon (photo: Ingvar Svanberg, 1972).

immigration was actively encouraged in order to meet the needs of reconstruction and industrial expansion. Between 1954 and 1968 alone, France welcomed more than 1 million North Africans. Most of them were unskilled workers: a third were employed in the building industry and another third in manufacturing cars.

Before 1962, the majority were Algerians, but after Algerian independence the French government attempted to diversify the work force by encouraging immigration from Morocco and Tunisia. In addition, in the late 1960s, workers from West Africa, including Mali and Senegal, started to come in larger numbers. Finally, the early 1970s saw the arrival of Turkish workers, especially in Alsace. In 1974, however, in response to the economic crisis caused by the oil embargo the previous year, an attempt was made to suspend all immigration and to encourage voluntary repatriation by offering grants of 10,000 F. When this met with a poor response, plans were drawn up to repatriate 500,000 foreigners within five years, principally by refusing to renew residence permits for Algerians. Because of the combined opposition of the Council of State and one of the parties in the conservative coalition, these plans were not implemented. Nevertheless, the Bonnet law, which was adopted in 1980, introduced stricter control of foreign residents and led to an increase in the number of expulsions, especially of children born in France to Algerian parents.

When the Socialist Party came to power in 1981, the new government rejected this repressive policy and forbade the expulsion of foreigners who were born in France or had arrived there before reaching the age of ten. It also regularised the situation of 130,000 illegal immigrants. In addition, in 1983, it introduced ten-year renewable work permits. However, the socialists fared badly in the 1986 elections, and Mitterand, the socialist president of the Republic, was forced to call upon the conservative Chirac to be prime minister. Bowing to pressure from the extreme right wing and overtly racist Front National, which had polled an astonishing 9.8 per cent of the votes and gained thirty-five seats, Chirac introduced a series of draconian measures. These included making it more difficult for immigrants to renew their work permits; rounding up illegal immigrants and forcibly repatriating them; and proposing to expel young delinquents brought up in France.

The 1993 elections strengthened the position of the conservatives who immediately proceeded to modify the laws on nationality. It had previously been possible for foreign nationals to apply for French nationality for young children born to them in France, thereby affirming their own intention to settle and protecting themselves against expulsion. In any case, if they did not do this, the children used to gain French nationality automatically on reaching the age of eighteen. Now, however, as a result of the Pasqua law (named after the minister of the interior), the children have to wait until they are between sixteen and twenty, when they must declare their wish to become French nationals. Since June 1997, France has had another 'cohabitation', this time with a conservative president and a socialist prime minister, but it is too soon to tell whether the Pasqua law will be rescinded.

Figures for the number of Muslims currently living in France should be treated with caution. Although the 1990 census does not mention religious affiliation, it gives statistics concerning resident foreign nationals, distinguishing between those born outside France and those born in France. The figures for foreign nationals from Muslim countries are shown in the table below:

	Born outside France	Born in France
Algerians	473,400	140,800
Moroccans	396,500	176,200
Turks	146,700	51,000
Tunisians	135,500	70,800
Senegalese	33,900	9,200
Malians	27,200	10,500
Iranians	14,300	900
Pakistanis	8,300	1,500

By adding up these figures, we arrive at a total of 1,700,000 nominal Muslims of whom 461,000 were born in France. This total excludes illegal immigrants; foreigners who have become naturalised; and Muslims from the Comoro Islands. It also excludes the grandchildren of immigrants, for under French law they automatically have French nationality provided both their parents were born in France. In addition, we must take into account the *harkis* – Algerians who served as auxiliaries in the French army during the War of Independence and were given French citizenship. In 1962, they and their families numbered some 60,000, but it is estimated that that number is closer to 500,000. Finally, there are about 30,000 French converts to Islam. On this reckoning, there must by now be well over 3 million Muslims in France. This grand total is, however, somewhat misleading. Forty-eight per cent of the Algerian immigrants, 36 per cent of the Moroccans and 31 per cent of the Turks all claim that they have no religion; Senegal and Mali are not exclusively Muslim countries; and only 11 per cent of the Algerians attend places of worship.

Although Muslims are found in significant numbers in almost every industrial town, they are especially in evidence in five regions. The highest concentration is in Ile-de-France (Paris and its environs), followed in decreasing order by Nord-Pas-de-Calais (especially in and around Lille and Roubaix in the *département* of Nord), Rhône-Alpes (especially in and around Lyon in the *département* of Rhône), Alsace-Lorraine (especially in and around Strasbourg in the *département* of Bas-Rhin), and Provence-Alpes-Côte-d'Azur (especially in and around Marseille in the *département* of Bouches-du-Rhône). Algerians, Moroccans, Tunisians and Turks live in all these regions, but the highest concentration of Turks is in Bas-Rhin. In contrast with the United Kingdom, where immigrants have populated the derelict inner-city areas, in France they are more often in the *banlieues* – run-down, high-rise estates in the outer suburbs.

Mosques and Prayer Rooms

Apart from archaeological evidence of an eighth-century mosque in Narbonne (the converted atrium of the basilica, mentioned earlier), no traces have survived of the places of worship constructed by the first waves of immigrants. At the beginning of the thirteenth century a crusader built a mosque at Buzancy in the Ardennes, in gratitude for his release from captivity, but it is unlikely that it was ever used and it now lies in ruins. In the seventeenth century there was a mosque in Marseille which was frequented by corsairs who had been taken prisoner and forced to serve as galley slaves on the king's ships. In the eighteenth and nineteenth centuries, a room in the Château de Versailles was set apart for the use of Ottoman ambassadors who wished to perform the ritual prayers. During the First World War, the government created prayer rooms in warehouses and hospitals for France's Muslim troops, and imported *imams* from Algeria to service them. Moreover, there was a purpose-built wooden mosque in the

The Paris Mosque, inaugurated in 1926 (photo: Ingvar Svanberg, 1995).

military camp at Zossen which was subsequently moved to the colonial garden at Nogent-sur-Marne. Between the two wars, the Muslim immigrants were relatively lax in their religious observance. Hence there was little call for places of worship, although employers sometimes took the initiative in providing them; for instance, a wooden mosque was erected in Toulouse.

Construction of the Paris Mosque began in 1922 and was completed in 1926. It was ostensibly built in recognition of the many Muslims who had lost their lives fighting for France. However, the idea of establishing a large mosque in Paris had been mooted long before the First World War, and the real motive seems to have been the desire to give architectural expression to the conviction that, by reason of its overseas territories, France was a great Muslim power. The purchase of a prime site near the botanical gardens in the fifth *arrondissement* was financed by the City of Paris, and the state made a substantial contribution to the building costs. By law, however, public money could not be spent on a place of worship. This problem was circumvented by channelling funds through a charitable organisation based in Algiers, on the understanding that they were intended for the creation of a 'Muslim Institute' which would comprise Turkish baths, a shop and a library, as well as a mosque. The mosque was inaugurated by Moulay

343

Youssef, the Sultan of Morocco; the lecture theatre was opened by Sidi Mohammed al-Habib Pasha, the Bey of Tunis; a Persian prayer carpet was donated by Reza Shah Pahlavi; and Muslims from many other countries, including Egypt and Turkey, gave generous support to the project. From 1926–54, the Director of the Muslim Institute was Si Kaddour Ben Ghabrit. Although born in Algeria, he had close links with Morocco where he had been both the Sultan's director of protocol and the French consul. His death in 1954, only months before the outbreak of the Algerian War of Independence, precipitated a crisis. He was succeeded, in accordance with his wishes, by his nephew. The latter persistently refused to condemn the Algerian insurrection. In 1957, the French government therefore intervened, appointing an Algerian director who was more to its liking and bringing the Institute under the control of the Ministry of the Interior. In 1962, when Algeria became independent, the registered office of the charitable foundation was transferred to Paris. It continued to receive subsidies from the French authorities until 1982. In that year, the Algerian government gained control of the Mosque and assumed sole responsibility for the running costs of the Institute. Since that time, successive Rectors of the Mosque have striven to make it the unifying focus for all Muslims in France, attempting to heal the divisions between Algerian immigrants and *harkis*, and to gain the respect of Moroccans and Tunisians. To this end, since 1985 they have organised and chaired a number of national gatherings in other cities including Marseille and Lyon. More recent developments will be discussed below in the section on Islam and the Republic.

Even during the colonial period, many Muslims had an ambivalent attitude to the Paris Mosque. As migrant workers, often from backward rural areas, they were ill-at-ease in this sumptuous showpiece and would have preferred a more modest structure situated nearer where they lived and better suited to their needs. Nevertheless, for forty-three years it was the only building in France to be officially recognised as a mosque apart from the small edifice complete with minaret which was built for Senegalese infantrymen in the military camp at Fréjus during the Second World War, but which was closed after their departure. Then in 1967, the newly-founded Association Culturelle Islamique opened the Belleville Mosque at 15 rue Belleville, in the north of Paris. In 1974, when the building was no longer large enough to accommodate the worshippers, they met on church premises as an interim measure. Eventually, in 1979, the association acquired a large building near the Stalingrad *métro* station. The Stalingrad Mosque, or 'Mosquée ad-Dawa' as it is officially called, is a disused cloth warehouse which can accommodate 4,000 worshippers. Planning permission to replace it with a purpose-built mosque has been granted, but the Mayor of Paris has so far refused to give the final authorisation. Members of Jamaat al-Tabligh originally frequented the Belleville Mosque, but in

1972 they moved to their own premises in Clichy and founded the association Foi et Pratique (Faith and Practice). The association has since opened several mosques of which the largest is Mosquée Omar in rue Jean-Pierre Thimbaud at Belleville. It was opened in 1979 and can accommodate 1,500 worshippers.

The relatively late advent of these metropolitan rivals to the Paris Mosque is hardly surprising. During the 1950s and 1960s, most of the Muslims in France were migrant workers who intended to stay only for a few years before returning home. If they practised their faith at all, they were content to do so inconspicuously. It was not until the economic crisis of 1973 that they began to demand prayer rooms. Because of the crisis, the rent was increased in the state-run hostels where many of them lived. This resulted in a rent strike at Bobigny, where the workers pressed for better living conditions including the provision of facilities for them to perform their prayers. The attempt to suspend immigration in 1974 resulted in further protests and the demand for more mosques and prayer rooms. Convinced that if they now left France they would not be allowed to re-enter, the immigrants began to put down roots and to look for ways of giving institutional expression to their faith. In 1976, the agitation spread from the hostels where the immigrants lived to the factories where they were employed, when Muslims successfully petitioned Renault for a prayer room in the car factory at Billancourt. Then, in 1978, Citroën and Talbot took the initiative in providing prayer rooms in their factories at Aulnay-sous-Bois and Poissy. By 1990, Muslims had 1,035 places of worship scattered throughout most of France, although there were none at all in the *départements* of Côtes-d'Armor and Lozère. These figures, given by the minister of the interior in reply to a question addressed to him in the National Assembly, deserve some comment. France is far from being a land of over a thousand mosques. Apart from the Paris Mosque, there are only four large purpose-built congregational mosques in the whole country: in Mantes-la-Jolie, Evry, Lille and Lyon. The one in Mantes-la-Jolie was built in the 1980s, but construction of the other three began after 1990. In addition, there are a handful of large buildings which have been converted into mosques, including the two in Paris, and a hundred or so that are of more modest proportions. The remaining places of worship are prayer rooms in hostels, blocks of flats and factories, with a capacity of between eight and forty worshippers. They are serviced by some 500 *imams*, only 4 per cent of whom have French nationality.

Nationwide Associations

In 1939, in order to prevent the formation of organisations and parties directly controlled by Nazi Germany and Fascist Italy, the French government prohibited foreign residents from forming associations without the prior approval of the Ministry of the Interior. This law remained in force until 1981, which explains why Islamic associations were rare before that date but have since multiplied exponentially. On a national level, the oldest association is the AEIF (Association des Etudiants Islamiques en France) founded in 1963 by Muhammad Hamidullah, a Paris-based scholar born in the Indian subcontinent. It caters principally for students from a North African background who ascribe to the views of Rached Ghannouchi, the moderate Tunisian Islamist.

The UOIF (Union des Organisations Islamiques de France) was founded in 1983. In 1986, there were only thirteen local associations of North African Muslims affiliated to it, but now there are over 220, of which the largest is the predominantly Tunisian GIF (Groupement Islamique en France) based in Paris. Every Christmas since 1988, the UOIF has organised an annual congress at Le Bourget. In 1996, it attracted 35,000 participants over three days. The UOIF also controls a company called Euro-Médias which makes and distributes videos of Muslim preachers in Arabic and French, and in 1992 it opened a theological institute (Institut Européen des Sciences Humaines) in the Nièvre *département* to train *imams* equipped to work in France. Ideologically, the UIOF is close to the Muslim Brotherhood.

The FNMF (Fédération Nationale des Musulmans en France) was founded in 1985 by a French convert to Islam, but its leaders are mostly Moroccans. It is backed by the Muslim World League and since 1993 has run an 'open university' in the League's premises. With over 100 affiliated associations, the FNMF is sufficiently powerful to challenge the Paris Mosque's claim to represent Islam in France. Most of the local Turkish associations are affiliated to the UIF (Union Islamique en France), which was founded in 1983, or the FAIF (Fédération des Associations Islamiques en France) which broke away from it the following year. The local associations representing West African Muslims left the FNMF in 1989 to form the FNAIACA (Fédération Nationale des Associations Islamiques d'Afrique, des Comores et des Antilles).

French Perceptions of Islam and Muslims

The French have a habit of confusing race and religion. Thus, for example, they are likely to refer to anyone from the Indian subcontinent as *un hindou* (a Hindu), despite the fact that India has a large Muslim minority and almost all the inhabitants of Pakistan and Bangladesh are Muslims. Similarly, they tend to use the words *arabe* (Arab) and *musulman* (Muslim) interchangeably. Few outside Alsace are aware that most Turks are at least nominally Muslims, and even fewer know that Islam is the religion of many Malians and Senegalese. An added complication is that French people usually think of all North Africans as Arabs, although half the Moroccans and a third of the Algerians in France are actually Berbers. Hence, the non-

Muslim French are for the most part unaware of the racial and linguistic diversity of France's Muslim population.

Apart from the almost universal tendency to think of the Muslims in France as an undifferentiated mass of (North-African) Arabs, perceptions of Muslims and Islam vary considerably and are affected by factors such as age, social class and educational background. Nevertheless, in the light of newspaper and television coverage it is legitimate to speak of widespread stereotypes. In the course of the present century, these have undergone a series of modifications. In the 1920s, because of the way in which North Africans had rallied to France's help in the First World War, Muslim immigrants were generally considered to be likeable, intelligent and patriotic. In the 1930s, however, because of the recession and because France had to take a number of repressive measures to maintain order in its North African territories, attitudes rapidly changed and the popular press began to portray the immigrants as lazy, and inclined to criminality and vice. During the Algerian War of Independence (1954–62), when the FLN (*Front de Libération Nationale*) made Islam a rallying cry, the fact that North Africans were Muslims was seen as a further reason for viewing them with mistrust. Since 1962, there has been increasing resentment of 'Arabs' desiring to live and work in France despite having fought so ferociously to shake off the colonial yoke. Here, Moroccans and Tunisians, whose countries gained independence relatively peaceably in 1956, tend to be tarred with the same brush as Algerians, while the *harkis*, who sided with France against the FLN, are simply forgotten.

During the Arab–Israeli conflicts in 1967 and 1973, the French government criticised Israel's expansionist policy, but public opinion was generally pro-Zionist and resentment of the 'Arab' presence in France increased. Matters were made worse when, in the wake of the 1973 conflict, the Arab oil-producing countries demonstrated their disapproval of Western support for Israel by imposing an oil embargo on Europe and the United States. As mentioned earlier, in France this caused an economic crisis which prompted an attempt to suspend immigration and led in turn to Muslims seeking to practise their religion openly and demanding the right to have mosques and prayer rooms. It is widely assumed that these demands were orchestrated by foreign agencies. There is an element of truth in this. For instance, the Muslim World League, which has its headquarters in Mecca, opened an office in Paris in 1977. It distributes free literature to local associations and has helped finance a number of building projects. Moreover, the construction of the mosque at Mantes-la-Jolie was heavily subsidised by Libya, Saudi Arabia and the Gulf States, and that at Evry by Saudi Arabia and Morocco. Nevertheless, as indicated earlier, this is not the whole story: the re-Islamisation of the long-standing immigrants, which began in the 1970s and continued through the 1980s, represents a fundamental change in their attitude to the host society and their relation to it.

In addition to the desire for prayer rooms and mosques, there have been increasing demands for the provision of *halal* meat and Muslim burial grounds. Although both have met with local resistance, neither has caused public outcry on the scale of that provoked in October 1989, when Muslim girls attended school wearing Islamic headscarves. The practice, which began with three girls at Creil on the outskirts of Paris and rapidly spread throughout the country, was widely condemned as an attack on the Republic, an affront to the dignity of women, and a threat to the secular status of the educational system. In order to understand the intensity of the hostility, it is necessary to see the headscarf affair in historical context. One of the greatest blows to France's national pride to have occurred in living memory was the loss of Algeria in 1962. In that year, in the final stages of the conflict, schoolgirls and students in Algeria defied the French authorities by veiling for classes. In addition, 1989 was the tenth anniversary of the Iranian Revolution which had imposed the veil on Iranian women, and in February that year Ayatollah Khomeini, the leader of the revolution, had issued his *fatwa* against Salman Rushdie. Finally, earlier in the 1980s, there had been a clash between secularists and Catholics over the public funding of Catholic schools. This had opened old wounds caused by the battle between Church and State in the nineteenth century.

Only three weeks before the schoolgirls made the French headlines with their Islamic scarves, the Algerian government had reluctantly legalised the FIS (Islamic Salvation Front). Then, on December 21, 1989, more than 100,000 women demonstrated in Algiers against the upsurge of aggression against Islam. Hence, although the Muslim schoolgirls in Creil were Moroccans, the headscarf affair was perceived to be linked with the growth of 'Islamic fundamentalism' in Algeria. Two years later, on December 26, 1991 the FIS gained an overall majority in the first round of the Algerian elections. The Security Council refused to accept the results; the two leaders of the FIS were arrested and, after being detained for five months, they were condemned by a military tribunal to twelve years in prison. Since that time, Algeria has sunk deeper and deeper into civil war and anarchy, but the French government has continued to support the Algerian military junta.

With Algiers only an hour's journey by plane, there were understandable fears that the conflict might spread to France. This eventually happened on December 24, 1994 when an Air France airbus, which had been hijacked by the GIA (Groupe Islamique Armé) in Algiers, landed in Marseille. The plane was stormed by French commandos who killed all four hijackers. Then on July 11, 1995, two gunmen killed the *imam* of the Khaled Ibn el-Walid Mosque in Paris. Two weeks later, on July 26, a bomb exploded in the St Michel *métro* station killing eight people and injuring a hundred others. Between then and September 7, there were two more explosions and two unexploded bombs were defused. The security forces traced the incidents to a group of North African youths in Lyon. The principal suspect, Khaled

Kelkal, had no known links with the FIS or GIA, but had begun to practise Islam a few years earlier while serving a prison sentence for stealing cars. On September 30, millions of viewers saw television coverage of him being hunted down and shot by the police. At the time of the bombings, over 2,000 Muslims were arrested on suspicion of involvement in terrorist organisations. Most of the suspects were eventually released without charges being pressed. There were two more bomb attacks in October, but after that the wave of bombings ceased, although over a year later on December 3, 1996 there was a further explosion in Paris which killed four people.

These incidents have increased public hostility towards Muslims, and in many people's minds Islamic revival is now equated with violence. This simplistic equation is sometimes encouraged by the media. During Ramadan, Larbi Kechat, the Rector of the Stalingrad Mosque, gave a television interview on the spiritual significance of fasting. Without his permission, a brief extract from it was broadcast at peak viewing time on February 27, 1997 as part of a programme on Islamist terrorist networks in Europe, giving the misleading impression that he condoned terrorism. Three weeks later, a bomb exploded outside the mosque causing extensive damage; the security forces searched the building; and the Front National distributed leaflets opposing the granting of planning permission.

The situation is not as bleak as the above chronicle of events makes it appear. Non-Muslims from various walks of life have spoken out in support of the Stalingrad Mosque and its Rector, proving that not all French people are Islamophobic. In 1987, the Institut du Monde Arabe opened in Paris. This prestigious institution, which has a fine library and organises exhibitions and public lectures, is financed jointly by the French government and the majority of the Arab states. It has done much to improve French people's understanding of Arabic culture and Islamic civilisation. The distinguished Catholic islamicist Louis Massignon (d. 1962) popularised the notion that Islam is an Abrahamic religion like Judaism and Christianity, and it is largely due to his efforts that the Catholic Church's official policy towards Muslims is now one of cooperation and conciliation. In recent decades Church authorities in France have allowed Muslims to use their premises and have been vocal in opposing racism and discrimination. This has occasionally raised the hackles of secularists, as for instance when the Archbishop of Paris defended the rights of Muslim girls to wear head scarves but used this as a pretext to remark on the need to reconsider the place of religion in schools.

Islam and the Republic

The status of Islam in France is affected by three pieces of legislation, none of which was framed with Muslims in mind. The first and most ancient of these is the Napoleonic Concordat of 1802. Under the terms of the Concordat, Catholicism was recognised as the religion to which the majority of the population adhered, and Catholic priests were paid by the state, as were Protestant pastors and Jewish rabbis. The second is the 1901 law on the right of associations. Because of this, freedom of association is a legal right subject to a simple declaration. The third is the 1905 law on the separation of religion and state. Article 1 of this law guarantees freedom of conscience and the free exercise of religion subject to certain restrictions in the interests of public order, thus endorsing the earlier law on the right of associations. Article 2, however, stipulates that, 'the Republic does not grant recognition to, pay the salaries of, or provide subsidies for any religion', hence annulling the Concordat of 1802. Nevertheless, the Concordat is still in force in Alsace, because in 1905 this region was part of Germany, and when it was reunited with France in 1918, it was reinstated under the terms of the Concordat that had been in force when it was lost to Germany in 1870.

The law of 1905 was the culmination of the long struggle between the Church and State which had divided French society throughout the nineteenth century. The law was intended to guarantee religious freedom, not least for non-Catholics, by making religion a private affair and excluding it from the public domain. In the case of state schools, this meant that religious symbols such as crucifixes and statues were to be removed; there were to be no classes for religious instruction, no religious assemblies and no proselytising. On this basis, some school principals believe that they are right to suspend Muslim girls who refuse to remove their headscarves. That was the attitude of the headmaster in Creil who provoked a national crisis by suspending three girls in 1989. After deliberation, the Council of State decided to leave the decision in the hands of the school principals but ruled that girls should not be suspended for wearing scarves unless there was a health risk or evidence that they were trying to proselytise. Most principals have chosen to avoid confrontation and by 1993 about 2,000 Muslim girls were wearing scarves in class. However, every autumn there have been problems in some schools. For instance a Moroccan girl in Grenoble reacted to suspension by going on a hunger strike, which culminated on February 5, 1994 with 1,500 Muslims from all over the country attending a demonstration to draw attention to her plight. On September 20, 1994 François Bayrou, the conservative minister of education, issued a circular declaring that pupils were permitted to wear discreet signs indicating their personal religious convictions but that ostentatious signs which constituted elements of proselytism or discrimination were forbidden. The prime minister subsequently confirmed that the small skull-cap worn by Jewish boys was not an ostentatious sign but said nothing about the Islamic scarf. Some principals interpreted this as giving them the green light to continue banning headscarves in their establishments. There have since been several court cases and the problem is far from resolved.

The position of religious associations is equally unclear. Article 1 of the law of 1905 permits their creation, but Article 2 denies them official recognition. In practice, local authorities have differed in their interpretation of the law. Until recently, the majority have adopted a militant secularist stance, refusing any institutional links with Islamic associations and frequently blocking planning permission for mosques. On occasions, this militant secularism has verged on persecution. For example, in August 1989, a prayer room in a disused factory at Charvieu-Chavagneux, twenty miles from Lyon, was 'accidentally' demolished early one morning when there were Muslims inside it. Some local authorities have, however, given implicit recognition to Islamic associations by subsidising their cultural activities and negotiating with their officials over matters of public concern.

There is, as we have seen, a precedent for the more generous interpretation of the law of 1905 in the way in which the state indirectly financed the building of the Paris Mosque. Despite the existence of this institution, however, France has traditionally resolved problems with her Muslim inhabitants by negotiating directly with their countries of origin, rather than with the Rector of the Muslim Institute or other local spokespersons. Nevertheless, in November 1989, Pierre Joxe, the socialist minister of the interior, summoned the then Rector, Tedjini Hadam, along with five other well-known Muslim figures of various persuasions, to a meeting in which he charged them to reflect on the creation of a body with which the state could liaise. These six became the kernel of CORIF (Conseil de réflexion sur l'islam en France) which was formed in 1990. Although CORIF's fifteen members mirrored the diversity of Islam in France, its sole *raison d'être* was that it had been willed into existence by the state. Differences of opinion soon surfaced and little was achieved apart from agreements on the demarcation of Muslim burial plots in public cemeteries and the provision of *halal* food for Muslim soldiers. Some of the members had Islamist sympathies and were suspicious of the Paris Mosque's close links with the Algerian government. Their suspicions proved justified in January 1992 when the Algerian Security Council, which had just annulled the elections, announced that Tedjini Hadam was a member of the five-man committee which it had appointed to run the country. He resigned from CORIF, leaving it in disarray, but held on to his position as Rector of the Muslim Institute until he was ousted by its committee.

In the run-up to the spring elections in France, the Mayor of Paris authorised a large subsidy to pay for repairs to the Paris Mosque. After the elections, the newly appointed conservative minister of the interior, Charles Pasqua, decided that he had no use for CORIF and that he would put all his weight behind the new Rector, Dalil Boubakeur. The latter responded positively by taking two initiatives. First, he laid plans for an institute of higher studies to train *imams* to work in France. The minister of the interior and the minister of culture attended its opening on October 4, 1993, but as yet it has attracted far fewer students than its rivals in the Nièvre and at the office of the Muslim World League. Second, he created the CRMF (Conseil représentatif des musulmans de France). This body presented the minister of the interior with a charter in January 1995, in which it explained who the Muslims were and what they wanted. The charter is based on the assumption that France is *dar al-ahd* (the land of contract or alliance) and that Muslims should be good republicans and cooperate fully with the secular state. Although bound to please the government, it is unlikely to meet with more than a lukewarm response from those Muslims who belong to associations which oppose the hegemony of the Paris Mosque.

In the present state of affairs, it is unrealistic to expect the fragmented Muslim community in France to create a truly representative body capable of entering into dialogue with the authorities. Within a generation, however, the situation may be very different. By then, the scars left by the Algerian War of Independence should have healed and the majority of the Muslims in France will be French. In the meantime, the government is understandably anxious to foster the emergence of a distinctively French Islam. One card which it has not yet played, but which it might conceivably play, is the extension of the Concordat to include Muslims. It could then open a state-funded Faculty of Islamic Theology in Strasbourg, alongside the existing Catholic and Protestant Faculties. The creation of such an institution would help to counter the pervasive influence of North African and the Middle Eastern ideologies.

Diversity of Belief and Practice

Although there is an extensive literature on Islam in France, the bulk of the research has been undertaken by political scientists. Their primary concern has been with institutional structures and the status of Islam in an overtly secular society. The distinctive beliefs and practices of France's Muslims have unfortunately attracted far less interest. These beliefs and practices naturally vary from one ethnic group to another. For instance, in matters of jurisprudence most of the North Africans and West Africans adhere to the Maliki school, whereas the Turks are predominantly Hanafis. Similarly, those who follow a Sufi *tariqa* (mystical path) are likely to belong to the Alawiyya, Shadhiliyya or Qadiriyya if they are North Africans; the Tijaniyya or Mouridiyya if they are West Africans; and the Naqshbandiyya if they are Turks. However, the differences between generations are equally striking and it is with them that I propose to conclude.

Most of the first generation Muslim immigrants came to France from North Africa in the 1950s and 1960s. There were two important currents in North African Islam at that time: the reformist Islam of Abdelhamid Ibn

A Muslim butcher's shop in Paris (photo: Ingvar Svanberg, 1997).

Badis (d. 1940), and popular religion with its emphasis on the intercessory and healing powers of entombed saints and living holy men. The Paris Mosque at times served as a vector for the thought of Ben Badis, but the majority of the immigrants retained their attachment to elements of popular religion. This was particularly true of their women folk, who often joined them later. Even when they neglected the prayers, the women wore headscarves out of respect for their husbands, fasted in Ramadan, and obtained amulets from *marabouts* (Sufi leaders). The men at first found it difficult to practise their religion in France, but have experienced a re-Islamisation since the early 1970s.

In the 1980s, second generation North African immigrants prided themselves on their secularism. They described themselves as *beurs* (part of the vocabulary of *verlan*, a type of slang in which the syllables of a word – in this case *arabes* – are transposed and deformed) and they rarely practised Islam. The minority who belong to the middle classes are still, on the whole, non-practising although many of them have internalised Islamic values. Since 1990, however, there has been a noticeable shift in attitude and an increasing number of young people now openly claim to be Muslims. Although most of them have derived a rudimentary knowledge of Islam from being brought up in Muslim households, their religion differs from that of their parents in a number of respects. It has nothing to do with preserving Algerian, Moroccan or Tunisian identity. It eschews the wearing of amulets, using the Quran for divinatory purposes, and other 'superstitious' practices imported from the North African rural setting. Most important of all, it is not based on inherited traditions but is something which they have consciously chosen.

The reasons for this change are complex. Undoubtedly, the *dawa* activities of local associations have played an important part in Islamic revival. Nevertheless, it is clear that in many instances their message is heeded because it meets a deeply-felt existential need. The media portray the high-rise suburban estates, in which the poorer immigrants live, as violent places where crime and drug addiction are rife. Hence, city-dwellers rarely visit them for fear of being attacked, and when youth from the estates go into the cities their presence is resented. In addition, there has been a marked increase in unemployment. Many second and third generation immigrants thus feel doomed to a meaningless, ghettoised existence characterised by ostracism and economic deprivation. In short, they have lost faith in the republican myth of integration and social advancement. Their Islam is therefore an Islam of the excluded. By becoming practising Muslims, they acquire a sense of dignity and purpose. Through participation in local associations, they attempt to create a new Islamic community which transcends ethnic barriers. If they have a sense of ethnic identity at all, it is as 'Arabs' in the broadest sense, because they recite the Quran and pray in Arabic, although their grasp of that language is often superficial.

The Islam of France's youth is one of ethical conformity rather than social activism. Through it, they seek salvation from their own unstructured lives and the moral chaos which they perceive around them. Nevertheless, the puritanical zeal of new converts often gives way to a more flexible and tolerant stance. For example, the initial desire to eat only *halal* food may evolve into a minimalist and unostentatious avoidance of pork and alcohol. Similarly, young women who wear the Islamic headscarf come to terms with friends who observe very different dress codes. Most important of all, strict segregation of the sexes, which was the norm alike for traditionalists and earlier generations of Islamists, is frequently regarded as unnecessary by France's young Muslims.

Although the media stigmatise women in headscarves as 'Muslim fundamentalists', those who wear them do so for a variety of reasons. For older women who are immigrants, it is a matter of keeping up traditions and maintaining a link with their country of origin by doing as their mothers and grandmothers did before them. For pre-adolescents and adolescents between the age of twelve and sixteen, on the other hand, the headscarf is often a passport to freedom, because wearing it reassures their parents that they can be trusted outside the home. When these girls leave school and become independent, as often as not they stop wearing it. In their case, it thus serves as a way of bridging the gap between home and society. For other girls of this age, however, the headscarf is a cruel imposition which their fathers or older brothers force them to wear against their will. In their case, it aggravates the gap between home and society. Finally, as a result of the media coverage of the controversy, still others wear the headscarf as an attention-seeking act of bravado. With post-adolescents between the age of sixteen and twenty-five, the motives for wearing the headscarf are different again. In the majority of instances they wear it to affirm their desire to be both French and Muslim. For them, it is a sign of Islamic modesty which they are *at liberty* to wear. Paradoxically, this attitude reveals that they have internalised the very republican values which on the surface they appear to have rejected. For other young women of this age, the headscarf is little more than a fashion accessory. Only very rarely do post-adolescents wear the headscarf out of a desire to identify themselves with radical Islamist groups which seek to impose Islamic law on society.

Because of the bombs which were planted in France from July 1995 onwards, and the almost daily reports of atrocities in Algeria, there is a widespread fear of radical Islamists infiltrating France and establishing terrorist networks. There is, however, little evidence that this is happening on a large scale. Young Muslims are often reluctant to condemn Algerian Islamism, but this does not mean that they are willing to adopt the tactics of the GIA. It is simply that they perceive the Algerian government as being supported by French neo-colonialism, and that they suspect the media of blackening the Islamists just at it blackens them. In most instances, their own Islam is apolitical. They are seeking to give meaning to their lives in the midst of the society which has rejected them, but they have not declared war on society. Moreover, they are too preoccupied with their own problems to become embroiled in those of their Algerian cousins.

Literature

This chapter was researched while the author was on study leave funded by the British Academy Research Leave Scheme. For introductory surveys of Muslims in France, see Annie Krieger-Krynicki, *Les musulmans en France* (Paris: Maisonneuve Larose, 1985) and Jocelyne Cesari, *Etre musulman en France aujourd'hui* (Paris: Hachette, 1997). Gilles Kepel, *Les banlieues de l'Islam* (Paris: Seuil, 1987) is a magisterial if somewhat unsympathetic study by a political scientist. See also the last section of his more recent book, *A l'ouest d'Allah* (Paris: Seuil, 1994), pp. 205–319. Bruno Étienne (ed.), *L'Islam en France* (Paris: Editions du CNRS, 1990) is wide-ranging and interdisciplinary.

On the colonial period and decolonialisation, see Jacques Frémaux, *La France et l'Islam depuis 1979* (Paris: PUF, 1991). The best general introduction to immigration is Philippe Bernard, *L'immigration* (Paris: Le Monde-Editions, 1993), but for a more detailed account of the present conditions of France's immigrants, see Michèle Tribalat, *De l'immigration à l'assimilation* (Paris: La Découverte, 1996). The question of whether and to what extent there is a place for Islam in republican France is explored in detail in Bruno Étienne, *La France et l'Islam* (Paris: Hachette, 1989), while the specific issue of the wearing of the Islamic scarf in state schools is examined in Françoise Gaspar and Farhad Khosrokhavar, *Le foulard et la République* (Paris: La Découverte, 1995).

The standard work on the Paris Mosque is Alain Boyer, *L'Institut Musulman de la Mosquée de Paris* (Paris: Centre des Hautes Etudes sur l'Afrique et l'Asie modernes, 1992). For the full text of the Muslim Charter with a commentary by the present rector, see *Charte du culte Musulman en France*, ed. D. Boubakeur (Monaco: Editions du Rocher, 1995). Nation-wide associations are put into European and global context in Antoine Sfeir, *Les réseaux d'Allah* (Paris: Plon, 1997), and local associations are discussed in Jocelyne Cesari, *Etre musulman en France: Associations, militants et mosquées* (Paris: Karthala, 1994). There are two recent studies of young Muslims written by Muslim sociologists: Farhad Khosrokhavar, *L'islam des jeunes* (Paris: Flammarion, 1997) and Leïla Babès, *L'Islam positif* (Paris: Ouvrières, 1997). On the issue of how Muslim youths are occasionally recruited by terrorist networks, see David Pujadas and Ahmad Salam, *La tentation du Jihad* (Paris: J-C. Lattés, 1995).

There is a dearth of studies on Muslims in specific localities other than the Paris region, but see P. Aziz, *Le Paradoxe de Roubaix* (Paris: Plon, 1996) and Franck Fregosi, 'L'islam en terre concordataire', *Hommes et Migrations*, 1209 (1997), pp. 29–48. Sub-Saharan African Muslims in France have received little attention, but the following articles are useful: Alloui Said Abasse, 'Itinéraires biographiques de quatre membres de l'élite comorienne de Marseille: éléments pour une sociologie de l'islam comorien', *Islam et Sociétés au sud du Sahara*, 9 (1995), pp. 99–116; A. Moustapha Diop, 'Immigration et religion: les musulmans négro-africains en France', *Migrations Société*, 1:5–6 (1989), pp. 45–57; A. Moustapha Diop, 'Les associations islamiques sénégalaises en France', *Islam et Sociétés au sud du Sahara,* 8 (1994), pp. 7–15; and Victoria Ebin. 'Making Room versus Creating Space: The Construction of Spacial Categories by Itinerant Mouride Traders', pp. 92–109 in *Making Muslim Space in North America and Europe*, ed. Barbara Daly Metcalf (Berkeley: University of California Press, 1996).

Chapter Sixteen

Britain

Ron Geaves

The Muslim presence in Britain is at least three centuries old and can be traced to the activities of the East India Company which recruited seamen known as 'lascars' from the subcontinent. The sailors were often taken on board ship in India for the duration of a single voyage. Consequently they found themselves stranded in British ports while they searched for a passage home. Some of the lascars formed relationships with British women and opened hostels and cafés to serve the itinerant dockside communities. These shifting settlements of seamen expanded considerably after the opening of the Suez canal in 1869 when large numbers of Yemenis and Somalis were recruited in Aden. The Yemenis, in particular, began to open boarding houses in Cardiff and South Shields and the Somalis settled in Liverpool. Numerically, the population of these two communities is currently no more than 15,000, but significantly, they were certainly the first permanent settlements of Muslims in Britain. The Yemeni community is particularly significant as it focused its development around the inspiration of a *shaykh* belonging to the Alawi Sufi order who arrived in Britain in the early twentieth century. The centres or *zawiyas* of the order began in the ports and spread inland to the Yemini communities in Sheffield and Birmingham. This is the earliest evidence of a Muslim community achieving cohesion and stability through organised religion.

In addition to the Yemeni community the principal centres of organised Islam in the early part of the twentieth century were in Liverpool, London and Woking. These small congregations of mainly subcontinent Muslims were comprised of businessmen, members of the Indian aristocracy, students and a handful of high profile converts. These centres of religious activity often depended on the efforts of these individuals and tended to disappear when they returned to their homelands or on their death. Jørgen Nielsen notes in his book, *Muslims in Western Europe*, that for a considerable period the personal physician to Queen Victoria was a Muslim. These prominent late-nineteenth-century Muslims were responsible for the foundation of the first mosques to be established in Britain. In 1887 a Liverpool solicitor named Henry William Quilliam converted to Islam whilst travelling in Morocco. Known as Shaykh Abdullah, he organised prayers, the celebration of festivals, weddings and funerals,

The mosque in Woking (photo: Pia Karlsson, 1997).

religious evening classes, and a day school in a group of converted terraced houses in Liverpool. He wrote several essays and pamphlets on Islam and claimed to have personally converted 150 members of the British public. The Ottoman sultan appointed him *Shaykh al-Islam* (the senior member of the *ulama*, religious scholars, in a country) to Britain, and the *amir* (military commander or governor) of Afghanistan provided him with the funds to purchase a building to be used as the Islamic Institute in Liverpool.

The oldest mosque in Britain is the Shahjehan mosque built in Woking in 1889. The Hungarian orientalist, Dr Leitner, persuaded the ruler of the Indian state of Bhopal to fund a complex which was envisaged to incorporate a library, hostel and eventually a Muslim university. Only the mosque and the hostel came to fruition. After Leitner's death in 1899 the mosque fell into disuse but was purchased in 1913 by the Ahmadiyya movement to be the centre of their missionary activities in Britain. The English convert Lord Headley and a Lahore barrister, Khwaja Kamal-ud-Din, who had come to England in order to challenge misconceptions of Islam, were responsible for the re-emergence of the Woking centre, but they were both increasingly criticised by orthodox Sunni Muslims for their connections with the Ahmadiyya movement. However, the Woking Muslim Mission sponsored the Muslim Literary Society and carried out welfare work on behalf of widows and orphans of Indian Muslim soldiers who died in the Second World War. Marmeduke Pickthall and Abdullah Yusef Ali, who have produced two of the best-known translations of the Quran into English, were both members of the Muslim Literary Society. After the death of Lord Headley in 1932 the management committee of the mosque broke all connections with the Ahmadiyya movement.

At the end of the First World War Lord Headley and other prominent Muslims in Britain had discussed the idea of a central mosque in London. In 1928 the London Nizamiah Trust was established but progress was very slow until the Second World War. Land was donated in Regents Park by King George VI in return for a site in Cairo intended for a new Anglican cathedral. In November 1944, the Islamic Cultural Centre was opened by the King himself. In 1947, thirteen ambassadors from Muslim nations created the Central London Mosque Trust to raise the funds to begin construction. The foundation stone was laid in 1954 but funding problems and disagreements over the design delayed the project. The mosque was finally opened in 1977 and is considered to be the most prestigious mosque in the country. However, by the time of its opening the Muslim presence in Britain had been dramatically transformed.

The subcontinent Muslim communities

Along with populations from various parts of the Arab world, Iran, Malaysia, Turkey, Cyprus, Morocco, East and West Africa who have arrived in Britain as a result of political upheaval or as students and businessmen, since the 1950s Britain has received tens of thousands of Muslim immigrants from the subcontinent. They came in response to the host nation's demand for cheap labour and to join their family members already living in Britain. At first, only men seeking employment on offer in manufacturing industries based in the cities and towns of the West Midlands and northern England travelled to Britain. The first communities developed around the efforts of the early settlers who had worked in the merchant navy during the Second World War. Philip Lewis, in his book *Islamic Britain*, notes that by the beginning of the war seamen recruited in the subcontinent formed 20 per cent of the merchant navy. A handful of others had come to Britain inspired by the British presence in India to better themselves economically and worked as market traders or travelling salesmen selling cheap goods out of suitcases. These pioneer settlers had often married British women and were in a position to assist the newly-arriving migrants. They had all risked leaving their country of origin to find work with higher wages, often intending to return home eventually. In the early 1960s there was concern over changes in the immigration legislation which was to tighten controls on entry to the country. Some of the migrants had begun to invest their wages into cheap terraced properties to accommodate their compatriots, but they were also experiencing some loneliness and a sense of alienation. As a consequence of these factors, the men began to reunite their families by bringing their wives and children to Britain. Others returned to the subcontinent to visit their families and returned with new brides. Once children began to be born in Britain the reality of return became more and more unlikely and therefore most have remained to form themselves into communities established around their religion, places of origin and kin networks (*biradari*).

It is difficult to determine exactly how many Muslims there are in Britain today as the census does not have a category to distinguish people by religion. Even if one should take the trouble to sift arduously through the categories of ethnic origin in the 1991 census in search of Muslim surnames, the results are likely to be highly inaccurate. Many will have refused to identify themselves by ethnic origin as they strongly identify themselves with a common Islamic identity. Others may not reveal their presence on the census as their presence in the country is not legal. To estimate the total Muslim population in Britain it is necessary to combine information derived from the ethnic category with the country of birth information for people who originate in Muslim nations. This will not include Muslims born in non-Muslim nations such as India or the number of converts amongst the Afro–Caribbean and indigenous white population. The estimate of the total Muslim population in 1991 is shown in the table below:

Country/Region of origin	Population
Pakistan	477,000
Bangladesh	163,000
India	134,000
East Africans of Indian origin	80,000
Arab nations	150,000
African Muslims	115,000
Turkish Cypriots/Turkey	70,000
Iran	50,000
Malaysia	30,000
Other Muslim countries	148,000
Total	1,517,000

These figures are calculated from those reproduced in *Muslims in Britain: 1991 Census and other Statistical Sources* by Muhammad Anwar (Birmingham, 1993) and *Muslims in Western Europe* by Jørgen Nielsen (Edinburgh: Edinburgh University Press, 1992).

It is clear from these figures that the dominant Muslim presence originates from the subcontinent. Philip Lewis notes that in addition to this numerical dominance it has to be taken into account that the subcontinent communities are not merely resident in Britain but have formed permanent communities where most of the members possess British nationality. As with all the other subcontinent communities, the first notable Pakistani presence appeared in the 1951 census. With the arrival of dependants beginning in the 1960s, the population of subcontinent Muslim migrants increased substantially. The figures shown below, which are derived from the 1981 census calculated on the basis of the place of birth of the head of the household, demonstrate this rapid growth of the Muslim population from the subcontinent.

Census	Population
1951	5,000
1961	24,900
1971	170,000
1981	360,000

Source: Jørgen Nielsen, *Muslims in Western Europe* (Edinburgh: Edinburgh University Press, 1992).

The significant figure, however, is not so much the total estimate but the ever-increasing proportion of Muslims born and educated in Britain as compared to the proportion of migrants born in Pakistan and Bangladesh. The percentages for this proportion of the population are shown below.

Census	Total population	Proportion born in Britain
1951	5,000	–
1961	24,900	1.2%
1971	170,000	23.5%
1981	360,000	37.5%
1991	640,000	47%

Source: Muhammad Anwar, *Muslims in Britain: 1991 Census and other Statistical Sources* (Birmingham, 1993) and Jørgen Nielsen, *Muslims in Western Europe* (Edinburgh: Edinburgh University Press, 1992).

If the immigration laws continue to make it increasingly difficult for subcontinent migrants to enter Britain, this figure will increase to almost 100 per cent within the duration of one generation's lifespan as the first generation migrants die, although parents are still seeking marriage partners in their countries of origin.

The other significant statistic amongst those born in the subcontinent is the diversity of regional place of origin. This is confined, however, to a few well-defined regions. A survey carried out in 1974 showed the following regional breakdown of subcontinent Muslims.

Pakistan	Punjab	37%
	Kashmir	37%
	Karachi	6%
	N.W. Frontier	4%
	Other	7%
Bangladesh (then East Pakistan)		9%
India	Punjab	49%
	Gujarat	16%
	Other	35%

Source: College de France, 'Muslim Immigration and Settlement in Britain', *Colloquium on Islam in Europe Today* (Paris: Association pour l'Avancement des Sciences Islamique, 1983).

Even these categories are too broad. The actual patterns of migration indicate that the Kashmiris originated from the district of Mirpur and the Punjabis came from the Cambellpur district. The majority of Bangladeshis were from Sylhet and the district of Chittagong. There is also a smaller but significant population of migrants from East Africa who had been brought over from India in the nineteenth century by the British as indentured labourers. The processes of chain migration have in reality limited the actual places of origin to clusters of specific villages in the above places.

Although often defined inaccurately by the receiving culture as a homogeneous minority usually labelled as Pakistani, the self-definition of the subcontinent Muslims has tended to revolve around the customs and beliefs inherited from these localised extended family groupings confined to small areas of rural Pakistan, Bangladesh and, to a lesser extent, India. It is, however, becoming increasingly difficult to pass on the values and traditions of these villages of origin to a generation born and educated in Britain who identify themselves as British Muslims. This cultural clash of values that manifests itself across the generations is central to the various dichotomies that Muslims in Britain need to resolve in order to form a communal self-identity based on religious unity.

The growth of mosques

The strong sense of a shared faith enables individual Muslims to cope with the difficult experience of living as a minority in Britain and it could be argued that the universal symbols of Islam become even more powerful in what is perceived to be a hostile environment by many of the Muslim population. However, ethnic identity which also embraces all the symbols of religion in order to affirm itself becomes an important factor too. There can be no doubt that the Muslim migrants passed through a stage of entrenchment in which ethnic identity was reinforced. This process can be observed in the rapid increase in the number of mosques. Nielsen (in *Muslims in Western Europe*) states that the growth of mosques in Britain

362

can be linked to the immigration process. The arrival of wives and families brought a dramatic increase in religious practices, and a new awareness of religious life. In 1966, there were only eighteen mosques but for the next ten years they increased at the rate of around seven mosques a year. From 1975, this annual rate of mosque registration more than doubled. This certainly reflects the developing awareness of the need for religion and a new assertiveness amongst Muslims to establish Islam in Britain. There were certainly some Muslim groups who benefitted from the Arab states' oil wealth and were able to construct purpose-built mosques in Britain's major cities, and throughout the 1990s more communities are building mosques rather than converting existing buildings. By 1985 there were 338 registered mosques in Britain and in 1997 this figure must be closer to 1,000 Muslim places of worship. It must be considered that the mosques function, however, not only as places of worship, but also as centres to maintain and reinforce shared memories, values and goals located in the place of origin. This function of the mosque is likely to slowly change as a younger generation of British Muslims take over the leadership and the older first generation migrants disappear. The mosques are more likely to become centres that reflect the needs of Muslims trying to resolve the issues of reconciling Islam's beliefs and practices with British secular life rather than maintaining shared memories of the subcontinent.

At first sight the increase in mosque numbers between 1966 and 1975 appeared to be a part of a religious revival or renewal of commitment to Islam but it is more likely that these phenomena of religion manifested themselves to reinforce ethnic or group identity. Certainly it can be observed that this gathering around Islamic symbols, which was used by the first generation migrants to sanctify the customs of their culture of origin, does not always sit easy with the younger generation of British-born Muslims. Many of them have utilised religion to attack the ethnic customs of their parents as un-Islamic. These young Muslims often seek a different kind of Islam which is freed from perceived South Asian cultural accretions. Central to the problems of Muslims in Britain is the distinction between the ideals and values of Islam on the one hand and the cultural mores of particular time–space milieus on the other.

Organising the community

It must be remembered that no single view of Islam is held by all members of the community. The process of organising the Muslim community on a national basis is as old as its presence in Britain, but the pattern of chain migration reinforced by *biradari* networks has significantly strengthened ties to extended families that originated in small locales of Pakistan and Bangladesh. This is reflected in the ways that the community has organised

Barelwi Muslims in Birmingham, followers of *shaykh* Sufi Abdullah from Zindapir in Pakistan, on the occasion of the Prophet Muhammad's birthday (photo: Ron Geaves, 1997).

itself in Britain. Virtually all the religious divisions prominent in Pakistan have their localised expression in Britain: Deobandi, Barelwi, Ahl-i Hadith, Ahl-i Quran, Jamaat al-Tabligh and the variety of organisations based on the inspiration of Jamaat-i Islami have all been successfully transplanted to Britain. Neither of the two largest movements, the Deobandis and the Barelwis, have been able to organise themselves nationally in spite of the fact that they claim the widest support amongst the subcontinent Muslims. More significant to the development of the community is the fact that the key movements and traditions have a history of mutual recrimination. Indeed, even excommunication has characterised their relationship with each other in the subcontinent and this has spilled over into Britain. There have been conflicts over control of mosques and each movement proclaims its brand of Islam as the only orthodoxy. This has resulted in the division of some small communities since the different groups are intensely suspicious of each other and do very little to integrate amongst themselves, all retaining strong links with their parent organisations in the subcontinent.

Mosques and welfare organisations proliferated throughout the 1970s and 1980s, each representing small subgroups within the community. Any attempts to create umbrella organisations to represent the community on a

The tomb and shrine of Pir Wahhab Siddiqui, a Naqshbandi *shaykh* buried in Coventry (photo: Ron Geaves, 1997).

national level were relatively unsuccessful and this is reflected in the large number of Muslim organisations in Britain. In 1986 it was estimated that there were over 4,000, mostly concerned with local welfare. Tensions between the universal and the particular are ever-present. Any move towards establishing the kind of national organisation based on the universals of Islam which would represent the whole community is likely to be seen as a critique of traditional, localised values which many Muslim migrants still hold dear as expressions of a former life in the villages where they originated.

In this context Sufism has always been a major influence in the subcontinent as well as other parts of the Muslim world although strongly opposed by organisations which assert a more orthodox brand of Islam. In particular, this has been the source of the conflict between Deobandis and Barelwis. The major Sufi orders, Naqshbandiyya, Qadiriyya and Chishtiyya, are all influential at a local level in Britain amongst most of the Muslim communities. The Sufi orders are found not only amongst the subcontinent communities but are also influential in the Turkish, Malaysian, West African and even some Arab communities. In the subcontinent, the *pirs*, the charismatic leaders of the Sufi orders, have always been the bearers of regional culture and language. They have taught in the vernacular, and carried the message of Islam deep into the hearts and minds of rural people who were often illiterate. There are many *pirs* teaching in Britain and some of the prominent ones are resident in the country and beginning to have large national followings.

This custom-laden version of Islam, upheld in Britain by the Barelwis, emphasises popular devotion, the intercession of saints, *baraka* (the power to bless), shrines, tombs of holy men, peculiar powers and miracles, singing and dancing and, above all, the importance of the *pir/murid* (master/ disciple) relationship. Asian food, candles, incense, rosewater offerings, holy water and amulets are all used in religious worship. Any of these may be used to cure the sick, secure the birth of male children, or protect the worshipper from magical forces such as evil *jinns* (spirits of fire and air). Obviously this form of Islam, unique as it is to the villages of the subcontinent, evokes very powerfully for many migrants the feeling of cherished places of origin. It is debatable in what form this strand of the faith will survive beyond the generation of migrants that was born in the subcontinent. Its powerful link with the villages of the migrants' past may have no association for British-born Muslims, and they may well ally themselves with the reformist critique of the Sufi tradition. Their need to distance themselves from their parents' Asian origin and to assert their British identity may leave them disenchanted with this folk form of Islam. On the other hand, the spirituality of the Sufi path may become attractive for those seeking their fulfilment away from the materialist ethos of late-twentieth-century Britain.

It must be remembered that prior to the creation of Pakistan in 1947, Muslims had always been a minority in the subcontinent. Muslims in India long regarded themselves as separate and distinct from other religious and social groupings. The various movements mentioned above all developed strategies to deal with living alongside a Hindu majority, and later to deal with being ruled by the British. Essential to these strategies was the message of return to the basics of Islam in order to revitalise the community, which had found itself in danger of being relegated to a minor position. Many of the nineteenth- and early-twentieth-century theological/political groups such as Deobandi, Ahl-i Hadith and Ahl-i Quran emerged in the subcontinent in response to the decline of the Muslim community and the successful spread of European culture. The central tenet of their message was a return to the fundamentals of Islam based on the Quran and Sunna, and a stripping away of anything that was seen to be cultural accretion or innovation. The influence of these groups has increased as a result of the general resurgence of Islam throughout the Muslim world.

It is not surprising that these theological/political movements have become much more influential in Britain than have the locally organised welfare organisations. The apparent emphasis on the universals of Islam, the history of Islamic revival, and the fact that many of the first generation Muslims have existing loyalties to one or other of them, has enabled them to flourish in Britain. On the other hand, the ideas of the twentieth-century ideological movements associated with Jamaat-i Islami and other revivalist organisations are more likely to be attractive to young Muslims of both sexes born in Britain. Perhaps even more attractive is the fact these groups were formed partly in opposition to British colonialism and Western values. Muhammad Anwar points out that the relationship betwen Muslims and the indigenous population can best be understood against the background of the colonial encounter, and the unequal economic and political power relationships generated by colonialism both in British India and now in Britain. If this is true, then the success of these groups must be attributed to the fact they have developed historical strategies to cope with Muslims being a minority ruled over by the British. The confrontation with British colonialism and Western values has been transplanted to Britain from the subcontinent by the economic processes of capitalism. The Muslim minority of the subcontinent, once ruled by a British colonial minority, now finds a part of itself to be an economically and socially deprived minority in the land of its old rulers. The major difference here in the new situation is that the old rulers are now the majority population.

It has yet to be ascertained whether any of these revivalist organisations can really fulfil the expectations of British-born Muslims. One has to examine critically their proclamation of a culturally-free emphasis on the universals of Islam. This may have been true at the time of their foundation and within the context of their creation, but they may now be too embroiled in the history of subcontinent Muslim sectarian conflict to be of any use in helping to create a unified British Muslim community. There is a strong possibility that they are in danger of imparting divisions which developed in the history of subcontinent Islam which could seriously undermine any efforts they might make towards developing a truly native version of Islam in Britain.

Very often the ideal of the *umma* (worldwide Islamic community) is seen to be betrayed by any degree of integration with the host community. Some Muslims go as far as to question whether a truly Islamic life is even possible in the West when Muslims are in a minority. Up until now the mosques have not responded positively to the challenge of modernity. This has resulted in their inability to attract young people and a neglect of a public participation of women in religious activities. It is amongst these two groups that the search for identity is most acute.

The intergenerational conflict

Muslims in Britain are undergoing a crucial change of self-identity amongst the British-born descendants of the original settlers. The first generation migrants had used 'the Myth of Return' to legitimise continued adherence to the values of the homeland, and to condemn any assimilation of British cultural values as irrelevant and destructive. Most of the first generation migrants come from rural areas in the subcontinent and were not educated. They have tried to maintain a world outlook which is foreign to the values of the receiving culture. Very often this has resulted in a conservatism that even in the original homeland many would find rigid and old-fashioned. The countries of origin have undergone considerable changes since the departure of the original migrants to Britain, but they often continue to hold an emotive attachment to the way things were at the time of migration. This outlook can become idealised and mythologised; the values brought over are not allowed to be challenged. Many migrants find it difficult to understand their children who were brought up and educated in Britain. Sometimes attempts to question or break away from the parents' values is seen as corruption by the host nation's un-Islamic values and as a move towards godlessness and the disintegration of the community. The children can find it equally difficult to understand the beliefs and lifestyle of their parents.

Despite their greater contact with the values of the indigenous culture through the medium of education, the family still remains tremendously important to the majority of young subcontinent Muslims. The concept of *izzat* (family honour) acts as a powerful agent of reinforcement for the passing down and maintenance within the family of the rules and customs of the community. There are powerful emotive inhibitions against disgracing the family or letting down the family honour. The most important part of the *sharia* is family law, which insists that religious duty governs personal relations. Consequently, *izzat* is maintained and sanctified by a complicated pattern of behaviour evolved from Islam and the time-honoured customs of the family's place of origin and social status. To the older generation who find themselves struggling to maintain their ethnic/religious identity as a minority group, *izzat* becomes of great significance. Very often the particular and the universal have equal importance. Their Islam is not only based on the study of Quran and Sunna, but has been formed by the rites and ceremonies of family and village life. Religion is indistinguishable from their way of life, and these traditions are zealously guarded in the alien and often hostile environment of Britain.

There are signs that young Muslims in Britain are increasingly rejecting both assimilation into the mainstream indigenous culture and the ethnocentricity of their parents. Thus both generations are affirming the values of religion. The earlier migrants use Islam to affirm their cultural inheritance and allegiance to life in the subcontinent. Old customs and traditions are reinforced by sanctifying them as prescribed by religion. Increasingly, however, there are signs that the later generations are developing a religious awareness which has little to do with ethnic solidarity. An attempt is taking place to discover an Islamic identity based on the universals of the faith. Some are beginning to believe that it is not enough to be born a Muslim. For them religion has to be more than an accident at birth, subservient to culture. It has to be founded on knowledge and experience. Many young Muslims in Britain are confounding their parents by their attempts to separate the essentials of the faith from cultural or historical additions. Values cherished by parents as part of their cultural and religious identity are now coming under attack, not from the expected directions of the indigenous culture, but from their children who declare them to be un-Islamic.

The impact on women

These changes are also having an impact on Muslim women. Many Muslim women in Britain, although apparently not desiring to achieve the freedoms won by British women, are questioning traditional images of Muslim womanhood. These include gender roles, *purdah* (seclusion of women), dress-customs, the issue of work outside the home, and certain kinds of arranged marriage which are seen as typical to South Asian culture.

Initially, the arrival of Muslim women in Britain led to a consolidation of ethnic identity. Ironically, this resulted in the women themselves facing stricter rules on dress, *purdah* and employment than any other group of Asian migrant women. The fragmentation of the traditional family, the isolation created by fear of moral contamination from the receiving culture, the prestige given to *purdah* as a mark of middle-class status, and finally the climate of Britain, all had severe consequences for women. *Purdah* was not only retained but strengthened in response to insecurity and the threat perceived from 'immoral' Britain. In the process, *purdah* increasingly lost its function as protection and became a prison. Many women have not learnt to speak English, and it is not uncommon to see them using their children as interpreters when out shopping. Unlike their husbands, who come in contact with the indigenous culture through employment, or their children (both male and female) through school, many older Asian Muslim women have minimal contact with a world outside their immediate family and close relatives.

There has been a lack of encouragement for women to organise and participate fully in public religious life in Britain. In many Muslim communities there has been outright rejection of South Asian female participation in public worship and many mosques still have no facilities for women. This is particularly the case with Deobandi mosques where there is a rigid interpretation of the Hanafi school of law favoured in the subcontinent. Women often find themselves the victims of South Asian gender attitudes which are rigidly disguised as the strictures of Islam. As with the boys, although taught to recite the Quran in mosque schools, they do not understand the Arabic and are likely to accept that everything that their parents say is according to Islamic prescriptions. The girls are often brought up to be submissive and not to confront their parents or elders. In many homes even dialogue and discussion by girls is discouraged as un-Islamic behaviour. Thus any attempt by women to challenge cultural norms concerning employment, dress, education, or marriage patterns is often attacked on the grounds that these are unalterable tenets of Islam.

South Asian men may well be afraid of the impact of Western culture on their wives and daughters, and can to some degree isolate them from contact with it. They cannot, however, isolate them from Islam and recent studies are showing that more young Muslim women are distinguishing between cultural traditions and the central tenets of Islam. Many parents and husbands have found that their religion itself is being used as an effective weapon against certain forms of ethnic oppression, as some women begin to redefine themselves and their role in society by studying the fundamentals of Islam. These women have argued that it was men, and not Islam, that had put them in a subordinate position. This new awareness has come about not only because of the need for Muslim women to redefine themselves in Britain but also because of an increased awareness of religion brought about by the resurgence of Islam worldwide. Many daughters and wives are arguing that there is no incompatibility between being British citizens and Muslim women. Dress does not have to be Asian to be in conformity with the prescriptions of the Quran. Many women are justifying the pursuit of education and careers by reference to religious ideology, arguing that their critics' understanding of Islam is outdated and narrow.

As devout Muslims, more and more young British-born women are looking to the Quran and the Sunna of the Prophet for the answer to all questions. Often they find that the teachings of Islam directly contradict hallowed customs and traditions regarding the status and place of women in society. They defend both Islam and themselves from the abuses of a rigidly patriarchal society by arguing that the poor standing of women that is often associated with Islamic prescription is a cultural accretion having no basis in the Quran itself. On the contrary, they can claim that true Islam is pledged to equality of the sexes, albeit respecting the essential differences between them.

Others are discovering that the emancipation of women was apparently a matter of importance to the Prophet. They refer to his wives, particularly Khadija, who was a successful businesswoman, and Aisha, who became a stateswoman in the early years of Islam's development. They claim that 1,400 years ago women were liberated by the establishment of Islam. They were given inheritance rights, the right to keep their earnings, the right to divorce and the right to retain their own surnames. Subsequently, they argue, various cultures have superimposed their own variation of gender inequality onto Islam as it spread through Asia.

370

The whole issue of the rights of Muslim women born in Britain is beginning to centre upon the challenge Islam is posing both to ethnicity and Westernisation. The opposition to uncritical acceptance of Western values is central to the ideology of Islamic resurgence throughout the world. By incorporating this into their view of British life, many young Muslim women are able to feel both solidarity with the Islamic movement globally and to develop a critique towards the dominant culture's attitude towards them. At the same time they can utilise the revivalists' stance against cultural accretion entering into Islam to defend themselves against attitudes which often belong more to the traditions of the village than the teachings of the Quran. This strategy enables young Muslim women born and educated in Britain neither to feel torn between two cultures or to switch back and forth between two opposed worlds, but to find a way forward utilising their religion.

The dilemma of education

Having looked briefly at young people and women, it becomes apparent that the issue of education is very important amongst Muslims in Britain. Many Muslims feel uneasy about the presence of their children in British state schools since it is the place where Muslim society and British society most deeply interact. It is this interaction between values that leads Muhammad Anwar to state that young Muslims are 'caught between two cultures'.

If education is viewed as a means of cultural engineering, then it will sometimes clash with an equally powerful form of socialisation that takes place within the family. Parents themselves are often torn between their loyalty to traditional value systems incorporating religious and social authority on the one hand, and a desire to see their children succeed in the educational system on the other. Distrustful of a Western secular society which is popularly viewed as corrupt and blatantly sexually promiscuous, they attempt to counteract this influence of school by nurturing their children into the overarching belief system of Islam. This last will include views of European culture, perceptions of education, the right behaviour between the sexes and between the generations, as well as codes of moral behaviour and appearance. All of these will be reinforced by the code of *izzat*, which is likely to be imposed more on the girls than the boys. Women are put under stricter surveillance after the onset of puberty as it is considered that too much freedom will ruin a girl's reputation. Even British teaching methods based on enquiry and the development of freedom of thought is highly suspect.

The Quran or mosque school is used to support this framework of the family and its values. Several nights a week the children will attend two-hour sessions. They will be taught by rote the Arabic of the Quran, basic religious instruction, and sometimes the mother-tongue of their parents. Usually the instruction is by the *imam* (prayer leader or qualified religious scholar), who is normally imported from the country of origin. Often he will be suspicious not only of the influence of British secular education on the children but also of the influence of their parents, whose knowledge of Islam he may not trust.

The main purpose of the mosque school is to inculcate into the children the awareness that they belong to a Muslim community. In fact, the children's education at mosque schools will ultimately depend on the calibre of the *imam* and the brand of Islam that he himself follows. Part-time religious schools run alongside the English system of education was the pattern under the British administration in colonial India. At the time it considerably disadvantaged Muslim youth, and it will continue to do so. At best it gives a very elementary knowledge of the faith; at worst it defeats its own object by turning the children against their own religion. The extra studying hours placed upon small children could well be to the detriment of their education at school. It could also create a clash of values as described by Anwar.

Some Muslims believe the solution to be the establishment of Muslim schools which teach academic subjects alongside religious instruction in Islam, and consequently there has been a proliferation of private schools in British cities. Many Muslims are campaigning for these schools to be state funded on the same lines as Jewish, Anglican and Roman Catholic schools, and it can only be a matter of time before this right is conceded by the British government.

The major religious movements are increasingly establishing *dar al-ulums* (higher institutions of Islamic religious education) which provide full-time religious education combined with a few core subjects from the British curriculum. Essentially these schools are based on the subcontinent Islamic curriculum which was established to train the *ulama*. The demand for places in the *dar al-ulums* is growing rapidly especially amongst Muslim parents with Deobandi sympathies. The major problem here is that there is hardly any agreement on which 'Islam' should be taught. Muslims with loyalties to Deobandi, Barelwi, Jamaat al-Tabligh and Jamaat-i-Islami brands of Islam each want to teach their children according to their own ideology, and consequently consolidate divisions within the community. Many Muslims in Britain originate from the rural areas of the subcontinent and received little informal education themselves. The education of girls was not considered important as marriage was thought to be their destiny and training in running a home is regarded as more important than formal education. As a consequence the parents often expect girls to concentrate on housework, cooking and looking after children, rather than schoolwork. Many of the girls are sent to single sex schools to protect them from the perceived sexual promiscuity of British culture. Despite this difference in attitude and closer control of girls, many find that the school provides them with opportunities to be more critical in their thinking, and to develop the ability to differ with their parents. Many parents are not able to sympathise or even be aware of the ethos of individual fulfilment and development offered to both sexes in school since it is not a part of their cultural background. This conflict of values has led many parents in Britain to become more repressive. Higher education by girls is rarely achieved without struggle although there are recent indications that more Muslim girls are attending British universities. On the other hand, many religious parents see that the solution is to provide girls with a *dar al-ulum* education only. In the meantime there is considerable evidence that Muslim children of subcontinent origin are not doing as well in school as they should be. Young Pakistanis and Bangladeshis have a much higher unemployment rate than either the indigenous population, or indeed any other minority group.

Status within British society

Any analysis of class in the Muslim community must take place on two levels. Within British society Muslims are likely to be perceived as working-class or even as an underclass. Their economic position has changed very little in the last thirty years; the majority are still concentrated in the semi-skilled and unskilled sectors of industry. Subcontinent Muslims, in particular, suffer disproportionately from unemployment due to their concentration in manufacturing industries and the continuation of racist attitudes in job allocation.

The most noticeable change is in the growing number of self-employed Muslims. This may reflect a shift away from focusing on the country of origin and an acknowledgement that the future is in Britain. Money that was once sent home to relatives in the subcontinent may now be used to establish small businesses. Essentially these enterprises are set up to serve the requirements of the growing communities. This is facilitated by the way in which various migrant groups gathered together in relatively small areas of particular towns and cities. These entrepreneurs concentrated on providing goods and services that reinforced the ethnic identity of their customers and this has resulted in a further closing of ranks amongst the Muslim populations. As the community becomes more autonomous, Muslim men and women can define their status within their own group. Thus the class position thrust upon them by the indigenous community becomes largely irrelevant in terms of self-esteem.

Amongst fellow-Muslims class status can be derived from several sources. Community leaders are provided with considerable prestige based on their education, their economic status, the length of time their family has been in Britain (original settlers are well-respected as community elders), the status of their family in the country of origin, Islamic scholarship, and membership of voluntary organisations such as welfare organisations and mosque committees. The membership of the latter is likely to be dominated by those with high status in the community. The committee which runs each mosque in Britain is usually controlled by businessmen and the professional middle class. Very often these are also the original settlers in the area. This control of the mosque will have important consequences for the development of Islam in Britain. The firm grip of the older generation is often resented by the generation born in Britain as the latter feel that the issues which are important to the old people are not relevant to them.

It is often in the interests of local Muslim entrepreneurs to maintain ethnic identity and this has sometimes resulted in conflict with the *imam* if he represents a movement attempting to promote Islam as a universal faith. This conflict, however, can also happen in reverse. Sometimes the *imam* will be entrenched in a more tradition-based form of Islam that is influenced by Sufi beliefs and village practices. This may not please all the members of the mosque committee. The bulk of the migrants were small landholders in their place of origin, people who considered themselves a class above landless labourers. In migrating to Britain they have not hesitated to take on work as labourers in mills, factories and foundries. Despite this apparent loss of status and their low position *vis-à-vis* the receiving culture, it can be argued that all migrants improve their class position by the actual process of migration to cities. This, in turn, has a radical effect on the kind of Islam they practise, since religion can be used to improve standing in the Muslim community. Thus British Muslim communities are likely to be in considerable flux with regard to their religious position. These changes are unequal in different parts of the community, and can generate considerable tension and intercommunal rivalry.

The pull towards Islamic militancy

One of the options open to disenchanted British-born Muslims is to join one of the numerous movements often described as 'fundamentalist'. Many of these organisations are addressing the problems discussed above. Islamic 'fundamentalism' has to be seen as a protest movement promulgating an ideology which evokes a response from those groups which are the most acutely aware of the tensions presented by the contemporary world. Although British, many Muslims still feel exploited by Western colonialism. They also face unequal opportunities even though promised success if they achieve the academic goals of education. Some of them can feel let down by both the culture of their birth and the culture of their parents. 'Fundamentalism' attracts them because it is quintessentially modern; that is to say, it constitutes a response to events and conditions in the present. In Britain, the values of modernity call for increasing assimilation into the cultural mainstream of the society into which the Muslims have settled. At the same time, opportunities to do this on an equal footing are denied. On the other hand the emergence of migrant communities which preserve group solidarity by defining identity ethnically cannot offer very much to young Muslims who firmly feel themselves to be British. Islamic revivalist movements, in their affirmation of religious authority as absolute and holistic, offer one solution to this dilemma. Although the establishment of an Islamic state is clearly an unrealistic goal in a British inner city where Muslims are a small minority, it should be apparent why it still remains the ideal for some. In this context a variety of organisations have developed in Britain but none has been able to provide a unified umbrella for this kind of Islamic commitment. After the extensive publicity at the time of the Rushdie affair several individuals were prepared to exploit the media's tendency to sensationalise and stereotype the Muslim presence in Britain. Foremost among these was Kalim Siddiqui who had been a journalist himself. He had been a member of the little-known Muslim Institute in London who throughout the 1980s identified with the cause of the Islamic revolution in Iran. He had supported Ayotollah Khomeini's *fatwa* (an opinion concerning Islamic law given by a member of the learned scholars) calling for a death sentence on Rushdie, and in 1990 issued the Muslim Manifesto which called for a parliament run on the lines of the Board of Deputies which represents the needs of the Jewish community in Britain. However, in spite of achieving considerable publicity and presenting himself as a leader of the 'Islamic Movement' in Britain, Kalim Siddiqui did not succeed in uniting even those Muslims who agreed with his ideology.

This ideology presents religion as not merely an individual commitment entailing personal piety nor a group loyalty which requires the formal ecclesiastical membership implicit in the arguments of secularisation theorists but a complete way of life. The phenomenon of 'fundamentalism' indicates that religion can be the corporate public action of religiously motivated individuals to change the social system on behalf of what they perceive to be their deepest spiritual loyalties. Thus for some Muslims in Britain the concept of the *umma* becomes of central importance in their religious ideology. It is able to provide some British-born Muslims with an identity which transcends both their allegiance to nationality and the culture of their parents. The indigenous culture which is so often unaccepting of the Muslim presence can be opposed by the concept of the *umma* used as a challenge to the overriding secular view of the world dominant in Britain.

Before a clear direction for a uniquely British Muslim community can be ascertained, it will be necessary to resolve the issues which have been the subject of this analysis. The form that the community takes will be forged out of the process of resolving these thorny problems. For most Muslims in Britain, this is not a simple transformation. It is extremely hard for them to find, in the midst of ethnic differences, a religious/cultural consensus which is simultaneously based on Islamic principles and capable of encompassing full participation in the cultural resources of the receiving culture. It is a balancing act which, if not successful, could divide the community on religious as well as ethnic grounds. Failure could lead either to extreme forms of Islam with the community alienated from both the indigenous and the migrant cultures; or else to assimilation into Britain's secular society, thus reducing Islamic belief and practice to the private sphere.

In spite of the problems involved in dealing not only with major ethnic and geographical divisions but also with the important regional, linguistic, social and political differences within the major groupings, there are signs that Islam is becoming the dominant mark of identity for the Muslim population. This is not only the product of the shift from the villages of the subcontinent to major urban/industrial centres of Britain but is also influenced by the worldwide resurgence of Islam. Certainly there is evidence that religious identity in the British Muslim community is becoming the sharpest focus for establishing a sense of selfhood. The early migrants experienced a sense of loss but the second generation often voice a protest at a feeling of denial of self or confusion of identity.

Islam is, in one form or another, the heritage of all Muslims who have come to live in Britain. Initially, the society they joined was virtually devoid of all symbols of Islam. Many of these symbols have now appeared in Britain and Muslims can observe the familiar outlines of mosques complete with dome and minarets on the skylines of British industrial cities and take pride in their achievements. Islam is now the second largest religion practised in Britain and is there to stay. Along with the symbols have come the controversies. The Islamic world is involved in the process of rediscovering what it means to be Muslim; this too is the focus for British Muslims. It is imperative to evolve and generate a new pattern of life which is in harmony with the values and norms of Islam but which, in the context of life chances, is based firmly in Britain. Many have already discovered that minorities need distinctive or alternative systems of resources to give them a greater degree of resistance. They are finding this in their common Islamic identity, but the process will involve continuous bargaining and negotiating between

(a) the British social, economic and cultural environment;
(b) the ideals and expectations of various components derived from the countries of origin; and
(c) the ideational forces of orthodox Islam in its several forms.

There is clearly no one group or grouping which on its own has the strength to impress itself on the majority of the Muslim population.

So far, there are no real indications that Muslims in Britain are following that path towards complete assimilation that has already been trodden by the majority of Britain's Catholics and to a lesser extent British Jews. Many young Muslims claim that assimilation is not a genuine choice since the indigenous white culture will always discriminate against them on the grounds of colour. Integration is criticised by many in the receiving culture as remaining separate. It is seen as a critique of the British 'way of life', and very often it is. Some young Muslims see three choices being presented to them by the receiving culture:

(i) to develop individuality and avoid group identity which would leave them even more isolated than they are now;
(ii) to adopt the cultural norms of the indigenous culture; or
(iii) to be more subservient and obedient which is perceived to be a form of internal colonialism.

Embracing Islam as a religious experience rather than a cultural heritage is providing increasing numbers of young Muslims with an alternative to the pressure to assimilate into British culture on the one hand, and on the other to respond to parental persuasion to conform to various strands of imported ethnic culture. Thus it can be seen that the situation is not a straight choice between assimilation and integration. The indigenous culture will have to come to terms with two major groups demanding the right to integrate: one on ethnic/racial grounds, the other on purely religious grounds. This can create considerable confusion. Both will call on Islam to support their case, and it will not always be easy for the receiving culture to distinguish between the two.

Literature

For an introduction to the development and growth of the Muslim community in Britain see the relevant chapters in Jørgen Nielsen, *Muslims in Western Europe*: (Edinburgh: Edinburgh University Press, 1992) and Philip Lewis, *Islamic Britain* (London: I.B. Tauris, 1994). The former shows the origins, present-day ethnic composition, distribution and organisation of the community along with the political, legal and cultural contexts in which the British Muslims exist. The latter explores some of the problems facing the Muslim community after the Rushdie affair and the Gulf War by focusing on the situation in the city of Bradford. A Muslim perspective of the situation can be found in Mohammad Raza, *Islam in Britain* (Leicester: Volcano Press, 1991).

A discussion of the choices of assimilation, integration and isolation facing the Muslim communities is in the chapter by John Wolfe, 'Fragmented Universality: Islam and Muslims', in *The Growth of Religious Diversity*, I, ed. Gerald Parsons (London: Routledge, 1993). The Rushdie Affair and its impact on British Muslims are discussed in Malise Ruthwen, *A Satanic Affair: Salman Rushdie and the Rage of Islam* (London: Chatto and Windus, 1990). An exploration of the relationship between Muslims and the British state is found in Steven Vertovec, 'Muslims, the State, and the Public Sphere in Britain', in *Muslim Communities in the New Europe*, eds. Gerd Nonneman, Tim Niblock and Bogdan Szajkowski (Reading: Ithaca, 1996). A similar area is covered at local government level by Jørgen Nielsen, 'Muslims in Britain and Local Authority Responses', pp. 53–77 in *The New Islamic Presence in Western Europe*, eds. Tomas Gerholm and Yngve Georg Lithman (London: Mansell, 1988).

The history of the various subcontinent Islamic movements at work in Britain and an exploration of their possible impact on the development of the community can be found in Ron Geaves, *Sectarian Influences within Islam in Britain* (Leeds: University of Leeds, 1996). An excellent history of the early Yemeni communities is explored in Fred Halliday, *Arabs in Exile: Yemeni Migrants in Urban Britain* (London: I.B. Tauris, 1992). The incidence, motivations and impact of conversion to Islam in Britain is explored in Ali Köse, *Conversion to Islam: A Study of Native British Converts* (London: Kegan Paul, 1996). The importance of Sufism in the development of the Muslim community is explored in a forthcoming book by Ron Geaves, *Sufis in Britain* (Cardiff: Cardiff Academic Press, 1999). Finally, a statistical analysis of the Muslim populations can be found in Muhammad Anwar, *Muslims in Britain: 1991 Census and Other Statistical Sources* (Birmingham, 1993).

Chapter Seventeen

The Nordic Countries

Ingvar Svanberg

The Nordic countries are, according to sociologist David Martin's research, among the most secularised in the world. Only a very small minority of the population are regular churchgoers. Apart from participation in religious activities, secularisation may also be defined by the role that religion is allowed to play in society. The majority regard religion as a personal matter of conscience that does not have any major social dimensions or implications. There is certainly a prevailing Lutheran tradition that still permeates the Nordic societies, but the concepts of being Swedish, Norwegian, Finnish or Danish are more closely associated with democracy, modernity and other non-religious concepts.

Since World War II Sweden, Denmark and Norway in particular have experienced a religious revival in at least two different ways. Parallel with a steadily decreasing religiosity in the traditional sense, new religions have entered the scene. The more marginal variety has been the interest among young people in various so-called sects, sometimes originating in the United States, sometimes in India and other Asian countries. Satanism, Veganism and Neo-Paganism are new elements on the religious scene. Of particular importance is the spread of New Age ideas and practices. However, an apparently more substantial change on the Swedish, Norwegian and Danish religious maps has come with immigration from other countries and cultural spheres.

As a result of this influx, well-established religious congregations such as the Roman Catholic Church and the Mosaic congregations have experienced an important revival and a substantial increase in the number of active members. Other churches and religions have been established for the first time as a result of adherents moving to Scandinavia. Today there are congregations of various Oriental churches and Muslims, Buddhists, Hindus and Sikhs exercise their religion within Nordic societies. These congregations thus exist in environments where religion essentially is a part of the private sphere. Religious practice has become individualised and its symbolic values have become transformed.

In Finland the presence of Islam goes back to the nineteenth century – the first Muslims came with the Russian army – while organised Islamic activities reckons around fifty years in Sweden. In Denmark and Norway its arrival is somewhat more recent. Its comparatively brief history, the marginality of its followers and the lack of unity between the Muslim organisations have all contributed to the low profile of Muslims in the Nordic countries until ten to fifteen years ago. Since the mid 1980s the Islamic presence in the Nordic countries has become increasingly noticeable. The labour immigrants of the 1960s and 1970s have strengthened their positions as minorities with an intensifying self-confidence. They have also aged, and both the immigrant generation and their Nordic-born children have become more interested in religious matters. Due to the influx of refugees from so-called Third World countries in the 1980s and early 1990s, foreigners dressed according to Muslim practice can be seen in public in almost every town and city in Sweden, Norway and Denmark. Youth descending from the labour immigrants from Turkey of the 1960s can also be seen in such attire. Even in Finland some people can be identified as Muslims due to their dress code.

This new visibility, together with the on-going discussions around the construction of mosques, religious schools and ritual slaughter, have caused debates about the Islamic presence, or threat, as some people view it. Some populist politicians – especially Mogens Glistrup in Denmark, who nowadays also uses Internet to spread his *islamophobic* messages – have, together with the small Neo-Nazi groups, tried in vain to use this fear in their political propaganda. Nevertheless, local resistance against mosque-building has sometimes been very strong, and politicians have responded to these public opinions despite the fact that religious freedom is granted in the constitutions of the Nordic countries. On the other hand, the existing mosque in Uppsala, the only one in the Nordic countries with a real minaret and probably the northernmost purpose-built mosque in the world, is a tourist attraction included in city tours. There is also a positive view of Islam manifested in culture and music festivals and sometimes an uncritically positive attitude among some intellectuals.

Historical background

With the exception of Denmark, the Nordic countries lack a tradition of having colonies. Despite a short period of ruling Tranquebar in India, the Nicobars and some of the Virgin Islands, the Danish experience as a colonial power is also restricted to Greenland and the Faroe Islands. In contrast to other parts of Western Europe, the Nordic countries thus do not have a long tradition of contacts with Muslims. However, exhibitions and books on Islam, as well as some Muslims who present their religion for a larger audience, sometimes stress that the Nordic countries have had a long tradition of contacts with Islamic cultures. During the Viking Age, there were frequent contacts with the Caliphate as a result of the Norsemen's journeys to the south and east. A great number of mainly Abbasid and Samidic coins with Arabic inscriptions have been found on the islands of Öland and Gotland in the Baltic Sea, bearing witness to these contacts. In his *Risala*, the emissary of the Baghdad Caliphate, Ibn Fadlan, gives an exhaustive description of a Nordic chief's burial on the bank of the Volga in 922. Ibn Fadlan's description is perhaps the most important narrative source concerning the pre-Christian Norsemen's customs and habits.

While Denmark allowed Jews and Catholics some religious freedom as early as in the 1680s, the clergy at the same time was opposed to all kinds of non-Lutheran believers in Sweden. In the Swedish Church Law of 1686 it is stated that 'Jews, Turks, Morians and Pagans entering the country should be informed about the right belief and baptised as Christians'. Once baptised, however, they were permitted to settle in Sweden. In fact, a few Muslims were baptised at the end of the seventeenth century. Some 'Turks' were baptised in Stockholm, in Storkyrkan in 1672 and in the German Church in 1695. During Sweden's period as a Great Power from the accession of Gustavus II Adolphus in 1611 until the death of Charles XII in 1718, the Lutheran orthodoxy ruled out virtually all immigration of non-Protestants to Sweden. However, an exception was made under Charles XII, who in 1718 issued a royal letter permitting Muslim religious services to be held within Sweden's frontiers. This permission related to Charles XII's creditors from the Sublime Porte who were staying in Karlskrona. A few early converts are mentioned in biographical literature. In the 1680s, Johan Hjulhammar, sergeant of the Life Guards, converted to Islam. The author and diplomat Gustaf Noring (1861–1937) from Malmö moved to Constantinople and converted in 1884, simultaneously adopting the name Ali Nouri. When the Turkish name reform was passed in the 1920s, he added the family name Dilmeç. The artist Ivan Aguéli (1869–1917) was another well-known convert, who assumed the name Abdul Hadi al-Maghrabi. During many years he published a daily newspaper in Arabic in Cairo. Contacts with Muslims were, furthermore, established because of Swedish, Danish and Norwegian Christian missionary work in Islamic areas. Attempts were made to convert, among others, the Bashkirs in Russia in the 1890s, Muslims in northern Iran at the beginning of the twentieth century, Uighurs in southern Xinjiang up to the 1930s, and continue among the Pathans in Pakistan. These missions never met with any great success. On the other hand, they increased knowledge and understanding of Islam, at least among individual missionaries.

Needless to say, moving from one country to another cause strains and doubts about basic assumptions and values. The essence of uprooting is the challenging of the stability of the plausibility structure. In this context the role of religion may be described as a tool to actualise the culture of the native country and to make that culture plausible in a foreign environment. Religion may serve to maintain a totality of beliefs and values. According to the sociologists Albert Bartenier and Felice Dassetto, the relationship between immigrants and religion can be discussed in different perspectives: 'national religion', i.e. transplanting religious congregations to the country of immigration; 'indigenous religion', implying assimilation into congregations in the new environment; 'para-religion' in which the congregations act as social and psychological aid organisations and intermediaries between immigrants and the majority population; 'folk religion', i.e. the development of non-orthodox religious behaviour in an emigration context; and, finally, 'sect religion' with missionary activities on the part of various 'sects'. The Muslim adaptation to the Nordic societies demonstrates most of these characteristics.

The contemporary presence of Islam in the Nordic countries is primarily a result of post-war labour and refugee immigration. The Muslims arrived as labour immigrants during the 1960s and 1970s, particularly from Turkey, Yugoslavia and Pakistan. In the 1970s and 1980s many Muslims arrived as asylum-seekers and refugees from the Middle East and various African countries. Most Muslims are therefore first or second generation immigrants. In the late 1990s there were around 80,000 organised and practising Muslims in Sweden, 50,000 in Norway, 67,000 in Denmark and 10,000 in Finland. Muslims are found also in Iceland and the Faroe Islands. As mentioned above, the first Muslims of Finland migrated there as early as in the nineteenth century, while the country was still under Russian rule. Tatar soldiers and merchants spent varying periods in Finland. There is a Muslim burial-place for soldiers on the islands of Åland that still bear witness to their presence. After Finland became independent in 1917 some Tatars remained in the country, and the first Islamic congregation was established in Helsinki in 1925. In Finland, Muslims are therefore regarded as an indigenous ethno-religious minority rather than as a recent immigrant group as they are in other Nordic countries.

There are no exact figures on how many Muslims actually live in the Nordic countries. No official registration of the population's religious affiliation exists. Such statistics are probably impossible to gather. One problem is the definition of the term 'Muslim'. Many emigrants from Turkey and Iran in the Nordic countries regard themselves as secular, without any close contact with Islamic traditions and the performance of religious rituals. Well-educated citizens from Turkey and Iran, as well as many nationalistic Kurds from these countries, do not want to be connected with Islam, which they see as an expression of under-development and archaic cultural traditions. Some Iranian immigrants have even protested about being called Muslims in various contexts. In, for instance, the Persian–Swedish periodical *Hambastegi* an editorial writer considered it a mockery for Iranians, who risked their lives in the struggle for a democratic and secular society in Iran, to be classified as Muslims in Sweden. A new concept – introduced by some scholars together with immigration bureaucrats – in this context is 'ethnic Muslim'. However, according to other scholars the term 'ethnic Muslims' belongs to the category of meaningless terms of the 1990s, which have gained strong ground in administrative language use. All those who have immigrated from Muslim countries or have parents from these countries are regarded as Muslims. Using that method, it has been calculated that 200,000 or even 300,000 Muslims live in Sweden. How many of these people really are Muslims, that is, believe in God and the Prophet Muhammad and carry out their obligations as believers is difficult to say. Freedom of religion, however, must encompass the right not to be called a Muslim, as well as the right to be a Muslim. The fact that everyone who has roots in a Muslim country is automatically termed an 'ethnic Muslim' is probably a hideous expression of the alienation mechanisms in the Nordic countries. The only reasonable figures are registered members in religious organisations.

Research on Islam

Although actual contacts with Muslims have been limited, there has been a scholarly interest in Islam among historians of religion, philologists and theologians in the Nordic countries over the centuries. The Swedish diplomat Claes Rålamb (1622–98) was perhaps one of the first Westerners to give a non-polemic description of Islam. Swedish contacts with the Ottoman Empire also resulted in the acquisition of many Islamic *objets d'art*, which may be found today in public museum collections. During the eighteenth century, Cornelius Loos (1686–1738) and Michael Eneman (1676–1714) were among those who contributed to the knowledge of Islam. A unique map of Mecca that was brought to Sweden by Eneman in 1713 is still owned by the Uppsala University Library. One of the world's oldest existing Quran manuscripts was brought back to Sweden by Jacob Jonas Björnståhl (1731–1779) and is still stored at Uppsala University Library. Mathias Norberg (1747–1826), professor in Lund, presided over several dissertations on Islam and Muslim belief. Herman Almqvist (1839–1904), produced popular works on the Quran; and Johan Theodor Nordling (1826–90), besides the exegesis of the Old Testament, also taught the Quran. Carl Johan Tornberg (1807–77) produced important Arabic manuscripts. He is also considered to be the most prominent Swede in the field of Islamic numismatics. The university libraries at Uppsala and Lund, and also the Royal Library in Stockholm, contain a large number of Oriental manuscripts brought from Muslim countries in Western and Central Asia. These manuscript collections are utilised by researchers worldwide. Jacob Jacobsen Dampe (1790–1867) may be remembered as a political martyr in Denmark, a victim of a justice scandal in Denmark, and held for life as a prisoner on Christiansø. However, he must also be remembered for his doctoral thesis *Conspectus et æstimatio ethicæ Corani*

(1812), which dealt with the ethical values of the Quran. A classic work is the famous Danish author Hans Christian Andersen's (1805–75) description from 1842 of the religious dance of the Mevlevi *dervishes* in the Ottoman Empire. The Norwegian author Henrik Ibsen (1828–1906) let his famous character Peer Gynt travel to North Africa, Timbuktu and Egypt to encounter Islam in various ways and appear in the role as prophet. The Åland islander Georg August Wallin (1811–52) was an exceptional Arabist of his time. He studied Bedouin nomads, lived among Arab town-dwellers and was among the first non-Muslim scholars to undertake participant observation as a pilgrim to Medina and Mecca. Eric Hermelin (1860–1944) of Lund carried out the remarkable task of translating, in the 1930s, works of Mawlana Jalal al-Din Rumi and other Sufi authors into Swedish. Hermelin's Rumi translations are being published in new editions, and still arouse great interest. The works of Tor Andrae (1885–1947), professor of history of religions and later bishop in the Lutheran Church of Sweden, reflect an unusual understanding of Islamic philosophy and ideology. His studies and biography of Muhammad have been translated into many languages. During the 1990s, we have witnessed an increasing interest in research on Islam in the Nordic countries. Today, wide-ranging research on Islam in many disciplines of the humanities and social sciences is underway at many Nordic universities. Recently a large number of books and scholarly theses on various aspects of Islam and on Muslims have been published, witnessing to the growing interest. Muslims are engaged in this research and the expanding presence of Islam has boosted the increase in public interest.

Who are the Muslims?

Today, Islam is the largest non-Christian religion in all Nordic countries. Most Muslims are immigrants from various geographical backgrounds, although the number of local-born Muslims is increasing. The core group of Muslims in Finland is the Mishär Tatars, who number some 900 persons, according to recent estimates. They have their own prayer and community premises at Fredriksgatan in the city centre of Helsinki. Others are living in Turku (Åbo), Tampere (Tammerfors) and Järvenpää. During the 1980s and 1990s Egyptians, Somalis, Bengalis and Kurds have emigrated to Finland. Contact between the newcomers and the more secularised and integrated Tatars is limited. Recent immigrants have therefore founded their own congregations.

The first Islamic congregation in Stockholm was founded by a handful of Tatars and Turks in the late 1940s. When the labour immigrants from Turkey began to arrive in the mid 1960s the congregation increased and the Islamic community started splitting up. The contemporary Muslims in Sweden have disparate geographical, national and social backgrounds, and there are many different ways of being religious. The Turks still constitute a

The Tatar mosque in Helsinki (photo: Ingvar Svanberg, 1998).

substantial part of the Muslim population in the country. They have to a large degree continued to have their own congregations, some of them sponsored by the Directorate of Religious Affairs (Diyanet Işleri Başkanligi) in Istanbul. Those who are not members of congregations connected with Diyaneti are members of new movements with Turkish background. However, one must bear in mind that Turks of urban background are often atheists or at least agnostics. Substantial numbers of Muslims originate from Uganda, Kosovo, Iran, Eritrea, Somalia, Gambia, Bosnia, Morocco, Pakistan, Iraq and Bangladesh. The largest concentrations live in Stockholm, Gothenburg and Malmö, although Muslims today can be found all over the country.

Most Muslims in Denmark, as in Sweden, are labour and refugee immigrants. The first Muslims arrived in the late 1960s. The labour immigrants of Muslim background came primarily from Turkey, Pakistan, Morocco and Macedonia. The largest group are of Turkish origin.

The demographic background of the Muslims in Norway is similar to Sweden and Denmark. In the late 1960s and early 1970s labour immigrants arrived from Turkey and Pakistan. Although the Turkish group is significant, the Pakistani community already outnumbered them in the 1970s and is still the largest and most dominant Muslim group in Norway. They are concentrated in Oslo and Akershus. Since the 1980s an increasing number of refugees has arrived, including Muslim Iranians, Iraqis, Kurds, Somalis, Bosnians and Kosovo Albanians. The largest concentrations of these Muslims are found in and around Oslo and Drammen.

Although it is impossible to know how many converts there are, figures nevertheless sometimes appear in various publications. On Internet the following figures may be found: Sweden, 5,000; Denmark, 1,000–2,000; Norway, 400; and Finland, 200.

Organisational structure

In Finland there are two national Muslim organisations: Finland's Islamic Congregation (Suomi Islam Seurakunta) with mainly Tatar members, and Finland's Islamic Community (Suomen Islamilainen Yhdyskunta) with about 250 members of refugee background from the Middle East and the Horn of Africa. It seems to organise both Shia and Sunni Muslims. A smaller organisation is the Islamic Centre of Finland (Suomen Islam-keskus), which has around 300 members. The newly established Helsinki Islam Centre (Helsinki Islam-keskus) has mainly Arab and Somali members. According to one source there are between fifteen and seventeen Muslim prayer rooms distributed throughout the country.

In 1944, when there was a large influx of Estonian refugees to Sweden, a handful of Mishär Tatars and a few other Muslims originating from the Soviet Union came along with them. The formation of the first congregation in 1949, the Turk–Islam Society in Sweden for Religion and Culture (Turk-islamföreningen i Sverige för religion och kultur), is attributed to Ali Zakerov, Osman Soukkan and Akif Arhan. The first meeting place for the Swedish Muslims was the Kjellson's café on Birger Jarlsgatan in central Stockholm. For many years the congregation remained relatively anonymous, using public premises as prayer and meeting halls, although its members developed their own institutions and rituals. The number of Muslims was estimated at 500 in 1953. In 1959, the Swedish convert Bengt Ismail Ericsson founded the Muslim Club and a small prayer hall in Kärrtorp, Stockholm. In 1964, another Swedish convert, Mohammad Bashir (= Göran Granquist), published a pamphlet about the history of Islam in Sweden, probably the very first printed manifestation of Swedish Islam.

Due to the Swedish traditions of popular associations (*folkrörelser*) and a system providing the Islamic organisations with economic support from the state, a kind of 'church structure' has developed. Islamic associations have thus become incorporated into an organisational structure that resembles that of Swedish free churches. There are several officially recognised national Islamic federations in Sweden. The oldest national federation is the United Islamic Communities in Sweden (Förenade islamiska församlingar i Sverige). The government approved financial support for this organisation in 1975. In 1997 it had thirty-nine congregations with 21,900 members.

Political rather than theological differences among some of the Islamic communities were the reason for the establishment of the Swedish Muslim Federation (Sveriges muslimska förbund) by some congregations in the larger cities. This national organisation was declared eligible for financial support in 1983. In 1997 it included twenty-three congregations with a total of 34,000 members. The Islamic Federation of Bosnia–Herzegovina (Bosnien-Hercegovinas Islamiska Riksförbund) has nineteen associations. It is not recognised by the authorities as a national federation by the Commission for State Grants to Religious Communities (Samarbetsnämnden för statsbidrag till trossamfund). However, it cooperates with the Swedish Muslim Federation. Many of the local Muslim associations represent a single major ethnic group. There are, for example, associations for Somalis, Gambians, Turks, Kurds and Albanians. Most of the associations are, however, local organisations representing the Muslims in a particular town.

In 1981 an additional nationwide organisation, the Union of the Islamic Culture Centres in Sweden (Islamiska Kulturcenterunionen i Sverige), appeared. It is an offshoot of the so-called Quran School Movement (Süleymanli) in Turkey and has its roots in the Naqshbandi brotherhood. The origin of this movement is still somewhat obscure. It grew strong in the 1970s among Turkish *Gastarbeiter* in Germany and had its first religious centre in Cologne. The movement was apparently formed by Süleyman Hilmi Tunahan (1888–1959), the son of a Naqshbandi *shaykh*, who settled in Istanbul in the 1920s. The founder preached that, wherever he was working, every brother should start one Quran class and provide for another five to be opened. In the 1970s the movement made its breakthrough in Europe, where it developed into a very hierarchical organisation. At the outset it was particularly militant: its followers did not want to cooperate with other religious groups. In the mid 1980s it existed in Germany, Belgium, the Netherlands, Austria, France, Denmark, Switzerland, Norway and Sweden. During recent years the members have changed their approach and now work for more dialogue with the surrounding community. In 1997 the Swedish members had eleven local congregations claiming a total of 21,000 members. In Sweden, the movement has a very clear church structure. Its leaders keep close contacts with the European centre of the movement, located in Cologne. The Islamic Cultural Centres are probably the best-organised Muslim organisations in Sweden. Their leaders very often act as spokespersons for the Muslim community in the mass media. They also have good contacts with authorities in Sweden. Today, the organisation seeks contact with all areas of society. The members collaborate with Christian organisations with regard to religious issues, and they are eager to stress that they represent a Swedish organisation.

A fifth organisation, the Islamic National Federation in Sweden (Islamiska Riksförbundet i Sverige) has recently been established in Spånga, near Stockholm. It claims to organise local congregations in five places in central and southern Sweden. This federation lacks support from the Commission for State Grants to Religious Communities.

It was not until 1992 that the Norwegian Muslim associations developed an umbrella organisation similar to those in Sweden. The Norwegian national organisation is called the Islamic Council. Before that the Muslim associations were quite autonomous with little contact between them. The first Muslim congregations in Norway were founded in the 1970s in the Oslo area. The number has increased and in the early 1990s there were nearly forty Muslim associations, more than half of which were located in Oslo. According to a survey by Richard Natvig most congregations seem to follow various ethnic or national groupings. Due to political or religious differences the Moroccan community in Oslo is divided into Masjid Attaouba, Masjid Hassan II and Center Rahma, the latter being oriented toward the Jamaat al-Tabligh. The Sunni Turks in Drammen are members of the Islamic Cultural Centre or the Turkish Religious Society. In Oslo they are found in the Turkish Islamic Union and the Islamic Cultural Centre. The cultural centres are probably branches of the Süleymanli movement. Somalis, Yugoslavs and Kashmiris all have their own associations. In Sarpsborg there is an association for Muslims from Uganda. As mentioned previously, Pakistanis are the dominant group and they have established numerous associations. Central Jamaat-e Ahl-e Sunnat, founded in 1976, with more than 5,000 members is the largest Pakistani association in Norway. Outside Oslo, there are branches in Sandvika, Bærum, Drammen, Kristiansand as well as in northern Norway. It is a local association of the international Barelwi movement. Another Pakistani Barelwi association in Oslo is the World Islamic Mission of Norway with around 3,800 members. Yet another international movement represented among the Pakistanis in Norway is the Jamaat al-Tabligh with local associations in Oslo, where their first association, Anjuman-e-Islahul Muslemeen, was created in 1977. Other local al-Tabliq organisations are found in Drammen, Moss, Mandal, Stavanger and Trondheim. Pakistanis also dominate the Islamic Cultural Centre, founded in 1973 and one of the earliest Muslim religious associations in Norway, although it also has North African members. It reckons around 1,800 members. Moreover, there are two modern reform movements among the Pakistanis in Norway with mostly intellectual members. The Tulu al-Islam movement was founded in Delhi in 1938 by Ghulam Ahmad Parwiz, which is represented by the association Basm-e Tolu-e Islam in Oslo. In 1995 it had around 500 members. The other Pakistani movement is Idara Minhaj ul-Quran, founded in 1980 in Lahore by Muhammad Tahir ul-Qadri. In 1994, this association had 2,500 members in Norway.

The Muslims of Denmark follow the same organisational pattern as in Norway. Thus, they are organised mainly according to ethnic groups and subdivisions relate to political or religious differences. The Turkish Diyanet supports mosque associations with mainly Turkish members. In 1989 they were, according to Jørgen Bæk Simonsen, represented in Copenhagen and nine small towns (Ishøj, Holbæk, Slagelse, Farum, Tåstrup, Hvidovre, Hedehusene, Brabrand and Køge). Diyaneti seems to control the majority of the religious organisations used by Turkish immigrants.

There are also a couple of Islamic congregations in Denmark, in Helsingør and Århus, belonging to Milli Görüş ('National View'), an Islamic organisation with its headquarters in Cologne, Germany. Milli Görüş was originally founded in 1975 in Germany. From there it has spread to other European countries, including Denmark, Norway (Oslo) and Sweden (Malmö). Apparently, it had close contacts with the now outlawed Refah Partisi ('Welfare Party') in Turkey. Most members of the Milli Görüş movement in Scandinavia are of Turkish background.

The Pakistanis in Denmark are divided into several Islamic associations. The Muslim Institute on Vesterbrogade in central Copenhagen represents the Barelwi movement. As is the case in Norway, some Pakistani immigrants in Denmark are organised in the Minhaj ul-Quran movement which is represented in Amager as well as in Ishøj, Gladsakse and Lyngby-Tårbæk. The Libyan Al-Dawa al-Islamiyya for furtherance of Islam is present in Oslo and in Copenhagen. In Malmö the organisation supported the building of the mosque financially.

Shia Muslims and Alevites

Sunni Muslims make up the overwhelming majority in all Nordic countries. Muslims from Iran are, however, usually Shia Muslims, as are many from Iraq and East Africa. In Sweden a federation for the Shia Muslims was founded in the mid 1990s. Local Shia organisations are found in Trollhättan in southern Sweden, where there is a purpose-built Shia Muslim mosque, in Märsta north of Stockholm and in Jakobsberg, a suburb of Stockholm. Organised Shia groups seem to be of Pakistani, East African and Iraqi background. Jönköping in southern Sweden also has a small group of Muslims, mainly Gujarati-speaking Shiites from Uganda, who have lived there since the 1970s. According to estimates the local Muslim population amounted to 1,000 persons at the end of 1990. They have one local organisation, but the Shiites and the Sunnites both have their own prayer rooms. Because of the Uganda Muslims, the Shia proportion is rather high, comprising almost 40 per cent of the Muslim community in Jönköping.

The Shia Muslims of Oslo have their own association, Anjuman-e-Hussaini, founded in 1974, with members from Pakistan and other countries. In 1995 it had about 700 members. Another Shia organisation, Tawheed Islamic Centre, was founded in 1994 in Oslo. The members originate from Iraq and south Lebanon. A third Shia organisation in Oslo, Sader Islamic Centre, was founded in 1997. The Shia Muslims of Finland are usually of Iraqi background and are mostly found in Turku (Åbo).

A high percentage of Turkish immigrants in Uppsala have Kurdish as their mother tongue. Many of them are Alevites with their origin in the Kahramanmarash area of southeastern Turkey. Due to their labour market within so-called ethnic business in Sweden many Alevites from Uppsala have settled in other towns and cities as well. Kurdish-speaking Alevites are also found in Denmark, particularly in Esbjerg and Roskilde. In Drammen in Norway, the Turkish immigrants to a large degree consist of Turkish-speaking Alevites from central Anatolia. Most of them came originally from Demirköyü in Konya district.

For a long time the Alevites did not develop any religious activity. In Sweden and Denmark they instead stressed the national struggle for the Kurds. The persistence of the importance of religious boundaries among these Kurds, however, is shown by the fact that marriage across religious boundaries is rare. One known case caused strong indignation within the community and the couple had to leave for another country. However, during the last few years there has been an increasing mobilising activity among Alevi immigrants in Germany. After the Sivas massacre in 1993 this activity gained momentum, and Alevites in many other countries began to organise themselves into cultural organisations. In 1995 the Alevites in Sweden formed their first organisation. This was achieved mainly by a younger more educated Swedish-born generation, that has begun to organise themselves. The organisation claims the number of Swedish Alevis at around 5,000 people. A few Ismailis, originally from Pakistan, live in Sweden and there is one Ismaili congregation established in Gothenburg.

Sufism

With the recently arrived refugees from Kosovo, Bosnia and Africa several Sufi groups have come to Scandinavia, although our knowledge of them is still very limited. However, organised Sufism has been present in Sweden since the 1920s. In 1925 the universalistic Indian Sufi leader Inayat Khan (1882–1927) visited Sweden and attracted some upper-class women in

Stockholm. In 1997 most members of Inayat Khan's Sufi movement in Sweden where a handful of ageing women. There is also a branch of this movement in Norway. Criticism against the Sufi movement from other groups exists, and many Muslims see it as a pseudo-Sufi group.

In Gothenburg there is a group of converts called the Sophia Foundation. These Sufi converts follow the teaching of Shaykh Fadhlalla Haeri, who was born in Karbala, Iraq. After many years in England he became interested in Sufism. He founded the Zahra Trust UK and published several books that were translated into many languages. Haeri now lives in South Africa, Mallorca and England. Around 1990 he met a Swede who invited him to Sweden, which was the beginning of the Swedish Sophia Foundation. In 1997 there were about twenty members. The Gothenburg group is now part of a worldwide Sufi network. They often travel to visit Sufis in other countries. They also collaborate internationally with a group of Rifaiyya under Shaykh Assaf in the United States. In 1998 this group opened a Sufi centre near Gothenburg.

The interest in Sufism also prevails among New Age-influenced people, and since the 1970s among the adherents of Baghwaan. Sufism has inspired several Swedish intellectuals, and one of Sweden's foremost modern poets, Gunnar Ekelöf (1907–68), was among those who were keenly interested in its wisdom. In his collections of poems *Diwan över Fursten av Emgión*, *Sagan om Fatumeh* and *Vägvisare till underjorden* – now also translated into Turkish and Arabic – the reader can discern many influences from the mystics of Sufism. The contemporary author Torbjörn Säfve has taken the full step of converting to Sufi Islam. He has also issued Sufi texts by Ibn al-Arabi and others in Swedish translation. Several modern forms of music are heavily Sufi-influenced; this applies both to arabesque music from Turkey, which is widespread in certain circles, and to hip-hop, which has inspired a whole youth generation.

Within the immigrant population several Sufi orders exist, although our knowledge of their presence is still limited. The Naqshbandi order is active among Turks in Stockholm as part of an international network. A Naqshbandi *shaykh* is living in southern Sweden. Basm-e Naqshband has around 600 members in Oslo. Other Naqshbandi groups seem to be active among both Turkish and Pakistani immigrants in Norway. In the Stockholm suburb Duvbo there is a Sufi-house owned by a group of Iranian Nimatullahiyya headed by Nadir Kohani. In Norway Sufism plays an important role among the Pakistani immigrants. The largest Muslim congregation in Norway, Jamaat e-Ahl e-Sunnat, has had *imams* who have been recruited from Chistiyya and Qadiriyya. Another Oslo-based Sufi organisation is the Ghousia Muslim Society for Qadiri Muslims. In Turku (Åbo) in Finland there is a tiny group of Bektashi Sufis. Another Finnish Sufi community is called Islam and Love (Islam ja Rakkaus). It was founded in 1994 in Helsinki, and now has about 30 members.

The Ahmadiyya mosque in Hvidovre outside Copenhagen (photo: Ingvar Svanberg, 1997).

The Ahmadiyya in the Nordic countries

In organised form the Ahmadiyya movement, which was established in India 1889, has been active in the Nordic countries at least since 1956, when the Pakistani Kamal Yousof came as a missionary. The movement now has an active mission in all Nordic countries and a number of converts, although most members seem to be of Pakistani or East African Asian background. When Zia ul-Haqq seized power in Pakistan in 1977 many Ahmadiyya members fled from the persecution to Western Europe, mainly to England, but also to Germany and Scandinavia.

In Denmark, an Ahmadiyya mosque was inaugurated in Hvidovre outside Copenhagen in 1967. This was the first proper mosque built in the Nordic countries. In Norway, the first Ahmadiyya congregation was founded in Oslo in 1974, and in 1980 the members converted a house into a mosque, the Nor Mosque, at Frogner in Oslo. At present there are around 850 members in Norway. Most of them have a Pakistani background, but a Norwegian convert, Truls Bølstad, heads the group. The community has a local radio station in Oslo. The spiritual leader of the movement, the Khalif, visited Gothenburg in 1975 in order to place the cornerstone for a mosque and in the spring of 1976 the Nasir Mosque was dedicated. Today there are Ahmadiyya congregations in five other Swedish places, among others in Malmö and Stockholm.

Although they see themselves as Muslims, the Ahmadiyya supporters are excluded from other Muslim communities and are not regarded by the majority of Muslims as part of the Islamic community in the Nordic countries. In Sweden, the authorities seem to accept this point of view and never list Ahmadiyya among the Muslim organisations. In Norway especially the conflicts have been rather fierce between Ahmadiyya and non-Ahmaddiya Pakistani Muslims. In the 1960s, the movement published the periodical *Aktiv Islam* in Swedish, and a Danish version is still published in Hvidovre.

Quran translations

In Denmark Frants Buhl and Owe C. Krarup translated parts of the Quran in the 1950s. A full translation, made by the Ahmadiyya convert A.S. Madsen, was published in 1967. It has been reprinted several times, although it has been criticised by many Danish Muslims. A Norwegian translation was made available in part in 1952, while an unabridged translation by the linguist and Arabist Einar Berg was published in 1980 and again in 1989. Parts of a new translation by the Shiite Trond Ali Lindstad into Norwegian were published in 1996. The Norwegian Ahmadiyya published a translation in 1996.

There are several complete translations of the Quran into Swedish. The first was Fredrik Crustenstolpe's translation from 1843, followed in 1874 by Carl Johan Tornberg's. Still available in bookshops is Karl Vilhelm Zetterstéen's translation, which was published for the first time in 1917. With its reverent tone, in archaic and Bible-influenced Swedish, it has been considered one of the best translations. The internationally renowned Swedish scholar H.S. Nyberg even argued that it was 'by far the best and most accurate in any European language'. In recent years, there have been new translations of the Quran into Swedish. Qanita Sadiqa, who is a Swedish Ahmadiyya convert, assisted in a translation that appeared in 1988. In 1994 the Bilal Mission of Scandinavia published a Quran translation by Jan Åhlander. Another translation has been prepared by Knut Mohammed Bernström, a former Swedish diplomat and convert residing in Morocco. In April 1998 the Swedish government decided to subsidise the printing of this translation into Swedish.

Islamic publications and institutions

During recent years, the Muslims of the Nordic countries have become better organised and developed various institutions. Since the 1970s Swedish Muslims have, for example, published several magazines. Nowadays, the most important Muslim journal in Sweden is *Salaam*, which is published in Swedish by the Islamic Information Association in Stockholm. The Muslim Youth Organisation in Uppsala (Muslimska ungdomsförbundet i Uppsala/MUFU) publishes *MUFU-bladet,* a periodical pamphlet. Swedish Muslim organisations are also very active on Internet with their own homepages and information bulletins both in English and Swedish. In Finland there are two magazines, *An-Nur* and the simpler *Al-Islam.* The Central Jamaat-e Ahl-e Sunnat of Oslo has published the monthly *Tarjaman-e Islam* in Urdu. The Shia convert Trond Ali Linstad publishes the *Muslim magasin* in Norwegian, Arabic and Urdu. Both in Denmark and Norway local radio broadcast stations exist, for example Radio al-Fatah in Denmark and Radio Islam Ahmadiyya in Oslo.

An Islamic bank was founded in Denmark in 1983. It is used by various Muslim organisations for economic transactions. The Islamic Relief Organisation is active in Sweden, gathering money for Muslim relief work in Bosnia and elsewhere. The civil war and genocide in Bosnia, where Muslims were left unprotected by the Western world, became an important catalyst for many Swedish-born youth with immigrant parents from Muslim countries. They became increasingly engaged in relief activities as well as in Muslim affairs in general.

Being a Muslim

Studies in various contexts such as schools, the work place and the military service show that being a Muslim in the Nordic countries is relatively easy. Employers and military officers allow Muslims to pray according to their faith, and special food is served in mess halls and schools. The legal traditions of the Nordic countries do not permit special legal regulations for a particular religious group. Viewing religion as a private matter provides a new perspective on religious life for many Muslim immigrants. In Germany the selling of food classed as *halal* has prompted a rapid and very successful establishment of Islamic business chains that provide various kinds of in-group service, from different provisions (including *halal* bread!) to package tours to Turkey. The people who are active in this process have been equally important for the promotion of religious and political groupings. However, this kind of Muslim entrepreneurship does not seem to exist in the Nordic countries.

Today public opinion generally accepts the fact that certain articles of food are forbidden for Muslims. Institutions such as schools and hospitals have adapted to the need for special menus, not only for Muslims, but also for vegetarians, or people with food allergies. Since pork products are included in many food additives, however, it has become more difficult to decide what food may be considered acceptable. The Swedish National Food Administration (Svenska Livsmedelsverket) has, for example, compiled a list of food additives that contain pork products as a guide for Swedish Muslims and Jews. Major Swedish chocolate and candy factories have also compiled such lists.

Halal meat is readily available in grocery shops runned by immigrants of Turkish, Arab or Pakistani background. In Denmark there are *halal* butcheries, while Sweden and Norway together with Switzerland are the only three countries in Europe that do not allow religious slaughter without preceding anaesthesia. Since 1929 and 1937, respectively, it has been prohibited in Norway and Sweden to slaughter larger animals without preceding anaesthesia. The demand for compulsory anaesthesia was part of reforms aimed at protecting animals. However, an important part of the argumentation centred on the distrust of 'foreign' habits. The debate about *kosher* slaughter before the prohibition often contained anti-Semitic elements. Slaughtering according to Jewish and Muslim tradition has been discussed in the Swedish parliament several times, but the decision-makers have been unwilling to change their attitude to the prohibition of such slaughter.

Muslims in Norway and Sweden who demand *halal* meat therefore have to rely on import products. Increasingly such meat is imported from Denmark, New Zealand and Australia. In 1996 Denmark exported to Norway and Sweden almost half of its produced *halal* meat (between 5,000 and 6,000 cattle and sheep). The Middle East is also a very important market for the Danish meat industry, and around 90 per cent, or 10 million, of the religiously slaughtered poultry were exported to the Middle East in 1996. However, as in many other countries allowing religious slaughter according to Jewish and Islamic rules, there is also a polemical debate in the Danish media about it.

Some Muslims in Norway and Sweden slaughter lambs themselves, according to Islamic rules, especially around the Festival of Sacrifice (*Id al-Adha*), although this is illegal. Since many of the Muslims come from rural backgrounds, where people often slaughter themselves, they have the necessary skills. There are also farmers who are willing to sell lambs to them. In Sweden some of these illegal slaughters have been reported to the police and some Muslims have been prosecuted. In the long-run the familiarity with slaughtering will probably be lost. Having meat slaughtered according to religious prescriptions is, however, not an imperative for all Muslims in Sweden and Norway. In 1995 the Turkish Diyaneti issued a *fatwa* (legal decision) allowing Muslims, obviously with Turks living in the diaspora in mind, to slaughter after electric shocks have been used as anaesthesia. In December 1996 a Muslim congregation in Stockholm declared that they accepted anaesthesia with injections before the throat of the animal is cut. Also a couple of Islamic organisations in Denmark have approved stunning in an agreement with the Danish Livestock and Meat Board.

Mosque issues

Debates about mosques are very similar in Denmark, Norway, Sweden and Finland. Despite early plans, Danish Muslims have not been able to build a mosque in Copenhagen due to protests from the surrounding people. Attempts to build a city mosque in Oslo met with protests from various Christian groups, feminists and others. It was not until 1995 a purpose-built mosque was inaugurated in the Norwegian capital. In a report published by the Democratic Audit of Sweden (Demokratirådet) in 1995, it is stated that 48 per cent of the Swedish population claim to be against the building of proper mosques, despite the constitutional law on freedom of religion. The mosque appears to be a loaded symbol in a conflict between acceptance or denial of a visible Muslim presence in Sweden. Reactions have been forecast in Stockholm and Gothenburg, but feelings have been voiced in many other parts of the country too. Nevertheless, four major mosques – in Malmö, Trollhättan, Uppsala and the Ahmaddiya mosque in Gothenburg – were built in Sweden before 1998. A former pentacostal church has been transformed into a mosque in Västerås. Moreover, advanced plans for building projects exist in a number of places. Yet the debates and stormy campaigns against planned mosques which have been going on over the last decade imply that there is a hostile and xenophobic undercurrent in all social strata. When a mosque was planned in Turku (Åbo) in Finland in 1997, an outcry similar to those in other Nordic countries occurred.

One of the most frequently recurring arguments against mosques in the Nordic countries is that they would cause more traffic, and therefore increase pollution, noise and the need for parking space. Mosques and parking spaces are regarded as intruders upon open green spaces and all sorts of culture relics. Many react spontaneously and claim that a mosque would be an alien element in their familiar local environment. Several arguments reveal anxiety and ignorance about the multi-cultural society. The most common reasons against the building of mosques are due to the fact that people are frightened of or dislike Islam as a religion. This aversion feeds on ignorance and misconceptions about Islam.

The Rushdie Affair and Radio Islam

In Scandinavia there were few public Muslim protests against Rushdie's *Satanic Verses* and many Muslims felt uneasy only about the publicity it caused. Approached by journalists, some Muslims commented upon the Rushdie affair. Apparently without any deeper knowledge about the book they condemned Rushdie. In Sweden, the matter became a kind of meta-discussion among intellectuals, and the weak support Rushdie and his freedom to write received from the Swedish Academy prompted three

Facilities for ritual washing before prayer in a suburban mosque outside Stockholm (photo: Pia Karlsson, 1998).

famous Swedish authors to leave the Academy, a protest from which that institution has not yet recovered. The *Satanic Verses* were sold openly in Sweden and no special precautions were taken. One Muslim convert reviewed the book quite negatively in a major newspaper. Another author, who is a Sufi convert, had no understanding for the banning of the book. However, the publishing house that published a Swedish translation of Rushdie's book invited a Muslim organisation to write a book about their beliefs and promised to market it. This book *Islam: vår tro* (*Islam: Our Belief*) includes general information concerning Islam, and the discussion on Rushdie is very brief and unsophisticated. The book maintained that Rushdie's book was offensive, but that it was difficult to understand the content of the critical message. The hope was expressed that 'the problem could be resolved peacefully', but that no notice had been taken of Muslim demands.

The situation in Norway was more critical. In February 1989 an Islamic Resistance Council was set up with the aim of stopping the publication of a Norwegian translation of the *Satanic Verses*. Nearly thirty associations, the first ever united attempt among Norwegian Muslims, took part in the campaign. They tried to use the legal system to stop the book on the grounds that it was blasphemous. In 1995 the Norwegian publisher was the victim of an attempt on his life.

The broadcasts from Radio Islam in Sweden have been very provocative. In the summer of 1987 this local broadcasting station in Stockholm began to attract attention because many of its programmes contained extreme anti-Semitic elements. In the late 1990s, Radio Islam is probably one of the most active anti-Semitic and openly history-revisionist institutions in Europe. Nowadays, it is very active on Internet. The rights of freedom of speech guaranteed by the Swedish constitution gives the authorities very limited powers to stop it. The Islamic messages in the broadcasts from Radio Islam seem to be non-existent. It is difficult to know how Muslims regard the programmes. However, the repudiations of them from various Muslim organisations have been few or non-existent, although at least some individuals have condemned them.

Circumcision

Muslim tradition expects that male children be circumcised. This takes place in ritual forms, and the age varies according to local traditions within the Islamic world. Probably circumcision is among the most tenacious of Muslim practices and is even applied among secularised persons from Muslim countries. Many immigrant Muslims in Scandinavia have been able to arrange circumcision in connection with vacation trips to their countries of origin. However, this is not possible for many refugee families, and in Sweden there has been debate as to what extent hospitals should provide circumcision service. Swedish Jews have already developed a tradition around circumcision, and a Jewish doctor in Stockholm has for a long time helped Muslims with the circumcision. In connection with the increasing stream of Muslims, however, there are queues at hospitals, and there is an ethical debate among doctors whether or not the performance of circumcision is in accordance with good medical practice.

Since circumcision is not regarded as a medically motivated treatment, many hospitals charge high fees. This would, however, not present a great problem for practising Muslims, as some *imams* in Sweden have pointed out. Even in Muslim countries there is a fee for circumcision, and in connection with circumcision rather expensive feasts are often held. The problem remains that many doctors refuse to do the operation, since they regard it as an unnecessary cosmetic treatment. However, some private medical doctors specialise in circumcision. A couple of unauthorised circumcisions, performed by traditional specialists, have been brought to trial in Sweden.

Lars Pedersen reports from Denmark that the option of having boys circumcised has gradually disappeared from the hospital services in recent years. This seems to be due to cuts in expenses.

Religious schools

Especially among social democrats, there has been an official resistance to private schools in Sweden and Norway. In the political culture of Sweden and Norway the official authorities have had the main responsibility for education of children, while Danish politicians have stressed the rights and responsibilities of the parents. The right of the parents to organise their children's education has been granted by the Danish constitution since 1849. Despite this fact, Muslim independent schools in Denmark seem to provoke the same debate and critique as in Sweden and Norway.

In 1992, a non-socialist Swedish government decided to change the school system, thereby facilitating the development of independent schools. Since then, a large number of so-called free schools have been founded. In 1997 there were around 350 such schools. Most of them are either Christian or stress alternative pedagogical movements. However, some Muslim schools have also been founded. The first such school in Sweden started in Malmö in 1993. In 1997, there were a handful Muslim schools in Sweden. The Foundation for the Islamic School (Stiftelsen Islamiska skolan) at present has two schools, one in Uppsala and one in Stockholm. Some local school boards have been reluctant to allow Muslims to open schools within the new system. Despite the fact that the national board confirmed the Islamic school Al Elowm Alislamia in Örebro, the local authorities refused to accept it. They regarded this school as a counterforce against integration and the tolerance fostered in the public school system where children of various social, ethnic and religious background meet each other. An Islamic school was seen as a threat against integration. Resistance from local school boards is also found in Malmö, Jönköping, Botkyrka as well as other places.

According to Lars Pedersen, Denmark has the highest percentage of private, publicly funded, Muslim schools in Europe, followed by the Netherlands. In 1995 there were fourteen Islamic schools in Denmark, the majority of them based in the Arab and Pakistani communities. However, a similar criticism exists in Denmark as in Sweden. The most common argument is that the underlying motive behind the schools is to avoid integration, and that the teaching does not promote an open, tolerant or democratic mind.

At present (1998) there is no Muslim school in Finland, although one is planned to open soon.

Literature

A general bibliography on Islam in Sweden and Norway has been published by Åke Sander, 'Sweden and Norway', pp. 151–73 in *Muslims in Western Europe: An Annotated Bibliography*, eds. Felice Dassetto and Yves Conrad (Paris: L'Harmattan, 1996). See also Oddbjørn Leirvik, *Islam i Norge: Oversikt, med bibliografi* (Oslo 1997).

Islam in Denmark is presented in a comprehensive work by Jørgen Bæk Simonsen, *Islam i Danmark: Muslimske institutioner i Danmark* (Aarhus: Statens humanistiske forskningråd, 1991) and in Mehdi Mozaffari, 'Les musulmans au Danemark', pp. 357–84 in *L'islam et les musulmans dans le monde, I. L'Europe occidentale*, eds. Mohammed Arkoun, Rémy Leveau and Bassem El-Jisr (Beyrouth: Centre Culturel Hariri, 1993). See also Lars Pedersen, 'Islam in the Discourse of Public Authorities and Institutions in Denmark', pp. 202–17 in *Muslims in the Margin: Political Responses to the Presence of Islam in Western Europe*, eds. W.A.R. Shadid and P.S. van Koningsveld (Kampen: Kok Pharos, 1996). Contemporary Islam in Sweden is dealt with in Ingvar Svanberg, 'Les musulmans en Suède', pp. 384–419 in *L'islam et les musulmans dans le monde, I. L'Europe occidentale*, eds. Mohammed Arkoun, Rémy Leveau and Bassem El-Jisr (Beyrouth: Centre Culturel Hariri, 1993); Leif Stenberg, 'Islam,' pp. 79–152 in *Världsreligionerna i människornas dagliga liv* (Stockholm: Brevskolan, 1998); and Åke Sander, 'Islam and Muslims in Sweden', *Migration: A European Journal of International Migration and Ethnic Relation*, 8 (1990), pp. 83–134. A good overview of the current situation in Norway is presented in Richard Natvig, 'Les musulmans en Norvège', pp. 423–33 in *L'islam et les musulmans dans le monde, I. L'Europe occidentale*, eds. Mohammed Arkoun, Rémy Leveau and Bassem El-Jisr (Beyrouth: Centre Culturel Hariri, 1993). For a brief account on Islam in Finland, see Harry Halén, *A Bibliographical Survey of the Publishing Activities of the Turkic Minority in Finland*, Studia Orientalia, 51:11 (Helsinki: Societas orientalis Fennica, 1979) and Ilkka Kolehmainen and Marja-Leena Marjamäki, 'Tatarian Music in Finland', *Antropologiska Studier*, 25–26 (1978).

For a full treatment of the discussions connected with construction of mosques, see Pia Karlsson and Ingvar Svanberg, *Moskéer i Sverige: en religionsetnologisk studie av intolerans och administrativ vanmakt* (Uppsala: Svenska kyrkans forskningsråd, 1995). See also Åke Sander, 'From Musalla to Mosque: The Process of Integration and Institutionalization of Islam in Sweden', pp. 62–188 in *The Integration of Islam and Hinduism in Western Europe*, eds. W.A.R. Shadid and P.S. van Koningsveld (Kampen: Kok Pharos, 1991) and Kirsti Kuusela, 'A Mosque of Our Own?

Turkish Immigrants in Gothenburg Facing the Effects of a Changing World,' pp. 43–55 in *Religion and Ethnicity: Minorities and Social Change in the Metropolis*, ed. Rohit Barot (Kampen: Kok Pharos, 1993). Folk religion among Norwegian Muslims is dealt with in Nora Ahlberg, *New Challenges – Old Strategies: Themes of Variation and Conflict among Pakistani Muslims in Norway* (Helsinki: Finnish Anthropological Society, 1990). Alevi immigrants in Norway have been studied by Ragnar Næss, 'Being an Alevi Muslim in South-western Anatolia and in Norway', pp. 174–95 in *The New Islamic Presence in Western Europe*, eds. Tomas Gerholm and Yngve G. Lithman (London: Mansell, 1988). Studies of Swedish Muslims have been published by Ingrid Lundberg and Ingvar Svanberg, 'Turkish Voluntary Associations in Metropolitan Stockholm', *Migration: A European Journal of International Migration and Ethnic Relations*, 19/1991:2 (1992), pp. 35–76, and Ingvar Svanberg, 'Turkish Immigrants in Sweden', pp. 215–27 in *Turcs d'Europe . . . et d'Ailleurs*, eds. Marcel Bazin, Michel Bozdémir, Altan Gokalp and Stephane de Tapia, Les Annales de l'Autre Islam, 3 (Paris: INALCO, 1996).

Chapter Eighteen

Russia and Transcaucasia

Svante Cornell and Ingvar Svanberg

The Russian Federation, founded in 1991 as one of the successor states of the disunited Soviet Union, is the largest country in the world with a population of some 150 million. Russia is officially a multi-ethnic and multi-confessional state, although the ethnic Russians count for almost 82 per cent of the total population. There are no official records of religious affiliation in contemporary Russia. Although pre-Soviet Russians usually were Orthodox Christians, it is very likely that a large number of their contemporary descendants are religiously indifferent. During the Soviet era the Communist Party conducted an intensive anti-religious propaganda, the nation was socialised in an atheist atmosphere and religious holidays were replaced with secular festivals. Most of the churches, mosques, temples and monasteries were closed down, the religious leaders were harassed and had difficulty in acting openly, religious literature was almost impossible to obtain and many people had to hide their religious affiliation. The anti-religious propaganda was especially harsh during the Stalinist era in the 1930s, when many religious leaders were sent to prison camps or murdered. However, during World War II, both the Russian Orthodox Church and the Russian Muslim organisations were able, to a limited extent, to re-establish themselves and were again allowed to conduct religious services and act openly in the Soviet Union. This new public presence continued after the war.

Since the Russian Orthodox Church had to work within the Soviet framework and under state control, many people nowadays distrust this church for having been too closely linked with the Soviet communist regime. Other Christian groups, such as Pentecostal and Baptist churches, were illegal during the Soviet time and their followers were often victims of persecution. Today Russia is experiencing a Christian revitalisation. Lutheran and Orthodox churches are given back their premises, monasteries are rebuilt and Christian festivals are celebrated again. The Russian Orthodox Church is prospering in the new Russian Federation as an important part of the new national identity for many Russians and non-Russian minorities. However, in many places the Church has been connected with ultra-nationalist forces. Although some handbooks report that 85 per cent of the population are Christians, this must be taken with a large grain of salt. Seventy years under Marxist control together with the general modernisation caused a considerable secularisation. It is likely that many people are non-believers. The communist regime also left a country marked by political instability and unsuccessful economic reforms. This has left room for mafia organisations, corruption and a very poor standard of living. The ideological vacuum has only partly been replaced by traditional religiosity. As in the West we can observe an increasing interest in various kinds of new religious movement, often labelled New Age.

Like Christianity, Buddhism, Islam and indigenous religions belong to the traditional religious heritage of Russia. The Buddhists are estimated to number around 1 million in Russia. There are more than eighty Buddhist communities, most of them found in Buryatia, Tuva and Kalmykia, where Buddhism has a long historical tradition. Other communities are found in major Russian cities – including Moscow, St Petersburg and Vladivostok – and as small groups all over the country. Indigenous religions are found mostly among minor ethnic groups in northern Russia and Siberia. Also part of the Mari people, living north of the Volga knee in the very heartland of Russia, still practise an aboriginal religion.

According to some estimates, the Muslim groups number nearly 10 per cent of the population or 15 to 17 million people of the Russian Federation. The famous Russian Islamist Gejdar Jemal even claims the figure of 30 per cent, while a recent socio-demographic study sticks at 2 per cent, or 3 million citizens, in Russia that identify themselves as Muslims. Sociological studies show unequivocally that believers are a minority among people who, on ethnic grounds, are identified as Muslims. The strength of Islam also varies regionally. As in the case of Christianity, a rediscovery of Islamic roots has taken place in many parts of Russia, as well as in other Soviet successor states. Thus, Islam has become an increasingly important part of the national identity in many areas. Many ethnic groups within Russia are again defined because of their religious background, although language differences seem to play a major role as ethnic identifiers. Tatars, Bashkirs and the various Caucasian peoples belong to these language-based groups.

A history of conquest and co-existence

Islam has a long tradition in Russia and Transcaucasia. During the Arab conquest of eastern Caucasus in the middle of the seventh century, Islam was imposed in the area. The Islamisation of what is today Azerbaijan and southern Daghestan was rapid, and in the eighth century the majority of the population was already Muslim. Between the ninth and thirteenth centuries, Islam expanded along the trade routes. Along the Volga River, Muslims have been present since the ninth century, and during the mediaeval time Muslims penetrated as far west as into the regions that today constitute Poland, Lithuania and Belarus. Their descendants are the so-called White Russian Tatars still living in Eastern Europe. As a result of this settlement in the fifteenth century, and of the immigration within the Russian Empire and the Soviet Union, the Baltic States, Ukraine, Belarus and Poland today have their own native Muslim populations. Estonian Muslims are probably mostly of Mishär Tatar background and settled in the country during the nineteenth century and later. Lithuania has a small Muslim population of White Russian Tatar origin, mainly located in Vilnius. According to recent estimates they number around 3,000. The oldest Muslim settlers in Belarus have the same background as the Lithuanian and Polish Tatars. In addition there are many Muslims who migrated into area during the Russian Empire and the Soviet period. Apparently, there are more than 100,000 Muslims in the now independent Belarus. The number of Polish Muslims, almost all of whom are of White Russian Tatar origin, is estimated at 2,200 and distributed over seven religious communities: Gdansk, Gorzow, Wielkopolskiego, Warzsaw, Bohoniki, Kruszyniany and Białystok.

During the Mongol period Sufi missionaries were important for the distribution of Islam within the steppe region of southern Russia, north of the Black and Caspian Seas. The Mongol Empire left several Muslim khanates as its successors in the region. From the mid-fifteenth century the young Muscovite State began to expand southward and eastward, and Muslim territories were incorporated into the Russian Empire. The Kazan khanate was conquered in 1552, followed by the Astrakhan khanate in 1556 and the Sibir khanate in 1598. Forcible conversion to Christianity took place during this time. The Bashkirs continued to resist the Tsarist armies, and they were not fully conquered until the late eighteenth century. During the uprising of Pugachev in 1773 many Bashkirs and Tatars joined his troops. After the defeat of the Bashkirs and the annexing of the Crimean khanate, Russia began a new policy toward Islam within its borders. In the 1780s, the Muslim population was given the right to practice their religion and were given the same rights as the Russians. Furthermore, a Muslim Spiritual Assembly was established in Orenburg, which was later moved to Ufa. The Tsarist authorities appointed the *muftis*, or chief judges of Islamic law. At the beginning of the eighteenth century a university that became important in the education of Muslims within the empire was established in Kazan. After the conquest of the Tatar Khanates the Russian Empire continued to expand towards Central Asia. During this period Islam actually advanced within the Russian Empire. Tatar *mullas* (minor religious leaders) and merchants became important, not only as leaders for the Muslims in Russia, but also for spreading Islam into areas conquered by the Tsarist troops.

After the Russo–Turkish war 1768–74, Russia began more seriously to expand southward. The conquest of the Crimean Khanate in 1784 was followed by extensive mass migration of Muslims to the Ottoman empire. It was caused by a policy that must be described as a regular ethnic cleansing. Christian peasants who moved in from the west replaced the Muslim Tatars. These conquests and the pacification of the southern steppe area of Russia opened up the road to annexing of the Caucasus and Transcaucasia. However, the Russian army encountered resistance from mountain warriors under Mansur Ushurma, a Chechen Naqshbandi *shaykh* who had begun a holy war against the Russians in 1773. In 1785 the warriors of Shaykh Mansur surrounded an important Russian force on the banks of Sunia river and wiped out the whole army, probably the worst deathblow that ever struck the army of Catherine II. A few years later the Russian troops crushed the Chechen warriors. Shaykh Mansur was captured in 1791 and sent to prison in Schlusselborg where he died in 1793. He left behind a memory showing that resistance and gathering around Islam was possible. Later generations of Chechens and other Caucasians have found inspiration in the memory of the resistance struggle of Shaykh Mansur and his troops. He represented the beginning of the Sufi resistance to Russian conquest, which continued until the early twentieth century and is known as the Murid movement.

Extensive mass evacuations, massacres and actual genocide among the conquest peoples mark the expansion of Tsarist Russia towards the south and the east. Especially affected were the many peoples of the Caucasus, who also resisted the Russian troops most fiercely. The conquest of the Caucasus was an extremely long and bloody campaign, marked by forced and voluntary mass migrations, penal expeditions, attempts to divide the mountain peoples, outrages from Russian Cossack troops, rivalry between mountain and plains peoples and between Muslims and Christians. The Russian offensive southward continued after 1791. Georgia was conquered in 1801, Ossetia in 1806, Abkhazia in 1810, northern Azerbaijan came under Russian control in 1813 and Armenia was conquered in 1828.

However, the mountain peoples continued to resist the Russians. Another important Sufi leader, Imam Shamil from Daghestan, appeared as a unifying figure for the Caucasian people in their resistance and, once more, the Naqshbandi brotherhood led the struggle against the Russians. Imam Shamil and his troops fought the Russians from 1824 for several decades. In 1846 the Russians tried to subjugate the mountaineers by extensive terror. Villages were burnt down, cattle were destroyed and captives were deported as prisoners to other parts of Russia, but Imam Shamil was not defeated until 1859. He spent his years as a prisoner of the Russians in Moscow and Kiev, far from his mountain home. After being released he conducted a pilgrimage to Mecca and Medina, where he died in 1871. Imam Shamil is probably the best-known Muslim hero of Russia, not only among the Muslims mountain peoples of the Caucasus, but also outside this region. His name has become a symbol for many people during

Caucasian Muslims using a car with Imam Shamil depicted on the door (photo: Jens A. Riisnaes, 1990).

the last 100 years, and he is an important example for the contemporary peoples of Daghestan and north Caucasus.

In the western Caucasus the resistance continued until 1864. Every group that was defeated had to choose between full subjection under the Tsar government or expulsion. Hundred of thousands of people were forced to escape from their mountains and cross the Black Sea to ports of the Ottoman empire. Many Circassians, Chechens, Lezgins, Ossets, Abkhaz and Daghestanis chose to leave. According to recent estimates, about 1.2 Million Muslim Caucasians were forced into exile between 1855 and 1865. Thousands of people died from hardship and epidemics. One Muslim group, the Ubykhs, fiercely resisted the Russians. When they finally were crushed the entire population had to leave their valley in the mountains. They did not survive the exile and the whole ethnic group disappeared. Their language is now extinct.

The Chechens also resisted the Russian troops but were finally defeated. Around 40,000 Chechens chose to migrate to the Ottoman Empire and another 20,000 were forced by the Russian authorities to leave in 1865. As has been pointed out by the Norwegian Slavist Alf Grannes, the conquest of the proud Muslim mountain peoples is a vast and colourful theme in the

Russian literature. The Russian colonisation of the Caucasus continued after 1865. Muslim Ossets revolted several times, which caused new forced migration. Revolts took place in Daghestan in 1877 and later also in Chechnya. The Naqshbandi brotherhood continued to be anti-Russian and they supported revolts against the Russians as late as in the early 1920s, when Shaykh Uzun Haji inspired an uprising in Chechnya. The nineteenth century was also a period when the Ottomans and Russians fought for the loyalty of the Muslims of Russia. Just as the Tsar declared himself to be the protector of all Christians living in Ottoman domains in this century, the Ottoman leaders began to stress their position as the protectors of Muslims living in Christian empires. The Ottomans followed the process of Russification of the Muslims of Russia through secret agents, and the Ottoman consulates tried to maintain their cultural and religious ties with these Muslims and to protect their identities.

The Russians continued to use Islam and Muslim leaders to gain the support of the Caucasians. In the Muslim areas which were directly under Tsarist rule, Islamic organisations were supported and controlled. In 1887 the Russians passed new building regulations regarding mosques. Muslims were free to practise their religion as long as they did not damage the Orthodox faith. Only communities with 300 or more members were allowed to build mosques, and these had to be maintained by each community itself. Apparently the *mufti* of the Caucasus, Hüseyin Efendi Gayabov, was collaborating to the extent of aiding the Russians in enforcing their policies. The Tsarist regime controlled the appointment of *muftis* and local religious leaders. The government paid their salaries, watched over their activities, and ensured that they were loyal to the regime. Thus the Russians promoted the development of a Muslim hierarchy, which was in turn controlled by them.

As a response to the attempts of Tsar Aleksander III to convert the Tatars, but also due to the impact of modernist influence from the West, the Jadid movement developed among the Kazan Tatars and soon spread into other Muslim areas as well. The Jadidists stressed the need for education of the population in order to develop their society. When, in 1905, Russia granted religious liberty in the country, Tatars who had converted to Christianity returned to Islam. They also began to do missionary work among various neighbouring peoples, and many Chuvash, Maris and Udmurts converted to Islam at the beginning of the century. At the beginning of the Russian Revolution, Jadidists and Bolsheviks cooperated. A Sufi brotherhood, the so-called Vaisovtzy, also cooperated and fought alongside with the Russian Bolsheviks on the eve of the Revolution in 1917. However, from 1928 the Soviet authorities began an anti-religious campaign, which continued more or less intensively until the *perestroika* of Mikhail Gorbachev in the mid 1980s. Muslim intellectuals, including the Jadids, were persecuted and murdered by the Bolsheviks. Due to events during World War II, an official Islam was again established in the Soviet Union. However, Muslims kept a relatively low profile and were very closely connected with the authorities. With the collapse of the Soviet Union at the beginning of the 1990s, Islamic institutions were again able to function and develop, this time entirely without state control.

In July 1997 the Duma of Russia passed a new Bill of religious freedom. The bill caused some controversy, since it restricted the rights of new foreign religious denominations to work in Russia. They had to prove that their religion had been practised in Russia for at least fifteen years. This affected many small religious entities, such as Bahai, Kadianism and the Unification Church, and Russia was heavily criticised by the United States senate, since it affected the possibility for many evangelical missionaries from the United States to work within the country. The major religions of the Russian Federation, the Russian Orthodox Church and Islam, were not affected by the restrictions, and their leaders therefore also favoured the bill.

A renewal of Islam

Most Muslims in the Russian Federation are Sunnites of the Hanafi school, but in Daghestan the majority of the Muslims follow the Shafii school. Pockets of Shia Muslims are found in Daghestan, especially among the Tats, a small ethnic group speaking an Iranian language. Since the Sunnites and the Shiites cooperated very closely within the Soviet Union, few differences remained between them. The differences between Sunnites and Shiites are nowadays little-known among common people. Due to the atheist policy of the Soviet regime, most people have very little knowledge of the theology of Islam. It has survived mostly as a kind of folk religion, and contemporary Muslim leaders are working hard to restore Islam again in Russia.

In post-Soviet Russia, a renewal of Islam is manifest all over the country. Several Islamic organisations and parties developed on the eve of, or after, the communist period came to an end. Twenty per cent of all officially registered religious organisations and associations in the Russian Federation are Muslim, and in 1997 the number of Muslim congregations was estimated at 3,000. The Islamic Rebirth Party was founded in 1990 and had its core members in Tajikistan, but branches were also reported in Daghestan, Chechnya and Ingushetia. This party includes both Islamists and more moderate members. A radical member of the party is Geydar Jemal, an outspoken Islamist who is said to be closely associated with the Muslim Brotherhood in Egypt and Jamaat-i-Islami in Pakistan. He also maintains close ties with rightist movements. Local Muslim political parties are found in North Caucasus and in Tatarstan. An Islamic Cultural Centre, headed by Abdul Vahed Niyazov, was founded in 1991 in Moscow aimed at founding Muslim universities in Russia.

Although Russians have lived for centuries with their Muslim fellow-citizens, strong anti-Muslim feelings have developed in recent decades. Before the war in Chechnya in 1994–95, a poll conducted in St Petersburg indicated that over 70 per cent of the young people felt resentment toward Islam. Incidents have occurred many times during the 1990s. During the war in Chechnya, the police and militia of St Petersburg and Moscow harassed many Caucasians, and in October 1996, special interior ministry troops raided a Moscow mosque and detained the worshipers. Some of them were Chechens and Ingush, many of whom were beaten before being released. A notorious move was the ordered expulsion from Moscow of 'persons of Caucasian nationality', which in reality meant all Muslims. It was implemented by the city militia and the interior ministry forces, and this major attack against human rights was seen as a way to blame the Muslims for the many problems in the city. In November 1995 a regular pogrom on Meskhetian refugees took place in Krasnodar Krai, when ultra-nationalist Cossacks attacked and assaulted Muslim settlers in a small village. Hate-groups and ultra-nationalist Russians also feed strong anti-Muslim sentiments that affect the relations between Russians and Muslims in many areas. Hostilities have become especially common in North Caucasus.

Sufism

Just as in Central Asia, Sufi groups are openly active in Muslim areas of contemporary Russia. Although the Naqshbandiyya reached the Tatars in the eigthteenth century – and a dissident branch, the so-called Vaisovtzy, was founded in Kazan by Bahauddin Vaisov in 1862 – Sufism is probably extinct in contemporary Tatarstan and Bashkortostan. Our knowledge of Sufi orders in the Caucasus and Transcaucasia is still very scant. Yet, it is obvious that during the Soviet period they played an important role as a counterbalance to the communist atheist influence and in the development of a religious subculture and unofficial Islamic force in those regions. The French scholar Alexandre Bennigsen even characterised the activities of the Sufi brotherhoods as a dynamic, parallel Islam, which acted beyond the control of the official and Soviet-supported Muslim spiritual directorates. Despite the fact that the orders were illegal during the Soviet era, Soviet sources claimed as late as in the 1970s that half of the population in the North Caucasus, that is the Chechen–Ingush and Daghestan republics, belonged to Sufi brotherhoods.

The current centres of Sufism in Russia are found in the Caucasus, particularly in Ingushetia, Chechnya and Daghestan, but also in northern Azerbaijan. Two brotherhoods are active in the region, the Naqshbandiyya and the Qadiriyya. In the spring of 1997, the world leader of a Naqshbandi branch, As-Sayyid Shaykh Mohammed Nazim al-Haqqani, visited a Quranic Conference in Moscow. This visit gave him the opportunity to meet with Naqshbandi scholars and *shaykhs* from various parts of the former Soviet Union. On his return journey to Cyprus, he visited Daghestan, which is one of the strongholds of Naqshbandiyya in Russia. The Qadiri order is dominant in Chechnya and Ingushetia. It was introduced into the region in the 1850s from Baghdad. The Ingush people were converted by Qadiri missionaries only in the late nineteenth century. It is believed that five branches of the Qadiri order are still active in north Caucasus: the Kunta Haji in Daghestan and Chechnya, the Bammat Giray in Chechnya, the Batal Haji in Ingushetia, the Chim Mirza in Chechnya and Ingushetia, and, finally, the Vis Haji branch, which was founded in the 1950s when the then deported Chechens and Ingush were living in Kazakstan. This new branch of the Qadiriyya has also found its way into northern Daghestan, Muslim Ossetia and into the Kabardin territory. According to a recent study by the American sociologist Susan Goodrich Lehmann, interviewees from Sufi areas in Russia were much more likely to report that they practised Islam than were the Muslims in areas were Sufi brotherhoods were not active.

Modern forms of Sufism are also present in Russia. For instance, the International Sufi Movement, founded by Inayat Khan in the 1920s, has its Russian centre in Novosibirsk. However, no data are available on the number of members. Also more New Age-inspired types of Sufism have found their way to contemporary Russia.

Russia and Siberia

Muslims are found throughout Russia. Provinces such as Astrakhan, Chelyabinsk and Orenburg have large percentages of Muslims in their population, as have Penza and Ulyanovsk. Moscow, the capital of the Russian Federation, is believed to have a Muslim population of around 10 per cent of the total population. Moscow's main mosque looks like a Russian Orthodox cathedral. It is painted in blue and white in the nineteenth-century neo-Baroque style. Also St Petersburg has an old nineteenth-century mosque located in the centre of the city. New so-called 'cathedral mosques' are mushrooming all over the country and are today found in many Russian cities. According to some sources, there were only 192 mosques in Russia in 1985. Ten years later the figures are closer to 2,500. Large Islamic centres with cathedral mosques, colleges and business centres are reported from many places. For example, a main mosque has been built in Samara, and another one has been built in Volgograd. These construction projects have been made possible through foreign aid. Muslim organisations in Russia have even used Internet to appeal to the Muslim world for financial support in their efforts to reconstruct and develop the Islamic heritage of the country. The new situation in Russia has opened up the opportunity for the modernisation of the Islamic service on a broad scale. For instance, solemn sermons in connection with the Festival of Sacrifice, *Id al-Adha*, are nowadays broadcast on major television networks all over Russia. Still, however, the Muslims of the Russian Federation remain far behind the various Christian organisations in the use of television.

The administrative organisations of the Muslims in Russia are now being transformed. During the Soviet era, the Muslims of European Russia, the western Soviet republics and Siberia were administered under the Spiritual Board of European Russia and Siberia. It was located in the city of Ufa in Bashkiria. This organisation has survived, although the former Soviet-appointed leaders have been replaced. Nowadays its leader or *Shaykh-ul-Islam,* Talgat Tadjuddin, a Tatar born in Kazan in 1948 and educated at Al-Azhar in Cairo, heads the muftiate of Russia and Siberia, and he is viewed as the grand *mufti* of Russia. However, with the increasing autonomy or independence of many areas, this spiritual board has been under pressure to subdivide into smaller units. The Muslims of Tatarstan have developed their own muftiate, although Talgat Tuadjuddin's organisation is found in that republic too, and the two muftiates compete with one another. A Spiritual Office of the Muslims of the Central European Russia was established in early 1994 around the main mosque of Moscow. This muftiate covers eleven regions with approximately 3.5 million Muslims living in or near the capital, including the Muslims of the Russian exclave Kaliningrad. Mufti Ravil Gainutdin was elected as its chairman. In the summer of 1997, the Muslims of Siberia and Russia's Far East voted to establish their own separate spiritual board for Muslims in these areas. It opened up its headquarters in Tobolsk and Shaykh Nafiula Ashirov was elected as its chairman and *mufti* of Siberia and Russia's Far East. Beside these, there are several other muftiates in Russia, many of which compete with each other over jurisdiction. There are now around eighteen muftiates in Russia. Most probably, the Muslims of the vast area that constitutes Russia will subdivide into further muftiates in the near future.

With the re-establishment of religious centres and new mosques the demand for educated religious leaders or *ulama* has increased. The number of religious leaders with any theological training was extremely low under the Soviet era. Most local leaders had only a limited knowledge of theology. Very few of them could even read the Quran, and many of them were not officially recognised. To compensate for this shortage of theologically trained leaders, the Spiritual Board of Moscow in 1994 opened a college with a four-year programme to train such leaders.

Tatarstan and Bashkortostan

In 1920, Tatarstan was created as an autonomous republic within Russia. During the eve of the final breakdown of the Soviet Union, the Tatar parliament declared Tatarstan's sovereignty in the early autumn of 1990. The contemporary republic of Tatarstan has a population of more than 3.7 million inhabitants, and about half of the population has a Muslim cultural background. Separation of religion and state is part of the new constitution. During the 1990s, Tatarstan has obviously reached far-reaching autonomy with its own international contacts. In particular, it has oriented itself towards Turkey, a country that has investments in Tatarstan and increasing bilateral trade.

Today we can observe an increasing Tatar nationalism, not only in Tatarstan but also among Tatars living in other parts of Russia and in the Tatar diaspora spread throughout the world. The language is restored, literature in the native language is published and Tatarstan encourages Tatars outside the republic to immigrate. With this cultural revitalisation, an increasing interest in the religious heritage has also developed. Most Tatars are by tradition Sunni Muslims. Although during this century the Tatars have been largely secular, there has been a religious revival in Tatarstan since the *perestroika* in the late 1980s made it possible for religious communities to function more openly. Institutional Islam has increased considerably in Tatarstan since the mid 1980s. Many religious organisations and political parties have been established in Tatarstan, among them Saf Islam ('Real Islam'), the Marjani Society (1988), the Bulghar National Congress (1990), and the Islamic Democratic Party (1992). Moreover, former at least nominally Christian Tatar groups, such as the so-called Kryashen Tatars that were baptised in the late sixteenth century, are nowadays turning to Islam because of missionary activities in the areas where they live. In 1998 the two major Islamic boards of Tatarstan were gathered under the United Clerical Board of Muslims of the Republic of Tatarstan. Mufti Gusman-hazret Ishkakov was elected chairman. Reports from Tatarstan claim that there were 700 Muslim religious organisations in the area in 1997. An Islamic university is planned to open in Kazan in 1999. Despite the increasing presence of Islamic institutions, Tatarstan still has a quite secular character. Among those who characterise themselves as 'believers', over two-thirds never visit mosques or even pray at home. To most Tatars, Islam seems to be more a matter of national identity than of religious conviction. As Goodrich Lehmann points out, active religiosity in Tataristan is still confined to older rural women with little education.

The neighbouring Bashkortostan is a republic with around 4 million inhabitants, with the Bashkirs as a minority. The majority groups are Tatars and Russians. It was founded as an autonomous republic in March 1920 and, when Tatarstan declared its sovereignty in 1990, Bashkortostan did the same. Its current autonomy is dependent on Tatarstan. Governmental authorities in both republics have suggested that Tatarstan and Bashkortostan could become a unified state, although this would probably create ethnic conflicts between the Tatars and Bashkirs. The common Muslim heritage will not bridge the different national aspirations of the two ethnic groups, nor will their common 'Turkic' roots. The Bashkir capital Ufa played an important role and was the administrative centre for the Muslims of European Russia and Siberia during the Soviet era. Nominally, it has retained this position and is the location for the main muftiate of Russia. The portion of Muslims is much higher in Bashkortostan, but they are ethnically divided. However, the people of Bashkortostan also show the same pattern as in the case of Tatarstan. There has been an increase in Institutional Islam, but at the same time, active religiosity is still to be found mainly among low-educated rural women.

Northwest of Tatarstan is the little known autonomous republic of Chuvashia. Many of the Chuvash converted to Islam in the nineteenth century, but there is very little information about the contemporary situation. However, as in many other minority areas of Russia, we can observe a cultural revitalisation and an increasing nationalism in Chuvashia. The Chuvash are to a large degree russified, although a renewed interest in their original language is noticeable. Moreover, it seems that Muslim Tatars are conducting missionary work among the Chuvash in order to convert them to Islam. The Chuvash National Congress also encourages this activity. Mari-el is another republic bordering on Tatarstan where a high level of conversion to Islam has been observed during the last few years due to the missionary endeavours of Tatar preachers.

North Caucasus

While the Muslims of Tatarstan, Bashkortostan and other places in Russia and Siberia have for centuries lived in close contact with Christians, the Muslims of Caucasus have always maintained close links with Islamic centres of the Middle East. The Islamic revival in North Caucasus started long before Michail Gorbachev's advent to power and can be traced back to the 1970s. Admittedly, even in the heyday of Soviet atheism, Islamic practices were never eradicated – above all they flourished in underground Sufi forms. The Naqshbandi and Qadiri brotherhoods, which are strong in the North Caucasus, became the focal point of Islam in the Soviet period, as the authorities persecuted official religion. What happened in the late 1980s was that religious practice became visible, in the end even encompassing many members of the indigenous Soviet élite. As Fanny Bryan has noted, the Islamic opposition underwent a strategic change due to *glasnost*. It became an active, aggressive movement against the system. Daghestan was one of the main scenes of this revival. In 1989, the first religious demonstrations took place in Buinaksk and Makhachkala, the capital of Daghestan. The primary demand was the building of new mosques and the restoration of old ones. Before 1989, there were officially twenty-seven

Carpet dealers outside the city wall of Derbent, Daghestan (photo: Jens A. Riisnaes, 1990).

functioning mosques in Daghestan, while the estimated number in 1994 was over 5,000. The *mufti* of the Makhachkala spiritual directorate, accused of collaborating with the state security agencies, was ousted by a popular revolt in May 1994. It is believed that many of these revolts were initiated and conducted by the powerful Sufi brotherhoods of the region. Furthermore, the *hajj* or pilgrimage to Mecca has been renewed on a large scale. Today, Arabic and Quran classes exist in the schools of Daghestan, and political leaders, riding on the Islamic wave, have proclaimed their intention of making Islam the state religion of the republic. The Islamic wind is blowing in the politics of Daghestan, too. The leading Islamic–Democratic Party decided to rename itself the Islamic Party, and its leadership has become more religiously coloured.

As Vladimir Bobrovnikov has noted in a rare field study on Islam in Daghestan, the Islamic revival has not taken place in a homogeneous way. It has affected the northwestern part of the republic, populated by Avars, Dargins and Kumyks, to a much larger extent than the central and southern parts, chiefly inhabited by Laks, Lezgins and Tabasarans. The majority of newly opened mosques and *madrasas* (Islamic colleges) are found in the northern and western parts of the country. The fact that the Sufis have been strongest in these areas is probably an important reason for these regional differences. As we shall see in the next section, the religious movement, far from being united, is divided along national lines, with each of the larger peoples setting up a spiritual directorate, or muftiate, of its own. Nevertheless, this tendency is counteracted by strong voices arguing for unity in the name of Islam.

The Islamic revival in Daghestan is important, as it is instrumental in tying the Daghestanis and other north Caucasians to the larger world of Islam. In particular, the performance of the *hajj* plays this role. The pilgrims who return to their native lands often work for the establishment of Islamic education there. Moreover, as has been the case in other areas such as in Turkey, their devotion entails a long-term objective of strengthening religion, completely independent from the short-term political struggle in the country – a strategy, which has seen considerable success elsewhere. Open conflicts between so-called Wahhabis, that is Islamists of various kinds, and Sufis have recently been reported. The 'Wahhabis' leader, Mullah Bagaudin Muhammad, heads the Kizilyurt mosque. Repeated accusations from the Daghestani authorities claim the 'Wahhabis' are paid agents of foreign Islamic organisations.

In terms of identity, Islam – just as it has been in the past – might become the unifying force of the north Caucasians. Whether this is seen as a positive or negative development naturally depends on one's views on political Islam. Russia is likely to counteract this tendency, and even to use it as a pretext for re-establishing its hegemony over the region, reiterating its claim to be the defender of Europe and Christianity in the face of an expansionist Islam. In Daghestan, however, through its unifying power and in view of the fragile multi-ethnic stability of the republic, Islam might become the main and crucial element in sustaining multi-ethnic peace and stability in the future.

Chechnya has also been the scene of an Islamic revival. The Chechens are, to an even greater degree than the Daghestanis, tied to the Sufi orders mentioned above. The adherence to Sufism was strengthened during the period of the Chechens' thirteen-year deportation to Central Asia during and after the Second World War. In exile, the Chechens retained a remarkable unity, compared to other deported peoples. They rallied around the Naqshbandi and Qadiri brotherhoods, which provided an informal mode of organisation where Chechen culture could be preserved, and was naturally instrumental in maintaining and furthering the religiosity of the people. In a deeper way, the independent-minded Chechens, while embracing Islam, were drawn to the decentralised Naqshbandiyya, which, at least in the version practiced in Chechnya, imposes few restrictions on its members.

Nevertheless, Islam in today's Chechnya is different from that of Daghestan with respect to its role in society. In Chechnya, the main determinant of a person's identity is Chechen ethnicity. This is significant as the north Caucasian rebellions against Russia in the nineteenth century and

Muslim graveyard outside a Caucasian village (photo: Jens A. Riisnaes, 1990).

even as late as in the 1920s were rarely confined to one sole ethnic group, but were carried out as holy wars (*ghazawat*) in the name of Islam. In the 1990s, however, Chechnya's rebellion was a rebellion of the Chechen nation, although certain Islamic elements were used by the leaders, and not even the close kin of the Chechens, the Ingush, were part of it. Historically too, the Chechen brand of Islam differs from that of the Daghestanis. The Chechen lineage society's traditions have seldom been superseded by Islamic traditions but rather preserved. This is particularly true for the position of women in society. Women enjoy equal rights to men in cases of divorce and can even reach the highest positions in the Sufi brotherhoods. Traditional law, moreover, takes priority over Islamic law. This comparatively weak position of Islam was related to the fact that the Chechens were not totally Islamicised until the nineteenth century – the last Ingush tribe being converted to Islam in the 1860s, whereas Islam had come to Daghestan as early as in the eighth century.

It was indeed under the rule of Imam Shamil, a Daghestani Avar, that a theocratic state was introduced in Chechnya during the long rebellion against Russia. This attempt at creating a centralised state was vehemently opposed by many Chechens, which presented an obstacle to the unified struggle against Russia. Nevertheless, in present-day Chechnya, Shamil's image is untarnished and great respect for his principles can be observed. Hence religiosity today is widespread, a fact which has only been enhanced by the recent war. At the end of the war in August 1996, there were voices calling for an Islamic state. Briefly, there were some instances of implementation of Islamic law, but this quickly disappeared, and the strength of the underlying secularised society became clear. Thus the fears often expressed about a 'fundamentalist' state emerging in Chechnya are highly exaggerated.

In 1998, thousands of people protested in the Chechen capital Groznin against the increasing presence of Wahhabism in the country. Wahhabism began to spread in Chechnya during the war, when Wahhabi volunteers arrived from the Middle East. A Jordanian citizen, Emir Khattab, who set up an Islamic Battalion in Chechnya, has become the leader of the Chechen Wahhabis. Not only the *mufti* of Chechnya has been alarmed by the new presence of Wahhabis in the country, but also the Chechen field commander Salman Raduev, who organised the rally in Grozny, has demanded that the authorities outlaw the movement.

Azerbaijan

In the Transcaucasus, the main Islamic grouping is the Azeri population, estimated at a total of 25–30 million people, of whom 7 million live in the former Soviet Republic of Azerbaijan, 300,000 in Georgia and the remainder in Iran. The Azeris, very much due to their historical connection with Persia, embraced the Twelver Shia version of Islam. With the Russian and Soviet rule over the Transcaucasus, the Azeris under Russian control became heavily secularised, an aspect which can be readily observed today. Azerbaijan's first period of independence was between 1918 and 1920. Significantly, there were hardly any signs then that the state was moving in Islamic direction, despite the fact that the Azeri national consciousness was in its incipient stage. The Azerbaijani Democratic Republic was in fact a secular republic characterised by the building of the Azeri nation, where Islam played a part as a component of national culture. It is interesting to note that this state was the first republic as such to be founded in a Muslim society – the Turkish republic did not see the light of day until 1923.

In Soviet times, the already weak Islamic identity was watered down even further. It should come as no surprise if an Azerbaijani, asked whether he is Sunni or Shia – there is a Sunni minority – answers that he has heard these terms but does not know what they mean.

Since 1991, religion has re-emerged in public life, but no remarkable religious revival has taken place. In a certain sense, the place of religion in Azerbaijani society can be said to be similar to the case of Turkey (despite recent events in that country), as opposed to Iran. In 1992, this orientation was confirmed in what has been so far the only democratic change of government in a Caucasian or Central Asian state. As the Soviet period leader, Ayaz Mutalibov, was forced to resign, the intellectual Abülfaz Elchibey was elected president with slightly over 60 per cent of the votes. Elchibey was heavily pro-Turkish, even Pan-Turkic, vehemently anti-Iranian and a firm secularist. His coming to power showed the weakness of Islam in Azerbaijan. When Elchibey was deposed after a year, he was replaced by the old Politburo member Heydar Aliyev. Aliyev, in order to improve relations with Iran and to diversify Azerbaijan's external relations, tried to improve his Islamic credentials, even performing the pilgrimage to Mecca. Nevertheless, this should not be seen as a deviation from Azerbaijan's secular route, although Islamic sentiments do exist among a minority of the population, and Islamic movements sponsored by Iran are operating in Azerbaijan. The popular support of these groups remains very limited. It should be noted that Islam is in a much stronger position south of the Araxes river. The Iranian Azeris have a much more highly developed Islamic consciousness whereas their national consciousness remains relatively limited. Hence, in the case of a future unification of the Azeri nation, it is likely that religion and its place in society would become a major point of discord.

In the Russian Empire, and especially during the Soviet era, Islam in Russia and Transcaucasia had to survive in relative isolation from the Islamic currents in other parts of the world. The collapse of the Soviet Union made it possible to re-establish contacts with brothers and sisters abroad. With the opening of the borders to the outside world, Islamic organisations and religious leaders have developed their own relations with international Islamic bodies. The American leading personality of Islam, Louis Farrakhan, has visited Russia several times. When he conducted a world tour in the early spring of 1998, he also included visits to Muslims in European Russia, Siberia and Daghestan. Prominent international Sufi leaders regularly visit Muslim communities in Russia. Saudi, Egyptian and Turkish Muslims and organisations, in particular, have established contacts with various Muslim organisations in Russia. The Muslims of Russia still cooperate to a large degree with their brothers and sisters in the Soviet successor states of Central Asia. The well-organised and international Ahmadiyya movement is also active, especially in spreading their own Russian and other translations of the Quran. Other Russian translations have appeared during the last few years too. For instance, a local printer has published an edition for the Muslims of St Petersburg. Traditional Muslim organisations in Russia fear that they may have difficulties in competing with the much better-organised and better-off Ahmadiyya and try to condemn its activities in the country.

During the Soviet era very few people were able to conduct their pilgrimage to Mecca and other holy places. The Soviet government in the 1970s and 1980s sent only a handful of carefully chosen individuals. This has now changed radically. The number of pilgrims has increased drastically during the 1990s. Several planes leave the main Muslim cities of Russia every year. From Azerbaijan it is also possible to reach Saudi Arabia by bus, an opportunity taken by a few hundred pilgrims every year.

Literature

The presence and development of Islam in contemporary Russia is to a large degree a blank spot in the scholarly literature. Our information on Islam in Russia and Transcaucasia is therefore largely based on reports from local and international news agencies and newspapers. Historical and demographic aspects of Islam in the Soviet Union are described in Alexandre Bennigsen and S. Enders Wimbush, *Muslims of the Soviet Empire: A Guide* (London: Hurst, 1985). For general aspects of Islam in Russia, see also Alexandre A. Bennigsen and S. Enders Wimbush, *Muslim National Communism in the Soviet Union: A Revolutionary Strategy for the Colonial World* (Chicago: The University of Chicago Press, 1979); *Central Asia and the Caucasus after the Soviet Union: Domestic and International Dynamics*, ed. Mohiaddin Mesbahi (Gainesville: University of Florida Press, 1994); *Muslim Eurasia: Conflicting Legacies*, ed. Yaacov Ro'i (London: Frank Cass, 1995); *Gamla folk och nya stater: det upplösta sovjetimperiet*, eds. Sven Gustavsson and Ingvar Svanberg (Stockholm: Gidlunds, 1992); and *The Nationalities Question in the Post-Soviet States*, ed. Graham Smith (London: Longmans 1996). Sufism in Russia is also discussed in Chantal Lemercier-Quelquejay, 'Le Caucase', pp. 300–08 in *Les voies d'Allah: Les ordres mystiques dans le monde musulmans des origines à aujourd'hui*, eds. Alexandre Popović and Gilles Veinstein (Paris: Fayard, 1996).

Specific works on Islam and its religious importance in the 1990s Russia are few. The best overview is Uwe Halbach, 'Islam in Rußland', *Orient*, 38 (1997), pp. 245–75. A recent comparative sociological study of five Islamic autonomous republics of Russia has been published by Susan Goodrich Lehmann, 'Islam and Ethnicity in the Republics of Russia', *Post-Soviet Affairs*, 13 (1997), pp. 78–103. There are also a few studies dealing with the specific situation in the Caucasus see especially Vladimir Bobrovnikov, 'The Islamic Revival and the National Question in Post-Soviet Dagestan', *The Keston Journal*, 24 (1996), pp. 220–34 and Anna Zelkina, 'Islam and Society in Chechnya: From the Late Eighteenth to the Mid-Nineteenth Century', *Journal of Islamic Studies*, 7 (1996), pp. 240–64. The modern history of Islam is discussed in *The North Caucasus Barrier: The Russian Advance towards the Muslim World*, eds. Abdurahman Avtorkhanov and Marie Bennigsen Broxup (London: Hurst, 1992). For a study of the recent war in Chechnya, see Carlotta Gall and Thomas de Waal, *Chechnya: A Small Victorious War* (Basingstoke: Pan Original, 1997).

Chapter Nineteen

North America

Mattias Gardell

With the fall of the Iron Curtain an era in global politics came to an end, as the Western world no longer could define itself in opposition to communism. During the past few years, we have witnessed a return to a previous pattern in which the Occident seeks its *raison d'être* by placing itself in opposition to Islam. The United States still portrays itself as the defender of liberty against totalitarian barbarism, but the symbols of evil are no longer taken from what Ronald Reagan called 'the Evil Empire' (i.e., the Soviet Union) but from the Muslim world. 'For a millennium, the struggle for mankind's destiny was between Christianity and Islam; in the twenty-first century, it may be so again', Pat Buchanan argues. 'For as the Shiites (in Iran and Lebanon) humiliate us, their co-religionists are filling up the countries of the West.' Far from being an isolated voice in the wilderness of American far-right politics, Buchanan's cry is echoed by mainstream Americans. Invited by Congress to give the 1990 Jefferson Lecture, the distinguished American Islamologist Bernard Lewis presented the Islamic challenge against the West as 'a clash of civilisations – the perhaps irrational but surely historic reaction of an ancient rival against our Judeo–Christian heritage'. A 1992 Pentagon report identified radical Islam as the sole remaining threat against a United States-led New World Order. President Bill Clinton's qualification that the West did not have problems with Islam, only with its wing of violent extremists, was sharply rebuked by the Harvard professor Samuel P. Huntington. Describing Islamic civilisation as inherently militarised and aggressive, Huntington in his 1996 study of the changing face of global politics, *The Clash of Civilizations and the Remaking of World Order*, urged the West to unite, maintain its global military superiority and restrict Muslim immigration. Huntington concludes with a dystopian thesis describing the end of Western civilisation if it maintains its present multi-cultural, multi-religious orientation.

In the context of an emerging 'new cold war' between an American-led Western world and Islam, it may be interesting to observe Islam as an *American* religion with an American history of at least some 500 years. Estimate of the number of Muslims residing in the United States varies between 2 and 9 million. The huge discrepancy depends in part on the lack of reliable statistics and in part on different definitions favoured by researchers. Should one include 'cultural' Muslims or only religiously active practitioners? Should Ahmadiyya be included or excluded? Should a black hip hop teenager who calls himself 'God Islam' and claims a black Islamic divine identity be disqualified as a heretic or be included in the statistics? Many observers lean towards a middle ground, suggesting that American Islam is well on the way to overtaking Judaism as the second largest religion in the United States. The Muslim expansion in the United States is mainly due to immigration, although a significant number of converts is found in the African–American community. Again depending on shifting definitions, the latter is estimated to make up for between 30 and 40 per cent of the total Muslim American community. Among non-black American converts, the most significant impact has been made by Sufi orders in the New Age milieu. There are more than 1,300 mosques of all sizes dotted all over the United States, although some seventy per cent of the Muslim population is concentrated in ten states: California, New York, Illinois, New Jersey, Indiana, Michigan, Virginia, Texas, Ohio and Maryland.

Black Muslim Sailors, Scholars and Slaves

Islam has a long but hidden history in America. Some researchers trace the first Muslims in the Americas to pre-Columbian times. Clyde Winters argues that Muslims from Mali may have been the first to establish colonies in the New World. Ivan van Sertima proposes a pre-Islamic African settlement in Central America, and the historian Kofi Wangara finds it likely that Islam made its first contact with the Americas through one or two pre-Columbian expeditions sent out by the Mali emperor Abubakari II in the early fourteenth century. Wangara and Leo Weiner both argue that a pre-Columbian African trade was established with the Americas and discuss possible African, particularly Muslim Mandigoan, influences on Central Amer-Indian language, religion and art. In a 1992 speech, the Libyan leader Muammar al-Qaddafi supported the thesis of a pre-Columbian Muslim link with the New World, adding that the continent was named after its 'discoverer' Amir Ka. Speculation aside, we find Muslims among the early Spanish explorers. African Muslims, either enslaved or hired, worked as navigators, guides and sailors for the Christian conquistadors. Some of these Muslim pioneers opened new avenues to the New World. The first known non-Indian to enter present-day Arizona and New Mexico was a black Muslim known as Estevanico. Linguistically talented, he established the first documented contacts with the Pueblo civilisations and became a renowned healer among several southwestern Amer-Indian peoples.

The vast majority of African Muslims who arrived in what today is the United States were not adventurers but captives, brought to the continent in the holds of slave ships. Allen D. Austin calculates that 10 per cent of the slaves exported to the colonies were Africans. After the War of Independence, the Muslims increased to an estimated 15–20 per cent, due to the new Americans' preference for slaves from Senegambia, an area with large Muslim populations. Some of the traded Muslims were well-educated *ulama* (Islamic scholars) and *fuqaha* (Islamic jurists), while others were ordinary members of the *umma* (community of Muslims). Most of these Muslims fade into anonymity through the dehumanisation process of chattel slavery, but a limited number of individuals emerge from the mist of contemporary indifference to be tangible for later historians. These individuals share a dramatic life-story with their anonymous co-religionists, but they have managed to attract the attention of some philanthropist, abolitionist, journalist or slave-owner who cared to put their story on paper. A few outstanding Muslims wrote their own autobiographies, in English or Arabic, for the world to know. Unfortunately, space limitations exclude the possibility for them all to be animated here, but a few exemplary voices from the past will illustrate the early presence of Islam in North America.

Abdul Rahahman, a Fulbe military leader and well-educated Muslim scholar, was ambushed in 1788, brought to the coast, and sold to a British slave trader. He was sold to a Louisiana farmer who renamed him 'Prince', because a Mandingo translator told of his royal family. Returning to his masters after a brief period as a runaway, he was put in charge of the farmer's cattle and made an overseer. Around 1807 Rahahman met an old acquaintance, John Coates Cox, while in Natchez on an errand. Cox had been given asylum and medical treatment by Rahahman's father, the commander in the great city of Timbo. After having been restored to health, Cox was safely escorted to the Gambia River, where he boarded a British ship and sailed home. Although Cox's efforts to purchase and free Rahahman failed, Prince became a local celebrity when Cox's story became publicly known. Southern papers published his autobiography, and the American Colonization Society (ACS) took an interest in him. Would not this royal scholar be a perfect agent for this society, spreading the gospel in West Africa? Rahahman wisely played his part in the game. When asked to write in Arabic, Rahahman wrote, he said, the Lord's Prayer, to the amusement of his audience. Under the guise of evangelising Africans living under the Islamic yoke, he raised enough money to purchase his family's freedom. To the disappointment of the ACS, Rahahman never abandoned his faith. Upon reaching the shores of Africa, he openly resumed his Islamic identity, and the Lord's Prayer proved upon examination to be the *Fati*, the opening *sura* of the Quran.

On Selapo Island, Georgia, we find another Muslim slave, Bilali, who was a Fulbe from Timbo and an Islamic scholar who must have completed a high level of education in Islamic jurisprudence, judging from the manuscripts he left behind. One document proved not to be the diary the researchers had expected to find but a series of excerpts from the *Risala*, a legal treatise of the Malaki school, the Islamic legal school dominant in West Africa. Furthermore, the excerpt dealt with the prescribed relations between masters and slaves, which indicates that Bilali compared his experience as slave in Christian hands with the substantially different Islamic view on the subject. In 1813, during the second American war with England, Bilali was entrusted with military leadership over eighty armed slaves. He pledged to defend the island if attacked, and assured his master that he could 'answer for every Negro of the true faith, but not for the Christian dogs you own', a statement indicating a Muslim congregation in the area. When he died many years later, Bilali was buried with his Quran and his prayer rug.

Omar Ibn Said was born around 1770 in Futa Toro, a town by the Senegal River. He worked as a teacher in Keba, west of the Niger, before he was captured and brought to North Carolina. His owner treated him with great cruelty, and Omar ran away into the woods. He was later captured and imprisoned in Fayetteville, North Carolina, where he astonished his jailer by writing a succession of lines in 'strange characters' with coal on the prison walls. The news of this remarkable inmate reached the governor's brother, who purchased Omar and gave him a relatively better future. Omar Ibn Said is then believed to have converted to Christianity, but some signs indicate that this was either a fake conversion, as was the case with Rahahman, or a blending of the two Abrahamic faiths. For instance, several of the Christian texts written by Omar, such as the Lord's Prayer or the twenty-third Psalm, are all preceded with the *Bismillah*, the introduction to the *suras* of the Quran: 'In the name of Allah, the Beneficent, the Merciful'.

Another slave, Job Ben Solomon, managed to write at least two complete copies of the Quran from memory, which proves that the words of God through his Prophet could be kept intact in the *dar al-kufr* (the abode of unbelievers). But did Islam survive as an organised religion? Could Muslim slaves establish an Islamic tradition, kept alive through the generations? Was the rise of a black Muslim movement among southern migrants in the northern cities in the 1930s the surfacing of a hidden tradition? Based on the scant sources available, the writer's assessment is that this did not happen. With the possible exception of isolated areas, the material suggest that Islam in North America's slave communities slowly faded into a memory. The Christianisation of African Muslims may have passed through a syncretistic stage in certain areas. Reverend Charles Colcock Jones of Georgia wrote in 1842 that slaves in his district 'have been known to accommodate Christianity to Mohammedanism. "God", they say, "is Allah, and Jesus Christ is Mohammed – the religion is the same, but different countries have different names".' Unlike the situation in Brazil, northern South America and the Caribbean, the slaves in North America (except for South Carolina) were a minority population and the direct import from

Africa was proportionally less in numbers. These combined factors explain in part why the African religions, including Islam, did not survive to the same extent in North America. The rise of Islam in twentieth-century black America cannot be attributed to the surfacing of an unbroken, underground tradition, although the existence of black Muslim slaves has a given role in the rhetoric of modern black Islamic preachers.

An Islamic religious text, written by a Muslim slave, is for Imam Isa of the Ansaaru Allah Community 'evidence that the first language of the black slaves residing today in America was Arabic and that Al Islaam was their true way of life when in Africa'. This notion of Islam as an *African* religion is a key factor in the Muslim revival in contemporary black America. When black intellectuals in search for their roots rediscovered their African heritage, they also encountered Islam. They found great Islamic civilisations in West Africa and made note of the relatively harmonious integration of Islam in the various local African cultures. In Islam, they found a faith traditionally opposed to European expansionism, a creed in which blacks often held leadership positions, and in which the archetype for wisdom is a black man, Luqman the Wise, as is told in the thirty-first *sura* of the Quran. The single most powerful symbol for the connection between Africa and Islam is Bilal Ibn Rabah. He was a black slave of Abyssinian origin owned by Ibn Khalaf of the mighty Ummayya clan in Mecca. Bilal was one of the first Muslims recorded in history and was severely brutalised when his master tried in vain to force him to become an apostate. Abu Bakr then ransomed Bilal, who became a close companion to the Prophet Muhammad. Bilal had a melodious voice and became Islam's first *muadhdhin,* the reciter of the call to prayer. This fact, that a black former slave is the prototype for the Muslim call that five times a day resounds from the minarets of the mosques, is given a tremendous symbolic significance: it is the black man who leads humanity to God.

Black Islam

A significant feature of Islam in North America is the development of distinct black Islamic theologies of liberation. Represented by a number of competing black Muslim organisations, Islam has come to be a vehicle for a separate national quest as well as an Afrocentric spiritual path for a growing body of African–Americans. They all argue that Islam is the nature of the black man, the pristine religion of Africa, and that black Americans could be identified as the Chosen People. Characteristically, Black Islam incorporates mystic elements from Christianity, Islam and Judaism, interpreted racially to form the basis of a racial gnosis informing the black man that he is divine.

The first movement to fuse black nationalism and Islam was the Moorish Science Temple, established in 1913 by Noble Drew Ali, born Timothy

A Muslim selling Islamic literature in Manhattan, New York (photo: Kristina Gardell, 1987).

Drew (1886–1929). Presenting himself as an 'Angel of Allah', Ali claimed to have made a pilgrimage to Africa where he obtained permission from the King of Morocco to revert all African–Americans to Islam and their true Moorish American nationality. The Moorish Science Temple combined the legacy of populist black nationalist Marcus Garvey with the notion of Islam as the old-time religion of the black man. Noble Drew Ali taught that the aboriginal black culture was the cradle of civilisation. All the Muslim prophets were black sages, and before its fall, the original Moorish Empire was said to encompass all of Africa, Asia and the Americas in mythical antiquity prior to the separation of the continents. Blessed by Allah as long as it honoured its racial God and traditions, the Moorish civilisation crumbled when it began to admire the gods and principles of the white man. Loosing racial consciousness, the black world was colonised and its former leaders turned into inferior 'Negroes' or 'coloured' deprived of knowledge of self and God. These tribulations were but material reflections of a spiritual battle. To assist His Chosen People, God manifested in the Moorish prophet Jesus who was then reincarnated in the prophet Muhammad. Completing the quest of racial redemption, God then decided to make North America His headquarters. Noble Drew Ali is thus Jesus Christ and Muhammad Ibn Abdullah reincarnated, the third and final carnal manifestation of Allah. In 1927, the Moorish Science Temple published the *Holy Koran*, which is not to be confused with the Holy Quran of the mainstream Islamic world. Ali claimed that its esoteric contents had been kept secret by a Silent Brotherhood of Islamic sages until the time appointed by Allah to free the secrets and deliver them to the black Muslims of America. In fact, the theological part of the *Holy Koran* was an abridged plagiarism of the *Aquarian Gospel of Jesus the Christ* published in 1907 by the Gnostic Christian, Levi H. Dowling, (1844–1911) slightly altered to fit a black nationalist quest. The black man is, according to the Moorish gospel, an eternal, infinite thought of Allah, temporarily in carnal hide at the plane of things made manifest. As a seed of Allah, man's true ontology is divine and his quest is to re-ascend into a perfected being as One with Allah.

The racial gnosis combined with black separatist pursuits. Dressed in Turkish and/or Northern African style, the Moorish Americans adopted the Moorish flag, changed their names by adding an 'El' or a 'Bey' and carried the Moorish national and identity card issued by Noble Drew Ali. Following Marcus Garvey, identified as a 'forerunner' of Ali, a 'Moorish Industrial Group' was established to achieve an independent black economy. It operated small business ventures, like barber shops and restaurants, and the Moorish Science Temple slowly became lucrative. In 1929, a number of top officials made considerable profits, selling religious paraphernalia, and when Ali disapproved of further advancement in that area he was challenged by the business manager and real estate broker Shaykh Claude Green who ousted Ali from the Chicago headquarters. Five days later, Green was butchered by a hit squad. The police arrested a number of suspects, among them Noble Drew Ali, provoking several days of racial unrest in the city. Perhaps brutalised in custody, Ali was ill when released and died a few days later, on July 20, 1929. In the aftermath, the Moorish Science Temple split over the issue of successorship into several competing factions. Only two, led by Ali reincarnated in John Givens El and Charles Kirkman Bey respectively, gained more than local following. In 1994, the El faction led by Shaykh Richardson Dingle El as Noble Drew Ali III had some thirty affiliated chapters while the reformed Kirkman branch is reportedly larger, claiming more than a 100 temples in Black America. The most successful of the new Moorish organisations was established in 1975, when the notorious 5,000-man-strong street gang Black P. Stone Nation (renamed El Rukn) adopted a Moorish identity when its leader Jeff Fort became Imam Malik when in prison. In 1987, police raided its South Side Chicago headquarters mosque, confiscated an entire arsenal including an anti-tank rocket. Charged with having established a 'terrorist connection' with Libya, Imam Malik and two co-defendants were convicted for conspiracy and weapon possession.

The single most important of the Black Islamic organisations is the Nation of Islam, often referred to as *the* Black Muslims. The Nation of Islam originated among southern migrants in the rapidly expanding inner city ghettos of the industrial north. Founded during the Great Depression in the 1930s by a mysterious prophet later identified as God in Person, it was led by the Last Messenger of God, Elijah Muhammad (b. 1897) until 1975. He was succeeded by his son Imam Warithuddin Muhammad (b. 1933), who initiated a rapid transformation process aimed at merging the movement with mainstream Sunni Islam. This period is known as 'the Fall of the Nation' among the followers of Minister Louis Farrakhan (b. 1933), who heads by far the most successful of the various 'resurrected' Nations that operate in black America. A former night club entertainer, Farrakhan is the epitome of black preacher artistry, who, with inflammatory rhetorical skill, has succeeded in making the Nation the centre of radical black racialist aspirations. Under his leadership, the Nation of Islam today enjoys a popularity unsurpassed in its history and black militant Islam has become an integral part of a contemporary black youth culture with its message rhythmically pumped out through popular hip hop stars. Though constantly controversial, Farrakhan has made a remarkable breakthrough in national politics after leading the greatest demonstration in US history in the Million Man March of 1995. The Nation of Islam had in 1997 established mosques and study groups in every state, and began its expansion internationally, with chapters in Canada, the Caribbean, England, France, Ghana, Nigeria and South Africa. Its weekly, the *Final Call,* reported a circulation exceeding 500,000 copies an issue, and Farrakhan could be seen on more than 100 television stations across the United States.

The Nation teaches that the black man is not an inferior creature whose future is necessarily as a welfare recipient in the black urban ghettos, but the Original Man, in himself a locus of all the divine creative powers. Blacks are 'gods of the universe'. In the Beginning of Time, a first emanation of divine intelligence took the form of Primordial Man, who took the colour from the black space out of which he emerged. The divine energy and creative powers can only manifest themselves in man, and a succession of Man–Gods took charge in creating the world as we know it. In the original divine civilisation, the black Man–God mastered all disciplines from mathematics to architecture, symbolised by the pyramids that were placed as a sign of this magnificent past, in itself containing parts of the keys to unlock the secrets of the universe. What is in the Bible described as the Fall of Adam represents an event of cosmic significance at which mankind fell into its present beast-like state. 'God in His fallen state is man, and man in his exalted state is God.' The black gods 'died' mentally, a metaphor used to describe the black man's unawareness of his true identity. World supremacy was given over to a white race of evil, grafted through a process of gene manipulation out of the black man. In essence, the white man is the abstracted and concentrated potential for evil that was present in the first black man, as all creation is composed of the negative and the positive. Ruled by his inner negative side, manifest as the blond, blue-eyed devil, the black man was to suffer in his effort to learn how to master the Quranic imperative 'enjoining what is right and forbidding what is wrong'. The true secrets of the universe were concealed to a closed circle of divine gnostic sages, 'the hidden imams' of Shia Islam, or the 'four and twenty elders' of Christianity, and was not to be revealed until the cycle of confusion ends and the cycle of unveilment commences. Reconnecting with the roots implies embarking on a black path of gnosis, and as knowledge of Self equals knowledge of God, the spiritual journey ultimately guides the black man and woman back into the exalted state of divinity defined as the *raison d'être* of mankind. This is symbolised in the concept of 'I.s.l.a.m.', which if one breaks it down stands for I-Self-Lord-Am-Master. The blackosophic rationale is reflected in the hip hop culture, where artists frequently adopt names such as 'Divine Justice', 'Supreme Intellect' or 'God Islam', and is carried further by splinter groups such as the East coast-based, youth-dominated Nation of Gods and Earths, founded by Clarence 13X as Father Allah in 1963.

The reign of the devil explains the phenomena of colonialism, slavery, racism, economic hardship and oppression that blacks have experienced in recent history. The white devil was commanded by God to subdue the world and establish his supremacy in fulfilment of Revelations 6:8: 'And behold a pale horse; and his name that sat upon him was Death, and Hell followed with him'. A pale horse rode into Africa, America, Asia and Australia, Farrakhan exclaimed, and 'wherever you Caucasians went you brought Death to the people. Wherever you went you brought Hell to the people.' But, as Revelations also informs us, there will be an end to the righteous' suffering. The white devil was to rule for 6,000 years, and that era is now rushing to its end. The count-down to Armageddon started in 1555, when a white devil named John Hawkins arrived at the shores of Africa onboard the slave ship *Jesus* to capture the black tribe of Shabazz and bring them as slaves to the 'wilderness of North America'. With this, God's words to Imam Shabazz (known Biblically as Abraham) in Genesis 15:13–14 came true: 'Thy seed shall be a stranger in a land that is not theirs, and they shall serve them; and they shall afflict them for four hundred years; and also that nation, whom they will serve, will I judge'. The fulfilment is stressed by the Nation as irrefutable evidence that identifies blacks as the principal actors of the Scriptures, reducing to impostors any other nation with claims to be the Chosen People. As is obvious from the above, the Nation makes frequent use of the Bible, counting as holy scriptures the Old, the New and the Final Testament – the latter, of course, being the Quran. In effect, slavery brought the original man as a Trojan horse into the fortress of evil, giving the African–American a key role in the approaching apocalypse.

Close to the expiry of the 400 years, a self-fulfilled God and member of the Gnostic circle named Master Farad Muhammad came to Detroit on the July 4, 1930. He raised a poorly educated son of a Georgia share cropper to become His Messenger, and then departed to the abode from which God supervises the destiny of mankind. Elijah Muhammad spread the gospel and embarked on the black path of divinity until he was elevated into a black Messiah and taken to God. The Nation thus denies the 1975 death of Elijah Muhammad, and keeps an empty coffin in its Chicago mother mosque as a symbol of the miracle. Elijah the Messiah entrusted Minister Farrakhan to guide the lost–found Nation of Islam through the turbulent times to come, and will imminently return to judge the wicked as the sun sets over the devil's world.

Far from being an escapist movement, passively awaiting God's intervention, the Nation is a *religion of practice* that teaches blacks to use their inherent divine powers to create their own destiny. Sharply criticising the black Church, which at that time had gone from its earlier activist position to become largely politically quietist and other-worldly, Elijah Muhammad taught that Islam was the aboriginal religion of the black man. Christianity was said to be a slave religion, a pie-in-the-sky philosophy, that taught the blacks to turn the other cheek to oppression and set all hopes for a dead white man nailed on a cross to give them compensation beyond the grave. Islam restored black self-respect, and in its demand for social justice turned into a creed of black empowerment. Inspired by black Islamic theology as preached by Elijah Muhammad and Malcolm X, black Christians in the late 1960s began developing a black theology of liberation, reasserting the activist standpoint of the early church. Today, black nationalist Christianity and Islam cooperate freely, with black as a theological concept bridging the manmade borders of different creeds.

The black-man-is-god concept can be seen as a psychological level, an extreme version of a very American *positive thinking,* destined to break the mental chains of inferiority by which the black man is said to be chained to the bottom ladder of society. The Nation urges the black man to stop whining over injustice past and present. Nothing good can be expected from the devil. The government of the United States is one of the most

A black Muslim interpretation of the statue of liberty.

powerful on earth and would have solved all its domestic problems long ago had it been genuinely interested. The United States is equated with Babylon and any demand for assimilation with the foul spirits in the city of evil at its brink of destruction is an insane suicidal policy. Aloof from the civil rights struggle for desegregation, the Nation taught separation from evil. Blacks were not Americans, but a *separate nation* with legitimate claims of self-determination in a territory of its own. In compensation for centuries of unpaid slave labour, the Nation demanded land, in America or Africa, and reparations in equipment and cash to get the new nation started. It adopted its own flag, which is red with a white star and crescent, and composed its own national anthem. Elijah Muhammad, and later Farrakhan, regard themselves as the head of a theocratic shadow cabinet, governing a rightfully independent nation state from its headquarters, 'the Black House', in Chicago. Organisationally, the Nation is modelled as a sovereign state administration, with departments for finance, education, health, defense, law, foreign relations and so on. Its disciplined members are clean-living, non-drinking, hard-working and law-abiding national soldiers, kept in shape by a strictly hierarchical and un-democratic chain of command. Farrakhan is elected by God and not the black citizens, and can according to the NOI Constitution appoint and discharge his Ministers and other officials at will. Their efforts to 'rebuild' an economic black national infrastructure have been remarkably successful. During the time of Elijah Muhammad, the Nation evolved into the most potent economic force in black America. They owned tens of thousands of acres of farm and grasslands, a modern transport fleet including trucks and a jet plane took care of distribution, and in the cities there were restaurants, supermarkets, real estate, bakeries, hotels, print shops, a bank and numerous other ventures. Due to legal suits in probate court and Imam Muhammad Warithuddin's sweeping privatisation of the Nation of Islam companies, the economic empire fell apart following the death of Messenger Muhammad, but has slowly been rebuilt during the present government.

Emphasising re-education as a key to national liberation, Muslim schools are now mushrooming throughout the country, but still fall short of meeting the national demand. The health ministry, presently headed by Minister Dr Alim Muhammad, not only runs programmes for better diet and exercise, but also operates a chain of AIDS clinics. The defense department is in charge of a black Muslim army which gained national attention when its soldiers started to intervene in down-trodden neighbour-hoods to clear the streets of drug dealers and prostitutes in the late 1980s. Later incorporated as Nation of Islam Security, the Islamic patrols today have contracts in at least five different states and are employed as guards at black housing projects. This could partly be seen as the Nation's first serious effort to expand its jurisdiction in black America. Its prison ministry has won great prestige for its outreach efforts, and is also responsible for what is held to be the most effective rehabilitation programme for criminals and drug addicts. Internationally, the Nation engages in trade and Farrakhan is today greeted as a head of state when he travels across Africa and Asia. Charges of having working relations with dictatorial governments counted as foes of the United States are brushed aside as interventions in the affairs of a sovereign state, and besides, who is the United States to criticise other nations for friendly relations with foreign dictatorships?

Long at the margins of black America, the Nation of Islam grew out of its sectarian position during the 1980s and gradually gained wider acceptance for its separatist message. For a long time, black America was largely caught up in the civil rights struggle and kept the dream of Martin Luther King, Jr. alive. A gradually diminishing gap in income, standard of

The Malcolm Shabazz Masjid (mosque) in Harlem, New York (photo: Kristina Gardell, 1987).

living and health and education seemed to confirm the vision of a multi-racial American nation as a realistic possibility. Affirmative action placed individual blacks in visible positions of power, and blacks made inroads into public affairs as elected representatives at county, city, state and federal levels. Reaganomics marked a dramatic reversal of this trend, and during the 1980s and early 1990s whites and blacks effectively moved apart, economically, socially and politically. The blacks in the United States are the only Western population whose life expectancy rate is *declining*. With 50 per cent of black children raised in poverty, a dramatic school dropout rate, high unemployment numbers, one third of black males either in prison or out on parole, and a crime rate that makes black inner cities war zones deadlier than the Vietnam War, Farrakhan is by many blacks considered more a realist than an extremist when he, paraphrasing the Kernel Commission, concludes that 'there already exist two nations in the United States. One black and one white. Separate and unequal'. Since 1995, the black-on-black crime rate has dropped dramatically. Besides all credit that might be given to the Clinton administration, the Muslim impact deserves recognition. Farrakhan's unique rapport with young blacks in concert with black Islamic rappers is a part of the picture. Touring the nation with a 'stop the killing' campaign, Farrakhan in 1992 succeeded in effecting a

432

truce between the notorious Los Angeles-based gang federations Bloods and Crips. Expanding the peace process, increasingly more gangs with a total membership of several hundred thousand signed up. The extent to which this effort will have a lasting effect remains to be seen. The Million Man March of 1995 encapsulated much of the same spirit as more than 1 million black men atoned for their failure to take responsibility for their own families and communities. Denouncing the path of self-destruction, they pledged to rebuild their neighbourhoods, renounce drugs and violence, become educated and take charge of their own future. This 'spirit of the Million Man March' should be considered when trying to explain the falling crime rates in black America.

Mainstream Islam in the United States

It should be emphasised that not all African–American Muslims adhere to the Nation of Islam or its black Islamic competitors, such as the Lost Found Nation of Islam led by Silis X Muhammad or the Ansaaru Allah Community led by Imam Isa. Although all estimate must be seen more as qualified guess work than rock solid statistics, it seems as if mainstream Islam has made an impact in the black community at least on a par with black Islam. Most scholars in fact claim that a huge majority of black Americans belong to more conventional Muslim congregations, although this development is fairly recent and reliable statistics are yet to be presented. Many of these African–American Muslims belong to mosques or Islamic networks with a predominantly black membership, such as Darul Islam, Al Fuqra or those who followed Imam Warithuddin Muhammad's reformation of the Nation, as was indicated above. Imam Muhammad is one of the leading Muslim theologians in the contemporary United States, whose message can be heard on local radio and television stations in most American states. Sharply criticising Farrakhan's path of black Islam, Imam Muhammad points out that the Black Muslims have gone from a position of being victims of racism to advocating racism themselves. True Islam, Muhammad argues, is a religion for all people and is therefore universal, not racial. Rejecting the merger of Islam and black nationalism as being in 'conflict with the open society and democratic order of an Islamic community', Imam Muhammad has tried to counter the anti-Muslim sentiments in American society by claiming its compatibility with basic American values. 'The Constitution of the United States is basically an Islamic document', Muhammad suggests. 'Its principles were presented to the world over 1,400 years ago by Prophet Muhammad (PBUH).' His efforts to expand the Judeo-Christian foundation of American society to include the latest partner in the Abrahamic triad was granted a gesture of recognition when Imam Muhammad became the first Muslim invited to offer morning prayers in the United States Senate in 1992. Imam

433

Dawa work in downtown New York (photo: Kristina Gardell, 1987).

Muhammad's instrumentality in spreading mainstream Sunni Islam in the African–American community has frequently been applauded by conventional Muslim leaders in the United States and abroad, especially by those involved in the Saudi led *dawa* (mission) machinery. In 1978, Imam Muhammad was chosen by a number of rich Persian Gulf states to be the sole consultant and trustee for the recommendation and distribution of their economic support to Muslim movements in the United States. A further sign of his rising international status came in 1986, when Imam Muhammad was elected to the prestigious Supreme Council of Masajid of the Muslim World League, with responsibility for the American mosques.

The large majority of Muslims in North America is comprised of immigrants and guest students derived from more than 60 different nations. Muslim immigration to the United States follows, like most other immigration, a wave-like pattern. The first wave commenced in 1860 with migration from what was then Greater Syria and lasted up to the outbreak of the First World War. There followed three other major waves: from the mid 1920s to the Second World War; from the early 1950s to mid 1960s; and from the 1970s to present. The latter wave has been the most significant due to a 1965 change in immigration policy that previously greatly restricted immigration for individuals of non-European descent. During the present wave, the number of Muslim immigrants has doubled in proportion to other categories of immigrants. In the previous waves, Muslims from Asia and Africa south of the Sahara were significantly under-represented, while Muslims from Eastern Europe were over-represented. During the latest wave, this trend has been reversed, with a significant increase in the number of Muslim immigrants from Asia and black Africa. A general feature of immigration is voluntary geographic concentration. If there is a choice, statistics show that immigrants tend to move into areas where they expect to find relatives, friends and other people from the same country, city, ethnicity and/or religious affiliation. This strategy facilitates establishment in the new country and has successfully been adopted by Muslim migrants to the United States. More than 30 per cent of the sum total of Muslims in the United States are concentrated in the three states of California, New York and Illinois. Iranians tend, for instance, to settle down in California where they comprise roughly one Muslim in ten. Muslims of East European origin favour New York, where they in 1980 made up for 40 per cent of the Muslim community, and Illinois, a state with a basically tripartite Muslim population consisting of African–Americans, East Europeans and West Asians/North Africans, divided into blocs of about equal size.

Major Mainstream Muslim Organisations

The early Muslim immigrants kept a low profile, religiously and politically. Their motives for leaving their homes in *dar al-Islam* to settle down in *dar al-kufr* were mostly pragmatic, based on uncertain conditions in their native countries, and they sought primarily individual fortunes in the United States. Religious ambitions before the Second World War were limited to discreet mosque constructions, with the first in Ross, a remote rural town in North Dakota. It should be noted that the first mosques were established on private initiatives by successful migrant families, such as the Diabs, the Igrams and the Khalids. Voluntary associations for mutual support and assistance had not yet been organised on religious grounds, but had an ethnic foundation. Thus the National Association of Arab–Americans was pan-Arabian and embraced Christian, Muslim and secular Arabs. A nationwide Islamic organising move, supported by religious communities rather than individual families, did not commence until after the end of World War II.

In 1952, the war veteran Abdullah Igram summoned a conference in Cedar Rapids, Iowa, with the intention of establishing a continental Muslim organisation. Some 400 delegates, representing local Muslim communities from the United States and Canada, gave birth to the International Muslim Society and elected Igram as its first president. Two years later, it was reorganised as the Federation of Islamic Associations of the United States and Canada (FIA) in an ambitious effort to include all North American Islamic communities, Shiites not excluded, and once again Abdullah Igram was elected as president. Although the activities of FIA were limited to organising meetings and conferences, it was a significant development that gave American Muslims a first semblance of belonging to a Western *umma*. The typical FIA leader was a second generation immigrant of West Asian parents. He was educated, had served in the military, had a successful professional career and was well-integrated in American society. A decade later, domestic and international developments made the time ripe for an Islamic organising move of higher profile, initiated by an increasing number of guest students with a more radical Islamic outlook.

In 1963, the Muslim Student Association was established by students from North Africa and Asia, who had been members or supporters of the Muslim Brotherhood (al-Ikhwan al-Muslimun) or the Pakistani-based Jamaat-i-Islami. Demanding radical transformation of society and government, the Muslim Brotherhood had mainly been forced underground in Syria and Egypt and would be further repressed in the years to come. The radical Islamic Jamaat-i-Islami had been outlawed by the Pakistani authorities and its founder, Abul Ala Mawdudi, had received his death sentence (later revoked). Following a modest start, the Muslim Student Association grew dramatically after the Arab–Israeli war of June 1967, and increased again after the October War of 1973, reflecting the general rise of Islamist sentiments and the dissatisfaction with the overtly pro-Israeli, anti-Muslim foreign policy of the United States government. In 1975, the members decided to employ a full-time secretariat and moved its headquarters to farmland owned by the Muslim Student Association (MSA) in Plainfield, Indiana. The MSA expanded in several directions. Gradually moving into new areas of activity, this association began to overshadow other Islamic organisations. It established Islamic teaching seminars, prison outreach ministries, publishing houses, newspapers, mosques, local community associations, propaganda arms and funds to support Muslim entrepreneurs. Many students who stayed in America after graduation continued their MSA activities through its professional leagues, like the American Muslim Social Scientist or the Islamic Medical Association. Later, the Muslim Student Association claimed 45,000 student members at 310 universities and had a roughly equal number of non-student members. It was obvious that the MSA had evolved into something larger than a student association and the need for reorganisation led to the establishment of the Islamic Society in North America in the early 1980s. The Islamic Society in North America is a federation of Muslim associations based on profession, local communities, country of origin, age, gender and specialisation (such as publishing, cooperatives or prison ministries). Among the various newspapers published are *Islamic Horizons, Al-Ittihad, American Journal of Islamic Studies* and *Muslim Scientist.*

Until the Iranian revolution and the subsequent war between Iraq and Iran, American Sunni and Shia Muslims generally co-existed in the same organisations. Four of the early Muslim Student Association presidents were Shiites, and so was the editor-in-chief of *Islamic Horizons*, Kaukab Siddiq. The war and the anti-Islamic fervour that Ayatollah Khomeini and the Islamist revolution unleashed in the United States, contributed to a split along Sunni–Shiite lines in the North American mainstream Muslim community. On various university campuses, Shiite student associations were established, and the International Islamic Society was founded in Virginia by long-time Shiite propagandist Yasin al-Jibouri. Financed by Saudi Arabia, the Muslim Student Association, the Islamic Society in North America and its affiliate, the Muslim Arab Youth Association, began distributing anti-Shiite literature. Shiites and Islamic pro-Khomeini revolutionaries countered by accusing these organisations for being corrupt puppets in the pocket of conservative and affluent Wahhabi oil princes. Siddiq accepted the post as editor of the Maryland-based Shiite paper *New Trend* which, together with the Canadian *Crescent International* and *Islamic Forum*, became a pro-Iranian voice, and Iran distributed free propaganda material through its office at the Algerian embassy and the Mostazafan Foundation in New York. Sunni strategists began legal preparations to ensure that Shiites would be unable to rule, should they win local *masajid* (*masjid*, mosque) elections, by statues stipulating that the Islamic Society in North America in such a case could assume control of the property. Outside the pro-Iranian Imamiyya Shiite community is the Nizari Ismailiyya, which grew from a few hundred to 25,000 in Canada and 5,000 in the United States when Idi Amin expelled all Asians from Uganda in 1972.

Muslim immigration and the black Islamic gospel of African–American independence have been the two major sources of Islamic presence in North America. There is, however, a third route represented by the Sufi connection with the New Age community. Sufism has, of course, also been a significant factor in the immigrant and black Muslim communities. A number of successful Sufi orders are found in the former, and in the latter, Sufism has informed the blackosophic black path to divinity and been manifest in separate organisations, such as the black racialist Order of the Sons of the Green Light. Besides these Sufi avenues, its presence can be noted by anyone who cares to browse through some of the many thousand bookstores that cater for the community of seekers in the New Age milieu. Instrumental in this history is the Sufi Order of the West, founded in 1910 by the Indian Sufi Hazrat Inayat Khan and revived in the 1960s by his son Vilayat and his early American disciple Sam (Sufi Ahmed Murad) Lewis. The latter felt his call as a 'teacher to the hippies' and attracted a large following in the flower power era, creating the immensely popular Dances of Universal Peace. Michael A. Köszegi argues that the Sufi Order of the West 'helped give both form and philosophy to the New Age movement' since its start in the 1960s and points out that leading New Age figures, such as G.I. Gurdieff and Oscar Ichazo had Sufi training. Among the many achievements of the Sufi Order of the West is the Omega Institute, a major vehicle for the New Age community in America and abroad. On its huge annual gatherings, Omega has attracted a great number of leading New Age propagandists and has turned into an outstanding forum for the exchange and development of 'movement' ideas.

Islam in Canada

Chattel slavery has no recorded history in Canada. Thus, we do not find any documented Muslims in Canada until 1871, when the Canadian census recorded thirteen Muslim residents. Prior to the Second World War, Muslim immigration was limited due to Canadian efforts to restrict immigration from Asia. The pre-war Muslim presence remained small, numbering not more than 3,000 residents in a Canadian *umma* dominated by Turks and Syrians/Lebanese. The first and only pre-war mosque was built by Lebanese Muslims in Edmonton, Alberta, in 1938. In the post-war period, Islam expanded due to a heavy influx of immigrants of various ethnic origins and the slow but steady spread of Black Islam. Estimations of Canadian Muslims varies, but could roughly be set at no more than 200,000, primarily living in metropolitan centres. Serving the community are some 200–300 mosques and Islamic associations, including Black Muslim, Ahmadiyya and Ismaili chapters. Local Canadian Muslim associations are in general affiliated with the above-mentioned Islamic confederations with headquarters in the United States, following a logic established by other mainstream American organisations, such as the labour movement. The one exception is the Nizari Ismailiyya, composed of 20,000 immigrants of Asian origin who were ousted from Uganda by then president Idi Amin in 1972.

Ambassadors of God in the Abode of Unbelievers

How, then, do American Muslims perceive their place and their role in the United States? Are they striving to assimilate? Are they trying to maintain a separate Islamic identity? Are they trying to create islands of peace in the house of war? Do they want to win America over to Islam? These questions may be tentatively answered if one avoids viewing the American Muslims as a monolithic entity in favour of identifying a number of distinct strategies of orientation.

The idea of the American society as a melting pot, into which immigrants of different ethnic and religious background from all over the world are assimilated or turned born-again Americans, has long been part of public ideology. In the light of reality, the theory can be severely questioned, and the controversy over what it means to be an American, and who should be included and who should be excluded as an alien, has characterized much of its history. The extent to which you can be a Muslim and an American is far from resolved, as was indicated in the introduction. Pakistani and Indian Muslims have found a niche in low-budget motel business, which has provoked white Christian motel owners to advertise their business as 'American owned and operated', thus rejecting that a United States citizenship makes an Asian Muslim an American. Research reports show that few Muslims chose the path of assimilation by playing down their Islamic identity, other than as an individual or temporary strategy. A great majority seem to favour the maintenance of Islamic norms and values in cases where these are perceived as conflicting with the norms harboured by the dominant culture.

At a speaking engagement during a United States tour, the internationally renowned Islamic theologian Sayyed Abdul Hasan Ali Nawdi reminded his Muslim audience that:

> For us Muslims, it is permitted to live only in a country where we can live with our distinctive qualities and observe our duties. If it is not possible in this environment or you feel you cannot carry out your religious obligations, it is not permissible for you to stay. It is your duty to see that you live here distinctly as Muslims. You should build your own society and ensure that your children remain Muslim after you.

Efforts to increase the possibilities for living as a Muslim in the United States have, with varying degrees of success, been made on different areas. The president of the Federation of Islamic Associations of the United States and Canada and war veteran Abdullah Igram in a successful plea made it permissible for Muslims enroled in the United States military to have the letter 'I' as a religious identification on their dog tags. Some American high schools have set aside facilities for students to observe *salat* (the Muslim prayer). Through successful legal battles, an increasing number of Muslim prison inmates have been entitled to a pork-free diet and to participate in Islamic activities, although few prisons allow attendance at the communal Friday service.

Politically, a number of Islamic strategies could be identified and correlated in relation to how the United States is perceived. A minority tendency seems to agree with Imam Warithuddin Muhammad, who see the

United States as 'blessed by Allah' to become 'the greatest country on the face of the earth'. For some, religion and politics should be separated and they see no contradiction in running for political office on a conventional party ticket while reducing their Islamic identity to a private matter. Most Islamic tendencies seem to harbour more critical attitudes and condemn the United States for placing man and Mammon above God. An overwhelming majority seem moreover greatly concerned with the 'anti-Muslim' and 'pro-Israeli' foreign policy of the United States governments.

The Islamist-oriented American groups seem to concentrate their activities on mobilising support for the cause fought for by their brethren in the various countries of origin. This has been of some concern for Israel, and in 1993 Israel urged the Federal Bureau of Investigation to take measures against Palestinian Americans involved with Hamas, claiming that several Hamas actions against Israel had been planned and directed from Virginia and California. It should perhaps be noted that Palestinians have accused Jewish–Americans of similar tactics.

Since the early 1980s, several Islamic lobby groups, such as the Muslim League of Voters and the All American Muslim Political Action Committee, have been established in concerted efforts to influence the decision-making process in United States foreign policy. Modelled on the successful pro-Israeli lobby, a handful of Islamic Political Action Committees (PACs) have organised think-tanks, sponsored candidates and arranged meetings with congress members. Explicitly Islamic candidates have run for offices at town, county or state level, some on the small Islamic Party ticket, although none to the best of the writer's knowledge have been even remotely successful. Any Islamic expectation of rapidly achieving an effective political mobilisation has been frustrated by the fundamental lack of unity that characterises the American Muslim community. Besides the obvious disagreement with Black Islam, the Islamic–American mainstream is torn apart by internal divisions in sharp contrast to the Islamic ideal of unity. Saudi-oriented, well-financed groups have clashed with both Ikhwan sympathisers and pro-Libyan groups. The Muslim Brothers not only fight the latter but also suffer from great internal divisions. In addition to the above-mentioned Sunni–Shia division, the Shia community is split into pro-Iranian revolutionaries and its foes. The Black Islamic world has its recurrent internal conflicts that occasionally have violent eruptions. A huge part of the Islamic community in the United States avoids participation in the arena of conventional politics. Spokespersons for Jamaat al-Tabligh, a numerically strong, mainly Indo-Pakistani and African–American, move-ment have sharply distanced themselves from any political involvement in North America, arguing that a system based on *kufr,* such as the American democracy, can never give rise to an Islamic state.

What then should a Muslim living in *dar al-kufr* do? He should, ideally, follow the example put forward by the Prophet Muhammad. When he realised that his God-given mission was frustrated by the unbelievers in power in Mecca, he moved to Medina and established an independent Islamic society. Muslims in the United States should thus perform *hijra* (migration) and build the foundation of a society in accord with God's plan for humanity. However, this imperative has no given interpretation and at least two ideal types could be contrasted, each leading to distinct strategies. The first method, termed 'the sectarian-hijra response' by John O. Voll, represents a separatist orientation, aiming to withdraw from the outer American society and establish an Islamic society within the United States. The Nation of Islam belongs to this category and represents its majority subdivision in its effort to establish a society within a society, wherever members might live. Another solution worked out on this basis is found in the several communal settlements that have been established. In 1987, followers of Imam Warithuddin Muhammad inaugurated its New Medina in rural Mississippi. Adherents of Imam Isa of the Ansaaru Allah Community have established a number of communal settlements, and the Atlanta-based Lost Found Nation of Islam, led by the Farrakhan critic Silis X Muhammad, has founded Project Exodus in Georgia with a similar purpose. Another, but multi-racial, all-Muslim communal township called Dar al-Islam is located outside Abiquiu, north of Santa Fe, in the New Mexican desert.

The other method is to identify the migration *to* the United States as the *hijra*, and thus intensify the *dawa* zeal in an effort to make the whole country the New Medina. The distinguished Arab–American Muslim scholar–activist Ismail R. al-Faruqi (1921–86) argues that it cannot be a coincidence that so many Muslims have migrated to the Western world. It must be by the design of God. Muslims should see themselves as 'ambassadors of Islam, with a mission to bring Islam to Western society'. Addressing Muslims living in the West, al-Faruqi suggested:

> This is our Medina, we have arrived, we are here. Now that you are in Medina, what is your task? [It is] the saving, the salvation of life, the realizations of the values of dignity, of purity, of chastity, all the nobility of which humans are capable.

As Voll points out, this vision is powerful and 'goes beyond the suggestions of traditional Muslim teachers who urge emigration from non-Muslim societies' if it proves difficult to live an Islamic way of life. It sets Islamisation of society as a goal without insisting that it should be accomplished immediately, and thus 'makes it possible for Muslims to have a sense of Islamic mission while participating in a non-Islamic social order'. It should perhaps be emphasised that al-Faruqi called for a Christian–Islamic dialogue, based on mutual respect and understanding, arguing that it should be possible to develop an Abrahamic ethic as the basis of moral society.

441

Literature

For an introduction to different aspects of Islam in the United States and Canada, see the excellent anthologies *The Muslims of America*, ed. Yvonne Y. Haddad (Oxford: Oxford University Press, 1991); *Muslim Communities in North America*, eds. Yvonne Y. Haddad and Jane Smith (Albany, NY: State University of New York Press, 1994); *The Muslim Community in North America*, eds. Earle H. Waugh, Baha Abu-Laban and Regula B. Qureshi (Edmonton: University of Albany Press, 1983); and *Islam in North America*, eds. Gordon J. Melton and Michael A. Koszegi (New York: Garland, 1992). Stephen E. Barboza's *American Jihad* (New York: Doubleday, 1994) is a brilliant compilation of interviews with American Muslims, immigrants, converts, Sufis and Black Muslims, including early disciples of Elijah Muhammad. An important study of Islam in Black America is *African American Islam* by Amirah McCloud (London: Routledge, 1995). For arguments of a pre-Columbian link with the Americas, see the anthology *African Presence in Early America,* ed. Ivan van Sertima (New Brunswick, NJ: Transaction Books, 1987). Albert J. Raboteau's awarded *Slave Religion* (Oxford: Oxford University Press, 1978) contains valuable information on Islam in the slave communities, as does Allan D. Austin's *African Muslims in Antebellum America* (New York: Garland, 1984).

Black Islam has begun to receive considerable scholarly attention. Two outstanding studies, C. Eric Lincoln's *The Black Muslims in America* (Trenton, NJ: African World Press, 1996) and E.U. Essien-Udom's *Black Nationalism* (Chicago: University of Chicago Press, 1962) present the Nation of Islam during the leadership of Elijah Muhammad. An eminent Elijah Muhammad biography is *An Original Man: The Life and Times of Elijah Muhammad* (New York: St Martin's Press, 1997), written by Claude Andrew Clegg III. Peter Goldman's *The Death and Life of Malcolm X* (Urbana, Il: University of Illinois Press, 1979) and Karl Evanzz's *The Judas Factor: The Plot to Kill Malcolm X* (New York: Thunder's Mouth Press, 1992) add valuable information concerning the Nation of Islam in that era. The Islamisation process initiated by Imam Warithuddin Muhammad is described by Clifton E. Marsh in *From Black Muslims to Muslims: The Transition from Separatism to Islam* (Metuchen, NJ: Scarecrow Press, 1984). For a comprehensive study of the Nation of Islam with a focus on the Second Resurrection during the leadership of Louis Farrakhan, see Mattias Gardell's *In the Name of Elijah Muhammad: Louis Farrakhan and the Nation of Islam* (Durham, NC: Duke University Press, 1996). The latter also includes some information on other Black Islamic tendencies. Arthur J. Magida sheds new light on Farrakhan's early life in his Farrakhan bibliography *Prophet of Rage* (New York: Basic Books, 1996).

Chapter Twenty

The Caribbean and Latin America

Muhammed Abdullah al-Ahari

For centuries Muslims have claimed that there were Arab and African Muslim explorers in the so-called New World long before Columbus. The discovery of a medieval Turkish map drawn in March 1513 by the cartographer Piri Muhyil-Din Reis has been put forward as one possible proof on numerous occasions since its initial discovery in October 1929 by Khalid Edhem Bey at the Topkapi Saray Library in Istanbul. Other explorers from Europe are said to have heard or read of Muslims finding strange, wonderful, distant lands across the Atlantic and felt that it was a shortcut to India. One such person was Vasco da Gama. He learned about the compass and the East Indies from Moorish navigators of the coast of Mozambique. There are rumours of other travellers using Muslims or their books as guides. The most famous is, of course, Christopher Columbus. During Columbus's first voyage, he had a Moor, Luis de Torres, as his navigator. Some writers have claimed that de Torres was a Jewish convert to Catholicism (as Columbus probably was). On his voyage, Columbus had a journal of a voyage to the New World written in the twelfth century. The narrative by al-Sharif al-Idrissi (1097–1155) was called *The Sea of Tears*. In it al-Idrissi discusses the voyage of eighty *muhajarin*, explorers from Lisbon, Portugal during the reign of al-Murabit Amir Yusuf ibn Tashufin. The narrative mentions visits to fourteen islands, half of which have been identified as belonging to either the Canary Islands or the Azores. However, the ones not traced could have been as far away as the Caribbean. An even earlier voyage, in 942, is mentioned by al-Masudi in his *Annals*.

Spanish Muslims and African Moors frequently were guides during the settling of the American southwest, the Caribbean and Latin America. Istafan the Arab, known in Spanish sources as Estevano, was guide to the Spanish settlers in Arizona in 1539. He was from Azamor, Morocco and had previously been to the Americas on Panfilo de Narvaez's ill-fated expedition to Florida in 1527. Istafan was a guide to a Franciscan friar, Marcos de Niza, and was invaluable in this capacity until he disappeared in an Indian attack in present-day Arizona or New Mexico. The influence of African Muslims prior to Columbus is harder to trace, but it is often claimed that Mandingos, Malis and other Muslims had settled in the New

World before Columbus. In fact, some Moorish Science Temple Muslims, who will be discussed below, claim descent from the Moorish settlers before Columbus and that the importation of slaves never existed and was a lie made to separate them from their land. The Muslims who came here left mostly a legacy of architecture and iron-work. All over Latin America traces of their craftsmanship still exist as do loan words from Arabic into Spanish. These artistic and linguistic traces of Muslim influence in America have been particularly documented by several Brazilian scholars.

The century before Columbus's voyages saw the conversion of all of Spain to Catholicism. Jews, Muslims and non-Catholic Christians were killed, exiled or forced to convert. When the exiled Muslims and Jews made it to the New World, the Catholic Church wanted to ensure that they would not set up Muslim colonies. Largely in vain, the Church issued proclamations against the importation of Muslim slaves and forbade any religion in their territories other than Catholicism. Still, there were numerous Muslim slaves imported and several Muslim insurrections in South America. In Latin America all who did not submit to Catholicism were killed, tortured or enslaved. The Inca, Aztec and Mayan empires all fell due to Spain's desire to import the inquisition to the New World.

Before the writer leaves this general introduction, brief mention of contact between North and South American Muslims during the time of slavery and afterwards is needed. During the War of 1812, around 1,000 southern slaves had been recruited by the British. Of these 240 ended up in the West Indies and became Muslims (some joined Trinidad's Free Mandingo Society). In the Muslim slaves' narratives in America we find that Muhammad Said (formerly of the 55th regiment during the Civil War) and Muhammad Baquaqua (a convert to Christianity and a minister) had both been slaves in Brazil. Furthermore, several dozen Muslims had been slaves in the Bahamas before arriving on the North American mainland. The most important of these are Salih Bilali and Bilali Muhammad of St Simon's Island and Sapelo Island, respectively. Bilali Muhammad was responsible for much of the Islamic influence upon the African–American languages of Gullah and Geechee. He also passed on a small thirteen-page text on prayer, fasting and beliefs loosely based on the tenth century Tunisian scholar Abi Zaid al-Qairawani's work *Al-Risalah*.

In the twentieth century we find several North American Islamic groups setting up centres in the Caribbean, Central America, Mexico and South America. The earliest of these is Noble Drew Ali's Moorish Science Temple. Drew Ali was born in 1886 in North Carolina as Timothy Drew to a share-cropping family. As a youth he became a circus magician and a Pullman porter. Sometime before the age of twenty-seven, according to Moorish American historiography, he travelled to the Middle East as a merchant seaman. During these travels he came upon the idea that Islam and reclaiming an Islamic identity/nationality was the only solution for the problems of the African–Americans, then only a few generations from slavery. He proposed a Moorish nationality and gave them a religious text called the *Holy Koran of the Moorish Science Temple* (based on Levi Dowling's *Aquarian Gospel* and the Rosicrucian text *Unto Thee I Grant*). In 1927 he travelled to Cuba and Mexico, where he set up branches of his Moorish Science Temple. He died on July 20, 1929 in mysterious circumstances possibly related to a power struggle within his organisation. His legacy includes his religious text, reclaiming nationality and establishing temples in many of the ghettoes across North America.

As shown in the chapter on North America by Mattias Gardell, the Nation of Islam was started in 1930 by Wali Farad Muhammad. When he vanished in late 1933 or early 1934, his student Elijah Muhammad took over the reins of leadership. They taught that the Black Man was 'god', descended from the Tribe of Shabazz, that the White Man was a grafted devil, and that the Black Man was the true inheritor of the earth. These teachings helped to take many individuals off drugs and out of prostitution and a way of life that was destroying family life in many inner cities. Elijah lead the organisation till his death in 1975. His students included his son and successor Warithuddin Muhammad, boxer Muhammad Ali, Malcolm X and Minister Louis Farrakhan. In 1977 Farrakhan would re-establish the Nation of Islam after a split with Imam Warithuddin Muhammad over the so-called Orthodox Sunni direction his American Muslim Mission was taking. As we shall see, Warithuddin Muhammad, Louis Farrakhan and Elijah Muhammad all established temples in the Caribbean, Central America and South America.

The Caribbean Islands

Most writers on eighteenth century Caribbean life neglect to mention the existence of Islam. Bryan Edwards and Richard Robert Madden were two exceptions. Edwards considered the Muslim to be a superior slave and tells us in his *The History, Civil and Commercial, of the British Colonies in the West Indies* (1794) book that, 'an old and faithful Mandingo servant . . . stands at my elbow while I relate this'. That Mandingo servant told Edwards about circumcision, memorising the Quran, prayer times, the *shahada* or creed, fasting and Friday prayers. Edwards also tells of another Mandingo servant who wrote Arabic exercises from the Quran but relates that this servant died shortly after being purchased before more could be learned about him. Madden is our main source for Islam in nineteenth century Jamaica. He was one of six special magistrates sent to the island in 1833 to ensure a smooth passage of former slaves to freedom. He stayed nine months and recorded his experiences in *Twelve Months' Residence in the West Indies* (1835). Like Edwards, he called all the Muslims Mandingos. In a letter to J.F. Savory at St Andrews, Jamaica he writes of a slave who wrote the Quran from memory, a self-trained doctor named Benjamin Cockrane, and half a dozen other Muslims he met. Madden recalls that when he mentioned the name of the Prophet Muhammad these so-called converts to Christianity all gave *salaams* (blessings) to him. In his narrative, Madden publishes letters sent between the Muslims he met. In one letter the young doctor Benjamin Cockrane writes that his African name was Anna Musa and that he had a warrior name, Gorah Condran. Cockrane mentioned that he was from the Carsoe nation and that its ruler was Demba Saga. That letter of November 1, 1834 was sent to another Muslim, Abu Bakr Sadiqa. In his reply, dated September 20, 1934, Abu Bakr Sadiqa writes that he was born in Timbuktu and raised in Jenne. Abu Bakr was captured in a fight with the Ashanti of Ghana and sold into slavery. This former slave was also a supposed convert to Christianity, but he writes that 'nothing shall fall on us except what He ordains; He is our Lord, and let all that believe in Him put their trust in Him'.

After the abolition of slavery, Muslims either converted to Christianity, went back to Africa or to other places in Latin America where there were Muslims, or hid the fact that they were Muslims. Until the last quarter of the present century, Islam was almost unknown in Jamaica outside the small indentured East Indian Muslim community. Today, most Muslims in Jamaica are of African descent but a fair number of Indians and Arabs have settled there. In 1981 the Islamic Council of Jamaica was founded. Today it is the umbrella organisation for this small Caribbean nation's eight mosques. In 1994 it was estimated by the Centre for Muslim Minorities Affairs in Saudi Arabia that there were 3,000 Muslims in Jamaica. They were, for the most part, found in Kingston, St Catherine, St Mary and Westmore.

The Muslims in Barbados number around 3,000. A third of these are East Indians and the rest are converts. They have four mosques and have contact with Muslims in Trinidad. An Islamic Centre was built in Christchurch with money from Trinidad and Saudi Arabia in 1981. There are two mosques in the capital. Besides the Saudi and Trinidadian influence, the Indian Jamaat al-Tabligh is extremely influential amongst the Muslims. In Barbados there are also some followers of the Nation of Islam. The number of Muslims in the Bahamas is over 1,000 of whom most are converts. The Nation of Islam and Warithuddin Muhammad both have a presence there. In the early 1990s the government of the Bahamas tried to ban Farrakhan from speaking to his supporters. The Muslims in the Bahamas are organised as the Jamaat-us-Islam. At one time in the 1970s a Spanish Sufi group, the Murabitun, had a centre ran by Abdul Haqq Bewley. They held a Maliki law conference there in the early 1980s. However, most Murabitun eventually left the Bahamas. There are between 500 and 1,000 Muslims, mostly converts, organised in Bermuda. Most are of African–Bermudian origin and congregate at an Islamic Centre in the capital. There are about 2,000 Muslims in the Virgin Islands. Most are of Arabic origin and they have a centre at Saint Croix. The Ansarullah, Islamic Party and the Nation of Islam have also made inroads there.

Before the revolution of 1959 there were more than 5,000 Muslims in Cuba. A large number of these were Chinese Muslims. The Moorish Science Temple also had a centre there, as in Mexico, but the one in Cuba has apparently been defunct for quite a while. It is estimated that more than 80 per cent of the Muslims emigrated after the revolution, but several small mosques still operate and *National Geographic* and *Aramco Magazine* have both had articles on the Muslims in Cuba.

About 2,000 Muslims existed in 1982 in the Netherlands Antilles. They established an Islamic association in 1964 and built a mosque in the capital. There are about seventy African and thirty East Indian Muslims in Grenada, and they have close contact with Trinidadian Muslims. A few hundred Muslims live on St Kitts. The 500 Muslim converts of Martinique were organised in 1982. The island of Dominica is a favoured site for students training to be doctors. The students of Indian and Arab origin have a Muslim organisation and the hundred or so other Muslims meet at each others' homes.

In the early 1980s Puerto Rico had a community of 3,000 Palestinian Muslims. Recently the number of Muslims has swelled due to the conversion of Puerto Ricans to such groups as the Ansarullah, the Nation of Islam and the Jamaat al-Tabligh. The Palestinians are organised into an Arab Social Club and an elder acts as *imam* for the community.

Trinidad and Tobago

Today most Africans live on the island of Tobago and most East Indians and Javanese on the island of Trinidad. The East Indian Muslims have segregated themselves from their African co-religionists. This was not always the case. Indians were indentured servants and the African Muslims were primarily free due to the efforts of the Free Mandingo Society. In fact, in the 1830s the chief *imam* of Trinidad was Jonas Bath, a Susu by birth. The Muslims in Trinidad established schools at Port of Spain and an organisation of free Mandingos led by Yunus Muhammad Bath. One of his descendants, Dr Patricia Bath, recently formed the Jonas Muhammad Bath Foundation in Los Angeles. A number of Africans that fought Napoleon in the British West Indian Regiment also joined Bath's organisation. Other soldiers settled in the south of Trinidad and in Manzanilla, on land given them as reward for their service to the crown. The main focus of Bath's organisation was to free Muslim slaves. The members even petitioned King William IV to that effect. The petition explained that Muslims saved their earnings and did not waste money on intoxicants and gambling. It was sent three times but refused each time it was received. This forced the Muslim slaves to settle in Trinidad after being freed. One former leader of the Free Mandingo Society, Muhammad Sesei (1788–838), did eventually return together with his wife to his native village Niyani-Maru on the Gambia River 100 miles from the Atlantic coast.

In 1814 a proposal for the importation of workers from India to Trinidad was put forward by William Burnley. He wanted men with habits and culture who could stand on their own, and since importation of new slaves from Africa was a closed door, he turned his eyes to India. Between 1838 and 1924 nearly half a million Indians immigrated to Trinidad, Guyana, Jamaica, Guadeloupe, Surinam, the Virgin Islands and other locations. The indentured servant could not lay down the terms of the contract upon which his immigration to the Caribbean from India depended. The controlling party in this venture was the British Government through the Colonial Office in India. Eventually, by 1840, the terms were as follows: work for five years as a day servant, one shilling per day wages, free housing and medical care, food free for first three months and then a third of daily pay per day, and after five years the indentured servant could resign or get free passage back to India. Among these Indian immigrants, most were Hindus but one in six was Muslim. The Indian Muslims came primarily from the lower and illiterate classes in India. They were forced to co-exist with the Hindu migrant workers in the New world. The Hindus called them 'Madingas' as an ethnic slur to show that they had more in common with their African co-religionists than with their fellow Indians who were Hindus. This was also true in Guyana where the Hindus called Indian Muslims 'Fulas' after the Fula people of West Africa.

Trinidad and Tobago consists of several islands. The largest being Trinidad and Tobago. The smaller of these main islands, Tobago, has always been the more African of this nation of Trinidad and Tobago. Most Indians and Javanese settled in Trinidad. There are few Muslims on Tobago. Less than 200 are estimated to live there. These islands are only seven miles from Venezuela and have close commercial ties with South America. Althogether there are approximately 115,000 Muslims in Trinidad and Tobago out of an overall population of 1.1 million. Most are of Indian origin. Muslims from other ethnic origins are also found in Trinidad. At least 500 Chinese Muslims are there and another 4,000 Chinese Muslims are spread between Mexico, Cuba, Panama and Ecuador. These Chinese Muslims are not well organised and are primarily service-oriented business people.

In 1985 the Muslims in Trinidad and Tobago had seventy mosques with Quranic schools. They are well-organised and some hold cabinet posts and are members of parliament. The Muslims from India were traditional Hanafi Muslims, but early in this century the Ahmadiyya movement was able to gain control of some of their centres. In 1935 the Anjuman Sunnatul Jamaat Association was founded to combat this new form of Islam. A similar organisation called the United Sadr Islamic Anjuman was organised

The Jinnah Memorial mosque in St Joseph, Trinidad (photo: Justin Ben-Adam, 1997).

in Guyana the following year. The government of Trinidad and Tobago is controlled by Africans, but the Indians have frequently sided with them in order to have a share of power. A Muslim, Dr Wahid Ali, has been president of the senate, and Muslims such as Kamaluddin Muhammad have held cabinet posts in the past. Since 1976, the American leader Warithuddin Muhammad has had an *imam* in Trinidad. The first was Sunni Ahmad. Warithuddin Muhammad also has mosques in Belize, Jamaica, Bahamas and Barbados. The adherents of Deen Muhammad number around 300 in their centre at Port of Spain, Trinidad.

Since most Muslims are of the Hanafi school and of Indian origin, some details about their organisation should be presented. The Islamic Missionaries Guild of South America and the Caribbean, founded in

1960 by Maulana Fazlur Rahman Ansari, has branches in all English-speaking Caribbean areas. They built a mosque in the mid 1980s at Kelly Village Caroni. The other areas where they have centres are Guyana, Surinam, Venezuela, Barbados, Jamaica, Saint Vincent, Dominica, US Virgin Islands and Brazil. Every year they hold a regional conference with a special theme. The Guild publishes *The Torch of Islam* (formerly *The Islamic Herald*) and has published several works by Abul Ala Mawdudi and other Indian Muslim writers. They have built a public Islamic Library, helped Muslims to perform the *hajj*, the pilgrimage to Mecca, and have sent students to study abroad in India, Pakistan, Egypt and Saudi Arabia. They also have a half-hour radio programme called the 'Voice of Islam', which goes on air every Friday night. The Muslims of Trinidad have to contend with the influence of Saudi Arabian-salaried *dawa* (missionary) workers from the University of Medina. The Saudi workers are connected to the Muslim Missionary Guild.

Tackweyatul Islamic Association (TIA), founded in 1927, was the first Islamic organisation in Trinidad. Today it is largely inactive but runs five secular schools with a total of 1,700 students. Like all other denominational schools, the government pays teachers' salaries and funds 75 per cent of other expenses. The principal in 1985 was the Al-Azhar trained Trinidadian Shaykh Muhammad Shakir. Islamic instruction is only for one hour a week at these schools. They control four mosques: Bamboo Settlement Mosque at Valsyn, Charlie Village Mosque, Freeport Mosque and Lengua Princetown Mosque. They have around 2,000 members and like to celebrate traditional holidays such as the birth of the Prophet Muhammad (*mawlid*), Islamic holidays and the fortieth day of remembrance after the death of a relative.

More than 80 per cent of Trinidadian Muslims belong to the Anjuman Sunnatul Jamaat Association of Trinidad and Tobago (ASJA), which was founded in the 1930s. It now controls fifty-three mosques, seven primary schools and two secondary schools. The schools are all government-supported. The members of the ASJA are for the most part traditional Hanafi Muslims, although Wahhabis have sought to influence their organisation. The Trinidad Muslim League, founded in 1947 by Ameer Ali, was one such Wahhabi-inspired organisation that grew from the ASJA. It runs three schools with around 1,000 students of whom 65 per cent are Muslim. Originally this organisation also had a number of Ahmadiyya followers as board members. However, in 1977 all of them were purged from the organisation in order to make it acceptable to the larger Muslim *umma* (community of Muslims).

The Islamic Trust, a charity founded in 1975, runs an Islamic bookstore, publishes a newspaper called *The Muslim Standard*, and established the first Muslim Credit Union in Trinidad. Members meet regularly for Islamic study circles. The Islamic Funeral Services Trust, registered in 1984, provides inexpensive funeral services for Muslims. They receive funds from most of the Muslim organisations in Trinidad. Its yearly budget in 1985 was $100,000. The Abdul Aziz Trust was established in 1978 by the son of Abdul Aziz Kudrat (d. 1952). They run free medical clinics at Dow Village, California and Samson Village, Clarkson. They also have a monthly periodical. Jamaat al-Tabligh is an Indian immigrant group that seeks to bring Islam to back-sliding Muslims. The present leader in Trinidad is Mufti Shabil. They have close contact with members of their group all around the world. An estimated 500 Muslims belong to this group.

Jamaat al-Muslimeen was founded in 1979 by former members of the Islamic Party of North America, Dar-ul-Islam, and the Ansarullah. The first elected leader was Yasin Abu Bakr, an African Trinidadian who went to college in Canada. The Jamaat al-Muslimeen has a mosque at Macurapo, a school with all grades (primary and secondary) and a residence for their *imam*. The schools have an Islamic curriculum, are not government funded and have students who do well on government school exit exams. Since 1982 the members of the Jamaat al-Muslimeen have published a newspaper called *Al-Nur*, but it has no regular publishing schedule. In 1983 they were accused of an attempted government coup, but no member of the Jamaat was formally charged. They have perhaps 300 members. A splinter group was started in 1982 by a member who felt it un-Islamic to participate in politics. That group, with fewer than fifty members was called Jamaat al-Muminin. The Saudis have given them funds to build a mosque in Levantine and to publish a newspaper called *The Voice*. Moreover, international organisations such as the Muslim World League, Rabitat al-Alami al-Islami, are influential in Trinidad. In 1977 it held a Muslim minorities conference and in 1980 directed an *imam* training course for Caribbean Muslims. As stated above, foreign Muslim organisations and leaders from North America, such as the Islamic Party, Dar-ul-Islam, Ansarullah, Warithuddin Muhammad and the Nation of Islam have been active *dawa* participants. However, Saudi Arabia has surpassed all organisations in its spending to spread its version of Islam.

One great boon for Muslims is that the government supports Muslim schools, holidays and personal laws. Since the early 1980s it has passed laws to make it easier to have Islamic schools, banks and other organisations in Trinidad. One such measure was to allow a tax-deductible $2,500 investment in Muslim Credit Unions. It appears that Islam will continue to grow and spread in Trinidad, but it may not spread to the Africans until the Indian Muslims accept converts from among them as equals. A strong reason to believe the likelihood of this assumption occurred in 1983 and 1990, when the African–American and African–Trinidadian Muslims took over the parliament building and staged unsuccessful coups. The coups were attempts on their part to establish a Muslim brotherhood, equality and an Islamic state. The leaders of these coups were former members of the Dar-ul-Islam, Islamic Party, Ansarallah and other non-Trinidadian groups. Some of the coup participants are still (1998) in prison.

Central America

Perhaps 1,000 Muslims live in Belize, the majority of whom are of African origin. This century some Muslim groups from the United States (mainly the Nation of Islam and the Ansarullah) established centres. The first Nation of Islam leader in Belize was Imam Nuri Muhammad. The Nation had earlier introduced the message of Elijah Muhammad to Jamaica, Bermuda, Trinidad and Tobago, Barbados, Nassau and other Caribbean islands. After the death of Elijah Muhammad, most of these new Muslims followed Warithuddin Muhammad's lead, but Farrakhan has rebuilt much of the pioneering work done to spread the message of the Nation of Islam. The Islamic Party of North America also established sites in Guyana, Belize, Grenada, the Dominican Republic and Surinam. The sites established by the Islamic Party collapsed after the death of one of the founders, Yusuf Muzaffar Hamid, from leukemia in 1992. Besides the Muslims of African origin and the followers of Louis Farrakhan and Warithuddin Muhammad, there are some 500 Muslims in Belize divided between the Arab and Indian immigrants.

Islam first arrived in 1552 in Panama when a group of 400–500 escaped slaves lead by a Muslim named Bayano settled there. He was arrested by the then governor of the Spanish territory Ursua. Bayano and forty of his men were killed by poisoning at the hands of Ursua. Islam virtually faded from Panama until migrant workers came from the Indian subcontinent in the nineteenth century. There are a number of manuscripts, which date from the time of slavery, written in Arabic. At the end of the nineteenth century, a number of Bangladeshis arrived in Panama. However, there was never a sufficiently large number of Muslims to organise until 1930 when Indian Muslims founded the Islamic Mission. One of the earliest leaders of this group was a Lebanese merchant in Colon named Muhammad Majdob. Abdul Jabbar Babu and his brother Ali Akbar lead the Islamic Mission group. Their numbers rarely exceeded twenty to twenty-five individuals. In 1967 they changed their name to the Indo–Pakistani Islamic Association and to the Panama Islamic Association in 1974. This organisation has an Islamic Centre, cemetery and school in Panama City. Recently Islam has begun to spread more widely in Panama. Much of the growth has been among African–Panamanians. In 1982 there were 1,000 Muslims in Panama; 400 were Palestinian, 200 Panamanians and 400 were of Indian origin. Since then, Warithuddin Muhammad, Farrakhan and the Saudis have all secured some influence there, and today there are almost 4,000 Muslims in Panama. The earliest Nation of Islam missionaries were Abdul

Wahab Johnson, Abdul Kabir Abdul Malik Reid and Suleyman Johnson. They established centres in Panama City and Colon. After the death of Elijah Muhammad, this group eventually disintegrated and faded from existence. However, their work was continued by followers of Warithuddin Muhammad and Farrakhan.

Among the Muslim communities of Latin America, it was only in Panama, Cuba, Venezuela and Brazil where Middle Eastern and Arab Muslim immigrants showed any great influence. Most of them became totally absorbed in business and had little to do with religion. In Panama, Venezuela and many South American countries, the central mosque is Saudi sponsored. In several areas the first mosques were built by the Ahmadiyya. This is especially true in Central America. In fact, the first mosque in Panama was built by the Ahmadiyya in 1930. Other than in Belize and Panama, there is little Islamic activity in Central America. A small number of Muslims exist among the Arab businessmen in the Dominican Republic and in El Salvador. Guatemala has a few 100 recently immigrated Palestinian businessmen, while Honduras has around hundred Arab Muslims. Nicaragua has 150 temporary resident Arab Muslims with no organisation and Costa Rica has a 100 recent immigrant Muslims among its 2,000 Arabs and Asians. There is an Islamic Centre in San Jose, Costa Rica.

The number of Muslims in Mexico is rapidly growing. There were several thousand Iranians shortly after the Iranian revolution and several hundred connected with foreign diplomats. The Moorish Science Temple and the Nation of Islam have centres there. It is estimated that there are at least 10,000 Muslims in Mexico including converts and immigrants. Islamic Centres are found in Mexico City and some of the larger northern cities. There is no national organisation and most of the *dawa* work is carried out by Mexican–American converts to Islam.

Venezuela, Guyana and Surinam

In 1983 there were 50,000 Muslims in Venezuela, of whom 45,000 were of Lebanese, Syrian and Palestinian origin. Around 20,000 now live in Caracas. Most are small retailers but some are professionals. The year 1968 saw the establishment of an organisation named the Committee for the Formation of Mosques in Venezuela. It established an Islamic Centre in the same year with a mosque in Alparaiso (a suburb of Caracas). The members have drawn up plans for an Islamic Centre and a school. In 1970 they built their first mosque in Caracas, and in 1972 a school was being run for sixty-four students.

According to Internet information, Muslims in Venezuela today remain a small unorganised community and are heavily influenced by an influx of funds from Gulf State nations. At present there is a battle between Wahhabi influence and traditional Sunni- and Sufi-oriented Islam. A large mosque in Caracas built by the Saudis is almost always empty, while small Sufi meetings in neighbourhood homes are always crowded. In addition to these problems, the Arabs have not been united in the past and have often grouped themselves along nationalist lines.

Guyana is a former British colony that was granted independence on May 26, 1966. The official language is English, but 55 per cent of the population is of Indian and 33 per cent of African origin. The first Muslims were of African origin. The African-origin Muslims either converted to Christianity or migrated to Africa, and by the 1880s they were almost non-existent in Guyana. However, Indian Muslims immigrated after 1835 as indentured servants. Until 1965, Muslims of both Indian and African origin were forbidden by law to practice the rites of Islam (including Islamic marriage). After the end of British rule, both Hinduism and Islam became state-recognised religions by Guyana's constitution.

Between 1835 and 1917 about 240,000 East Indians came to Guyana. Among these Indian indentured servants were some 40,000 Muslims. The Indian Muslims in Guyana organised in 1865 and built mud and thatch mosques with associated schools for rudimentary education in Urdu, Islam and Arabic. Most of the Muslims were not trained in Muslim schools in India but did the best they could to pass on their traditions. In 1935 the United Sadr Islamic Anjuman (USIA) was founded in order to unite Guyanese Muslims against the threat of being taken over by the Ahmadiyya. The USIA split in 1972 into two groups, one identifying itself with the governmental party and one with the opposition. The Muslims are divided between those who feel they need to side with Hindus, those who side with Africans and those who wish to remain neutral. Efforts at forming an Islamic political party have failed. Since then an umbrella group, the General Congress of Islamic Brotherhood, established 1973, has come into existence. The USIA groups now have 120 local organisations.

In 1982, there were 130,000 Muslims in Guyana (15 per cent of the population). Over 90 per cent of these were of Indian origin. Muslims in Guyana have more than 130 Islamic centres, the ability to apply Muslim personal laws and a secular Muslim Trust College in Georgetown. Africans control Guyanese politics, but Indians struggle to have a share of the power. Since 1964 the African-dominated People's National Congress Party has been in control. In 1978, the Muslims held four ministerial posts and ten seats in the National Assembly. The Muslims in Guyana struggle to retain their Muslim identity, although they have little contact with the larger Muslim world.

The Muslims in Surinam resented being slaves and fought against the Dutch on numerous occasions. The most successful slave revolt was led by Arabi (born in Senegal) and Zam-Zam. In 1761, the latter forced the Dutch to sign a peace treaty with his co-religionists. The area they controlled is still ruled by their descendants. East Indians were imported as indentured servants to Trinidad. They proved so valuable there that they, as of 1873, began to be brought to Surinam. By 1916, some 24,000 East Indians had been imported and among them were some 6,000 Muslims. The Surinamese Indians follow the Hanafi law school and have the *khutba* (Friday sermon) in the Urdu language. About a third of the Indians follow the Ahmadiyya, a fact which has caused a split in the community.

A group of Indonesians from Java began to arrive in 1890, and by 1907 they numbered 33,000. The 50,000 Javanese there today remain aloof from Muslim affairs in Surinam, the Caribbean and the rest of Latin America. Since the 1940s, the Javanese segregated themselves from the Indians and many returned to Indonesia after its independence or obtained dual citizenship. The Javanese mosques are distinct from other centres in Surinam in that they face west for prayers (as in Java) and are Shafii instead of Hanafi. Many writers on Javanese Islam point to its eclectic nature and its use of pre-Islamic Javanese native religious rites such as magic and spirit worship. Most of the Javanese who came as workers to Surinam stayed and did not take the return provision of their contract. About 7,000 of the Javanese live in Paramaribo where they are employed in commerce, industry or as domestic servants. However, the close kinship lines of traditional Javanese society remain in Surinam so that even if the people in general are poor, no member of the Javanese community there can be found to be hungry or homeless.

In all there are some seventy mosques in Surinam. Until 1978, the Ahmadiyya held control in many centres and the national Muslim organisation, Surinamese Islamic Organisation (established 1929), was dominated by them. The Muslims broke away from this organisation in 1978 and founded the non-Ahmadiyya-controlled Surinam Islamic Association. There are three Dutch translations of the Quran used in Surinam, two Ahmadiyya ones and one by Professor J.M. Krammer. The Muslims in Surinam stand on the verge of possibly establishing the only Muslim majority country in the Western hemisphere. In 1982 they were 150,000 in number and 35 per cent of the country's population. The Muslims are 33 per cent Indian, 55 per cent Javanese, with the remainder of African and other origins. Despite their diversity, they have a nationwide umbrella organisation, the Surinam Islamic Council.

Muslims in Surinam have been able to follow Islamic personal laws for themselves and establish more than fifty Islamic centres. Some of them perform the *hajj* every year and about twenty full-time Muslim schools exist. *Id al-fitr* (the feast of breaking the fast of Ramadan) is a national holiday, and in 1973 Muslims held two cabinet seats (out of thirteen) and eight legislative seats (out of thirty-nine). Politically, most Indian Muslims belong to the opposition party, Vereenigde Herormings Partij. Recently, one of the major political parties in Surinam has been the Moslim Partij. Since attempts at *coups d'état* in February and August of 1980, the implicit discrimination against Muslims has increased and an estimated 30 per cent of the Indian Muslims have emigrated to the Netherlands. Likewise with the Javanese, a large number of them emigrated since the coups of the early 1980s.

Brazil

Most of the early Muslims in Brazil were of African origin. Today the majority are of Middle Eastern background. The area where the early Muslims were most numerous was the state of Bahia. In the sixteenth century African slaves formed an independent state in Northern Brazil called Palmares. Little has been written about this slave empire that lasted almost a century. Researchers have assumed that it was an African 'pagan' empire, but more un-biased researchers such as Clyde Ahmad Winters have pointed to a more likely Muslim power-base for the Brazilian–African Palmares Republic. Most of the literate slaves in Brazil were Muslims (primarily Yoruba and Hausa).

The Brazilian authorities called the Muslims Malis or Males (inhabitants of Mali). The Muslims in Brazil had secret schools and often had trained *imams*. They called God Allah or Olurum-ulua. Lessons were taught to Muslims (*alufos*) by the teacher (*lessano*) and assistant (*ladano*). The beliefs of the Muslims in Brazil were those of traditional West African Muslims of the Maliki school of law. They used amulets containing passages from the Quran and believed in *baraka* (blessings) that were contained in that Book of God. The most vocal of the eighteenth and nineteenth century Brazilian Muslims were the Yorubas. It was these Yorubas who kept Islam alive until the forced assimilation of the late nineteenth and early twentieth centuries after slavery and segregation ended in Brazil. Throughout much of South America the Yoruba-speaking Muslims were known as 'Hausas'. In Brazil, these 'Hausas' were often the leaders amongst slaves, and the most feared by the slave owners. Because Islam requires basic literacy in its active practice, a fairly large number of the 'Hausas' were literate. This gave them a unique edge in a society where even many of the slave owners were unable to read or write. The slave owners were very suspicious of the Muslims and often treated them harshly, in many cases outlawing the practice of the Islamic faith in order to punish the Muslims.

Their constant oppression coupled with their often educated minds made the Muslims very likely to participate in subversive activities. This combination proved true in Bahia, a section of Brazil heavily populated by Yorubas. In 1835, a slave rebellion took place in the city of Salvador (a city in Bahia) that was the biggest of its kind in the Americas. Despite the fact that the Yoruba Muslims contributed great numbers and provided much of the planning for the uprising, it is important to note that many non-Muslims, and non-Yorubas for that matter, participated in the rebellion. Although others did take part, the role of Muslims should not be overlooked. They were central in the planning phase. During slavery the masters took many measures to keep the slaves separated. However, much of the planning was done without arousing the suspicion of the owners. It remained secret largely because the meetings were held under the auspices of religion. In this manner the planning was completed. The Muslims, with their superior education, were able to lead the preparations and devise a sound plan.

The Islamic spirit was crucial in the uprising. Many of the captured slaves who had participated in it were found to possess amulets or talismans filled with Quranic verses. They believed that the spirit of Allah would protect them and lead them to success. Clearly the Yorubas, who formed a majority among the Brazilian Muslims, played an important role in the rebellion of 1835. After the *jihad* ('holy war') of that year, numerous Arabic texts were found on the bodies of the Muslim combatants. The Portuguese authorities in Brazil considered them to be plans for *jihad*. However, when translated, they proved to be one of the following: prayers, verses from the Quran, Arabic alphabetic exercises or amulets. The most popular portions from the Quran were 12:64, chapters 109–14 and various short passages. These proved a love of God and his Prophet and a belief in their protection rather than a plan for *jihad*.

After the abolition of slavery, the number of Muslims in Brazil of African origin diminished dramatically. Many of them returned to Africa. Other factors which led to a decline in the number of Muslims were public education, inter-marriage and desegregation. A further factor in the declining number of Muslims was the appearance of the Ahmadiyya in 1924, which had a divisive effect. For such reasons, immigrant Muslims today form the largest sector of the Muslims of Brazil. Around 1890, Muslims from Syria, Lebanon and Palestine began to arrive. Most of them settled in Rio de Janeiro and São Paulo. Some decided to use their pen to aid the cause of Arabs and Islam. These writers included Fawzi Ma'luf (d. 1930) and Illyas Farhat (d. 1893). It was estimated that in 1908 there were 100,000 Muslims of African origin in Brazil, most were centred in Bahia. As late as the 1940s the Brazilian police would often harass and arrest the Muslims when they gathered. Consequently, the number of Muslims was probably underestimated.

Today, there are approximately 500,000 Muslims in Brazil. The majority are of Lebanese origin, with a large number of Syrians and Palestinians also. About half of the Muslims live in the state of São Paulo. A Syrian Muslim runs a television station in Manaus, Amazonia, but there is no local Muslim newspaper. The first non-African mosque was built in São Paulo in 1950. In 1985, there were fifteen mosques in Brazil with plans for more. Several Islamic organisations have been established to work between these mosques. The Brasilia Islamic Centre was started in 1977 and the Federation of Muslim Associations in 1979.

Argentina

The first Muslims to set foot in what would later become Argentina were the so-called Moriscos – the forcibly baptised Christian Moors – expelled from Spain in the sixteenth century. These early immigrants had little lasting impact, but numerous Argentinian writers (especially those who represent the Gaucho tradition) have an affinity for Islamic subjects. Domingo Sarmiento, a nineteenth century author, even claimed descent from Turk Ali Kaka Ben Al-Bazin in eastern Spain. His most famous works are *Recuerdos de Provincia* and *Facundo*. The Egyptian Sayf al-Din Rahhal was a fine Arab poet who wrote elegant Spanish prose. Many see him as the poet laureate of Argentina. Of course, there were also much earlier Spanish writers who used Islamic themes, such as Cervantes in his *Don Quixote*.

The Muslims in Argentina were able to establish a lasting presence with immigration from Greater Syria between 1880 and 1955. Most of the Syrians were Christian, but Syrians still make up over half of the Muslims in Argentina. By 1982, 300,000 Muslims of Syrian origin lived in Argentina. These and other Muslims numbering 100,000 formed 1.5 per cent of the country's population at that time. Around 80 per cent of the 400,000 Muslims were Sunnis, 10–12 per cent were Lebanese Shias and the rest were mainly Druse. Very few of the immigrants returned to Syria and, as a result, the Muslim population of Argentina is stable and growing. The vast majority of the Muslims are now second or third generation Arab–Argentinians and have heavily intermarried among Christian Argentinians.

About half the country's Muslims live around Buenos Aires. The majority of the others live in the northern provinces. Muslims in Argentina suffer the humiliation of having to have Christian names, although they are allowed freedom of congregation and religion by the constitution. In addition, Islamic marriages are not recognised by the government and, as a result, Muslims are forced to marry in Catholic churches or in civil ceremonies. Despite laws such as this that have the practical aim of effacing Islam in Argentina, many military and political leaders have come from the Muslim ranks. In fact, a coup attempt was lead in the early 1980s by a general of Druse ancestry. The most important Muslim military and political leader of Arab ancestry was Carlos Saul Menem, president of Argentina from 1989, who converted from Islam to Catholicism during his imprisonment in the late 1970s.

Outside Buenos Aires, Arabic is practically a dead language among the younger generation and there is little contact with the larger Muslim world. The Syrian Muslims are successful economically, however, since most are engaged in commerce of some sort. Most Muslims of Syrian origin belong to Arabic social clubs organised along Syrian village origins of both Christian and Muslim immigrants. In Buenos Aires, the first Islamic centre was established in 1918. In 1968 it left its rented space for a permanent location. Since then the centre has been directed by an Al-Azhar-trained *imam*. In 1960 another Islamic organisation, called the Arab Argentinian Islamic Association, was established by Argentinian Muslims. Muslims in Buenos Aires have an Islamic school for 250 students, and they also have a cemetery. Centres were established in Mendoza in 1926, Cordoba in 1929 and later in Rosario and Tucuman. The centre in Cordoba has had an Iraqi-trained *imam* since 1973. Tucuman saw the organisation of their local Arab Club into an Islamic centre by the Muslim World League in 1974 when a Saudi-trained *imam* was sent there. However, most Arab Muslim centres outside Buenos Aires are more like social clubs than true Islamic centres because they have no regularly trained *imams*. Some Argentinian Christians have converted to Islam, including one nun from New York, but Islam in Argentina remains Arab-inspired, and the lack of Spanish language materials for converts and Arabs who were born and raised in Argentina does not help to spread Islam.

Other South American countries

The Muslims in Columbia are mostly Arabs. The Christian Arabs began to organise shortly after Columbian independence. At the beginning of the nineteenth century, Syrians arrived and after 1947 Palestinians came. An Islamic Club was organised by the Palestinians in Bogota in 1964. In 1971 there were about 10,000 Muslims in Columbia, and of these some 2,000 were living in Bogota. A decade later centres were located in rented apartments in Bogota, Maco and Bona Vintura. In 1948 the first Lebanese family came to Bolivia. The first member of that family to settle in Bolivia was Ahmed Sabagh. In 1971, 100 Muslims lived in Bolivia, of whom some fifty lived in the capital. The Muslims are unorganised and hold no communal festival or Friday prayers. There are about 20,000 Arabs in Ecuador, and it is estimated that around 100 are Muslim. There are approximately 5,000 Arabs in Paraguay and at best 1,000 of them are of Muslim origin. They are unorganised and have no Islamic centres or organisations. A small population of Muslims, of Syrian and Palestinian origin, also exist in Uruguay.

The 500 Muslims of Peru are not organised religiously and have no schools for their children but carry a great deal of political clout. Most are wealthy Arab businessmen who live in the capital Lima. They were organised in 1924 by the Palestinian importers Talib Ahmed Humaida and Mutih Abdullah Humaida into an Arab Social Club. The influence of Islam is also literary, like the literature of Argentina and Colombia. Thus, several writers in Peru have also touched on Muslim themes. In the mid 1980s, a convert to Islam from Peru, Muhammad Ali Louis Castro, went to study at the Islamic University of Medina in Saudi Arabia.

The Muslims in Chile have had a considerable influence on the literature, music and art there. In 1921 the Chilean writer Pedro Prado wrote a series of poems patterned after Omar Khayyam under the pen-name Karez-I-Roshan. These poems were extremely popular and praised by the likes of Bernard Shaw and Khalil Gibran. Another famous writer was Benedicto Shawqi. Today around 2,000 Muslims live in Chile. They are divided between Syrian, Lebanese, Palestinian and Bosnian origin. Palestinians have a weekly radio programme. Christian Arabs run orphanages and hospitals. They are actively trying to convert the Muslims of Chile to Christianity. The first Islamic organisation was founded on July 25, 1926. In 1955 Tewfiq Romiah, a translator for the Syrian embassy, reactivated the organisation. He was also active in helping to buy land to establish a cemetery. A Union of Arab Nations exists, but there is no fully functioning Islamic centre. The children have the benefit of a trained teacher, Abdullah Mustafa Idris, who was born in 1921 to a Chilean mother and a Syrian father in Chile. He was raised in Syria and thus know both Arabic and Spanish well.

The slave trade in past centuries and mass immigration from Europe and the Near East to the New World have brought Muslims to the United States, the Caribbean, the British Colonies, Brazil and Latin America. Since the majority of these new immigrant Muslims were slaves or held little political or social influence, it was a rarity to find any detailed inclusion of them in the history of the New World, no matter how extensive their contributions may have been toward building a society there. The travesty of exclusion from historic record has been turning around to a point where most recent history texts mention Muslims in the New World. However, they still have to contend with inaccurate presentations of Islam in the mass media. This is particularly the case for Muslims in Latin America where they exist in small numbers, have little literature in the vernacular languages and rarely have formal Islamic education. It is hoped that this small effort at writing some notes on the Muslim minorities in the Caribbean and Latin America will help to change this situation.

Literature

Material on Islamic history in Latin America and the Caribbean can be found in Allan Austin's *African Muslims in Antebellum America* (New York: Routledge, 1997); Thomas Ballentine Irving's *The World of Islam* (Brattleboro, VT: Amana Books, 1984); Ivan van Serima's *They Came before Columbus* (New York: Random House, 1976); and Abdullah Hakim Quick's *Deeper Roots: Muslims in the Caribbean from before Columbus to the Present* (London: Ta-Ha, 1996). See also the writer's own study of

American Islamic history entitled 'The historical development of the Islamic community in the United States', *Fountain Magazine*, 2:10 (April–June 1995), pp. 18–22, which has material on early Muslim immigrants to Latin America. Expulsion notices and similar documents can be found in Rafael Guevara Bazan's 'Muslim immigration to Spanish America', *The Muslim World*, 53:3 (July 1966), pp. 173–87. Interested readers should look there for further information and bibliographic sources. Recently the Islamic Circle of North America's *Message Magazine* has had articles on Islam in South America, but they are polemic, not scholarly, in content. Material on nineteenth century Islam in Jamaica can be found in Richard Robert Madden's *A Twelve Months Residence in the West Indies* (Philadelphia: Carey, Lea and Blanchard, 1835) and Bryan Edward's *The History, Civil and Commercial, of the British Colonies in the West Indies* (London: John Stockdale, 1794).

Articles on Trinidad and Tobago, Argentina, Surinam, Guyana and Brazil have appeared in the *Journal of Muslim Minority Affairs* published by the Institute for Muslim Minority Affairs in Saudi Arabia. Muslims in Trinidad, The Bahamas, Jamaica, Brazil, Venezuela, Argentina, Surinam and Guyana also have an Internet presence, for this essay and some of the more recent material, was derived from Muslim web pages for these areas. General survey material on Islam in Brazil and the Caribbean can be found in articles by Clyde Ahmed Winters in back issues of *al-Ittihad*, published by the Islamic Society of North America. Articles in Portuguese dealing with the 1835 slave revolts and Arabic writings by captured Muslim combatants can be found in issues of *Afro–Asia* 1965–67. Similar articles by Reichart are in French in the *Bulletin de l'I.F.A.N.*, published by L'Institut Fondamental d'Afrique Noire. See also Raymundo Nina Rodrigues' *Os africanos no Brasil* (São Paolo: Companhia editora nacional, 1932).

Index